SIXTH EDITION

Management

ALLYN AND BACON

Management

Concepts, Practices,

and Skills

Concepts, Practices, and Skills

R. WAYNE MONDY
McNeese State University

SHANE R. PREMEAUX
McNeese State University

Boston   London   Toronto   Sydney   Tokyo   Singapore

Editor-in-Chief, Business and Economics: Rich Wohl
Editorial Assistant: Sarah Carter
Editorial-Production Services: Leslie Anderson Olney
Text Designers: Ronald Kosciak and Melinda Grosser
Cover Administrator: Linda Dickinson
Cover Designer: Paradise Designs
Composition Buyer: Linda Cox
Manufacturing Buyer: Louise Richardson

Library of Congress Cataloging-in-Publication Data
Mondy, R. Wayne, 1940-
    Management--concepts, practices, and skills / R. Wayne Mondy,
  Shane R. Premeaux. —6th ed.
        p.   cm.
  Includes bibliographical references and index.
  ISBN 0-205-13854-3
  1. Management. I. Premeaux, Shane R., 1954-
  HD31.M616 1992
  658.4—dc20   92–25673
                                                   CIP

Printed in the United States of America
10 9 8 7 6 5 4 3 2 1   94 93 92

To Marianne Elizabeth,
my T-ball player and
love of my life.
R. Wayne Mondy

To my beautiful baby girl,
Paige Elizabeth Premeaux.
I will always love you "PEP"
Shane R. Premeaux

Brief Contents

Contents

Preface xvii

● ● ● ● ● ●

Chapter 3: Social Responsibility and Business Ethics *74*

PART TWO: DECISION MAKING AND PLANNING

● ● ● ● ● ●

Chapter 4: Managerial Decision Making *104*

CONTENTS

PART FOUR: INFLUENCING

Chapter 10: Motivation 292

Chapter 11: Leadership 330

••••••

Chapter 12: Communication 358

••••••

Chapter 13: Group Performance, Intergroup Behavior, and Conflict 388

PART FIVE: CONTROLLING

• • • • • •

Chapter 17: Total Quality Management *522*

PART SIX: SPECIAL TOPICS

• • • • • •

Chapter 18: Management in the Multinational Enterprise *546*

Preface

Like the five previous editions, the sixth edition of *Management: Concepts, Practices, and Skills* is written for an audience that expects management theory to be linked with actual management practice. Although it is essentially pragmatic in approach, the text is balanced throughout with current management theory. A common theme—a "real-world" approach to management—exists throughout the book. Each of the management functions—planning, organizing, influencing, and controlling—is discussed from the standpoint of how each function interrelates to the management process. The book puts the student in touch with reality through the extensive use of company examples and exercises. A major feature of the sixth edition is the further development of a theme which emphasizes how management is practiced. The following material is presented to show how management is practiced: extended company examples, many new company examples, Management In Practice exercises, Ethical Dilemma exercises, and Self-Assessment exercises. The lead-off vignettes are completely new or updated and revised.

Features of the Chapters

- **Management.** This chapter presents an overview of the book and shows how the management functions are integrated throughout the book to develop an effective management approach.
- **The Manager's Environment.** This chapter shows the many environmental factors which impact top level managers. It also stresses that the environment of lower-level managers in the organization is different from that of upper-level managers. New sections that have been added include "Managing Diversity," and "The Economy".

- **Social Responsibility and Business Ethics.** This chapter covers the areas of social responsibility and ethics. The information in this chapter permits the discussion of ethics throughout the remainder of the text. Ethical Dilemma exercises are presented in the remaining chapters.
- **Managerial Decision Making.** The traditional decision making topics are included in this chapter.
- **The Planning Process.** This chapter describes not only the planning process, but also includes contingency planning, and a discussion of management by objectives from both a positive and negative standpoint.
- **Strategic Planning.** This chapter includes current topics in the field and the organizational aspects which impact strategic planning.
- **The Organizing Process and the Informal Organization.** This chapter discusses the organizing process, specialization of labor, departmentation, organizational differentiation, and the informal organization.
- **Organizing Concepts and Organizational Structure.** This chapter focuses on such topics as responsibility, authority, delegation, accountability, organizing principles, centralization versus decentralization, and types of organizational structures. Also included is a section on how managers can become better at working with committees.
- **Human Resource Management and the Staffing Function.** In addition to the traditional topics on this subject, a current section on laws and executive orders affecting equal employment opportunity has been added to the sixth edition. Other topics such as the "Glass Ceiling," "Drug Testing," "Negligent Hiring and Retention," and "Sexual Harassment," have been added.

- **Motivation.** The chapter focuses on philosophies of human nature, needs theory, equity theory, reinforcement theory, expectancy theory, goal setting and motivation, how managers can be better at motivating, and possible rewards a first level manager can dispense.
- **Leadership.** Established topics such as the trait approach to leadership, behavioral leadership theories, and situational leadership theories are discussed in this chapter.
- **Communication.** Traditional topics such as the communication process, communication channels, barriers to communication, how managers can become better communicators, communication networks and their characteristics, barriers to effective group communication, and directing are discussed in this chapter.
- **Group Performance, Intergroup Behavior, and Conflict.** This chapter includes such topics as groups, group formation, group development, factors influencing group effectiveness, increasing group effectiveness, work-team effectiveness, and conflict management.
- **Power, Organizational Politics, and Stress.** This chapter includes such topics as power and reasons for exerting power, sources of power, how managers can increase their power, power configurations, power differences, strategies for obtaining power, significance of power to the manager, resisting intimidation, political actions in organizations, and stress and burnout in organizations.
- **Corporate Culture, Change, and Development.** Traditional topics are addressed in this chapter such as factors that influence corporate culture, participative versus non-participative cultures, the change sequence, sources of resistance to change, approaches to reducing resistance to change, organizational development, and evidence of culture.
- **The Controlling Processes and Techniques.** Topics discussed include: the controlling process, strategic control points, ways of overcoming negative reactions to controls, and disciplinary action. Topics such as budgetary control, quality control, inventory control, network models are also discussed in this chapter.
- **Total Quality Management.** A new chapter is provided in the sixth edition which stresses the importance of a commitment to excellence by everyone in an organization through the TQM process.

- **Management in the Multinational Enterprise.** This chapter provides students with a realistic understanding of the operations of multinational companies. The chapter illustrates how different environments can affect the operation of the multinational. New topics to the sixth edition include: the transnational company, orientation, performance appraisal, financial compensation, and employee relations.
- **Production and Operations Management.** Traditional topics include graphic methods, work measurement, site selection, physical facilities layout, maintenance control, learning curves, financial planning techniques, and simulation.
- **Management Information Systems.** Traditional topics included in this chapter are information needs of a firm, characteristics of an effective MIS, the MIS at different organizational levels, computer selection, possible information subsystems for managers, computer advancements affecting productivity, creating the MIS, guidelines for effective MIS design, and implementation of the MIS.

Features of the Appendices

- **Planning a Career in Management.** In this appendix the student is provided with meaningful information regarding planning for a career in management. The authors stress the need for a thorough self-assessment, addresses the types of entry level management positions that are available, and career paths.
- **History of Management and Organizational Behavior.** In this appendix, the student is provided information which is both informative and interesting. Mistakes of the past are prone to be repeated, and therefore, students of management must understand and appreciate the history of management so they will have a better frame of reference with which to make critical decisions.

Features of the Book

The following features are included to promote the readability and understanding of important management concepts.

- An introductory vignette involving management is provided at the beginning of each chapter to set the tone for a discussion of the major topics included within the chapter. All of these cases are completely new or updated and revised.
- An "Ethical Dilemma" is provided in Chapters 4–20. These Ethical Dilemmas provide instructors with an opportunity to allow students to experience some realistic situations in a classroom setting.
- Management In Practice exercises are provided in each chapter. They are designed to literally put students "on the spot," to let them think through how they might react in typical management situations.
- A "Global Perspective" is provided in each chapter. These perspectives provide instructors with an opportunity to allow students to experience some realistic global experiences.
- A section entitled Self-Assessment Exercise is provided at the end of each chapter. These are exercises designed to assist in the actual implementation of the subject matter.
- Two extended examples are provided in each chapter to illustrate how the material discussed in the chapter is used in the real world.
- Two case studies involving management are provided at the end of each chapter to highlight material covered in the chapter.
- An end-of-section Self-Assessment exercise is provided so that students can measure their ability in such areas as ethics, decision making, organizing, leadership, time management, and cultural attitudes.
- Learning objectives are listed at the beginning of each chapter to highlight the general purpose and key concepts of the chapter.
- Review questions appear at the end of each chapter to test the student's understanding of the material.
- Key terms are listed at the end of each chapter. In addition, a key term is presented in the margin, in bold print the first time it is defined or described in the chapter.
- A glossary of all key terms appears at the end of the book.
- A subject index is provided at the end of the book.
- Finally, a comprehensive list of references is provided.

Improvements to the Sixth Edition

The first, second, third, fourth, and fifth editions of this book enjoyed considerable success. Many of our adopters provided us with suggestions for improving the sixth edition. Topics which have been added or have been given additional coverage are provided below.

- The practitioner base of the book has been expanded. The Self-Assessment Exercises provided at the end of each chapter give practical appreciation regarding the subject matter of each chapter.
- Because of the impact of the multinational environment on management, multinational topics are extensively discussed throughout the book. Major multinational topics are covered under the heading of "A Global Perspective" in each chapter.
- Over 70 percent of the lead-off company examples are new and the remainder have been revised somewhat.
- Because of the movement in some quarters toward Total Quality Management, a TQM chapter was added.

All these features were designed to promote and stimulate student interest. We sincerely hope that students of management derive as much pleasure from reading the book as we did in writing it.

Ancillary Materials for the Instructor

- Annotated Instructor's Edition
- Instructor's Resource Manual
- Transparencies
- Test Bank
- Computer Test Bank
- Computer Simulations in Management
- Videotapes
- Study Guide

R. Wayne Mondy, McNeese State University
Shane R. Premeaux, McNeese State University

Acknowledgments

The assistance and encouragement of many people is normally required in the writing of any book. It is especially true in the writing of *Management: Concepts, Practices, and Skills.* Although it would be virtually impossible to list each person who assisted in this project, we feel that certain people must be credited because of the magnitude of their contribution. Our sincere thanks go to the many members of the faculty and staff at McNeese State University. We would also like to thank Pat Simmons and Marianne Hartman, both very competent and professional individuals who were always available to ensure that our deadlines were met. We would also like to thank our reviewers for their many excellent suggestions during the preparation of the sixth edition of *Management: Concepts, Practices, and Skills:*

Dennis G. Allen, *Grand Rapids Community College*
William Anthony, *Florida State University*
Debra A. Arvanites, *Villanova University*
Gary Blau, *Temple University*

David Blevins, *University of Mississippi*
Allen Bluedorn, *University of Missouri–Columbia*
Don B. Bradley, III, *University of Southern Arkansas*
Roosevelt D. Butler, *Trenton State College*
Michael Cicero, *Highline Community College*
Janice Feldbauer, *McComb Community College*
Paula Funkhouser, *Truckee Meadows Community College*
Florence Heffron, *University of Idaho*
Dewey E. Johnson, *California State University–Fresno*
G. Scott King, *Sinclair Community College*
Robert J. Kovachev, *California State University–Fullerton*
Richard D. McAfoose, *Indiana University of Pennsylvania*
Gerald Melnick, *New Jersey Institute of Technology*
Bruce Meyers, *Western Illinois University*
Herff L. Moore, *University of Central Kansas*
Eugene C. Murkison, *Georgia Southern College*
Duane Schecter, *Muskeegon Community College*
James Swenson, *Moorhead State University*
Mary S. Thibodeaux, *University of North Texas*
William N. Thompson, *University of Nevada—Las Vegas*
Paul Tiffany, *Wharton School of the University of Pennsylvania*
Joseph Weiss, *Bentley College*

Management

Concepts, Practices,

and Skills

1

Management: An Overview

LEARNING OBJECTIVES

After completing this chapter students should be able to

- Define *management*.
- Explain the management functions of planning, organizing, influencing, and controlling.
- Describe management at different organizational levels and explain the work of managers at those levels.
- Discuss the importance of conceptual, technical, and human managerial skills.
- Explain the desirability of entering management.
- Define *productivity* and state why it is important to managers.

At age twelve R. David Thomas launched his fast-food career as a twenty-five-cents-an-hour cook at a Knoxville, Tennessee lunch counter. He became a successful restaurant manager after learning all aspects of the restaurant business from his mentor Colonel Harland Sanders, of Kentucky Fried Chicken fame. While assisting Sanders, Thomas revived several chicken restaurants and helped Sanders found the Arthur Treacher's Fish and Chip chain. In 1969, Thomas opened his first Wendy's restaurant. In spite of its late entrance into the market, Wendy's was the first fast-food-service chain to surpass $1 billion in annual sales within ten years. Sales tripled, to $3 billion, in the eighties. Even with Wendy's successes, there was a consensus among industry analysts that giant McDonald's would remain the industry leader in the foreseeable future. But with nearly 4,000 restaurants, Wendy's remained a formidable competitor.

Wendy's was able to play in the same league as McDonald's because of its solid management and productivity advantage. On the basis of labor and materials cost per hamburger, Wendy's had the most efficient production system of any quick-service restaurant company. The hamburgers were produced on hamburger assembly lines, similar in principle to those in Detroit. Each worker had a specific job. However, the key to Wendy's success was management's emphasis on speed and efficiency. A survey indicated that on average Wendy's served customers twice as fast as competitors.

But managers never sacrificed quality for efficiency. Thomas said, "Quality is our recipe." A number of Wendy's policies supported this motto. Wendy's used only fresh, locally purchased beef. There were no heating lamps, microwave ovens, or steam cabinets to keep food hot, and every hamburger was produced when ordered. If a meat patty was not sold within two minutes, rules required that it be put into the chili pot.

As the hamburger market became more competitive, Wendy's diversified its product line, making the production process more complicated. Managers were challenged to maintain efficiency in the face of increasing complexity. To help meet the challenge, Wendy's boosted its research and development expenditures to five times the 1980 level. The company invested in computerized cash registers, which compile data for sales analyses, inventory projections, cash control, and even labor scheduling. Customer-count and product-mix data were rapidly communicated to regional and corporate offices so that opportunities to improve the system would not be missed. Wendy's saved millions of dollars through new building designs, resulting in better operations control and lower energy costs.

With its large competitors using similar sophisticated techniques, Wendy's continually had to seek more efficient ways to make and market hamburgers and related products. Drops in per-restaurant sales and profits in 1986 forced Robert Barney, the chairman and CEO who took over from Thomas, to initiate a "back to the basics" plan. The main elements of the plan were simple: "Better service and red meat." By 1989, the per-restaurant sales were back on the rise. And after a brief dip into red ink, Wendy's management team created a profitable operation once again. Even in hard times, Wendy's margins were up 27 percent largely because of changed operations, improved quality, speed, consistent service, and retrained management personnel.[1]

What accounts for Wendy's success? Most would agree that effective management played a major role in Wendy's ability to compete with much larger competitors such as McDonald's. This book is about management, which consists of getting things done through the efforts of other people. At Wendy's, effective management was so critically important that Wendy's accelerated its national expansion and founded a Management Training Institute to properly train its managers. In his 1991 autobiography, *Dave's Way*, Dave Thomas stated that these individuals must be "willing to sacrifice, confident, focused, and above all patient." Through effective management, R. David Thomas managed to make Wendy's into the third-largest chain of quick-service hamburger restaurants.

Many managerial situations do not end with the level of success that Dave Thomas was able to realize with his restaurants. According to the Small Business Administration information, 24 percent of all new businesses fail within the first two years of operation, and only 48 percent last beyond four years.[2] In many of these cases, the cause of failure is ineffective management, but through effective management, companies like Wendy's can be successful. The costs of poor management to individuals and to society are great. Not only are financial and physical resources wasted, but individuals often suffer psychological damage from a business failure. Therefore, it is vitally important that effective management techniques be instilled into every individual who wishes to enter the world of business.

We live in a society of large and small organizations. Within these organizations people work together to accomplish goals that are too challenging to be achieved by a single individual. Throughout life, each person has experiences with a variety of organizations—hospitals, schools, churches, the military, businesses, colleges, government agencies, and other types of institutions. More and more it is being recognized that the most significant factor in determining the performance and success of any organization is the quality of its managment.

The job of managing is likely to become even more challenging. Foreign competition, coupled with the large number of corporate takeovers and restructurings,

We live in a society of large and small organizations. Within these organizations people work together to accomplish goals that are too challenging to be achieved by a single individual. Here, a group of men from various walks of life build a playground in Anne Arundel County, Maryland. Such efforts are often headed by a volunteer manager from the community.

Source: © Jim Pickerell

has resulted in new "lean and mean" organizations. Many companies like Chrysler, USX Corporation, BankAmerica, and General Electric have cut out layers of managers and made greater demands on those who remained. Similar efficiency measures were necessary at thousands of smaller firms. For example, Cotton's Bakery in Monroe, Louisiana, and Vermont Cider, near Montpelier, were forced to retrench when national firms opened branches to compete with them. No longer will managers succeed because they master the bureaucracy, but only if they add real value to their organizations.[3]

Why are some managers successful and others not? The reasons are as diverse as individual personalities. In this book, we talk about the concepts and techniques used by good managers, such as David Thomas. We present ideas, concepts, and practices that can aid effective management. We emphasize human behavior in organizations. Our primary focus is for-profit businesses; however, we include not-for-profit examples, since most of what can be said about one applies to the other.

In this first chapter, we discuss management as a concept and describe the four management functions. We then present decision making as a topic that relates to all of them. The manner in which management differs at various levels in the organization and the skills managers need come next. Then, we examine the desirability of entering management and the global perspective of management. Finally, we address the productivity challenge management faces.

What Is Management?

Unless you inherit a fortune, you will probably choose to be employed by some type of organization. Many of you will become managers, and those who do not are likely to be professional and technical employees such as engineers, salespeople, systems analysts, accountants, marketing researchers, and computer programmers. In any case, all of you will be managed and will likely manage others at various times in your lives. Thus, it is important to address the question: What is management?

Management is *the process of getting things done through the efforts of other people.* This often involves the allocation and control of money and physical resources. Thomas's position gave him extraordinary power over those with whom he worked. He could hire and fire managers and employees, fund or not fund the activities his subordinates favored, shut down restaurants, and carry out his purposes at Wendy's in dozens of other ways. The definition of *management* includes all of these activities. What is excluded is the action of an individual working alone. A person who is not involved in getting things done through others is not a manager. This concept will be highlighted throughout the text in the form of many company examples, Management in Practice exercises, Ethical Dilemma exercises, and Self-Assessment exercises.

Management

The process of getting things done through the efforts of other people.

The Management Functions

Management's job is to see the company as what it can become. Fulfilling such a vision requires effective planning, the first of the management functions. Basically, a **function** is *a type of work activity that can be identified and distinguished from other work.* By general agreement, the management process is said to consist of four functions:

Function

A type of work activity that can be identified and distinguished from other work.

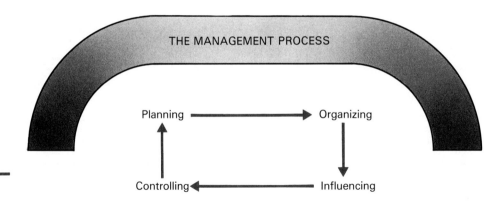

FIGURE 1–1

The Management Process

planning, organizing, influencing, and controlling. Figure 1–1 illustrates the management process. The arrows connecting planning, organizing, influencing, and controlling indicate that the functions are interrelated and interdependent; a significant change in one often affects the others.

Planning

Planning

The process of determining in advance what should be accomplished and how it should be realized.

The process of determining in advance what should be accomplished and how it should be realized is **planning.** Ideally, plans should be stated in specific terms in order to provide clear guidance for managers and workers. For example, from the front profile, when drops in per-restaurant sales and profits occurred in 1986, Robert Barney, the chairman and CEO who took over from Thomas, initiated a "back to the basics" plan. The main elements of the plan were simple: "Better service and red meat." The Wendy's example is one of strategic planning—the determination of overall organizational purposes and objectives and how they are to be achieved—a topic which is the focus of Chapter 6.

How Management Is Practiced

In most chapters are sections entitled Management in Practice: A Skill-Building Exercise, Ethical Dilemma, and Self-Assessment Exercises. The purpose of these sections is to provide a practical understanding of the concepts presented in the chapter. The Management in Practice exercises permit you to make decisions about situations that could occur in the real world. They are designed to put you on the spot, to let you think through how you would react in typical management situations. The Ethical Dilemmas provide you with an opportunity to experience some realistic ethical dilemmas in a classroom setting. The Self-Assessment Exercises are placed at the end of each chapter. These exercises permit you to analyze how well you will deal with the subject matter.

The Wendy's story is an example of top-level planning, but the planning process is similar at all levels of an organization. For example, suppose at the first of the week a supervisor is given a production list for completion by Friday. Since the list tells the supervisor what should be accomplished, part of the planning has already occurred. The supervisor, however, still has to determine how the required production can be completed on time. After analyzing all available information, the supervisor may schedule one-fifth of the output for Monday, one-fifth for Tuesday, and so forth. Analyzing all information available and making decisions are major aspects of the planning process.

Planning frequently requires updating and sometimes means abandoning many aspects of the overall plan to accomplish the mission of the organization. For example, when Federal Express Corporation went international, it ran head-on into entrenched overseas rivals and burdensome foreign regulations. The result was a loss of approximately $75 million over three years. The mission of Federal Express remained the same—to become a successful multinational—but the plans of chief executive Frederick Smith changed. The new strategy was to purchase Tiger International Inc., and with it the rights to the delivery routes Tiger had acquired over forty years. Tiger's routes and planes provided a much-needed boost for Federal's express package delivery service, helping Smith toward his ultimate goal of making Federal "the largest and best transportation company in the world."[4]

Planning is covered in greater detail in Chapters 5 and 6.

Organizing

The process of prescribing formal relationships among people and resources to accomplish goals is **organizing.** At Wendy's, hamburgers were produced on a hamburger assembly

Organizing

The process of prescribing formal relationships among people and resources to accomplish goals.

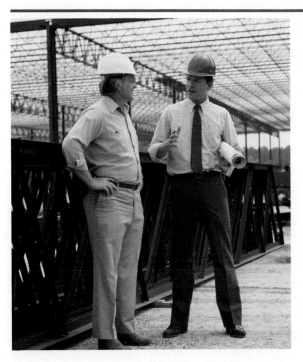

Volcroft sends engineers directly to the jobsite to assist in planning. This allows direct observation in deciding what needs to be done and how to do it. It also improves communication, which is vital to the planning process.

Source: Photograph courtesy of Volcroft

line, similar in principle to those in Detroit. Each worker had a specific job. Wendy's had to reorganize as did many companies during the 1980s. This was also the case at Lotus Development Corporation.

Lotus Development Corporation

Lotus Development Corporation spun out of control as it tried to develop release 3 of its popular 1–2–3 software. While confusion reigned at Lotus, Microsoft intensified the marketing of its new spreadsheet. Lotus CEO Jim P. Manzi recruited W. Frank King III to head the software products group and give it the direction it needed.

A veteran of IBM engineering, Manzi brought with him the discipline and structure of the mainframe world. He began to require each programmer to submit weekly schedules and progress reports, and he personally checked on progress each day. In addition, the release 3 programmers were confined just to the release project. As a programmer's part in release 3 was completed, that programmer would start work on 3.1. Previously, programmers had often moved from a completed product to an unrelated one or had worked on several projects at once.

Release 3 was introduced to hundreds of users—King had made it a reality. The joy at Lotus was dampened somewhat by the bloodletting required to get the release project back on track. Manzi had "cleared the underbrush" by getting rid of eight of Lotus's top seventeen executives, and by doing so he may well have changed the future of the company.[5] What was done must have been effective because soon after the introduction of version 3.0 came version 3.1.

The formal organization must take into account the informal organization, which is the set of evolving relationships and patterns of human interaction within the organization that are not officially prescribed. The informal organization is discussed in greater detail in Chapter 7 and more generally throughout the text.

A most important aspect of managing is ensuring that the right people with the right qualifications are available at the right places and times to accomplish the purposes of the organization. This is called staffing, an important human resource management topic that is covered in Chapter 9.

Influencing

Influencing

The process of determining or affecting the behavior of others.

Motivation

The willingness to put forth effort in pursuit of organizational goals.

The process of determining or affecting the behavior of others is **influencing.** A multitude of topics are placed under this heading, including motivation, leadership, communication, group dynamics, power, politics, and corporate culture. **Motivation** is *the willingness to put forth effort in pursuit of organizational goals.* Motivating workers often means simply creating an environment that makes them want to work. H. Ross Perot, founder of the highly successful Electronic Data Systems Corporation, places a high premium on creating such an environment. He once went to Iran to rescue subordinates being held hostage. Later, as a General Motors board member, he took on GM when he believed management was ignoring the people component of the organization. In these and other ways, Perot has served as a positive and motivating influence to those around him.

An essential element of motivation is the direction provided by the manager. Each worker may require a different means of motivation, and no manager can motivate a worker to produce if the worker chooses not to respond. Thus, the manager's challenge is to create a situation in which workers will want to be more productive (be motivated), as David Thomas and Robert Barney did at Wendy's. Motivation is the subject of Chapter 10.

Leadership is *the influencing of others to do what the leader wants them to do.* A good leader gets others to put forth their best efforts. Leaders depend in part on charisma and other personal attributes for their effectiveness. However, good leadership more often results from learning what motivates individual workers and using this knowledge to direct their activities. The leadership style that works best varies, depending on the characteristics of the leader, the led, and the situation. As the president of a top *Fortune* 500 firm said: "A leader must *lead*, not drive. People are unpredictable, different from one another, often irascible, frequently petty, sometimes vain, but always magnificent if they are properly motivated."

Leadership
Influencing others to do what the leader wants them to do.

According to *Fortune* magazine, the top companies in terms of excellent management, high-quality products, and superior financial performance are Merck, Rubbermaid, Wal-Mart Stores, Liz Claiborne, and Levi Strauss Associates. These companies had one thing in common: chief executives who thoroughly understood their business and their people. These leaders inspire their employees to exert the extra effort necessary for collective success.[6] Leadership is discussed in Chapter 11.

Communication is *the transfer of information, ideas, understanding, or feelings among people.* Much of a manager's day is spent communicating. Supervisors, for example, tell workers what needs to be done. They also report to managers, summarizing their units' activities, seeking support and guidance, and representing subordinates. Lack of good communication skills can hurt productivity. Communication is the subject of Chapter 12.

Communication
The transfer of information, ideas, understanding, or feelings among people.

MANAGEMENT IN PRACTICE: A Skill-Building Exercise

Imagine that you are a member of the board of directors of General Motors before GM chairman Robert C. Stempel took over. GM's market share has been sliding dramatically for three years. Profits have fallen below Ford's. Analysts frequently describe GM cars as low-quality look-alikes. At the time industry experts blamed former GM chief executive Roger B. Smith and his too-quick move toward automation. You know Smith to be something of an efficiency expert and a somewhat abrasive person. You consider him exceptionally competent as an administrator. Smith understands and respects the huge GM bureaucracy and has many close relationships with other senior executives at the company.

A concerned group of board members have nominated Ross Perot to replace Smith. Perot, a self-made billionaire and a Johnny-come-lately on the board, appears to agree with the experts on the cause of GM's problems. He has said GM must balance the human component with technology. Perot has complained of the many layers of management at GM and of the headlong rush to robotize. He often talks of the need for an "entrepreneurial spirit" in big companies. Perot has just requested your support and has reminded you again of his emphasis on the human element in business.

How would you respond?

Group

Two or more people having a unifying relationship, such as common objectives or physical proximity.

Power

The ability to influence behavior.

Politics

A network of interactions by which power is acquired, transferred, and exercised on others.

Corporate culture

The system of shared values, beliefs, and habits in an organization that interacts with formal structure to produce behavioral norms.

A **group** is *two or more people having a unifying relationship, such as common objectives or physical proximity.* We all belong to many groups—at work, in the community, and even at home (the family is a group). There are formal work groups, of course, made up of managers and subordinates. There are also informal groups, which consist of two or more persons associated with one another in ways not prescribed by the formal organization. The focus of Chapter 13 is the many aspects of groups that affect the management job.

Power is *the ability to influence behavior.* It is the ability to get things done the way one wants them to be done.[7] **Politics** can be described as a *"network of interactions by which power is acquired, transferred, and exercised on others."*[8] Power and politics, the subjects of Chapter 14, are immensely important to managers.

The ways in which managers motivate and lead workers and communicate with superiors and subordinates affect, and are affected by, **corporate culture**—*the system of shared values, beliefs, and habits in an organization that interacts with formal structure to produce behavioral norms.* The culture can be one of openness and support. It also may be one of autocracy and fear. Whatever the corporate culture, it will have an impact on those in the organization. Corporate culture is discussed in Chapter 15.

Controlling

Controlling

The process of comparing actual performance with standards and taking any necessary corrective action.

The process of comparing actual performance with standards and taking any necessary corrective action is **controlling.** Controls help ensure performance in accordance with plans. If performance is unsatisfactory, corrective action can be taken. For instance, if a company's production costs are higher than planned, management must have some means of recognizing and correcting the problem. For example, when Wendy's control system reported a drop in per-restaurant sales and profits, management was able to make appropriate adjustments so that by 1989 profits and sales were back on the rise. Controlling is discussed in Chapter 16. An aspect of the controlling function that relates uniquely to human resources is disciplinary action. This action is taken to correct undesirable behavior. It can range from a verbal warning to outright dismissal, as will be discussed in Chapter 16.

Decision Making and the Management Functions

Decision making

The process of generating and evaluating alternatives and making choices among them.

Decision making is *the process of generating and evaluating alternatives and making choices among them.* As Figure 1–2 illustrates, each management function involves decision making. In fact, management is one continuous string of decisions. Planning involves, for example, setting the company's overall direction as well as determining tomorrow's job assignments. In a similar way, organizing requires choices among basic organizational forms as well as between tight or loose reporting relationships. There are many ways to influence, and leaders must choose which approach to use in each case. Finally, choices must be made between tight and loose controls and among the many possible standards and tolerances to employ. Of course, the decisions mentioned here for each management function only scratch the surface.

FIGURE 1–2

Decision Making and the
Management Functions

CEO Scott G. McNealy, of computer maker Sun Microsystems, continually talked up the great value of effective decision making, both inside and outside his company. The practice was to seek consensus, if possible, and always to allow participation by subordinates in decisions affecting them. Other Sun executives caught the fever. The quality decisions that resulted made Sun a leader in its fiercely competitive industry.[9]

August Busch III is another corporate executive who is considered to be an effective decision maker, one who makes decisions in unlikely ways. As chairman of Anheuser-Busch, the United States' largest brewer, Busch employs an unusual means for arriving at answers to tough, complicated decisions. He arranges debates in which managers are assigned opposing positions. Each manager is given staff support and several weeks to prepare. After listening to the debates, Busch makes the final decisions. Decision making is the topic of Chapter 4.

Management at Different Levels

Sometimes managers are thought of as being only the top-level individuals in large organizations. But most managers do not have responsibility for an entire company. Although the distinctions are by no means clear, it is useful to think of three levels of managers, as Figure 1–3 shows.

Supervisory managers are *the managers who directly oversee the efforts of those who actually perform the work.* Most supervisory managers have titles such as supervisor, foreman, leadman, and office manager. Department heads at universities are supervisory managers because they oversee the activities of professors, who actually do the jobs of research and teaching. At most fast-food chains, the person responsible for a particular store is a supervisory manager.

Middle managers are *managers above the supervisory level but subordinate to the firm's most senior executives.* Most major companies have a number of levels of middle managers; for example, a district manager may oversee ten sales offices. Division or area managers may be responsible for a number of district managers.

Top managers are *the organization's most senior executives.* They usually include the chairman of the board and the president, along with vice-presidents who are in charge of major subdivisions of the organization. Top managers are responsible for providing the overall direction of the firm.

Supervisory managers

The managers who directly oversee the efforts of those who actually perform the work.

Middle managers

Managers above the supervisory level but subordinate to the firm's most senior executives.

Top managers

The organization's most senior executives.

```
┌─────────────────────────────┐
│       TOP MANAGERS          │
│    Chairman of the Board    │
│         President           │
│   Chief Executive Officer   │
│   Chief Operating Officer   │
│       Vice-President        │
└─────────────────────────────┘

   ┌───────────────────────────────┐
   │       MIDDLE MANAGERS         │
   │      Division Directors       │
   │        Area Managers          │
   │        Plant Managers         │
   │     Department Managers       │
   └───────────────────────────────┘

 ┌───────────────────────────────────┐
 │      SUPERVISORY MANAGERS         │
 │           Supervisors             │
 │         Office Managers           │
 └───────────────────────────────────┘

┌─────────────────────────────────────┐
│             WORKERS                 │
│        Operators, Laborers,         │
│  Artisans, Professionals, Technicians│
└─────────────────────────────────────┘
```

FIGURE 1–3

Managerial Levels

In sum, a *manager* is anyone, at any level of the organization, who gets things done through the efforts of other people. Wherever a group of people work together purposefully, a manager is usually present. School principals, meat market supervisors, and service station operators are managers, as are the presidents of Porsche, Prudential Insurance, and Bank of America. The president of the United States is a manager too. Managers set goals, plan operations, organize various resources — personnel, materials, equipment, capital — lead and motivate people to perform, evaluate results against goals, and train and develop people so the organization's goals can be met.

Unfortunately, managers are often judged exclusively on short-run performance, being considered effective if a unit is earning a profit, reducing costs, or increasing the market share for the company's products — right now. Naturally, such accomplishments are important to a business; however, a major challenge and obligation of all managers is the training and development of subordinates. The quality of a manager's subordinates is perhaps the main variable that determines the long-term success and effectiveness of that manager.

Managerial Skills

To be effective, a manager must possess and continually improve several essential skills. Figure 1–4 illustrates three categories of such skills and their relative significance at each level of management. Effective managers know the importance of each of these skills. They dare not concentrate on only one, even though it may be the most important at their level in the organization. With this in mind, let us consider each of the three categories of skills.

Conceptual Skill

The ability to comprehend abstract or general ideas and apply them to specific situations is **conceptual skill.** Managers with conceptual skill understand the complexities of the overall organization, including how each unit contributes to the accomplishment of the firm's purposes. The most successful firms are good at tapping the conceptual skill of people at all management levels. All managers, and even workers, are encouraged to see their jobs in the context of the company's broader purposes. At Ford, for example, "Quality Is Job 1" is a topic at every employee meeting, and signs in the factories proclaim the slogan.

Conceptual skill is especially crucial for top-level executives, who must keep the "big picture" clearly in focus. Certainly, R. David Thomas, Wendy's founder, was one such manager. Competing with a giant such as McDonald's and being successful takes a truly conceptual thinker.

The farther down the organization one looks, the less need one finds for conceptual skill. Middle managers need a moderate level of conceptual skill, but not as much as top managers. Supervisors typically have relatively less need for this skill because they usually are given fairly specific guidelines. They are concerned primarily with their own and other closely related departments, and their relationships and functions tend to be clearly defined. A fast-food restaurant manager, for example, does not have to trade off aesthetics, construction costs, and efficiency considerations to arrive at an appropriate restaurant design. That has been done at higher levels.

Conceptual skill
The ability to comprehend abstract or general ideas and apply them to specific situations.

Technical Skill

The ability to use specific knowledge, methods, and techniques in performing work is **technical skill.** This skill is important for supervisors, who must use it in training new workers and monitoring daily work activities. If corrections are needed, the technically skilled supervisor is qualified to direct them. The Boeing Company realizes the value of technically skilled employees. Many Boeing employees must read blueprints. Some assemble critical components. Others install wiring systems in airplanes. And Boeing engineers must know how to use computer-aided design (CAD) systems to make sure complex avionics systems fit neatly together.[10]

Technical skill
The ability to use specific knowledge, methods, and techniques in performing work.

FIGURE 1–4

Skills at Various Levels of Management

As one moves to higher levels of management, the relative importance of technical skill usually diminishes. Managers at those levels have less direct contact with technical operating problems and activities. Unlike supervisors, many upper-level managers generally use their technical skill only indirectly. For instance, the president of an engineering firm, although trained as an engineer, is not likely to design a new machine personally. On the other hand, some chief executives, such as Wendy's Robert Barney, are highly respected by subordinates for their technical expertise. This undoubtedly makes them better managers, even though their primary organizational mission is not technical.

Human Skill

Human skill

The ability to understand, motivate, and get along with other people.

The ability to understand, motivate, and get along with other people is **human skill.** As was previously mentioned, H. Ross Perot, founder of the highly successful Electronic Data Systems Corporation (EDS), said management success is people success. He became openly critical of the management at GM for ignoring the people component of the organization. Perot's extraordinary human skill is given credit for the respect his former employees at EDS had for him and for the impressive productivity record of that firm. Human skill is about equally important at all levels of management. Middle managers who can understand, motivate, and get along with supervisors while wielding influence with top managers are sure to be effective. The same is true of supervisors who relate well to their subordinates and superiors.

Activities requiring human skill include communication, leadership, and motivation. For example, a typical store manager must interact with workers, customers, and suppliers. And more senior executives must communicate with and influence

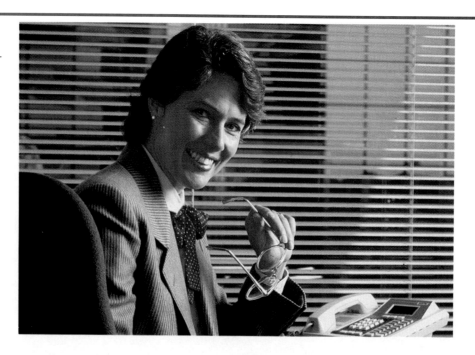

The ability to understand, motivate, and get along with other people is human skill. At Honeywell, as at most major companies, managers must be able to relate well to their subordinates and superiors.

Source: Photograph courtesy of Honeywell, Inc.

other managers and directors in the company as well as people outside it, such as investment bankers. Harvey Mackay, known in Minnesota as "Mr. Make-Things-Happen," preaches a gospel of learning, along with caring and hard work.

● ●

Mackay Envelope Corporation of Minneapolis employs 350 workers and makes one simple product. But chief executive Harvey Mackay has said he could not learn enough about the art of making envelopes. "Hire people who are still learning," said Mackay. "Show them you want them to grow—and your business will grow too." Mackay dotes on his people—"Your long-term success depends on their performance. . . . Show genuine personal concern. . . . Make them your friends." Mackay's top staff members are rewarded—and locked into the company—with gifts of stock.

Mackay Envelope Corporation

"Perfect practice makes perfect" is Mackay's recurrent theme. In his famous book, *Swim with the Sharks,* he wrote, "The minute I persuade myself that I have learned all there is to learn about the subject and can relax, that's the moment my competition will find a way to [make envelopes] better than I can and will hand me my head." As the decade of the nineties began, Mackay clearly had an edge over his competitors. Costs were down and profits were up. But the real source of success at Mackay Envelope was hard work. Although one needs to know when to "throttle back," according to Mackay, "you have to be able to work very, very hard." Mackay has the ability to impart those kinds of values to the people around him.[11]

● ●

The Desirability of Entering Management

Many students have thought about the possibility of becoming managers. Advancement of excellent people into management is important not only to those who are involved but also to the organization as a whole. Let us consider some of the pros and cons of becoming a manager (see Figure 1–5).

Pros Associated with Entering Management

First, an obvious reason to seek a management position is the increased salary. Although there are isolated cases where lower-level managers make no more than senior workers, a manager's pay is usually better. Even if the pay is only a little better at first, entering management may open the door to future promotions, which may involve large pay increases. Most companies prefer to promote managers from within. Even in companies that hire managers from outside, the management trainee often begins as a supervisor.

Second, many people desire the respect and influence that normally go with a managerial job. It is natural to want to have influence over others.

Third, the manager's job offers special opportunities for accomplishment. Instead of just doing mechanical or technical tasks, supervisors perform the much more

CONS
Not enough difference in pay
Involvement with problems of others
Responsibility for actions of others
Inadequate authority
Necessity for making tough decisions

PROS
Higher pay and opportunity
for advancement
Respect and influence
Special opportunities for accomplishment
More freedom and flexibility
Better working conditions
Opportunity to help others

FIGURE 1–5

Pros and Cons of Entering
Management

complex job of managing people. Each day, they face new and different situations. Handling these situations successfully enhances their self-esteem. Accomplishing the job of managing gives a special feeling that is simply not available at the worker level.

Fourth, managers typically have greater freedom than workers. They are usually paid a salary rather than on an hourly basis and are often allowed some flexibility in their working hours. Managers usually do not have to formally request a few hours off; they just keep their superiors advised.

Fifth, a manager's working conditions are often better than those of workers. Many have private offices and are given other advantages, such as secretarial help. Practically all managers have some control over conditions around them, including privacy and comfort.

Finally, managers have special opportunities to help people. Workers have personal problems that can sometimes be solved through counseling. These may involve conflicts with the organization. No one is in a better position than the manager to go to bat for workers or to help them understand the organization's needs. Managers are also able to train workers and help them prepare for advancement or for additional responsibilities. Most managers find it a special thrill when a subordinate is promoted.

Cons Associated with Entering Management

Certainly, the job of a manager can be challenging and exciting. But as with anything worthwhile, there are certain trade-offs. Some managers have even returned to their nonmanagerial jobs. They commonly give reasons such as: "There is just too much hassle involved." Although the negatives of management are often matters of perception rather than actuality, they have been mentioned by practicing managers as trade-offs that must be considered.

First, some managers think their pay is low in relation to that of subordinates. Workers usually just come to work, do the job, and go home. The manager, however, often is on the job before regular working hours and is still there after the workers have gone. In some instances, the difference in pay is insignificant. In fact, as suggested earlier, some beginning managers make less than their most senior subordinates.

Second, in addition to their own concerns, managers must struggle with the problems of others. Workers may bring to the job a variety of off-the-job problems. Perhaps one worker is going through a divorce and simply wants to talk. Another might be having financial problems. Workers may have the option of worrying only about their own problems. Managers do not have that choice. They have people working for them who have different personalities, aspirations, and problems. To some, this can be a burden.

Third, managers are held answerable not just for their own actions but for the actions of others. Workers need only be concerned about meeting individual quotas. Managers must make sure that members of the work group cooperate to achieve departmental goals. Daily, weekly, monthly, and even annual production standards must be met. For some, it is not easy to keep a positive attitude under such pressure.

Fourth, managers are sometimes not given enough authority to get the job done. Often they can only recommend certain actions. For instance, a supervisor may think a certain worker should be fired immediately for loafing or insubordination. But upper management may require a formal request for such a drastic measure.

Finally, some managers do not enjoy making the tough decisions that go with the job. Decisions about performance appraisals, pay raises and cuts, and layoffs are tough enough. But disciplining a worker, especially a former co-worker, is even harder. Firing someone can be traumatic. And management decisions can seldom be made intuitively; they should be systematic and rational, and the manager's reasoning often must be a matter of record.

The negative aspects described here will keep some people from wanting to enter management. For others, however, they will increase the challenge and excitement of a management career.

MANAGEMENT IN PRACTICE: A Skill-Building Exercise

Peggy Turnage was excited and also a bit frightened. She worked at Saint Francis Medical Center, a large general hospital in Schenectady, New York, and had just become the new supervisor of the patient records section. Peggy had eight years' experience in patient records, five of them at another hospital. She had no experience as a supervisor. But she had recently completed a supervision course at Central State College, near the hospital. Peggy was eager to use the skills she had learned.

Peggy came to work early that morning. Sitting alone in the cafeteria, she thought about her new job. Many special cases required the supervisor's attention. For example, patients often checked out earlier than expected, and the records had to be updated. Accuracy in maintaining the records could be a matter of life or death. Imagine what could happen, she thought, if test results got into the wrong folder. When Peggy was handling the records personally, she didn't worry. But now she would be responsible for what others did.

Peggy also knew that she had been promoted over Rod Mabry, who had worked in the records office for ten years. Rod was disappointed, Peggy knew, because he felt he deserved the promotion. She also knew it would be hard for her to gain the acceptance of the other workers. Before, she had been just one of the gang, but now she was the boss. It was a thrilling feeling, but a little scary.

As Peggy was finishing her breakfast, Rod came in. "Mind if I sit down?" he asked. "Of course not. Nice to see you, Rod," said Peggy.

Rod placed his food on the table and set the tray aside. Smiling, he said: "Peggy, I want to congratulate you on the promotion. You sure deserve it. If you hadn't been here, I think I would have gotten the job. But management apparently felt you would make a better supervisor. I certainly can't question your knowledge of the job, and you seem to have a lot of patience. Anyway, what's done is done, and I'm going to try to do the best job I can."

"Thank you, Rod," Peggy said. "I was worried about how you would feel. I should have known we could work together."

Do you believe that the anxiety Peggy was experiencing is typical of many who enter management? Explain.

A Global Perspective

Member countries of the European Community are on an adventure in deregulation that aims to sweep away obstacles to the free movement of goods, services, capital, and people. Barriers were dismantled in favor of a unified market of millions of consumers. This single market should produce $4.5 trillion in goods and services, putting it just behind the United States and far ahead of Japan in economic might.

Over the next decade, removal of internal trade barriers is expected to revive an ailing European economy and result in a more challenging and demanding situation for managers. As the world becomes a much smaller place, more and more businesses will be competing worldwide. Global competition, air travel, and satellite communication technology have made doing business abroad both necessary and feasible, and companies continue to establish multinational operations. When one considers that managers of mid-sized multinational companies expect their international sales to jump 15 to 20 percent a year for at least the next five years, and that 95 percent of the planet's population is outside the United States, it becomes evident that the number of multinational firms will increase dramatically in the next decade.[12] Clearly, the majority of business opportunities in the future will be outside U.S. borders. American managers must learn not only to cope with the multinational environment but to thrive in it.

Unfortunately, many American managers have fallen back on their own limited management experiences and treated overseas assignments much like assignments in the States. More and more managers, however, are beginning to realize that this attitude is wrong. Still, some managers assume that international businesses can simply force foreign countries to conform to the companies' usual ways of operating. Cornelius Van Der Klugt, president and chairman of the Dutch electronics giant Philips NV, knows better. According to him, domestic managers operating overseas must be adaptive and must appreciate the nature of the environment they are operating in.[13] Fortunately, American managers are beginning to recognize that the challenge of engaging in multinational operations is not easily met. They are finding that the manager who succeeds is the manager who deals effectively in the assigned multinational environment.

The Productivity Challenge

Management knowledge is not an end in itself. Increasing the quality and quantity of goods and services produced is a major goal of most managers and of the country as a whole. **Productivity** is *a measure of the relationship between inputs (labor, capital, natural resources, energy, and so forth) and the quality and quantity of outputs (goods and services)*. Note from this definition that outputs must be measured in terms of both quality and quantity.

Productivity is usually expressed in terms of output per person-hour or output per employed person. What causes it to be high or low? Productivity is a result not only of the capability and motivation of workers but also of technology, capital investment, capacity utilization, scale of production, and many other factors. Wendy's was able to play in the same league as McDonald's because of its solid management and productivity advantage. On the basis of labor and materials cost per hamburger, Wendy's had the most efficient production system of any quick-service restaurant company.

How does productivity in the United States compare with that in other countries? Historically the United states had the highest worker productivity level of all major countries. Figure 1–6 shows productivity in terms of gross domestic product per

Productivity

A measure of the relationship between inputs (labor, capital, natural resources, energy, and so forth) and the quality and quantity of outputs (goods and services).

1989 dollars

FIGURE 1–6

Gross Domestic Product per Employed Person, Selected Countries, 1989

SOURCE: *U.S. Department of Commerce*

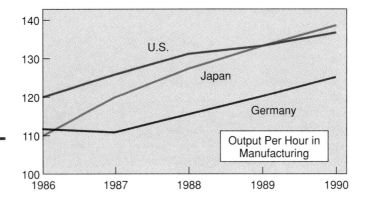

FIGURE 1–7

Output per hour in
Manufacturing

SOURCE: *Bureau of Labor Statistics*

employed person in the major industrialized countries in 1989.[14] Gross domestic product, as used in national income accounting, "measures the output of production attributable to all labor and property located in a country."[15] The figures shown are corrected for exchange rate variations. Note that the United States had a commanding lead over most of these other countries.

In recent years, the productivity trend has begun to change. As may be seen in Figure 1–7, Japan has pulled ahead of the United States in terms of output per hour in manufacturing. Manufacturing firms of all types are moving to alter this trend. As will be seen in Chapter 16, total quality management is being used by many firms to achieve greater quality and more efficiency.

Effectiveness

The capability of bringing about an effect or accomplishing a purpose, sometimes without regard to the quantity of resources consumed in the process.

Efficiency

The capability of producing desired results with a minimum of energy, time, money, materials, or other costly inputs.

Closely related to productivity are effectiveness and efficiency. **Effectiveness** is *the capability of bringing about an effect or accomplishing a purpose, sometimes without regard to the quantity of resources consumed in the process.* **Efficiency** is *the capability of producing desired results with a minimum of energy, time, money, materials, or other costly inputs.* In general, we can say an organization is effective if it gets the job done; it is efficient to the extent that it gets the job done cheaply. For instance, the Jeep plant in Toledo, Ohio used 5,400 workers to produce 750 cars per day in a recent period, an average of 7.2 employee-days per car. At the same time, the Honda plant at Marysville, Ohio made 870 cars per day while employing 2,423 workers, an average of 2.8 employee-days per car.[16] The Jeep plant was effective but not efficient while Honda was effective and efficient.

Purposes and Organization of This Text

Effective management is critical for every firm's success. To be effective, managers must plan, organize, influence, and control. They should keep in mind how individuals, groups, and the entire organization are affected. Basically, managers must understand management concepts and properly apply the management functions to achieve organizational goals. This book is designed to provide students with the following:

- A greater knowledge of and insight into the art and science of managing people and other resources.
- A better understanding of the problems of directing a business organization.
- An opportunity to learn to be better decision makers.
- An understanding of basic principles of management.
- A better understanding of individual behavior and its relationship to management.
- A better understanding of group behavior and its relationship to management.
- A better understanding of how organizations, especially business firms, behave as interactive systems.

The book is organized into six parts, as outlined in Figure 1–8.

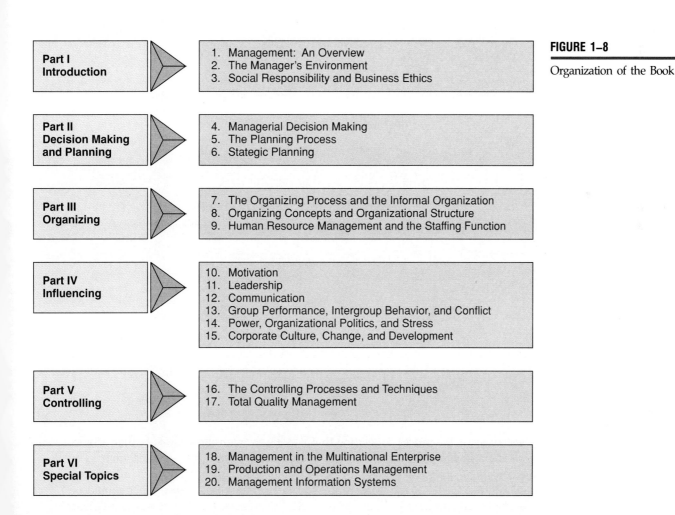

Part I
Introduction

1. Management: An Overview
2. The Manager's Environment
3. Social Responsibility and Business Ethics

Part II
Decision Making and Planning

4. Managerial Decision Making
5. The Planning Process
6. Stategic Planning

Part III
Organizing

7. The Organizing Process and the Informal Organization
8. Organizing Concepts and Organizational Structure
9. Human Resource Management and the Staffing Function

Part IV
Influencing

10. Motivation
11. Leadership
12. Communication
13. Group Performance, Intergroup Behavior, and Conflict
14. Power, Organizational Politics, and Stress
15. Corporate Culture, Change, and Development

Part V
Controlling

16. The Controlling Processes and Techniques
17. Total Quality Management

Part VI
Special Topics

18. Management in the Multinational Enterprise
19. Production and Operations Management
20. Management Information Systems

FIGURE 1–8

Organization of the Book

Self-Assessment
Exercise

Should You Enter
Management?

---

1. Are you willing to get things done through the efforts of others under your direction?

   ☐ Yes ☐ No

2. Are you willing to accept responsibility for the actions of others?

   ☐ Yes ☐ No

3. Are you willing to learn to be a good decision maker?

   ☐ Yes ☐ No

4. Are you willing to master the skills of planning?

   ☐ Yes ☐ No

5. Are you willing to learn to get organized?

   ☐ Yes ☐ No

6. Are you willing to learn what turns people on?

   ☐ Yes ☐ No

7. Are you willing to be prepared to take corrective action?

   ☐ Yes ☐ No

8. Are you willing to develop good communication skills?

   ☐ Yes ☐ No

9. Are you willing to learn to be a good leader?

   ☐ Yes ☐ No

10. Are you willing to master the appropriate conceptual or technical skills?

    ☐ Yes ☐ No

Summary

Management is the process of getting things done through the efforts of other people. This often involves the allocation and control of money and physical resources. The management process consists of four functions: planning, organizing, influencing, and controlling. Planning is the process of determining in advance what should be accomplished and how it should be realized. Organizing is the process of prescribing formal relationships among people and resources to accomplish goals. Influencing is the process of determining or affecting the behavior of others. It involves motivation, leadership, communication, group dynamics, power, politics, and corporate culture. Controlling is the process of comparing actual performance with standards and taking any necessary corrective action. Each management function involves and is affected by decision making, the process of generating and evaluating alternatives and making choices among them. At all three managerial levels, from supervisory to top management, managers must motivate and lead workers and communicate with superiors and subordinates.

To be effective, a manager must possess and continually develop several essential skills. Conceptual skill is the ability to comprehend abstract or general ideas and apply them to specific situations. Technical skill is the ability to use specific knowledge, methods, or techniques in performing work. The ability to understand, motivate, and get along with other people is human skill.

There are both pros and cons in becoming a manager. The pros include the following. First, an obvious reason to seek a management position is the increased salary. Second, many desire the respect and influence that normally go with a managerial job. Third, the manager's job offers special opportunities for accomplishment. Fourth, managers typically have greater freedom than workers. Fifth, a manager's working conditions are often better than those of workers. Finally, managers have special opportunities to help people.

The cons include the following. First, some managers think their pay is low in relation to that of subordinates. Second, in addition to their own concerns, managers must struggle with the problems of others. Third, managers are held answerable not just for their own actions but for the actions of others. Fourth, managers are sometimes not given enough authority to get the job done. Finally, some managers do not enjoy making the tough decisions that go with the job.

Managerial skills are developed for the purpose of increasing the quality and quantity of goods and services produced in the economy. Productivity is a measure of the relationship between inputs (labor, capital, natural resources, energy, and so forth) and the quality and quantity of outputs (goods and services). Productivity is usually expressed in terms of output per person-hour or per employed person. The major challenge facing American management is to attain levels of productivity growth that will ensure that the United States remains the most productive major industrialized nation in the world.

Closely related to productivity are effectiveness and efficiency. Effectiveness is the capability of bringing about an effect or accomplishing a purpose, sometimes without regard to the quantity of resources consumed in the process. Efficiency is the capability of producing desired results with a minimum of energy, time, money, materials, or other costly inputs.

Review Questions

1. Define *management*. Why does the definition exclude the action of an individual working alone?
2. List and briefly describe the functions of management.
3. Distinguish by definition and example among supervisory managers, middle managers, and top managers.
4. List and briefly define the types of skills important to managerial effectiveness.
5. Discuss the pros and cons of entering management.
6. Define *productivity*. How does the United States rank among industrial nations with regard to levels of productivity? Productivity growth?

Key Terms

Management	Group	Top managers
Function	Power	Conceptual skill
Planning	Politics	Technical skill
Organizing	Corporate culture	Human skill
Influencing	Controlling	Productivity
Motivation	Decision making	Effectiveness
Leadership	Supervisory managers	Efficiency
Communication	Middle managers	

CASE 1.1	PEOPLE EXPRESS GOES FROM RICHES TO RAGS

People Express Airlines was founded in 1981. For a few short years, the company grew and prospered. It operated out of Newark Airport, which is close to New York City. The People Express formula for success was simple: Keep costs and prices below those of competitors. One way People Express did this was by flying used planes, some bought at fire-sale prices. And the company's aircraft flew an average of thirteen and one-half hours a day, twice the industry average.

People Express also used second-rate airports—Newark instead of La Guardia and West Palm Beach instead of Miami, for example—because landing fees and other costs were lower at those airports. Many People executives did their own paperwork—and therefore kept it to a minimum.

The main reason for low cost at People Express, though, was not cheap airports, cheap planes, or lack of executive secretaries. "You don't keep costs down by counting pencils and paper clips," said Leroy Martin, a People Express general manager. "You have to squeeze massive productivity out of people and planes." Donald Burr, president and CEO, said the organization was filled with young people "having a blast." Pilots earned under $40,000 their first year, less than some airlines paid senior ticket agents. There was no union at People, even for pilots. All employees switched jobs when necessary—pilots worked the ticket counter at times, and ticket agents loaded baggage. Even top executives, from Chairman Burr on down, filled in as dispatchers, schedulers, and baggage handlers.

Every employee was required to buy a hundred shares of stock, but at a 70 percent discount. Many of the early participants in this program accumulated shares valued above $50,000. Burr explained that the people work hard because stock ownership "gives them a sense that they have a significant stake in the entity, a piece of the rock." "To be a winner," Burr claimed, "you have to have the ultimate frill—nice people."

But it all came apart in the mid-eighties. In 1984, People bought Frontier Airlines, a unionized carrier of comparable size, for $100 million. Frontier lost an estimated $70 million in the nine months following the merger. This began a slide that forced Burr to negotiate a sale of People Express to Texas Air Corporation in 1986. The selling price was about $6 a share, less than one-fourth the price in 1983.

People employees had accepted lower wages than their counterparts at other airlines, expecting that stock ownership and other benefits would make up the difference. But by 1987 the stock was gone, sold at a fraction of its earlier value. And People's manager-employees were soon stripped of their manager titles. People Express is no longer an entity in itself; it has been absorbed into Continental Airlines.[17]

Questions

1. Would you rather be a manager at a company like People Express or at a more traditional one? Explain.
2. Evaluate Burr's performance in terms of his human and conceptual skills.

Wharton Products was a New Brunswick, New Jersey, maker of valve actuators for the petrochemical industry. On her first day as president of Wharton, Gloria Phillips allowed herself a moment of nostalgia. Gloria had known that she was the likely choice for president when the previous president resigned. She had worked hard over the years and knew she was respected for her competence in the field and for her ability to work with employees at all levels. As she sipped her coffee, her thoughts raced back over the twenty years she had been with Wharton.

Gloria had come to Wharton as a young college graduate with a degree in industrial management but no business experience. She was hired as an assistant supervisor in the air-actuated assembly area. "I don't see how I got by," she thought. "I knew so little about the operations and even less about management. It seemed that every day was filled with one brush fire after another." Thanks to procedures manuals, other technical publications, and a patient superior, Gloria was able to stay out of trouble. In fact, she was soon competent enough to handle the supervisor's job.

She did not get to do that, though. After just six months on the job, she had a chance to become assembly manager, with responsibility for three assembly areas, air-actuated, electromechanical, and hydraulic. The supervisor who had been her boss became one of her subordinates. As assistant supervisor, Gloria had been concerned mainly with daily operations. In her new job, she found it necessary to plan weeks and even months in advance. She also had to complete more reports and attend more meetings, and she found herself with less time for the technical responsibilities she had enjoyed earlier.

She chuckled as she thought about the time, just after she took over as assembly manager, when she discovered that the operating procedures manuals were grossly out-of-date and inadequate. Several new machines had been installed, and the whole hydraulic area had been added since the last revision to the manuals. It took Gloria more than a year to put the manuals in order. In the process, she learned a lot about how the assembly division fits into the overall plant operations. She also visited several other plants and discovered a number of new and better ways of doing things, which she incorporated into the procedures manuals.

Because the company was growing and because changes in the manufacturing technology Wharton used were occurring frequently, the procedures manuals had to be modified often. Soon Gloria was able to turn this work over to an assistant and spend more time on planning and on helping her subordinates do their jobs better. She also spent much time in meetings and discussions with superiors and in reviewing and completing reports.

When Gloria was twenty-eight, just five years after she had become assembly manager, Wharton lost its vice-president for planning to a competitor. Gloria applied for the job and, in competition with five others, got the promotion. Gloria had thought she was well qualified, but the complexities of her new position were overwhelming at first. It was difficult enough to forecast production requirements a year in advance, but the typical lead time for a new plant or even a new production line was several years. Also, in the new job, Gloria had to consider the interrelationships among marketing, finance, personnel, and production. The higher Gloria rose in the organization, the less she was able to depend on standard operating procedures.

From the planning job, Gloria was promoted to senior vice-president for manufacturing, and later to chief operating officer, before her advancement to president.

"Surely," thought Gloria, "at some point one begins to feel fully competent to handle any situation that might arise." Gloria knew that she had not reached that point, however; she felt nervous and apprehensive about how things would go over the next few months.

Questions

1. What specific skills will be most important to Gloria's success as president of Wharton Products? Do you believe she possesses these skills? Explain.
2. How would you imagine Gloria's managerial responsibilities changed as she progressed up the management hierarchy?

Notes

1. This case is a composite of a number of published accounts, among them: "Wendy's International," *Standard & Poor's Corporate Daily News*, June 6, 1989, p. 2445; Stephen Phillips, "A New Chef Lights a Flame Under Wendy's," *Business Week*, May 8, 1989, p. 70; "The Fast-Food War, Big Mac under Attack," *Business Week*, January 30, 1984, pp. 44–46; "Burger Wars: Round 3," *Marketing and Media Decisions*, July 1983, p. 42; Verne Gay, "Brand Report 59: Fast Foods," *Marketing and Media Decisions*, November 1980, pp. 137–150; Hume Scott, "Major Fast Fooders Locking Horns Again," *Advertising Age*, September 12, 1983, p. 94; Richard Greene, "Specialty Retailers," *Forbes*, January 3, 1983, pp. 208–209; Ken Smikle, "Golden Nuggets," *Black Enterprise*, October 1986, p. 26; Wendy's International, Inc., *Annual Report* (various years); and numerous articles in the *Wall Street Journal; CNN Inside Business:* Dave Thomas and Wendy's, September 29, 1991.

2. "The 1990 Guide to Small Business," *U.S. News & World Report*, October 23, 1989, p. 72.

3. Peter Nulty, "How Managers Will Manage," *Fortune*, February 2, 1987, p. 47.

4. "Mr. Smith Goes Global," *Business Week*, February 13, 1989, p. 66.

5. Geoff Lewis, "The Spreadsheet That Nearly Wore Lotus Out," *Business Week*, July 3, 1989, pp. 62–64.

6. "The Five Best," *Business Month*, December 1988, pp. 30–31.

7. G. R. Salancik and J. Pfeffer, "Who Gets Power—and How They Hold on to It: A Strategic-Contingency Model of Power," *Organizational Dynamics* 5 (Winter 1977): 3–21.

8. John M. Pfiffner and Frank P. Sherwood, *Administrative Organization* (Englewood Cliffs, N.J.: Prentice-Hall, 1960), p. 311.

9. "Sun Microsystems, Inc.," *Business Week*, July 18, 1988, p. 15.

10. Anthony Ramirez, "Boeing's Happy, Harrowing Times," *Fortune*, July 17, 1989, pp. 40–48.

11. Lisa Cross, "Swim with the Sharks," *Graphic Arts Monthly*, April 1988, pp. 116–118; and Harvey Mackay, *Swim with the Sharks without Being Eaten Alive* (New York: Ivy Books, 1988).

12. Christopher Knowlton, "The New Export Entrepreneurs," *Fortune*, June 6, 1988, p. 87.

13. On "Inside Business," Van Der Klugt shared his perspectives about certain realities of operating in the multinational environment, with the CNN business news team of Kandel, Hartley, and Young.

14. Ed Rubenstein, "Still Number One," *National Review*, July 23, 1990, p. 15.

15. U.S. Bureau of the Census, *Statistical Abstract of the United States: 1989*, 109th ed. (Washington, D.C.: Government Printing Office, 1989), p. 417.

16. John Merwin, "A Tale of Two Worlds," *Forbes*, June 16, 1986, pp. 101–106.

17. This case is a composite of a number of published accounts, among them: "Full Trade in the Sky," *Economist*, June 4, 1983, p. 14; "People Power," *Forbes*, April 25, 1983, p. 170; Peter Nulty, "A Champ of Cheap Airlines," *Fortune*, May 22, 1982, pp. 127–128; "Real PEOPLE, Real Profits," *Newsweek*, April 4, 1983, p. 16; "Icarus Rebounds," *Economist*, August 13, 1983, p. 59; Henry Lefes, "People Express Slashes Its Way into Market with 'Cheaper than Driving' Fares," *Air Transport World*, June 1981, pp. 26–27; "Is People Express Stock Flying Too High?" *Business Week*, May 30, 1983, pp. 79–82; and "Let the People Fly Smart," *Economist*, April 16, 1983, p. 77.

A P P E N D I X

Planning a Career in Management

A career is a general course of action a person chooses to pursue throughout the person's working life. Career planning is a process whereby an individual sets career goals and identifies the means to achieve them. In this appendix, we will first attempt to identify whether a person has aspirations for a career in management. Then, we will offer a section on gaining insight that will allow access to true interests and abilities. We will follow this section with a presentation of the types of entry-level management positions that are commonly available. We will then present possible career paths, and we will follow them with a discussion of tips individuals can use in advancing their careers.

Aspiration To Be in Management

All of us have different aspirations, backgrounds, and experiences. Our personalities are molded, to a certain extent, by the results of our interactions with our environments. Edgar Schein's research identified five motives that account for the ways people select and prepare for a career, and he called them *career anchors:*

1. *Managerial competence.* The career goal of managers is to develop qualities of interpersonal, analytical, and emotional competence. People using this anchor want to manage people.
2. *Technical/functional competence.* The anchor for technicians is the continuous development of technical talent. These individuals do not seek managerial positions.
3. *Security.* The anchor for security-conscious individuals is the stabilization of their career situations. They often see themselves tied to a particular organization or geographical location.
4. *Creativity.* Creative individuals are somewhat entrepreneurial in their attitude. They want to create or build something that is entirely their own.
5. *Autonomy and independence.* The career anchor for independent people is a desire to be free from organizational constraints. They value autonomy and want to be their own boss and work at their own pace.[1]

After considering these career anchors, you should have some notion of the desirability of a management career. For instance, if you enjoy interpersonal contacts management may well be an appropriate career option. To determine the feasibility of a career in management, you may find it useful to gain additional insight into yourself.

Gaining Insight into Yourself

Learning about oneself is referred to as *self-assessment.* Anything that could affect one's performance in a future job should be considered.[2] Realistic self-assessment may help a person avoid mistakes that could affect the entire career progression. An individual may accept a job without considering whether it matches personal interests and abilities. This approach often results in failure. A thorough self-assessment will go a long way toward matching specific qualities and objectives with the right job or profession.

Two useful tools are the strength/weakness balance sheet and the likes and dislikes survey. However, any reasonable approach that enhances self-understanding is helpful.

Strength/Weakness Balance Sheet

The self-evaluation procedure developed by Benjamin Franklin that helps people become aware of their strengths and weaknesses is called the *strength/weakness balance sheet*. People who understand their strengths can use them to maximum advantage. Those who recognize their weaknesses can avoid overutilizing their weaker qualities or skills. Furthermore, by recognizing their weaknesses, they will be in a good position to overcome them. This attitude is summed up by the statement: If you have a weakness, understand it and make it work for you as a strength; if you have a strength, do not abuse it to the point where it becomes a weakness. The first step in self-assessment, then, is to recognize both strengths and weaknesses.

To use a strength/weakness balance sheet, the individual lists the perceived strengths and weaknesses. This perception is important because believing that a weakness exists can equate to a real weakness. Thus, people who believe they will make a poor first impression on meeting someone will probably do just that. The perception of a weakness can become a self-fulfilling prophecy.

The mechanics for preparing the balance sheet are simple, although you will need to do the job several times. To begin, draw a line down the middle of a sheet of paper. Label the left side "strengths" and the right side "weaknesses." Record all perceived strengths and weaknesses. You may find it difficult to write about yourself. Remember, however, that no one else need see the results. The primary consideration is complete honesty.

Typically, weaknesses will outnumber strengths in the first few iterations. However, as the process is repeated, some items that first appeared to be weaknesses may be recognized as strengths and should be moved from one column to the other. A person should devote sufficient time to the project to obtain a clear understanding of strengths and weaknesses. Typically, the process should take a minimum of one week. The balance sheet will not provide all the answers about a person's strengths and weaknesses, but many people have gained a better understanding of themselves by completing it.

Likes and Dislikes Survey

Individual likes and dislikes should also be part of a self-assessment. A *likes and dislikes survey* helps people recognize the restrictions they place on themselves. It is prepared much like the strength/weakness balance sheet. Some people aren't willing to live in certain parts of the country, and that information should be noted as a constraint. Some positions require a person to spend a considerable amount of time traveling. Thus, an estimate of the amount of time a person is willing to travel would also be helpful. The recognition of self-imposed restrictions may reduce future career problems.

Other limitations involve the size or type of firm an individual will consider working for. Some people like a major organization whose products are well known. Others prefer a smaller organization, believing that the opportunities for advancement may be greater or the environment better suited to their tastes. All factors that could affect work performance should be listed in the likes and dislikes survey.

This type of self-assessment helps people understand their basic motives, thereby setting the stage for pursuit of a management career or of further technical competence. A person with little desire for management responsibilities should probably not accept a promotion to supervisor or enter management training. People who know themselves can more easily make the decisions necessary for successful career planning. Many people get sidetracked because they choose careers based on haphazard plans or on the wishes of others rather than on what they believe to be best for themselves.

Getting to know oneself is a lifetime project. As individuals progress through life, their priorities change. They may think they know themselves well at one stage of life and later may begin to see themselves quite differently. Therefore, self-assessment should be viewed as a continuous process. Those who desire a career in management must realize that much of what is done in management, especially at higher levels on the career ladder, is abstract and requires ongoing personal growth and development. Career-minded managers must heed the Red Queen's admonition to Alice: "It takes all the running you can do, to keep in the same place."[3] Once you have gained insight into yourself and can appreciate the career anchors that apply to you, you may find it useful to talk to professionals in management.

Talking to Professionals

People who are successful in their jobs are a valuable resource for career information. It is likely that students, their parents, or close friends know managers who would be willing to share information about careers. Most likely, these people would be willing to discuss the demands of a particular job. Before setting up an interview with such a person, it would be wise to identify some questions that need to be answered, for example:

1. What type of entry-level position would be available to a person with my education and experience?
2. If I didn't start off in a managerial position, how long would it take me to be promoted into management?
3. What type of training does your firm provide management trainees?
4. What is the typical salary range for a person like me starting with your firm?
5. What are the typical duties of a new employee?
6. What is the firm's policy regarding promotion from within?
7. What type of preparation or qualifications does a person need for a career with this firm?

The list could go on and on. The point is that professionals should be asked the questions that concern the student the most. The benefits are numerous. The questioner is in a position to discover if a particular job might be interesting and rewarding. The professional is not under the pressure of conducting an interview and will likely answer questions candidly. Also, valuable information that can be used in future job interviews can be gained. Confidence is also gained because the job seeker can talk intelligently about the position later on in an interview. An additional benefit of this approach is that typical salary ranges for specific positions may be obtained. This information is important because prospective employees need to be realistic about salary expectations.

College or University Testing Center

A resource that goes unused by many students is the college or university testing center. The unique feature of the testing center is that students can discover many things about themselves prior to going for an interview. They can be absolutely honest when taking a test because only they and the counselor will see the results. Since many companies give similar tests to job applicants, students may feel more relaxed if they first used the testing center. The purpose of using the testing services is to gain personal insight that may prove beneficial in seeking a job. Some of the topics students may explore in detail relate to interests, aptitudes, and personality.

Interest Tests

A large number of college students do not know what they want to do once they graduate. *Interest tests,* which help people identify career fields, may help. If the test interpretation supports a person's belief in what constitutes a desired career, there is a good chance that the situation has been properly assessed and the person's belief that the proper decision has been made is reinforced. On the other hand, the person may discover areas that were not initially recognized. Knowledge of these additional interests can provide the stimulus to evaluate other alternatives.

Aptitude Tests

At times, our abilities and our interests do not match up. A person may have an interest in being a brain surgeon but no aptitude for the career. *Aptitude tests* help individuals determine if they have the natural inclination or talent needed for a particular job. These tests are valuable in establishing the likelihood of success in a particular career.

Personality Tests

There are jobs for which certain personality types will be more successful. *Personality tests* help people determine if they possess the right personality for a particular job. Although it is difficult to generalize about which qualities may be beneficial on a particular job, individuals often benefit from the test result interpretations. Corporations, like individuals, have personalities. People tend to be attracted to organizations that provide the means for meeting their objectives and aspirations. A person may be successful in one firm and a failure in another merely because of personality differences.

Tests should not be expected to provide all the answers. The results should be viewed only as indicators. However, if the results suggest that an alternate career path would be warranted, it may be beneficial to reevaluate personal objectives. A conference with a respected instructor may provide some assistance. Often, individuals are pushed into careers not of their choosing because of well-intentioned but perhaps misinformed friends and associates. If at this point a management career seems appropriate, it should prove beneficial to review the possible avenues for obtaining entry-level management positions.

Types of Entry-Level Management Positions Available

Students need to know much more than that they desire a career in management. There are a large number and many types of managerial positions. Following are four avenues for obtaining entry-level management positions.

Entry-Level Management

Sometimes a person with limited or no work experience can enter immediately into management. This is most often the case for individuals possessing a college degree. When that happens, the person typically makes decisions under the supervision of an experienced manager. These jobs offer recent graduates the opportunity to learn without the fear of making a wrong decision that could be detrimental to a career. Many of these positions are in retail management and offer titles such as assistant manager of a department.

Management Training Programs

Some entry-level management positions involve a formal management training program. In such a program, a college graduate is formally trained for a period of three months to two years in the job the person ultimately will be filling. The trainee often receives both classroom and experiential training so as to get the overall picture of the firm's operations. Along with formal training, the individual may work in production one month, marketing the next, and accounting the following month. In that way, the person is exposed to the many different aspects of the firm that could affect performance. Once the training program is completed, the individual is placed in a managerial position.

Formal management training programs are often expensive, and the firm may not receive much benefit from the employee until training is complete. Thus, it is likely that firms will use a highly competitive screening process to make sure the individual to be trained will become a productive long-term employee. Graduates who wish to enter formal programs must convince company representatives of their potential.

From Professional to Management

Many people graduate in technical fields such as accounting, computer science, and engineering and later see their future in management. Such people usually must prove their ability at the technical aspects of the job before they are considered for management.

At times, this path can be a delicate one to follow. People who have always been associated with the technical aspects of a job may have difficulty moving into management. A successful engineer or accountant may not be an effective manager. But because many firms believe that their supervisors should be technically competent, managers often are promoted from the ranks of technical and professional staff members.

From Sales to Management

An avenue used increasingly by college graduates is to achieve success in sales and then move into management. A salesperson is in a position to learn the operations of the entire company. Thus, many graduates have found that the quickest path to a managerial position is through sales. It is likely this situation has occurred because many entry-level positions open to graduates are in sales.

Some firms make it mandatory for employees to progress through sales before entering management. For instance, one large insurance company initiated a program to attract bright graduates into its management ranks. In this program, new employees spent three months at the home office working in various departments and another three months observing in the field. They were then required to do well as salespeople for one year. At this point, they had the option of going into management or remaining in sales.

A sales position can lead to managerial positions in areas other than sales—for example, production. Because salespeople deal with customers, they can provide valuable input in the production area of the business.

Now that you have an appreciation of the possible avenues for obtaining entry-level management positions, it may be beneficial for you to learn about the nature of career paths.

Career Paths

Career paths are flexible lines of progression through which employees typically move during their tenure with a company. Customarily, the paths involve upward mobility within a particular occupation. However, their focus may depend on the organization and the nature of the jobs involved. Three types of career paths may be used: traditional, network, and dual.

Traditional Career Path

The career path by which an employee moves along a vertical line of progression from one specific job to the next is the *traditional career path*. It is assumed that each job is essential preparation for the next higher level of job. Therefore, an employee must move, step by step, from one job to the next to gain experience. This type of career path is most likely to be found in clerical or production operation functions.

One of the biggest advantages of the traditional career path is its straightforwardness. The path is clearly laid out, and the employee knows the specific sequence of jobs through which to progress. Today, however, the traditonal approach has become flawed because of business trends and changes in the workforce. Some of these factors include:

- "Thinning of middle-management ranks due to mergers, downsizing, growth and ungrowth cycles.
- Extinction of paternalism and job security.
- Erosion of employee loyalty to a company.
- Fluctuations in employees' hierarchy of needs as careers are progressed.

- Predisposition to assignments that continously challenge, educate, and encourage skill expansion.
- Turbulence in business and technology demands, with oscillations in the skill mix requirements of employers."[4]

The certainties of yesterday's business methods and growth have vanished in many industries, and neither organizations nor individuals can be assured of ever regaining them.

Network Career Path

The career path that contains both a vertical sequence of jobs and a series of horizontal opportunities is the *network career path*. This path recognizes the interchangeability of experience at certain levels and the need to broaden experience at one level before promotion to a higher level. It is a more realistic representation of jobs in an organization than is the traditional career path. Moreover, it provides more opportunities for employee development. Because of the vertical and horizontal options in the network, the problem of a particular employee blocking the progression for other employees is lessened. One disadvantage of this type of career path is the difficulty of explaining to employees the specific route their careers may take in a given line of work.

Dual Career Path

The dual career path was originally developed to deal with the problem of technically trained employees who had no desire to move into management—the normal procedure for upward mobility in an organization. The *dual career path* is the career path that recognizes that technical specialists can, and should be allowed to, continue to contribute their expertise to a company without having to become managers to increase their pay. Consequently, it provides an alternate progression route for such employees as scientists and engineers. Individuals in these fields can increase their specialized knowledge, make contributions to their firm, and be rewarded for their efforts without entering management. Managers and technical people in such firms receive comparable compensation at each level.

The dual career path is becoming increasingly popular. In a high-tech world, specialized knowledge is as important as managerial skill. Rather than creating poor managers out of competent technical specialists, the dual career path permits an organization to retain both skilled managers and technical people.[5]

Notes

1. Edgar Schein, "How 'Career Anchors' Hold Executives to Their Career Paths," *Personnel*, May–June 1975, pp. 11–24.

2. Paul Frichtl, "Keep Score," *Industrial Distribution* 75 (August 1986): 37.

3. Lewis Carroll, *Through the Looking Glass* (1872; New York: Norton, 1971), p. 127.

4. Mike Hawkins and Milan Moravec, "Career Paths Discourage Innovation and Deflate Motivation," *Personnel Administrator* 34, (October 1989): 112.

5. Donald L. Caruth, Robert M. Noe, III, and R. Wayne Mondy, *Staffing the Contemporary Organization* (New York: Quorum Books, 1988), pp. 253–254.

2

The Manager's Environment

LEARNING OBJECTIVES

After completing this chapter students should be able to

- Explain how the business system operates.
- Describe the major factors in the external environment that can affect an organization.
- Describe the major factors in the internal environment that can affect an organization.
- Describe the basic transformation process that may occur in any organization.

Subway Sandwiches: Aiming for Number 1 in the World of Fast Food

The president and CEO of Subway Sandwiches and Salads, Fred DeLuca, failed to realize that he was operating in an open system when he opened his first sandwich shop, Pete's Submarines. In fact, in the beginning DeLuca ignored his environment almost totally. He did no advanced planning, had no clear strategy, and had little working knowledge of the industry. With all this going for him, DeLuca responded by opening a second store when the first store was failing. However, luck and enthusiasm can only carry an entrepreneur so far. Soon the Subway management became quite aware of their environment, and they realized that the impact of the environment must be taken into account if success is to be assured, and competition effectively dealt with. There have been a lot of changes since then. Now, as head of the world's fastest-growing franchise chain, DeLuca recognizes that selling a good sandwich is not enough to make a business grow and remain profitable.

Subway was confronted with the same realities as many of their competitors: labor problems, various economic pressures that specifically impact franchising, and less than totally effective management. Overcoming the disadvantages of part-time employees required Subway managers to exercise extraordinary leadership. At 11 Colorado Subway Sandwiches restaurants employee turnover was reduced to 50 percent, much less than the 300 percent experienced in most fast-food chains. Staff members were allowed to set their own hours around other priorities in their lives, and tasks were rotated to help prevent burnout.

Because economic pressures were negatively impacting the franchise operation, strategic changes were made in the franchising program. To offset the tough economic times, DeLuca reduced capital requirements for new franchisees by more than $20,000 by adding the option of leasing equipment. Additionally, the franchise fee was limited to $7,500, making it the lowest in the industry. This change allowed Subway's sales to increase, due to franchise expansion. Subway grew by 66.7 percent, with an average of 25 new stores opening each week. Subway began franchising in 1974, and now has more than 4,000 shops across the country.

All of these problems and those yet to surface are effectively dealt with by the unusual management style set up by DeLuca. Referred to as "super-highway" management, it lets the manager set up the highway, allowing for different speeds and exits, but bars people from interfering with others on the highway. This management style allows people to work independently and provides great opportunities. By properly dealing with their environment, Subway is experiencing annual sales increases at a time when sales growth for the fast-food industry has been running well below 10 percent. The system-wide sales for the chain were $600 million, up 60 percent, and store volumes were also up. The future for Subway may well be extremely challenging since DeLuca's goal is to overtake McDonald's in the fast-food market. One can be assured that this will not be accomplished by the luck of the draw, but rather by effectively dealing with the manager's environment.[1]

It is somewhat surprising that Fred DeLuca could have succeeded even for a short period of time, since he virtually ignored his environment. The company was suddenly successful, but also became a participant in a ruthlessly competitive environment. Subway was now aware of the problems associated with environmental pressures and worked to deal with them as they occurred. Subway responded to its environment so effectively that it is profitable and shooting for number one, McDonald's. To help ensure success in the future, DeLuca set up an unusual management style that allows managers to work independently and provides great opportunities to cope with the company's ever-changing environment.

This chapter starts with an overview of the business system. Next, it describes major external environmental factors. This description is followed by a discussion of the internal environment. Finally, the chapter describes the transformation process, by which inputs are converted to outputs within the business system, and ends with a global perspective.

The Business System: An Overview

Systems approach

The viewing of any organization or entity as an arrangement of interrelated parts that interact in ways that can be specified and to some extent predicted.

Open system

An organization or assemblage of things that affects and is affected by outside events.

Closed system

An organization or assemblage of things that neither affects nor is affected by outside events.

The Subway Sandwiches story shows that management must understand the interrelationships between the firm and its environment. Middle and lower managers at Subway Sandwiches were forced to think of external environmental factors. And, in difficult straits, they had to pay renewed attention to how their units interacted inside the organization. The **systems approach** is *the viewing of any organization or entity as an arrangement of interrelated parts that interact in ways that can be specified and to some extent predicted.* It provides a rational means for examining interactions between a company and its environment and within the company. Use of the systems approach inevitably leads to the conclusion that every organization, indeed every system, is an open system. An **open system** is *an organization or assemblage of things that affects and is affected by outside events.* On the other hand, a **closed system** is *an organization or assemblage of things that neither affects nor is affected by outside events.* Of course, there are no completely closed systems, only systems that exhibit various degrees of openness. Still, some managers make the mistake of failing to consider outside events; that is, they treat their organizations as closed systems. This is what the president and CEO of Subway Sandwiches and Salads, Fred DeLuca, did when he opened his first sandwich shop, Pete's Submarines.

Figure 2–1 illustrates the business system. Note that the organization is affected by a number of forces, both external and internal. Top management has perhaps the greatest concern for external forces, while management at all levels must confront forces inside the organization. Lower-level managers face an internal environment markedly different from that of more senior managers.

As indicated in Chapter 1, the U.S. business system is directed more and more at providing services, as opposed to manufactured products. Quality is vital to the success of manufacturing companies, and it is just as important for service-oriented ones.

FIGURE 2–1

The Business System

The External Environment

The manager's job cannot be accomplished in a vacuum within the organization. Many interacting external factors can affect managerial performance. The **external environment** consists of *those factors that affect a firm from outside its organizational boundaries.* The external factors include the labor force, legal considerations, society, unions, stockholders, competition, customers, and technology. As head of the world's

External environment

Those factors that affect a firm from outside its organizational boundaries.

fastest-growing franchise chain, DeLuca recognized that selling a good sandwich was not enough to make a business grow and remain profitable. Subway was confronted with the same external environmental realities as many of their competitors: labor problems and various economic pressures that specifically impact franchising.

As another example, Frederick W. Smith, founder of Federal Express Corporation, was reminded of how important the external environment could be as he tried to expand his firm's international operations in the late 1980s. Federal Express ran headlong into entrenched overseas rivals and onerous foreign regulations. Smith's lesson on the external environment was a costly one, resulting in a $75 million loss over three years. But he was undaunted. He arranged for Federal Express to acquire Tiger International Inc., the world's largest heavy-cargo airline, to get rights to the international routes and relationships Tiger had built over forty years. This acquisition promised to help Smith cope with the external environment.[2]

The Labor Force

The capabilities of a firm's employees determine to a large extent how well the organization can perform its mission. Since new employees are hired from outside the firm, the labor force is considered an external environmental factor. The labor force is always changing. This inevitably causes changes in the work force of an organization. In turn, changes in individuals within an organization affect the way management must deal with its work force. In short, changes in the country's labor force create dynamic situations within organizations.

By 1995, the U.S. labor force is projected to be about 129 million people, 14 percent more than the 1984 level of 114 million. Figure 2–2 shows actual and expected labor force growth rates through 1995. Size alone, however, does not tell the whole story. The labor force now includes more women and older persons than ever before.

FIGURE 2–2

Labor Force Growth Rate

SOURCE: *U.S. Department of Commerce, Bureau of the Census.*

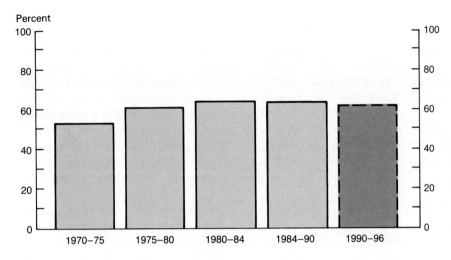

Percent

FIGURE 2–3

Women as a Percent of Labor Force Growth

SOURCE: *U.S. Department of Labor, Bureau of Labor Statistics.*

Many companies are hiring part-time workers, and the use of temporary and leased employees is increasing. Employees with disabilities are being included in increasing numbers. Many immigrants from developing areas, especially Southeast Asia and Latin America, are joining the labor force. In the late 1980s, immigration was proceeding at the highest rate since the 1920s.[3]

The Hudson Institute, an economics think tank, projected that there would be the following mix of new entrants into the labor force between now and the year 2000: 15 percent U.S.-born white males, 42 percent U.S.-born white females, 7 percent U.S.-born nonwhite males, 13 percent U.S.-born nonwhite females, 13 percent immigrant males, and 10 percent immigrant females.[4]

Further complicating the labor force outlook is the estimate that there will not be enough people in the next five to ten years to fill the jobs that the U.S. economy is expected to generate. During the 1990s, the United States will add about 20 million new jobs. For the first five years of this period, the number of 18- to 24-year-olds available will be about 500,000 less than in 1980.[5] Adding to this problem is the fact that foreign companies are employing more and more U.S. employees. In 1991, the number of U.S. workers employed by foreign companies rose to 4.6 million.[6]

The Nontraditional Household There are an increasing number of nontraditional households in the United States. These households include those headed by single parents and those in which both partners work full time. Women who formerly remained at home to care for children and the household, today need and want to work outside the home. In fact, women are expected to account for over 60 percent of labor force growth during the period 1984–1996 (see Figure 2–3). Business is having to adapt to employees' requirements for flexibility and innovation in child-care services, benefit plans, and work practices.

Traditionally, child-care needs were viewed as being outside the realm of the business world—a responsibility that workers had to bear and manage alone. This was particularly difficult for single parents, but even working parent couples generally cannot afford a full-time live-in housekeeper. For many workers, child care has been managed with the help of family or friends. The need for alternative arrangements is evidenced by the fact that in 1950, only 12 percent of women with children under age six were in the labor force. That figure has now risen to almost 60 percent.[7]

Today, business has begun to see that providing child-care services and workplace flexibility may influence workers' choice of employers. Many companies have begun providing day-care services for employees. Some companies located in the same building or facility provide joint day-care service. Other companies, such as IBM, provide day-care referral services. More and more companies provide paid maternity leave, and some offer paternity leave. Still other firms give time off for children's visits to doctors, which can be charged against the parents' sick leave or personal time. Managers need to be sensitive to the needs of working parents. At times, they also need to be creative in accommodating this most valuable segment of the work force.

The increasing number of dual career couples presents both challenges and opportunities for organizations. Some firms have revised their policies against nepotism to allow both partners to work for the same company. Other firms have developed policies to assist the spouse of an employee who is transferred. When a firm wishes to transfer an employee to another location, the employee's spouse may be unwilling to give up a good position or may be unable to find an equivalent position in the new location. Firms have begun to realize that forcing a transfer can lead to the loss of valuable employees. Some companies are offering assistance in finding a position for the spouse of a transferred employee.[8] Overall, the trend is toward "nontraditional" households, and firms must develop programs to accommodate employees' needs.

Older Workers The U.S. population grew older through the 1980s, a trend that is expected to continue through the year 2000. Life expectancies continued to increase through the 1980s, and the baby boom generation (people born from the end of World War II through 1964) had only half as many children as their parents did.

The trend toward earlier retirement reversed itself in the mid-1980s. This may have been due mainly to the 1986 amendment to the Age Discrimination in Employment Act of 1967. As amended in 1978, the act prohibited age discrimination against individuals between the ages of forty and seventy. The 1986 amendment removed the upper age limitation. Firms cannot force employees to retire because of age, no matter how old they are. And many older persons do not want to retire, or even slow down. As many as one-third of retirees want to return to full- or part-time work.[9]

The "graying" of the work force has required some adjustments. Some older workers favor less-demanding full-time jobs, others choose semiretirement, and still others prefer part-time work. Many of these individuals require retraining as they move through the various stages of their careers. According to Ernie Morris, president of Fred Jones Manufacturing Company in Oklahoma City, "The single most important item in this country for the next ten years will be employee education and retraining."[10]

Part-Time Workers More and more companies employ part-time workers. These employees have been estimated to be the fastest-growing segment of the work force.[11] Of course, the use of more part-time workers is not without disadvantages. For example, it means more workers to do the same job. This increases the burden on management, especially in the area of communication. Part-time employees tend to be less dependent on the firm and therefore less committed to it. Remember that overcoming the disadvantages of part-time employees required Subway managers to exercise extraordinary leadership. At 11 Colorado Subway Sandwiches restaurants employee turnover was reduced to 50 percent, much less than the 300 percent experienced in most fast-food chains. Needed training for part-timers is often hard to justify economically. The manager has only part of a workweek to get a return on the training costs; besides, part-time workers tend to be less permanent than full-time ones. Some problems may be eased if part-time workers are given first shot at full-time job openings.

Temporary Employees   The corporate takeover fervor in the late 1980s caused many firms to cut work forces to the bare minimum, making it necessary for gaps to be filled with temporaries.[12] In addition, there is an increasing availability of skilled professionals who desire to work on a temporary basis. Often these individuals desire the excitement of working in a wide variety of organizations while others like the flexibility of choosing their work schedule. Some companies use a substantial portion of their compensation budget, as much as 20 percent, on temporary workers in a wide variety of skills.[13]

Leased Employees   **Leased employees** are *individuals provided by an outside firm at a fixed hourly rate, similar to a rental fee, often for extended periods.* Using this approach, a firm formally terminates some or most of its employees. A leasing company then hires them, usually at the same salary, and leases them back to the former employer who becomes the client. The employees continue to work as before, with the client supervising their activities. The leasing company, however, assumes all responsibilities associated with being the employer, including personnel administration.

Leased employees
Individuals provided by an outside firm at a fixed hourly rate, similar to a rental fee, often for extended periods.

Use of employee leasing is growing. Currently, about 75,000 employees are being leased. It is estimated that 20 percent of the 4.4 million businesses in the U.S. with fewer than 35 employees will be attracted to employee leasing, resulting in 10 million leased employees by the year 2000. Larger companies have also begun using employee leasing to a greater extent. It provides them with a body of well-trained, long-term employees which can expand or contract as the business conditions dictate.[14]

Persons with Disabilities   Laws pertaining to workers with disabilities define *disability*, or *handicap*, quite broadly. In general, a disability is a disadvantage that limits the amount or kind of work a person can do or makes achievement unusually difficult. According to one estimate, 36 million persons with disabilities, not including mentally handicapped ones, are employed in the United States. Among the more common disabilities are limited hearing or sight, limited mobility, mental or emotional disabilities, and various nerve disorders. Recent studies indicate that workers with disabilities can do as well as workers without impairments in areas such as productivity, attendance, and average tenure. In fact, in certain high-turnover occupations, disabled workers were found to have lower turnover rates.[15]

A serious barrier to effective employment of disabled persons is bias, or prejudice. Managers should examine their own biases and preconceived attitudes toward such persons. Many individuals experience anxiety around workers with disabilities, especially if the disabilities are severe. Fellow workers may show pity or feel that a disabled worker is fragile. Some even show disgust. Most disabilities affect specific parts of the body—eyes, ears, arms, legs. Except for the disorder, the affected people are usually normal and healthy. Most are not pitiful; nor are they heroes. They should be treated accordingly. The manager can set the tone for this treatment. If someone is unsure about how to act or how much help to offer, the disabled person should be asked for guidance. Managers must always strive to treat employees with disabilities as they treat other employees and must hold them accountable for achievement.

MANAGEMENT IN PRACTICE: A Skill-Building Exercise

Duane Roberts, a paraplegic, has just been assigned to your division as radio dispatcher for your delivery trucks. The personnel department has given you only limited information about Duane. But you know he is thirty-two years old and has held similar jobs before. You are in the dispatching office when you see a person you assume to be Duane coming up the sidewalk in his wheelchair. You think he might have a problem getting through the double glass doors in his path, which open against his direction of travel.

How would you handle the situation?

Immigrants from Developing Areas   Large numbers of immigrants from developing areas, such as Southeast Asia and Latin America, have settled in many parts of the United States. They have brought with them attitudes, values, and mores particular to their home-country cultures. As corporations employ more foreign nationals in this country, managers must work to understand the different cultures and languages of their employees.

Young Persons with Limited Education or Skills   Each year, thousands of young, unskilled workers are hired, especially during peak periods such as holiday buying seasons. These workers generally have limited education, sometimes even less than a high school diploma. Those who have completed high school often find that their education hardly fits the work they are expected to do. Most, for example, lack familiarity with computers. Many of these young adults and teenagers have poor work habits; they tend to be tardy or absent more often than are experienced or better-educated workers.

Although the negative attributes of these workers at times seem to outweigh the positive ones, the workers are a permanent part of the work force. There are many jobs they can do well. And more jobs can be "de-skilled," making it possible for lower-skilled workers to do them. A well-known example of de-skilling is McDonald's substitution of pictures for numbers on its cash register keys. Managers should also look for ways to train unskilled workers and to facilitate further their formal education.

Managing diversity

Having an acute awareness of characteristics common to a culture, race, gender, age or sexual preference, while at the same time managing employees with these characteristics as individuals.

Managing Diversity   Largely because of this changing work force, a new concept is weaving its way through many of the leading business organizations. **Managing diversity** is *having an acute awareness of characteristics common to a culture, race, gender, age or sexual preference, while at the same time managing employees with these characteristics as individuals.*[16] This philosophy recognizes that individuals of a particular culture may have general characteristics. But, in the work environment employees are treated as individuals, while still taking into consideration cultural differences.

Legal Considerations

Managers must comply with federal, state, and local legislation and the many court decisions interpreting this legislation. Table 2–1 lists some of the federal laws that

TABLE 2–1

Sample of Federal Laws Affecting Business

Laws	Major Provisions
Sherman Antitrust Act of 1890	The federal government's first large-scale intervention in private business, aimed at controlling trusts and preventing monopolies.
Pure Food and Drug Act of 1906 as amended	Protection of consumers by requiring inspection of food and drug products.
Clayton Antitrust Act of 1914 and Federal Trade Commission Act of 1914	The Clayton Act made tying contracts, exclusive trading, and price discrimination illegal. The Federal Trade Commission Act established the Federal Trade Commission to enforce the Clayton Act.
Securities Exchange Act of 1934	Protecting investors from fraud and swindles and regulating securities markets.
National Labor Relations Act of 1935	Protecting rights of employees to form unions and placing bargaining responsibilities on management.
Social Security Act of 1935 as amended	Establishment of a federal insurance program to provide retirement and survivor benefits, disability payments, Medicare, and unemployment insurance.
Fair Labor Standards Act of 1938	Requiring firms to pay minimum wages and extra compensation for overtime.
Air Pollution Control Act of 1962 as amended by the Clean Air Acts of 1970 and 1977	Establishment of air quality standards to promote the public health and welfare and the productive capacity of the nation.
Equal Pay Act of 1963	Requiring males and females on the same job get equal pay.
Civil Rights Act of 1964 as amended in 1972 by the Equal Employment Opportunity Act	Prohibiting discrimination in hiring, training, promotion, and pay on the basis of race, color, religion, nationality, and sex.
Age Discrimination Act of 1967 as amended in 1978, 1986	Prohibiting age discrimination.
Occupational Safety and Health Act of 1970	Setting safety and health standards and enforcing them through inspections and fines.
Consumer Products Safety Act of 1972	Setting safety standards for consumer products and banning products that create undue risk of injury.
Employee Retirement Income Security Act of 1974	Protecting employee rights in private pension plans.
Employee Polygraph Protection Act of 1988	Prohibiting employers from requiring employees or prospective employees to submit to lie detector tests.
Worker Adjustment and Retraining Notification Act of 1988	Requiring firms employing a hundred or more workers to give sixty days' notice to employees and local government officials when a plant closing or layoff affecting fifty or more employees for a ninety-day period is planned.

govern management policies. A number of the laws that have had the greatest impact on business date from the 1930s and before. Among them are the Social Security Act of 1935 as amended, the National Labor Relations Act of 1935, the Pure Food and Drug Act of 1906 as amended, and the Sherman Antitrust Act of 1890. Among the laws passed in recent decades, the Civil Rights Act of 1964 as amended has probably affected business managers most extensively. This act has been largely responsible for bringing many more women and minorities into the work force and for giving them opportunities for advancement.

Laws that limit the actions a firm may take continue to be passed. For example, the Americans with Disabilities Act was passed in 1990, prohibiting discrimination against qualified individuals with disabilities. A new Civil Rights Act was passed in 1991.

Future legislation will also affect businesses. For example, a move by President George Bush to clean up the environment could cost industry and consumers up to $19 billion a year by the mid-1990s.[17] Today, managers must be alert to the ever-changing U.S. legal environment. Likewise, when a firm's operations extend into other countries, the laws and regulations of those countries must be taken into account.

Society

Members of society may also exert pressure on management. The public no longer accepts the actions of business without question. People have learned that their voices and votes can produce changes. The large number of laws that have been passed since the early 1960s is testimony to the public's influence. The firm that is to remain acceptable to the general public must accomplish its mission within the range of societal norms.

When a firm responds effectively to societal interests, it is said to be socially responsible. **Social responsibility** is *the implied, enforced, or felt obligation of managers, acting in their official capacity, to serve or protect the interests of groups other than themselves.*[18] Many companies develop patterns of concern for moral issues through policy statements, practices over time, and the leadership of morally strong employees and managers. Open-door policies, grievance procedures, and employee benefit programs often stem as much from the desire to do what is right as from a concern for productivity and for the avoidance of strife.

Many firms strive to be good corporate citizens. They work cooperatively with other members of the community to control pollution, drug abuse, unemployment, and other ills. They participate in fund drives. Many executives are encouraged to be involved in civic clubs and to seek ways to support local government. Such activities enhance a firm's image in the community and in the long run may improve the firm's profitability.

A firm's work force is part of the society the firm must accommodate. Also, employees provide a conduit to the broader community and a source of information about society's concerns. Each employee communicates with dozens of family members and friends. If management maintains clear and honest communications with its employees, the company will be able to get its own message out more effectively. It will also know of developing problems in time to take corrective action.

Social responsibility

The implied, enforced, or felt obligation of managers, acting in their official capacity, to serve or protect the interests of groups other than themselves.

Social responsibility is closely related to **ethics**—*the discipline dealing with what is good and bad, or right and wrong, or with moral duty and obligation.* Social responsibility and business ethics are discussed in Chapter 3. Ethical dilemma exercises are presented in Chapters 4 through 20.

Ethics

The discipline dealing with what is good and bad, or right and wrong, or with moral duty and obligation.

Unions

Wage levels, benefits, and working conditions for millions of employees now reflect decisions made jointly by unions and management. A **union** is *a group of employees who have joined together for the purpose of dealing with their employer.* Unions become essentially a third party when dealing with the company. For example, it is the union rather than individual employees that negotiates agreements with a firm.

Although unions are a fairly powerful force, union membership as a percentage of the nonagricultural work force slipped from 33 percent in 1955 to about 16.4 percent in 1990.[19] The emphasis in the future will likely shift to a management system that deals directly with individual workers to satisfy their needs and allow the company to compete more effectively. United Auto Workers president Owen Bieber, at least, seems inclined to help management compete in an environment marked by global competition.

Union

A group of employees who have joined together for the purpose of dealing with their employer.

• •

United Auto Workers president Owen Bieber called it "jointness," an effort to work with auto company management in its fight against Japanese competitors. A central aspect of the joint effort was the employee involvement (EI) programs undertaken at Chrysler, Ford, and General Motors in the late 1980s.

Under EI, workers were asked to learn several skills and to manage themselves as teams. This called for dramatic changes in job classifications, seniority, and work rules. The payoff was supposed to be job security. But one GM plant in Pontiac, Michigan, got union help in cutting costs and then laid off hundreds of workers. EI skeptics pointed to several other auto plants that they said were closed after workers caved in and cooperated. In mid-1989, GM had two plants on "indefinite idle"—the union contract forbade shutdowns—and 43,000 GM workers were on layoff. But GM and Ford had made it clear that more layoffs might come if the teamwork did not continue.

Advocates of EI said work teams and other mechanisms of cooperation were needed to match Japanese productivity and quality. Opponents said such mechanisms illustrated management's "hidden agenda to erode the collective bargaining system." Bieber and his followers are winning the debate, but there is growing foment within the union about EI.[20]

United Auto Workers

• •

Stockholders

The owners of a corporation's stock are called **stockholders,** or **shareholders.** In general, stock is of two types, common and preferred. Only the common stockholders typically have the right to vote. They vote in proportion to the numbers of shares they own.

Stockholders (shareholders)

The owners of a corporation's stock.

Technically, they elect directors, who make up the board of directors. The directors then elect the company's top managers and make various other decisions. As a practical matter, however, stockholders of publicly traded firms usually assign their voting rights to management or just fail to vote. Most of them see their ownership of the company as a purely financial investment.

Still, stockholders are wielding increasing influence. There are frequent stockholder lawsuits against managers and directors, claiming they failed to look out for stockholder interests. For example, a stockholder lawsuit was filed in Contra Costa County, California, against Lane Nemeth, chief executive of Discovery Toys, Inc. The suit alleged Nemeth had been using corporate funds for personal expenses and paying herself bonuses while refusing to pay dividends to shareholders. The shareholders claimed Nemeth had "run the company as if she were its sole owner."[21]

Also, takeovers and attempted takeovers are now common. A group or individual accumulates large blocks of common stock and tries to buy the rest or use its current holdings to influence management to take actions beneficial to shareholders.

Competition

Companies must compete with one another not only for sales but also in other areas. For example, each firm must have competent employees, and good employees with appropriate skills are often in short supply. An easy solution is to raise pay, but this may result in a bidding war when several competitors need people with the same skills. Besides, competition in product and service markets force employers to keep labor costs low. So managers often combine other benefits and working conditions to get "more bang for the buck" in terms of recruitment and retention. Probably because of such competition, pay, benefits, and working conditions tend to be comparable within an industry.

In global markets, competitors often gain advantage by seeking government support, both financial and regulatory. The superconductor industry provides an example.

Superconductor Industry

By the year 2000, revenue in the superconductor industry is expected to exceed $20 billion a year. In February 1987, a researcher at the University of Houston discovered a ceramic that would superconduct at −195 degrees Centigrade, a much higher temperature than was previously known to be possible. This discovery set off a furor of superconductivity research worldwide.

Bills were quickly introduced in Congress to subsidize superconductivity research so as to give U.S. researchers an advantage. Dozens of research labs in the United States, mostly corporate research and development divisions, sprang into action. New developments were closely guarded, with each research team aware of the proprietary nature of its work and therefore unwilling to share results with others. Apparent early leaders in the race were IBM, which had actually abandoned research on superconducting in 1983, and AT&T. The congressional action seemed to have little impact.

In Japan, on the other hand, the Ministry of International Trade and Industry (MITI) sprang into action. A forty-member superconductivity research team was formed; a superconductivity advisory group, made up of executives from Toshiba, Hitachi, and several other major companies, helped steer MITI policy. The effort quickly became the central focus of MITI's Office of Basic Technologies for Future Industries. But, as the composition of the advisory group suggests, the work did not rely solely on government initiative for its direction. The Japanese effort instead combined the research strength of private industry with that of the government to advance the technology rapidly. As a result, the Japanese made several quick advances: Toshiba developed superconducting wire, and NEC Corporation made a new computer chip using the ceramic discovered in Houston. One reporter termed superconductivity "a national obsession" in Japan. In this case, private U.S. industry seemed hardly able to compete with "Japan, Inc."

Customers

The people who use a firm's products and services are an important part of the external environment. Because sales are critical to a firm's survival, management must take care not to antagonize customers. When firms misbehave, customers sometimes show their displeasure through collective action. For example, after the Exxon *Valdez* Alaskan oil spill, environmentalists organized a boycott of Exxon products.

Technology

Change is occurring at an ever-increasing pace, and few firms operate today as they did even a decade ago. Products not even imagined in the sixties are now being

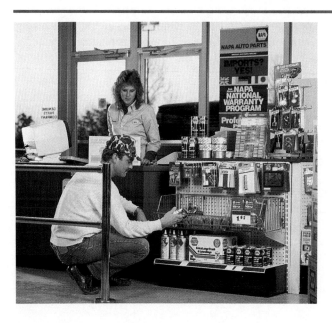

The modern concept of marketing requires that every manager focus on fulfilling customer needs. Genuine Parts tries to help its franchisees turn consumers into patrons through its NAPA (National Automobile Parts Association) warranty program. Here, a customer gets advice from a trained NAPA parts store employee.

Source: Photo courtesy of Genuine Parts Company

mass-produced, and new skills are continually needed to meet new technological demands. Word processing, for instance, has substantially changed the traditional role of the secretary. Many managers now keyboard and print their own letters using a word processor instead of handwriting or dictating them.

At the same time, the advance in technology has rendered some skills obsolete, requiring periodic retraining of affected employees. It has been estimated that half of all existing jobs will be substantially changed within the next decade, with 30 percent of them being eliminated because of technological advances.[22] Furthermore, by the year 2000, 75 percent of all jobs are expected to involve the use of computers.[23]

At times, the need for new technology results from changes in other environmental factors. Fast-food chains, for example, had increasing difficulty attracting reliable workers during the eighties and turned to automation to reduce the numbers of workers required. Self-service drink dispensers were being installed to eliminate the need to have employees pour soft drinks.[24] Several fast-food chains were also studying the feasibility of selling self-service hamburgers and other fast foods.

The trend toward a service economy also affects the type and amount of technology needed. Figure 2–4 shows that employment in service-producing industries has been increasing faster than employment in goods-producing ones. As incomes and living standards have risen, largely because of technological change, people's desires for services have grown more rapidly than their desire for goods. By the middle of 1991, 75 percent of all U.S. jobs were service related.[25] A major portion of Chapter 21 is devoted to technological advances affecting management.

The Economy

The economy of the nation and of various segments of the country is a major environmental factor affecting a manager's job. As a broad generalization, when the economy is booming, it is often more difficult to recruit qualified workers. On the other hand, when a downturn is experienced, more applicants are typically available. Remember that because economic pressures were negatively impacting the franchise operation at Subway Sandwiches, strategic changes were made in the franchising program. To offset the tough economic times, DeLuca reduced capital requirements for new franchisees by more than $20,000 by adding the option of leasing equipment.

FIGURE 2–4

Projected Growth of Service-Producing versus Goods-Producing Industries

[1] *Includes wage and salary workers, the self-employed, and unpaid family workers.*

Source: U.S. Department of Labor, Bureau of Labor Statistics.

Workers (millions)[1]

The work place today is often far different from that of just a few years ago. The rapid advance of information technology creates a need for employees to continually adapt. The equipment being used by these Gelderman employees did not exist in 1980 and will be obsolete long before it is worn out.

Source: Photograph courtesy of Con Agra, Inc.

Additionally, the franchise fee was limited to $7,500, making it the lowest in the industry.

Complicating this even further is the fact that one segment of the country may be experiencing a downturn, another a slow recovery, and another a boom. Such was the situation existing in some areas of the U.S. in the early 1990s. While some of the northeastern states were facing a downturn, Houston, Texas was gradually recovering, and Salt Lake City was booming.[26]

Responding to the External Environment

Managers approach changes in the external environment proactively or reactively. A **proactive response** is *taking action in anticipation of environmental changes*. A **reactive response** is simply *reacting to environmental changes after they occur*. For example, while the Occupational Safety and Health Act (OSHA) of 1970 was traveling its way through Congress, some companies had already implemented its anticipated provisions. Managers of these companies were being proactive. Those who waited until the law went into effect to plan the required changes were being reactive.

Organizations exhibit varying degrees of proactive and reactive behavior. When OSHA was enacted, some firms did only what the letter of the law required. Others went far beyond that and sincerely tried to create a safe and healthful environment for employees. Title VII of the Civil Rights Act of 1964 provides another illustration. Prior to passage of that law, most firms were reactive with regard to equal employment opportunity. However, many of these companies later became aggressive in promoting equal opportunity. Convinced that the national agenda was to eliminate employment discrimination based on race, color, sex, religion, or national origin, they went well beyond the explicit requirements of the law.

A firm may be either reactive or proactive in any matter, legal or otherwise. For example, reactive managers may demonstrate concern for employee welfare only after the start of a union organizing attempt. Proactive managers try to spot early

Proactive response

Taking action in anticipation of environmental changes.

Reactive response

Reacting to environmental changes after they occur.

signs of discontent and correct the causes of that discontent before matters get out of hand. Proactive managers also prevent customer complaints rather than "handle" them. In the markets they serve, they tend to set the prices competitors must match. They install scrubbers on exhaust stacks before environmental groups begin picketing the plant and before federal regulators file suit. In all matters, proactive managers initiate rather than react.

The Internal Environment

Internal environment

Those factors inside an organization that affect the organization's management.

The internal environment of an organization, as illustrated in Figure 2–5, is quite different from the external one. The **internal environment** consists of *those factors inside an organization that affect the organization's management.* Aspects of the internal environment include the organization's mission, corporate culture, the management style of upper managers, policies, employees, the informal organization, other units of the organization, and unions.

Mission

Mission

A unit's continuing purpose, or reason for being.

A unit's continuing purpose, or reason for being, is its **mission.** Each management level should understand the overall mission of the firm. And each unit (division, plant, department) should have clearly understood objectives that coincide with the organizational mission.

FIGURE 2–5

The Internal Environment

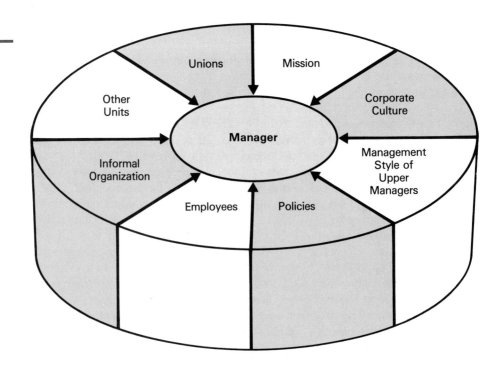

Corporate Culture

The system of shared values, beliefs, and habits within an organization that interacts with the formal structure to produce behavioral norms is **corporate culture.**[27] It is a firm's social and psychological climate. Managers can, and should, determine the kind of corporate culture they wish to work within and strive to make sure that kind of culture develops. Dennis L. Nowlin, manager of executive development at 3M Corporation, said his company was challenged with "managing a large firm with the value system of a small business." Nowlin added, "We work in a highly technical organization with many technical, research and development, and manufacturing specialists. . . . My personal vision is to get every manager within 3M thinking from a general management perspective."[28]

Corporate culture, like the culture of a society, has many dimensions. For example, it is common to speak of corporate culture as being either closed and threatening or open, considerate, and participatory. In a closed and threatening culture, decisions tend to be made higher up in the organization; managers tend to lack trust and confidence in subordinates; secrecy abounds throughout the firm; and workers are not encouraged to be creative or to engage in problem-solving activities. In an open, considerate, and participatory culture, decisions tend to be made at lower levels in the organization; management has a high degree of trust and confidence in subordinates; open communication is advocated; and workers are encouraged to be creative and to solve problems with other team members. Corporate culture will be discussed in considerable detail in Chapter 15.

Corporate culture
The system of shared values, beliefs, and habits within an organization that interacts with the formal structure to produce behavioral norms.

Management Style of Upper Managers

Closely related to corporate culture is the way in which the attitudes and preferences of superiors affect how a job is done. This deserves special emphasis here because of the problems that can result if the managerial style of upper-level managers differs from that of lower-level managers. In general, a lower-level manager must adapt to the style of the boss. It is hard to be open and considerate when the boss believes in just giving orders and having them followed. A lower-level manager's concern for involving employees in decision making and giving them freedom may be seen as a lack of decisiveness. Even the company president must deal with the management style and attitudes of superiors, in this case the board of directors.[29] The president may be a risk taker and want to be aggressive in the marketplace, but the board may prefer a more conservative approach.

MANAGEMENT IN PRACTICE: A Skill-Building Exercise

Lee Roy Howard, a supervisor in the hard surfacing department at Ampex Corporation, had just received a report from the cost accountant. It showed that his unit costs had gone up 10 percent. He knew that the plant manager, Alton Williams, had also received this report.

Lee Roy expected trouble. The plant manager was the brother-in-law of company president Byron Smith. Alton had recently been assigned to the plant after many years as a "driller" in the oil field. Lee Roy knew that one of his good friends, a supervisor in another department, had been fired by Alton for failing to get an order out on time.

Lee Roy was considering how he might explain and correct the cost increase when Shelton Lewis, one of the workers, approached. Shelton angrily said: "Lee Roy, my machine is broken again. That's the third time this week. Do you think purchasing will get us a new one now?"

How is Lee Roy's environment different from that of top management?

Policies

A predetermined guide established to provide direction in decision making is a **policy.** Policies set limits on decisions. They are usually established formally, often in writing. Policies may concern important matters, such as the safe operation of equipment, or minor ones, such as how people dress. Managers at every level may often set policies for subordinates, but they must live within the policies of managers higher in the organization. Policies are often designed to assure consistent practice among organizational units. For example, there are often companywide policies about when shifts change, when pay periods end, and when and how performance is appraised. Sometimes, policies arise informally, from consistent practices over time. A manager may call a meeting of subordinates every Thursday afternoon for years. At some point, the Thursday meetings become a matter of policy. Finally, policies are sometimes established to eliminate conflicts. A supervisor may complain of too many "emergency" orders. Upper management may resolve the conflict by requiring that any order submitted with less than a two-day lead time be submitted to the plant manager for approval.

Effective implementation of policies often requires monitoring field activities by head-quarter's personnel. Honeywell managers spend a lot of time in customer plants checking instrumentation the company makes and installs. Honeywell believes its process control systems give customers the tools to solidify their competitive advantage and improve financial returns.

Source: Photograph courtesy of Honeywell, Inc.

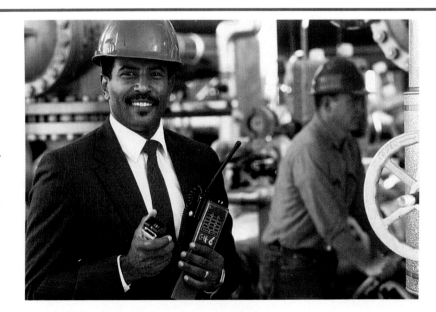

Employees

Employees differ in many areas, among them capabilities, attitudes, personal goals, and personalities. As a result, the behavior a manager finds effective with one worker may not be effective with another. In extreme cases, employees can be so different that it is virtually impossible for them to be managed as a group. In order to be effective, the manager must consider both individual and group differences. A supervisor of experienced workers, for instance, may pay little attention to the technical details of the job and more to encouraging group cooperation, while a supervisor of inexperienced workers may focus mainly on the technical aspects of the task.

Informal Organization

New managers quickly learn that there are two organizations they must deal with in the firm—one formal, the other informal. The formal organization is usually delineated by an organization chart and job descriptions. Managers know the official reporting relationships. But alongside the formal organization exists an informal one. The **informal organization** is *the set of evolving relationships and patterns of human interaction within an organization that are not officially prescribed.* Such relationships are powerful. Assume, for instance, that top management has expressed total commitment to equal employment opportunity. An all-male or all-white work group may still resist the assignment of women or blacks to the group. Unwanted workers may be ostracized, refused the usual friendly assistance in adapting to a new job. In extreme cases, derogatory jokes may be told within earshot of such employees. This kind of behavior places the supervisor in a difficult position, caught between a formal policy and aggressive action arising from the informal organization. As we will discuss in Chapter 7, the informal organization can have positive effects too.

Informal organization
The set of evolving relationships and patterns of human interaction within an organization that are not officially prescribed.

Other Units

Managers must be keenly aware of interrelationships that exist among divisions or departments and should use such relationships to best advantage. Some of the possible relationships among departments are presented in Figure 2–6. The personnel department helps maintain a competent work force; the purchasing department buys materials and parts. Because one department precedes another in the flow of work, that department's output becomes the other department's input. Most managers soon discover that cooperation with other departments is necessary if the job is to get done efficiently. Managers who make enemies of other managers may jeopardize the productivity of several departments.

Unions

Upper management typically negotiates labor-management agreements with unions, but managers throughout the organization must implement the terms of the agreements. In most instances, agreements place restrictions on the managers' actions. For example, a manager may want to shift a maintenance worker to an operator's

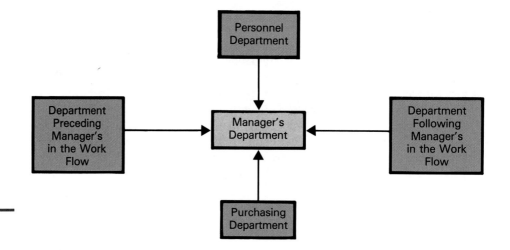

FIGURE 2–6

Possible Relationships with
Other Departments

job temporarily. But if the labor-management agreement specifies the tasks that can
and cannot be performed in each job, the manager may not be able to make the
temporary assignment.

The Transformation Process

In any organization, management's job is to use resources (inputs) in an efficient
manner to produce desirable goods or services (outputs). Management's role in
transforming inputs to outputs is illustrated in Figure 2–7.

FIGURE 2–7

The Transformation Process

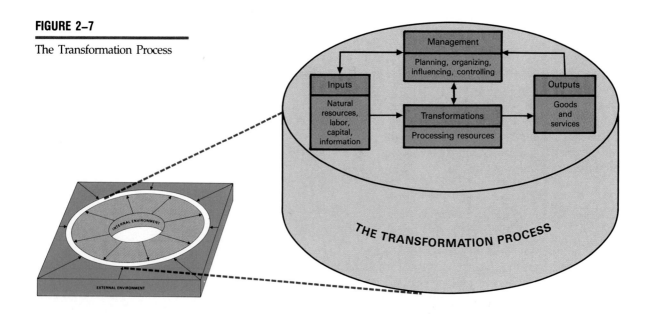

Inputs

Just as humans cannot live long without food and water, a dynamic business system cannot survive without resources to sustain it. Managers must assure that the inputs needed to complete the transformation process exist in sufficient quantity and quality. These inputs—categorized as natural resources, labor, capital, and information—will vary according to the type of business a firm conducts and its particular goals. For example, the manufacturer of Rolex Oyster Perpetual watches emphasizes high-quality watches. The inputs needed, therefore, are likely to be highly trained workers, highly specialized equipment, and high-quality materials. A manufacturer of low-price watches will need different inputs, such as mass-production equipment and less-skilled employees.

Processing Resources

Managers are responsible for assuring that resources are properly processed. Resources (inputs) are processed (transformed) within the organization to create desired outputs in the form of goods or services. There are three main kinds of production operations:

1. Inputs may be *combined* to form significantly different outputs, as when sand, gravel, and Portland cement are mixed together to make concrete.

2. Something useful may be *extracted* from inputs. An example of extraction is iron smelting, a method whereby usable iron is obtained from iron ore.

3. The form of inputs may be *changed*. This occurs when iron is rolled into sheets, logs are cut into boards, and glass is spun into fiberglass.

Processing for service industries is more difficult to describe because service firms do not produce tangible goods. Rather, they create, produce, and distribute services. Service industries include banking, insurance, transportation, real estate, medical care, beauty, and education. Government agencies are also considered part of the service segment of the economy. About two thirds of the U.S. work force was employed in service-producing industries as the 1990s began.

The fundamental process that service industries follow, however, is the same as that for manufacturing industries. Hospitals try to convert ill patients into healthy ones, schools try to turn uninformed students into knowledgeable ones, and beauty salons try to transform individuals into more attractive ones.

Top management is responsible for the overall transformation process and must be concerned not only with the interrelationships among departments involved in the process but also with those among internal and external environmental factors. The foregoing analysis of the elements in Figure 2–7 suggests the complexity of the job faced by top management. In actuality, Figure 2–7 is a gross simplification designed to foster a greater understanding of the infinite complexities of the business system.

Outputs

Goods and services are the end result of the transformation process. Once inputs are converted to outputs, the products are returned to the environment. The output of IBM is largely information processing, whereas Consolidated Edison produces energy. As mentioned in Chapter 1, the capability of producing desired results with a minimum of costly inputs is efficiency; and the capability of bringing about an effect or accomplishing a purpose, sometimes without regard to the quantity of resources (inputs) consumed in the process is effectiveness. The overall objective of the manager in managing the transformation process is to obtain a high level of effectiveness and to do so efficiently.

Management

The operation of the transformation process shown in Figure 2–7 is the responsibility of those in management, who must plan, organize, influence, and control. As the arrows indicate, management receives feedback from the output of the production process and monitors the inputs and the process itself. Inputs are then controlled or changed and the production process is adjusted to provide the desired results in the form of outputs.

A Global Perspective

Regardless of whether a firm operates in a domestic or global environment, management must use company resources in an efficient manner to produce desirable goods or services. Faced with the ever-increasing difficulties of global competition, managers are searching for the key to being competitive globally. Many American companies have had problems competing with foreign competitors, especially the Japanese. American and Japanese competitors differ as to the reasons for lackluster success by many American firms in relation to their Japanese counterparts. Representatives of American companies often complain that the Japanese do not play the game fairly, and many Japanese officials respond that American manufacturers do not add value to the goods they produce.

According to Akio Morita, the co-founder of Sony, the Japanese compete better because they have a different perspective regarding the transformational process. Morita believes that to be competitive, American manufacturers should concentrate on adding extra value to goods. They should create new and better goods from basic technologies and should focus on producing goods that both American and foreign consumers really want to buy. Morita claims that the lack of global competitiveness by many American firms is because Americans do not build things as well as the Japanese do.

Morita buttressed his assertion with the story of an American friend who continually complained about unfair competition by the Japanese. He and his friend were playing golf together in the United States. Morita took out his MacGregor driver, and his friend took out his (Japanese-made) Yonex club, claiming that the Japanese club gave him better control. After golf, they went back to his friend's home. In his American friend's garage were a Japanese snowmobile, a Japanese motorboat, and a Japanese four-wheel-drive vehicle. In the friend's house were a Sony television and a Sony stereo system. Upon a full evaluation, and being unable to locate any U.S.-made products, Morita told his friend, "Time and again you have angrily claimed that Japan does not buy American products, but if you yourself use only Japanese-made things, what do you suggest we can buy from you?"[30] This story may address the true nature of the problem. Americans often use the transformational process to produce goods whose desirability is limited, while the Japanese transformational process produces goods with added value that are highly sought after by consumers worldwide. American companies must better utilize the transformational process to produce superior products, so they can be more competitive in the global arena.

Self-Assessment Exercise

Can You Deal with the Manager's Environment?

1. Are you willing to learn to be aware of the nature of the top, middle, and lower-level manager's environment?

   ☐ Yes ☐ No

2. Are you willing to learn to not try to deal with factors beyond your control?

   ☐ Yes ☐ No

3. Are you willing to familiarize yourself with the policies related to your job?

   ☐ Yes ☐ No

4. Are you willing to know the rules that govern your workplace and enforce them?

   ☐ Yes ☐ No

5. Are you willing to be aware of how work in your department affects work in others, and how their work affects yours?

   ☐ Yes ☐ No

6. Are you willing to be familiar with the labor-management agreement if one exists?

   ☐ Yes ☐ No

7. Are you willing to understand how your boss's style of management affects your own and be able to work with him or her?

   ☐ Yes ☐ No

8. Are you willing to learn how to deal with the formal and informal organization?

   ☐ Yes ☐ No

9. Are you willing to learn to adapt to the new work force and not resist it?

   ☐ Yes ☐ No

10. Are you willing to learn to be socially responsible?

    ☐ Yes ☐ No

Summary

The systems approach—the viewing of any organization or entity as an arrangement of interrelated parts that interact in ways that can be specified and to some extent predicted—provides a rational means for examining these interactions. Use of the systems approach inevitably leads one to conclude that every organization, indeed every system, is an open system. An open system is an organization or assemblage of things that affects and is affected by outside events.

The business system is affected by many forces, both external and internal. Top management has perhaps the greatest concern for the external forces, while management at all levels must be concerned with the forces of the internal environment. Managers at lower levels of the organization, however, confront an internal environment that is markedly different from that encountered by management at more senior levels. Within these complex external and internal environments, the business system operates; inputs are converted to outputs through a transformation process directed and controlled by managers.

Factors that management must consider in the external environment include the labor force, legal considerations, society, unions, stockholders, competition, customers, technology, and the economy. Managers approach changes in the external environment proactively or reactively. A proactive response is taking action in anticipation of environmental changes. A reactive response is simply reacting to environmental changes after they occur. Organizations exhibit varying degrees of proactive and reactive behavior. A firm may be either reactive or proactive in any matter, legal or otherwise.

Factors to be considered in the internal environment include the firm's mission, its corporate culture, the management style of upper managers, policies, employees, the informal organization, other units of the organization, and unions.

Management's job is to direct the transformation of resources (inputs) in an efficient manner to produce desirable goods or services (outputs). In the course of this process, managers plan, organize, influence, and control. They monitor the input and the transformation process and, upon analyzing feedback from the output, make the adjustments necessary in the production process to obtain the desired results.

Review Questions

1. Define *systems approach*. Why does a manager need to understand the systems approach?

2. Identify and describe the major external environmental factors that can affect top managers.

3. How is the work force expected to change by the year 1995?

4. What are the major internal environmental factors that can affect the jobs that managers do?

5. What are the components of an organization's transformation process?

Key Terms

Systems approach	Social responsibility	Reactive response
Open system	Ethics	Internal environment
Closed system	Union	Mission
External environment	Stockholders	Corporate culture
Leased employees	(shareholders)	Policy
Managing diversity	Proactive response	Informal organization

CASE 2.1   FIGHTING AGAINST THE ENVIRONMENT

Pan American World Airways, Inc. was a leader in U.S. aviation for more than fifty years. But a string of losses from 1981–1989 brought the company to its knees. And it was showing scant signs of recovery when Donald Trump bought Eastern's Washington-to-New-York-to-Boston shuttle. The flamboyant Trump announced plans to go head-to-head with Pan Am's shuttle, its most profitable operation. Beleaguered Pan Am managers must have thought, "What next?"

The 1978 deregulation of the airline industry had brought new challenges to all of the major airlines. At about the same time, a major recession began, and airline travel was hit particularly hard. International travel was dampened by unfavorable exchange rates. Through 1981, fuel prices, a major part of air carrier costs, continued the upward trend that had begun in 1973 with the Arab oil embargo.

To add to the chaos, PATCO (the Professional Air Traffic Controllers Organization, a union) walked out in 1982. There was a lengthy strike and President Ronald Reagan fired the strikers. Civil Aeronautics Board Chairman Dan McKinnen remarked, "Nobody in his wildest imagination could dream of such negative factors all coming together at once."

The managers of Pan Am believed the company had to grow to survive in the marketplace. So Pan Am acquired National Airlines, hoping to use it to build a major domestic hub. But stung by $700 million in losses in 1981–1982, the managers were forced to gut most of National's domestic system. Then the managers tried a new tack. They restructured the company's routes and introduced a discount fare program that undercut competition by 17 to 33 percent. To get operating cash, they sold Pan Am's Intercontinental Hotels Corporation subsidiary and some of its planes. Ten vice-presidents, 112 staff managers and 5,000 other employees were laid off.

Pan Am was able to fly 60 percent full in 1983, but profits remained elusive. More than a third of the company's revenues were paid in foreign currencies, and foreign exchange losses were $11.5 million just for the 1984 second quarter. Another $8 million went to pay for overtime and for free drinks for passengers during air traffic control delays. Finally, 11 percent of Pan Am's second-quarter 1984 air travel represented free rides, granted under the WorldPass program. The credits were to expire on June 30 that year, so passengers rushed to use them. Still, Pan Am did better than Braniff International and Continental Airlines, which both filed bankruptcy petitions. Even high-flying Delta saw losses in 1983. Eastern Airlines survived only by threatening bankruptcy, a threat it would carry out in 1989, and by paying wages partly with company stock.

In late 1984, Pan Am managers thought they had weathered the storm. In the words of a Shearson Lehman/American Express analyst, "Pan Am certainly has built enough strength to eliminate any concern that they may be in dire circumstances." But stockholders were not at all confident of the company's survival. Pan Am's stock was down to 7¼ in October 1983, a fraction of its historic value. Though the stock recovered to over 9 in 1986, it would crash to below 4 in 1989.

A number of airline-industry takeovers and mergers in 1986–1989 brought Pan Am face to face with giant carriers several times its size. Texas Air, for example, had gobbled up Eastern and People Express to become the nation's largest airline, with nearly 20 percent market share. Delta had acquired Western. Pan Am's 22,000 employees were petrified as the company's managers actively sought bids. They knew mergers invariably brought layoffs and other retrenchments. To make matters worse, OPEC agreed in 1987 to escalate oil prices to near $20 a barrel, where they would stay through 1989. And the crash of Pan Am flight 103 near Lockerbie, Scotland, in November 1988 brought the company the kind of publicity it did not need. While commerical aviation in general was surging into the 1990s, Pan Am was still trying to shake off the effects of the "dismal decade" it had just experienced. In December of 1991, Pan Am ceased to exist.[31]

Questions

1. Describe the environmental factors affecting Pan Am.
2. Did Pan Am respond appropriately to these environmental factors? Explain.

CASE 2.2	SINGING THE SMALL BUSINESS BLUES

"There seems to be a conspiracy out there to keep me from making money and to increase my stress level," said James Sharplin, the sole owner of Sharpco, Inc. James's small company manufactures steel items for heavy equipment and rebuilds the heavy tracks and related components of crawler tractors, or "dozers."

James went on to explain the elements of the conspiracy. "The workers," he said, "try to get as much pay as they can for doing as little as possible. Customers want us to repair their equipment for less than our cost. Then they bring it back a year later, expecting warranty work. Half of the customers try to pay a little late—and if I don't hound them, they'll pay a lot late, or not at all. Suppliers try to give us inferior merchandise at premium prices—everything from paint that doesn't cover to steel that has flaws.

"And government! I'd swear half of my time is spent filling out forms, worrying about income taxes, trying to keep a worker I fired for stealing from collecting unemployment compensation, meeting with the fire marshal to explain why we don't have a fire extinguisher on every column—it just goes on and on. Sometimes I think even the equipment is involved in the conspiracy. Yesterday I was just getting ready to load a rush job on a customer's truck and the crane broke down. Mother used to say, 'If it's not one thing, it's another.' I've become convinced that it's five or six others."

Questions

1. How does James's environment differ from that of a manager in a larger company?
2. Evaluate James's view of the various environmental factors to which he is subjected.

Notes

1. "Nice Guys Finish First," *Inc.*, October 1989, p. 79 and CNN Pinnacle Program: Subway Sandwiches.
2. "Mr. Smith Goes Global," *Business Week*, February 13, 1989, p. 66.
3. Elizabeth Ehrlich and Susan B. Garland, "Where the Jobs Are Is Where the Skills Aren't," *Business Week*, September 19, 1989, p. 120.
4. Bruce Nussbaum, "Needed: Human Capital," *Business Week*, September 19, 1988, p. 103.
5. Jac Fitz-enz, "Getting—and Keeping—Good Employees," *Personnel Journal* 67 (August 1990): 26.
6. John Hoerr, Leah Nathans Spiro, Larry Armstrong, and James B. Treece, "Culture Shock at Home," *Business Week*, December 17, 1990, pp. 81–84.
7. Dan Cordtz, "Hire Me, Hire My Family," *Finance World* 159 (September 18, 1990): 77.
8. "Corporate Women," *Business Week*, June 22, 1987, pp. 72–80.
9. Joan L. Kelly, "Employers Must Recognize That Older People Want to Work," *Personnel Journal* 69 (January 1990): 44.
10. Nancy J. Perry, "The New, Improved Vocational School," *Fortune*, June 19, 1989, pp. 127–138.
11. Harry Bacas "Desperately Seeking Workers," *Nation's Business*, February 1988, p. 20.
12. Max Messmer, "Strategic Staffing for the '90s," *Personnel Journal* 69 (October 1990): 94.
13. Ibid.
14. John Ross, "Effective Ways to Hire Contingent Personnel," *HR Magazine* 36 (February 1991): 53.
15. Susan Goff Condon, "Hiring the Handicapped Confronts Cultural Uneasiness," *Personnel Journal* (April 1987): 28.
16. Stephenie Overman, "Managing the Diverse Work Force," *HR Magazine* 36 (April 1991): 32.
17. Edmund Faltermayer, "Air: How Clean Is Clean Enough?" *Fortune*, July 17, 1989, pp. 54–60.

18. Kenneth E. Goodpaster and John B. Matthews, Jr., "Can a Corporation Have a Conscience?" *Harvard Business Review* 60 (January–February 1982): 132–141.

19. Gene Koretz and Celeste Whittaker, "More Picket Lines, Fewer Rank-And-Filers," *Business Week*, May 7, 1990, p. 24.

20. Wendy Zellner, "The UAW Rebels: Teaming Up Against Teamwork," *Business Week*, March 27, 1989, pp. 110–114; and "For Auto Workers, It's Team Spirit vs. Suspicion," *Business Week*, July 10, 1989, pp. 60–61.

21. Richard B. Schmitt, "Bow-Firm Investor Gripes He Ventured but Didn't Gain," *Wall Street Journal*, August 28, 1989, p. B2.

22. Eric G. Flanholtz, Yvonne Randle, and Sonja Sackmann, "Personnel Management: The Tenor of Today," *Personnel Journal* 66 (June 1987): 64.

23. Marilyn Joyce, "Ergonomics Will Take Center Stage During '90s and into New Century," *Occupational Health and Safety* 60 (January 1991): 31.

24. Aaron Berstein, Richard N. Anderson, and Wendy Zellner, "Help Wanted," *Business Week*, August 10, 1987, p. 50.

25. Eva Pomice, "Shaping Up Services," *U.S. News & World Report*, July 22, 1991, p. 42.

26. Patricia Sellers, "The Best Cities for Business," *Fortune*, October 22, 1990, p. 49.

27. Arthur Sharplin, *Strategic Management* (New York: McGraw-Hill, 1985), p. 102.

28. Stephanie Lawrence, "Voices of HR Experience," *Personnel Journal* 68 (April 1989): 71–72.

29. Judith H. Dobrzynski, Michael Schroeder, Gregory L. Miles and Joseph Weber, "Taking Charge," *Business Week*, July 3, 1989, pp. 66–71.

30. Gene Bylinsky, "A Japanese View: Why America Has Fallen Behind," *Fortune*, September 25, 1989, p. 52.

31. This discussion is a composite from a number of sources, among them: Gray Weiss, "The Airline Rally Wows Wall Street," *Business Week*, May 1, 1989, p. 119; Seth Payne, "War of the Shuttles," *Business Week*, February 20, 1989, p. 38; Christopher Power, "Pan Am Needs a Partner, But Does Anybody Need Pan Am?" *Business Week*, April 10, 1989, pp. 92–94; John Greenwald, "Turbulence in the Skies," *Time*, February 21, 1983, pp. 52–53; "Can Pan Am Weather Another Storm?" *Newsweek*, February 14, 1983, pp. 69–70; Louis Krasas, "Putting Pan Am Back Together Again," *Fortune*, December 28, 1981, pp. 42–47; "Lenders Ease Pan Am Debt/Equity Need," *Aviation Week and Space Technology*, January 3, 1983, p. 25; "The Surgery Pan Am Hopes Will Save It," *Business Week*, June 15, 1981, pp. 36–37; numerous articles from the *Wall Street Journal;* and various reports by Standard and Poor's Corp., and Moody's Investors Services, Inc.

A P P E N D I X

History of Management and Organizational Behavior

Mistakes of the past are likely to be repeated. Virtually everyone has heard this statement, but many unfortunately ignore its message. It is important that managers understand and appreciate the history of management and organizational behavior in order to gain a better frame of reference within which to make critical decisions.

Historical Perspectives

In order to fully understand the current state of management in the world, it is useful to review the historical perspectives that dominated management thought during this century. Certain aspects of earlier viewpoints, philosophies, and schools of thought remain relevant today and can provide the careful observer with valuable insight into present-day management.

Since 1900, each of a dozen major schools of thought has fallen within one of three general areas, or historical perspectives, of management thought: structural, human, and integrative. The *structural perspective,* which evolved around the turn of the century, encompasses the theory of scientific management, classical theory, bureaucracy theory, and decision theory. The *human perspective,* which first appeared in the 1920s, eventually included schools of thought focused on human relations, group dynamics, and leadership research. Since the 1960s, however, the schools of thought that have prevailed have integrated the human perspective with the structural perspective to form the third major area of organizational thought, the *integrative perspective.*

This appendix examines these three perspectives and their major schools of thought. Table A2–1 groups the schools into the three historical perspectives and provides a brief description of the thinking that characterized each school.

Structural Perspectives

The earliest theorists expressed concern primarily for the structuring and design of work within the organization.

Organizational Theory Prior to 1990

The emphasis in this book is on the current state of management and organizational behavior. However, just as political science students cannot fail to consider the history of government, management students should have at least a moderate familiarity with the history of management thought. This history obviously extends several thousand years into the past. Moses, for example, is credited with having employed the first management consultant—his father-in-law—to help design the organization through which Moses governed the Hebrews. Before the early 1900s, however, little formal business theorizing took place. Few industrial organizations of the types that exist today were around during that time, and the basic organizational models were the military and the Roman Catholic Church.

Economists such as Adam Smith sowed the seeds of later theory. In his book *An Inquiry into the Nature and Cause of the Wealth of Nations* (1776), Smith included a chapter on the division of labor that laid the groundwork for the later introduction of assembly-line processes. Smith spoke approvingly of a pin manufacturer who divided the work into a number of "branches," causing pin making to be separated into eighteen different operations. This separation of operations permitted workers to concentrate on only one task and thus radically increased the quantity of pins that could be manufactured in a day. Smith also emphasized the importance of proper machinery to facilitate labor.

Scientific Management

Not until the early twentieth century did management emerge as a concentrated field of study. Frederick W. Taylor, who made major contributions to management

Perspectives and Schools	Decade	Description
Structural Perspectives		
Organizational theory prior to 1900	Before 1900	Emphasized the division of labor and the importance of machinery to facilitate labor.
Scientific management	1910s	Described management as a science, with employees having specific but different responsibilities; encouraged the scientific selection, training, and development of workers and the equal division of work between workers and management.
Classical	1910s	Listed the duties of a manager as planning, organizing, commanding employees, coordinating activities, and controlling performance; basic principles called for specialization of work, unity of command, scalar chain of command, and coordination of activities.
Bureaucracy	1940s	Emphasized order, system, rationality, uniformity, and consistency in management; led to equitable treatment of all employees by management.
Decision theory	1960s	Suggested that individuals "satisfice" when they make decisions.
Human Perspectives		
Human relations	1920s	Focused on the importance of the attitudes and feelings of workers; informal roles and norms influenced performance.
Group dynamics	1940s	Encouraged individual participation in decision making; noted the impact of the work group on performance.
Leadership	1950s	Stressed the importance of groups having both social and task leaders; differentiated between Theory X and Theory Y management.
Integrative Perspectives		
Sociotechnical	1960s	Called for considering technology and work groups in understanding a work system.
Systems theory	1970s	Represented organizations as open systems with inputs, transformations, outputs, and feedback; stated that systems strive for equilibrium and experience equifinality.
Contingency theory	1970s	Emphasized the fit between organizational processes and characteristics of the situation; called for fitting the organization's structure to various contingencies.
Management roles	1970s	Emphasized that managerial work encompasses ten roles and three focuses: interpersonal contact, informational processing, and decision making.

Frederick Winslow Taylor (1856–1915). Supported in his efforts by Henry Gantt, Frank and Lillian Gilbreth, and Harrington Emerson, all of whom became famous in their own rights, Taylor is credited with developing the theory of scientific management.

Source: Historical Pictures Service, Inc., Chicago

thinking around the turn of the century, is often called the father of scientific management. Supported in his efforts by Henry L. Gantt, Frank and Lillian Gilbreth, and Harrington Emerson, all of whom became famous in their own right, Taylor is credited with developing the theory of scientific management.

Scientific management is the name given to the principles and practices that grew out of the work of Taylor and his followers and that are characterized by concern for efficiency and systematization in management. Taylor was convinced that the scientific method, which provides a logical framework for the analysis of problems, could be applied to the management process. The method consists of defining the problem, gathering data, analyzing the data, developing alternatives, and selecting the best alternative. Taylor believed that use of the scientific method would direct the manager to the most efficient way work could be performed. Thus, instead of abdicating responsibility for establishing standards, for example, management could scientifically study all facets of an operation and carefully set a logical and rational standard. Instead of guessing or relying solely on trial and error, management could go through the logical, though time-consuming, process of scientific research to develop answers to business problems. Taylor's philosophy is summarized as follows:

- Taylor proposed applying the scientific method to the practice of management to find the "one best way" to perform work.

- He suggested the use of scientific approaches to select employees who are best suited to perform a given job.

- He advanced the proposition that employees should be provided with scientific education, training, and development.

- He encouraged friendly interaction and cooperation between management and employees, but with a clear separation of duties between managers and workers.

- He advocated that managers take charge of all work that they are better prepared to accomplish, ending the pattern of placing most of the work and the greater part of the responsibility on the workers.[1]

Taylor believed that scientific management practices would benefit not only the employer, through increased output, but the workers as well, through increased income. But he stressed that scientific management would require both managers and employees to undergo a revolution in thinking.

The greater part of Taylor's work was oriented toward improving the management of production operations. The classic case of the pig iron experiment at the Bethlehem Steel Company illustrates his approach.[2] Laborers would pick up 92-pound pigs (chunks of iron) from a storage yard, walk up a plank onto a railroad car, and place the pigs in the car. Studying a group of seventy-five laborers, Taylor determined that the average output was about 12.5 tons per man per day. By applying the scientific method, he developed (1) an improved method of work, (2) a prescribed amount of rest on the job, (3) a specific standard of output, and (4) payment by the unit of output. After Taylor's recommendations were implemented, the average output per worker rose to 48 tons per day, and daily pay rose from $1.15 to $1.85 under the incentive system.

Taylor's dedication to the systematic planning and study of processes of all kinds pervaded his life. With a specially designed tennis racket, he played on a national doubles tennis championship team. When playing golf, he used clubs he designed

Lillian Gilbreth (1878–1972) and Frank Gilbreth (1868–1924). Frederick Taylor disciples Frank and Lillian Gilbreth concentrated on motion study to develop more efficient ways to pour concrete, lay bricks, and perform many other repetitive tasks. After Frank's death, Lillian continued their work alone, eventually becoming a professor of management at Purdue University. Until her death in 1972 she was considered the first lady of management.

Source: The Bettmann Archive

individually to achieve a predictable lie; his friends reportedly refused to play with him when he used a particular putter because of its accuracy.

Frank and Lillian Gilbreth concentrated on motion study to develop more efficient ways to pour concrete, lay bricks, and perform many other repetitive tasks. After Frank's death in 1924, Lillian continued their work alone, eventually becoming a professor of management at Purdue University. Until her death, in 1972, she was considered the first lady of management.

Henry Gantt developed a control chart that is used to this day in production operations. The Gantt chart is considered by some to have been the forerunner of modern PERT (program evaluation and review technique) analysis.

Henry L. Gantt (1861–1919). Henry L. Gantt, a colleague of Frederick W. Taylor, developed a control chart that is used to this day in production operations. The Gantt chart is considered by some to have been the forerunner of modern PERT (program evaluation and review technique) analysis.

Source: Historical Pictures Services, Inc., Chicago

Harrington Emerson set forth "twelve principles of efficiency" in his 1913 book of that title. Certain of Emerson's principles state that a manager should carefully define objectives, use the scientific method of analysis, develop and use standardized procedures, and reward employees for good work. His book remains a recognized management classic.

General Management Theory: The Classical School

In contrast to the proponents of scientific management, Henri Fayol and Chester I. Barnard developed a broader theory of general management that is identified today as the *classical* view of organizational theory. Fayol was a French manager who wrote at about the same time as Taylor, although his works were not widely available in English until 1930. Fayol's major contribution to management literature, *General and Industrial Management*, was not translated into English until long after both Taylor and Fayol had died. Once translated, however, it became very popular in the United States. Fayol's view of management theory complemented Taylor's scientific approach in many ways. Fayol listed the duties of a manager as planning, organizing, commanding employees, coordinating activities, and controlling performance.[3]

Barnard's ideas, expressed in his 1938 classic, *The Functions of the Executive*, have significantly influenced the theory and practice of management.[4] Barnard, who for years was president of New Jersey Bell Telephone, believed that the most important function of a manager is to promote cooperative effort toward realizing the goals of the organization. He believed that cooperation depends on effective communication and on a balance between rewards to and contributions by each employee.

Other proponents of general management, or classical, theory have identified four features of organizations. First, organizations should *specialize*, meaning workers should be organized according to logical groupings such as client, place of work, product, expertise, or functional area. Second, *unity of command* dictates that each organizational member should have exactly one supervisor. Third, the *scalar chain of command*, or the reporting relationships, should be clearly defined within a formal organizational structure, beginning with the chief administrator and extending to the least-skilled employee. Fourth, managers should *coordinate activities* using mechanisms that will ensure good communication among specialized groups.[5]

A Classical Theory of Bureaucracy

Max Weber, a German sociologist, addressed the issue of organizational administration in a somewhat different fashion. He studied European organization during the late 1800s and described a prototype form of organization that emphasizes order, system, rationality, uniformity, and consistency—a *bureaucracy*. Weber's writings were not widely read in the United States, however, until their English translation was published in 1947.[6] For many people, the term *bureaucracy* conjures up an image of massive red tape and endless unneeded details. Weber, on the other hand, believed bureaucracy led to the equitable treatment of all employees by management.[7] To the extent that bureaucratic organizations are impersonal and have strict rules, Weber saw these characteristics as ensuring fairness to all workers.[8]

In a bureaucracy, each employee has specified and official areas of responsibility that are assigned on the basis of competence and expertise. Like the classical schools, bureaucracy calls for an orderly system of supervision and subordination, a unity of command that specifies a single supervisor for each subordinate. Managers in a bureaucracy use written documents extensively in managing employees. Not only do rules and regulations exist, but they are translated into detailed employment manuals. Office managers and work groups also receive extensive training in their job requirements. Within this system, management must use rules that are consistent, complete, and learnable.

Decision Theory

In the 1950s, Herbert A. Simon and James G. March introduced the decision-making framework for understanding organizational behavior.[9] They elaborated on the bureaucratic model by emphasizing that individuals who work in rational organizations behave rationally. But their model (for which Simon won the Nobel prize for economics) added a new dimension: the idea that a human being's rationality is limited. The model suggests that individuals generally make decisions by examining a limited set of possible alternatives rather than all available options. Moreover, they do so by drawing on the rules and experience they have at hand. The model states further that individuals "satisfice"; that is, they choose adequate solutions to problems rather than seeking optimal choices.

Human Perspectives

When the structural perspectives of scientific management and classical, bureaucratic, and decision theory are applied to management, many organizational problems can be solved; but much of workers' dissatisfaction and resistance to change is not addressed by these theories. Seeking answers to the remaining problems, researchers began to focus on the *human* side of organizations, specifically on human relations, group dynamics, and leadership theory. The classical theory of the human relations school provides some insight into solving these problems.

Human Relations School

Beginning in 1924, the Western Electric Company, in conjunction with the National Academy of Sciences, performed five studies of various work groups at Western Electric's Hawthorne plant.[10] The first study looked at the effects of lighting on the productivity of workers in different departments of the company. In the tradition of scientific management, the study considered whether various illumination levels affected output positively or negatively. Researchers first increased the light to an extreme brightness and then decreased it until the work area was so dim that assembly materials could hardly be seen. Results showed that the workers maintained or even exceeded their normal output regardless of whether illumination was increased or decreased. But what explains this behavior?

Subsequent studies by Elton Mayo, Fritz (F. J.) Roethlisberger, William J. Dickson, and their colleagues examined the impact on output of pauses for rest, shorter working days and weeks, wage incentives, and the nature of supervision.[11] They speculated that something other than the physical work environment was responsible for improved productivity among workers. By observing and interviewing the employees, the researchers discovered that the employees, by participating in experiments, felt that someone cared about them. Their morale improved and they produced more. The influence that behavioral researchers can have on the people they study became known as the *Hawthorne effect*, marking the first dramatic indication that the attitudes and feelings of workers could significantly influence productivity.

On the basis of these findings, Western Electric interviewed workers regarding their feelings about work. Results of the interviews suggested even more strongly the close relationship between morale and the quality of supervision and led to the creation of a new training program for supervisors.

In the final experiments of the Hawthorne series, researchers identified one other human feature of organizations: the tendency for workers to develop informal groups. When the researchers observed a group from the bank-wiring room, they found that the workers had established among themselves informal roles and norms (expected standards of behavior) through which they controlled and restricted their productivity level. For example, workers could be identified as leaders or followers; *rate-busters*—those who produced more than the level acceptable to the leaders—were ostracized by the group, as were those who produced too little.

Group Dynamics

Because of a shortage of meat during World War II, Kurt Lewin, a social psychologist at the University of Iowa, was asked to study methods of changing housewives' dietary habits to decrease meat consumption.[12] Lewin believed that the women were expected by their families, parents, and other housewives not to serve other kinds of food; this norm created a significant barrier to change. He suggested that the way to break down the barrier was to give the housewives the opportunity to discuss and make decisions themselves about the types of foods to serve. The results of the experiments conducted by Lewin and his associates supported his ideas about participation. Housewives who joined in group discussions were ten times more likely to change their food habits than were housewives who received lectures on the subject.[13]

Lewin's associates later extended these experiments to industrial settings. For example, Lester Coch and John R. P. French, Jr., found that employees at the Harwood pajama plant in Marion, Virginia, were much more likely to learn new work methods if they were given the opportunity to discuss the methods and to have some influence on how to apply them to their jobs.[14] Studies such as these led to a greatly expanded awareness of the impact of the work group and spawned research on the relationship between organizational effectiveness and group formation, development, behavior, and attitudes.[15]

Leadership

The 1950s marked the beginning of concentrated research in the area of leadership, as theorists such as Robert F. Bales and Douglas McGregor examined the roles of managers and leaders in organizations.[16] Bales postulated the importance of groups having both task and social leaders. The *task leader* helps the group achieve its goals by clarifying and summarizing member comments and focusing on the group's tasks.

The *social leader* maintains the group and helps it develop cohesiveness and collaboration by encouraging group members' involvement.

McGregor described two types of managers.[17] Those who adhere to Theory X believe that workers have an inherent dislike of work, must be controlled and threatened with punishment if they are to put forth adequate effort, and prefer to avoid responsibility. Managers who follow Theory Y, on the other hand, believe that employees find work as natural as play or rest, exercise self-direction toward the objectives to which they are committed (requiring less strict control), and can learn to seek responsibility. McGregor, together with other researchers, postulated that the assumptions managers hold affect the way they treat their employees and thus affect employees' productivity.

Integrative Perspectives

Organizational thought in the past few decades has emphasized the integration of structural and human perspectives. More recently, contingency theory has added an emphasis on fitting organizational features to the work situation.

Sociotechnical School

In the 1950s, several theorists began studying technology and its interaction with functioning work groups. The *sociotechnical school* assumed that managers could exclude neither technology (representing organizational structure) nor work groups (reflecting human relations) in trying to understand a work system. The most notable members of the sociotechnical school were E. L. Trist, K. W. Bamforth, A. K. Rice, and F. E. Emery.[18]

Trist and Bamforth described a change in technology in a British coal mine where workers were used to working independently in small, self-contained units in which they organized the work themselves.[19] When the technology for mining coal improved, management was required to increase job specialization and decrease the workers' participation in job assignments. According to scientific management and classical management traditions, greater job specialization should have increased productivity. But the coal miners hated the specialization; they much preferred working closely with one another and performing a variety of tasks.

Trist and Bamforth compared the performance of work groups whose jobs had become specialized to that of work groups that retained their original social structure when the new technology was introduced. They found that absenteeism was several times greater and productivity much lower in the specialized groups. Researchers concluded after a number of such studies that technological changes must be made in conjunction with a strong social system—that both social and technical aspects of jobs must be considered simultaneously.

Systems Theory

According to Harold Koontz, "The systems approach requires that the physical, human, and capital resources be interrelated and coordinated within the external and internal environment of an organization."[20] Systems theory, which offers an integrated and comprehensive view of organizational functioning, evolved from economic, sociological, psychological, and natural science theories and includes human, structural, environmental, technological, and other concerns.

The general systems model described by Daniel Katz and Robert L. Kahn, among others, represents an organization as an open system, one that interacts with environmental forces and factors, much like physical systems such as the human body, a microscopic organism, or a cell.[21] First, a system consists of a number of interdependent and interrelated subsystems; second, the organization is open and dynamic; third, it strives for equilibrium; and fourth, it has multiple purposes, objectives, and functions, some of which are in conflict.

Subsystems vary in size from the smallness of an individual cell to the largeness of a major division of an organization. To trace subsystems in organizations, the observer generally must specify significant individuals and groups and examine their interdependence. Typical subsystems include individual employees, work teams, departments, and management groups.

As described in Chapter 2, an organization as a system is also open and dynamic; that is, it continually receives new energy in the form of resources (people, materials, and money) or information (concerning strategy, environment, and history) from the environment. This new energy, called *inputs,* is then *transformed* into new *outputs.*

The key organizational components that change inputs into outputs are *transformation processes.* These processes include the interactions among the tasks, the individuals, the formal organizational arrangements, and the informal organization.[22] The transformation of inputs creates changes in individual, group, and organizational behaviors and attitudes.

When organizations receive new inputs or experience certain transformations, they simultaneously seek balance, or equilibrium. When organizations become unbalanced, or experience disequilibrium—for example, when changes in the environment make current staffing inadequate—they attempt to return to a steady state, which may mirror or significantly differ from the original state of equilibrium. They use information about their outputs, called *feedback,* to modify their inputs or transformations to attain the result of more desirable outcomes and equilibrium.

Assume, for example, that worker performance has declined significantly. This information cues the organization to examine the nature of its inputs and transformations for a cause. The feedback may subsequently pinpoint changes in employee training or reward systems as causes. It may also indicate which subsystems in the organization have similar goals and which have different ones.

Finally, organizations as open systems demonstrate equifinality. *Equifinality* suggests that organizations may employ a variety of means to achieve their desired objectives. No single structure results in a predetermined set of inputs, outputs, and transformations. Introducing a more open and participatory structure does not necessarily result in increased productivity; increasing the level of individual involvement in decision making does not necessarily change worker attitudes. Thus, organizations that survive *adapt* to a particular situation. They respond to changes in the environment with appropriate changes in the system.

Contingency Theory

The concept of management based on the idea that there are no universal rules but that the correct management technique depends on the surrounding circumstances is *contingency theory*.[23] It emphasizes the fit between organizational processes and characteristics of the situation.

Early contingency research looked at the fit between an organization's structure and its environment. Tom Burns and George Stalker described two radically different types of management systems: mechanistic (machinelike) and organic (living, human, and flexible).[24] Mechanistic systems have characteristics such as those described in the scientific and classical management traditions—for example, rigid structure and strict lines of authority. Organic systems are much more flexible and loosely structured and allow more employee influence over decisions.

Joan Woodward found that the type of structure an organization develops (and should develop) is influenced by the organization's technology, whether the technology is unit, mass-production, or continuous-process.[25] She suggested that a mechanistic type of organization fits best with mass-production technology—producing pins, lifting pig iron, or manufacturing heavy equipment. A more organic form of organization responds best to a unit (craft) or continuous-process technology (for example, that of a gas refinery).

Recent thinking in organization design has reemphasized the importance of fitting organizational structure to various contingencies. Thus, contingency theory has been extended to job design, leadership, group dynamics, and power relations. (See Chapters 10, 11, 13, and 14 for discussions of these areas.)

Management Roles Approach

Harvard professor Henry Mintzberg, in studying what managers do, observed that managerial work encompasses ten roles. Three of the roles focus on *interpersonal contact*: (1) figurehead, (2) leader, and (3) liaison; three involve mainly *information processing*: (1) monitor, (2) disseminator, and (3) spokesperson; and four relate to *decision making*: (1) entrepreneur, (2) disturbance handler, (3) resource allocator, and (4) negotiator.[26]

The roles that focus on interpersonal contact are described as follows:

1. *Figurehead.* The manager, acting as a symbol or representative of the organization, performs diverse ceremonial duties. By attending chamber of commerce meetings, heading the local United Way drive, or representing the president of the firm at an awards banquet, a manager performs the figurehead role.

2. *Leader.* The manager, interacting with subordinates, motivates and develops them. The supervisor who conducts annual performance interviews or selects training opportunities for subordinates performs this role.

3. *Liaison.* The manager establishes a network of contacts to gather information for the organization. Belonging to professional associations or meeting over lunch with peers in other organizations helps the manager perform the liaison role.

The roles that involve mainly information processing are described as follows:

1. *Monitor.* The manager gathers information from the environment inside and outside the organization. The manager may attend meetings with subordinates, scan company publications, or participate in companywide committees as a way of performing this role.

2. *Disseminator.* The manager transmits both factual and value information to subordinates. The manager may conduct staff meetings, send memorandums to staff members, or meet informally with staff members on a one-to-one basis to discuss current and future projects.

3. *Spokesperson.* The manager gives information to people outside the organization about its performance and policies. The manager who oversees preparation of the annual report, prepares advertising copy, or speaks at community and professional meetings fulfills this role.

The roles related to decision making are described as follows:

1. *Entrepreneur.* The manager designs and initiates change in the organization. The supervisor who redesigns the job of subordinates, introduces flextime to the workplace, or brings new technology to a job performs this role.

2. *Disturbance handler.* The manager deals with problems that arise when organizational operations break down. A manager who finds a new supplier on short notice for an out-of-stock part, replaces unexpectedly absent employees on a project, or deals with machine breakdowns performs this role.

3. *Resource allocator.* The manager controls the allocation of people, money, materials, and time by scheduling his or her own time, programming subordinates' work efforts, and authorizing all significant decisions. Preparation of a budget is a major aspect of this role.

4. *Negotiator.* The manager participates in negotiation activities. A manager who hires a new employee may negotiate work assignments or compensation with that person.

Not all managers perform every role listed here, but some diversity of role performance always occurs. The choice of roles depends on the manager's specific job description and the situation in question. An examination of the manager's work role suggests that leadership is only one of many roles, but one that is essential to effective management.

Mintzberg's view of managerial behavior offers a perspective that complements those of various organizational behavior theories, including theories of perception, attribution, motivation, communication, personal development, group dynamics, and leadership theory. The roles he identified emphasize the individual and motivation (interpersonal roles), communication (information roles), and leadership and decision making (decisional roles).

Notes

1. Frederick W. Taylor, *The Principles of Scientific Management* (New York: Harper & Bros., 1911), pp. 36–37.

2. Taylor, *Principles of Scientific Management*, pp. 41–47.

3. Henri Fayol, *General and Industrial Management*, trans. C. Storrs (London: Pitman, 1949).

4. Chester I. Barnard, *The Functions of the Executive* (Cambridge, Mass.: Harvard University Press, 1938; rev. eds. 1950, 1988).

5. L. Gulick and L. Urwick, eds., *Papers on the Science of Administration* (New York: Columbia University Institute

of Public Administration, 1937), and J. D. Mooney and A. C. Reiley, *Onward Industry* (New York: Harper & Bros., 1931), offered complementary views of management.

6. Max Weber, *The Theory of Social and Economic Organization*, ed. and trans. A. M. Henderson and T. Parsons (New York: Oxford University Press, 1947).

7. R. M. Weiss, "Weber on Bureaucracy: Management Consultant or Political Theorist?" *Academy of Management Review* 8 (April 1983): 242–248, argues that Weber was not concerned with prescribing the characteristics of an efficient organization but rather was solely offering political theory.

8. Max Weber, *Essays on Sociology*, ed. and trans. H. H. Gerth and C. W. Mills (New York: Oxford University Press, 1947), pp. 196–198.

9. Herbert A. Simon, *Administrative Behavior*, 2d ed. (New York: Macmillan, 1957); and James G. March and Herbert A. Simon, *Organizations* (New York: Wiley, 1958).

10. C. E. Snow, "A Discussion of the Relation of Illumination Intensity to Productive Efficiency," *Tech Engineering News*, November 1927; cited in F. J. Roethlisberger and William J. Dickson, *Management and the Worker* (Cambridge, Mass.: Harvard University Press, 1939).

11. Roethlisberger and Dickson, *Management and the Worker*.

12. Kurt Lewin, "Forces behind Food Habits and Methods of Change," *Bulletin of the National Research Council* 108 (1943): 35–65.

13. M. Radke and D. Klisurich, "Experiments in Changing Food Habits," *Journal of the American Dietetics Association* 23 (1947): 403–409.

14. Lester Coch and John R. P. French, Jr., "Overcoming Resistance to Change," *Human Relations* 1 (1948): 512–533.

15. See C. S. Bartlem and E. A. Locke, "The Coch and French Study: A Critique and Reinterpretation," *Human Relations* 34 (July 1981): 555–566, for another view of the significance of research about participation.

16. Robert F. Bales, "Task Roles and Social Roles in Problem Solving Groups," in *Readings in Social Psychology*, 3d ed., ed. E. Maccoby, T. M. Newcomb, and E. L. Hartley (New York: Holt, Rinehart & Winston, 1958), pp. 437–447; and Douglas McGregor, *The Human Side of Enterprise* (New York: McGraw-Hill, 1960).

17. McGregor, *Human Side of Enterprise*; and E. H. Schein, *The Hawthorne Group Studies Revisited: A Defense of Theory Y*, Working Paper #756–74 (Cambridge, Mass.: M.I.T. Sloan School of Management, December, 1974).

18. E. L. Trist and K. W. Bamforth, "Some Social and Psychological Consequences of the Long Wall Method of Coal Getting," *Human Relations* 4 (1951): 3–38; A. K. Rice, *The Enterprise and Its Environment* (London: Tavistock, 1963); and F. E. Emery and I. L. Trist, *Socio-Technical Systems*, vol. 2 of *Management Science: Models and Techniques* (London: Pergamon, 1960).

19. Trist and Bamforth, "Some Social and Psychological Consequences."

20. Harold Koontz, "The Management Theory Jungle Revisited," *Academy of Management Review* 5 (April 1980): 175.

21. D. Katz and R. L. Kahn, *The Social Psychology of Organizations*, 2d ed. (New York: Wiley, 1978).

22. D. A. Nadler and M. L. Tushman, "A Diagnostic Model for Organizational Behavior," in *Perspectives on Behavior in Organizations*, ed. J. R. Hackman, L. W. Porter, and E. E. Lawler III (New York: McGraw-Hill, 1977).

23. Koontz, "The Management Theory Jungle Revisited," p. 176.

24. T. Burns and G. M. Stalker, *The Management of Innovation* (London: Tavistock, 1961).

25. J. Woodward, *Industrial Organization: Theory and Practice* (London: Oxford University Press, 1965); and P. Lawrence and J. Lorsch, *Organization and Environment* (Boston: Harvard Business School Division of Research, 1967).

26. Henry Mintzberg, *The Nature of Managerial Work*, 2d ed. (Englewood Cliffs, N.J.: Prentice-Hall, 1979).

3

Social Responsibility and Business Ethics

LEARNING OBJECTIVES

After completing this chapter students should be able to

- Describe the concept of corporate social responsibility.
- Explain what is meant by stakeholder analysis and the social contract.
- Describe the changing values toward social responsibility and the business-goverment interface.
- Explain the concept of ethics.
- Describe business ethics and the social audit.

Sam Walton of Wal-Mart fame is praised for his many accomplishments in the field of retailing. Among these accomplishments is making Wal-Mart the number 1 retailer in the United States. Wal-Mart stock performance continues to amaze industry experts and some experts view Wal-Mart as unstoppable. Many aspects of the Wal-Mart operation contribute to their success, but none more than Wal-Mart's sense of social responsibility and proper ethical behavior.

These aspects may well be among the most important, but least mentioned, of Sam Walton's contributions to the business world. Wal-Mart has a very strong sense of social responsibility. Wal-Mart has ushered in the "green" era in retailing. They are looking for "Quality Products That Are Guaranteed Not To Last." Wal-Mart has challenged their manufacturers to "Improve Their Products, To Help Prevent Lasting Environmental Problems." Wal-Mart's goal is to provide their customers with the option of purchasing environmentally-improved products. Specifically, Wal-Mart is encouraging their manufacturers to: produce recyclable products or packaging, make products or packaging from recycled materials, produce packaging systems that are refillable or reusable, produce concentrated products that reduce package volume and waste, manufacture in a way that is safe for our land, air, and water, and produce products that are safe for the environment. In addition, employees are strongly encouraged to recycle. Wal-Mart is switching to recycled paper and is setting up recycling centers for paper, plastics, aluminum, and batteries. Wal-Mart is also involved in plans such as "Adopt-A-Highway" and "Adopt-A-Beach."

In addition to a strong sense of social responsibility, this retailer lives by a strict code of ethics. Wal-Mart is going above and beyond what is considered ethical, and is focusing on treating others as they would like to be treated. The retailer's code of ethics is part of their daily way of doing business. A few of the ways that Wal-Mart practices what they preach are listed in their ethical code. According to this code, associates will avoid any social contact with vendors; gifts and gratuities will never be accepted; harassment of any type will not be tolerated; company supplies and property will not be used for personal gain; managers will work at all times to control expenses and to do more with less; all employees are associate-partners and will be treated as such, and associates will at all times be friendly, committed to open communication, and will encourage the sharing of ideas, observations, problems, and concerns regarding the company.

Wal-Mart's Annual Report echoes this sense of social responsibility and ethical correctness. Sam Walton summed it all up this way, "We Care."[1] The world will truly miss Sam Walton who passed away in 1992.

Wal-Mart management believes that their position is clearly enhanced by being socially responsible and ethically aware. Wal-Mart management views social responsibility and ethical behavior as good business. Most questions regarding corporate social responsibility are not clear-cut, and seldom are answers simply right or wrong. However, Wal-Mart makes every attempt to be clear in their approach to social responsibility and is quite definitive about their ethical expectations. Wal-Mart has behaved responsibly and managed to produce profits for stockholders, preserve jobs for employees, comply with government regulations, and provide a product to consumers at everyday low prices.

This chapter examines a number of basic issues of corporate social responsibility and business ethics. First it explains the concept of corporate social responsibility. Then it discusses stakeholder analysis and the social contract that exists between the organization and other elements of society. Following that discussion is a description of traditional and modern views concerning the social responsibilities of business. The next three sections of the chapter discuss the business-government interface, present a model of ethics, and address the specific topic of business ethics. The last topics covered are the social audit, which is used to evaluate social performance, and a global perspective of business ethics.

Corporate Social Responsibility

Social responsibility

The implied, enforced, or felt obligation of managers, acting in their official capacity, to serve or protect the interests of groups other than themselves.

When a corporation behaves as if it has a conscience, it is said to be socially responsible. **Social responsibility** is *the implied, enforced, or felt obligation of managers, acting in their official capacity, to serve or protect the interests of groups other than themselves.* Remember that Wal-Mart is encouraging their manufacturers to: produce recyclable products or packaging, make products or packaging from recycled materials, produce packaging systems that are refillable or reusable, produce concentrated products that reduce package volume and waste, manufacture in a way that is safe for our land, air, and water, and produce products which are safe for the environment.

A corporation's approach to social responsibility is usually determined by its top executives.[2] More frequently than ever, corporate executives appear to be making decisions that closely parallel the expectations of society.[3] One *Business Week* study indicates that senior executives have begun to increase their emphasis on corporate social responsibility. The same seems to be true of boards of directors. The reporters found that "rubber-stamp boards" were on the wane. They unearthed a number of examples of directors correcting irresponsible decisions, firing inept and unethical CEOs, and, in general, behaving in a socially responsible manner.[4]

Many companies take action that tends to promote a corporate culture that emphasizes concern for moral issues. This is done through policy statements, practices over time, and the leadership of morally strong individuals. Some companies have programs of community involvement for their employees and managers. They cooperate with fund drives such as the United Way's. Open-door policies, grievance procedures, and employee benefit programs often stem as much from a desire to do what is right as from a concern for productivity and the avoidance of strife. In fact, some argue that a corporation itself can have a conscience, which could result in socially responsible behavior on a consistent basis.[5]

Some companies have programs of community involvement for their employees and managers. It is important that top-level managers set the example. Here, a senior Citgo official lends a hand during the Jerry Lewis MDA Telethon. A major portion of charitable giving is by corporations.

Source: Photograph courtesy of CITGO Petroleum Corporation

It appears that the larger the number of stockholders a corporation has, the more committed management is to a sense of social responsibility. For example, the environment service department at Allied Chemical, a major publicly held company, is charged with controlling air and water pollution and with maintaining safe and healthful working conditions for employees. The manager of that department reports directly to the company president. Koppers Company, which manufactures foam insulation and also sells tar, wood, and coke, has two committees of outside directors, one concerned with the environment and the other with human resources. At least twice a year, company management must account to these two committees about the company's efforts in the area of social responsibility.

Others believe a sense of social responsibility cannot be segmented and compartmentalized into departments and committees but should pervade all levels of the company. When Coca-Cola's treatment of migrant field workers made national headlines because of an investigative reporter's articles, a special project was established at the direction of the president of Coca-Cola's food division. Expenditures on housing, education, and health services for migrant workers have now been integrated into the company's regular activities.

It is interesting to consider how managers of many U.S. corporations like Dow Chemical, AT&T, BankAmerica, Federal Express, 3M, and Whirlpool are beginning to realize that economic and social values can at times be co-aligned. Dow Chemical invested $20 million in pollution control in a plant in Michigan. The yearly cost to run the pollution control equipment was $10.5 million. Dow claims to have recovered its costs through reduced corrosion on cooling towers and by the saving of valuable chemicals previously pumped out as waste. In three years' time, over $6 million was saved in recovery of these wasted chemicals alone. Another example of such a co-alignment involved the recycling of paper by several U.S. corporations. AT&T,

BankAmerica, Federal Express, 3M, and Whirlpool are finding that recycling is good for society, saves them disposal costs, and also pulls in profits.[6] In the future, even more corporate managers are likely to realize that responsible behavior is also good business, and they will probably search for additional ways to be socially responsible and save money.

Most Americans would not have predicted the kind of socially responsible actions described here. In fact, during the 1980s, managers and the corporations they worked for were subjected to considerable criticism and received low levels of approval from the public. Hardly a week passed without news headlines of corporate misconduct. Pollster Louis Harris found that 70 percent of the public believed "business *does not* see to it that its executives behave legally and ethically."[7]

Chrysler Corporation was indicted on charges it had disconnected the odometers of more than 60,000 vehicles driven by company managers before selling them as new automobiles. On Wall Street, insider trading scandals did much to lower the trust of the general public in the stock market. It is not surprising that a survey by Opinion Research Corporation found that 75 percent of the public agreed that business neglects the problems of society and 65 percent believed business executives "do everything they can to make a profit, even if it means ignoring the public's needs."[8] Business executives were considered less ethical than doctors and lawyers, although more ethical than members of Congress.[9] Clearly, the public had little confidence in the goodness of business.

Some experts believe businesses are increasingly willing to accept their societal responsibilities and that managers are becoming more ethical. They find that managers are more socially responsible and ethical than were their counterparts a generation ago. According to social theorist Archie B. Carroll, however, the demands made on business and the expectations of what is considered proper conduct have risen faster than the ability of business to raise its standards. Carroll suggests that the ethical level of "actual business practices" will continue to rise, but not as quickly as "society's expectations of business."[10] Because of this discrepancy, the public's esteem for business will probably remain low, while business actually becomes more and more socially responsible. In order to meet the expectations of society, future managers will need to strive to be more ethical and socially responsible.

Today, business organizations are expected to assume broader and more diverse responsibilities to the various groups in society. However, critics argue that there is more lip service than action, more public relations programs than concrete socially responsible activities. Nevertheless, social responsibility is an area on which the modern business firm must take a stance, accompanied by appropriate policies and activities. Social responsibility can be understood in terms of the social contract that exists between a firm and its environment.

Stakeholder Analysis and the Social Contract

Organizational stakeholder

An individual or group whose interests are affected by organizational activities.

Most organizations, whether profit or nonprofit, have a large number of stakeholders. An **organizational stakeholder** is *an individual or group whose interests are affected by organizational activities.* Although all stakeholders are affected by the organization, managers may not acknowledge responsibility to all of them. As was mentioned earlier, corporate boards of directors increasingly hold management accountable for

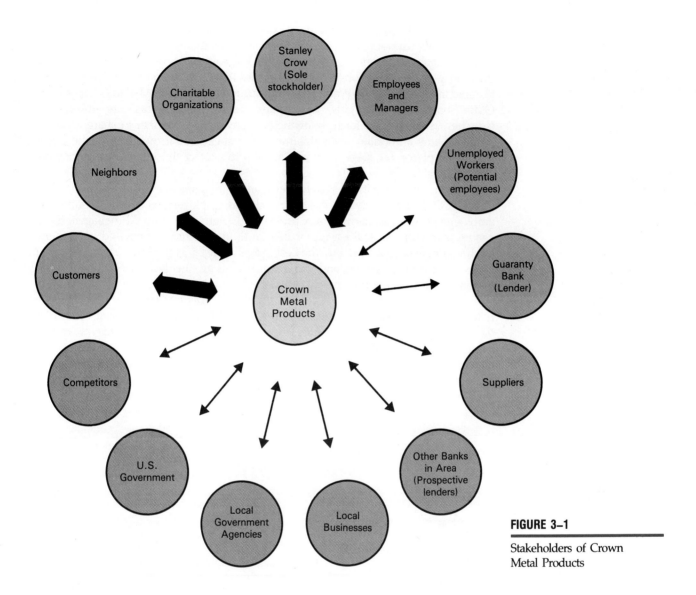

FIGURE 3–1

Stakeholders of Crown
Metal Products

putting the interest of stakeholders first. In the 1970s, noted management writer Peter Drucker stated, "There is one thing all boards have in common . . . they do not function." That statement is less true today than when he uttered it. According to Kenneth A. Macke, CEO of Dayton-Hudson Corporation, boards "are thinking through the process of corporate governance—what they are responsible for—and going into more detail about it." Drucker readily admitted that boards were changing, but he maintained that they were not responsible enough and that they worked well only "in the case of a catastrophe."[11]

Some of the stakeholders for Crown Metal Products, a small manufacturer of metal furniture near Boise, Idaho, are shown in Figure 3–1. But only a few, identified by bold arrows, are viewed as constituencies by Crown management.

The actions of many corporate executives are designed to serve interests other than those of the common shareholder. For example, a number of managements have recently placed large amounts of company stock in employee stock ownership trusts for the purpose of avoiding takeover attempts that were clearly in the interests of common shareholders. This benefited the employees, of course, but it also helped the managers keep their jobs. Major companies that have taken these kinds of actions to avoid takeovers include Walt Disney Productions and Martin Marietta Corporation. Other companies make gifts of company resources, often cash, to universities, churches, clubs, and so forth, knowing that any possible benefit to shareholders is remote. Some authorities favor this trend and suggest that members of the public should be placed on major corporate boards to protect the interests of nonowner stakeholders.[12]

Protecting the diversity of stakeholder interests requires answering such questions as these: During an economic downturn, should employees be afforded continuous employment, even if this will hurt profits in the long run? Should managers try to ensure that suppliers make a reasonable profit on the items purchased from them, or should managers simply buy the best inputs available at the lowest price possible? Should a company go beyond the requirements of the law in cleaning up the environment if competitors barely comply with the law?

Answering such questions is termed *stakeholder analysis.* One approach to stakeholder analysis involves consideration of the social contract. The **social contract** is *the set of written and unwritten rules and assumptions about acceptable interrelationships among the various elements of society.* Much of the social contract is embedded in the customs of society. For example, in integrating minorities into the work force, society has come to expect companies to do more than the law requires. When a company such as Wal-Mart behaves in an especially commendable way, its actions tend to increase the expectations society has concerning other companies.

Social contract

The set of written and unwritten rules and assumptions about acceptable interrelationships among the various elements of society.

FIGURE 3–2

The Social Contract

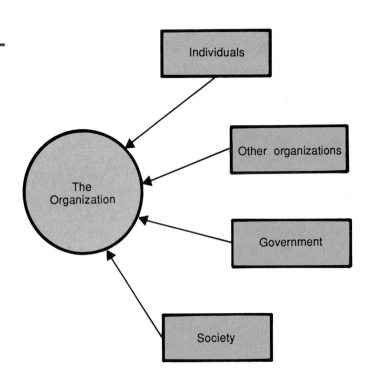

Some of the "contract provisions" result from practices of the parties to the contract. Like a legal contract, the social contract often involves a quid pro quo (something exchanged for something). One party to the contract behaves in a certain way and expects a certain pattern of behavior from the other. For example, a relationship of trust may have developed between a manufacturer and the community in which it operates. Because of this, each will inform the other well in advance of any planned action that might cause harm, such as the phasing down of a plant's operations by the company. The widespread belief that such a relationship was rare prompted Congress to pass the Worker Adjustment and Retraining Notification Act of 1988. That law requires firms employing a hundred or more workers to give sixty days' notice to employees and local government officials when a plant closing or layoff affecting fifty or more employees for a ninety-day period is planned.

The social contract concerns relationships with individuals, government, other organizations, and society in general, as Figure 3–2 illustrates. Each of these relationships will be considered individually in the following sections. First, though, it is interesting to consider how Exxon Corporation found itself constrained by the social contract as it tried to manage the aftermath of its huge oil spill near Valdez, Alaska.

• •

On March 24, 1989, the *Exxon Valdez* oil tanker ran aground in Alaska's Prince William Sound, spilling 10 million gallons of crude oil. The oil spoiled hundreds of miles of the pristine coastline. Tankers carried a fourth of the U.S. crude oil supply from the Trans-Alaska pipeline to other states. But there was no plan, and little equipment available, to handle such a large spill.

The **Exxon Valdez** *and the Alaska Oil Spill*

The spill was clearly Exxon's fault. The ship was being illegally piloted by a third mate while the captain, who had been drinking, stayed below. A judge later said of the incident, "These are misdemeanors of such magnitude they have never been equaled in this country." Yet, according to former Alaska governor Steve Cowper, "There was almost [no cleanup equipment] on the scene for the first 18 hours." A huge public outcry in the United States and elsewhere brought presidential and congressional intervention. The Coast Guard took charge of the area, demanding that Exxon prepare to pay the bill. A partial boycott of Exxon products throughout the United States increased the pressure on the company. Environmental groups and the international press highlighted the company's slow and bungling actions. Exxon yielded and began to sponsor the frantic cleanup effort, which would eventually cost over $1.25 billion. Less than a third of the cost was covered by insurance.

And the fray was far from over. In July 1989, an internal Exxon memorandum was leaked to the press. The memo said the company intended to unilaterally suspend the cleanup on September 15 of that year, with much of the coast still befouled. The resulting verbal assault came from all sides. Senior Exxon officials were soon sheepishly explaining that they would continue testing through the winter and continue consulting with all interested parties. Still, federal prosecutors rejected plea bargain proposals by Exxon, and a federal grand jury indicted the company on several criminal counts related to the spill in early 1990. Exxon announced in March that year that its crews were renewing the cleanup effort.[13]

• •

Obligations to Individuals

Individuals often find healthy outlets for their energies through joining organizations. From the church, they expect guidance, ministerial services, and fellowship, and they devote time and money to its sustenance. From their employers, they expect a fair day's pay for a fair day's work—and perhaps much more. Many expect to be paid for time off to vote, perform jury service, and so forth. Clubs and associations provide opportunities for fellowship and for community service. Customers expect to be catered to. To some degree, most of society still subscribes to the notion that the customer is king. To the extent that individuals' expectations are acknowledged as responsibilities by the organization, they become part of the social contract.

Obligations to Other Organizations

Managers must be concerned with relationships involving other organizations—both organizations that are like their own, such as competitors, and very different ones. Commercial businesses are expected to compete with one another on an honorable basis, without subterfuge or reckless unconcern for their mutual rights. Charities such as the United Way expect support from business, often including the loan of executives to help with annual fund drives. At the same time, such institutions are expected to come hat in hand to business managers, requesting rather than demanding assistance.

In the traditional view of social responsibility, which we discuss later in the chapter, business best meets its obligations through pursuit of its own interests. Some companies view the social contract mainly in terms of the company's interests. For example, FMC Corporation, a major diversified manufacturer, has firm policies about how it will direct its contributions. The basic criteria FMC applies are that contributions must help areas around company facilities or where its employees live and that gifts must improve the corporation's business environment.[14] FMC might contribute to a

Gifted high school seniors in the Pittsburgh area meet leading scientists to learn about latest developments in science and technology. Scientists from the Westinghouse R & D Center volunteer to present lectures at twelve Saturday sessions. Nearly 300 students participated in this "Honors Institute." Here, Dave Moon is shown working with a student.

Source: Photograph courtesy of Westinghouse Corporation

business college in an area where it has a plant, but it would not make gifts to distant universities.

Obligations to Government

Government is an important party to the social contract for every kind of organization. Under the auspices of government, companies have a license to do business, along with patent rights, trademarks, and so forth. Churches are often incorporated under state laws and given nonprofit status. Many quasigovernment agencies, such as the Federal Deposit Insurance Corporation, regional planning commissions, and school boards, have been given special missions by government.

In addition, organizations are expected to recognize the need for order rather than anarchy and to accept some government intervention in organizational affairs. On the international scene, many businesses got very disturbed when the move toward democratic reform in China was sidetracked. In fact, the 1989 massacre of students and other dissidents in Tiananmen Square in Beijing raised fears of civil war. But top CEOs predicted that U.S. companies would remain in China and help resolve the problems. The market in China is so massive that businesses were apparently willing to take considerable risk to remain there. By doing so, they certainly accepted some chance of anarchy or government intervention in their affairs.[15]

Obligations to Society in General

The traditional view of business responsibility has been that businesses should produce and distribute goods and services in return for a profit. Businesses have performed this function effectively, giving the United States one of the highest overall standards of living in the world. A high percentage of the population has its basic needs for food, clothing, shelter, health, and education reasonably well satisfied. And most citizens are afforded some leisure time. Profitable firms are able to pay taxes to the government and make donations to charities. All this should be a matter of some pride for business owners and managers.

The main reason for the exceptional productivity of the United States is perhaps the manner in which the free enterprise economic system operates. The profit motive provides incentive to businesses to produce goods and services efficiently. Practically every firm tries to curb costs in order to keep prices low enough to attract customers and still allow for profit. Some believe this focus on profits through cost cutting causes quality to be neglected as a competitive tool.[16]

Businesses operate by public consent with the basic purpose of satisfying the needs of society. As those needs are more fully met, society demands more of all of its institutions, particularly large business firms. Here are some of the goals businesses are expected to help society meet:

- Elimination of poverty.
- Provision of quality health care.
- Preservation of the environment by reductions in the level of pollution.
- Provision of a sufficient number of jobs and career opportunities for all members of society.

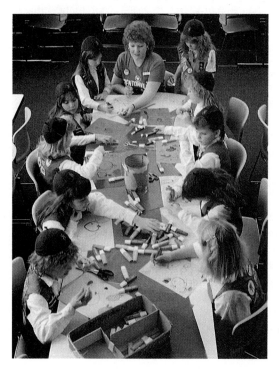

Companies like Wal-Mart carefully monitor their interactions with society. The Helen Robson Walton Award is given annually to the two most deserving Wal-Mart stores. Selections are based upon the number and quality of projects, the level of community support, and the financial success of the project. In tiny Bentonville, Arkansas, where Wal-Mart is headquartered, a local Brownie chapter benefits from the spirit of volunteerism fostered by Wal-Mart founder, Sam Walton.

Source: Photograph Courtesy of Wal-Mart Stores, Inc.

- Improvement in the quality of working life of employees.
- Provision of safe, livable communities with good housing and efficient transportation.[17]

As responsible corporate citizens, businesses should follow the spirit of the law as well as the letter. Many companies that created huge hazardous waste dumps throughout the country now defend themselves by saying that the dumps were legal when created. But the fact is that the laws and regulations controlling hazardous waste dumping were meant to protect the public health, and the dumping of certain concentrations of substances was prohibited. In many cases, dangerous but unregulated substances and harmful (though legal) concentrations of other substances were dumped over an extended period of years. For example, in the notorious Love Canal incident, property previously used by Hooker Chemical Company as a waste dump was sold to developers, who built houses and public buildings on it. The result is that the public health in the affected areas has been endangered. It is clear that society now considers this unacceptable.

In the sixteenth century, Sir Thomas More said, "If virtue were profitable, common sense would make us good, and greed would make us saintly."[18] More knew that virtue is not profitable, so people must make hard ethical choices from time to time. Common sense hardly makes one good. Still, some social theorists continue to believe that social responsibility is just a matter of "managerial self-interest."[19] In the United States today, the consensus is clear. Corporate strategists are being held to a higher standard than just pursuing their own interests, or even those of stockholders; they must consider the interests of other groups too.

Society's broadening expectations of business are illustrated in Figure 3–3. The inner circle, Level I, represents the traditional economic function of business. The economic function remains the primary responsibility of businesses to society. Businesses produce needed goods and services, provide employment, contribute to economic growth, and earn a profit. Level II recognizes the responsibility of business to perform the economic function but with an awareness of changing social goals, values, and demands. Management must demonstrate concern for, among other things, the efficient utilization of resources, the reduction of environmental pollution, the employment and development of disadvantaged minorities and women, and the safety of employees and customers. The actions of Hershey Chocolate Company following the Three Mile Island nuclear incident provide an example of Level II concern. Located near the nuclear plant, Hershey immediately instituted a careful testing program for milk received from within seventy-five miles of Three Mile Island and isolated all milk coming from within ten miles. A Hershey executive said, "While we have no indication of anything wrong with any product, if we are going to err, we want to err on the safe side."[20]

Level III, the outer circle, illustrates corporate responsibility for assisting society in achieving such broad goals as the elimination of poverty and urban decay through a partnership of business, government agencies, and other private institutions. Although the responsibilities in Level III are not primary obligations of business, business has shown increasing interest in such voluntary social actions. By encouraging

FIGURE 3–3

Primary Roles of Business

recycling, Wal-Mart went beyond simply carrying out economic functions. This is an example of Level III concern.

Changing Values and Social Responsibility

Numerous associations of respected business leaders, including the American Management Association and the Committee for Economic Development, have encouraged corporations and managers to become involved in socially responsible activities. In a climate of changing social values, these groups have stressed such programs as the following:

- Better jobs and promotion opportunities for minorities and women.
- Financial support for education.
- Financial and managerial help aimed at improving health and medical care.
- A safer working environment.
- Leadership and financial support for urban renewal.
- Reduction of environmental pollution.

Iron law of responsibility
The rule, first stated by Keith Davis, that "in the long run, those who do not use power in a manner society considers responsible will tend to lose it."

The major arguments for the acceptance of social responsibility by business appear in Table 3–1. These arguments can be summarized by the **iron law of responsibility,** *the rule, first stated by Keith Davis, that "in the long run, those who do not use power in a manner society considers responsible will tend to lose it."* Thus, if business firms are to retain their social power and social role, they must be responsive to society's needs.[21]

The Traditional View of Social Responsibility

In 1776, Adam Smith published *The Wealth of Nations,* sometimes called the "capitalist manifesto." In it, he described a system in which individuals and businesses pursued their own self-interests and government played a limited role. This system became the model for capitalism in the United States. Adam Smith wrote:

TABLE 3–1

Arguments for the Acceptance of Social Responsibility

1. People expect businesses and other institutions to be socially responsible.
2. Business will benefit if it is socially responsible, so social responsibility is just a matter of enlightened self-interest.
3. Responsible businesses have better images, both as honorable corporate citizens and as desirable places to work.
4. Business should be involved in social programs because it controls the necessary resources.
5. Business exists only with the sanction of society, so it should serve society's interests.
6. If business does not respond to society's needs, the public will press for more regulation.
7. Socially responsible actions may increase profits in the long run.

[An individual or business] generally, indeed, neither intends to promote the public interest, nor knows how much he is promoting it. . . . He intends only his own gains, and he is in this, as in many other cases, led by an invisible hand to promote an end which was no part of his intention, nor is it always the worse for society that it was no part of it. By pursuing his own interest he frequently promotes that of the society more effectively than when he really intends to promote it.[22]

This idea—that capitalism allows the serving of the public interest by individuals and businesses seeking maximization of satisfaction or profit—is considered by some to be the foundation of the U.S. economic system. Traditionally, companies were not expected to serve social goals, except indirectly. For example, until the mid-1930s, it was illegal for U.S. corporations to make charitable contributions. This was based on a precedent set in an 1883 lawsuit in Great Britain, *Hutton v. West Cork Railway Corporation*. The court in that case ruled that the corporation should be concerned only with the equitable distribution of its earnings to its owners. This distribution could not include corporate philanthropy, the court said.[23]

In 1935, the Federal Revenue Act provided for the tax deductibility of corporate charitable contributions. Under that provision, corporations could deduct up to 5 percent of net income for charitable contributions. By 1953, the right of businesses to make extensive charitable gifts was clearly established. That year, in *A. P. Smith Manufacturing Company v. Barlow et al.*, the New Jersey Supreme Court concluded that business support of higher education was in society's best interest.[24] Corporations today are expected to go far beyond corporate philanthropy in serving society's interests.

Economist Milton Friedman, who received a Nobel prize in economics, called the idea of corporate social responsibility a "fundamentally subversive doctrine." Friedman said, "There is one and only one social responsibility of business—to use its resources and engage in activities designed to increase its profits so long as it stays within the rules of the game, which is to say engages in open and free competition without deception or fraud."[25]

Friedman's statement is often quoted as an example of a radical view and an excuse for corporate irresponsibility. Friedman's followers, however, say he simply subscribes to the idea that, in the long run, the public interest is served by individuals and businesses pursuing their own best interests, primarily financial well-being, through participation in a relatively free economy. It is true that Friedman sets a rather high standard when he suggests that businesses should operate within the "rules of the game," practicing neither deception nor fraud. The rules of the game obviously include accepted ethical practices, in addition to international, national, and other laws. How many corporations are willing to tell the absolute truth in their advertisements and to engage in open and fair competition, avoiding collusion, price fixing, and so forth? The fact is that few subscribe to Friedman's hard-line views today. Let us look at how values concerning social responsibility are changing.

Trend Toward Social Responsibility

More and more U.S. corporate executives see themselves as legitimate servants of a variety of constituencies. In a political sense, a constituency is a body of citizens or voters who are entitled to elect a representative to a legislative or other public

Organizational constituency

Any identifiable group that organizational managers either have or acknowledge a responsibility to represent.

body. An **organizational constituency** is *any identifiable group that organizational managers either have or acknowledge a responsibility to represent*. The intention of political constituencies is that they will be represented by the person they elect. Unlike political constituencies, constituencies of corporate managers may or may not have the power to choose those managers.

For some executives, the common shareholder is only one of many constituencies to be served—and not even the primary one. This is the situation at Lincoln Electric Company.

Lincoln Electric Company

At Lincoln Electric Company, the world's largest producer of arc welding products, corporate executives see the customer as their primary constituency. Employees are in second place, with stockholders a distant third. James Lincoln, the company's founder and president until his death, in 1965, said, "The last group to be considered is the stockholders, who own stock because they think it will be more profitable than investing money in any other way."

To some degree, though, the Lincoln employee and stockholder are one and the same. More than half the company's stock is owned by employees, who can buy a limited number of shares each year at well below market prices. Lincoln also has a profit-sharing program, which adds to employees' ownership interest. Of course, all the top executives own Lincoln stock.[26]

The Business-Government Interface

The influence of business firms and other private organizations on government is understandably a matter of concern to the general public. However, the pervasive involvement of government in business activities is of more importance to most managers. The trend during the Reagan years was toward lessening regulation and reducing government interference in both business and private activities. The airline, trucking, and banking industries are now largely deregulated. It is ironic that it is the deregulated industries that tend to be the most vehement opponents of deregulation. Once companies have adapted to a regulated environment, they apparently are not sure they will be able to compete in a freely competitive one.

There is always a concern that political contributions can subvert government processes. This is especially true for contributions made by political action committees. **Political action committees (PACs)** are *tax-favored organizations formed by special interest groups to accept contributions and influence government action*. The growth of PACs has created an avenue through which corporations can contribute hundreds of millions of dollars to political candidates. Much of the money is obviously aimed at serving the special interests of those corporations. Billions of dollars in subsidies and price supports have been approved for the dairy industry after PACs representing them made large contributions to key legislators.

Political action committees (PACs)

Tax-favored organizations formed by special interest groups to accept contributions and influence government action.

FIGURE 3–4

A Model of Ethics

Type I Ethics

Type II Ethics

A Model of Ethics

Closely related to social responsibility, but not identical to it, is the concept of ethics. **Ethics** is *the discipline dealing with what is good and bad, or right and wrong, or with moral duty and obligation.* A *Time* magazine article argued, "Large sections of the ethical roofing has been sagging badly from the White House to churches, schools, industries, medical centers, law firms, and stockbrokers—pressing down on the institutions and enterprises that make up the body and blood of America."[27]

Whether ethics in the United States is sagging or not, the topic is certainly of increasing concern to us all. Everyone makes ethical (or unethical) decisions every day. Do you tell the clerk when you get too much change? What if your professor errs in your favor in computing your grade? You may think these minor private decisions are unimportant. But decisions in small matters tend to set a pattern for the more important ones you may make as managers.

Nearly 40 percent of managers in a multi-industry survey said that their superiors had at some point told them to do something unethical.[28] Such statistics may not be as meaningful as they seem, because what is or is not ethical is so much a matter of perception. But, despite the ambiguity, ethics appears to be moving up on the corporate priority list.[29] An increasing number of companies have codes of ethics. Remember that Wal-Mart has a strong code of ethics. Many industry associations adopt such codes, which are then recommended to members. Some consultants specialize in helping companies embed ethical principles in their corporate culture. And most business schools now teach business ethics in their courses. A *Fortune* magazine survey suggested that teaching ethics will be one of the six most important priorities for business schools in the next decade. According to this report, business school graduates must have a "strong grasp of ethics."[30]

A model of ethics is presented in Figure 3–4. It can be seen there that ethics consists mainly of two relationships, indicated by the bold horizontal arrows. A person or organization is ethical if these relationships are strong and positive.

Ethics

The discipline dealing with what is good and bad, or right and wrong, or with moral duty and obligation.

MANAGEMENT IN PRACTICE: A Skill-Building Exercise

Suppose for a moment that you have a goal that is critically important to you. Your friends are very supportive and are determined to assist you in the accomplishment of your goal. You later attain your goal. You then learn that your friends did some illegal things to help you. Your friends' actions did not help, and no one was hurt.

You have two options: You can cover for your friends and possibly get caught, or you can turn your friends in and allow them to suffer the consequences of their actions. (This is one version of a story involving President Richard M. Nixon and his friends, the Watergate burglars.)

What would you do?

The first element in the model is *sources of ethical guidance.* One might use a number of sources to determine what is right or wrong, good or bad, moral or immoral. These sources include the Bible, the Koran, and other holy books. They also include the "still, small voice" that many refer to as conscience. Millions believe that conscience is a gift of God or the voice of God. Others see it as a developed response based on the internalization of societal mores. Another source of ethical guidance is the behavior and advice of the people psychologists call "significant others"—our parents, friends, and role models and members of our churches, clubs, and associations. For organized professionals, especially, there are often codes of ethics that proscribe certain behavior.

Laws also offer guides to ethical behavior, prohibiting acts that can be especially hurtful to others. If a certain behavior is illegal, most would consider it to be unethical as well. There are exceptions, of course. For example, through the 1950s, laws in most southern states relegated black persons to the backs of buses and otherwise assigned them inferior status. Martin Luther King, Jr., resisted such laws and, in fact, engaged in civil disobedience and other nonviolent forms of resistance to their enforcement. King won the Nobel Peace Prize for his efforts and is today considered by most Americans to have been a highly moral person.

Notice in Figure 3–4 that the sources of ethical guidance should lead to our beliefs or convictions about what is right or wrong. Most would agree that people have a responsibility to avail themselves of these sources of ethical guidance. In short, individuals should care about what is right and wrong and not just be concerned with what is expedient. *The strength of the relationship between what an individual or an organization believes to be moral and correct and what available sources of guidance suggest is morally correct* is **Type I ethics.** For example, suppose a student believes it is acceptable to copy another student's exam, despite the fact that almost everyone condemns this practice. This student is unethical, but perhaps only in a Type I sense.

Simply having strong beliefs about what is right and wrong and basing them on the proper sources may have little relationship to what one *does.* Figure 3–4 illustrates that **Type II ethics** is *the strength of the relationship between what one believes and how one behaves.* Everyone would agree that to do what one considers wrong is unethical. For example, if a student knows that it is wrong to look at another's examination answer sheet but does so anyway, the student is being unethical in a Type II sense. If a business manager considers it wrong to damage the environment, yet dumps poisonous waste into a nearby stream, this behavior is unethical also. Generally, a person is not considered ethical unless the person possesses both types of ethics.

Business Ethics

One can usually provoke a lively discussion by simply mentioning business ethics. **Business ethics** is *the application of ethical principles to business relationships and activities.* Reading the newspaper or watching the evening news provides ample illustration

Type I ethics

The strength of the relationship between what an individual or an organization believes to be moral and correct and what available sources of guidance suggest is morally correct

Type II ethics

The strength of the relationship between what one believes and how one behaves.

Business ethics

The application of ethical principles to business relationships and activities.

of illegal or unethical practices of individuals in large corporations. Business ethics has come into sharp focus during the decade of the eighties and should become even more important in the nineties.

Nowhere has unethical and illegal business behavior been more apparent than on Wall Street. Former U.S. Attorney Rudolph Giuliani, who later ran for mayor of New York, waged a remarkably successful fight to curb Wall Street's unethical and illegal practices. He is the man who prosecuted stock manipulator Ivan Boesky. Of the fifty-three cases of insider trading Giuliani prosecuted, forty-six resulted in convictions. Giuliani's avowed goal was to create on Wall Street a "culture of compliance" in which integrity would be more important than profits.[31]

Practices that are particularly ethical seldom make the news. When Southland Corporation executives were accused of bribing New York State tax officials, the story made every major newspaper. Yet, the company's support of Olympic athletes received scant coverage.

Deciding what is ethical is often difficult. Following are examples of business activities that are usually considered unethical:

- Falsifying information on an application blank.
- Trading stocks on the basis of inside information.
- Padding expense accounts and otherwise seeking reimbursement for questionable or nonexistent business expenses.
- Divulging confidential information or trade secrets to competitors.
- Taking company property or materials for personal use.
- Giving or receiving gifts in return for orders.
- Quitting a job without giving adequate notice.
- Firing someone without giving adequate notice.
- Stealing.
- Soliciting or offering kickbacks.

As mentioned earlier, many companies have developed specific codes of ethics. For example, Texas Instruments furnishes its managers with a handbook entitled *Ethics in the Business of TI*. The book summarizes the company's philosophy of business as follows:

> It is fundamental to TI's philosophy that good ethics and good business are synonymous when viewed from moral, legal and practical standpoints. The trust and respect of all people—fellow workers, customers, consumers, stockholders, government employees, elected officials, suppliers, competitors, neighbors, friends, the press, and the general public—are assets that cannot be purchased. They must be earned. This is why all of the business of TI must be conducted according to the highest ethical standards.[32]

In the handbook, TI sets forth many specific ethical guidelines on a wide range of issues. The areas covered include truthfulness in advertising, gifts and entertainment, improper use of corporate assets, political contributions, payments in connection with business transactions, conflicts of interest, and trade secrets and proprietary information.

There are reasons to encourage industry associations to develop and promote improved codes of ethics. It is difficult for a single firm to pioneer ethical practices if its competitors take advantage of unethical shortcuts. For example, U.S. companies must comply with the 1979 Foreign Corrupt Practices Act, which prohibits bribes of foreign government officials or business executives. Obviously, the law does not prevent foreign competitors from bribing government or business officials to get business, and such practices are common in many countries.[33] This sometimes puts U.S. companies at a relative disadvantage. Several multinationals, including Switzerland's Ciba-Geigy, have encouraged other multinationals to band together and adopt policies on corrupt practices that will resemble those in the U.S. law. Perhaps such voluntary codes will be effective in upgrading the standards of ethics practiced in international business.

As was mentioned earlier, the concern for ethics in business appears to be increasing. One researcher concluded, "Business behavior is more ethical than it was in 1961, but the expectations of a better educated and ethically sensitized public have risen more rapidly than the behavior."[34] Managers surveyed in the study claimed they were more ethical than the average manager and their department and company were more ethical than others. They believed written codes of ethics would improve business practices. A survey of 611 companies found that 77 percent already had codes of conduct or of ethics. Of the largest companies (those with $400 million or more in sales), 97 percent had such codes.

Guidelines for Dealing with Ethical Dilemmas

Pagano and Verdin developed a list of guidelines that future managers can use to resolve difficult ethical dilemmas. The guidelines are not intended to provide hard and fast answers to ethical questions, but should assist future managers in evaluating ethical dilemmas by examining their own values and those of the organization. When future managers answer the following questions, they are forced to carefully consider the ethical consequences of alternate decisions.

1. Is the problem or dilemma really what it appears to be? If you are not sure, find out.
2. Is the action you are considering legal? Ethical? If you are not sure, find out.
3. Do you understand the position of those who oppose the action you are considering? It is reasonable?
4. Whom does the action benefit? Harm? How much? How long?
5. Would you be willing to allow everyone to do what you are considering doing?
6. Have you sought the opinions of others who are knowledgeable on the subject and who would be objective?
7. Would your action be embarrassing to you if it were made known to your family, friends, co-workers, or superiors? Would you be comfortable defending your action to an investigative reporter on the evening news?

There are no absolutely correct answers to these questions, but they can help clarify ethical aspects of tough managerial decisions. Moreover, answering them is likely to improve the quality of management decisions from a purely practical standpoint.[35]

1. The company may not have specific objectives in social areas.

2. Specific criteria or units of measurement may not be agreed upon.

3. It may be difficult to determine how an action today might affect society's interests tomorrow.

4. The business system, which previously focused on economic variables, may not have control points or measurement techniques appropriate to measuring social variables.

5. Auditing implies the collection of complete, objective, and accurate data, not usually available in social areas.

TABLE 3–2

Reasons for Not Applying
Financial Auditing in
Social Areas

The Social Audit

Many firms acknowledge responsibilities to various stakeholder groups other than corporate owners. Some even set specific objectives in social areas. Over the last two decades or so, a number of organizations have recommended that firms attempt to formally measure their contributions to various elements of society and to society as a whole. A **social audit** is *a systematic assessment of a company's activities in terms of their social impact.* Despite the efforts of the American Institute of Certified Public Accountants and a number of management societies, it has not been possible to do rigorous auditing in social areas. As Table 3–2 shows, there are a number of possible reasons for this failure.

Despite the difficulty, or impossibility, of conducting a rigorous social audit, most firms make some effort to inform themselves and the public about their social performance. A survey of the annual reports of five hundred large companies in the United States showed that over 90 percent of them contained social responsibility disclosures.[36]

Three possible types of social audits are currently being utilized: (1) simple inventory of activities, (2) compilation of socially relevant expenditures, and (3) determination of social impact. The inventory is generally a good starting place. It consists of a listing of socially oriented activities undertaken by the firm. Here are some examples: (1) minority employment and training, (2) support of minority enterprises, (3) pollution control, (4) corporate giving, (5) involvement in selected community projects by executives, and (6) a hard-core unemployment program. The ideal social audit would go well beyond a simple listing and involve determining the true benefits to society of any socially oriented business activity.

Social audit

A systematic assessment of
a company's activities in
terms of their social impact.

A Global Perspective

Business ethics came into sharp focus during the decade of the eighties and will become even more important in the nineties. Deciding what is ethical is often difficult, and that difficulty is compounded when the firm is competing in a multinational environment. It is hard for a single multinational firm to pioneer ethical practices if its competitors undercut it by taking advantage of unethical shortcuts or socially irresponsible actions. For instance, cigarette manufacturers are attempting to eliminate all trade barriers with Japan. These barriers currently limit the manufacturers' ability to export American cigarettes to Japan. If the barriers are lifted, competitive forces will be greatly intensified, and American cigarette manufacturers will be under pressure to use promotional methods long banned in the United States, such as television advertising. Certain methods were banned because of the claim by some experts that they caused individuals to start smoking. There is no such ban in Japan; therefore Japanese cigarette manufacturers use such promotional methods.

This sort of situation raises several ethical questions: Should the United States dictate the code of ethical conduct for cigarette manufacturers headquartered in America but operating in Japan? Should American cigarette manufacturers feel obligated to observe the U.S. promotional ban overseas, thereby forfeiting a substantial portion of the Japanese cigarette market? Do the competitive realities of marketing products overseas override the health considerations of foreign consumers? Can American business ethics be exported along with products? As globalized markets become a reality—with the eroding of Japanese trade barriers and trade barriers in the European Community—the question of globalized ethical behavior must be addressed. However, in addressing such behavior, it is important to keep in mind the need for all firms to compete on an even plane.

MANAGEMENT IN PRACTICE: A Skill-Building Exercise

Leroy Hasty was faced with a dilemma. He supervised twelve process technicians at the Indestro chemical plant in El Dorado, Arkansas, but was being transferred to a new job. The production manager, Jack Richards, had just asked Leroy to nominate one of his subordinates as a replacement. Two possible choices immediately came to mind, Carlos Chavez and James Mitchell.

Carlos was a very capable worker. He was twenty-four years old and married, and he had earned his bachelor's degree in management by attending night school. His heritage was Mexican-American. He had done an excellent job on every assignment Leroy had given him. He had all the qualifications Leroy believed a good supervisor should have, including solid technical expertise. Leroy considered him punctual, diligent, mature, and intelligent. A serious sort, Carlos often came to work early and stayed late and seemed to spend most of his spare time with his family.

James was a twenty-five-year-old high school graduate. He was single, and Hasty knew he often went hunting or partying with several of the other technicians. Like most of his fellow workers, James was a WASP (white Anglo-Saxon protestant). He was a hard worker and was liked and respected by the others, including Carlos. On the basis of objective factors, Leroy believed James ran second to Carlos, although the call was a close one.

But then there was the race issue. Several times Leroy had heard fellow workers refer to Carlos as "spic" and "wetback." Leroy believed some of the workers would prefer to have James as supervisor, purely because of his national origin. In fact, he thought one or two of them might resist Carlos's authority or try to make him look bad. And if productivity in the section fell off because of administrative problems, Leroy knew his own record with the company might be tarnished.

At that moment, the phone rang. It was Jack Richards. "Leroy," he said, "I need to see you. Could you come to my office in a few minutes?" As Leroy hung up the phone, he thought, "I know Jack is going to want to talk about my replacement."

What decision would you recommend that Leroy make? Discuss.

1. Are you willing to be socially responsible?

   ☐ Yes   ☐ No

2. Are you willing to promote a corporate culture which emphasizes concern for moral issues?

   ☐ Yes   ☐ No

3. Are you willing to assume broader and more diverse responsibilities to the various groups within society?

   ☐ Yes   ☐ No

4. Are you willing to follow the spirit of the law as well as the letter?

   ☐ Yes   ☐ No

5. Are you willing to see yourself as a legitimate servant of a variety of constituencies?

   ☐ Yes   ☐ No

6. Are you willing to care about what is right and wrong and not just be concerned with what is expedient?

   ☐ Yes   ☐ No

7. Are you willing to work toward making ethical decisions every day?

   ☐ Yes   ☐ No

8. Are you willing to accept the fact that ethics appears to be moving up on the corporate priority list and work toward acting in an ethical manner?

   ☐ Yes   ☐ No

9. Are you willing to abide by your organization's code of ethics?

   ☐ Yes   ☐ No

10. Are you willing to accept the fact that deciding what is ethical is often difficult, and still try to be ethical?

    ☐ Yes   ☐ No

Summary

Social responsibility is the implied, enforced, or felt obligation of managers, acting in their official capacity, to serve or protect the interests of groups other than themselves. Some experts believe businesses are increasingly willing to accept their societal responsibilities and that managers are becoming more ethical. They find that managers are more socially responsible and ethical than were their counterparts a generation ago.

Most organizations, whether profit or nonprofit, have a large number of stakeholders. An organizational stakeholder is an individual or group whose interests are affected by organizational activities. Although all stakeholders are affected by the corporation, managers may not acknowledge responsibility to all of them.

The social contract is the set of written and unwritten rules and assumptions about acceptable interrelationships among the various elements of society. Much of the social contract is embedded in the customs of society. Some of the "contract provisions" result from practices between parties. Like a legal contract, the social contract often involves a quid pro quo (something for something) exchange. The social contract concerns relationships with individuals, government, other organizations, and society in general.

Numerous associations and groups of respected business leaders have encouraged corporations and managers to become involved in socially responsible activities. Their arguments for this kind of involvement can be summarized by the iron law of responsibility, first stated by Keith Davis, which says "In the long run, those who do not use power in a manner society considers responsible will tend to lose it." Thus, if business firms are to retain their social power and role, they must be responsive to society's needs. However, Nobel laureate economist Milton Friedman called the idea of corporate social responsibility a "fundamentally subversive doctrine."

More and more U.S. corporate executives see themselves as legitimate servants of a variety of constituencies. In a political sense, a constituency is a body of citizens or voters who are entitled to elect a representative to a legislative or other public body. An organizational constituency is any identifiable group that organizational managers either have or acknowledge a responsibility to represent. The intention of political constituents is that they will be represented by the person they elect. Unlike political constituents, constituents of corporate managers may or may not have the power to elect those managers.

There is always a concern that political contributions can subvert government processes. This is especially true for contributions made by political action committees (PACs). These committees are tax-favored organizations formed by special interest groups to accept contributions and influence government action. The growth of PACs has created an avenue through which corporations can contribute hundreds of millions of dollars to political candidates. Much of the money is obviously aimed at serving the special interests of those corporations.

Closely related to social responsibility is the concept of ethics. Ethics is the discipline dealing with what is good and bad, or right and wrong, or with moral duty and obligation. Business ethics is the application of ethical principles to business relationships and activities.

Over the last two decades or so, a number of organizations and individuals have recommended that firms measure the degree to which they contribute to the welfare of various elements of society and to that of society as a whole. When this effort is formalized, it is called a social audit. This audit is a systematic assessment of a company's activities in terms of their social impact.

Review Questions

1. Define *social responsibility*. In general, how is U.S. business viewed by the public?

2. What is the social contract? Describe the various relationships involved with the social contract.

3. Contrast the traditional view of social responsibility with the recent trend concerning social responsibility.

4. What are political action committees?

5. What is ethics? Distinguish between Type I and Type II ethics.

6. Are the ethics of business and its managers changing? Discuss.

7. What is the purpose of the social audit?

Key Terms

Social responsibility

Organizational stakeholder

Social contract

Iron law of responsibility

Organizational constituency

Political action committees (PACs)

Ethics

Type I ethics

Type II ethics

Business ethics

Social audit

THE BHOPAL GAS LEAK TRAGEDY

December 2, 1984, began as a typical day in the central Indian city of Bhopal. In the shadow of a Union Carbide India Limited (UCIL) pesticide factory, tens of thousands of India's poorest citizens milled about the shantytown they called home. Inside the plant, an all-Indian crew operated the systems that produced the mildly toxic pesticide Sevin. Sevin is a patented product of Union Carbide Corporation (UCC), UCIL's U.S. parent. In a failing market, the plant had been allowed to run down. Some of the safety equipment was in disrepair, and personnel standards had been lowered substantially.

About 60 tons of poisonous methyl isocyanate (MIC), used in making Sevin, was stored in two tanks in the plant. Sometime before midnight, several hundred gallons of water entered one of the tanks from an unknown source. The water reacted violently with the MIC and a relief valve soon lifted.

The cloud of deadly white gas drifted toward the shanties. As the gaseous tentacles reached into the huts, there was panic. Many of the weak and elderly died where they lay. More than 2,000 died and 200,000 were injured. Bhopal's mayor said later: "I can say that I have seen chemical warfare. Everything so quiet. Goats, cats, whole families—father, mother, children—all lying silent and still. And every structure totally intact. I hope never again to see it."

UCC chief Warren Anderson rushed to India, only to be arrested and briefly detained. He said UCC took moral responsibility and offered medical and financial aid, but the offers were rejected. Several American lawyers also flew to Bhopal, to recruit clients. The lawyers quickly brought lawsuits in the United States. But a U.S. court ordered the case back to India. The Indian government declared itself the representative of all the victims. India demanded that UCC pay damages and later offered to settle for $650 million. The government pointed out that Sevin was a patented UCC product and that Indian engineers had traveled to UCC's U.S. plant for training. Also, UCC employees had helped in the plant startup in 1979–1980. A government lawyer said, "In reality, there is but one entity, the monolithic multinational [UCC], which is responsible for its subsidiaries."

But UCC, which owned 50.9 percent of UCIL's stock, said UCIL was independent. Although UCC had helped in designing the plant, few Americans had ever worked there. And the last one had left Bhopal in 1982. Still, UCC offered to pay $350 million. After more than four years of legal wrangling, the Indian Supreme Court ordered a $474 million settlement. UCIL paid 10 percent, and UCC paid the rest. And it was uncertain when, or if, the bulk of the money would be distributed.[37] And, it is still not over. In March 1992, the government of India requested extradition for the homicide of retired UCC chairman Warren Anderson.

Questions

1. Was Anderson correct in taking "moral responsibility" for the incident? Explain.
2. Discuss the actions of the U.S. lawyers who flew to Bhopal to recruit clients. Was this "ambulance chasing"?

"YOU CAN'T FIRE ME"

Norman Blankenship came in the side door of the office at Consolidation Coal Company's Rowland mine, near Clear Creek, West Virginia. He told the mine dispatcher not to tell anyone he was there. Norman was general superintendent over the Rowland operation. He had been with Consolidation for twenty-three years, having started out as a mining machine operator.

Norman had heard that one of his section bosses, Tom Serinsky, had been sleeping on the job. Tom had been hired two months earlier and had been assigned to the Rowland mine by the regional personnel office. He had gone to work as section boss on the midnight to 8:00 A.M. shift. Because of his age and experience, he was the senior person in the mine on his shift.

Norman took one of the battery-operated jeeps used to transport personnel and supplies in and out of the mine and proceeded to the area where Tom was assigned. Upon arriving, he saw Tom lying on an emergency stretcher. Norman stopped his jeep a few yards away from where Tom was sleeping and approached him. "Hey, you asleep?" Norman asked. Tom awakened with a start and said, "No, I wasn't sleeping."

Norman waited for Tom to collect his senses and then said, "I could tell that you *were* sleeping. But that's beside the point. You weren't at your work station. You know that I have no choice but to fire you." After Tom had left, Norman called his mine foreman and asked him to come in and complete the remainder of Tom's shift.

The next morning, Norman had the mine personnel officer officially terminate Tom. As part of the standard procedure, the personnel officer notified the regional personnel director that Tom had been fired and gave the reason for firing him. The regional personnel director asked the personnel officer to put Norman on the line. The regional personnel director said, "Norm, you know Tom is Eustus Frederick's brother-in-law, don't you?" Frederick was a regional vice-president.

"No, I didn't know that," replied Norman, "but it doesn't matter. The rules are clear. I wouldn't care if he was Frederick's son."

The next day, the regional personnel director showed up at the mine just as Norman was getting ready to make a routine tour of the mine. "I guess you know what I'm here for," said the personnel director. "Yeah, you're here to take away my authority," replied Norman. "No, I'm just here to investigate," said the personnel director.

By the time Norman returned to the mine office after his tour, the personnel director had finished his interviews. He told Norman, "I think we're going to have to put Tom back to work. If we decide to do that, can you let him work for you?" "No, absolutely not," said Norman. "In fact, if he works here, I go." A week later, Norman learned that Tom had gone to work as section boss at another Consolidation coal mine in the region.

Questions

1. What, if anything, would you do now if you were Norman?
2. Do you believe the personnel director handled the matter in an ethical manner? Explain.

Notes

1. This is a composite of a number of published accounts, among them: John Huey, "Wal-Mart: Will It Take Over the World?" *Fortune*, January 30, 1989, pp. 52–64; Sharon Reier, "CEO of the Decade: Sam Walton," *Financial World*, April 4, 1989, pp. 56–62; Bill Saporito, "Is Wal-Mart Unstoppable?" *Fortune*, May 6, 1991, p. 50; "Trendcheck—Wal-Mart: Starting It All," *Stores*, October 1990, p. 69; John Huey, "America's Most Successful Merchant," *Fortune*, September 23, 1991, pp. 46–47; and the 1991 Wal-Mart Annual Report.

2. Keith B. Murray and John R. Montanari, "Strategic Management of the Socially Responsible Firm: Integrating Management and Marketing Theory," *Academy of Management Review* 11 (October 1986): 816.

3. Archie B. Carroll, *Social Responsibility of Managers* (Chicago: Science Research, 1984), p. 14.

4. Judith H. Dobrzynski, Michael Schroeder, Gregory L. Miles, and Joseph Weber, "Taking Charge," *Business Week*, July 3, 1989, p. 2.

5. Kenneth E. Goodpaster and John B. Matthews, Jr., "Can a Corporation Have a Conscience?" *Harvard Business Review* 60 (January–February 1982): 132–141.

6. "Cash from Trash," *Fortune*, June 19, 1989, p. 16.

7. Louis Harris, *Inside America* (New York: Vintage Books, 1986), p. 236.

8. Edward L. Hennesy, Jr., "Business Ethics: Is It a Priority for Corporate America?" *FE* (formerly *Financial Executive*) 2 (October 1986): 14–15.

9. Roger Ricklefs, "Public Gives Executives Low Marks for Honesty and Ethical Standards," *Wall Street Journal*, November 2, 1983, p. 33.

10. Carroll, *Social Responsibility of Managers*, p. 14.

11. Ibid.

12. Thomas M. Jones and Leonard D. Goldberg, "Governing the Large Corporation: More Arguments for Public Directors," *Academy of Management Review* 7 (October 1982): 603–605.

13. Allanna Sullivan, "Exxon Discloses Oil-Spill Expenses over $1.25 Billion," *Wall Street Journal*, July 25, 1989, p. A3; George Hackett, " 'They'll Never Get It All,' " *Newsweek*, May 8, 1989, pp. 25–26; Julia Lieblich, "Exxon Befouled," *Fortune*, April 24, 1989, p. 16; George Hackett, "Environmental Politics: As the Alaska Oil-Spill Cleanup Proceeds, Activists Gain New Clout," *Newsweek*, April 17, 1989, pp. 18–19.

14. Louis F. Boone and David L. Kurtz, *Principles of Management*, 2d ed. (New York: Random House, 1984), p. 547.

15. Alan Farnham, "Ready to Ride Out China's Turmoil," *Fortune*, July 3, 1989, pp. 117–118.

16. Robert Luchs, "Successful Businesses Compete on Quality—Not Costs," *Long Range Planning* 19 (February 1986): 12.

17. Adapted from the Committee for Economic Development and from Sandra L. Holmes, "Corporate Social Performance and Present Areas of Commitment," *Academy of Management Journal* 20 (September 1977): 435.

18. Quoted in Robert Bolt, *A Man for All Seasons* (New York: Random House, 1962).

19. William J. Byron, "In Defense of Social Responsibility," *Journal of Economics and Business* 34 (1982): 190.

20. Dennis Montgomery, "Candy Firm Monitoring Atomic Risk," *Detroit News*, April 2, 1979, pp. 3A, 6A.

21. Keith Davis, "The Case for and against Business Assumption of Social Responsibilities," *Academy of Management Journal* 16 (June 1973): 36.

22. Adam Smith, *The Wealth of Nations* (1776; reprint ed., New York: Modern Library, 1937), p. 423.

23. Daniel Wren, *The Evolution of Management Thought*, 2d ed. (New York: Wiley, 1979), p. 109.

24. Ibid., p. 453.

25. Milton Friedman, *Capitalism and Freedom* (Chicago: University of Chicago Press, 1962), p. 133; also see Theodore Leavitt, "The Dangers of Social Responsibility," *Harvard Business Review* 36 (September–October 1958): 41–50.

26. James F. Lincoln, *A New Approach to Industrial Economics* (New York: Devin Adair, 1961), pp. 38, 122. The Lincoln story is told in some detail in Arthur Sharplin, "The Lincoln Electric Company (1985)," in Arthur A. Thompson, Jr., and A.J. Strickland III, *Strategic Management: Concepts and Cases* (Plano, Tex.: Business Publications, 1987), pp. 874–895.

27. E. Bowen, "Looking to Its Roots," *Time*, May 27, 1987, p. 26.

28. Roger Ricklefs, "Public Gives Executives Low Marks for Honesty and Ethical Standards," *Wall Street Journal*, November 2, 1983, p. 33.

29. John A. Byrne, "Businesses Are Signing Up for Ethics 101," *Business Week*, February 15, 1988, pp. 56–57.

30. Jeremy Main, "B-Schools Get a Global Vision," *Fortune*, July 17, 1989, pp. 78–86.

31. **INSIDE BUSINESS:** CNN correspondent Lou Dobbs discusses these, and other issues, with Mr. Giuliani.

32. *Ethics in the Business of TI.* (Dallas: Texas Instruments, 1977).

33. Bernard J. White and B. Ruth Montgomery, "Corporate Codes of Conduct," *California Management Review* 22 (Winter 1980): 80.

34. Steven N. Brenner and Earl A. Molander, "Is the Ethics of Business Changing?" *Harvard Business Review* 55 (January–February 1977): p. 60.

35. Anthony M. Pagano and Jo Ann Verdin, *The External Environment of Business* (New York: Wiley, 1988), chap. 5.

36. *Social Responsibility Disclosure: 1977 Survey of Fortune 500 Annual Reports* (Cleveland: Ernst and Ernst, 1977).

37. This case is a composite of a number of published accounts, among them: Arthur Sharplin, "Union Carbide of India Limited: The Bhopal Tragedy," in Joe G. Thomas, *Strategic Management: Concepts, Practice, and Cases* (New York: Harper & Row, 1988), pp. 955–966; "India to Pay Bhopal Heirs," *New York Times*, April 9, 1989, p. D13; Sanjoy Hazarika, "For Bhopal Gas Victims, the New Enemy Is Fraud," *New York Times*, April 11, 1989, p. A13; Arthur Sharplin, "Union Carbide India Limited, 1989," management case distributed by the North American Case Research Association, July 1989; *Illustrated Weekly of*

India, December 30, 1984, pp. 6–9; "Pesticide Plant Started as a Showpiece but Ran into Troubles," *New York Times*, February 3, 1985, p. 8; Stuart Diamond, "The Disaster in Bhopal," *New York Times*, January 28, 30, 31, and February 3, 1985; Rajendra Prabhu, "Flaws Revealed in Bhopal Plant," *Hindustan Times*, January 5, 1985, pp. 1, 8; "CBI Team to Probe All Aspects," *Times of India*, December 4, 1984, pp. 1, 12; "India's Night of Death," *Time*, December 17, 1984, pp. 22–31; various articles from the *Wall Street Journal*; Union Carbide Corporation statements and press releases; and Resa W. King and Jerome Zukosky, "An Offer That Shareholders Can't Refuse?" *Business Week*, November 17, 1986, p. 67.

Management Skills

Are your ethical skills honed to a fine edge, or are there unanswered issues you must confront prior to facing real-world ethical situations? To assess your ethical values and better determine where you stand on the ethical plane, take the self-assessment exercise "How Do Your Ethics Stack Up?" Then, turn to page 632 to evaluate yourself.

How Do Your Ethics Stack Up?

INSTRUCTIONS: For each statement answer as follows.

Strongly Agree = **SA**	Disagree = **D**
Agree = **A**	Strongly Disagree = **SD**

	SA	A	D	SD
1. Employees should not be expected to inform on their peers for wrongdoings.	—	—	—	—
2. There are times when a manager must overlook contract and safety violations in order to get on with the job.	—	—	—	—
3. It is not always possible to keep accurate expense account records; therefore, it is sometimes necessary to give approximate figures.	—	—	—	—
4. There are times when it is necessary to withhold embarrassing information from one's superior.	—	—	—	—
5. We should do what our managers suggest, though we may have doubts about its being the right thing to do.	—	—	—	—
6. It is sometimes necessary to conduct personal business on company time.	—	—	—	—
7. Sometimes it is good psychology to set goals somewhat above normal if it will help to obtain a greater effort from the sales force.	—	—	—	—
8. I would quote a "hopeful" shipping date in order to get the order.	—	—	—	—
9. It is proper to use the company WATS line for personal calls as long as it's not in company use.	—	—	—	—

	SA	A	D	SD

10. Management must be goal oriented; therefore, the end usually justifies the means. — — — —

11. If it takes heavy entertainment and twisting a bit of company policy to win a large contract, I would authorize it. — — — —

12. Exceptions to company policy and procedures are a way of life. — — — —

13. Inventory controls should be designed to report "underages" rather than "overages" in goods received. (The ethical issue here is the same as that faced by someone who receives too much change from a store cashier.) — — — —

14. Occasional use of the company's copier for personal or community activities is acceptable. — — — —

15. Taking home company property (pencils, paper, tape, and so on) for personal use is an accepted fringe benefit. — — — —

Source: Lowell G. Rein, "Is Your (Ethical) Slippage Showing?" *Personnel Journal* 59 (September 1980): 743. Reprinted by permission.

4

Managerial Decision Making

LEARNING OBJECTIVES

After completing this chapter students should be able to

- Describe the decision-making process and identify major factors that can have an impact on managerial decision making.

- Describe the group methods used in decision making.

- Explain the requirements that must be present for the decision-making process to be carried out.

- Relate how models are used in decision making.

- Describe worker participation in the decision-making process.

- Explain how managers can handle decision making in a crisis situation.

"Management doesn't get paid to make shareholders comfortable. We get paid to make shareholders rich," said Coca-Cola chief executive Robert Goizueta. After being rated as the 6th "Most Admired Corporation" Goizueta restated his position that "Increasing shareholder value over time is the bottom line of every move we make." Coca-Cola is the world's largest soft-drink company, a leading fruit-juice marketer (Minute Maid), and owner of 49 percent of Columbia Pictures Entertainment. Cuban-born Goizueta took the helm at Coke in 1981. An admitted workaholic, he takes only one week of vacation a year, and that reluctantly. He demands similar devotion from the other top managers at Coke.

Shortly after Goizueta became CEO, he began to shake up the organization. Cost-cutting—in every division—was a continuing theme. Coke's share of the sugar-cola market had been declining for 20 years. "You can extrapolate that out and eventually you end up with zilch," said Goizueta. The priceless Coca-Cola trademark was extended to six variations on the basic soft drink and later to clothing and other items. Pepsi-Cola had been gaining market share, so Coca-Cola brought out New Coke, a bit sweeter cola more like Pepsi. Three months later Goizueta stood in the glare of TV lights and confessed his error. Classic Coke, with the old, secret formula, was restored to store shelves and soon outsold New Coke ten to one. Although the experience was considered a fiasco, the error paid off. Classic Coke soon displaced Pepsi-Cola as the best-selling soft drink.

Each decision rankled corporate conservatives, although Goizueta worked hard at building consensus. And when Goizueta decided to take on debt to acquire companies, many at Coke became even harder to convince. The company invested $2 billion to buy its biggest bottlers. Half of the stock in the bottling division was later sold to the public. Another $1.5 billion was spent on Columbia Pictures. Then, plans were announced to start buying back 10 percent of Coke's common stock. Long-term debt quintupled from 1981–89. The Coke balance sheet had begun to look like that of many other major companies—half debt, half equity. No longer a beverage company, Coke was a conglomerate.

But Goizueta kept making stockholders rich. Net income was up every year from 1981–89, as were dividends. Share price quadrupled. It seems likely that shareholders were also becoming more comfortable with Goizueta. However, even though Coca-Cola has had a higher total stockholder return over the last ten years, it is interesting to note the PepsiCo is ranked 5th and Coca-Cola is ranked 6th among the "Most Admired Corporations." Despite this rating Coke is emerging from its strongest decade ever, and holds a solid market share lead over Pepsi—41 percent to 33 percent.[1]

Decision making

The process of generating and evaluating alternatives and making choices among them.

The Coca-Cola story suggests the extensive need for decision making in business. **Decision making** is *the process of generating and evaluating alternatives and making choices among them.* As Goizueta would attest, many decisions are hard to make, especially when a manager is departing from past patterns.

A managerial decision typically affects a great number of people—customers, stockholders, employees, and the general public. Coca-Cola, for example, has more than 100,000 shareholders of record and nearly that many employees. Professional managers see the results of their decisions reflected in the firm's earnings report, the welfare of employees, and the economic health of the community and the country. To survive and prosper, managers must be able to make professional decisions.

This chapter first discusses the decision-making process and several important factors that affect decision making. Next it describes group methods of decision making. Then it presents the requirements for decision making, followed by the use of models in decision making. The final sections are devoted to how worker participation is involved in the decision-making process, how managers can handle decision making in a crisis, and the global perspective of decision making.

The Decision-Making Process

Companies do not want dynamic failures; they want individuals who are properly equipped to make decisions. This does not mean that managers must be right 100 percent of the time; no one is perfect. It does suggest that successful managers have a higher batting average than less successful managers. Robert A. Lutz, Chrysler's top operating executive, is one individual who makes a wide range of decisions every day.

Chrysler Corporation's Robert A. Lutz

Robert A. Lutz must make many decisions each day in order to deal with the multitude of situations that occur. According to former Chrysler chairman Lee Iacocca, "Lutz has got the difficult job of trying to get the factories, engineers, and suppliers together to do our new cars." He must make sure that Chrysler plants produce 10,000 cars and trucks each day and figure out ways to entice consumers to buy them. He must also dream up new models that won't be on the market until 1993. At any given time, his concerns range from the correct audio speakers for the Dodge Daytona to the effects of future engine design on global warming.

Lee Iacocca is convinced that Lutz can do the job. He considers Lutz "a proven operating officer who has continually demonstrated extraordinary decision-making ability, which sets him apart from less successful managers." In the news conference to announce his replacement Iacocca once again praised Lutz, but decided to go with Eaton because he was more qualified. However, it remains to be seen if Iacocca's replacement, Robert J. Eaton, also views Lutz as one of the best in the industry.[2]

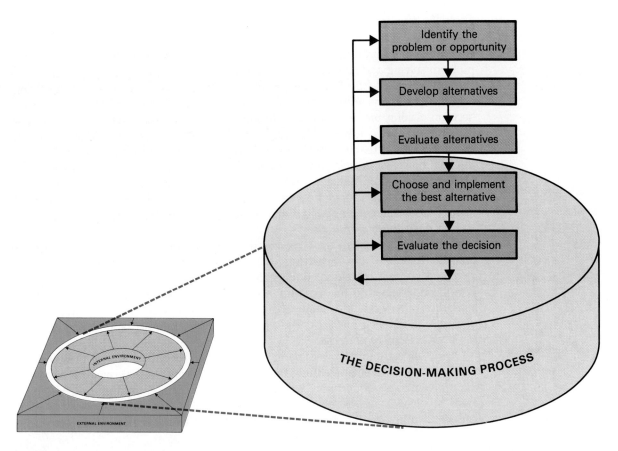

FIGURE 4-1

The Decision-Making Process

Managers are evaluated primarily on the results of their decisions. Some apparently successful executives follow an intuitive approach to decision making, basing their decisions on hunches and gut feelings. However, a more formalized approach, such as that illustrated in Figure 4–1, can usually increase a manager's batting average.

Environmental Factors

Decision making does not occur in a vacuum. Notice in Figure 4–1 that the elements of the organization's external environment are the same as those identified in Chapter 2. Variations in any of these factors can affect decision making. In a similar manner, the internal environment helps determine what decisions are made and who makes them. For example, the success of Pepsi-Cola in gaining market share while Coca-Cola lost it helped convince Goizueta that change was needed. And price competition surely influenced his decision to cut costs. Goizueta had to overcome the resistance of conservatives at Coke as he made and implemented all of these decisions. The steps in the decision-making process, shown in Figure 4–1, will be discussed next.

Identify the Problem or Opportunity

According to Harold Leavitt, "A business leader must have three major talents: problem solving and subsequent decision making, implementing, and visionary and entrepreneurial talents.[3] Some people view decision making only as problem solving; however, problems are usually better treated as opportunities. The first step in the decision-making process should be to look more for decision-making opportunities than for problems. Eventually, problems will make themselves evident. Goizueta knew the loss of market share to Pepsi would eventually lead to disaster. Opportunities, however, usually must be sought out. In purchasing Columbia Pictures, Coke was taking advantage of what seemed an opportunity. Within a few years, Coke had gotten its money back by selling stock in Columbia to the public and still owned about half the company. Often, however, the distinction between a problem and an opportunity is not clear.

In defining a problem (or opportunity), it is important to consider not just the problem itself but the underlying causes. For instance, the problem may be an increased number of defects coming off a production line. Untrained workers may have been assigned to the department. Maintenance people may have been doing a poor job of servicing the equipment. Or materials may have been defective because of sloppy purchasing practices. The causes of a problem must be understood before the problem can be corrected.

Often, solving a problem or taking advantage of an opportunity requires working with other departments. Defining the problem in terms of what caused it or seeing the problem as an opportunity will help identify the persons and groups who need to be involved. If a problem is due to poor maintenance, for instance, it may be necessary to involve the maintenance supervisor in deciding how to correct it.

MANAGEMENT IN PRACTICE: A Skill-Building Exercise

Wilson Trahan had been the postmaster at Balcomville, Utah, for seven months when he received notice of a 20 percent reduction in force, effective immediately. At first, Wilson was distressed by the news. He had only ten employees in the post office and was not sure he could do the job with eight.

However, after some thought, Wilson decided that this cutback might really be an opportunity in disguise. He had tried in the past to rearrange the work area, but to no avail. He had drawn up several alternative arrangements of the work flow. All of them would have been better than the present arrangement. But the postal workers were comfortable with the arrangement of the stamp machine, the sorting boxes, and the counters just where they had been for years. They resisted each change he tried to make.

Wilson seized on the opportunity created by the reduction in force. He decided to let the remaining workers help him select the best work space arrangement. The workers cooperated this time. Within a few months, the post office was providing better service than ever. And Wilson, although he had already lost two people, decided that he would not hire a replacement when the next worker quit or retired.

Did Wilson encounter a problem or an opportunity? Discuss.

Develop Alternatives

A problem can usually be solved in any of a number of ways. *The choices that the decision maker has to decide on* are **alternatives.** The only alternative that really counts is the one judged best among those considered. At this point in the decision-making process, however, it is important to consider all feasible ways by which the problem can be solved. Naturally, the number of alternatives generated is limited by the amount of time available for the decision, as well as by the importance of the decision itself. And the best alternative cannot be chosen if no one thinks of it. Finally, until all the alternatives have been evaluated, it is best not to eliminate any alternative from consideration.

Alternatives
Choices that the decision maker has to decide on.

Evaluate Alternatives

Usually, advantages and disadvantages can be found in every possible solution. One alternative may be clearly superior, but it may also have some weak points. The alternative of producing a new Coke carried with it the risk of alienating Americans who liked the old Coke. It is essential that managers realistically appraise arguments for or against a particular alternative. Sometimes, an idea sounds good initially, but taking time to weigh the pros and cons of alternatives usually pays off. It prevents the manager from having to say, "I wish I had put more effort into making that decision."

There are a number of ways of evaluating alternatives. One way is to list the pros and cons of each. This often results in one alternative being identified as clearly superior to the others. Care should be taken, however, not to place too much emphasis on the number of pros and cons, but rather to consider the overall importance of those relating to each alternative.

Another way to evaluate alternatives is to determine the expected payoff associated with each alternative. This "payoff relationship" (which will be discussed later in

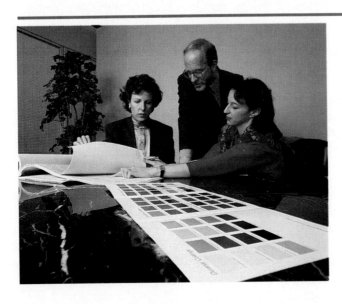

PPG representative Margaret Russell assists clients in the selection of coating systems for a manufacturing operation. Once selected, the system will be used for a long period of time. Margaret's job is to present alternatives and offer information to help client executives make a proper choice.
Source: Courtesy of PPG Industries

the chapter) requires consideration of both costs and benefits. It is also necessary to consider the probability of occurrence of the expected payoff. For example, an alternative that offers a 50 percent probability of a $1 million payoff generally will be chosen over one with a 10 percent probability of a $2 million payoff. Mathematical techniques to calculate expected payoffs are available, but they are beyond the scope of this chapter.

Choose and Implement the Best Alternative

The ability to select the best course of action from several possible alternatives often separates successful managers from less successful ones. The alternative offering the highest promise of attaining the objective, taking into consideration the overall situation, should be selected. This step may sound easy, but for managers it is the toughest part of the job. However sophisticated the selection technique followed, a manager can never be sure that the results of a decision will be favorable. Perhaps Goizueta's decision to market New Coke seemed logical at the time; nevertheless, the decision had to be altered.

Fear of making a wrong decision sometimes causes a manager to make no decision at all. It is no wonder that relatively high salaries are paid to managers with a reputation for having the fortitude to make decisions and for making correct ones most of the time. It is easy to be a Monday morning quarterback and criticize the coach's decisions. The coach, however, has to make decisions on the football field under pressure of time; no coach has the luxury of knowing how those decisions will turn out.

It is easy to see how managers feel a responsibility not only to make correct decisions but also to ensure that those decisions are implemented properly. Even if the decision making is not done in a crisis situation, the responsibility for implementation cannot be avoided. No matter how technically correct a decision and how faithfully a manager follows the recommended process, the decision has no value except through its implementation.

Evaluate the Decision

No decision-making process is complete until the decision has been exposed to the realities of the business environment. Evaluation requires an objective assessment of how the decision has solved the problem or taken advantage of the problem-turned-into-opportunity. This is particularly important for firms that stress decentralized management. In these companies, lower-level managers are allowed to become more involved in decision making. This provides junior managers with decision-making experience, improving their intuition and judgment.

The implementation of a decision does not complete the decision-making process. The arrows in Figure 4–1 indicate that there is constant reevaluation of and feedback to every phase of decision making. The outcome—whether good or bad—provides information that can contribute to future decisions. For example, it will be a long time before executives at Chrysler Corporation forget their Italian adventure.

Former Chrysler chairman Lee Iacocca usually distinguished himself as an effective decision maker. After all, Iacocca is well known as the savior of Chrysler Corporation. He is also the man who decided to purchase American Motors for its hot-selling Jeep line, which gave Chrysler added profits and respectability during the late 1980s. But at about the same time, Iacocca struck a deal with his buddy Alejandro de Tomaso, the boss of Maserati, which he would just as soon forget. The idea was to upgrade Chrysler's image for class and style while gaining a toehold in the European two-passenger coupe market—by building the Chrysler-Maserati "TC." The outcome was humbling for those involved.

Iacocca and the Maserati Fiasco

Prospective customers considered the TC "an inelegantly styled Chrysler with a Maserati emblem." Car magazines complained that the new car was underpowered, noisy, and marred by cheap plastic accoutrements. "Such inattention to detail in a car that cost almost as much as the Porsche," raged *Automobile Magazine*, "is grotesque—like finding a lava lamp in William F. Buckley's reading room."[4] Chrysler dropped an option to increase its Maserati stake to 51 percent. In 1989, TC production plans, already long delayed, were shoved further back. By the early 1990s, several other joint Maserati-Chrysler projects died on the vine.

Factors Affecting Decision Making

Many factors can have an impact on the manager's decision making. Some of the more important ones, shown in Figure 4–2, are described here. All of these factors influence managers as they make decisions, though some are more important at higher levels than at lower levels and vice versa.

Routine Versus Nonroutine Decisions

Management decisions may range from minor ones such as picking a supplier of bathroom tissue (routine decision) to major ones such as whether to build a new plant or to enter a new business (nonroutine decisions).

Routine Decisions   Most managers make numerous routine decisions in the performance of their jobs. These decisions are governed by the policies, procedures, and rules of the organization, as well as by the personal habits and preferences of managers. Managers certainly should not devote as much time to making routine decisions as they would to making nonroutine or more serious ones. It would be silly, for example, to follow a formal procedure in deciding whom to assign to a certain machine on a given day. Managers should be flexible in their decision making, just as in any other aspect of their job. They are little more than clerks if they simply adhere to the rule book and do not exercise some personal judgment for the betterment of all concerned.

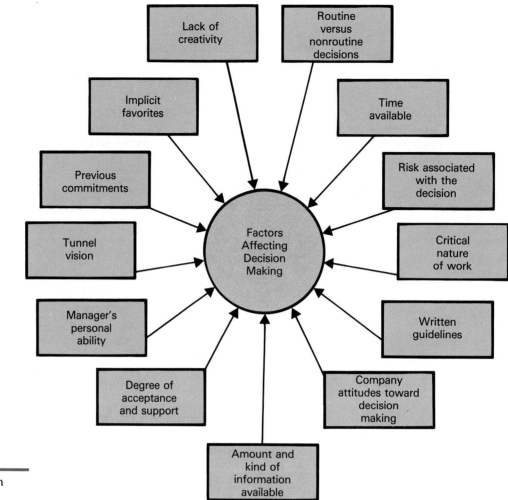

FIGURE 4-2

Factors Affecting Decision Making

Nonroutine decisions

Decisions that are designed to deal with unusual problems or situations.

Nonroutine Decisions Even though routine decisions may take up a considerable portion of a manager's time, individuals succeed or fail as managers on the basis of their nonroutine decisions. **Nonroutine decisions** are *decisions that are designed to deal with unusual problems or situations.* Whether or not to expand to foreign markets, to build a new production plant, or to buy a more advanced computer system—all are nonroutine decision situations. Nonroutine decisions are made by managers at all levels in the organization. Decisions made by a first-line supervisor might involve firing an employee or changing the layout or procedures in the department. But the nonroutine decisions that will result in the success or failure of the organization must be made by upper-level managers, including individuals such as the CEO, the president, and the owner.

Figure 4–3 illustrates the relationships of three levels of management and the amounts of routine and nonroutine decisions. As a manager progresses to higher levels, the number of nonroutine decisions increases. Nonroutine decisions require that managers exercise creativeness and good judgment.

Time Available

The amount of time that can be devoted to decision making is often a critical factor. Managers would prefer to have sufficient time to thoroughly evaluate and analyze all alternatives prior to making a decision, but few have this luxury. Decisions frequently must be made in time-pressure situations. When New Coke sales failed to take off, Goizueta could not wait a year to bring back the old formula. The sales loss was costing millions each month. As another example, assume that a customer of yours offers to make a large purchase at a low, though profitable, price. Assume further that the order must be accepted today or the buyer will go to another supplier. Even if you have good reasons to prefer taking your time with such decisions, you dare not do so.

Risk Associated with the Decision

Decision risk is *exposure to the probability that an incorrect decision will have an adverse effect on the organization.* It is a factor that all managers consider, consciously or unconsciously, in decision making. For instance, Betty Harris, president of a small book publishing company, is considering paying $100,000 to a well-known author to write a book. If the book sells well, the firm could make $500,000. But if it doesn't sell well, the company could lose the $100,000 plus an additional $75,000 in development and promotion costs. Harris may decide not to take the risk if the loss of $175,000 could seriously harm the company.

On the other hand, the purchasing manager for General Motors often signs contracts for automobile parts that greatly exceed $1 million. The risk in such decisions is low because of the size of the organization. Even the loss of $1 million for General Motors would not have a disastrous effect on the firm. As the decision risk increases, more time and effort are often devoted to individual decisions.

Decision risk

Exposure to the probability that an incorrect decision will have an adverse effect on the organization.

FIGURE 4-3

Managerial Levels and the Relative Amounts of Routine and Nonroutine Decisions

Critical Nature of the Work

Some managers are in charge of a section that is critical to the success of the organization or to human life and health. Even where health is not involved, a mistake in one department may be quite costly or may adversely affect the work of several other departments. Adverse effects may also be especially important when a department produces a good or service that is a vital input to other units of the organization. Managers in such departments often find their operations under close scrutiny by upper-level managers.

Managers in critical areas should be especially careful and systematic in making decisions. They should, for example, document their decision-making processes, since they may be called on to explain them. A manager who is asked "Why did you do it that way?" will find it more comfortable to say, "We considered these three options and decided the first one was best on the basis of this written analysis," than to say, "It just seemed like a good idea at the time."

Written Guidelines

Some firms have extensive written guidelines covering virtually any situation. (These guidelines, which are referred to as policies, procedures, and rules, are discussed in Chapter 5.) A manager in a large organization may need only to check a written document to determine the proper course of action. A major part of the manager's decision-making effort is then constrained. Situations of this sort should not be viewed negatively, though. There is always room for creativity in areas where decisions have not been made by upper-level managers.

In a unionized firm, many of the supervisor's decisions are restricted by the labor-management agreement. For example, promotions may have to be based largely on seniority, making it hard for the supervisor to consider merit. When written disciplinary guidelines are present, disciplinary action decisions must be made in accordance with the agreement. The manager has little discretion in matters covered by the union agreement.

Company Attitudes toward Decision Making

Some organizations encourage highly systematic decision making. Others lean toward a less formal approach. When the company's attitude is informal, a manager will probably not earn any credit by talking about the systematic decision process described early in this chapter. However, if top management follows and promotes a formal decision-making process, lower-level managers should certainly do the same. Many upper-level managers prefer to know the thought processes involved in a supervisor's decision. Given a choice, systematic decision making is usually best.

Amount and Kind of Information Available

The manager is either helped or hindered in decision making by the availability of information. Making decisions without knowing enough about the situation is risky.

Certainly, simple decisions do not require exhaustive information. But specific information is necessary to decide how to handle a complex problem.

Managers can protect themselves from the problems caused by a lack of information by actively keeping up with everything related to their area of responsibility. Paying careful attention to communications of all kinds often pays off. Time spent reading technical manuals about equipment may be helpful. Discussing potential problems with workers and getting their input on possible solutions could lead to what will seem a stroke of genius later on.

Information should be formally catalogued in some manner if it is to be available when needed. Managers cannot remember everything. Critical information should be put where it can be found quickly and easily. Of course, personal computers offer a handy way for managers familiar with their use to maintain ready access to a vast body of information.

Degree of Acceptance and Support by Equals and Superiors

At times, new managers are not immediately accepted. Reasons for lack of acceptance vary. Perhaps the manager is in a division where most of the other managers are much older, or perhaps the work group does not like outsiders. A similar concern may exists for a female manager who is in a male-dominated organization. If the acceptance and support by other managers is lacking, decision making will be affected; and it is up to the individual manager to overcome the problem.

A lack of acceptance on the part of subordinates can limit a manager's ability to make decisions and get them implemented. Solutions requiring close cooperation may not be feasible if subordinate acceptance is lacking. Perhaps the best way for a manager to gain acceptance is to earn subordinates' respect. Making an effort to improve communication and to involve workers in the decision-making process helps develop a feeling of mutual respect. The extremely successful Wal-Mart stores are distinguished by a top management that keeps employees closely informed about company plans and practices and includes them in corporate decision making.[5] When former CEO Lee Iacocca came to Chrysler, he kept his reputation for working harder than anyone else, coming to work early and staying late. It was also clear that he knew his job and was willing to put out extra effort to get the work done. Any manager who wishes to gain subordinate acceptance may have to work hard to get it.

The Manager's Personal Ability as a Decision Maker

Perhaps the most important factor affecting decision making is a manager's own ability and attitude. No matter how willing a manager is to make decisions and be responsible for them, it is the person's ability to make correct decisions that is essential for success. To some degree, this ability depends on following an appropriate decision-making process.

A manager's own experiences and level of understanding also help determine the quality of decisions. Experience tends to be a good teacher. For example, many college recruiters emphasize the experience a student has gained from business and extracurricular activities. They believe the learning process for a particular job may be shortened if a student has been active in other endeavors while in college. But decision makers who rely only on their own experience may base their judgments mainly on their feel for the situation; and if they are confronted with unfamiliar situations, faulty decisions may result. Basing decisions only on experience has several obvious shortcomings, among them:

1. Learning from experience is usually random.
2. Although we may have experience, there is no guarantee that we have learned from it.
3. What we learn from experience is necessarily circumscribed by the limits of our experience.
4. Conditions change, and the past may not be a good indicator of current or future conditions.[6]

The question might be asked: Do you have twenty years of experience, or do you have one year of experience twenty times? Ralph C. Davis's classic statement summarizes the need for a bond between experience and intellect for a professional decision maker: "A person who has nothing but background is a theorist. An individual who has nothing but practical experience is a business mechanic. A professionally trained executive is one in whom there is an effective integration of these two general types of experiences, combined with adequate intelligence regarding the types of problems with which the person must deal."[7]

Tunnel Vision

Tunnel vision

The extremely narrow viewpoint of people who have mental blinders, such as individual biases, that restrict the search for a solution to a narrow range of alternatives.

The extremely narrow viewpoint of people who have mental blinders, such as individual biases, that restrict the search for a solution to a narrow range of alternatives is **tunnel vision**. For example, a male manager who has a bias against female managers will not even consider a well-qualified woman for such a job. To the extent that tunnel vision inhibits identifying additional and worthwhile alternatives, it has a detrimental effect on the decision-making process.[8]

Previous Commitments

Another barrier to effective decision making is previous commitments. Decisions usually occur in sequence and therefore affect other decisions. Possibly the most difficult decision a person can make relates to choices about the fate of an entire sequence of decisions. Research indicates that people who feel personally responsible for a bad decision often tend to commit additional resources to that alternative. This escalating commitment makes it increasingly difficult to objectively evaluate other alternatives and to change the already initiated course of action.[9]

Implicit Favorites

One researcher has shown that many people select a favorite alternative early in the decision-making process but continue to evaluate additional solutions. Subsequent alternatives are therefore distorted perceptually—evaluated using decision criteria that emphasize the superiority of the preferred solution. The decision maker will process information in such a way that final selection of the implicit favorite is virtually guaranteed.[10]

You are the personnel director for a manufacturing firm that is undergoing a major change in direction. This change involves the hiring of young, energetic workers, and you have some difficult decisions to make. The firm is building two technologically advanced plants in the state of Tennessee, and it will close four of its five old plants in Michigan and Ohio. John Morrow is a fifty-six-year-old production worker who has been with your firm ten years. In your opinion, he is not capable of being retrained; but he is not old enough to receive any retirement benefits. You must decide whether to place John in the only remaining old plant the company has left or fire him.

What would you do?

Lack of Creativity

Most people possess creative ability, which can be developed through training and application.[11] **Creativity** is *the ability to generate ideas that are both innovative and functional.* This ability is an obvious requirement for managerial effectiveness, and it is especially important in making nonroutine decisions.

Unfortunately, creativity rarely receives adequate attention in organizations. The first reason for this neglect is that organizational policies and procedures are usually designed to promote order, consistency, and uniformity, thereby limiting creativity. Second, managerial work is fast paced and action oriented, whereas creativity requires time for preparation, incubation, inspiration, and validation.[12] Finally, most individuals do not understand creativity and therefore overlook it rather than advocating or reinforcing it.

Creativity
The ability to generate ideas that are both innovative and functional.

Group Methods Involved in Decision Making

Up to this point, decision making has been discussed as if it were a process carried out by the individual manager. In most organizations, individuals are responsible for the outcomes of decisions under their control. Effective decisions generally combine high quality with acceptance by those affected by the decision.[13] Groups bring different resources to the decision-making task. For example, studies indicate that plants with work team systems that allow auto workers real participation in decision making produce better-quality cars more efficiently than do plants with traditional work systems.[14]

There are several techniques through which groups can be involved in any stage of the decision-making process. Three of them are brainstorming, nominal grouping, and the Delphi technique.

Brainstorming

Brainstorming

The idea-generating technique wherein a number of persons present alternatives without regard to questions of feasibility or practicality.

The idea-generating technique wherein a number of persons present alternatives without regard to questions of feasibility or practicality is **brainstorming.** Through this technique, individuals are encouraged to identify a wide range of ideas. Usually, one individual is assigned to record the ideas on a chalkboard or writing pad. Brainstorming may be used at any stage of the decision-making process, but it is most effective at the beginning, once a problem has been stated. Sometimes, the alternatives produced through brainstorming may be rather bizarre. For example, if a brainstorming group were to consider how Coke might respond to a new Pepsi ad campaign, someone might suggest buying out PepsiCo. Building on this, another participant might suggest selling out to PepsiCo. No criticism is allowed, because the purpose of brainstorming is to come up with innovative possibilities. Evaluation can wait until later. It is not part of brainstorming.

Although brainstorming is useful for all types of decisions, it is most effective for simple, well-defined problems. It encourages enthusiasm and competitiveness among group members in generating ideas. It also prevents group members from feeling hopeless about the range of possibilities in a given situation.[15] Brainstorming can result in many shallow and useless ideas, but it can spur members to offer terrific ideas as well.

Nominal Grouping

Nominal grouping represents an attempt to move toward a structured approach, which encourages individual creativity.[16] *Nominal* refers to the fact that members, acting independently, form a group in name only. An important feature of this technique is that it allows the members to meet face-to-face but does not restrict individual creativity, as traditional group discussions do. **Nominal grouping,** then, is *the approach to decision making that involves idea generation by group members, group interaction only to clarify ideas, member rankings of ideas presented, and alternative selection by summing up the rankings.* The steps, which are shown in Figure 4–4, are as follows:

Nominal grouping

The approach to decision making that involves idea generation by group members, group interaction only to clarify ideas, member rankings of ideas presented, and alternative selection by summing up the rankings.

1. *Statement of the problem.* After the nominal group is assembled, the group leader states the decision problem clearly and succinctly. No discussion is allowed, although group members may ask questions to clarify the problem.

2. *Idea generation.* Group members silently record and number their ideas for solving the problem.

3. *Round-robin recording.* The group members alternate in presenting their ideas while the group leader lists the ideas presented on a flip chart or chalkboard. This process continues without discussion until all of the ideas have been recorded.

4. *Clarification of ideas.* Under the leader's guidance, group members question one another to clear up any confusion about what each idea means. No evaluation is allowed yet.

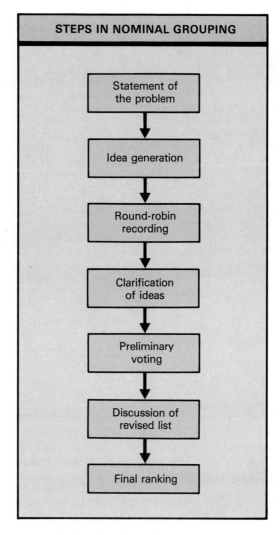

FIGURE 4-4

Steps in Nominal Grouping

5. *Preliminary voting.* Each group member independently ranks what are considered the best of the decisions presented. The ideas that receive the lowest average ranking are eliminated from further consideration.

6. *Discussion of revised list.* Individual group members question one another to clarify the ideas that remain. The purpose is not to persuade but to understand.

7. *Final ranking.* Group members rank all of the ideas. The one with the highest total ranking is adopted.

Delphi Technique

The formal procedure for obtaining the consensus of a number of experts through the use of a series of questionnaires is the **Delphi technique.** The procedure is similar to nominal grouping, but participants do not meet. In fact, ideally the experts do not

Delphi technique

The formal procedure for obtaining the consensus of a number of experts through the use of a series of questionnaires.

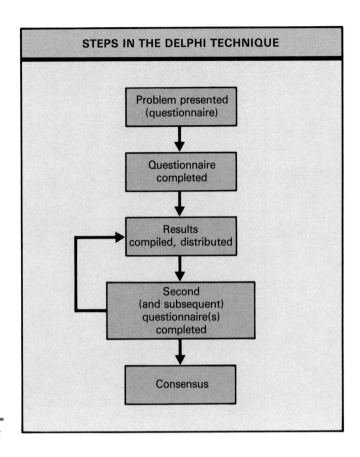

FIGURE 4-5

Steps in the Delphi Technique

know who else is involved. The steps in the Delphi technique, which are shown in Figure 4–5, are as follows:

1. The problem is presented to group members by means of a questionnaire that asks them to provide potential solutions.
2. Each expert completes and returns the questionnaire.
3. The results are compiled and provided to the experts, along with a revised and more specific questionnaire.
4. The experts complete the second questionnaire.
5. The process continues until a consensus emerges.

The Delphi technique prevents the respondents from being influenced by the personalities of the other participants and at the same time allows for the sharing of ideas. This method was conceived by the Rand Corporation to forecast how seriously a nuclear attack would affect the United States. It is expensive and time-consuming and generally has been limited to important and futuristic ideas. The Delphi technique is useful in instances where

- The problem does not lend itself to precise analytical techniques but can benefit from subjective judgments on a collective basis.
- The individuals needed to contribute to the examination of a broad or complex problem have no history of adequate communication and may represent diverse backgrounds with respect to experience or expertise.

- More individuals are needed than can effectively interact in a face-to-face exchange.
- Time and cost make frequent group meetings infeasible.
- The efficiency of face-to-face meetings can be increased by a supplemental group communication process.
- Disagreements among individuals are so severe or politically unpalatable that the communication process must be refereed or anonymity assured.
- The heterogeneity of the participants must be preserved to assure validity of the results; that is, domination by quantity or by strength of personality ("bandwagon effect") must be avoided.[17]

Decision-Making Requirements

Perhaps no other attribute so frequently distinguishes the excellent manager from mediocre ones as does the ability to make wise and innovative decisions. However, as Figure 4–6 shows, the good manager must also meet certain requirements if the decision-making process is to be carried out effectively.

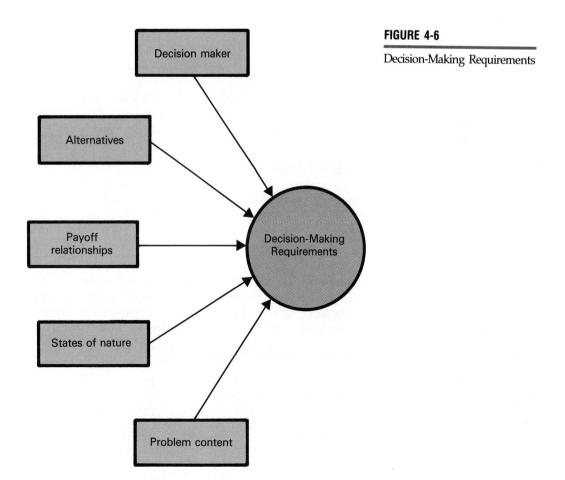

FIGURE 4-6

Decision-Making Requirements

Decision Maker

When Harry Truman was President of the United States, he kept on his desk a plaque that stated, "The buck stops here." He was the person responsible, and he made the final decision. The role of decision maker may be assumed by an individual or by a group of individuals, depending on how the organization is managed. The decision maker must choose from among a group of alternatives, a task many individuals do not like. Contrary to some thinking, not everyone enjoys making decisions, even when charged with the responsibility to do so. Certainly this is not the case with Coca-Cola chief executive Robert Goizueta.

Alternatives

To have a decision problem, the decision maker must have more than one alternative to choose from. Alternatives may be many or few in number. They may merely represent the option of doing something or doing nothing. A good decision maker, however, attempts to identify and evaluate as many alternatives as possible within time and resource restrictions.

Payoff Relationships

Payoff relationship

Evaluating alternatives in terms of their potential benefits or costs.

Evaluating alternatives in terms of their potential benefits or costs is the **payoff relationship.** Ultimately, the decision maker should be attempting to choose the decision that will either maximize benefits or minimize costs. When the profits and costs associated with a particular alternative cannot be expressed in dollar amounts, the decision maker suffers. For example, decision making is much easier if one can state that a particular decision will result in a savings of $50,000, as compared with one's merely expressing the opinion that costs will be lowered.

States of Nature

States of nature

The various situations that could occur and the probability of each of them occurring.

The various situations that could occur and the probability of each of them occurring are **states of nature.** For example, we have all heard weather forecasters say, "There is a 20 percent chance of rain." The 20 percent chance of rain is one state of nature, and the 80 percent chance of no rain is the other.

Choice may be required in either of two situations: (1) when the precise relationships among alternatives are known and the problem is merely to define what the relationships mean in terms of an objective or (2) when there is uncertainty about the future environment or the precise relationships among alternatives. Good decision makers study situations thoroughly in the hope that their decisions will be correct more often than not. Because of the state of doubt, it is likely that decision makers will never be 100 percent correct.

Problem Content

Problem content

The environment in which the problem exists, the decision maker's knowledge of that environment, and the environment that will exist after a choice is made.

The environment in which the problem exists, the decision maker's knowledge of that environment, and the environment that will exist after a choice is made are the **problem content.**

Because the environment is taken into consideration in decision making, a decision that may be considered proper in one organization may be improper in another. For example, managers in two firms producing similar products and presented with the same problem may make different decisions because of the internal environment each faces. One firm may stress maximum risk taking for managers, thereby permitting even lower-level managers to make important decisions. Another firm may want to have this type of decision approved by upper-level management. Even though a lower-level manager in the second firm might be perfectly capable of making the decision, the situation does not permit it.

MANAGEMENT IN PRACTICE: A Skill-Building Exercise

You have been put in charge of phase 1 of the new production process. This phase makes or breaks the rest of the production operation. If production quality and quantity standards are not met, the entire process will fail to meet the rigid time and quality restrictions placed on it by the client. You have been given two alternatives by the vice-president of operations. You can get a new semiautomated machine that will replace seven of the twelve people on your line and will assure the success of the project. (The machine has allowed three of your competitors to exceed the standards you will be required to meet.) Or you can keep all twelve employees on the line and attempt to retrain and motivate them to achieve the standards. These employees have never been able to meet such high standards, but they have never been formally trained either. If you fail to assure that phase 1 of the production process is successful, you will seriously jeopardize your career. If you get rid of seven employees, morale will be hurt, and you will be firing several people you have known for many years.

What is your decision?

A Decision-Making Problem

To understand how the components of decision making interact, imagine how a student (the decision maker) might choose a part-time job. Suppose the student needs to take a job to supplement her financial aid. She needs to analyze each element of decision making with regard to its requirements. The only available jobs are at a recently opened pizza restaurant. The two job alternatives are pizza baker and assistant manager.

The payoff for each position is different. The baker receives an hourly wage of $4.35, no matter what the level of sales. However, the assistant manager's payoff is $8 an hour for high sales, $6 an hour for average sales, and $1 an hour for low sales.

Because the restaurant is relatively new, its sales potential has not been established. However, the student, relying on her experience in the community, estimates that there is a 20 percent chance of high sales, a 50 percent chance of average sales, and a 30 percent chance of low sales. These states of nature will have a major impact on the amount of money the assistant manager will receive.

Now the student is in a position to evaluate the two alternatives. One technique for doing so is known as "determining expected value," and the computation is as follows:

Expected earnings (pizza baker) = .2($4.35) + .5($4.35) + .3($4.35) = $4.35

Expected earnings (assistant manager) = .2($8) + .5($6) + .3($1) = $4.90

If the student prefers the alternative with the higher expected value, she should accept the assistant manager position (expected value of $4.90 per hour, versus the $4.35 per hour guaranteed by the other position).

But one factor remains to be examined—the problem content. There may be other facts to consider before a decision is made. The student's financial situation may prevent her from taking the chance of receiving only $1 per hour if sales are poor. On the other hand, the individual may desire the status of being an assistant manager. Although numerous other considerations may also come into play, this example should provide some insight into the factors involved in decision making.

The Use of Models in Decision Making

Model

An abstraction of a real-world situation.

A technique that has proved beneficial to managers in the decision-making process is model building. A **model** is *an abstraction of a real-world situation*. It attempts to portray reality through various means without dealing directly with the real world. In business, models can be expressed in many ways and can have many meanings. This is true because managers often must deal with highly complex business systems that must be simplified to be understood. Model building provides the means for simplifying complex situations.

Model builders first determine the purpose of the model—how it relates to the real-world situation. Next, they decide which parts of the situation should be included in the model. This factor alone is a major advantage of model building. Components that exist in the real world but have no effect on the problem under consideration can be omitted. Finally, model builders must define the relationships among the parts. Understanding these relationships is vital in model building. Models are more widely employed than is commonly realized. Some of the most commonly used models are physical, schematic, and mathematical.

Physical Models

Physical models

Models that generally look like the systems they represent.

Models that generally look like the systems they represent are **physical models.** These models were among the first to be used in management and are the most familiar. Systems represented by physical models include people, ships, airplanes, automobiles, houses, dams, shopping centers, factories, and retail stores. Models can also be more abstract representations. A photograph captures the physical appearance of a person. So does a painting, but the portrait painted by the artist may deemphasize or exaggerate features.

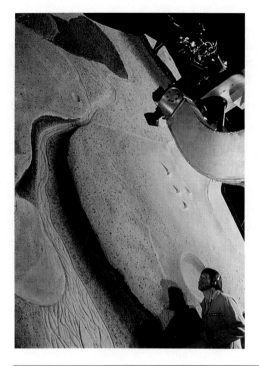

Models that generally look like the system they represent are called physical models. *A model attempts to portray reality through various means without having to work directly with the real world. This is a scale model of Martian terrain produced by Martin Marietta Corporation. The model is being used to test an unmanned space probe which employs artificial intelligence.*

Source: Photograph courtesy of Martin Marietta Corporation

Schematic Models

Line drawings, flowcharts, graphs, maps, organization charts, and similar items that represent the major features of a particular system are **schematic models.** These models may or may not be related in scale to the object being abstracted. Elements of a highway system are represented by road maps, which are two-dimensional scale models. On the other hand, the schematics depicting electrical circuitry that are found on the back of a radio or television set usually are not drawn to scale.

Schematic models have been widely used in management to describe components of the organization and to analyze problems. They are used to describe processes and procedures as well as physical components. For example, a computer programmer uses a schematic model—the flowchart—to illustrate the steps that must be taken in writing a program. Although schematic models are useful to managers in each major business function, the field of production and operations management has, perhaps, utilized them more than any of the others. Production and operations models are discussed in Chapter 19.

> **Schematic models**
>
> Line drawings, flowcharts, graphs, maps, organization charts, and similar items that represent the major features of a particular system.

Mathematical Models

Mathematical equations that define and represent the relationships among elements of a system are **mathematical models.** These models portray in quantitative terms the essential elements and interrelationships among elements of the systems they describe. The

> **Mathematical models**
>
> Mathematical equations that define and represent the relationships among elements of a system.

language used, mathematics, is a powerful one, because it is not subject to misinterpretation. However, for mathematical models to represent reality, we must know a good deal about reality. In many instances, this itself is a problem. The primary limitation to the use of mathematical models in assisting management is the constraint imposed by our inability to measure the relationships among elements of the environment.

Worker Participation and the Decision-Making Process

Worker participation

The process of involving workers in the decision-making process.

Although participation as a factor in corporate culture will be discussed in Chapter 15, participation as involved in the decision-making process is discussed here. **Worker participation** is *the process of involving workers in the decision-making process.* It is projected that worker participation will go far beyond the level of participation we know today. In the future, employees will not only participate in decision making but will also be encouraged to analyze and solve problems.[18] Most managers assume that they must be either participative or nonparticipative when involving workers in decision

FIGURE 4-7

Degrees of Worker Participation

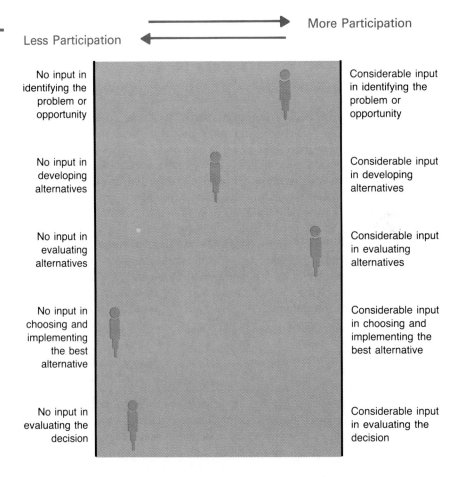

Less Participation → More Participation

No input in identifying the problem or opportunity	Considerable input in identifying the problem or opportunity
No input in developing alternatives	Considerable input in developing alternatives
No input in evaluating alternatives	Considerable input in evaluating alternatives
No input in choosing and implementing the best alternative	Considerable input in choosing and implementing the best alternative
No input in evaluating the decision	Considerable input in evaluating the decision

making. Also, some managers believe that if they involve workers in decision making, they will lose control over the work unit.[19] That is not necessarily the case, since the degree of worker participation differs in each step of the decision-making process.

As can be seen in Figure 4–7, worker participation may be high in some steps and low in others. In one situation, workers might participate extensively in identifying the decision-making opportunity and developing alternatives but take almost no part in making and evaluating the decision. In other situations or with other managers, the pattern of participation might be entirely different.

Virtually every manager receives some input from employees before making important decisions. From a motivational standpoint, encouraging input is probably useful only when the employees believe they play a meaningful part in the process. The manager should be completely honest about this. If a decision has already been made, the manager should not ask employees for advice about making it. Employees should be consulted only when they have information or insight that will help managers make better decisions.

How Managers Can Handle Decision Making in a Crisis

No matter how well managers plan, they often find themselves in crisis situations. Decisions in such situations are significantly more important, urgent, and risky than usual. For instance, suppose a piece of equipment has broken down on Thursday afternoon and the manager has to get a crucial order out by Friday. Or suppose the manager has just heard that a group of senior executives is going to inspect the work area and only one day is available to prepare. Effective managers should not be afraid of such crises. Rather, they should see them as providing opportunities to show exceptional competence. The successful handling of one crisis might earn a manager as much respect as would several years of good performance.

A few things should not be done (but often are) in a crisis situation. First, some managers pretend that nothing unusual is happening and conduct business as usual. They may prefer not to see the problem. Second, some managers overreact in crises. They take more extreme action than is needed to solve the problem. Calling everyone in on overtime when one worker would be sufficient is an example. Third, managers sometimes treat a crisis decision like any other decision. This type of decision is different, however, because of its importance, urgency, and riskiness. The manager must exert more than usual effort—perhaps working overtime, being more disciplined, or laying aside less urgent or less important matters.

What should be done? There are some guidelines that will help managers handle crises effectively. First, managers should be on the lookout for situations that could become critical. It may be possible to prevent a crisis from occurring. For instance, suppose a supervisor has heard that a large order is expected shortly. It might be worthwhile to alert workers about the expected overtime so they will not make other plans. Also, good machine maintenance will help prevent crises caused by breakdowns. In addition, proper attention to the needs of workers will help prevent people-related crises.

Second, managers should stay calm during crises. If the manager panics, workers may also panic. Managers can provide a calming influence. They should be careful to react appropriately, but not excessively, to any situation. Nowhere is this more important than in a hospital emergency room, where a doctor may supervise the work of several interns and nurses caring for accident victims.

Third, managers should accept the fact that in times of crisis there is additional risk—risk that may be understood by superiors. The solution to the problem may have to be an innovative one. Fear of making a mistake may prevent the manager from making the decision in time to do any good. There may not be time to go through a formal decision-making process. The manager may have to make a quick decision and live with it. It is likely that upper management will appreciate the decisiveness of the manager.

Finally, managers should remember Murphy's Law: If anything can go wrong, it will. Murphy's Law is not an excuse for pessimism. But managers who keep it in mind might be better prepared to handle the crises that inevitably occur. Managers should try to have plan B ready for the predictable crisis.

A Global Perspective

Decision making does not occur in a vacuum. Managers must consider both internal and external factors, because variations in any of these factors can adversely affect decision making. Operating in the multinational environment further complicates the

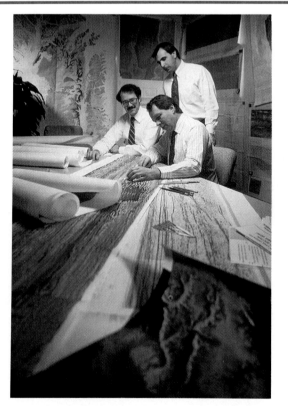

Managers must understand the nature of the market in which they compete. Consideration of both internal and external factors are important because variations in any of these factors can adversely affect decision making. The petroleum geologists shown here study a seismic "map" which shows the various density layers of the earth's crust represented in different colors. On a global perspective, it is equally as important for managers to consider the external environment in order to make the best decisions.

Source: Photograph courtesy of Atlantic Richfield Corporation

decision-making process. It is important for managers to understand the nature of the market in which they compete. Frederick W. Smith, founder of Federal Express Corporation, lost the company millions of dollars when he expanded into the overseas market because his decisions were based on competing in the American market. He decided to attack the competition directly, as he had done domestically, but he ran head-on into entrenched overseas rivals and foreign regulations.[20] By better investigating the nature of the overseas market he could have better approached his expansion overseas.

For many years, Procter & Gamble (P&G) managers decided to develop products for the U.S. market and to use American-style advertising and marketing to push the products in Japan. Such decisions led to more than $200 million in losses in sixteen years. Now P&G is hiring more Japanese, becoming more closely attuned to the local ways of the Japanese, keying in on doing what is necessary to capture market share from Japanese firms. For instance, P&G is capturing more of the Japanese diaper market by producing thin, superabsorbent diapers in blue for boys and pink for girls. P&G's diaper market share in Japan is now up to 20.5 percent.[21]

* *

Self-Assessment Exercise

Will You Be a Good Decision Maker?

1. Are you willing to be decisive when making decisions?

   ☐ Yes   ☐ No

2. Are you willing to not waste time regretting the failure of past decisions?

   ☐ Yes   ☐ No

3. Are you willing to learn from the results of past decisions?

   ☐ Yes   ☐ No

4. Are you willing to keep a little levity in your attitude?

   ☐ Yes   ☐ No

5. Are you willing to not reinvent the wheel?

   ☐ Yes   ☐ No

6. Are you willing to let the decision roll over in your mind?

   ☐ Yes   ☐ No

7. Are you willing to not let the desire to make a quick decision cause you to make a poor decision?

   ☐ Yes   ☐ No

(continued)

Summary

Decision making is the process of generating and evaluating alternatives and making choices among them. Some people view decision making only as problem solving; however, problems are usually better treated as opportunities. Often the distinction between a problem and an opportunity is not clear. In any event, no decision-making process is complete until the decision has been exposed to the realities of the business environment. The phases of the decision-making process are identifying the problem or opportunity, developing alternatives, evaluating alternatives, choosing and implementing the best alternative, and evaluating the decision.

Decisions may be routine or nonroutine. Many other factors may also affect a manager's decision making: the time available, the risk associated with the decision, the critical nature of the work, written guidelines, company attitudes toward decision making, the amount and kind of information available, the degree of acceptance and support by equals and superiors, the manager's personal ability as a decision maker, tunnel vision, previous commitments, implicit favorites, and lack of creativity.

Groups can be involved in any stage of the decision-making process. Three ways of involving groups are brainstorming, nominal grouping, and the Delphi technique.

There are certain decision-making requirements in addition to the decision maker. Evaluating alternatives is the payoff relationship. States of nature are the various situations that could occur and the probability of each of them occurring. The problem content is the environment in which the problem exists, the decision maker's knowledge of it, and the environment that will exist after the choice is made.

A technique that has proved beneficial to managers in the decision-making process is model building. A model is an abstraction of a real-world situation. Some of the most commonly used models are physical, schematic, and mathematical. Physical models generally look like the system they represent. Schematic models are line drawings, flowcharts, graphs, maps, organization charts, and similar items that represent the major features of a particular system. Mathematical models are equations that define and represent the relationship among elements of a system.

Most managers assume that they must be either participative or nonparticipative in involving workers in decision making. Also, some managers believe they will lose control if they involve workers in decision making. That is not necessarily the case, since the degree of worker participation may differ in each step of the decision-making process.

To handle crisis decision making, managers should watch situations that could become critical, should stay calm, should accept the possibility of additional risk, and should remember that if anything can go wrong, it will.

Review Questions

1. Define *decision making* and identify the steps in the decision-making process.
2. Explain what is meant by the following statement: The ability to select the best course of action from several possible alternatives often separates successful managers from less successful ones.
3. The text identifies several factors that affect decision making. Briefly discuss each factor.
4. Define each of the following terms:
   a. brainstorming
   b. nominal grouping
   c. Delphi technique
5. Briefly describe each of the requirements that must be present before the decision-making process can be carried out.
6. Define *model*. How can a model be used to assist in the decision-making process?
7. Describe how worker participation may differ in each step of the decision-making process.
8. How can managers handle decision making in a crisis situation?

Key Terms

Decision making	Brainstorming	Model
Alternatives	Nominal grouping	Physical models
Nonroutine decisions	Delphi technique	Schematic models
Decision risk	Payoff relationship	Mathematical models
Tunnel vision	States of nature	Worker participation
Creativity	Problem content	

CASE 4.1	**EXPANSION PLANS FOR THE TOGGERY**

Nan Rabinowitz, president of The Toggery, Inc., and a member of the board of directors, felt she already had two strikes against her. She knew expansion from Massachusetts into the other New England states was a good idea. But getting the mandate she needed from the rest of the board was going to be difficult. Nan thought two other members of the five-member board favored her position, but two were adamantly opposed. And Nan was unwilling to move ahead without unanimity.

The Toggery operated fourteen men's clothing stores in Massachusetts. It was a family business, owned equally by Audrey and Lewis Simone and Sheila and Marc Crown. Audrey and Sheila started the business in 1980 with just one store. By 1983, they had eight stores, all profitable. That year, Lewis left his job with Raytheon and joined The Toggery as vice-president and member of the board of directors. At that time, Audrey was president and Sheila was vice-president. Marc joined the board of directors that same year but continued to work full-time at BayBank Middlesex, where he was chief executive. Marc was a well-known community leader in Waltham, Massachusetts, the Boston suburb where The Toggery was headquartered. Among many other civic activities, he served as chairman of the United Way campaign in 1985 and president of the Waltham Chamber of Commerce in 1986.

Nan, a Harvard MBA, had worked as an executive with Filene's Department Stores for several years before joining The Toggery in 1985. She was hired when the Simones and Crowns could no longer agree that any member of the family should be chief executive. She directed the company as it grew from ten stores to fourteen, all in Massachusetts, and took credit for doubling The Toggery's profits. Her plan in early 1987 was for the company to open four new stores that year in Vermont and to move into other states later. All The Toggery stores were rental units in neighborhood shopping centers, and that was not expected to change.

As Nan planned for the August director's meeting, she remembered a recent conversation with Marc Crown. Marc had said, "I am not willing for us to borrow any more money until we have our present operation clear of debt." Nan had argued that expansion was not possible without more borrowing, but Marc had refused to budge. Nan did not understand how a banker could feel that way, especially because The Toggery had much less debt than most similar companies. But she knew that if she could convince Marc, the others would go along.

When the meeting night arrived, Nan had prepared a very professional presentation on her proposal. After she went over it with the other directors, the following interchange occurred:

Marc: I'm still opposed. What do you think, Audrey?

Audrey: Nan has put a lot of work into this. She has a tough job trying to mediate among all of us. I think we owe her a vote of confidence.

Sheila: Marc, I usually go along with you, and I will this time. But if Lewis and Audrey are in favor, I don't think we should stand in the way.

Marc: Lewis, you and Audrey have talked about this, haven't you? Are you in agreement?

Lewis: Well, when we came here tonight, I think Audrey and I both were inclined to stay concentrated in Massachusetts. But Nan's excellent analysis has obviously changed Audrey's mind, and I could go either way.

The discussion continued for about an hour, but no decision was made. It was clear to Nan that everyone except Marc really wanted to accept her proposal, although Lewis remained equivocal.

Nan called Marc the next morning and asked if they could have lunch together. "Of course, Nan," said Marc, "I think we need to talk. The others have given me their proxies on the expansion decision, and maybe we can lay that to rest." Nan resolved that if Marc was not willing to approve her plan, she would resign and go into the business herself. She had several wealthy friends who were aware of her excellent success in managing The Toggery and would probably jump at a chance to invest in any venture she started.

Questions

1. What factors should Nan consider in deciding whether to go into business for herself?
2. Evaluate the board of director's decision-making effort.

CASE 4.2	A REQUEST FOR SPECIAL FAVORS

"My husband has made plans for us to go, and he says we're going," said Barbara Kener. Barbara was a payroll clerk at Wellingham Corporation, a Brockton, Massachusetts, shoe manufacturer. Barbara had just asked Jerry Wall, the payroll department manager, if she could take a week of vacation the first week of January to visit her husband's family. Jerry had tried to talk her out of it because of the heavy workload

during that period, but Barbara clearly felt strongly about taking the time off.

It had been customary for payroll department clerical personnel to schedule their vacations at times other than during January, because it was then that the payroll department had the most to do. All of the individual payroll records had to be finished, and a wide range of reports, including the employee W-2 forms for two thousand employees, had to be completed. Jerry was not sure he would be able to meet the deadlines for preparation of the reports without Barbara's help. Barbara was an especially efficient worker; and although she had been employed only since March, Jerry had come to depend on her.

Jerry recalled that when Barbara was hired, he had failed to discuss the need for avoiding January vacations, telling her only that she would be eligible for one week of vacation for each six months of employment. Jerry felt somewhat responsible for the misunderstanding. But he knew that letting Barbara take her vacation as requested might hurt morale in the department, even if the workload could be handled. Not only would the others have to work harder, but Jerry remembered having turned down two special requests for January vacations in the past.

Questions

1. What should Jerry do about Barbara's request? In answering this question, use the decision-making process developed in the chapter.
2. What situational factors should Jerry consider in making the decision? Why?

Notes

1. This case is a composite of a number of accounts, among them: Standard and Poor's Corporation, "Coca-Cola," *Standard NYSE Stock Reports* 56, no. 89 (May 9, 1989): sec. 7; John H. Taylor, "Some Things Don't Go Better with Coke," *Forbes*, March 21, 1988, pp. 34–35; Thomas Moore, "He Put the Kick Back into Coke," *Fortune*, October 26, 1987, pp. 46–56; Peter Waldman, "Coke Enterprises had Disappointing Fourth-Period Net," *Wall Street Journal*, February 3, 1989, p. C14; Alison L. Sprout, "America's Most Admired Corporations," *Fortune*, February 11, 1991, pp. 57–58; Michael J. McCarthy, "Coca-Cola Is Facing New Pepsi Challenge: Avoiding Signs of Age," *Wall Street Journal*, October 1, 1991, p. A1.

2. Alex Taylor III, "How a Top Boss Manages His Day," *Fortune*, June 19, 1989, pp. 95–100.

3. Jeremy Main, "B-Schools Get a Global Vision," *Fortune*, July 17, 1989, pp. 78–86.

4. John Rossant and Wendy Zellner, "How Chrysler's $30,000 Sports Car Got Sideswiped," *Business Week*, January 23, 1989, p. 68.

5. Thomas J. Murry, "Wal-Mart Stores Penny Wise," *Business Month*, December 1988, p. 42.

6. Adapted from Alvar O. Elbing, *Behavioral Decisions in Organizations* (Glenview, IL: Scott, Foresman, 1970), p. 14.

7. Ralph C. Davis, *The Fundamentals of Top Management* (New York: Harper & Row, 1951), p. 55.

8. Donald D. White and David A. Bednar, *Organizational Behavior: Understanding and Managing People at Work* (Newton, MA: Allyn and Bacon, 1986), p. 285.

9. B. M. Staw, "The Escalation of Commitment to a Course of Action," *Academy of Management Review* 6 (October 1981): 577–587.

10. P. O. Soelberg, "Unprogrammed Decision Making," *Industrial Management Review* 8 (1967): 19–29.

11. D. J. Treffinger and J. D. Gowan, "An Updated Representative List of Methods and Educational Programs for Stimulating Creativity," *Journal of Creative Behavior* 5 (1971): 127–139.

12. C. Patrick, *What Is Creative Thinking?* (New York: Philosophical Library, 1955).

13. Maier, op. cit.

14. John Hoerr, "Is Teamwork a Management Plot? Mostly Not," *Business Week*, February 20, 1989, p. 70.

15. J. L. Adams, *Conceptual Blockbusting: A Guide to Better Ideas*, 2d ed. (New York: Norton, 1979).

16. A. L. Delbecq and A. H. Van de Ven, "A Group Process Model for Problem Identification and Program Planning," *Journal of Applied Behavioral Science* 7 (1971): 466–492.

17. Ibid.

18. Brian Dumaine, "What the Leaders of Tomorrow See," *Fortune*, July 3, 1989, pp. 48–62.

19. Larry Hatcher and Timothy L. Ross, "Gainsharing Plans —How Managers Evaluate Them," *Business* 36 (October–December, 1986): 30.

20. "Mr. Smith Goes Global," *Business Week*, February 13, 1989, p. 66.

21. Zachary Schiller, Ted Holden, and Mark Maremont, "P&G Global by Acting like a Global," *Business Week*, August 28, 1989, p. 58.

5

The Planning Process

After completing this chapter students should be able to

■ Describe the planning process and explain the function of a mission statement.

■ State the importance of objectives and describe plans.

■ Explain standing plans, explain the levels of planning, and describe the planning process for lower-level managers.

■ Describe contingency planning.

■ Describe management by objectives (MBO), explain the essential elements of the MBO process, state characteristics of performance objectives for the individual, and assess the overall effectiveness of MBO programs.

AT&T doubled its earnings from $1.37 billion in 1984 to $2.74 billion in 1990, and revenues rose 12 percent. This is excellent performance for a company that was shocked into a top management transition, which could have left it rudderless, at least for a while. It was two days before AT&T's 1988 annual meeting when chief executive James Olsen died. At 5:29 A.M., Mrs. Olson called Robert Allen, the president and chief operating officer; and he called other senior executives of the firm. Allen later talked about that day: "We were all terribly distraught, but there was so much to do. It was really not until later that we had time to mourn. Jim was such a vibrant and dynamic person. He really touched the lives of an awful lot of AT&T people, so it was a shock, and a particular emotional burden for me because he had also been a good friend. I was aware that I was Jim's choice [to succeed him] and that I would probably be the board's choice. But I really thought I had another year or two to prepare."

Allen was chosen by the board and took office immediately. He was thrust to the helm—with only the knowledge that he must hold it steady, without a plan for the course he would steer. He had no firm plan for dealing with the sudden void that was created at AT&T, and therefore he was not ready to act immediately. "Jim's death caused me to pause for a few months and rethink a lot of things about the business, about where we ought to go and how I ought to lead," said Allen. He found the direction he needed and, by all accounts, was very successful. Analysts give Allen credit for changing the corporate culture to a more adaptive one and for recruiting a cadre of good, young executives, ensuring smooth management succession into the twenty-first century. A former chairman said of Allen, "He is an orderly person. He knows the business well. It is good for AT&T to have a steady person now."

Allen is indeed a steady person who plans to accomplish AT&T's number 1 mission: growth. This mission is not a speculation, but a perfectly clear statement of what AT&T is going to do. Allen is not satisfied with the 12 percent increase in revenue, and therefore is focusing on growth. To achieve this mission, he recruited experienced top managers from outside the company. According to Allen, planning in the old Bell System was easy: Thick manuals spelled out procedures for every possible eventuality, and it didn't take a whole lot of strategy to succeed. However, today's competitive environment requires solid planning and effective management. Allen has put his plan into action, hiring a few top managers who were already successful, and working with them to plan a course for the future that will allow AT&T to achieve its mission of growth.[1]

Planning is central to the success of any company, including AT&T. As the AT&T example suggests, planning in a competitive environment is much more than following well-established procedures. The mission must be clearly understood, and effective managers must be in place to accomplish it. AT&T's chairman and CEO Robert Allen has a clear picture of the company's mission of growth. This is communicated throughout the organization. Specific objectives are established in each unit, and a proven manager is in place to keep all units of the organization contributing to AT&T's overall mission.

This chapter begins with a brief overview of the planning process. Next it discusses the elements of the planning process—mission, objectives, and plans—in detail. The remainder of the chapter is devoted to the following planning topics: standing plans, the levels of planning, the planning process, contingency planning, succession planning, a global perspective of effective planning, and management by objectives. This chapter is intended to instill an appreciation of the importance of effective planning, regardless of whether the planner is a company president, a supervisor, or a manager of a small business.

The Planning Process

Planning

The process of determining in advance what should be accomplished and how it should be realized.

Planning is *the process of determining in advance what should be accomplished and how it should be realized.* Figure 5–1 illustrates the planning process and serves as a guide for planning. The process applies to planning done by managers at all levels. As the figure indicates, planning begins with an understanding of the organizational mission. From the mission statement, specific objectives (or goals) can be established; then plans can be developed to accomplish them. Remember that AT&T's number 1 mission is growth. Plans then were developed to accomplish this mission. The

FIGURE 5–1

The Planning Process

The planning process often involves people from different organizations. For example, Westinghouse Credit Corporation provided financing for an affiliate of the Hillman Company to acquire real estate for development in the Los Angeles area. Westinghouse Credit vice president Daryl Carter (center) helps Hillman executives plan the project.

Source: Photograph courtesy of Westinghouse Corporation

planning process is dynamic. It must be continually evaluated and adapted to conform to the unfolding situation that management confronts.

Planning is vital to all firms. Effective planning can have a major impact on individual, group, and organizational productivity. Planning is becoming more and more complex as a global economy becomes a greater reality. While the United States was reeling under record trade deficits in the 1980s, major U.S. companies were seeking ways to become more competitive internationally. Foreign competitors, especially those in Japan, were chipping away at domestic markets—in automobiles, in electronics, in steel, and even in computer chips, where the United States had long retained dominance.

Planning provides direction, reduces the overall impact of change, increases productivity, and allows managers to organize, lead, control, and direct the activities necessary to accomplish organizational objectives. The need for planning exists at all levels, but it is extremely important at higher levels, where the potential for impact on organizational success is greater. Top-level managers like AT&T's Robert Allen plan for the future, thereby allowing the entire organization to crystallize its strategies. Once upper-level strategies are well defined and understood, lower-level managers can plan to accomplish the objectives of their units. If one were to isolate the most significant reason for planning, it would be the fact that most studies show that managers who plan outperform nonplanners on traditional financial measures, such as profits.[2]

The elements of the organization's environment, as shown in Figure 5–1, are dynamic. For example, the Boston city government decided to dismantle an old elevated railway (called "The El"). Underneath the railway, traffic was being disrupted during the project, and the merchants along the street had to make plans to remain in business. A fish market owner planned to take out a loan so the business could survive with lower profits for a time. And the manager of a grocery store rearranged his store so a side entrance could be used.

Mission

The **mission** is *a unit's continuing purpose, or reason for being*. The number one mission at AT&T's is growth in the communication field. The **mission statement** is *a broadly stated definition of the basic purpose and scope of a unit*.[3] A clear statement of mission serves to guide individuals, groups, and managers throughout the organization. The mission may not need to be published externally, but it should be understood by managers at all levels. A mission statement should be established for the entire company and for each department or unit in it. Naturally, the mission of each unit should be in agreement with the organizational mission. The question that needs to be answered to develop an appropriate mission statement is: For what reason is this unit in existence?

Each unit of an organization has a mission that guides its direction. For instance, the pharmaceutical company Merck is number 1 in the world, but that means a market share of only 4.4 percent. Managers at Merck are not resting on their laurels, but instead are working to double their current market share.[4] Merck's mission, its continuing purpose, is to be the untouchable number 1 pharmaceutical company in the world. In order for this mission to be accomplished, each unit has a mission that should work in harmony with the overall company mission. For instance, the research and development department for Merck might have a mission of developing an idea for a new drug each quarter and completing research on and obtaining Food and Drug Administration (FDA) approval for a new drug each year. (Organizational mission is a major focus of Chapter 6.)

MANAGEMENT IN PRACTICE: A Skill-Building Exercise

Cecil Ross was the maintenance supervisor for Devon Products Company, a Knoxville, Tennessee, producer of plastic pipe and fittings. In early December 1992, he was told by the plant manager to make plans to refurbish the number 3 extruding machine. This was to be done the weekend of January 13 and 14.

The extruding machine was a vital part of Devon's operation. Cecil had been keeping a checklist of needed repairs. But making the repairs had not been possible because the machine had not been shut down for a single day since July.

Cecil stayed on the job late that evening to inspect the machine and to update his checklist. He also checked the spare parts room and the toolroom and made up an order for additional parts and tools that would be needed for the job.

The next day, Cecil held a meeting with his maintenance workers so they would be prepared. Over the next several days, he looked at each repair item and prepared a written task assignment schedule. He assigned each task to the worker he considered most competent to do it.

Cecil knew that after the machine was shut down he would find some unexpected defects. Also, some of the jobs would not go exactly as planned. So he decided to use his best worker, Breece Gimler, as utility man. Breece would handle unexpected repairs and help the other workers when needed.

When the crew members returned from the Christmas holidays, Cecil gave each person a list of that person's repair tasks for the machine. On January 11, he held a final meeting to prepare for the shutdown. Cecil worked some extra hours that weekend. But because he had planned well, the machine was back on line in good repair on Monday morning.

Was Cecil an effective planner?

Objectives

Once the mission is understood, specific objectives can be established. **Objectives** are *the desired end results of any activity*. They should be set at each managerial level in the organization; however, lower-level objectives should be consistent with upper-level objectives (see Figure 5–2).

Objectives
The desired end results of any activity.

How Managers Establish Good Objectives

Objectives should have four basic characteristics: (1) They should be expressed in writing, (2) they should be measurable, (3) they should be specific as to time, and (4) they should be challenging but attainable (see Figure 5–3). Placing the objectives in written form increases people's understanding of and commitment to them.

Measurability suggests that the objectives should be quantified whenever possible. It would be much better to have an objective of increasing profits by 10 percent during a certain period than merely to say, "We want to increase profits." Any increase would meet the latter objective.

Objectives should be specific as to time. Individuals need and want to know when an objective should be accomplished. Also, an objective that is set without a time

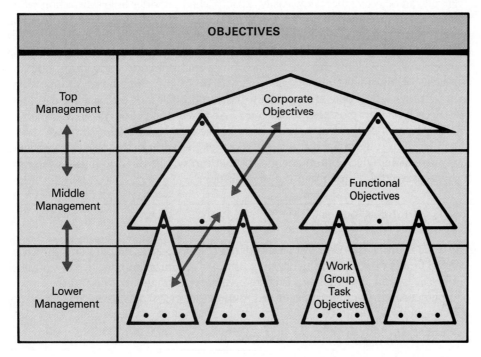

FIGURE 5–2

Consistency of Objectives

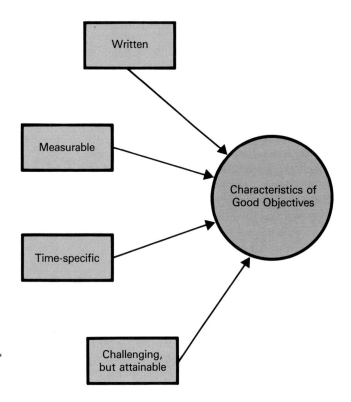

FIGURE 5–3

Characteristics of
Good Objectives

limit cannot be challenging. In the measurability example, are the profits to be increased by 10 percent this year or by the end of the century?

Finally, an objective that is too easily accomplished provides little satisfaction when it is met. On the other hand, an unattainable objective is more likely to frustrate workers than to encourage them. Therefore, objectives should be challenging but attainable. Objectives are established at each level of management. Those set by top management should be consistent with the overall mission of the firm. And the objectives of lower-level management should be in line with those of upper-level management. The people charged with the responsibility of establishing corporate objectives vary from business to business. At times, the president or chairman of the board provides the major thrust in objective creation. At other times, a group of top-level executives are consulted. Whatever the source, the objectives provide the course along which future energies of the firm will be directed and set the tone for objective setting throughout the organization.

Types of Objectives

The creation of specific organizational and unit objectives is no simple task. Numerous external factors exert their influence on a firm. An organization usually has a number of objectives, and the emphasis each receives may change according to the impact of a particular environmental factor or group of factors. At least three main types of objectives can be identified:

- *Economic*—survival, profit, and growth.

- *Service*—creation of benefit for society.
- *Personal*—objectives of individuals and groups within the organization.

AT&T is successful, and one reason may be that the company continually attempts to achieve all three types of objectives.

Economic Objectives   Survival is a basic objective of all organizations. Whether or not an organization is producing something of economic value to society seems to take second place to just staying alive. It is difficult for a firm to take into account higher social objectives when it is not known whether the next payroll can be met. As an anonymous statesman once said, "It is extremely difficult to think that your initial objective was to drain the swamp when you are up to your knees in alligators."

In order to survive, a firm must at least break even—that is, it must generate enough revenues to cover costs. But business firms want more than mere survival; they are in business to make a profit. Profit provides a vital incentive for the continued successful operation of the enterprise. An adequate profit depends primarily on the industry and the specific needs of an organization.

Growth—in sales, number of employees, or number of facilities—may also be a major objective of a firm. It may set the stage for long-term survival. A company may seek unrestricted growth, which sometimes becomes an end in itself. When this happens, the company may fail to give proper emphasis to profitability. There are, of course, certain economic advantages that come with size, and many companies see growth as a way of competing more effectively. AT&T's growth mission is one reason that AT&T continues to be successful.

Service Objectives   Profit alone is often viewed as the primary motive for being in business. Although it is true that a firm cannot survive for long without making a profit, many managers also recognize an obligation to society. Even those who feel

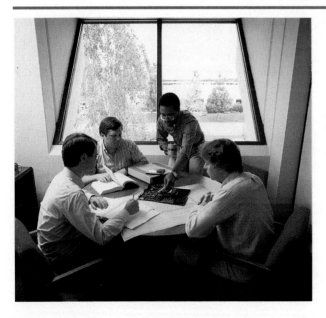

Objectives should be specific as to time. Individuals need and want to know when an objective should be accomplished. The creation of specific organizational and unit objectives is no simple task. Computers often assist managers to determine the best objectives.

Source: Photograph courtesy of Atari Corporation

no such responsibility know that if a firm cannot consistently create economic value for society, it will not stay in business long enough to make a profit. AT&T continually strives to offer its customers value in terms of quality personal service at competitive prices. AT&T therefore consistently creates economic value for society. Many firms have gone out of existence when they ceased producing goods and services desired by society.

Personal Objectives Organizations are made up of people who have different personalities, backgrounds, experiences, and objectives. Personal objectives are seldom identical to the objectives of the organization. If personal and organizational objectives are incompatible, an employee may choose to withdraw from the firm. But many employees do not feel financially able to leave their firms. A conflict between an employee's objectives and the organization's objectives can result in minimal work effort, absenteeism, and even sabotage. A conflict between group objectives and the organization's objectives can have the same negative effects. Employees are not the only ones whose objectives, when they differ from those of the organization, can affect the organization. For instance, a stockholder whose objectives conflict with the objectives of the organization could cease to provide support for the organization by selling stock.

Personal objectives also include the objectives of groups. If an organization is to survive, grow, and earn a profit, it must provide a reasonable match between its objectives and the objectives of powerful groups. Table 5–1 shows how the objectives of a business might differ from those of related groups. It is not unusual for particular groups or their members to experience actual or imagined conflict between their personal objectives and the objectives of the organization. For instance, some customers may believe that higher wages will make the price of products higher, whereas the union may believe that stockholders' profits are too high. Management has the difficult task of reconciling these conflicts, whether or not they are based on factual information.

Problems Encountered in Establishing Objectives

Conflicts among objectives can result from many sources. Three potential sources are the existence of real objectives that are different from the stated ones, the use

TABLE 5–1

Possible Objectives of the Organization and Related Groups

Groups	Possible Objectives
Organization	Maximizing profits.
Management	Promotions, higher salaries, and bonuses.
Employees	Increased wages and bonuses.
Government	Adherence of firm to all government laws and regulations.
Competition	Attaining a greater share of the market.
Customers	Quality product at lowest price.
Stockholders/owners	Higher dividends.
Society	Protection of the environment.
Unions	Greater influence for union members.

of multiple objectives, and the application of quantitative versus nonquantitative objectives.

Real versus Stated Objectives   The real objectives may be at odds with the stated objectives. Objectives are often the result of power plays and pressures that come from circumstances in the marketplace or from internal tensions. The personal objectives of the board of directors, outside creditors, lower-level managers, employees, stockholders, and labor unions are bound to be different. Stated objectives are often significantly altered by individuals and groups who seek to adapt the organization to their narrower purposes. Because of these differences, the stated objectives are at times different from the real objectives.

To determine the real objectives, one must look at the organization's day-to-day decisions and actions. A manager's actions speak louder than words. For example, Japanese corporations are normally polite, collective-rule companies. However, those who work for the Kyocera Corporation realize that the company founder and Chairman of the Board, Kazuo Inamori, does not believe in shared leadership through quality circles. His actions have shown him to be a military-style disciplinarian. Employees at this company would do well not to question the objectives of the company, since Inamori is setting those objectives.

Other clues as to the actual direction of the organization may be discovered by asking these questions: What functions or groups receive the major share of the resources? What type of behavior is accorded the greatest rewards by management? The top managers of a prison may specify its major objective as being rehabilitation of prisoners. But if the prison employs only two counselors and has five hundred guards, the facts contradict the stated objective.

Multiple Objectives   All organizations have multiple objectives that must be recognized by management. For instance, what is the major objective of a university? Is it to provide education for students, to conduct research to advance the state of knowledge, or to provide community service? In some universities, research is given the first priority in money, personnel, and privilege. In others, the teaching objective is dominant. In still others, an attempt is made to be all things to all people. Given limited funds, however, priorities must be established. One can debate the priority of objectives for such institutions as a mental hospital (therapy or confinement), a church (religion or social relationships), a prison (rehabilitation or confinement), a vocational high school (skill development, general education, or keeping young people off the streets), a medical school (training medical students for clinical practice, basic research, or academic medicine), and an aerospace firm (research information or usable hardware). Seemingly conflicting objectives may not be mutually exclusive, but choices must be made as to how much emphasis each is to receive.

Quantitative versus Nonquantitative Objectives   In general, the more quantitative an objective, the greater the attention on and pressure for its accomplishment. The feasibility of quantifying objectives varies throughout the organization. Production managers, for example, often have specific quotas and schedules. It is easy to tell if either quantity or quality declines. Human resource managers, on the other hand, often have more subjective objectives. The fact that the human resource manager's objectives are more subjective does not mean that they are less important.

If the most important objective is also the most measurable, such as the objective of winning for a professional sports team, then little distortion will take place. But when important objectives are not so easily measured, organizations are likely to be pushed in the direction of the more quantitative, but perhaps less important, objectives. For example, in universities, research and publication are far easier to measure precisely than is excellence in teaching. Thus, the primary objective, excellence in education, may be replaced with the research emphasis.

When objectives at various levels in an organization conflict, ways must be found to correct the problem. Dairy Queen has struggled with the contrasting objectives of its franchisees for decades.

Conflicting Objectives at Dairy Queen

Among the top ten fast-food franchisers, Dairy Queen trailed the crowd in profitability, sales per store, and franchisee contentment. The Dairy Queen operation lacked clear, well-defined objectives, and therefore the operational plans were fragmented and at times did not seem to apply to many of the company's individual operations. The over 5,200 Dairy Queen restaurants run the gamut from large, well-run operations to ice cream stands that shut down in winter. The managers of these diverse restaurants do not appear to be overly concerned with the corporate image. The small units are often managed by owner-operators with one or two employees, while fifty-unit "mini chains" of Dairy Queens in several states may be run by one corporate franchisee.

As Dairy Queen's fortunes worsened in the late 1980s, statewide "operators' groups" became more aggressive. For example, the Texas group insisted on its own "Country Basket" special instead of the company's "Basket Deal." According to the Texas operators' group, Dairy Queen's approach has been "I'm right, you're dumb."

Planning was refocused, keying in on consistency, which is a basic rule of franchising, and Dairy Queen planned to make its system more uniform. It bought out a number of mini-chain operators who wanted to go their own way. It gave weaker franchisees low-interest loans to upgrade their restaurants. It also gave them a break on royalties on the increased sales the improvements produced. The number of management levels in the Dairy Queen organization was reduced to assure better communication and tighter control. And the company worked through its "National Council" of franchisees to sell its members on consistency.[5]

In the Dairy Queen situation, the company objectives were not very measurable and did not appear to filter down to the franchise level. The resulting problems at the franchise level caused problems throughout the Dairy Queen operation. Once the company formulated solid corporate objectives, communicated them to the franchisees, and provided oversight and financial support, the situation at Dairy Queen began to improve.

Plans

Plans
Statements of how objectives are to be accomplished.

The next step in the planning process is the creation of plans. **Plans** are *statements of how objectives are to be accomplished.* Planning is a task that every manager, whether a top-level executive or a first-line supervisor, must perform. Stating an objective does not guarantee its accomplishment. A plan must be developed to inform people what to do in order to fulfill the objective. There is usually more than one way to accomplish an objective. The plan states which approach is to be taken. Specifically, planning should answer the following questions:

1. What activities are required to accomplish the objective?
2. When should these activities be carried out?
3. Who is responsible for doing what?
4. Where should the activities be carried out?
5. When should the action be completed?

John Sculley, president and CEO of Apple Computer Inc., obviously was effective at carrying out these steps.

● ●

John Sculley planned a new course for the future by assuring that Apple Computer's top management team would develop a comprehensive product line strategy designed to keep Apple positioned as the technological and marketing leader in the fast-growing personal computer industry. The progression of Sculley's career—he was the youngest-ever president of PepsiCo, then moved on to the top leadership role at Apple Computer—was due in part to effective planning. Working very hard to control the technological atmosphere of the computer business, Sculley developed a plan to streamline Apple management, restore discipline to the corporation, and satisfy consumers in the company's primary markets. Since Sculley took over in 1983, Apple's sales have almost tripled, to $2.7 billion. Currently, the firm is seventh in size in the overall U.S. computer industry and number 2 in the personal computer market.[6]

John Sculley Plans for Apple Computer

● ●

Standing Plans

Plans that remain roughly the same for long periods of time are **standing plans.** The most common kinds of standing plans are policies, procedures, and rules.

Standing plans

Plans that remain roughly the same for long periods of time.

Policies

A predetermined guide established to provide direction in decision making is a **policy.** Policies should be based on thorough analyses of corporate objectives. Separate policies cover each of the important areas of a firm, such as personnel, marketing, research and development, production, and finance.

To formulate a policy, the manager must have knowledge and skill in the area for which the policy is being created. However, certain generalizations apply to the establishment of policies. The most important has already been stated: Policies must be based on a thorough analysis of objectives. Several other points can help the manager create appropriate policies:

Policy

A predetermined guide established to provide direction in decision making.

1. *Policies should be based on factual information.*

2. *Subordinate and superior policies should be complementary, not contradictory.* For instance, a policy for an individual department at AT&T should not conflict with the company's corporate policy.

3. *Policies of different divisions or departments should be coordinated.* Policies should be directed toward organizational optimization instead of toward optimizing a particular department, such as sales, engineering, purchasing, or production, to the detriment of the whole.

4. *Policies should be definite, understandable, and, preferably, in writing.* If a policy is to guide actions, the people concerned must be aware of its existence. This requires creating understandable directives in a definitive written form. In effect, policies are the memory of the organization, which it uses to help cope with future events.

5. *Policies should be stable and flexible.* The requirements of stability and flexibility are not contradictory. Stable policies change only in response to fundamental and basic changes in conditions. Government regulations can represent such a basic change and therefore have a major impact on a firm's policies. The higher the organizational level, the more stable the policy must be. Changing the direction of the enterprise is a much more complex and time-consuming task than changing the direction of a department or section. Armco Inc. provides an excellent example of a firm whose policies have been remarkably stable. First formulated in 1919, these policies, outlined in Table 5–2, are still applicable today.

6. *Policies should be reasonably comprehensive in scope.* Policies conserve the executive's time by making available a previously determined decision. The manager should organize the workplace in such a way that subordinates can handle the routine and predictable work in conformity with established policies while the manager's time is devoted to exceptional events and problems. If the body of policies is reasonably comprehensive, few cases arise that are not covered by policy.

Procedures and Rules

Procedure

A series of steps for the accomplishment of some specific project or endeavor.

Standard operating procedures (SOPs)

The stable body of procedures, written and unwritten, that govern an organization.

Rule

A specific and detailed guide to action set up to direct or restrict action in a fairly narrow manner.

Procedures and rules might be thought of as further restrictions on the actions of lower-level employees. They are usually established to ensure adherence to a particular policy.

Procedures　*A series of steps for the accomplishment of some specific project or endeavor* is a **procedure.** Many organizations have extensive procedure manuals designed to provide guidelines for lower-level managers and workers. *The stable body of procedures, written and unwritten, that govern an organization* are called **standard operating procedures (SOPs).** For most policies, there are accompanying procedures to indicate how the policies should be carried out.

Rules　*A specific and detailed guide to action set up to direct or restrict action in a fairly narrow manner* is a **rule.** There may be a rule that requires hard hats to be worn in a certain work area, for example.

TABLE 5-2

Armco Inc. Policies

Ethics	To do business guided and governed by the highest standards of conduct so the end result of action taken makes a good reputation an invaluable and permanent asset.
Square deal	To insist on a square deal always. To make sure people are listened to and treated fairly, so that men and women really do right for right's sake and not just to achieve a desired result. For everyone to go beyond narrowness, littleness, and selfishness in order to get the job done.
Organization	To develop and maintain an efficient, loyal, aggressive organization who believe in their company, to whom work is a challenge, and to whom extraordinary accomplishment is a personal goal.
Working conditions	To create and maintain good working conditions . . . to provide the best possible equipment and facilities . . . and plants and offices that are clean, orderly, and safe.
Quality and service	To adopt "Quality and Service" as an everyday practice. Quality will be the highest attainable in products, organization, plant, property, and equipment. Service will be the best possible to customers, to shareholders, to city, state, and nation.
Opportunity	To employ people without regard to race, sex, religion, or national origin. To encourage employees to improve their skills by participating in available educational or training programs. To provide every possible opportunity for advancement so that each individual may reach his or her highest potential.
Compensation	To provide not only fair remuneration, but the best compensation for services rendered that it is possible to pay under the changing economic, commercial, and other competitive conditions that exist from time to time. It is Armco's ambition to develop an organization of such spirit, loyalty, and efficiency that can and will secure results which will make it possible for individual members to earn and receive better compensation than would be possible if performing a similar service in other fields of effort.
Incentive	To provide realistic and practical incentives as a means of encouraging the highest standard of individual performance and to assure increased quantity and quality of performance.
Cooperation	To recognize cooperation as the medium through which great accomplishments are attained. Success depends more on a spirit of helpful cooperation than on any other one factor.
Objectivity	To always consider what is right and best for the business as a whole, rather than what may be expedient in dealing with a single, separate situation.
Conflict of interest	To prohibit employees from becoming financially interested in any company with which Armco does business, if such financial interest might possibly influence decisions employees must make in their areas of responsibility. The above policy does not apply to ownership in publicly owned companies. This is not considered a conflict of interest but, rather, is encouraged as part of the free enterprise system.
Citizenship	To create and maintain a working partnership between industry and community in this country and throughout the world. To support constructive agencies in communities where Armco people live and work in an effort to create civic conditions that respond to the highest needs of the citizens.

SOURCE: Used with permission from Armco Inc.

The differences among policies, procedures, and rules are shown in Table 5–3. As the table shows, procedures and rules may overlap. Taken out of sequence, a step in a procedure may become a rule.

Policies, procedures, and rules are designed to direct action toward the accomplishment of objectives. If it could be assured that people doing the work completely agreed with and understood basic objectives, there would be less need for policies, procedures, and rules. However, it is apparent that objectives at times are unclear

TABLE 5–3

Examples of Policies, Procedures, and Rules

POLICY	It is the policy of the company that every employee is entitled to a safe and healthful place in which to work and that accidents should be prevented from occurring in any phase of its operation. Toward this end, the full cooperation of all employees will be required.
	Management will view neglect of its safety policy or program as just cause for disciplinary action.
PROCEDURE	The purpose of this procedure is to prevent injury to personnel or damage to equipment by inadvertent starting, energizing, or pressurizing equipment that has been shut down for maintenance, overhaul, lubrication, or setup.

1. Maintenance persons assigned to work on a job will lock out the machine at the proper disconnect with their own safety lock and keep the key in their possession.
2. If the job is not finished before shift change, the maintenance person will remove the lock and put a seal on the disconnect. A danger tag will be hung on the control station, stating why the equipment is shut down.
3. The maintenance person who will be coming on the following shift will place his or her lock on the disconnect along with a seal.
4. Upon completion of the repairs, the area supervisor will be notified by maintenance that work is completed.
5. The supervisor and the maintenance person will check the equipment to see that all guards and safety devices are securely in place and operable. Then the supervisor will break the seal and remove the danger tag from the machine.

RULES   The following rules are intended to promote employee safety.

1. The company and each employee are required to comply with provisions of the Occupational Safety and Health Act (OSHA). You will be informed by your supervisor of specific OSHA rules not covered here that apply to your job or area.
2. Report all accidents promptly that occur on the job or on company premises—this should be done whether or not any injury or damage resulted from the incident.
3. Horseplay, practical jokes, wrestling, throwing things, running in the plant, and similar actions will not be tolerated, as they can cause serious accidents.

and even controversial. Thus, all organizations need policies, procedures, and rules—which should be more definitive and understandable than the objectives on which they are based.

ETHICAL DILEMMA

Your firm is one of the largest subcontractors in the toy assembly business. A couple of years ago, you moved one of your operations to a south Florida town where 100 older, well-qualified workers were willing to provide you with high-quality labor for minimum wages and no benefits. You leased a partially completed industrial park that includes three large assembly buildings, an office building, and an apartment complex whose units you could rent to up to 200 employees for only $200 to $300 per month.

You promised the town's industrial board members that if they could locate another 150 retired workers who were willing to work for no benefits and minimum wages, you would give these workers permanent jobs, good working conditions, and sub-

4. Observe all warning signs, such as "No Smoking," "Stop," etc. They are there for your protection.

5. Keep your mind on the work being performed.

6. Familiarize yourself with the specific safety rules and precautions that relate to your work area.

7. Approved eye protection must be worn in all factory and research lab areas during scheduled working hours or at any other time work is being performed.

8. Hearing protection is required when the noise level in an area reaches limits established by OSHA.

9. Adequate hand protection should be worn while working with solvents or other materials that might be harmful to hands.

10. Wearing rings or other jewelry that could cause injury is not allowed for persons performing work in the factory area.

11. Good housekeeping is important to accident prevention. Keep your immediate work area, machinery, and equipment clean. Keep tools and materials neatly and securely stored so that they will not cause injury to you or others.

12. Aisles, fire equipment access, and other designated "clear" areas must not be blocked.

13. Learn the correct way to lift. Get help if the material to be lifted is too heavy to be lifted alone. Avoid an effort that is likely to injure you.

14. Only authorized employees are allowed to operate forklifts and company vehicles. Passengers are not allowed on lift equipment or other material-handling equipment except as required in the performance of a job.

15. Learn the right way to do your job. If you are not sure you thoroughly understand a job, ask for assistance. This will often contribute to your job performance as well as your job safety.

16. Observe safe and courteous driving habits in the parking lot.

---

sidized low-cost housing. The retirees would be able to substantially increase their standard of living and quality of life by moving to the area. Your work force subsequently grew to 250 employees.

After nineteen months, all of your employees from other areas have sold their homes and moved to Florida. They are enjoying the location, their jobs, their new social relationships, and their increased income.

You have just received some bad news from your business adviser. Congress is about to pass a wage and benefits law that will increase the minimum wage by 65 cents an hour and will require employers with over 100 workers to offer a benefits package to each employee. If you provide such a pay and benefits package, your profits will be reduced by approximately 60 percent. Your adviser is sure the bill will pass. She recommends that you purchase a new subassembly machine that will allow you to eliminate the need for all but 75 employees. The lead time for getting the machine is nine to eighteen months from when the order is placed, so the decision must be made rather quickly. You can take a chance that the bill won't pass, or you can purchase the new machine and cut your staff.

What would you do?

Levels of Planning

Strategic planning

The process by which top management determines overall organizational purposes and objectives and how they are to be achieved.

Tactical plans

Plans designed to implement the strategic plans of top management.

Planning is critical at every level in the organization. At the top-management level, the primary concern is with **strategic planning,** *the process by which top management determines overall organizational purposes and objectives and how they are to be achieved.* (This is the subject of Chapter 6.) Strategic plans are designed to implement the broad-based plans of top management. Strategic plans must be broken down into less generalized operating, or tactical, plans. **Tactical plans** are *plans designed to implement the strategic plans of top management.* They often relate to limited functional areas, such as sales, finance, production, and personnel. Tactical plans also encompass a shorter time frame than strategic plans. The managers who are responsible for implementing tactical plans tend to be middle- and lower-level managers, rather than top-level managers.

The Planning Process for Lower-Level Managers

All too often, discussions of planning are limited to the benefits top management may derive from proper planning. Sometimes we forget that all effective managers engage in planning. The planning process for top-level and lower-level managers is quite similar. However, the environment of lower-level managers is mainly internal. Lower-level managers are constrained by overall company objectives and strategies, but the importance of planning remains. For example, no matter how grandiose

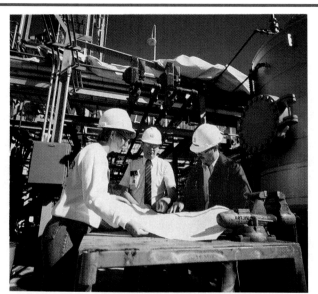

Strategic plans must be broken down into less generalized operating or tactical plans, *which are plans designed to implement or carry out the strategic-based plans of top management. In this scene, Phillips Petroleum employees at the company's Bartlesville Research Center discuss plans for a new pilot plant to make a special resin.*

Source: *Photograph courtesy of Phillips Petroleum Company*

AT&T's corporate planning, the company would fail without effective planning by lower-level employees thoughout the organization.

The amount of time spent in the planning function at lower levels of management may not be as great as at higher levels. For instance, as compared to a corporate executive, a hotel manager may devote a much larger percentage of time to influencing or controlling than to planning. However, this does not diminish the importance of planning for the hotel manager. Also, the time frame for planning may be shorter for lower-level managers than for senior executives. To be successful, top-level management must make decisions affecting operations far into the future. But to ask a lower-level manager to plan five years ahead may be unrealistic. Daily, weekly, monthly, and yearly quotas must be met.

It is quite possible that even long-range planning for some lower-level managers may encompass a relatively short time span. However, the shorter time span does not diminish the importance of long-range planning. Consider some of the types of plans that lower-level managers typically make:

- *Production plans.* The objective might be to meet a daily, weekly, or monthly production schedule. The production plan at the supervisor's level would involve scheduling jobs and assigning workers to do them.

- *Methods improvement plans.* The objective could be to find the best way to do a certain task. The plan might consist of a simple listing of the steps necessary to obtain the improvements.

- *Absences plans.* The objective might be to ensure that the work continues to get done when some workers are absent. Scheduling vacation time is an example of this form of planning.

- *Budget plans.* A budget is a statement of desired results expressed in financial or numeric terms. Although the budget itself is a plan, the supervisor's objective might be to stay within the budget. Therefore, the lower-level manager's budget plan would describe what is considered the most effective way to expend budgeted funds.

Contingency Planning

"The best laid plans of mice and men often go astray" (a paraphrase of a line from Robert Burns's poem "To a Mouse") is certainly applicable in today's business world. Events can occur so rapidly that plans may become useless before they can be fully implemented. External and internal disturbances resulting in the need for a change in plans often occur. **Contingency planning** is *the development of plans to be placed in effect if certain events occur.*

As Figure 5–4 shows, contingency planning is important at each level of management and for both strategic and operating planning. Even lower-level managers have a need for contingency planning. The manager of the production department undoubtedly has a contingency plan to cover breakdowns on certain pieces of equipment.

Contingency planning
The development of plans to be placed in effect if certain events occur.

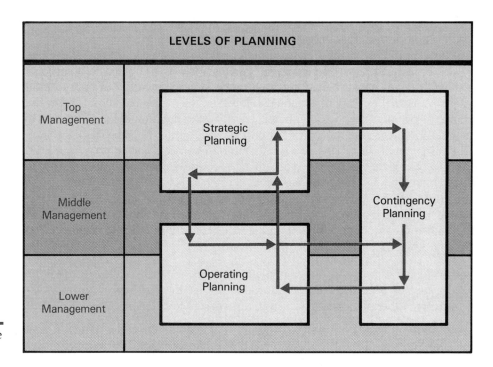

FIGURE 5–4

Contingency Planning and the Levels of Management

Contingency planning entails the recognition that events can alter the results of initial plans. Contingency planning makes it unnecessary for a firm to wait for a situation to occur before it prepares to respond. Naturally, not all situations can be anticipated, but the manager who tries to anticipate reasonably probable occurrences will stand a good chance of coping with future events. Separate plans cannot be made even for all probable situations, since such situations are usually far too numerous. So it is often useful to categorize events and link each category to fairly generalized plans.[7]

A disaster recovery plan for a computer installation is a common example of a contingency plan. Organizations that use computers become very dependent on them. This is true for practically every modern company. But what happens when the system fails? Sabotage and vandalism are human-made disasters to which computer systems may be vulnerable. Fires, floods, rainstorms, tornadoes, and hurricanes are natural threats that often disable such systems.

The plan for recovery typically involves provisions for backups, not only for the information contained in the computer but also for the functions the computer performs. The data-processing personnel for a large firm may make daily or weekly copies of master files and place them in a secure location. Contingency plans are made to obtain these files if they are needed. Some other aspects of a data-processing contingency plan might be site evacuation, damage assessment, emergency processing, and methods to keep system users informed about restoration efforts. Reciprocal emergency processing agreements between firms are often the subject of contingency plans. Because of the ever-changing external and internal conditions of many of today's businesses, contingency planning is becoming increasingly important.

After several weeks of careful planning, you have set up a job rotation schedule for your crew of twenty-one employees. Your boss has put you in charge of the first stage of a three-stage production process to create component parts for the new ultrasound machine your company has developed. The process is very sensitive to quality variances, so you have personally trained the three production supervisors under your direction. One of these individuals will be responsible for quality control in each of the three stages of component part production. Two days into this production program, your boss's boss, the production manager, "borrows" five of your people, including the three production supervisors, to help out on a special order. You are given five replacements from the company's pool of temporary help.

How could this affect your planning?

Succession Planning

Because of the tremendous changes that will confront management in the 1990s, succession planning takes on more importance than perhaps ever before. In view of these expected changes, organizations need to develop a profile of the type of individuals who will effectively lead the organization both now and in the future.[8] Apparently many are doing this; in a 1990 survey of over 400 boards of big American companies, nearly three-quarters of the firms questioned had a succession plan.[9]

An example of an effective succession plan occurred recently at NCR when a senior vice-president of finance retired. Following his departure, nine people moved up in the organization. At the end of the chain reaction, a young college student was hired as a financial analyst.[10] When Robert Allen ascended to the top management position at AT&T, there were likely many lower-level managment changes made.

A Global Perspective

Effective planning is essential for multinational success. For instance, construction companies in Japan, Korea, and other countries are planning to increase their share of the world's construction business. Their plan is to enter the market and build a better product and then use some of their revenues to continue their already impressive research efforts in order to be better future builders. In the United States, construction companies do little, if any, research. The Japanese and other foreign competitors are also planning to increase their market share by creating better construction equipment and techniques to solve construction problems in the markets they serve. The Big Five Japanese construction companies—Shimizu, Kajima, Taisei, Takenaka, and Ohbayashi—employ an average of four hundred researchers each, who are "doing imaginative work on earthquake-resistant concrete"; and the Japanese have developed a way of boring a 30-foot-wide tunnel with a computer-controlled machine that "turns the soil into slurry and pipes it to the surface."

Fortunately, some American firms are currently planning in a manner that may afford them a competitive advantage globally. Eleven Twenty Five productions, Zbig Vision, and Rebo High Definition Studio lead the world in high-density (superior picture quality) television programming. Because of their pioneering research in the area, they are producing for companies such as Sony. According to Larry Thorpe, vice-president of production technology for Sony, "U.S. companies are three to four years ahead of everybody else."[11] Regardless of a firm's country of origin, management must do whatever is necessary to compete, and planning is essential for global success. Effective global managers are appearing on all fronts with plans not only to do a better job of serving their global markets but to become better and more innovative than the competition.

Planning through Management by Objectives

Management by objectives (MBO)

The philosophy of management that emphasizes the setting of agreed-on objectives by managers and their subordinates and the use of these objectives as the primary bases of motivation, evaluation, and control efforts.

Management consultant Peter Drucker first described management by objectives (MBO) in 1954 in *The Practice of Management*.[12] During the past two decades, few other developments in the theory and practice of management have received as much attention and application as MBO. **Management by objectives (MBO)** is *the philosophy of management that emphasizes the setting of agreed-on objectives by managers and their subordinates and the use of these objectives as the primary bases of motivation, evaluation, and control efforts*. Above all else, MBO represents a way of thinking that concentrates on achieving results. It forces management to plan explicitly, as opposed to simply responding or reacting on the basis of guesses or hunches. It provides a systematic and rational approach to management and helps prevent "management by crisis." MBO emphasizes measurable achievements and results and may lead to improvements in organizational, group, and individual effectiveness.[13] It depends heavily on active participation in objective setting at all levels of management.

The MBO Process

The dynamics of an MBO system are illustrated in Figure 5–5. Notice that MBO requires top management support and commitment and involves five steps. These aspects of MBO are discussed in the following sections.

Top Management's Support and Commitment

An effective MBO program requires the enthusiastic support of top management. It is because of the lack of top-level commitment that many MBO programs fail. For MBO to be effective, the philosophy of top management must be consistent with its principles. MBO relies on the participative approach to management, requiring the active involvement of managers at all levels. The chief executive should trust subordinates and be personally committed to a participative style of management. Top management cannot introduce MBO by simply giving an order or a directive. Lower-level managers, too, must be convinced of the merits of the system and must want meaningful participation in the process.

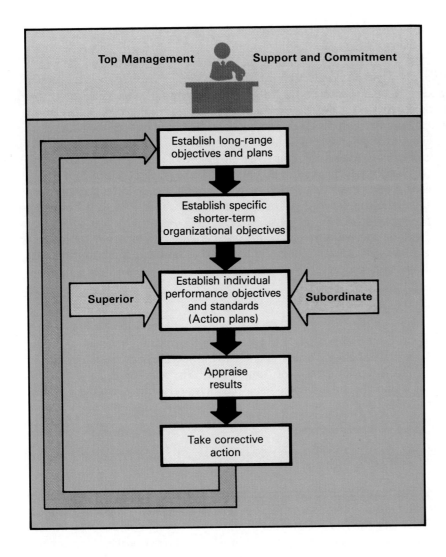

FIGURE 5–5

The MBO Process

Establishing Long-Range Objectives and Plans

A vital element of MBO is the development of long-range objectives and plans. These plans are developed through thoughtful consideration of the basic purpose, or mission, of the organization.

Establishing Specific Shorter-Term Organizational Objectives

After long-range objectives and plans are established, management must be concerned with determining specific objectives to be attained within a shorter time period. These objectives must be supportive of the overall purpose as well as the long-range objectives and plans. Usually, shorter-term objectives are expressed as specific and quantifiable targets covering such areas as productivity, marketing, and profitability.

Establishing Individual Performance Objectives and Standards (Action Plans)

The establishment of performance objectives and standards for individuals is known as **action planning.** This crucial phase of the MBO process requires that challenging but attainable objectives and standards be established through interaction between superiors and subordinates. Individuals jointly establish objectives with their superiors, who then give the individual some latitude in how to achieve the objectives. Jointly establishing objectives makes the employee an involved part of the process. This ownership of objectives increases the likelihood that they will be met.[14]

Action plans require clear delineation of what specifically is to be accomplished and when it is to be completed. For example, if a sales manager has a performance objective of increasing sales in his or her area by 38 percent next year, the action plan might include the employment of three experienced salespersons, six calls a week by the sales manager on major customers, and assignment of appropriate sales quotas to all the sales people.

Appraising Results

The next step in the MBO process is to measure and evaluate performance on the basis of progress toward objective attainment. Having specific performance objectives provides management with a basis for comparison. When objectives are agreed on by the manager and the subordinate, self-evaluation and control become possible. In fact, with MBO, performance appraisal can be a joint effort based on mutual agreement.

Taking Corrective Action

Although an MBO system provides a good management framework, it is left up to the managers themselves to take corrective action when results are not as planned. Such action may take the form of changes in personnel, changes in the organization, or even changes in the objectives. Other forms of corrective action may include providing additional training and development of individual managers or employees to enable them to better achieve the desired results. Corrective action should not necessarily have negative connotations. Under MBO, objectives can be renegotiated downward without penalty or fear of job loss.

Characteristics of Performance Objectives for the Individual

In order for MBO to achieve maximum results, the performance objectives for each individual should be carefully developed. They should be limited in number, highly specific, challenging, and attainable. The number of objectives for each manager should range from four to eight. Each objective should be assigned a priority, perhaps ranging from 1 to 3. Should time and resources prove to be more limited than anticipated, this ranking gives the individual a basis for deciding which objectives to pursue.

Perhaps the most important characteristic of good performance objectives is that they are stated in specific terms. In most instances, this means quantification. For example, objectives may have little impact when stated in such terms as "improve the effectiveness of the unit," "keep costs to a minimum," or "be alert to market changes." At the performance review, one should be able to answer definitely the question, Did I do it or not? An objective stating that production will be increased by 1,000 units during a given period is clear. Thus, in writing performance objectives, a special attempt should be made to state them in such terms as volume, costs, frequency, ratios, percentages, indexes, degrees, and phases. It is particularly important to place time limits on each objective. In ten of eleven studies that examined the impact of such specific objectives on performance, evidence supported the contention that specifically stated objectives increase the level of accomplishment.[15]

The development of challenging and attainable objectives requires a delicate balance. Obviously, supervisors want objectives to be set at levels that require special efforts on the part of subordinates. In attaining objectives, promotion and salary are and should be related to success. However, as some researchers have pointed out, in attempting a participatory approach to objective attainment, a subordinate may well be constructing a "do-it-yourself hangman's kit."[16] For instance, Dean Bishop, a hospital supply sales representative, might optimistically indicate to his sales manager that he plans to sell $1 million in surgical instruments and supplies during the next three months. However, since no one else in the company had ever reached this level of sales in a three-month period, and since Dean sold only $1 million in supplies the previous year, it is highly unlikely that he will attain his objective. It is much more likely that Dean has just hung himself, because his objective is unrealistic and probably unattainable.

In the initial phases of new MBO programs, one of the more common errors is the establishment of unattainable objectives. This is particularly the case if the time period for review is six months to a year. Anything seems possible with that much time. The superior must not allow excessively high objectives to be set. Specific attention must be given to obstacles that affect accomplishment, particularly the availability of resources. The impact of other personnel on the subordinate's performance must be recognized and discussed.

Challenging objectives lead to greater accomplishment only if the subordinate accepts the objectives as reasonable and only if objective accomplishment actually leads to rewards. Challenging objectives with a history of past success will lead to continued success. A series of failures creates a mental set that makes attainment increasingly less likely. Subordinates' assessment of the probability of success should be that they at least have a fifty-fifty chance of achieving each objective.

MBO: Assessing Its Overall Effectiveness

In a review of 185 studies, Jack N. Kondrasuk found numerous arguments relating to the effectiveness of MBO. Many organizations have adopted MBO on faith, often as a result of questionable case studies or unsubstantiated testimony. One researcher concluded, "There is relatively little empirical evidence to demonstrate the impact of MBO on any aspect of organizational or individual behavior, including job performance." According to Kondrasuk, "There are tendencies for MBO to be more effective in the short term [less than two years], in the private sector, and in organizations removed from direct contact with the customer. Basically, MBO can be effective, but questions remain about the circumstances under which it is effective."[17]

Although the evidence shows that MBO generally has not worked out well as a complete system, it still provides a good model for planning. Its central principles have been incorporated into all kinds of organizations and continue to have a major impact. These principles include specific and verifiable objectives, evaluation of performance on the basis of objective accomplishment, and integration of individual objectives with organizational objectives.

Self-Assessment Exercise

Will You Be a Good Planner?

1. Are you willing to make sure objectives are challenging but attainable?
   ☐ Yes ☐ No
2. Are you willing to become involved in objective setting with the boss?
   ☐ Yes ☐ No
3. Are you willing to consider planning as an ongoing process?
   ☐ Yes ☐ No
4. Are you willing to plan before it is time to do the activity?
   ☐ Yes ☐ No
5. Are you willing to write down important plans?
   ☐ Yes ☐ No
6. Are you willing to plan with numbers?
   ☐ Yes ☐ No
7. Are you willing to remember that plans affect people?
   ☐ Yes ☐ No
8. Are you willing to plan for results, not activities?
   ☐ Yes ☐ No
9. Are you willing to be innovative?
   ☐ Yes ☐ No
10. Are you willing to plan to prevent problems rather than solve them?
    ☐ Yes ☐ No

Summary

Planning is the process of determining in advance what should be accomplished and how it should be realized. Planning begins with an understanding of the organizational mission—a unit's continuing purpose, or reason for being. The mission statement is a broadly stated definition of the basic purpose and scope of a unit. From it, specific objectives (or goals) can be established; then plans can be developed to accomplish them. The planning process is dynamic. It should be continually evaluated and adapted to conform to the unfolding situation the organization confronts.

Objectives are the desired end results of any activity and should be set at each managerial level in the organization. Plans are statements of how objectives are to be accomplished. Those that remain roughly the same for long periods of time are standing plans. The most common kinds of standing plans are policies, procedures, and rules. All three are designed to direct action toward the accomplishment of objectives.

Planning occurs at every level in the organization. Strategic plans, relating to overall organizational purposes, are designed to implement the broader-based plans of top management. Tactical plans implement the strategic plans of top management. Those responsible for implementing tactical plans tend to be middle- and lower-level managers. Contingency planning is the development of plans to be placed in effect if certain events occur.

Management by objectives (MBO) is the philosophy of management that emphasizes the setting of agreed-on objectives by managers and their subordinates and the use of these objectives as the primary bases of motivation, evaluation, and control efforts. Above all else, MBO represents a way of thinking that concentrates on achieving results.

Review Questions

1. What are the steps involved in the planning process?
2. What is the purpose of a mission statement?
3. Describe the characteristics of good objectives. What are the three main types of objectives?
4. What are the specific questions that planning should answer?
5. Distinguish by definition among policies, procedures, and rules.
6. What is meant by the term *contingency planning?*
7. What is management by objectives (MBO)? Describe the basic steps in the MBO process.

Key Terms

Planning	Policy	Tactical plans
Mission	Procedure	Contingency planning
Mission statement	Standard operating procedures (SOPs)	Management by objectives (MBO)
Objectives		
Plans	Rule	Action planning
Standing plans	Strategic planning	

CASE 5.1	**CERTIFIED DEPARTMENT STORES' MBO PROGRAM**

Parker Neilson was irritated and confused after his meeting with Dale Simpson. Parker was the manager

of the Kansas City Certified Department Store, and Dale was the district manager for the company, in charge of stores in Missouri, Kansas, and Oklahoma. Three weeks earlier, Parker had received a letter from Dale explaining that top management had decided on an MBO program to help Certified Stores improve efficiency and increase profit contributions. In that letter, Dale had said that the objectives established would be used to measure the performance of store managers and that salary increases and promotions would be directly related to performance. The accompanying instructions required managers to list the objectives they believed were appropriate for their store and then to await the district manager's review visit.

Parker had done just what he was instructed to do. In a meeting with his five department managers, Parker had chosen objectives that they all agreed were appropriate. All of the objectives represented performance levels that were improvements over the past year and were reasonably attainable. The objectives they established were to

- Increase selling efficiency, as measured by the ratio of salaries to sales, by 10 percent.
- Reduce inventory losses to 2 percent of sales.
- Reduce cash register shortages to .05 percent of sales.

- Improve customer service to the point that 20 percent fewer complaint letters would be mailed to the home office.

Dale arrived late for the MBO review visit and stressed that there was little time. He quickly scanned the written statement of objectives Parker gave him, then explained that profit improvement was really what the home office was interested in. Senior management had decided that a 12 percent increase in profit would be a reasonable objective for Parker's store. This single objective, Dale said, would facilitate the monitoring of performance by the home office and would also reduce the amount of information the store would have to submit. The visit was cut short because Dale had to attend a meeting on the advertising budget back at the home office.

Questions

1. Does the MBO system at Certified meet the criteria for an effective program as discussed in the chapter? Explain.
2. How did Parker approach objective setting?

| CASE 5.2 | NUCOR STEEL |

As steel producers went during the 1980s, Nucor Steel was a high flyer. While giants such as USX Corporation (formerly U.S. Steel) and Bethlehem Steel suffered huge losses in the early 1980s, Nucor stayed prosperous. More than 100,000 steel workers remained out of work in 1987, but Nucor had not laid off a single hourly employee. Near the end of the decade, Nucor stock sold at nineteen times earnings, compared to eleven for USX Corporation, five for Bethlehem Steel, and eight for Armco.

Things were not always so rosy for this relatively small (if $1 billion in sales can be called small) steel producer. Nucor started off during the Great Depression as Reo Motors, Inc., a spinoff from the R. E. Olds Company. In 1938, the company filed for reorganization under the bankruptcy laws. It was briefly revived by World War II and then lingered until 1954, when liquidation seemed to have ended its suffering.

The only remnant that survived was Nuclear Corporation of America, the shares of which had been distributed to the former shareholders of Reo Motors. Nuclear Corporation was a hodgepodge of small, un-

related businesses, one of which was a steel bar joist maker. Bar joists are light steel beams made of angle iron and rods. They are used mainly to support elevated floors and roofs in commercial buildings.

Nuclear Corporation struggled along until 1965, posting a $2.2 million loss in that year alone. In the depths of Nuclear's despair, Kenneth Iverson took over as president and chief executive officer. Things began to change. By 1971, sales were $64.8 million and profits $2.7 million, healthy in comparison with the past. By 1980, sales had climbed, to $482.4 million. Profits had increased even more markedly, to $45.1 million. When the recession of the early 1980s decimated the rest of the steel industry, Nucor barely flinched. And the company remained continuously profitable through the last half of the decade.

What accounts for the success of Nucor while the rest of the steel industry stagnated? Opinions differ, but there are a number of possibilities. First, the company produces a narrow product line, using modern and highly efficient mini mills to melt scrap steel and shape it into angles, channels, and bars. Large, integrated producers such as those mentioned earlier mine iron ore and try to make every kind of steel plate and shape.

Probably the most significant single factor in Nucor's success is the productivity of its work force. Nucor located its mini mills in rural areas where the work ethic was strong and there was little prounion sentiment. This facilitated the company's use of certain innovative personnel policies designed to enhance productivity.

Iverson said two things are very important to most people: What am I going to be paid, and am I going to have a job tomorrow? Two fundamental Nucor policies grew out of this line of thinking. First, compensation is based on individual and group productivity and company profitability. Second, Nucor does not lay off hourly employees. "We had some short weeks last summer," Iverson said. "But nobody has ever lost a job here because business was bad."

Nucor also emphasizes communication with employees. There are only three layers of management. John Savage, manager of personnel services, said that, in communicating with employees, managers should "tell them everything or tell them nothing." He continued, "We definitely believe in telling employees everything about the company—about its successes, its failures, its mistakes, and its good and bad decisions." In sum, Savage said: "It has been Nucor's experience that the American worker is willing to work. Too many times, management gets in their way. Our employees take a great deal of pride in being as productive as we are." [18]

Questions

1. What is the mission statement of Nucor Steel?
2. What do you believe has been the effect of the two fundamental human resource management policies at Nucor?

Notes

1. This case is a composite of a number of published accounts, among them: Andrew Kupfer, "Bob Allen Rattles the Cages at AT&T," Fortune, June 19, 1989, pp. 58–66; Patricia M. Fernberg, "AT&T at Centennial Plaza," Modern Office Technology, April 1989, pp. 76–80; Paul B. Carrol, "AT&T Reports 18% Gain in Net for 2nd Quarter," Wall Street Journal, July 21, 1989, p. A6; Charles H. Granger, "The Hierarchy of Objectives," Harvard Business Review 42 (May–June 1964): 63–74; and Peter Coy, "AT&T Reaches Out and Taps Some New Talent," Business Week, September 2, 1991, p. 80.
2. Charles B. Shrader, Lew Taylor, and Dan R. Dalton, "Strategic Planning and Organizational Performance: A Critical Appraisal," Journal of Management 10, Summer 1984, p. 152.
3. Jerome H. Want, "Corporate Mission: The Intangible Contributor to Performance," Management Review, August 1986, pp. 46–50.
4. "Merck & Company Sheer Energy," Business Month, December 1988, p. 36.
5. Adapted from Barbara Marsh, "When Franchisees Go Their Own Way," Wall Street Journal, July 6, 1989, p. B1.
6. PINNACLE: Senior CNN correspondent Tom Cassidy discussed these, and other issues, with John Sculley.
7. Jane E. Dutton and Susan E. Jackson, "Categorizing Strategic Issues: Links to Organizational Action," Academy of Management Journal 12 (January 1987): 76.
8. James E. McElwain, "Succession Plans Designed to Manage Change," HR Magazine 36 (February 1991): 67.
9. "Heirs and Races," The Economist 318 (March 9, 1991): 69.
10. Ibid.
11. Rahul Jacob, "The U.S. Lead in High-Density TV," Fortune, September 25, 1989, p. 16.
12. Peter F. Drucker, The Practice of Management (New York: Harper & Row, 1954).
13. Anthony P. Raia, Managing by Objectives (Glenview, IL: Scott, Foresman, 1974), pp. 10–12.
14. Jay T. Knippen, "Boost Performance through Appraisals," Business Credit 92 (November–December 1990): 27.
15. Raia, Managing by Objectives, pp. 14–15.
16. Gary P. Latham and Gary A. Yuki, "A Review of Research on the Application of Goal Setting in Organizations," Academy of Management Journal 18 (December 1975): 829.
17. Jack N. Kondrasuk, "Studies in MBO Effectiveness," Academy of Management Review 6 (September 1981): 419–430.
18. This case is a composite of a number of published accounts, among them: Ruth Simon, "Nucor's Boldest Gamble," Forbes, April 3, 1989, pp. 123–124; John Savage, "Incentive Programs at Nucor Corporation," Personnel Administrator, August 1981, pp. 33–49; Richard I. Kirkland, "Petguims Profits at Nucor," Fortune, April 1981, pp. 43–46; Don Bedwell, "Nucor's Lean, Mean Management Team," South Magazine, August 1980, pp. 50–56; Thomas M. Roham, "The 'Others' U.S. Steel Industry Is Booming," Industry Week, July 13, 1981, pp. 56–62; George J. McManus, "Steel Industry Breaking Ranks," Iron Age, June 1983, pp. 23–25; and various 1989 reports by Standard & Poor's Corporation and Moody's Investors Services, Inc.

6

Strategic Planning

LEARNING OBJECTIVES

After completing this chapter students should be able to

- Distinguish between planning and strategic planning.
- State the importance of strategic planning and discuss strategic business units and the levels of strategic planning.
- Explain who the organizational strategists are.
- Explain the strategic planning and implementation processes.
- Describe the means of formulating corporate-level strategy.
- Explain the means of formulating business-level and functional-level strategy.

G. D. Searle and Company has spent millions annually on research and development— $200 million on drug research alone in one year. But the company's most exciting product, NutraSweet, was discovered by accident. The Searle scientist, who is credited with developing NutraSweet in 1965, was working on a product for ulcer treatment.

NutraSweet was introduced nationally in 1982 and accounted for about half of Searle's billion-dollar revenues in 1984. For the rest of the decade the product was the sweetener of choice for most artificially sweetened products. NutraSweet sales were $746 million in 1988 and recently topped $1 billion. Customers ranged from Coca-Cola and Pepsi, General Foods, Procter and Gamble, Heinz, and Wrigley to the millions of consumers who made the NutraSweet-based diet sweetener Equal an instant best-seller.

The path from the development of the product in 1965 to its domination of the artificial sweetener market in 1984–89 was not an easy one. Exceptional management skill and a great deal of strategic planning were required. First, the Food and Drug Administration (FDA) had to be convinced that the product was safe. Partial FDA approval came in 1981, sixteen years after the product was developed. It was not until 1983 that the government allowed carbonated soft drinks to be sweetened with NutraSweet. Despite FDA approval, some groups continue to question NutraSweet's safety.

Searle created a new division for NutraSweet in 1983. Donald Rumsfeld, Searle's chief executive, chose Robert Shapiro, the company's general counsel, to head this division. The multimillion-dollar marketing effort Shapiro initiated was aimed mainly at consumers, although NutraSweet was not sold to them directly. Because of the exceptional success of the advertising program, Shapiro faced another challenge. How could the company produce 3 million pounds and be ready for growth that was sure to come? While Shapiro was fighting off adverse publicity related to NutraSweet safety, he had to build a new organization involving thousands of workers and hundreds of managers and sales personnel. Two European companies were engaged to help make NutraSweet. Despite having a new $160 million plant in Augusta, Georgia, demand outstripped supply, and new customers were refused.

Competitors in West Germany and the United States had already patented innovative new sweeteners, and others were on the verge of doing so. So Shapiro had to intensify research and development efforts. "Our objective is to make sure that we're the people who make NutraSweet obsolete," he said.

Also, Shapiro knew that, at $90 a pound, NutraSweet, which is 200 times sweeter than sugar, would face continued cost pressure compared to $4 for saccharin, which is 300 times sweeter than sugar. Productivity had to be increased at the NutraSweet plants in Illinois, Michigan, and Georgia. Monsanto Corporation paid $2.8 billion for Searle—and Shapiro had access to the expert manufacturing help that was lacking inside Searle.

The overall NutraSweet strategy worked. NutraSweet is still producing roughly 20 cents profit on every sales dollar. However, when the exclusive patent rights are eliminated, the cost pressure will intensify even more. NutraSweet's strategy for continued success is to take advantage of its brand recognition and customer insistence, to continue its aggressive promotional campaigns, and to make every attempt to become more price competitive. Hopefully, this strategy will assure that NutraSweet remains an ingredient in over 4,000 products. Brand insistence and aggressive promotional campaigns are nothing new, but price competitiveness is a strategic element that may add the little extra needed to keep the strategy effective. Can this strategy make NutraSweet competitive with producers of the less-expensive sweetening ingredient in NutraSweet, aspartame? Will this strategy assure that NutraSweet continues to enjoy the sweet taste of success? Well, the strategy is in place, the previously successful management team is poised for action, and the future is now.[1]

Strategic planning

The process by which top management determines overall organizational purposes and objectives and how they are to be achieved.

The planning process remains essentially the same at each organizational level; however, managers today have access to a number of concepts and techniques that relate specifically to strategic planning. **Strategic planning** is *the process by which top management determines overall organizational purposes and objectives and how they are to be achieved.* NutraSweet is a division which practices strategic planning. NutraSweet's overall purpose is to stay number 1, and the strategy developed to accomplish this objective involves something old and something new, and hopefully something that will repeat that same sweet taste of success that NutraSweet experienced in the past.

In this chapter, the discussion begins with the difference between planning and strategic planning. Next, the importance of strategic planning is examined. The discussion then turns to the levels of strategic planning, identification of the organizational strategists, and a brief description of the strategic planning and implementation processes. This is followed by a discussion of the formulation of corporate-level strategies, business-level strategies, functional-level strategies, and a brief overview of global strategic perspectives.

Planning Versus Strategic Planning

In Chapter 5, *planning* was defined as the process of determining in advance what should be accomplished and how it should be realized. Planning involves selecting objectives and deciding how to achieve them. Strategic planning is a type of planning. But unlike tactical, operational, or short-term planning, strategic planning involves an extended time frame, the deployment of a substantial percentage of the resources of the organization, a wide spectrum of activities, and a major eventual impact. Basically, strategic planning is planning that is long term, wide ranging, and critical to organizational success in terms of the costs of the resources it affects and of the outcomes it envisions.[2]

Construction workers extend the Colorado Interstate Gas Pipeline for Coastal Corporation. Such major projects require extensive strategic planning. Unlike tactical, operational, or short-term planning, strategic planning involves an extended time frame, deployment of a substantial percentage of the resources of the organization, a wide spectrum of activities, and a major eventual impact.

Source: Photograph courtesy of The Coastal Corporation

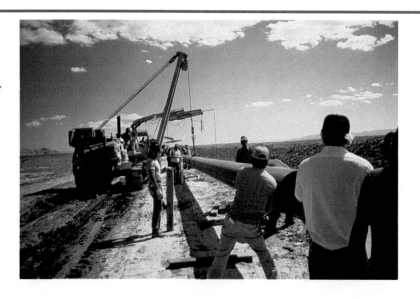

The Importance of Strategic Planning

There is a growing realization among professional managers of the importance of strategic planning to the growth and profitability of any company. It is also important to the job security and self-esteem of employees, to the welfare of communities, and to the financial security of investors.

When a firm's mission is clearly defined and its guiding principles are understood, employees and managers are likely to put forth maximum effort in pursuit of company objectives. The firm is also more likely to succeed in responding to a changing environment. Even if the existing plan does not envision a particular contingency that occurs, the plan can provide a good point of departure.

A number of research studies have compared organizations that use formal strategic planning with those that do not, and the studies have found that formal strategic planning pays off.[3] The advantage of strategic planning is most evident in firms with rapidly changing environments.[4] This fact should make strategic planning even more important as the Economic Community in Europe removes its barriers to trade, and as Asian markets, especially China's, open up even more. As the globalization of business becomes more pervasive, strategic planning may well provide the edge American companies need. It allows managers in changing environments to carefully chart their courses, and it helps their organizations expand and survive.[5] For example, Volvo management aims directly at the global market with a strategy that involves cultural sensitivity and possibly even cooperation with manufacturers in other countries. Apparently, Volvo subscribes to the notation that formal strategic planning is essential for success in the global market. Specifically, Volvo's global strategic plan is to grow as an independent company with integrity. This strategy allows Volvo managers to respond to the changing business environments of countries throughout the world.

However, strategic planning has its pitfalls too. There may be a danger of creating a bureaucracy of "planners" who lose touch with the various markets the organization is attempting to serve.[6] In addition, too much emphasis on formality in strategic planning may slow down the decision-making process. Managers may seem to make rational, risk-minimizing decisions, but their efforts may limit innovation and the exploration of lucrative business possibilities.[7]

The Levels of Strategic Planning

It is important to consider strategic planning according to the organizational levels at which it occurs, particularly in light of the growth in recent decades of such complex organizations as General Electric, United Technologies, Allied Corporation, and Textron. Figure 6–1 illustrates the organizational levels of a typical complex corporation, along with the corresponding levels of strategic planning. Since each level has its own distinctive characteristics, the tools and processes that are useful in formulating strategy at the three levels differ.

If an organization produced a single product or service, then a single strategic plan would encompass everything the corporation did. However, many organizations are in diverse businesses, some of which are only vaguely related. Because so many organizations are engaged in multiple activities, it is important to understand the

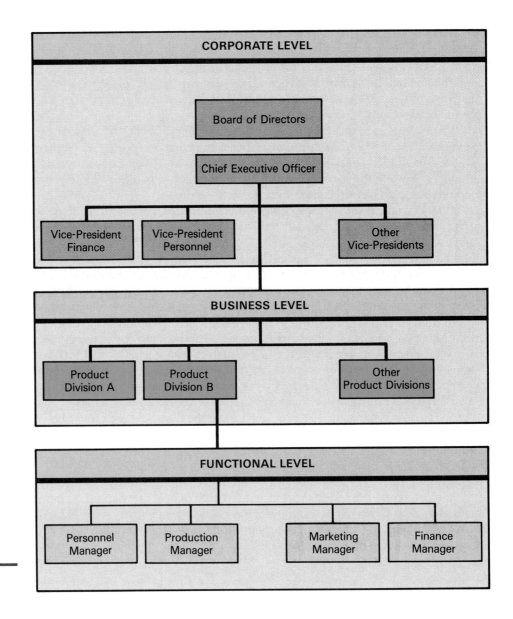

FIGURE 6–1

The Levels of Strategic
Planning

differences among corporate-level strategic planning, business-level strategic planning,
and functional-level strategic planning.

ETHICAL DILEMMA

Colgate-Palmolive Company's Asian market was solidified by the company's purchase of 50 percent of Hawley & Hazel Company. Hawley & Hazel markets an
extremely popular toothpaste called Darkie, which bears the logo of a smiling, top-
hatted black face. American critics were quick to charge the company with racism.

Among the more vocal critics is the Interfaith Center for Corporate Responsibility, a nonprofit New York organization of more than 240 church groups. According to Colgate research, Asians don't find Darkie brand toothpaste offensive. In fact, Darkie is a big seller in all the Asian markets.[8] Colgate has decided to stick with the brand.

You work for Colgate-Palmolive, and you have just been told you are being transferred overseas to manage the Asian toothpaste merchandising operation. Your wife is a member of one of the churches affiliated with the Interfaith Center for Corporate Responsibility. She has expressed concern that your company is continuing to sell the Darkie brand overseas. You too are bothered by Colgate's insistence on selling toothpaste with a logo of a smiling, top-hatted black face, but you have kept your feelings to yourself. You can either refuse the assignment and jeopardize your career with the company, or you can take the overseas assignment.

What would you do?

Corporate-level strategic planning is *the process of defining the overall character and purpose of the organization, the businesses it will enter and leave, and how resources will be distributed among those businesses.* This type of planning will determine what line of businesses the corporation should be in. Corporate-level strategy typically concerns the mix and utilization of business divisions called strategic business units (which will be discussed shortly). Corporate-level strategic planning addresses the actions the organization will take and determines the roles of each business in the organization's grand strategy. For example, G. D. Searle and Company's top management will develop a corporate-level strategic plan for the entire organization and will also develop business-level strategic plans for each business the company is engaged in, including NutraSweet.

Without advance and carefully considered corporate-level strategic planning, corporate managers will not fulfill their objectives. Corporate strategists can make the mistake of attempting business ventures that they are not capable of operating successfully. Companies often expand without having made a proper job of corporate-level strategic planning, and their expansions are unsuccessful. According to Wayne Calloway, chairman and CEO of PepsiCo, the company's mission has been, and continues to be, to do only what it can do best. PepsiCo is no longer in the transportation business and the sporting goods business. The company is now one-third beverage businesses, one-third snack businesses, and one-third restaurants. It is number 1 in the chicken category, number 1 in the Mexican foods category, and number 1 in the pizza category. It is not in the hamburger business because it could not buy McDonald's and therefore could not be number 1 in this category. The corporate-level strategic plan takes into account all of PepsiCo's separate businesses, and business-level strategic plans are developed for each one.[9]

Business-level strategic planning is *the planning process concerned primarily with how to manage the interests and operations of a particular business.* In the case of PepsiCo, different business-level plans would be appropriate for the beverage businesses, the snack businesses, and the restaurant businesses. Business-level planning determines how each of these businesses should compete, on the basis of conditions such as market variables and available resources. Since many organizations, like PepsiCo, have extensive interests in different businesses, top managers often have a difficult time organizing the complex companies and their varied activities. One approach for dealing with this problem is the creation of strategic business units, which are meant to facilitate the management of large organizations.

Corporate-level strategic planning
The process of defining the overall character and purpose of the organization, the businesses it will enter and leave, and how resources will be distributed among those businesses.

Business-level strategic planning
The planning process concerned primarily with how to manage the interests and operations of a particular business.

Strategic business unit (SBU)

Any part of a business organization that is treated separately for strategic planning purposes.

A **strategic business unit (SBU)** is *any part of a business organization that is treated separately for strategic planning purposes.* It can be a single business or a collection of related businesses. PepsiCo's beverage, snack, and restaurant businesses could all be treated as separate SBUs for planning purposes. The corporate-level strategy provides the general direction, and a business-level strategy provides the direction for each SBU. The business-level strategic plan is reviewed at the corporate level, changes are made if necessary, and the final business-level strategic plan for the SBU is approved. Each SBU has a unique mission and product line and its own competitors and markets.[10]

Many companies set up SBUs as separate profit centers, sometimes giving them virtual autonomy. Other companies have tight control over their SBUs, enforcing corporate policies and standards down to very low levels in the organization. In general, SBU business-level strategic planning is the responsibility of vice-presidents or division heads.

Functional-level strategic planning

The process of determining policies and procedures for relatively narrow areas of activity that are critical to the success of the organization.

Functional-level strategic planning is *the process of determining policies and procedures for relatively narrow areas of activity that are critical to the success of the organization.* Practically every large organization is divided into functional subdivisions, usually production, marketing, finance, and personnel. Military installations have supply, police, and maintenance departments, among others. Churches have preaching, education, and music ministries. Each of these functional subdivisions is vital to the success of the organization. Functional-level strategic plans conform to both the corporate-level and the business-level strategic plans.

During the 1980s, Philip Morris, Inc., and R. J. Reynolds Tobacco Company both invested their tobacco profits in "clean" businesses, especially foods. But tobacco products remain major strategic business units for these two mammoth companies.

RJR Nabisco Versus Philip Morris

Throughout the 1980s, R. J. Reynolds Tobacco Company's cigarette market share was declining. Throughout most of the eighties, the company's primary strategic business unit was the cigarette business. Then, R. J. Reynolds bought Nabisco, becoming RJR Nabisco, Inc., and adding another strategic business unit to its operation. As a result of the Nabisco purchase, RJR entered the decade of the 1990s seriously hampered by a huge debt burden. Competitor Philip Morris was having greater success in the cigarette market than RJR, and RJR executives formulated a plan to turn this situation around.

The new chief executive of RJR's tobacco division, James W. Johnston, planned to make the cigarette SBU successful by spending "whatever it takes to succeed." In spite of this approach, though, Philip Morris's Cambridge and Alpine brands gained a huge share of the "price-value" market segment (consumers who look for low prices but also high quality) previously dominated by RJR's Doral brand. While RJR's newly introduced "smokeless" cigarette flopped, Philip Morris introduced the first "very low nicotine" product. Next, Philip Morris hired nine hundred new salespeople and began calling on stores twice as frequently as it had before. The two companies' market shares, already near 40 percent for Philip Morris and just over 30 percent for RJR, continued to diverge, but at a faster pace.[11]

It appears that Philip Morris's business-level strategy provides better direction for the cigarette SBU than does RJR's. Because of the lack of success of RJR's business-level strategy, it might prove fruitful to review the company's business-level strategic plan at the corporate level. RJR's business-level strategic plan obviously must be changed, and the final business-level strategic plan for the cigarette SBU must be implemented as soon as possible. In addition to revising its overall mission, RJR should also reevaluate its cigarette product line and markets relative to competitors', especially Philip Morris.

• •

The Organizational Strategists

For most organizations, it is difficult to identify the organizational strategists. In ancient Greece, where the concept of strategy originated, strategy was determined by generals. For some companies today, strategy clearly comes from the top. For example, Robert Goizueta, president and chief executive officer of Coca-Cola, seems to call the shots. Boeing boardmember T. A. Wilson was once Boeing's greatest strategist. Wilson finalized the corporate-level strategic plan and then did whatever was necessary to accomplish overall organizational objectives. To accomplish these objectives, he fired 95,000 people, two-thirds of Boeing's employees.[12] One of the ultimate strategists of our time is Olive Ann Beech, who formed the Beech Aircraft company around the classic single-engine biplane created by her husband.[13]

Many companies use in-house **strategic planning staff specialists**—*specialists who assist and advise managers in strategic planning*. Strategic management involves planning and doing. Staff strategic management specialists are involved especially in planning.

Many organizations retain consultants to assist in designing and implementing strategy. Consultants are particularly useful in that they conduct marketing research and other kinds of research that provide an important information base for strategic decisions. Consultants can play an effective part in strategic planning, even for small firms.[14] In fact, most small firms cannot afford full-time staff specialists. For these companies, using consultants may be the most economical approach to strategic planning.

At least to a limited extent, every manager is an organizational strategist.[15] This is because every manager is responsible for activities related to continuing the company's business operations and to achieving vital corporate objectives. It should be recognized, however, that what may be an overwhelming matter to the human resource director—for example, the size of the annual departmental budget—may be a relatively incidental matter from the standpoint of the total organization. Whether or not a matter is important to any individual has nothing to do with whether or not it is strategic. Strategic matters are determined by answers to the question: How important is it to the organization as a whole, and to what degree does it have continuing significance? **Organizational strategists** are therefore *the people who spend a large portion of their time on matters of vital or far-ranging importance to the organization as a whole*. In general, they include the top two levels of management, in-house staff specialists in strategic management, and retained consultants who are experts in the areas in which strategic decisions must be made. General Motors' acquisition of Electronic Data Systems (EDS) in 1984 brought two organizational strategists with contrasting styles into direct conflict with each other.

Strategic planning staff specialists
Specialists who assist and advise managers in strategic planning.

Organizational strategists
The people who spend a large portion of their time on matters of vital or far-ranging importance to the organization as a whole.

General Motors and Electronic Data Systems

In 1984, General Motors Corporation purchased Electronic Data Systems, the country's largest computer services company. EDS was founded by Ross Perot. Perot had become a legend in his home state of Texas, mainly for such adventures as his rescue of two EDS employees from Iran during the 1978 Iranian crisis. At the time of the acquisition, EDS had about 15,000 employees.

GM wanted EDS to help it use sophisticated computer systems in its cars and production operations. GM paid Perot and the other owners of EDS $2.5 billion, mostly in GM stock. Part of the stock was a new issue (Class E) tied directly to EDS earnings.

Feuding soon started between GM management and Perot. GM wanted EDS to give it bargain prices. But it was to EDS's advantage to fatten its contracts as much as possible because EDS's profits would increase the value of the stock owned by the EDS employees.

There were also behavioral problems, mainly because of the clash of the two corporate cultures. Perot ran a tight but egalitarian organization. Managers and employees ate in the same cafeteria; executive perks, such as reserved parking spaces, were not allowed; and top management was very committed to its employees, as is evidenced by Perot's Iranian adventure. On the other hand, GM is a conservative manufacturing company, much more bureaucratic than EDS. Its president at the time, Roger Smith, had worked at GM for his entire career, as had most of the other top-level managers. The EDS managers were condescending toward their GM counterparts and openly contemptuous of them. Moreover, the EDS managers were paid much more than those at GM.

In 1986, Perot began to publicly criticize Smith's conservative approach to business. For example, he claimed GM under Smith had failed for some years to create any innovative car designs. Some commentators said Perot's behavior was self-serving, since a large amount of his own wealth was tied directly to the fortunes of EDS and the Class E stock. However, GM had lost 5 percent of its American market share between 1980 and 1985, so other commentators found Perot's criticisms justified.

Smith and the other GM directors eventually voted to buy back Perot's stock for $700 million, roughly twice its value in the acquisition. Perot and other top EDS managers agreed to leave EDS, and Perot gave up his seat on the GM board. The former EDS executives were forbidden to create a computer services company that would directly compete with EDS for at least three years. Perot also agreed to pay GM $7.5 million if he publicly criticized the company again. The agreement didn't stop him, however. He continued to ridicule GM management for, among other faults, giving large bonuses to top management while closing eleven plants and idling 29,000 workers. Even though Perot was out of GM, his ideas had some effect. In November 1989, GM announced that it would fire 5,000 managers and white-collar employees in each of the following five years. This was widely viewed as an effort to diminish the bureaucracy at GM. It will be interesting to watch and see if the GM bureaucracy changes substantially since Smith's retirement.

The Strategic Planning and Implementation Processes

Strategic planning at all levels of the organization can be divided into four steps: (1) determination of the organizational mission, (2) assessment of the organization and its environment, (3) setting of specific objectives or direction, and (4) determination of strategies to accomplish those objectives (see Figure 6–2).[16] The strategic planning

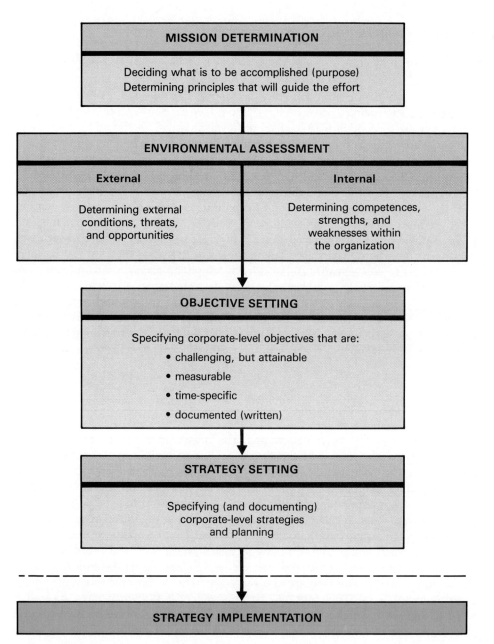

FIGURE 6–2

Formulating Strategy and
Implementation

process described here is basically a derivative of the SWOT (strengths, weaknesses, opportunities, and threats) framework that affects organizational performance, but it is less structured. We believe the step-by-step approach just described guides the understanding of the strategic planning process.

Despite its complexity, it is useful to think of strategic planning as a sequential process. By individually examining the four steps of the strategic planning process and the final step of strategy implementation, we will now bring into focus the desirability of a systematic approach to strategic planning and implementation.

Mission Determination

The first step of the strategic planning process is to determine the corporate mission. The corporate mission is the sum total of the organization's ongoing purpose. Arriving at a mission statement should involve answering the questions: What are we in management attempting to do for whom? Should we maximize profit so shareholders will receive higher dividends or so share price will increase? Or should we emphasize stability of earnings so employees will remain secure?

There are many other possibilities. Mission determination also requires deciding the principles on which management decisions will be based. Will the corporation be honorable or dishonorable, ruthless or considerate, devious or forthright, in dealing with its various publics? The answers to these questions, once arrived at, tend to become embedded in a corporate culture and to determine the organizational mission.

An example of a well-conceived mission is AT&T's visionary mission, which was developed some eighty years ago. The mission was described by a former chairman as "a dream of good, cheap, fast, worldwide telephone service. [This mission] . . . is not a speculation. It is a perfectly clear statement that you are going to do something."[17] In line with that mission, AT&T signed joint venture contracts with Philips, a Dutch telecommunications company, to bid together on the installation of large telephone systems in Europe, Asia, and the Middle East. It appears that AT&T's eighty-year-old mission to expand into international markets is still on course.

Environmental Assessment

Once the mission has been determined, the organization must be assessed for strengths and weaknesses, and the threats and opportunities in the external environment must be evaluated. Specific objectives can be established, and strategies can be developed for accomplishing those objectives. For example, through environmental assessment, BIC Corporation discovered an opportunity during the early 1980s to market disposable safety razors. Assessment within the organization revealed that BIC had a greater capability than almost any other U.S. company to mass-produce small plastic-based items. The company set sales, production, and profit objectives, designed strategies, and quickly became the world's leading marketer of disposable safety razors. In the late eighties, the razor segment of the business came under pressure from Gillette. Therefore, BIC began searching for other markets. It decided to go all out with a multinational ad campaign promoting an inexpensive cologne that would cost $4 for a quarter-ounce easy-to-carry spray bottle.

Making strategic plans involves information flows from both the internal and the external environment. From inside comes information about organizational competencies, strengths, and weaknesses. Scanning the external environment allows organizational strategists to identify threats and opportunities, as well as constraints. In brief, the job in the planning phase is to develop strategies that take advantage of the company's strengths and minimize its weaknesses in order to grasp opportunities and avoid threats.

Objective Setting

Explicitly stating objectives and directing all activities toward their attainment is not the only approach to strategic management. It may not even be the best approach for some organizations at certain times. However, since Peter Drucker coined the term *management by objectives* in the 1950s, it has been generally accepted that the use of objectives improves the process of management. This is no less true at the corporate level of strategic management than it is for the miler who wishes to better the existing world record.

Characteristics of Strategic Objectives Objectives should be challenging but attainable. If a miler capable of running at near world record speed set an objective of a five-minute mile, the objective could be easily achieved, but the miler would probably not run at maximum speed. On the other hand, if the objective were set at three minutes, no one in the world could come close. Anyone who attempted it would be frustrated. Corporate objectives, too, should offer a reasonable opportunity for accomplishment. To avoid frustration, the probability of accomplishment should not be zero, and to avoid suboptimal performance, it should not be nearly 100 percent.

Remember, too, that objectives should be specific, preferably quantifiable, and measurable. An objective to "maximize profits" offers little specific guidance. To earn $1.2 million in profits or to increase profits by 5 percent over last year's level is specific. The more specific objectives are, the more definite can be the strategies designed to accomplish them.

Satisficing Herbert Simon has suggested that managers in general do not attempt to optimize or maximize corporate results.[18] He believes the term *satisficing* more correctly describes what managers do. According to Simon's theory, managers typically accept the first satisfactory outcome they are offered. For example, one who believes that 10 percent is a reasonable return on invested funds is likely to approve any return on investment objective that exceeds that amount.

If Simon is right, many corporate strategists may be more concerned with establishing direction than with setting specific objectives. As long as this year's sales and profits are above last year's, that may be acceptable because the direction is upward. Many effective organizations have never set specific objectives. In fact, some have only a vague understanding of the direction in which they are headed. It appears likely, however, that any organization can improve its performance by setting objectives that are challenging but attainable and specific, preferably quantified.

You are a supervisor at a company that has initiated a big push to increase productivity. The company's market share is eroding, and Japanese competitors are expected to erode it even more in the near future. Top management is concerned with holding on to current customers. Its objective is not to innovate or grow but to increase internal efficiency and control to produce reliable products for regular customers. Your boss has just reviewed the corporate-level strategic plan and has asked you and other supervisors to submit new production objectives for your units. Your boss has indicated that "sizable increases" in production, ranging from 30 to 40 percent, are expected from each unit. Your unit has never produced more than 20 percent over established guidelines, regardless of how much you emphasized the importance of greater productivity.

What level of increase would you recommend?

Strategy Setting

Once objectives are established or direction is determined, strategies can be formulated. Many organizations limit their written strategic plans to financial budgets. And some do not even have budgets. Most authorities, however, consider it worthwhile to put strategies in writing. Whether or not strategies are written, it is the task of organizational strategists to clearly communicate how the organization intends to accomplish its goals. G. D. Searle is a company that practices strategy setting.

Strategy Implementation

Once the strategic planning process is complete, the strategy must be implemented. Some people argue that strategy implementation is the most difficult and important part of strategic management. No matter how creative and well formulated the strategic plan, the organization will not benefit if it is incorrectly implemented. Strategy implementation involves several dimensions of the organization, as is illustrated in Figure 6–3. It requires changes in the organization's behavior, which can be brought about by changing one or more organizational dimensions, including management's leadership ability, organization structure, information and control systems, production technology, and human resources.[19]

Leadership Getting others to do what the leader wants them to do is leadership. Managers must influence organization members to adopt the behaviors needed for strategy implementation. Top-level managers seeking to implement a new strategy may find it useful to build coalitions and persuade middle-level managers to go along with the strategic plan and its implementation. If leaders involve other managers during strategy formulation, implementation will be easier because managers and employees will better understand, and be more fully committed to, the new strategy. Basically, leadership is used to encourage employees to adopt supportive behaviors and, when necessary, to accept the required new values and attitudes.

FIGURE 6–3

Organizational Dimensions for Strategy Implementation

SOURCE: *Adapted from Jay R. Galbraith and Robert K. Kazanjian,* Strategy Implementation: Structure, Systems, and Process, *2d. ed. (St. Paul, MN: West Publishing, 1986), p. 115. Used with permission.*

Organizational Structure   A company's organizational structure is typically illustrated by its organization chart. This structure indicates individual managers' responsibilities and degrees of authority and incorporates jobs into departments. The structure also pertains to the degree of centralization and the type of department that will be utilized. One of the earliest studies of organizational structure examined historical changes at General Motors, DuPont, Standard Oil of New Jersey, and Sears, Roebuck.

As these companies grew large and prosperous, they altered their structures to reflect new strategies.[20]

Information and Control Systems   Among the information and control systems are reward systems, incentives, management by objectives systems, budgets for allocating resources, information systems, and the organization's rules, policies, and implementations. A proper mix of information and control systems must be developed to support the implementation of the strategic plan. Managers and employees must be rewarded for adhering to the new strategy and making it a success, or the intensity of implementation will be reduced substantially.

Technology   The knowledge, tools, and equipment used to accomplish an organization's assignments are its technology. If an organization adopts a strategy of producing a new product, managers must often redesign jobs and construct new buildings and facilities. New technology, because of its efficiency, may also be required for implementing a low-cost strategy. As with other aspects of strategy implementation, the appropriate level of technology must be found for proper implementation of the strategic plan.

Human Resources   The organization's human resources are its employees. The human resource function involves such tasks as recruitment, selection, training, transfers, promotions, and layoffs of employees to properly implement the strategic plan. In certain situations, employees simply are incompatible with a new strategy and may have to be replaced. The new strategy may foster resentment and resistance among both managers and employees, a matter that must be resolved quickly or it may hinder strategy implementation. In essence, a proper balance of human resources must be developed to support strategy implementation.

Formulating Corporate-Level Strategy

Corporate-level strategy typically concerns the mix and utilization of strategic business units. Executives generally define an overall strategic direction—a grand strategy—and then develop a portfolio of strategic business units to carry it out.

Several Grand Strategies

The nature of the strategic planning process has been discussed thus far in general terms. Strategic planning at the corporate level will now be considered in terms of three grand, or master, strategies that often grow out of the corporate-level strategic planning process: integration, diversification, and retrenchment.

Integration
The unified control of a number of successive or similar operations.

Integration   A commonly used term among organizational strategists is **integration**, *the unified control of a number of successive or similar operations*. The combining of companies is an example of integration. Integration also includes a company's taking over a portion of an industrial or commercial process that previously was accomplished by other firms. Integration need not involve ownership; it may include only

Southland Corporation, which sells gasoline and oil at its 7-Eleven convenience stores, vertically integrated backward when it bought an oil refinery from Citgo in 1983. In 1990, Southland completed the sale of the refinery to Petroleos De Venezuela, the Venezuelan national oil company. The purchase amounted to forward integration for the latter firm.

Source: © David Dempster

control. Thus, supply and marketing contracts are forms of integration. *Integration toward the final users of a company's goods or services*, as when Tandy Corporation opened its Radio Shack stores, is **forward integration.** *A company's taking control of any of the sources of its inputs, including raw materials and labor*, is **backward integration.** Southland Corporation's purchase of a petroleum refinery that supplies gasoline to the company's 7-Eleven stores is an example of backward integration. *Buying or taking control of competitors at the same level in the production and marketing process* is **horizontal integration.** For example, when Firestone, already in the auto service business, took over J. C. Penney's auto service centers, horizontal integration occurred.

Integration can extend beyond the boundaries of the United States. AT&T's joint ventures with Italtel, an Italian telecommunications company, and Philips, a Dutch telecommunications company, are examples of backward integration. These joint ventures established AT&T as a major player in the European telecommunications market.[21]

Following are some of the competitive advantages of integration:

- Improved marketing and technological intelligence.
- Superior control of the firm's economic environment.
- Product differentiation advantages.[22]

Each type of integration can be a strategy for accomplishing a different objective. For example, if the objective is to decrease the cost of inputs, a company could buy out suppliers that earn profits producing the inputs—an example of backward integration. If the objective is to increase market share, horizontal integration might be attempted. This was done when 7-Eleven's parent, Southland Corporation, bought the Pak-A-Sak convenience store chain.

Backward and forward integration are usually designed to accomplish one or both of two purposes: capturing additional profits and obtaining better control. Backward integration does this for the supply channels, and forward integration does it for the distribution channels. Obviously, if either a supplier or an intermediate customer

Forward integration

Integration toward the final users of a company's goods or services.

Backward integration

A company's taking control of any of the sources of its inputs, including raw materials and labor.

Horizontal integration

Buying or taking control of competitors at the same level in the production and marketing process.

is making exorbitant profits, vertical integration may be justified on this basis alone. Vertical integration may also be justified when a company believes it can perform the functions of suppliers or intermediate customers effectively and efficiently. But if better control of sources of supply or distribution channels is the only objective, it may be better not to buy the business. There may be better ways to ensure control, such as making franchise agreements with intermediate customers and long-term supply agreements with suppliers. Taking over customers or suppliers is costly, and it often involves the company in businesses with which its managers are unfamiliar.

Diversification

Increasing the variety of goods or services made or sold.

Conglomerate diversification

The development of businesses unrelated to the firm's current businesses.

Concentric diversification

The development of businesses related to the firm's current businesses.

Diversification *Increasing the variety of goods or services made or sold* is **diversification,** which may be conglomerate or concentric. **Conglomerate diversification** is *the development of businesses unrelated to the firm's current businesses.*[23] **Concentric diversification** is *the development of businesses related to the firm's current businesses.* As a grand strategy, diversification usually has risk reduction as its purpose. A company involved in a number of businesses avoids having all its eggs in one basket. Ideally, when some of a conglomerate firm's businesses decline, others will be on the increase. Some conglomerate firms are countercyclical; that is, they tend to see increasing sales when the economy in general is declining. Such businesses are hard to find. The do-it-yourself hand-tool market is one of the rare exceptions. When times are tough, people tend to repair their own automobiles, for example; and they need tools to do so.

About the best a conglomerate firm can hope for, in general, is a group of SBUs whose valleys and peaks occur at different times in the business cycle. Of course, concentric diversification may not appear to serve the risk reduction objective as well as conglomerate diversification does; however, this type of diversification tends to be more successful in improving profitability.[24] This is probably because the managers of concentrically diversifying firms know something about the businesses they are buying.

Diversification often occurs as a by-product of bargain hunting by corporate strategists. Even if the preference is for a related merger candidate, corporate-level strategists may opt for acquiring an SBU in an entirely different business because it is deemed to be greatly underpriced. Diversification can also be a product of a desire for growth.

Retrenchment

The reduction of the size or scope of a firm's activities.

Retrenchment Another grand strategy, usually applied only when failure is imminent, is retrenchment. **Retrenchment** is *the reduction of the size or scope of a firm's activities.* Most corporate managements resist this strategy. Although growth is often an objective, retrenchment seldom is. When a retrenchment strategy is followed, the objective is often survival.

Prompt elimination of losing businesses has been the hallmark of a number of successful managers of large corporations. For example, Baker Hughes, Inc. is quick to "lop off weak limbs" when a loser surfaces in the corporation.[25] Of course, smaller companies also may find themselves involved in activities that are unprofitable and that appear likely to remain so. For example, Superior Printing Company, a small printing operation in Columbus, Ohio, was losing money producing standard business forms. When Superior stopped doing the unprofitable work and sold the related equipment, profits improved markedly. In addition, the owner, Jeffrey Shuman, could then pay attention to what he really knew best, limited orders for custom-printed items such as fine letterhead and direct mail circulars.

Portfolio Strategy

Once the grand strategy has been determined—that is, once the organization has established the major action by which it intends to achieve long-term objectives—a portfolio strategy is developed. **Portfolio strategy** is *the process of determining how an SBU will compete in a particular line of business, with a concentration on the mix of business units and product lines that fit together in a logical way to provide maximum competitive advantage for the corporation.*[26] The technique was developed by General Electric in 1971 to integrate its many different businesses. Since then, the Boston Consulting Group (BCG) has refined the approach for use by other organizations. An organization that engages in many different businesses sometimes adopts a business portfolio approach to develop a comprehensive method for strategic planning. An individual may wish to diversify an investment portfolio with some high-risk stocks, some low-risk stocks, some growth stocks, and perhaps a few income bonds. In much the same way, corporations like to have a balanced mix of SBUs. In general, however, an SBU engages in just one line of business. The BCG matrix is probably the most popular portfolio strategy.

The BCG Matrix

Research shows that half or more of America's largest corporations practice some kind of formal business portfolio planning.[27] Most of them use a two-dimensional model to display the various attributes of their diversified group of businesses (or SBUs) in a concise way. The best-known model is the BCG matrix, which was developed by the Boston Consulting Group. The matrix is illustrated in Figure 6–4. Each circle in it represents a different SBU. Although the BCG matrix greatly simplifies the strategic planning process, to show the SBUs of a complex company such as General Mills (forty SBUs) would produce a rather cluttered diagram.

Placing SBUs on the BCG Matrix   The matrix shows three things about each SBU. First, the area of each circle is proportional to the sales revenue of its business. For example, SBU A is the largest in sales among those illustrated and SBU E is the smallest. Second, the relative position of a circle along the horizontal axis is determined by the SBU's market share as compared to that of the largest rival firm. Third, the vertical axis of the BCG matrix measures the market growth rate of the industry, not the growth rate in sales of the individual business. A business that is gaining market share will show a higher growth rate than the market in general.

Stars, Question Marks, Cows, and Dogs   An implicit assumption of the BCG analysis is that, in a given business, market share signifies strength and market growth rate signifies opportunity. Referring again to Figure 6–4, businesses with high market shares that are also in high-growth-rate industries are given the favorable designation Stars. Theoretically, Stars offer the best profit and growth opportunities for the company. SBUs with low market shares in low-growth industries are called Dogs, because their market shares suggest competitive weakness and because the slow industry growth rates suggest approaching market saturation. The steel industry, for example, is considered by many to be saturated.

Market Share

Relative Sales Growth of Market

Stars

Question Marks

Cash Cows

Dogs

FIGURE 6–4

The BCG Matrix

The major focus of the BCG analysis is on cash flows. SBUs that hold high market shares in low-growth-rate industries should not be rapidly expanding investment in those industries (because there are better investments available). Still, these high-market-share SBUs should be allowed to earn profits. Research suggests that the profitability of such companies depends mostly on employee productivity, capital utilization, and pricing policies—not on added investment.[28] Because there is no need for added investment in the business, the profits can be used to finance the corporation's other businesses, particularly Stars. These high-market-share, low-growth-rate businesses appear in the lower left-hand quadrant of the BCG matrix and are called Cash Cows.

Usually, when a company enters a new business, it will at first have a low market share. If the new business is part of a rapidly growing industry, such as the home computer industry, the business faces an uncertain future as a new entry into the market. So low-market-share businesses in high-growth industries are called Question Marks on the BCG matrix. Typically, it requires large amounts of cash to develop them into Stars. Sometimes, however, a Question Mark business grows rapidly and is so profitable it can generate the cash flows it requires for its own growth.

Implications of the BCG Analysis The corporate-level strategist who uses the BCG approach must ask: What are the strategic implications for the corporation as a whole? What does BCG analysis say about resource allocation and about disposition of the various SBUs? First, BCG proponents argue, the corporation's overall cash flow must be balanced. There should be enough Cash Cows in the business portfolio to fund the cash needs of the Stars and Question Marks, which offer the greatest promise. Second, the positions on the BCG matrix imply certain strategies. Sale or liquidation is recommended for Dogs and perhaps for weak Cash Cows. Growth is the right path for Question Marks and Stars. Efforts should be made to get back investment funds by utilizing Cash Cows.

Some researchers believe resource allocation is an important, but often ignored, use of the BCG matrix.[29] In other words, they think BCG analysis should not be limited to buy-sell and invest-disinvest decisions but should also be used to distribute funds within the corporation.

Formulating Business-Level Strategy

Strategy formulation at the business level—within the strategic business units—is concerned primarily with how to compete. The strategies of growth, stability, and retrenchment apply at the business level as well as the corporate level, but they are accomplished through competitive actions rather than by the acquisition or divestment of other business. Two frameworks in which business units formulate strategy are the adaptive strategy typology and Porter's competitive strategies.

Adaptive Strategy Typology

The adaptive strategy typology is based on a study of business strategies by Raymond Miles and Charles Snow.[30] The basic idea is that business-level managers seek to formulate strategies that will be harmonious with the external environment. Organizations strive to achieve a fit among internal characteristics, strategy, and external characteristics. Their strategies allow organizations to successfully adapt to the environment. The strategies based on the external environment are the prospector, defender, analyzer, and reactor strategies. These strategies, their environments, and their characteristics are summarized in Table 6–1.

TABLE 6–1

Miles and Snow's Adaptive Strategy Typology

Strategies	External Environment	Organizational Characteristics
Prospector—Innovate. Find new market opportunities. Grow. Take risks.	Dynamic, growing	Creativity, innovation, flexibility, decentralization.
Defender—Protect turf. Retrench. Hold current market.	Stable	Tight control, centralization, production efficiency, low overhead.
Analyzer—Maintain current market. Innovate moderately.	Moderate change	Tight control, flexibility, efficient production, creativity.
Reactor—No clear strategy. React to specific conditions. Drift.	Any condition	No clear organizational approach; depends on current needs.

SOURCE: Based on Raymond E. Miles, Charles C. Snow, Alan D. Meyer, and Henry L. Coleman, Jr., "Organizational Strategy, Structure, and Process," *Academy of Management Review* 3 (1978): 546–562.

One example of prospector strategy is United Parcel Service, which innovated in both services and production techniques in the rapidly changing overnight mail industry. In this promotional photograph, we see UPS's two main means of transport and get some idea of the number of countries to which the company delivers.

Source: Photograph courtesy of United Parcel Service

Prospector strategy

The business-level strategy that involves innovation through seeking out new opportunities, taking risks, and expanding.

Defender strategy

The business-level strategy that seeks to maintain current market share by holding on to current customers.

Analyzer strategy

The business-level strategy of attempting to maintain a stable business while innovating on the fringe.

Prospector   The business-level strategy that involves innovation through seeking out new opportunities, taking risks, and expanding is the **prospector strategy.** This strategy is well suited to a dynamic, growing environment, where creativity is more important than efficiency. The internal organization is flexible and decentralized to facilitate innovation. United Parcel Service's computerization of its entire operation so it would be able to react quickly to changing situations is one example of prospector strategy.

Defender   The defender strategy is almost the opposite of the prospector strategy in that it is concerned with stability or retrenchment rather than growth. The **defender strategy** is *the business-level strategy that seeks to maintain current market share by holding on to current customers.* The objective is neither to innovate nor to grow. The defender is concerned with internal efficiency and control to produce reliable products for regular customers. Defenders can be successful, especially when they exist in a declining industry or a stable environment.[31]

Analyzer   Analyzers are considered to lie midway between prospectors and defenders. The **analyzer strategy** is *the business-level strategy of attempting to maintain a stable business while innovating on the fringe.* Some products are targeted toward stable environments with a strategy designed to retain current customers. Others are targeted toward new, more dynamic environments, where growth is possible. The analyzer attempts to balance efficient production for current lines with the creative development of new product lines. One example is Anheuser-Busch, which has a stable beer line and the innovation of offering snack foods as a complementary line.

Reactor   The reactor has no strategy whatsoever. Rather than defining a strategy to suit a specific environment, reactors respond to environmental threats and opportunities in ad hoc fashion. They take whatever actions seem likely to meet their immediate needs and have no long-term plan for congruence with the external environment. Reactors exist in any environment but may have no strategy or internal characteristics suited to that environment. A reactor strategy seems almost random, because top management has not defined a plan or given the organization an explicit direction. Consequently, failing companies often are the result of reactor strategies.

Porter's Competitive Strategies

Management strategist Michael E. Porter studied a number of business organizations and proposed three effective business-level strategies: differentiation, cost leadership, and focus.[32] The organizational characteristics associated with each strategy are summarized in Table 6–2.

Differentiation *The business-level strategy that involves an attempt to distinguish the firm's goods or services from others in the industry* is the **differentiation strategy.** The organization may use such skills and resources as advertising, distinctive product features, exceptional service, and technology to achieve a product that could be perceived as unique. Successful differentiation strategy is often profitable because customers will usually be loyal and will pay high prices for the product. Examples of products that have benefited from a differentiation strategy include Porsche automobiles, Maytag appliances, and Ralph Lauren Polo clothing, all of which are perceived as distinctive in their markets.

Cost Leadership *The business-level strategy in which the organization aggressively seeks efficient facilities, pursues cost reductions, and uses tight cost controls to produce products more efficiently than competitors* is the **cost leadership strategy.** A low-cost position means that the company can undercut competitors' prices and still offer comparable quality and earn a reasonable profit. Quality Inns is a low-priced alternative to lodging outlets such as Holiday Inns and Ramada Inns.

Differentiation strategy

The business-level strategy that involves an attempt to distinguish the firm's goods or services from others in the industry.

Cost leadership strategy

The business-level strategy in which the organization aggressively seeks efficient facilities, pursues cost reductions, and uses tight cost controls to produce products more efficiently than competitors.

TABLE 6–2

Organizational Characteristics for Porter's Competitive Strategies

Strategy	Commonly Required Skills and Resources	Common Organizational Requirements
Differentiation	Strong marketing abilities. Product engineering. Creative flair. Strong capability in basic research. Corporate reputation for quality or technological leadership.	Strong coordination among functions in R&D, product development, and marketing. Subjective measurement and incentives instead of quantitative measures. Amenities to attract highly skilled labor, scientists, or creative people.
Cost leadership	Sustained capital investment and access to capital. Process-engineering skills. Intense supervision of labor. Products designed for ease in manufacture. Low-cost distribution system.	Tight cost control. Frequent, detailed control reports. Structured organization and responsibilities. Incentives based on meeting strict quantitative targets.
Focus	Combination of the above policies directed at a particular strategic target.	Combination of the above policies directed at the regular strategic target.

SOURCE: Reprinted with permission of The Free Press, a division of Macmillan, Inc., from *Competitive Strategy: Techniques for Analyzing Industries and Competitors* by Michael E. Porter. Copyright © 1980 by The Free Press.

Focus strategy

The business-level strategy in which the organization concentrates on a specific regional market, product line, or buyer group.

Focus *The business-level strategy in which the organization concentrates on a specific regional market, product line, or buyer group* is the **focus strategy.** When focusing on a single market segment, the company may use either a differentiation or a low-cost approach, but only for that narrow market. The company may be seeking either a competitive cost advantage or a perceived differentiation in the target segment.

Porter found that many businesses did not consciously adopt one of these three strategies and were therefore stuck in the middle of the pack with no strategic advantage. Without a strategic advantage, the businesses earned below-average profits and therefore were not in a position to compete successfully.

There is some similarity between Porter's strategies and Miles and Snow's adaptive typology. The differentiation strategy is similar to the prospector strategy, the low-cost strategy is similar to the defender strategy, and the focus strategy is similar to the analyzer strategy, which adopts a focus strategy appropriate for each product line. The reactor strategy, which is really not a strategy at all, is similar to what is used by the middle-of-the-pack organizations that cannot attain a competitive strategic advantage.

Formulating Functional-Level Strategy

Functional-level strategies are the action plans adopted by the major functional departments to support the execution of a business-level strategy. Major organizational functions include marketing, production, finance, human resources, and research and development. For example, strategic planning for the finance function at G. D. Searle and Company involves the establishment of budgeting, accounting, and investment policies and the allocation of SBU cash flows. In the human resource area, policies for compensation, hiring and firing, training, and human resource planning are of strategic concern.

Strategic planning is not concerned with day-to-day supervision. It is concerned mainly with providing general, longer-range direction and guidance. Many corporations are expanding their strategic planning range beyond the domestic front to the international arena. Coca-Cola, Kentucky Fried Chicken, Bausch & Lomb, Johnson & Johnson, RJR Nabisco, Seagram, and Procter & Gamble have established strategic joint partnerships with Chinese companies. Increasingly, companies are seeking potential overseas markets and making this objective part of their organizational mission. It is expected that the European Community will be a very attractive overseas market for U.S. firms. Senior managers adopt strategies that are coordinated with the business-level strategy to achieve the organization's strategic objectives.[33]

Consider a company that has adopted a prospector strategy and is introducing new products that are expected to experience rapid growth in the early stages of their life cycle. The human resource department should adopt a strategy appropriate for growth, which means recruiting additional workers and training middle managers for movement into new positions. The marketing department should undertake test marketing, aggressive advertising campaigns, and product trials by consumers. The finance department should adopt plans to borrow money, handle large cash investments, and authorize construction of new production facilities.

A company with mature products or an analyzer strategy will have different functional strategies. The human resource department should develop strategies for retaining and developing a stable work force, including transfers, advancements, and incentives for efficiency and safety. Marketing should stress brand loyalty and the development of established, reliable distribution channels. Production should maintain long-production runs, routinization, and cost reduction. Finance should focus on net cash flows and positive cash balances. Basically, functional-level strategies should support the execution of business-level strategies by developing an effective mix of the major organizational functions.

A Global Perspective

In order to compete globally, managers must find a way to achieve their overall organizational objectives overseas. South Korea's Daewoo Heavy Industries appears to have an overall organizational mission of expanding its share of the market for aircraft components produced for the world's major aircraft manufacturers. The company is using its major strengths—not low wages but instead new, efficient factories and a strong technological base—to attract an ever-expanding portion of the aircraft component parts market.[34]

Management at Ford Motor Company believes that to be competitive in the global market for cars, the company must have a premium image car. Top-level managers surmise that the onrush of competition by the Japanese trio of Honda, Toyota, and Nissan can be best countered by a Ford/Saab combination.[35] Companies in the airline industry also appear to agree that partnerships are strategically best for them. In order to compete globally, American airline companies such as United, Northwest, Delta, Continental, and American West have formed partnerships with foreign airlines.[36]

Strategically, many companies are opting to combine as partners with others that have certain strategic advantages overseas. Other companies are making inroads by doing an excellent job with what they know best. Daewoo, which is building and co-building component parts for major aircraft manufacturers, is one example. Still others are going global by acting like locals. Procter & Gamble, for example, hired more Japanese workers at its plants in Japan, became more closely attuned to the local ways of the Japanese, and keyed in on doing whatever was necessary to capture market share from the Japanese.[37] Strategically, both Daewoo and P&G appear to be on the correct course. Even though their methods of accomplishing their objectives differ, they have clearly isolated their overall organizational objectives.

· ·

1. Are you willing to recognize that strategic planning is important at all organizational levels?

☐ Yes   ☐ No

(continued)

Self-Assessment Exercise

Will You Be a Good Strategic Planner?

2. Are you willing to recognize that managers at all organizational levels should base their plans on the organizational mission?

☐ Yes ☐ No

3. Are you willing to work to understand the environment in which the decision is to be made?

☐ Yes ☐ No

4. Are you willing to recognize that objectives in the strategic planning process should be specific in nature?

☐ Yes ☐ No

5. Are you willing to recognize that at times it is not possible to maximize results?

☐ Yes ☐ No

6. Are you willing to realize that no matter how good a strategic plan is, it is worthless unless properly implemented?

☐ Yes ☐ No

7. Are you willing to learn the numerous grand strategies available in the strategic planning process?

☐ Yes ☐ No

8. Are you willing to understand that diversity may be necessary to achieve corporate objectives?

☐ Yes ☐ No

9. Are you willing to learn that a portfolio strategy may need to be developed to termine how to compete in a particular line of business?

☐ Yes ☐ No

10. Are you willing to understand how to formulate functional-level strategy?

☐ Yes ☐ No

Summary

Strategic planning is the process by which top management determines organizational purposes and objectives and how they are to be achieved. Corporate-level strategic planning is the process of defining the overall character and purpose of the organization, the businesses it will enter and leave, and how resources will be distributed among those businesses. Business-level strategic planning is concerned primarily with how to manage the interests and operations of a particular business. Functional-level strategic planning is the process of determining policies and procedures for relatively narrow areas of activity that are critical to the success of the organization. Many companies use in-house organizational strategists to assist and advise managers in strategic planning.

The strategic planning process is a four-step approach: (1) determining the mission, (2) assessing the organization and its environment, (3) setting objectives or direction, and (4) determining strategies to accomplish the objectives. Basically, the process is a derivative of the SWOT—strengths, weaknesses, opportunities, and threats—framework, which affects organizational performance. Once the strategic plan is developed, the next step is to implement the plan.

Corporate-level strategy typically concerns the mix and utilization of strategic business units. Executives in charge of the entire corporation generally define an overall strategic direction—called a grand strategy—and then develop a portfolio of strategic business units to carry out the grand strategy.

The two frameworks in which business units formulate strategy are the adaptive strategy typology and Porter's competitive strategies. Functional-level strategies are the action plans adopted by major functional departments to support the execution of business-level strategy. Major organizational functions include marketing, production, finance, human resources, and research and development.

Review Questions

1. Define *strategic planning*. What is a strategic business unit?

2. Distinguish among corporate-level strategic planning, business-level strategic planning, and functional-level strategic planning.

3. Who are the organizational strategists?

4. List and briefly describe each step in the strategic planning process.

5. Describe the concept of satisficing as suggested by Herbert Simon.

6. Identify and briefly describe the grand, or master, strategies that grow out of the strategic planning process.

7. Briefly describe the following business-level strategies:
   a. adaptive strategy typology
   b. Porter's competitive strategy

Key Terms

Strategic planning
Corporate-level strategic
  planning
Business-level strategic
  planning
Strategic business unit
  (SBU)
Functional-level strategic
  planning
Strategic planning staff
  specialists

Organizational strategists
Integration
Forward integration
Backward integration
Horizontal integration
Diversification
Conglomerate
  diversification
Concentric diversification

Retrenchment
Portfolio strategy
Prospector strategy
Defender strategy
Analyzer strategy
Differentiation strategy
Cost leadership strategy
Focus strategy

CASE 6.1	MASTER HARDWARE

Master Hardware is a chain of twelve retail outlets located in small towns in northern Kentucky and southern Ohio. The parent corporation, Master Merchandisers, Inc., is a Kentucky corporation owned by the Booker family of Louisville. The Bookers, led by Beatrice, who was eighty-five years old in 1992, have steadfastly refused to vary from the plan that Beatrice found successful when the first Master Hardware stores were opened during the 1940s. The plan is simple: Only one store is opened in each town, and the towns must be between 8,000 and 15,000 population at the time. Inventories are tightly controlled, and no item is stocked unless it turns at least four times a year. Each store is managed by a carefully selected local citizen, who is paid 50 percent of the profits the store generates. All purchasing is done by the central office in Louisville, although most items are shipped directly from hardware wholesalers and manufacturers to the individual stores. The store buildings are rented. After an initial infusion of capital, each store is required to pay its own way. If it does not, it is closed.

Master Merchandisers had opened no new stores for several years, although the existing stores were quite profitable. The company had never done much borrowing, so the high profits resulted in increasing cash balances, even after family members were paid director's fees, salaries, and so forth.

Until 1987, the excess funds were invested in U.S. Treasury securities, which are safe but yield low returns. That year, Beatrice Booker agreed with the board of directors—made up of two of her sons, a nephew, and a niece—that the company should go into the restaurant business. The Bookers decided that Master Merchandisers would invest $3 million and build at least five new seafood restaurants. They would feature pond-raised catfish and would be located in towns similar to those where the Master Hardware stores were.

The restaurant business was separately incorporated as Catfish Master Restaurants, Inc. By mid-1990, three Catfish Master Restaurants were opened. The system was patterned as much as possible after the Master Hardware chain. Restaurant managers were paid a percentage of the profits. Purchasing was done centrally, and each restaurant was required to support itself after the initial investment. It became clear within a year, however, that the first two restaurants would have to be closed unless additional funds were provided. The Bookers put up an additional $50,000 to help those two restaurants stay open, but both were still unprofitable two years later.

Questions

1. State what you believe to be the corporate mission of Master Merchandisers, Inc.
2. List the strategies discussed in the case that you consider business-level strategies. Explain your answer.
3. What kind of integration occurred when Master Merchandisers went into the restaurant business? Discuss.
4. Do you believe the Booker family is likely to be successful in the restaurant business? Explain.

The sign says "Free Ice Water, Wall Drug Store." But if you take the exit to the little town of Wall, near the Badlands of South Dakota, you will find a lot more than a drugstore and much more to do than drink ice water. In fact, Wall Drug Store is more than a store; it's a service station, a place of amusement, a family entertainment center, a gallery of South Dakota history, and a Western heritage museum.

With about $5 million in sales and seasonal employment as high as 200, Wall Drug Company may be the most widely known small business in the world. A series of Wall Drug Company case studies appear in a dozen or more management texts. The company has become familiar to thousands of students in hundreds of colleges.

As unlikely a site as Wall is for a $5 million business, it was even more unlikely in 1931. That year, Ted Hustead and his wife, Dorothy, bought a small drugstore in what was then a desolate crossroads town of three hundred people. The Husteads eked out a living for a few years, until Dorothy had the most important idea in Wall Drug's history: She and Ted would begin placing eye-catching signs next to the two highways leading to Wall.

As the customers came to sample the "free ice water," they bought other items as well—medicines, combs, and facial tissues. Shelves were no sooner filled than they were empty again. The Husteads expanded their line of merchandise and increased the size of the store every few years. Until 1971, they remained cautious, adding inventories and floor space only when the funds to pay for them were in sight. By that time, Wall Drug included a gasoline station, a coffee shop, an art gallery, and a hodgepodge of other attractions.

In 1972, the Husteads borrowed $250,000 to build what they called "the Mall," and sales jumped 20 percent the next year. The mall is patterned after the main street of a typical western town, the small shop buildings constructed of native timber and old brick. The street surface is made of rock hauled from the nearby Cheyenne River.

As Wall Drug expanded, so did the work force. The Husteads' son, Bill, was old enough to start working in 1951. The work force has never been stable because the business is so seasonal. South Dakota winters do not encourage tourism. Bill comments: "I really think there isn't anything more difficult than running a business with 20 to 30 employees in the winter and 180 to 200 in the summer. It's kind of exciting and fun for the first twenty-five years, but after thirty years you begin to think it's a tough racket."

Ted Hustead is over eighty, but he still exercises authority. A caller who asks for the public affairs department is likely to hear Ted's rasping voice. The third generation of Husteads began to be heard when Bill's son Rick joined the store in 1980. He was an "old hand" by 1987.

Some have asked about expanding such a successful operation to other towns. Bill's answer: "We will try to diversify within our own community." The Husteads have several hundred acres near the interstate highway. That is as far away as they have any thought of doing business. Among the possibilities are a motel and a modified drugstore. With pride in his voice, Bill indicates that Wall Drug is much more than a job to him. He says: "The place is so crazy, so different—it's the largest drugstore in the world. It may get in the *Guinness Book of Records* as the only drugstore with a church in it."[38]

Questions

1. On the basis of the information provided in this case, what do you believe the mission statement is for Wall Drug?
2. Who are the organizational strategists at Wall Drug?

Notes

1. This case is a composite of a number of published accounts, among them: Thomas N. Cochran, "The Right Chemistry," *Barron's*, March 20, 1989, p. 60; Standard and Poor's Corp., "Monsanto Co.," *Standard NYSE Stock Reports* 56 (June 28, 1989), sec. 15; Jennifer Alter, "Something Old, Something New Sweeten Searle's Sales Picture," *Advertising Age*, February 14, 1983, pp. 4, 64; Gene Bylinsky, "The Battle for America's Sweet Tooth," *Fortune*, July 26, 1982, pp. 28-32; Matt Clark and Mary Hager,

"A Sweet Sugar Substitute," *Newsweek,* July 27, 1981, p. 63; Jay Gissen, "Beginners Luck," *Forbes,* May 21, 1984, p. 240; "NutraSweet Business Unit," *Searle Annual Report* (1983), pp. 2–11; Robert Shapiro, "Masterminding Searle's Sweet Taste of Success," *Sales & Marketing Management,* January 16, 1984; Subrata N. Chakravarty, "Taking Risks Is What They Pay You For," *Forbes,* February 10, 1986, pp. 45–46; Judann Dagnoli, "NutraSweet Rivals Stirring," *Advertising Age,* June 26, 1989, p. 3; Stuart Elliot, "Better Identity for NutraSweet," *New York Times,* May 22, 1991, pp. C6, D16; Bruce Oman, "Bittersweet Success," *Beverage World,* January 1991, p. 58; Joanne Lipmann, "Nutra-Sweet's New Campaign," *Wall Street Journal,* May 22, 1991, p. 33; and numerous articles from the *Wall Street Journal.*

2. Robert H. Hayes and Steven C. Wheelwright, *Restoring Our Competitive Edge: Competing through Manufacturing* (New York: Wiley, 1984), pp. 27–28.

3. J. Scott Armstrong, "The Value of Formal Planning for Strategic Decisions: Review of the Empirical Research," *Strategic Management Journal* 3 (July–September 1982): 197–211.

4. Jay R. Galbraith and Daniel A. Nathanson, *Strategy Implementation: The Role of Structure and Process,* 2d ed. (St. Paul, MN: West Publishing, 1986), p. 12.

5. David M. Herold, "Long-Range Planning and Organizational Performance," *Academy of Management Journal* 15 (March 1972), pp. 91–102.

6. "The New Breed of Strategic Planner," *Business Week,* September 17, 1984, pp. 62–68.

7. Richard B. Robinson, Jr. and John A. Pearce II, "The Impact of Formalized Strategic Planning on Financial Performance in Small Organizations," *Strategic Management Journal* 4 (July–September 1983), pp. 197–207.

8. Ann Hagedorn, "Colgate Still Seeking to Placate Critics of Its Darkie Brand," *Wall Street Journal,* April 18, 1988, pp. 36–37.

9. *INSIDE BUSINESS:* Calloway's strategic planning vision, both in terms of the domestic and international business scene, came into full view when he was interviewed by the CNN business news team of Kandel, Hartley, and Perry.

10. Frederick Gluck, Stephen Kaufman, and A. Steven Walleck, "The Four Phases of Strategic Management," *Journal of Business Strategy* 2 (Winter 1982): 11–12.

11. Betsy Morris, "Philip Morris Jabs at Its Weakened Rival," *Wall Street Journal,* July 21, 1989, p. B1; "Is Bigger Better for Philip Morris?" *Fortune,* May 8, 1989, pp. 66–71; Colin Leinster, "Selling Cigarettes to Fewer Americans and More Japanese," *Fortune,* May 8, 1989, p. 69.

12. Walter Guzzardi, "Wisdom from the Giants of Business," *Fortune,* July 3, 1989, p. 84.

13. Ibid., p. 80.

14. Richard B. Robinson, Jr., "The Importance of 'Outsiders' in Small Firm Strategic Planning," *Academy of Management Journal* 25 (March 1982): 80–93.

15. James J. Polyczynski and Jason Leniski, "Inviting Front-Line Managers into the Strategic-Planning and Decision-Making Process," *Appalachian Business Review* 9 (1982): 2–5.

16. Ian Wilson, "The Strategic Management Technology: Corporate Fad or Strategic Necessity," *Long-Range Planning* 19 (April 1986): 21–22.

17. Quoted in Charles H. Granger, "The Hierarchy of Objectives," *Harvard Business Review* 42 (May–June 1964): 63–74.

18. Herbert A. Simon, *The New Science of Management Decision* (New York: Harper & Row, 1960).

19. Jay R. Galbraith and Robert K. Kazanjian, *Strategy Implementation: Structure, Systems, and Process,* 2d ed. (St. Paul, MN: West Publishing, 1986).

20. Alfred V. Chandler, *Strategies and Structures* (Cambridge, MA: M.I.T. Press, 1962).

21. Harris Collingwood, "In Business This Week," *Business Week,* February 13, 1989, p. 38.

22. Kathryn Rudie Harrigan, "A Framework for Looking at Vertical Integration," *Journal of Business Strategy* 3 (Winter 1983): 30–37.

23. In a technical sense, the term *related diversification* is better than *concentric diversification,* but the latter has found more widespread use.

24. Richard A. Bettis, "Performance Differences in Related and Unrelated Diversified Firms," *Strategic Management Journal* 2 (October–December 1981): 379–393.

25. Todd Vogel, "Baker Hughes Lops Off a Weak Limb," *Business Week,* May 29, 1989, p. 34.

26. Richard L. Daft, *Management* (New York: The Dryden Press, 1988), p. 140.

27. Philippe Haspeslagh, "Portfolio Planning: Uses and Limits," *Harvard Business Review* 60 (January–February 1982): 58–73.

28. Ian C. MacMillan, Donald C. Hambrick, and Diana L. Day, "The Product Portfolio and Profitability: A PIMS-Based Analysis of Industrial-Product Businesses," *Academy of Management Journal* 25 (December 1982): 733–755.

29. Frederick Gluck, "The Dilemmas of Resource Allocation," *Journal of Business Strategy* 2 (Fall 1981): 67–71; and Haspeslagh, "Portfolio Planning: Uses and Limits," pp. 58–73.

30. Raymond E. Miles and Charles C. Snow, *Organizational Strategy, Structure, and Process* (New York: McGraw-Hill, 1978).

31. Donald C. Hambrick, "Some Tests of the Effectiveness and Functional Attributes of Miles and Snow's Strategic Types," *Academy of Management Journal* 26 (1983): 5–26.

32. Michael E. Porter, *Competitive Strategy* (New York: Free Press, 1980), pp. 36–46.

33. Harold W. Fox, "A Framework for Functional Coordination," *Atlanta Economic Review* (now *Business Magazine*) 23 (November/December 1973): 8–12.

34. Laxmi Nakarmi, Maria Shao, and Dave Griffiths, "South Korea's New Destination: The Wild Blue Yonder," *Business Week*, September 11, 1989, p. 50.

35. Richard A. Melcher, James B. Treece, and A. Dunlap Smith, "Ford Is Kicking Saab's Tires," *Business Week*, September 18, 1989, p. 52.

36. Christopher Power and Seth Payne, "Birds of a Feather . . . Are Doing Deals Together," *Business Week*, September 11, 1989, p. 32.

37. Zachary Schiller, Ted Holden, and Mark Maremont, "P&G Global by Acting like a Global," *Business Week*, August 28, 1989, p. 58.

38. This case is a composite of a number of published accounts, among them: James D. Taylor, Robert L. Johnson, and C. Philip Fisher, "Wall Drug Store 1983," in Arthur Sharplin, *Strategic Management* (New York: McGraw-Hill, 1985), p. 102; "American Scene in South Dakota—Buffalo Burgers at Wall Drug," *Time*, August 31, 1983, p. 8; "Wall and Water," *Guide Post*, July 1982, p. 34.

Management Skills

Since effective decision making is so important in business, it is essential that you develop, and continually fine-tune, your decision-making skills. To assess your decision-making ability, take the self-assessment exercise "Are You a Good Decision Maker?" Then, turn to page 632 to evaluate yourself.

Are You a Good Decision Maker?

INSTRUCTIONS: For each statement answer either yes or no.

	YES	NO
1. Do you often try to avoid or delay making important decisions and even hope that problems will go away?	☐	☐
2. When required to make a decision fairly promptly, do you become flustered and fail to function at your best?	☐	☐
3. Would you consider it demeaning to consult your subordinates regarding a problem with which they have experience?	☐	☐
4. In deciding a complicated problem where strong arguments exist for either side, would you trust your "gut reaction"?	☐	☐
5. Do you often wish that you didn't have to make any decisions?	☐	☐
6. When faced with a serious decision, are your sleep and appetite usually adversely affected?	☐	☐
7. Do you secretly dislike making decisions because you lack self-confidence?	☐	☐

	YES	NO
8. Are you uneasy even when required to make unimportant decisions?	☐	☐
9. Would you fire a friend if his continued employment was against the welfare of the enterprise in which you held a high position?	☐	☐
10. When baffled by a problem within your jurisdiction, would you try to pass it off to others?	☐	☐
11. At home, do you participate in all or most of the important decisions?	☐	☐
12. Are you usually edgy both before and after making important decisions?	☐	☐

Source: Adapted from Walter Duckat, "Check Your Decisionmaking Skills," *Supervision* 41 (February 1979): 3. Reprinted with permission from *Supervision*. Copyright © 1979 by The National Research Bureau, Inc., 424 North Third Street, Burlington, Iowa 52601.

7

The Organizing Process and the Informal Organization

LEARNING OBJECTIVES

After completing this chapter students should be able to

- Describe what an organization is and explain the organizing process.
- Define *specialization of labor* and identify its benefits and limits.
- Identify and describe the primary means of departmentation.
- Describe organizational differentiation.
- Describe the informal organization and explain its benefits and costs.

In 1989, with over $20 billion in sales, Wal-Mart was the nation's third largest retailer, but by the end of January 1991 earnings had risen to $32.6 billion, and Wal-Mart became the nation's number 1 retailer. The company operated 1,650 discount department stores, 200 Sam's Wholesale Clubs, and several Discount Drug Stores and Hypermarket USA stores. A sweetheart of Wall Street, Wal-Mart stock quintupled in value in just six years, and stockholders realized nearly a 50 percent annual return in the previous decade. The company was consistently among *Fortune* magazine's "Most Admired Corporations," ranking fourth in 1991.

Wal-Mart is headquartered in the tiny town of Bentonville, Arkansas, where the Wal-Mart saga began with a single store in the early 1960s. The man credited with Wal-Mart's success is founder Sam Walton. Walton had been successful at everything he had tried, with the exception of retirement. Until his death in 1992, Walton continued to devote about four months a year to "barnstorming the heartland," visiting Wal-Mart stores. He spent several days a week going from store to store visiting with store managers and employees—who are called "associates"—about ways to improve the operation. Walton called this the "grass-roots management style." He was frequently found at the door of a Wal-Mart or Sam's store greeting customers.

Walton always stressed participation. Not only are managers expected to interact with their people on a daily basis, but there is a mandatory meeting once a year to gather suggestions that will be passed on to top management. Portraying employees as associates is more than window dressing. It is not uncommon to see a store manager or department chief cleaning up a spill or polishing handprints off the store's glass doors, and every employee is encouraged to own stock in the company.

Although management at Wal-Mart emphasizes individual initiative and autonomy, managers are accountable for results. Every store manager must prepare a monthly financial statement listing each expenditure, from taxes and rent to paper clips and telephone charges. District managers are required to review each report and discuss ways to reduce expenses.

Rex Chase, who oversees ten Wal-Mart stores in Texas, says that his group of store managers and associates is "like family." He continues, "The hardest part of my job is when I have to demote someone. If I can go an extra mile with him—and some people fault me because I go the extra mile—I can save that man. I've done him a favor and I've done the company a favor." Before his death, Sam Walton supported the concept of a "family operation" by personally visiting his family at every Wal-Mart store in the United States. With all of this success, the number 1 retailer is surely headed toward "decisive battles with its archrival, a smarter Kmart," but at the present time Wal-Mart appears to be unstoppable.[1]

The organizing process as it evolved at Wal-Mart is similar to that at many other firms, whether small or large, domestic or international, service or manufacturing. However, Wal-Mart is definitely an organization that has sucessfully prescribed formal relations among their people and the resources available to accomplish their objectives. Wal-Mart's organizing process is so effective that they open 150 or so stores annually.[2]

In this chapter, the organizing process is discussed first. Then, specialization of labor is presented, followed by a discussion of departmentation. Next, organizational differentiation, which becomes necessary as an organization grows, is discussed. Finally, the informal organization and its benefits and costs are addressed.

What Is an Organization?

The word *organization* is used widely. Most of us are reminded of it each day when we read newspapers, walk around campus, watch television programs, or listen to the radio. Some of us, when we hear the word, envision large companies such as Wal-Mart and General Motors. But few of us think of the local grocery store, service station, fast-food restaurant, or nursery school. Each of these, however, is an organization.

Organizations, large or small, have at least three characteristics:

1. They are composed of people.

2. They exist to achieve objectives.

3. They require some degree of limitation on member behavior.

Organization

Two or more people working together in a coordinated manner to achieve group results.

Thus, an **organization** is *two or more people working together in a coordinated manner to achieve group results.* Because most people spend a considerable part of their lives working in organizations, it is important to understand how organizations function and how they can be managed effectively. To be effective, a manager must be capable of organizing human resources, physical factors, and functions such as production, marketing, and finance, in a manner designed to ensure the achievement of the objectives of the firm. This process is crucial to the success of every organization where people work together as a group.

The Organizing Process

Organizing

The process of prescribing formal relationships among people and resources to accomplish objectives.

Organizing is *the process of prescribing formal relationships among people and resources to accomplish objectives.* The organizing process, as is illustrated in Figure 7–1, takes place within the constraints of the organization's external and internal environments. First, it is necessary to consider the organizational objectives and to determine the kind of organizing needed to accomplish those objectives. Next, the types of functions, or work activities, that will be required to meet company objectives must be determined. Finally, activities that are similar must be grouped together. A number of departments or otherwise separate organizational units need to be set up, each designed to carry out a different function or group of functions.

FIGURE 7–1

The Organizing Process

The External Environment

In Chapter 2, we saw how the external environment affects the management of corporations. The external environment also affects the organizing process. For instance, laws and public concern about clean water and air may create a need for a manufacturer to add personnel to monitor any possibly toxic substances that may be discharged. The necessity of dealing with a wide range of suppliers and of buying in large volumes requires a sophisticated purchasing department at company headquarters. Differences in legislation from state to state require that someone be responsible for helping individual managers stay within the law.

More than in the past, rapidly changing technological factors influence the organizing process. For example, new automotive technology required U.S. automobile manufacturers to make major changes in assembly lines, which had changed little from those developed by Henry Ford before 1920. Robots often do repetitive tasks previously done by humans. In some plants, cars are assembled at work stations rather than on mile-long assembly lines. Rapid technological change is occurring in virtually every industry segment. As changes in the manufacturing process occur, organizations must be able to respond with new and more flexible ways of assigning persons and machines to jobs.

Technology has also affected the way work is assigned. When the chairman of Mack Trucks was faced with a major contract dispute with the United Auto Workers, he turned to a nonunion plant to take advantage of more flexible work rules and recent technological advancements. He understood the problems associated with running a truck company. In order to deal with the external environment, he ushered in new technology and demanded plant closures, layoffs, and manufacturing consolidation.[3]

Surprisingly, even the once inflexible British labor unions have allowed changes in organizing. Japan-based British industries now have flexible work rules, and British

New automotive technology, mainly introduced by Japanese producers, has forced U.S. auto-mobile manufacturers to make major changes in assembly lines, which had changed little from those developed by Henry Ford before 1920. Robots, such as the automated welding system shown here, now do many of the repetitive tasks previously done by humans.

Source: © Jim Pickerell

companies have adopted the Japanese management style, just-in-time inventory, and quality assurance systems. Flexible ways of assigning people and machines to jobs apparently work for Japanese companies operating in Britain, so the British are adopting their methods. According to Roy Sanderson, national secretary of Britain's electricians' union, the Japanese have "set the pace for British manufacturing productivity and technology."[4]

At the General Motors Saturn plant in northern Tennessee, Japanese methods and machines are used to help produce the new compact model. The Japanese method of cooperation between employees and management is the norm at the Saturn plant. Union members work alongside managers in activities ranging from job-related matters to strategic planning. A number of heavy-duty Japanese machines have been installed in the plant, including two new 4,500-ton stamping presses made by Komatsu and Hitachi-Zozen.[5]

The Internal Environment

The organizing process is also influenced by the internal environment that individual managers face. The approach to organizing that an individual manager uses must be compatible with the internal environment. For example, a company's procedures manual may specify the manner in which machinery can be rearranged, and personnel regulations may restrict the reassignment of workers.

The boss's view of the company's strategic and operating plans will limit the way a lower-level manager can organize resources to carry out those plans. At Wal-Mart, it is well known that the company placed emphasis on individual initiative and autonomy and held managers accountable for results.

Considering Organizational Objectives

Everything the manager does should be directed toward accomplishment of objectives, and organizing is no exception. Organizing should have as its purpose arranging people and resources in the best way possible to support the organization's objectives.

It is important that every phase of the organizing sequence be directed at accomplishment of objectives. Wal-Mart's objective was to expand its basic business—offering name brand merchandise to a vast low- to middle-income population. Organizing for Wal-Mart therefore involved arranging people and resources in the best way possible to support that objective. One principle that distinguishes Wal-Mart from its competitors is the unusual depth of employee involvement in company affairs. Wal-Mart's highly motivated workers are the envy of its competitors. For example, employee suggestions resulted in the successful practice of installing official greeters in all Wal-Mart stores to offer advice, give directions, or just be friendly to customers. Wal-Mart also has an inventory control system that is recognized as one of the most sophisticated in retailing.[6] Simply by arranging its people and resources effectively, Wal-Mart remains the nation's largest retailer.

Determining Types of Work Activities

Once objectives and the kind of organizing needed to accomplish them are established, it is possible to determine the kinds of work activities that should be involved. On a typical baseball team, players perform the tasks of fielding, hitting, and pitching. A good team must develop competent specialists in each of these activities. Pitching can be further broken down into starting, long relieving, and short relieving. Fielding involves playing the infield and the outfield. And playing second base requires talents that are different from those needed to do the other infield jobs.

Similarly, the work activities required to accomplish the objectives of business firms can be identified. In a manufacturing concern, raw materials must be procured and the product must be made and sold. Each of these major phases involves hiring and supervising people, processing paperwork, and numerous other activities. So all these types of activities must be distinguished from one another before the organizing process can proceed. An important concept in specifying different kinds of tasks is specialization of labor.

MANAGEMENT IN PRACTICE: A Skill-Building Exercise

Jim Beck was the drawbench crew chief at Jamestown Tube Corporation's West Monroe, Louisiana, stainless steel tubing facility. The drawbench pulls, or draws, the welded tubing down to smaller sizes. Jim supervised six workers and often lent a hand himself, particularly when maintenance or adjustment was required.

In early 1992, the plant manager, Ken Kincaid, told Jim an additional drawbench was soon to be added. "Jim," said Ken, "we have approval to add six more workers for the new drawbench. But I want you to study the operation and see if we can cut that to five. It seems to me that with the two drawbenches right beside each other, we may be able to cut some of the labor costs." Jim said, "I'm sure we can, Ken. I'll see if I can find a way to do it." Jim continued, "I'm a little worried about supervising eleven people. I think that I can do it, but it's going to be kind of tough."

As Jim left the office, he thought about how things were always changing in the plant. Just two years earlier, when the plant was opened, he had helped plan the operation of the drawbench. Since Jim had two years' experience, he felt it would be easier the second time. As Jim approached the drawbench, Mike Robinson saw him and said, "Jim, Ed is going to have to be off this afternoon to take his baby to the doctor. That will leave us one operator short." "Okay, Mike," replied Jim. "Do you remember when I had you and Ed switch places a while back? I did that so you could learn each other's job. You can take up the slack when Ed is gone. We'll have to slow down the drawbench a little, but you can handle it."

Did Jim Beck properly determine the types of work activities? Explain.

Specialization of Labor

Specialization of labor
The division of a complex job into simpler tasks so that one person or group may carry out only identical or related activities.

In *The Wealth of Nations* (1776), Adam Smith explained how he was able to increase the productivity of a group of pin makers more than a thousandfold through the specialization (division) of labor. **Specialization of labor** is *the division of a complex job into simpler tasks so that one person or group may carry out only identical or related activities.* One purpose of organizing, like everything else a manager does, is to improve

FIGURE 7–2

Degrees of Specialization Associated with the Job of Producing Small Transistor Radios

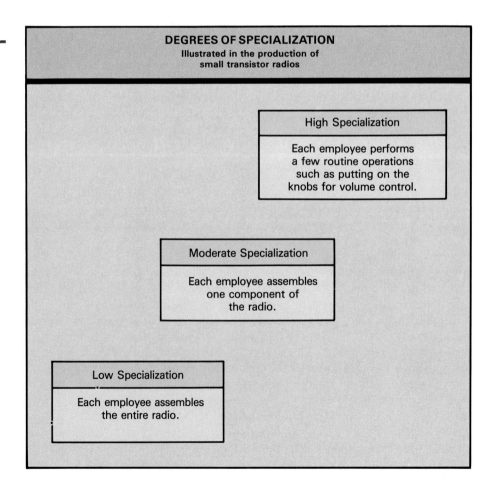

DEGREES OF SPECIALIZATION
Illustrated in the production of small transistor radios

High Specialization

Each employee performs a few routine operations such as putting on the knobs for volume control.

Moderate Specialization

Each employee assembles one component of the radio.

Low Specialization

Each employee assembles the entire radio.

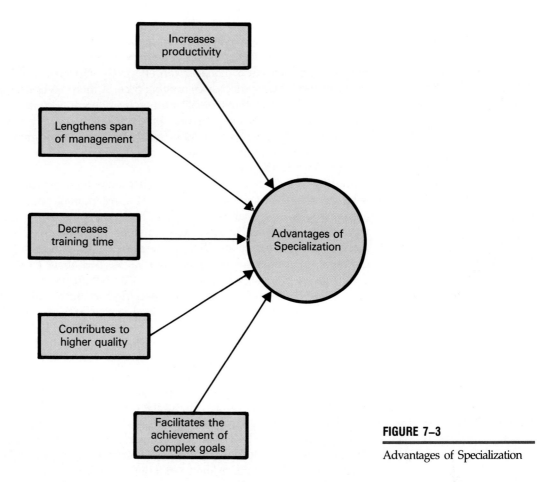

FIGURE 7–3

Advantages of Specialization

productivity. Through specialization of labor, it is possible for members of the organization to concentrate on a single area, thereby increasing output. To achieve
efficiency, specialization is especially essential in mass-production industries. But in
fact, most work activities in nearly all organizations are of a specialized nature.

Organizations have endless options as to the degree of specialization for each job.
For instance, if a company produces small transistor radios, several different approaches might be available (see Figure 7–2).

Advantages of Specialization

As Figure 7–3 shows, there are five specific advantages of specialization. First,
specialization often increases productivity. A worker who is allowed to concentrate
skill and effort on just a small number of tasks can usually achieve a higher level
of output. In the manufacture of electronic components, output per worker tends
to be much higher in situations where employees perform highly specialized work
activities. The same thing applies to many fast-food restaurants. At McDonald's,
employees efficiently perform such specialized functions as cooking hamburgers or
french fries.[7] This specialization contrasts with the work in more traditional restaurants, where employees may perform a wide variety of jobs.

Second, specialization permits managers to efficiently supervise a large number of employees. A manager may be able to supervise thirty workers who are performing the same specialized tasks. If workers are performing a number of diverse tasks, the number of employees a manager can effectively supervise will be much lower.

Third, specialization decreases training time. A more specialized job can be learned more quickly than a job that entails numerous different work activities. When training time is reduced, the workers become productive more quickly. For instance, the time required to train a worker to cook french fries or prepare milk shakes is minimal compared with the time required for an employee to learn all the jobs performed in a fast-food restaurant.

Fourth, specialization contributes to consistently higher-quality goods and services. It has been said that we live in an age of specialization, one in which most people are employed as specialists. Many students who pursue a degree in business administration specialize in accounting, management information systems, finance, management, or marketing. Few professions better demonstrate the move to specialization than does medicine. As more is learned about each phase of medicine, entire careers emerge, with concentrations on specific parts of the body or specific symptoms. Forty or fifty years ago, most doctors treated all of the ailments of all members of the family. Now, most physicians specialize, becoming gynecologists, pediatricians, cardiologists, ophthalmologists, and so forth. By specializing in a narrow range of medicine, a physician is able to offer the best diagnosis and treatment medical research and technology have available.

Finally, specialization can facilitate the achievement of highly complex objectives. Complex projects usually require large numbers of specialists. The U.S. space program would not have been possible without the contributions of the thousands of specialists assembled by the National Aeronautics and Space Administration. Teams of specialists, each knowledgeable in a particular phase of the project, contributed to its success. Similarly, the design and construction of airplanes and of large buildings require the contributions of many different specialists.

Disadvantages of Specialization

Despite its advantages, the specialization of labor is not always desirable. In some organizations, too much specialization has caused certain jobs to become over-simplified, leading to boredom and fatigue among employees. For example, some people find it very boring to tighten a thousand bolts every day. Typically, the highest degree of specialization is found in this kind of assembly-line work, and the result is often a high level of employee turnover and absenteeism and a deteriorating quality of output. These negative consequences may offset the advantages and increase the costs of specialization.

A number of companies have established programs to overcome the disadvantages of specialization. Others have reduced the degree of specialization. General Motors is using work teams and experimenting with team monitors assigned on a rotating basis.[8] This gives each worker a feeling of involvement in the company's efforts to increase the quality and quantity of output. Shaklee Corporation has a unique management philosophy for its plant in Norman, Oklahoma. There, small groups of employees make, inspect, and package a diverse array of products. The teams establish their own production schedules and working hours. They select new workers from a pool approved by the personnel department and can even initiate discharges.[9]

Of course, the need for specialization becomes more intense as organizations grow. The Limited Inc. found ways to combat the organizational problems size created.

• •

As The Limited's sales approached $4 billion in the late 1980s, the chief executive decided it was time to act. All kinds of problems related to size were cropping up. Profits were down, and the distribution system was strained. The Limited had set the pace for specialty retailing for years. But management felt it was no longer nimble and able to respond quickly to changes in the marketplace. The CEO remembered the counsel of Tom Peters, the famous co-author of *In Search of Excellence*. Peters said, "Size has become a paramount issue, and somewhat smaller is apparently becoming much more beautiful everywhere."

But with its upscale clothing stores in malls all over the country, The Limited was not ready to retrench. The CEO held a series of meetings at which he said to managers: "The Limited is beginning to look like General Motors. Do we act like them?" The solution that grew out of those meetings was simple: Axe layers of management and give more authority to lower-level managers. The changes were made, and, according to a *Business Week* writer, "he can now breathe a sigh of relief—at least until his company gets bigger still."[10]

The Limited

• •

Departmentation

The process of grouping related work activities into manageable units is **departmentation**. The purpose of departmentation is to contribute to more effective and efficient use of organizational resources. This section discusses first the ways functions should be grouped in an organization. Then it describes common types of departments.

Departmentation

The process of grouping related work activities into manageable units.

Functional Similarity

Ideally, each department or division in the organization should be made up of people performing similar tasks. This is the concept of *functional similarity*, a guiding principle in the creation of sections, departments, and divisions. Jobs with similar objectives and requirements are grouped to form a section, and the person with the background necessary to supervise these functions effectively is assigned as the manager. For example, a construction company might employ a plumbing crew, an electrical crew, and so forth. Each different crew performs a group of related functions. The achievement of functional similarity depends on a number of factors, several of which are shown in Figure 7–4 and discussed here.

Volume of Work   Sometimes the volume of work does not allow for specialization. In small firms, people have to cope with a wide assortment of jobs. For example,

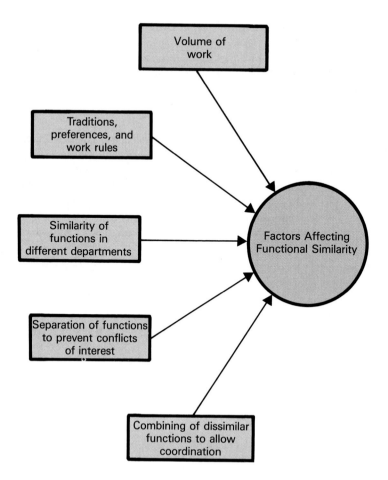

FIGURE 7–4

Factors Affecting Functional
Similarity

at a full-service gas station, workers have to do a variety of tasks ranging from pumping gas to fixing flat tires. But with increases in volume, the concept of functional similarity can be applied more rigorously. For example, compare the operations of a small grocery store with those of a large supermarket. In the small store, one person may perform such functions as setting out produce, stocking shelves, and checking out and bagging groceries. In the large supermarket, each worker may specialize in one or only a few of the basic functions. It is common for one manager to oversee the produce section, another the stocking, and another the checking out and bagging functions.

Traditions, Preferences, and Work Rules Although two tasks may be similar, traditions, personal preferences, and work rules may prevent their assignment to one individual. For example, the function of installing electrical conduit (the steel pipe that protects electrical wire) is similar to the function of running water piping; however, few plumbers would be willing to run conduit, and electricians would usually object to installing water pipes. This is because individuals associate a set of behavioral expectations, duties, and responsibilities with a given position.[11]

Similarity of Functions in Different Departments Another complicating factor is that a particular function often occurs in different departments. For example, inventory control would appear to fit logically in the purchasing department, which buys materials and thus has the need for records of inventory levels. However, the production department uses the same materials and, in scheduling, must work with the same inventory records. Inventory control could be placed in either department.

Separation of Functions to Prevent Conflicts of Interest Sometimes similar functions are not combined because doing so might create conflicts of interest. Quality control is intimately involved in production; inspectors frequently work side by side with production employees. Inspectors, however, should not be unduly influenced by the production manager's interest in quality and costs. Thus, inspection, although similar to production, should be separate from production, to protect its independence.

Combining of Dissimilar Functions to Allow Coordination Finally, there are occasions when two dissimilar functions must be combined for purposes of effective action and control. In a factory, purchasing is clearly differentiated from selling. But in department stores, buying and selling are so interdependent that one person is often made responsible for both. The theory is that a well-bought dress or hat is already half-sold.

Kinds of Departments

There is no standard way to divide an organization. Even companies in the same industry often have vastly different kinds of departments. It is possible, however, to identify five bases on which departmentation normally occurs: (1) function, (2) product, (3) customer, (4) geographic territory, and (5) project. Additionally, a combination approach may be used.

Departmentation by Function Departmentation by function is perhaps the most common means of dividing an organization. Under this approach, departments are formed on the basis of specialized activities such as finance, marketing, production, engineering, and personnel (see Figure 7–5). Grouped together, specialists become more efficient. Departmentation by function is especially useful in stable environments where technical efficiency and quality are important.[12] Undoubtedly, functional specialists also feel more comfortable working with others of similar background and experience.

Departmentation by function has several advantages and disadvantages. As mentioned, it is advantageous in a stable environment. In addition, it fosters the development of expertise, allows specialization, and requires little coordination and few interpersonal skills.[13] By and large, the advantages of functional specialization outweigh the disadvantages, but certain disadvantages are important.

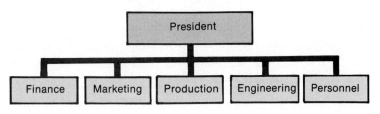

FIGURE 7–5

Departmentation by Function

FIGURE 7–6

Departmentation by Product

Employees in a specialized department may become more concerned with their own department than with the overall company. Because of the sometimes conflicting purposes of various departments, upper management must ensure that an effective means of coordination exists. An example of interdepartmental conflict occurred at Tennco Products Company's tubular products facility near Memphis, Tennessee. The personnel director asked the production manager to hire more women machine operators, thinking that this would be a simple task. The production manager argued that qualified women were not available and that top management's demand for increased efficiency made taking time to train women impractical. In the end, more women were hired, but only after the president became involved and encouraged production and personnel to settle their differences.

Functional departmentation may also result in a slow response time in large organizations. Bottlenecks may occur when sequential tasks are performed. And functional departmentation may not encourage innovation, could foster conflict over product priorities, and may limit the development of general managers.[14]

Departmentation by Product Product departmentation is concerned with organizing according to the type of product being produced or sold by the firm. This method, through which efficiency is enhanced by the application of specialized knowledge of particular goods or services, is often used by large, diversified companies. Figure 7–6 shows the organization of a large electronics firm divided into three product divisions. Firms manufacturing and selling technologically complex products are often set up in this way.[15]

Departmentation by Customer Departmentation by type of customer is used by organizations that need to provide different services to different types of customers. As Figure 7–7 illustrates, a diversified manufacturing company may have industrial, government, and consumer sales divisions. A USX salesperson who obtains government contracts simply maintains good relations with purchasing agencies and

FIGURE 7–7

Departmentation by Customer

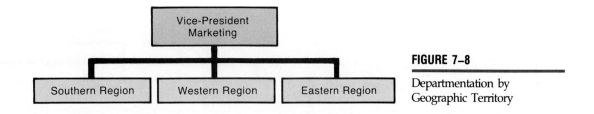

FIGURE 7–8

Departmentation by
Geographic Territory

makes sure that USX has opportunities to bid. Selling to industrial customers, in contrast, requires greater emphasis on personal persuasion and long-standing relationships. A person who does well in one area may be a failure in the other. Banks also use departmentation along customer lines. For example, commercial loan officers deal only with business customers, and consumer-lending specialists make personal loans. When client satisfaction is the main competitive issue, especially in an uncertain environment, customer departmentation is often appropriate.[16]

Departmentation by product and customer has several advantages and disadvantages. Among the advantages are that it enables people to cope with fast change, it allows high product visibility, it allows full-time concentration on the tasks, it clearly defines responsibilities, it permits the processing of multiple tasks, and it facilitates the training of general managers. Among the disadvantages are that it fosters politicking for resource allocation, it may not encourage coordination of activities among divisions, it could encourage neglect of long-term priorities, it may permit a decline in competencies, and it can create conflicts between divisional and corporate tasks.

Departmentation by Geographic Territory Grouping activities according to geographic territory is a method used by organizations with physically dispersed or noninterdependent operations or markets. For example, the marketing function of a company may be organized into southern, western, and eastern regional divisions (see Figure 7–8). Geographic departmentation offers the advantages of better service with local or regional personnel, often at less cost. Division by geography is the single most common scheme for international companies. For example, when Wendy's decided to expand into Europe, the company faced a competitive and legal environment very different from that in the United States and therefore established a separate division for the European operations. Geographic departmentation is most effective when the corporation's activities are widespread and there are few product lines.[17] Often, however, the advantages of geographic departmentation are outweighed by the advantages of functional, product, and customer departmentation.

Departmentation by Project When the work of an organization consists of a continuing series of major projects, departmentation by project normally occurs. This type of departmentation is especially common in the construction industry. Figure 7–9 shows how a typical construction operation might be departmentalized. In this example, each project superintendent, under the direction of the general superintendent, is responsible for a separate contract. Such an organization changes frequently as projects are completed and new ones are started. The superintendent in charge of Project A may transfer to a new project or back to headquarters or be laid off when Project A is finished. In addition, the plumbing supervisor currently working

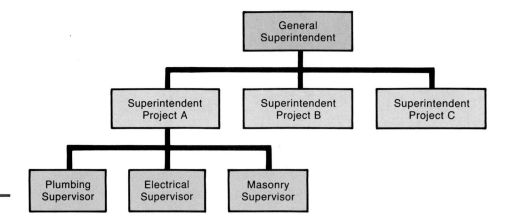

FIGURE 7–9

Departmentation by Project

Matrix departmentation

The form of departmentation that occurs when project departmentation takes on a permanent status designed to achieve specific results by using teams of specialists from different functional areas of the organization.

on Project A may move to Project C when the plumbing on Project A is complete. **Matrix departmentation** is *the form of departmentation that occurs when project departmentation takes on a permanent status designed to achieve specific results by using teams of specialists from different functional areas of the organization.*

Departmentation by project and matrix has several advantages and disadvantages. Among the advantages are that it offers increased flexibility and greater interdisciplinary cooperation, it involves and challenges people, it develops employee skills, it frees top management for planning, it motivates employees to identify with the end product, and it allows experts to be moved to crucial areas as needed. Among the disadvantages are that it may create a risk of anarchy, it can encourage power struggles, it may result in too much discussion and not enough activity, it requires interpersonal skills, it is costly to implement, it may cause duplication of effort by project teams, and it probably will affect morale negatively when people are reassigned.[18]

ETHICAL DILEMMA

You are a supervisor at a medium-sized high-tech manufacturing firm. Your company operates totally on the basis of project departmentation. The company recently bid on, and has a good chance of obtaining, a major federal government contract that will permit it to open up a second shift and even hire some new workers. The company will also gain great prestige in the industry if the contract is secured. Since the contract bid exceeded $1 million annually, your firm is required to analyze the composition of its labor force in relation to minority employees and to work toward correcting discrepancies if they exist. When the analysis was conducted, it was determined that few minorities were employed by the company.

Top management has stated that it intends to work toward increasing the number of minorities in the firm. However, there is considerable resistance to this policy throughout the firm and especially in your department, which has no minorities. You have a minority applicant and a Caucasian applicant for one job opening on the line. In your opinion, the minority applicant is slightly better qualified than the Caucasian applicant, and you are aware of the firm's policy toward hiring minority workers. You believe, however, that a minority worker on the line would cause you a lot of problems with the other workers. You can hire either the better-qualified minority applicant or the less-qualified Caucasian applicant.

What would you do?

Departmentation: A Combination Approach   Unless the organization is quite small, it is likely that several different bases for departmentation will be used in combination. No one form of departmentation can meet the needs of most firms, particularly of large companies such as General Motors, General Electric, and Exxon. In the product-type organization at GM, portions of the design function continue to be performed by the corporate staff rather than the product divisions. Also, GM still uses district managers in its marketing organization. Figure 7–10 shows an organization chart of a manufacturing company that uses three forms of departmentation: functional (engineering, production, marketing, finance, and personnel), product (industrial and consumer), and geographic (northern and southern parts of the United States). The precise forms of departmentation a firm chooses must be based on its own needs. For example, AT&T Chairman and CEO Robert Allen heads a large diversified company somewhat organized according to the type of products and services sold, but also having some functional departmentation. AT&T remains the major telecommunications giant and is departmentalized by long distance services, telecommunications equipment, computers, and their exceptional 800 service. Allen is now marketing an AT&T credit card similar to VISA and MasterCard. AT&T divides their organization into product lines to assure that they can apply specialized knowledge to market each of their products, and they combine this with functional departments similar to more conventional organizations.

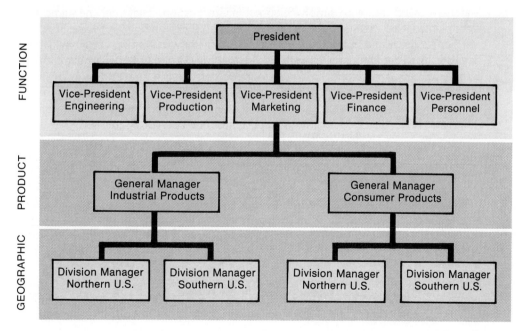

FIGURE 7–10

Organization Chart: A Combination Approach to Departmentation

Organizational Differentiation

In a newly formed small organization, a single owner-manager performs all the major functions of the business, such as financing, procuring materials, designing the product, and making and selling the product. This was the case with Woodrow Shepherd of Freeport Firestone when he opened his service station. But such simplicity did not last long.

Freeport Firestone

Freeport, Maine, is well known as the home of L. L. Bean, Inc., the famous catalog merchandiser of sporting goods and clothing. L. L. Bean also operates a 50,000-square-foot retail store in Freeport. The store is open day and night and attracts celebrities and others from all over the world.

Woodrow Shepherd, who owns Freeport Firestone, had started out as an L. L. Bean employee in 1969. Shepherd quit his job with L. L. Bean in 1974 and invested his life savings, plus $20,000 he borrowed, in a service station. At first, he worked from daylight to dark six days a week. He employed only one helper, Joe Gross, who pumped gas, fixed flats, and did whatever else Woodrow needed him to do. As Freeport grew over the next ten years, Shepherd's business did also. It was not long before the bookkeeping was too much for him, so he asked his wife to start coming in half-days to take care of that.

Shepherd added on to his service station and in 1976 got the Firestone tire franchise. The tire business was especially profitable, so he spent most of his time in the tire department, selling, installing, and repairing tires. By that time, Joe Gross had become a seasoned and dependable attendant. So Shepherd hired another man to help Gross take care of the service island. He also hired a helper in the tire department.

By 1980, Shepherd found it necessary to hire a full-time bookkeeper. He also employed an additional worker and a supervisor in the tire department. Until 1981, Shepherd called the place simply Shepherd's Gulf Station. That year, he had a nice sign painted and changed the name to Freeport Firestone. In 1984, he installed another service island and added a tire and battery showroom next to the tire service bays. He hired a night manager in 1986 to keep the service island open until midnight. By then, Freeport Firestone employed fourteen persons full time and two part time.

The town of Freeport had grown to about 35,000, and Shepherd thought about opening a smaller service station and tire center at the opposite end of Main Street. In August 1991, the new branch of Freeport Firestone opened. Many new challenges lay ahead.

The evolution of the organization at Freeport Firestone is typical of that at many other firms. As the volume of business grows, the work required increases beyond the capacities of one person. When Woodrow Shepherd decided to hire Joe Gross, he had to describe the tasks that Gross would perform; that is, he had to differentiate them from the other tasks of the organization. Gross was to pump gas and fix flats, among other duties. A new level in the organization had been created, even though Freeport Firestone was only a two-person firm (see Section A of Figure 7–11). The employment of additional people requires vertical and horizontal differentiation.

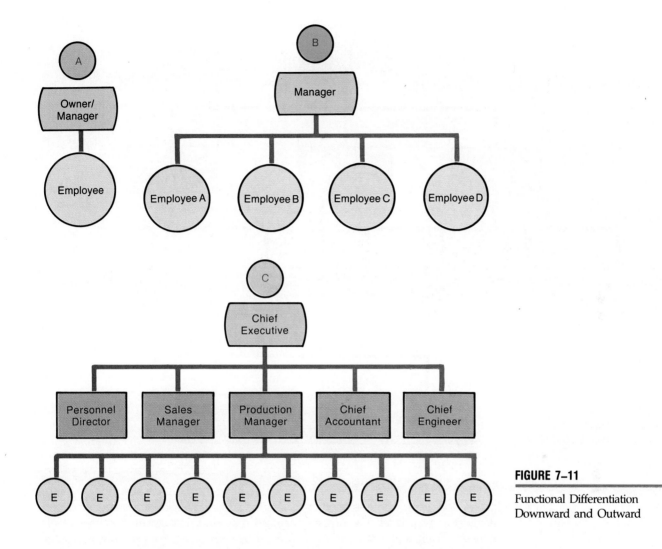

FIGURE 7–11

Functional Differentiation
Downward and Outward

The process of creating additional levels in the organization is **vertical differentiation.** Initially, there are just two levels, managerial and operative, but managers such as Woodrow Shepherd usually do not assign all the operative work to a subordinate. Shepherd continued to wait on customers and often worked alongside Joe Gross, in addition to supervising him. In the early stages of organizational growth, functions that are considered vital to success and that require special expertise, such as sales and finance, often continue to be done by the manager.

As the volume of business continues to grow, additional employees will be added and more operative functions will be differentiated and allocated. *The process of forming additional units at the same level in the organization* is called **horizontal differentiation.** The result is shown in Section B of Figure 7–11. For Freeport Firestone, this process occurred when Shepherd hired a person to help Gross on the service island and a helper for the tire department. Although Shepherd continued to do operative work for a time, he knew that the management job would soon become too demanding for him to continue.

Vertical differentiation

The process of creating additional levels in the organization.

Horizontal differentiation

The process of forming additional units at the same level in the organization.

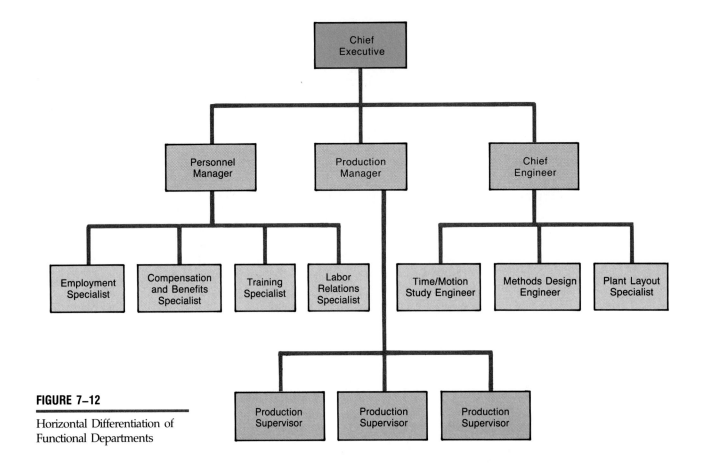

FIGURE 7–12

Horizontal Differentiation of
Functional Departments

Woodrow Shepherd employed horizontal differentiation because the workload became too great. There is another reason for adding additional workers or departments at a given level. The original manager may find that certain functions can be more effectively and economically performed by a specialist. For example, a manager may find sales a weak area, because of ineffective or inadequate training programs. Therefore, a sales trainer would be employed to take over that phase of the business, so the manager could devote more time to other areas. As in the case of Freeport Firestone, horizontal growth usually occurs at lower levels as additional workers are required. When the number of workers becomes too large for one manager to supervise, additional supervisors must be added. As the organization grows, horizontal differentiation usually results in the splitting off of the functions that are the most complex and the least similar to other functions of the firm.

As is shown in Section C of Figure 7–11, horizontal differentiation usually results in the creation of several functional departments. If the organization continues to grow, further differentiation will be needed, both horizontal and vertical. Figure 7–12 shows how personnel, production, and engineering might be further subdivided, resulting in an additional level of managers.

When differentiation occurs, coordination is required. **Coordination** is *the process of ensuring that persons who perform interdependent activities work together in a way that contributes to overall objective attainment.* Coordination assumes a greater importance

Coordination

The process of ensuring that persons who perform interdependent activities work together in a way that contributes to overall objective attainment.

as the organization becomes more complex. For example, the manager of the company illustrated in Figure 7–12 would have to be much more concerned with coordination than was Woodrow Shepherd when his only employee was Joe Gross. For large, multibusiness companies, separate business units are often set up. Usually, the more diverse the products such a company makes, the more authority will be decentralized.[19]

The Informal Organization

It is possible to identify many groups, of varying size, within a typical firm. Naturally, a number of these groups have a place in the formal organization. The groups also have a place in the informal organization. In fact, all the groups blend together to form the **informal organization**—*the set of evolving relationships and patterns of human interaction within an organization that are not officially prescribed.*

In the formal organization, managers establish what employees should do through formal organization charts and through formally writing out the duties and responsibilities associated with jobs. Traditional managers tend to emphasize the values of organizational and personal loyalty. Many will tolerate incompetence more readily than disloyalty. The formal organization represents management's attempt to specify the way things should be done in the various sections, departments, and divisions of the firm. But the official organizational structure is only part of the story. There emerges another structure, existing alongside the formal one, which consists of informal relationships created not by officially designated managers but by organization members at every level.

Because of the impact of the informal organization, an increasing number of firms are training their managers to cope with it. The director of corporate personnel for a large insurance company says, "We teach our managers/supervisors to be alert to the formation of 'informal work groups' and that such groups can be either a positive or a negative influence on a department or company objective." Corning Glass Works has an extensive management development program devoted to understanding how

Informal organization
The set of evolving relationships and patterns of human interaction within an organization that are not officially prescribed.

The official organizational structure is only part of the story. There emerges another structure, existing alongside the formal one, which consists of informal relationships created not by officially designated managers, but by organizational members at every level. Here, a group of Conagra employees from various levels in the company enjoy a fundraising activity to help children's charities.

Source: Photograph courtesy of Geldermann, Inc.

the informal group functions and to designing ways to have the informal group work in a positive manner.

The informal organization has the following definable characteristics:

- *Its members are joined together to satisfy needs.* They may have completely different reasons for developing informal relationships. One worker may want to make friends, and another may be seeking advancement. Progress toward either of these objectives might be furthered through interactions with the informal organization.

- *It is continuously changing.* The informal organization is dynamic. Relationships that exist one day may be gone the next.

- *It involves members of various organizational levels.* The informal organization does not abide by the boundaries established by the formal organization. A worker in one area may have close ties to a supervisor in another.

- *It is affected by relationships outside the firm.* Two workers might associate with each other because they are Masons or members of the Moose Lodge.

- *It has a pecking order.* Certain people are assigned greater importance than others by the informal group. Once workers adhere to group norms, their status within the informal organization tends to increase.

Because of factors such as the close proximity in which people work, the frequent interaction of group members, and the long time periods employees spend working together, there will always be informal groups and an informal organization. How managers deal with it can affect the productivity of their work unit.

Although an informal organization cannot be placed into a formal organization chart, it does have its own structure. Like the formally structured organization, the informal organization may have a chain of command, which is sometimes charted after the fact by management. Managers should recognize that informal work groups exist at all levels of the organization. A formal organization chart can be misleading in terms of who has real authority and influence.

The nature of the informal structure is dynamic and constantly changing. As different members enter and exit the group, the structure is modified. The structure is based heavily on the communication patterns that develop among group members. If many people attempt to gain the advice of one individual, this individual is often the informal leader around whom the structure develops. Just as formal organizations have vice-presidents, the informal group may have an equivalent counterpart. The informal structure evolves rather than being formally laid out, yet it is often as rigid as the formal structure.

The organizational structure of the informal work group may be studied by means of a contact chart. A **contact chart** is *a diagram showing various individuals in the organization and the numbers of interactions they have with others.* These charts are developed to identify the connections an individual has with other members of the organization. As may be seen from the contact chart in Figure 7–13, not all contacts follow the formal organization chart. In various instances, certain levels of management are bypassed; other instances show cross-contact from one chain of command to another. On the basis of the number of contacts in Figure 7–13, individual 19 appears to be very popular.

One difficulty with a contact chart is that it does not show the reasons for relationships. Also, it is never clear whether the contacts shown will work for or against

Contact chart

A diagram showing various individuals in the organization and the numbers of interactions they have with others.

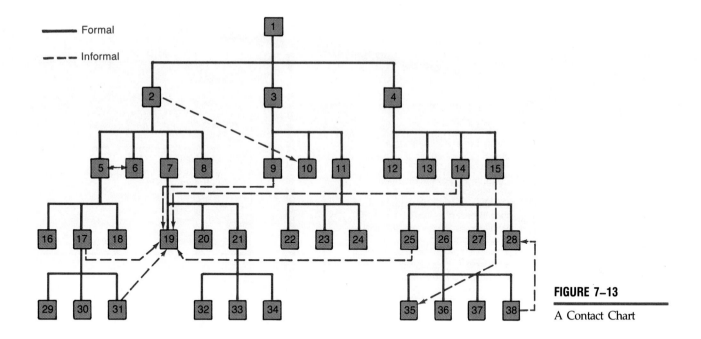

FIGURE 7–13

A Contact Chart

the organization. Individual 19 could be helping other employees accomplish their tasks. On the other hand, this individual could be badmouthing the organization and promoting disharmony among company employees. Once managers have identified the major contact points, they are in a position to either encourage or discourage the individual within the work group.

MANAGEMENT IN PRACTICE: A Skill-Building Exercise

John Higgins has recently taken over the accounting and finance department. He had been the number 2 person in the department for over five years. He has all the qualifications for the job, and that is why you selected him to take over from Thomas Magnum, the former head of the department.

As John's superior, you have received a memo from John about the behavior of a secretary who has been with the company for sixteen years. According to this memo, she is leaking information from John's department—and has been doing so for many years. She has most recently given out some informal information to the unit heads to allow them to begin their budgeting activities. When John took her to task about the leaks, she claimed that the information she gives out is really not confidential. Furthermore, she said that the unit heads need the information early because the formal reports come out too late to allow them to budget adequately. At the end of the memo, John noted, "Either she straightens up, or she has to go; I need your support." John has just walked in.

What would you do?

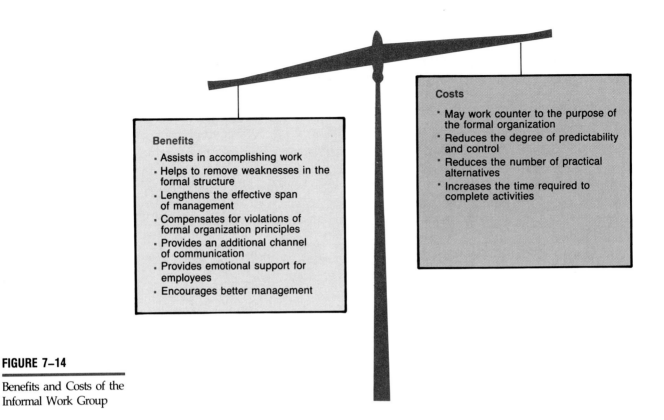

FIGURE 7–14

Benefits and Costs of the
Informal Work Group

Benefits and Costs of the Informal Organization

Managers often have mixed emotions about the informal organization. Although it is capable of contributing to greater organizational effectiveness, it is not without its costs. But if management is properly trained to understand and work with the informal organization, the benefits should exceed the costs, as Figure 7–14 suggests. If management is not careful, the reverse may be true.

Benefits of the Informal Organization

It is fortunate that managers cannot destroy the informal organization, because it is capable of contributing in significant ways to an organization's effectiveness. Following are several of the means by which the informal organization can benefit the work group.

Assists in Accomplishing Work   For managers to be effective, their subordinates must be permitted a certain degree of flexibility in accomplishing assigned tasks. Monitoring subordinates' every move is detrimental to their achieving success. If employees acted only when they were told to act, following standard instructions to the letter at all times and contacting others only when duly authorized, the business would have to cease operations. Still, there are traditionalists who tend to rely more heavily on formal decisions based on the scientific study of business problems.

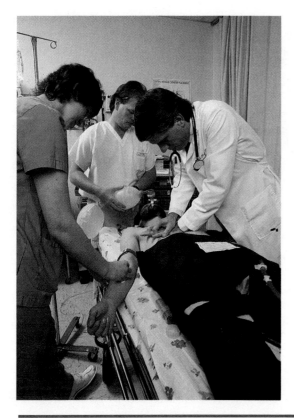

For managers to be effective, their subordinates must be permitted a certain degree of flexibility in performing their required tasks. It might be detrimental, for example, for the emergency room physician shown here to attempt detailed direction of the professionals who assist him.

Source: © Jim Pickerell

There are also decision-making situations for which the formal command is inadequate, even wrong. If the atmosphere is heavily traditional, subordinates may exhibit malicious obedience by executing commands faithfully despite personal knowledge that their actions will ultimately result in failure. Many managers have discovered that a subordinate can agree with them all day, follow every directive to the letter, and yet fail miserably. When managers place more faith in informal relationships, subordinates may voluntarily adapt the formal order to the requirements of the situation. Loosely structured groups are often more effective in achieving organizational objectives.

Helps to Remove Weaknesses in the Formal Structure   The formal organization often has a number of gaps that the informal group can fill. Consider a person who is promoted to a position that exceeds that individual's current capabilities. This is not an unusual occurrence in the armed services, for instance, where young officers may be appointed unit commanders. Without the advice and assistance of experienced sergeants, these officers might not survive their first assignments. In fact, most likely there are many officers who are unsuccessful in the military because they fail to recognize the power of the informal organization. Formal orders and regulations may state that someone is the commander, with certain responsibilities and authorities. But in reality that person may be deficient. By admitting temporary weaknesses, the commander might be able to obtain help from other officers and enlisted personnel. In such a case, deficiencies in the formal structure are overcome by shared decision making. In time, the informal organization may conform to the formal one more closely.

Span of management
The number of direct subordinates reporting to any manager.

Lengthens the Effective Span of Management *The number of direct subordinates reporting to any manager* is referred to as the **span of management.** As individuals and small groups learn to interact effectively and are permitted to do so by their supervisors, the manager should be able to devote less time to each worker. This may allow the manager's effective span of management to grow.

Compensates for Violations of Formal Organizational Principles Informal relationships can compensate for the ineffectiveness of certain traditional principles of formal organizations. For example, even though authority should equal responsibility, the principle is frequently violated. As a result, managers often try to develop informal contacts with people over whom they have no formal authority. As favors are traded and friendships formed, one quickly learns that the formal prescription of authority often is not sufficient. This does not negate the desirability of authority equaling responsibility. We discuss this organizing principle further in Chapter 8.

Grapevine
The informal means by which information is transmitted in an organization.

Provides an Additional Channel of Communication *The informal means by which information is transmitted in an organization is* the **grapevine.** To some managers, the grapevine constitutes an obstacle to be destroyed. They seek to channel and control most, if not all, communications through the official chain of command. However, the grapevine can add to organizational effectiveness if the manager uses it. The grapevine is fast and usually accurate in the information it transmits.

Use of the grapevine does not decrease the importance of maintaining an official channel of communication and command. Although the grapevine can spread much information in a short period, it cannot provide the authority necessary to ensure that action will take place. The grapevine is discussed in greater detail in Chapter 12.

Provides Emotional Support for Employees Over half of all voluntary resignations in many organizations occur within the first six months of employment. They are often the result of little help being provided the new employee in joining and being accepted by the group. Friendships, or at least speaking acquaintances, are essential to a satisfactory working environment for most people. In one hospital where the turnover rate of janitorial personnel was high, the formation of cleanup teams reduced turnover considerably. The janitors had felt isolated and uncomfortable working alone among physicians, nurses, and patients.

Encourages Better Management Awareness of the nature and impact of the informal organization often leads to better management decisions. The acceptance of the fact that formal relationships will not ensure full accomplishment of organizational tasks should stimulate management to seek other means of increasing motivation. Managers should seek to improve their knowledge of the nature of the people in general and subordinates in particular. They should realize that organizational performance can be enhanced by workers' cooperation and enthusiasm. Means other than formal authority must be sought to develop attitudes that support effective performance.

Costs of the Informal Organization

The informal organization is not without its drawbacks. Here are some of the possible detrimental effects of the informal organization.

May Work Counter to the Purposes of the Formal Organization   It is apparent to most managers that individuals in informal groups can and sometimes do work against the formal objectives of an enterprise. Few would object to the existence of the informal organization if its objectives could always be the same as those of the formal organization. However, informal groups sometimes pressure workers to exhibit disinterest in company requirements, disloyalty, and insubordination, or to engage in unauthorized actions that work at cross-purposes with the organization.

Reduces the Degree of Predictability and Control   An objective of most organizations is to ensure predictability and control of behavior so individuals will work effectively toward organizational objectives. This objective depends, however, on people interpreting and following the formal guidelines. If managers recognize and accept the possibility of a good outcome from permitted flexibility, they must also accept the risks that accompany this lesser degree of control. Informal relationships can and do add much to an organization's effectiveness; they also can and do add much to the degree of uncertainty.

Reduces the Number of Practical Alternatives   A study of the U.S. Army during World War II concluded that the natural unit of personal commitment is the informal group, not the formal organization.[20] For example, the soldiers reported that one of the major reasons for moving forward in combat was to avoid letting the other fellows down. In all organizations, business or military, the solidarity of the informal group can be a major constraint on management actions.

This solidarity may create problems in the reassigning of personnel. If informal groups are broken up by the moving of individual members, members may feel insecure and show decreased motivation and cooperation. This may suggest that management should think in terms of moving whole groups, rather than individuals. If management wishes to capitalize on the considerable value of informal relationships in work groups, it must be willing to accept some loss of flexibility in decision making.

Increases the Time Required to Complete Activities   If the cooperative efforts of informal work groups can be aligned with the objectives of the firm, management has the best of both worlds. The collective power generated can be phenomenal. But informal work group activities such as gossiping, betting pools, long coffee breaks, and general horseplay are time-consuming and may be detrimental to efficient operations. These acts often tax the patience of managers. However, if effective work groups are to be established, some of these activities will have to be permitted, possibly even encouraged. Managers must realize that, despite their concern for accomplishing objectives, they must allow the group time and opportunity to maintain itself in good working order. People can usually sustain action for a longer period of time in an informal atmosphere than they can when the situation is rigid, controlled, and formal.

A Global Perspective

An international alliance is an organization of sorts. Organizations bring people together in a coordinated manner to achieve group results. An effective organization is designed to ensure the achievement of the objectives of the firm. Similarly, an effective international alliance is designed to ensure and support achievement of the firm's common objectives. Specifically, an international alliance is a collaboration between two or more multinational companies that is developed to let them jointly pursue a common objective.

According to *Fortune* magazine, U.S. companies entered into some 2,000 alliances with European companies alone in the decade of the eighties. Most major multinational companies maintain numerous international cooperative arrangements. General Electric has formed eight alliances with companies in Europe, Japan, and South Korea. Corning, Inc. maintains more than a dozen joint ventures with multinational companies in Europe, Australia, China, Japan, and South Korea. General Motors has entered into separate partnerships with Toyota, Isuzu, Suzuki, and Daewoo. AT&T also has some twenty such major alliances throughout the world.

International alliances make it possible for companies to share the costs and risks of doing business. They enable companies to share financial resources, technology, production facilities, marketing know-how, and human resources. The major driving force behind many international alliances is the rapid development of technology and the globalization of markets and products. International alliances have become a competitive necessity for any firm that aspires to become a global player. In a sense, what an effective organization is to domestic companies, international alliances are to global firms.[21]

....

Self-Assessment Exercise

Will You Be Good at Dealing with the Organizing Process and the Informal Organization?

1. Are you willing to learn that all managers, from supervisors to top-level managers, are involved in the organizing process?

   ☐ Yes   ☐ No

2. Are you willing to understand that reorganization should only occur when it helps you better achieve your objective?

   ☐ Yes   ☐ No

3. Are you willing to work to get the maximum benefit from worker specialization?

   ☐ Yes   ☐ No

4. Are you willing to organize so that each worker has a full-time job?

   ☐ Yes   ☐ No

5. Are you willing to be unafraid to reorganize?

   ☐ Yes   ☐ No

(continued)

6. Are you willing to understand that you cannot eliminate the informal organization?

    ☐ Yes   ☐ No

7. Are you willing to understand that the grapevine often transmits information told in absolute confidence?

    ☐ Yes   ☐ No

8. Are you willing to learn when directives violate informal group norms?

    ☐ Yes   ☐ No

9. Are you willing to understand that you should not try to be a buddy and a boss?

    ☐ Yes   ☐ No

10. Are you willing to make a conscious attempt to understand the informal organization?

    ☐ Yes   ☐ No

Summary

An organization is two or more people working together in a coordinated manner to achieve group results. Organizing is the process of prescribing formal relationships among people and resources to accomplish objectives. It is affected by both the external environment of the firm and the internal environment that individual managers face. Organizing should be directed toward accomplishment of objectives; once objectives are established, work activities can be determined. Complex objectives are often achieved through specialization of labor, which offers a number of benefits, including increased productivity. Negative consequences of specialization may offset its advantages and increase costs.

The process of grouping related work activities into manageable units is departmentation. Ideally, each department should be made up of people performing similar tasks. This is the concept of functional similarity. In addition to function, there are four other ways to divide an organization: by product, by customer, by geographic territory, and by project. Unless the organization is quite small, it is likely that several different bases for departmentation will be used.

Additional levels in the organization are created through vertical differentiation. Additional units at the same level are created through horizontal differentiation. Coordination ensures that persons who perform interdependent activities work together in a way that contributes to overall objective attainment.

The informal organization is the set of evolving relationships and patterns of human interaction within an organization that are not officially prescribed. It has a number of definable characteristics and may be studied by means of a contact chart, a diagram showing various individuals in the organization and the numbers of interactions they have with others.

Managers often have mixed emotions about the informal organization. Although it is capable of contributing to greater organizational effectiveness, there are certain costs. But if management is properly trained to understand and work with the informal organization, the benefits should exceed the costs.

Review Questions

1. Define *organization*. What are the three common characteristics of an organization?

2. Describe the process of organizing. What tasks must managers perform in the organizing process?

3. In terms of the organizing process, what types of work activities are needed on a baseball team?

4. Define *specialization of labor*. What are its advantages and disadvantages?

5. What guidelines should be used in grouping work activities?

6. What are the primary means of departmentation?

7. Distinguish between vertical and horizontal differentiation.

8. What is the purpose of a contact chart?

9. Describe the benefits and costs that may be attributed to the informal organization.

Key Terms

Organization	Matrix departmentation	Informal organization
Organizing	Vertical differentiation	Contact chart
Specialization of labor	Horizontal differentiation	Span of management
Departmentation	Coordination	Grapevine

Shelton Lewis is production manager for Memorand, Inc., a maker of small components for the hydraulics industry. Shel, as his employees call him, came to Memorand in 1982 as a production foreman. He believes the company has been good to him, and he has chosen not to leave, even though he has had a number of offers of better-paying jobs with competing firms.

Gloria Honeycutt is in charge of the quality control section at Memorand and reports directly to Shelton. Gloria started out as Shelton's secretary five years ago. With his encouragement, she attended college and got a degree in industrial management with a concentration in quality control. She then was reassigned to the quality control job, but she continued to report directly to Shelton.

One day recently, a delicate situation arose, creating a strain on the usually excellent relationship between Shelton and Gloria. The problem began with the following conversation.

Gloria: Shel, I'm finding too many flaws in the cylinders we're making for Ingersol Rand. I know you're facing a deadline, but I believe we should slow down and inspect all the cylinder parts before they're assembled.

Shelton: Have you found more than the standard number of defectives?

Gloria: No, but a number of cylinders barely passed the leakage tests, and many of the mounting holes

are just within specs. If you don't slow down, we may miss a chance at future orders from Ingersol Rand. You know how quality-conscious they are.

Shelton: If we do slow down, we won't make the scheduled delivery date. If we don't do that, Memorand may not even be considered for future contracts. I don't expect you, of all people, to stand in the way of getting the order out on time.

Gloria didn't know what to do, so she just left the office. She still felt she was right. The contract with Ingersol Rand was a lucrative one, and it had been given to Memorand only because Shelton had guaranteed quick delivery. Pleasing Ingersol Rand could easily result in a 10 percent sales increase for the company as a whole. Ingersol Rand has a reputation for selecting suppliers carefully and sticking with them as long as delivery and quality are up to par.

Questions

1. Is there anything amiss with the organizational relationship between Gloria and Shelton? If so, what? How would you change it? Defend your answer.
2. What do you believe Gloria should do at this point? Explain.

Doris Prier had recently been hired as production planning manager for Royale Airlines. Immediately after starting her new job, Doris recognized that there were difficulties with the time control section. This section consisted of sixteen clerks and a supervisor who reported to her.

The basic function of the time control section was to maintain records on all rotatable parts used on a

fleet of eighty-five passenger airplanes. Records reflected the date a part was installed or removed and total aircraft flying time. To maintain identification, serial numbers were recorded for each controlled part. The Federal Aviation Administration (FAA) required strict control of life-limited parts. Parts that had operated beyond their approved limit had to be removed and overhauled.

The problem Doris noticed was that there were numerous instances of inaccurate records. The records were in violation of FAA regulations, and poor record-keeping resulted in excessive overhaul costs. When Doris studied the situation, she observed that the employees had formed an extremely strong informal work group. The members would accept or reject new employees on the basis of factors completely unrelated to the job. Some outsiders observed that if a new employee's bowling score was not above 175, the person had little chance for success within the group. The group members bowled three times a week and had a great time together. Those who did not like to bowl and socialize frequently were ignored and made to feel uncomfortable to the point where they would quit. This resulted in an annual turnover rate of about 200 percent. Doris realized that this problem had to be solved immediately or major problems could result for Royale Airlines.

Questions

1. How did the informal work group affect the operations of the production planning department?
2. What action should Doris take in coping with the informal group?

Notes

1. This case is a composite of a number of published accounts, among them: John Huey, "Wal-Mart: Will It Take Over the World?" *Fortune*, January 30, 1989, pp. 52–64; Sharon Reier, "CEO of the Decade: Sam Walton," *Financial World*, April 4, 1989, pp. 56–62; Bette Hendrix, "Wal-Mart Stock History," *Wal-Mart World* 13 (January 1983): 19; "Wal-Mart Discounts Everything but People," *Retailing*, January 18, 1982, pp. 32, 52; Howard Rudnitsky, "How Sam Walton Does It," *Forbes*, August 16, 1982, pp. 42–44; "Wal-Mart Reigns, Jamesway Second," *Chain Store Age*, June 1983, pp. 51, 53; "Rex Chase—Pure Wal-Mart Lore," *Chain Store Age*, March 1983, p. 35; "The Service 500," *Fortune*, June 11, 1984, p. 170; Stephen Taub, "Gold Winner: Sam M. Walton of Wal-Mart Stores Takes the Top Prize," *Financial World*, April 15, 1986, pp. 28–33; Bill Saporito, "Is Wal-Mart Unstoppable?" *Fortune*, May 6, 1991, p. 50; John Huey, "America's Most Successful Merchant," *Fortune*, September 23, 1991, pp. 46–47; Alison L. Sprout, "America's Most Admired Corporations," *Fortune*, February 11, 1991, pp. 57–58; Standard & Poor's Corporation, "Wal-Mart Stores," *Standard NYSE Stock Reports* 56, no. 106 (June 2, 1989): sec. 21; and a number of articles from the *Wall Street Journal*.

2. John Huey, "America's Most Successful Merchant," *Fortune*, September 23, 1991, p. 47.

3. PINNACLE: Various aspects of competing in an ever-changing business environment are discussed by CNN senior news correspondent Stuart Varney and Jack Curcio.

4. Richard A. Melcher, Mark Maremont, Amy Borrus, and Thane Peterson, "The Japanese Are Coming—And Thatcher Is All Smiles," *Business Week*, February 20, 1989, p. 46.

5. Jim Dunne, "Inside Detroit," *Popular Mechanics*, August 1989, pp. 30–32.

6. Thomas J. Murry, "Wal-Mart Stores Penny Wise," *Business Month*, December 1988, p. 42.

7. "The Fast-Food War: Big Mac under Attack," *Business Week*, January 30, 1984, p. 45.

8. Dunne, "Inside Detroit," p. 33.

9. "The New Industrial Relations," *Business Week*, May 11, 1981, pp. 85–98.

10. John A. Byrne, "Is Your Company Too Big?" *Business Week*, March 27, 1989, pp. 84–94.

11. W. G. Astley and A. H. Van de Ven, "Central Perspectives and Debates in Organization Theory," *Administrative Science Quarterly* 28 (June 1983): 248.

12. R. L. Daft, *Organization Theory and Design* (St. Paul, MN: West Publishing, 1983), p. 227.

13. Arthur A. Thompson, Jr., and A. J. Strickland, *Strategy Formulation and Implementation* (Homewood, IL: Irwin, 1983), p. 324.

14. Ibid.

15. Theodore T. Herbert, "Strategy and Multinational Organization Structure: An International Relationships Per-

spective," *Academy of Management Review*, April 1984, p. 263.

16. Daft, *Organization Theory and Design*, p. 23.

17. Herbert, "Strategy and Multinational Organization Structure," p. 263.

18. Harold Kerzner, "Matrix Implementation: Obstacles, Problems, Questions, and Answers," in David McCleland, ed., *Matrix Management System Handbook* (New York: Van Nostrand Reinhold, 1984), pp. 307–329; and William Jerkovsky, "Functional Management in Matrix Organizations," *IEEE Transactions on Engineering Management* 30 (May 1983): 89–97.

19. Vijay Govindaragan, "Decentralization, Strategy, and Effectiveness of Strategic Business Units in Multibusiness Organizations," *Academy of Management Review* 11 (October 1986): 844–856.

20. Samuel A. Stouffer et al., *The American Soldier* (Princeton: Princeton University Press, 1949), 2:1974.

21. Wayne F. Cascio and Manuel G. Serapio, Jr., "Human Resources Systems in an International Alliance: The Undoing of a Done Deal?" *Organizational Dynamics*, Winter 1991, pp. 63–66; and Leigh Bruce and Jack Burton, "Strained Alliances," *International Management*, May 1990, p. 29.

CHAPTER 8

Organizing Concepts and Organizational Structure

LEARNING OBJECTIVES

After completing this chapter students should be able to

- Describe the concepts of responsibility and authority.
- Explain delegation and accountability.
- Describe several important organizing principles.
- Contrast centralization and decentralization.
- Describe the basic types of organizational structures.
- Explain how managers can become better at working with committees.

Texaco acquired Getty Oil in 1983. Pennzoil, which had an earlier agreement to buy Getty, sued Texaco and won a $10 billion judgment. After fighting it out with Pennzoil for several years, Texaco filed for bankruptcy reorganization in April 1987. In the ensuing two years, Texaco settled with Pennzoil for $3 billion, sold $7 billion worth of plants and other assets, restructured itself, and avoided a take-over bid by corporate raider Carl Icahn. Even in the midst of this desperate situation chief executive James W. Kinnear addressed the worldwide staff of Texaco and made what sounded like a quixotic prediction. He predicted that "Texaco would ultimately emerge as one of the most admired companies in the world."

By 1990, Texaco had emerged from bankruptcy and bought off Icahn. Kinnear continued the job of reorganizing with the avowed goal of enhancing shareholder value. He said, "There's a lot of adrenaline running through Texaco. This is a new company." Kinnear cut 10,965 employees from the payroll. Salaries were pegged to performance and Texaco's tradition of promoting from within was violated to bring in "new blood." The 26 exploration and production divisions became 12 independent profit centers, each operating like a small company, and two layers of management were slashed. Decision-making authority was pushed down in the organization. Union-management work groups, which cut across organizational lines, were set up at selected plants.

The idea of submitting to the will of shareholders was new at Texaco. The 1987 proxy statement, issued by the board of directors, had imperiously said, "The Company strongly supports the role of corporate democracy and the right of stockholders to have their views submitted to, and considered by, the Company." A student of Texaco's history wrote, "Concern for shareholders' happiness is a marked reversal of attitude at Texaco, where haughty, autocratic leaders once ran the business however they pleased. . . ."

Kinnear preached the gospel of organizational transformation in 1989. In what he called "vision speeches," he told employees to cut through the "ozone layer" of corporate bureaucracy. He advised them to "just say no" when bosses assigned make-work duties, to "take risks" as if they were entrepreneurs, and to eliminate red tape. By 1991, Texaco had come a long way, but there was still more to do. The life of its oil reserves went from one of the shortest in the industry to almost 8.8 years, which is about 3 years behind Exxon and Amoco Corporation. Kinnear has more to do, but Texaco no longer has a "rather tight noose around its neck." For Kinnear and Texaco, it's been quite a reprieve. And what about Kinnear's prediction of being "One of the most admired companies in the world?" Well, Texaco appears to be well on its way. According to a recent *Fortune* poll, Texaco was the most-improved company for the second year in a row.[1]

$\mathbf{I}$n Chapter 7, the organizing process and the informal organization were discussed. Here, we take up organizing concepts and structure. The structure at Texaco was traditionally quite rigid, with many levels of management bound by strict rules. Chief executive Kinnear changed all that. Like many reorganizing attempts, Texaco's resulted largely from external pressure. The crisis atmosphere at Texaco gave Kinnear the opportunity to restructure the company in ways virtually impossible in normal times. It involved substantial costs within the company and met with resistance, but it appears that Kinnear is well on his way to "Transforming a rigid, oil-poor company into a focused, innovative, and growing force in the industry."[2]

In this chapter we first discuss four important management concepts: responsibility, authority, delegation, and accountability. Then, we review several organizing principles. Next, we discuss the trade-off between the needs of centralization and those of decentralization. Then we describe common types of organizational structures. In the final section of the chapter, we deal with a global perspective and the means by which managers can become better at working with committees.

Responsibility

Responsibility
The obligation to perform work activities.

In accepting a job, a person takes responsibility for performing the tasks involved in it. **Responsibility** is *the obligation to perform work activities*. Texaco's CEO James W. Kinnear is obviously responsible for everything that goes on within the company. But he is now apparently making those lower in the organization responsible for their units. Remember that two layers of management were slashed and decision-making authority was pushed far down in the organization. The degree to which a manager feels the obligation to perform is enhanced if responsibilities are clearly defined. Nothing is more frustrating to a manager or a worker than being confused about the nature, scope, and details of specific job responsibilities. For instance, suppose Susan James, a first-line supervisor for Texaco, has the following conversation with her boss, Phil Williams:

Susan: Am I responsible for processing the new drilling policies, or should Joe Davis's unit handle them?

Phil: I don't think it really matters too much which unit handles these policies so long as it's done correctly and thoroughly.

Susan: But what do you expect me to do?

Phil: I'll get back to you later on this—I'm busy at the moment.

Obviously, Phil's comments leave Susan unsure of her responsibility. In fact, in cases such as this, managers often assume that someone else will do what needs to be done. Therefore, Phil should not be surprised if the new policies do not get processed at all. When he finds out that nothing has been done, he may be upset with Susan, but the real fault is his own.

Authority
The right to decide, to direct others to take action, or to perform certain duties in achieving organizational objectives.

Authority

A common complaint of managers is that, although they have unlimited responsibility, their authority is often inadequate. **Authority** is *the right to decide, to direct others to take action, or to perform certain duties in achieving organizational objectives*. One person who seems to really appreciate the value of assigning responsibility and matching it with adequate authority is Bob Allen, AT&T's CEO. Allen realizes the advantage of putting authority in the hands of those who can best use it. When he took over from the former CEO, James Olson, he reached a major conclusion: "AT&T has the most entrenched corporate culture in America, and must finally change and change for the good." In the new AT&T, middle managers are gaining authority. Allen is eliminating petty procedures and placing power in the hands of those closest to the problem or opportunity at hand.[3]

The definition of *authority* suggests that it has at least three key characteristics:

1. Authority is a right.
2. Exercising authority involves making decisions, taking actions, or performing duties.
3. Authority is granted for the purpose of achieving organizational objectives.

Every manager must have some authority in order to organize and direct the use of resources to attain the objectives of the organization. For example, a supervisor made responsible for staffing a department may have the authority to do so at any of the levels of authority shown in Figure 8–1. At the lowest level, the supervisor will believe he or she lacks the authority to staff the department adequately. Various sources and types of authority will be discussed later.

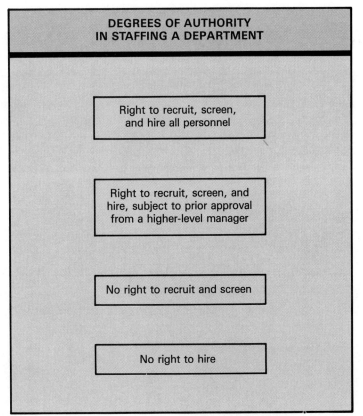

**DEGREES OF AUTHORITY
IN STAFFING A DEPARTMENT**

Right to recruit, screen, and hire all personnel

Right to recruit, screen, and hire, subject to prior approval from a higher-level manager

No right to recruit and screen

No right to hire

FIGURE 8–1

Degrees of Authority in Staffing a Department

You have been promoted to supervisor over the newly created third shift. The competition was intense for the job, but you were the one promoted. The department manager told you that the third shift is essential for the success of the entire restructuring of the manufacturing operation. He also said that he is counting on you to make sure that the third shift is every bit as good as the other two shifts. He specifically said, "It is your responsibility; that's the reason I selected you."

You will have twelve people working for you, and they will be performing three sequential assembly operations. You are to choose six people from the other two shifts. You must also train six new employees. The first person you thought of was your old buddy, John. He has worked all three assembly-line positions and could help you train the new employees for your line. Your former supervisor agreed to allow you to "draft" John for your shift, but the assistant manager of the department said that you cannot have John. The assistant manager normally has to approve all personnel changes. It may be just coincidence, but the assistant manager wanted someone else promoted to the supervisor's position. You really need John to complete your assignment.

What action would you take?

Delegation

Delegation

The process of assigning responsibility along with the needed authority.

The process of assigning responsibility along with the needed authority is **delegation.** Delegation is one of the most significant concepts affecting a manager's ability to get the job done. It creates a risk for managers, however, because the success or failure of an operation is ultimately their responsibility. When a manager delegates a responsibility to a subordinate, the relationship between the two is based on an obligation. Managers should remember an important point: One cannot relieve oneself of any portion of the original responsibility; delegation only allows for someone

Delegation is one of the most significant concepts affecting a manager's ability to get the job done. It creates a risk for managers, however, because the success or failure of an operation is ultimately their responsibility. In this typical construction scene, a great deal of authority has been delegated to the project superintendent, shown speaking. But managers at company headquarters are still responsible for the outcome.

Source: © Jim Pickerell

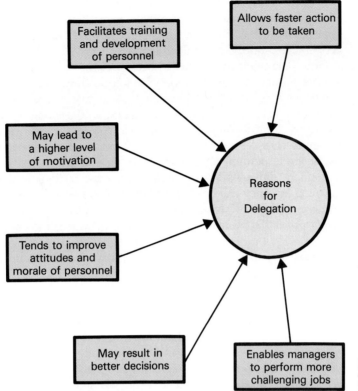

FIGURE 8–2

Reasons for Delegation

else doing the work. Some managers attempt to reduce risk by avoiding delegation and doing everything themselves.

Since Texaco cut two layers of management, it is likely that the managers who remain must be capable of delegating if they are to survive. Delegation of responsibility and authority is essential if managers are to provide opportunities for the development of their people. Also, few managers have the capability of personally performing all the duties for which they are responsible. A frequent cause of operational failure is the unwillingness or inability of some managers to delegate responsibility and authority.

Some of the more significant reasons that delegation is important are illustrated in Figure 8–2. First, delegation of authority often leads to quicker action and faster, better decisions. Action can be taken much faster if people can avoid going to a higher level in the organization for a decision.

Second, delegation tends to be an important factor in training and developing personnel in the organization. Managers cannot learn to perform a certain function or make decisions unless they are given the opportunity to do so. Delegation of responsibility and authority is essential if the firm is concerned about developing personnel to assume more challenging and demanding jobs in the future.

Third, delegation may lead to a higher level of motivation. People who are given authority and responsibility by their superiors often see this as a reflection of trust in their abilities. This may become a self-fulfilling prophecy as subordinates try to live up to that trust.

Fourth, closely related to improved motivation are the attitudes and the morale of employees. People who are given responsibility and authority tend to have a better attitude toward their superiors. They are often easier to manage and more cooperative, and their morale is higher.

Fifth, delegation may result in better decisions. The person who is closest to the job being done is often the one who knows how to do it best.

Finally, it is through delegation that managers are able to perform especially challenging jobs, such as putting a human on the moon. Delegation can be thought of as a way of extending the manager's capabilities. Evidence suggests that managers recognize this. A study of graduating MBAs and practicing managers revealed that the ability to perform a wide variety of tasks tends to be associated with increasing delegation.[4] Business leaders believe that organizations of the future will be flatter, meaning that they will have fewer layers of management between the chief executive and the supervisory level. Span of management will necessarily broaden. As one writer put it, "Tomorrow's manager should oversee the efforts of 300 people rather than 30."[5] With this expansion of the degree of span of management will come the inevitable situation where managers will have to delegate in order to accomplish all that they have responsibility for.

Despite these and other advantages of delegation, managers should consider certain limitations or potential problems of delegation. Table 8–1 mentions four such limitations.

Certain general guidelines should be followed in delegating. First, managers should not fail to delegate just because they personally enjoy doing a particular job. Many managers were specialists before being promoted. Some continue doing some of the tasks they particularly enjoyed. If a subordinate can satisfactorily perform the job, it should probably be delegated, no matter how much fun it is.

Second, managers should not be afraid to delegate the dirty work. They should recognize that at times less than desirable assignments have to be given out. Some managers feel guilty about assigning undesirable jobs and instead do the jobs themselves. This is not an efficient use of time. Both pleasant and unpleasant tasks should be considered for delegation.

Third, the manager's ability to perform a task better and faster than the workers in the unit is not a reason to fail to delegate. Most managers are better at doing certain tasks than the average worker and can get the job done faster themselves. But they could have accomplished more by spending the time on their main responsibility—supervising others. Besides, there are not enough hours in a day to perform tasks that others should be doing.

TABLE 8–1

Limitations or Potential Problems with Delegation

- If improper feedback is provided, the manager may lose control and may not have the time to correct the situation if a problem occurs.
- Delegation can fail if the level of responsibility and authority is not clearly defined and understood.
- If the delegatee does not possess the ability, skills, and experience to accomplish the job or to make decisions, delegation can prove disastrous.
- Problems can result if an employee is given responsibility but insufficient authority to perform the task.

Managers should delegate with finality. Workers should know that they are expected to do the jobs assigned and should know when completion is expected. Status meetings, such as the one shown here, give the manager a chance to query employees about their jobs and reinforce the expectation that delegated work will be completed on time.

© *Jim Pickerell*

Finally, managers should delegate with finality. Delegate and let workers know that you expect them to do the job you assign and to complete it by a certain time. Workers should not believe that they can bring jobs back at the first sign of trouble. Some workers are very good at managing their manager.

Accountability

No organization can function effectively without a system of accountability. **Accountability** is *any means of ensuring that the person who is supposed to perform a task actually performs it and does so correctly.* Situations can rapidly get out of control when people are not held accountable. By setting up twelve independent profit centers, Texaco's Kinnear was making the managers in charge accountable. As organizations become flatter and span of management is broadened, managers have responsibility and corresponding authority. Therefore, it is appropriate to hold managers accountable. When managers are given the resources necessary to accomplish assigned tasks, they will have to bear the inevitable burden of accountability.

Before a manager can be held accountable for results, certain conditions should be present, as Figure 8–3 shows. First, responsibilities must be thoroughly and clearly delineated. An individual who is unaware of what is expected cannot be properly held accountable. Second, the person must be qualified and capable of fulfilling the obligation. It would be inconceivable to assign the responsibility and authority for performing engineering or accounting functions to individuals having no educational background or experience in these areas. Finally, sufficient authority to accomplish the task must be delegated. Assigning a manager the total profit responsibility for a department but no authority to hire or fire employees might mean that insufficient authority has been delegated. The manager probably would object to being held accountable for results.

Because a manager's accountability is so closely related to responsibility, it cannot be delegated to someone else. Managers are usually accountable not only for their own actions and decisions but also for the actions of their subordinates. In navy tradition, the captain should go down with the ship, but this is an extreme case.

Accountability

Any means of ensuring that the person who is supposed to perform a task actually performs it and does so correctly.

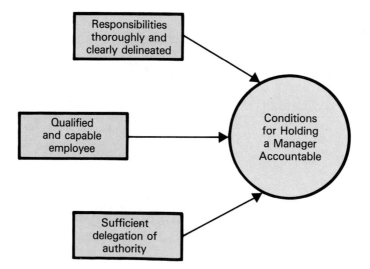

FIGURE 8–3

Conditions for Holding a
Manager Accountable

Accountability can be established in several ways. The first method is through personal inspection by the manager. After assigning a person to do the task, the manager checks to see that it is done properly. The second method is to have the subordinate complete reports and give them to the manager. It is likely that each of the profit center managers at Texaco will submit reports to Kinnear. However, because it is human nature to want to be seen in the best possible light, such reports might be biased in favor of the subordinate. A third method is through reporting done by others. A quality control inspector might report the number of defective units for each worker to the manager. Customers may report poor service or faulty products. This method of accountability is out of the hands of the person held accountable and is therefore reasonably free of bias. Finally, accountability may be obtained through a machine with a counter or some other measuring device. In a supermarket, a cash register tape of all sales serves this purpose. Most modern retailers, like Wal-Mart, use point-of-sale accounting systems, under which most mistakes are immediately logged for correction.

Organizing Principles

To accomplish organizational objectives, organizations may follow any or all of a number of important organizing principles. These principles, briefly discussed here, are summarized in Table 8–2.

Unity of Command

**Unity of command
principle**

The belief that each person
should answer to only one
immediate superior.

The belief that each person should answer to only one immediate superior is the **unity of command principle.** That is, each employee has only one boss. Unity of command allows better coordination and understanding of what is required and improves discipline. However, even though this principle is valid in theory, it is almost universally violated in practice. An important problem caused by its violation is that an employee with two or more bosses can receive contradictory orders.

Equal Authority and Responsibility

An important principle of management is that the degree of authority should equal the degree of responsibility. Following this principle ensures that work will be performed efficiently and with a minimum amount of frustration. If an adequate amount of authority is not delegated, energies and resources are wasted, and employee dissatisfaction often results. Unfortunately, many managers continue to give their subordinates more responsibility than authority.

Scalar Principle and Chain of Command

The philosophy that authority and responsibility should flow from top management downward in a clear, unbroken line is the **scalar principle.** If this principle is followed, there is a clear chain of command for every person in the organization. The **chain of command** is *the line along which authority flows from the top of the organization to any individual.* A clear chain of command clarifies relationships, avoids confusion, and tends to improve decision making, thus often leading to more effective performance. When the scalar

Scalar principle
The philosophy that authority and responsibility should flow from top management downward in a clear, unbroken line.

Chain of command
The line along which authority flows from the top of the organization to any individual.

TABLE 8–2

Organizing Principles

Principle	Definition of	Reason for	Possible Causes of Violation	Possible Results of Violation
Unity of command	A person should report to only one boss.	Clarity and understanding, to ensure unity of effort and direction and to avoid conflicts.	Unclear definition of authority.	Dissatisfaction or frustration of employees and perhaps lower efficiency.
Equal authority and responsibility	The amount of authority and responsibility should be equal.	Work accomplished more efficiently, people developed, and frustration reduced.	Fear on the part of some managers that subordinates might take over.	Waste of energies and dissatisfaction of employees, resulting in reduced effectiveness.
Scalar principle	There should be a clear definition of authority in the organization (going through channels).	Clarity of relationship avoids confusion and improves decision making and performance.	Uncertainty on the part of the employee or a direct effort by the employee to avoid the chain of command.	Poor performance, confusion, or dissatisfaction.
Span of management	There is a limit to the number of employees a manager can effectively supervise.	Increased effectiveness in direction and control of a manager.	Overloading of a manager because of growth in the number of employees.	Lack of efficiency and control, resulting in poor performance.

principle is followed, superiors and subordinates communicate by going through channels.

Span of Management

The number of direct subordinates reporting to any manager is the **span of management (control).** Although the span of management may vary greatly, there is a maximum number of employees a manager can effectively supervise in a given circumstance. Efficient use of managerial talent also dictates that there be a minimum number of subordinates assigned to each manager. The maximum effective span of management is determined to a large extent by the sophistication of reporting technology such as computerized reports, electronic mail, facsimile transmission of documents, and other technological advancements.

As was previously mentioned, business leaders believe that organizations of the future will be flatter, meaning that they will have fewer layers of management between the chief executive and the supervisory level. Span of management will necessarily broaden. This has been the case at Sears, IBM, and GM.

Management Shrinks at Sears, IBM, and GM

The trend toward downsizing management structures continues in the nineties. Sears' CEO Edward Brennan appears to believe that Sears is back on track, but admits that it is way behind the new leaders. In an effort to become more competitive Sears is eliminating management jobs and freezing the salaries of those who remain with the company. With return on investment falling and revenues sliding, IBM is wrenching its annual growth by downsizing in all areas including management.[6] Under Robert C. Stempel's leadership GM is focusing on things such as quality and doing the job right. However, it is quite evident that cost cutting and slimming down are essential parts of his plan to regain GM's competitive edge. By 1995, GM will be down to roughly half of their 1985 salaried workforce. According to GM they will concentrate on their core business and become a much leaner organization.[7] It appears that Sears and IBM are following a similar path. It will be interesting to see if shrinkage in management ranks will result in an effective span of management or have an adverse impact on management effectiveness, and in turn profitability.

Although it is not appropriate to attempt to specify what the correct span of management should be in every situation, it is useful to think about how relationships increase when a manager has more than about eight direct subordinates. This was the subject of research done by V. A. Graicunas, a management consultant of the 1930s. Graicunas derived a formula to determine the potential interactions or relationships possible when managers have a given number of employees.[8] The formula is as follows:

$$R = n + n(n - 1) + n(2^{n-1} - 1)$$

where R is the number of relationships or interactions and n is the number of subordinates reporting to the manager.

TABLE 8–3

Possible Relationships with
Two Employees

Relationships	Number of Relationships	Examples
Direct relationships	2	• Ed may meet and talk with John. • Ed may meet and talk with Susan.
Group relationships	2	• Ed may meet and talk with John with Susan present, or Ed may meet and talk with Susan with John present.
Cross-relationships	2	• John may interact with Susan without Ed being present, or Susan may meet with John without Ed being present.
Total	6	

According to the Graicunas formula, a manager with two employees would have six potential relationships. For example, if Ed Bishop has two subordinates, John and Susan, there would be six possible interactions, as Table 8–3 illustrates. Table 8–4 shows that each additional employee creates a substantial increase in the number of potential relationships.

Accepted spans of management have historically been relatively narrow, usually ranging from six to fifteen. Narrow spans of management permit closer supervision of personnel but tend to create tall organizational structures—structures with a large number of levels. This may cause difficulties in communication and result in managers and workers at lower levels feeling isolated. Wide spans result in relatively fewer levels, or flat organization structures, and greater freedom for the individual employee. As was previously mentioned, the trend is toward broader spans of management.

A number of factors affect the span of management:

1. In general, the more complex the work, the shorter the optimal span of management.

2. The span can be longer if the manager is supervising employees performing similar jobs.

3. If jobs are closely interlocked and interdependent, the manager may have greater problems with coordination, creating the need for a rather limited span of management.

4. If the organization is operating in an unstable environment, a narrow span may prove to be more effective.

TABLE 8–4

Possible Relationships with
Different Numbers of
Employees

Number of Employees	Potential Number of Relationships
1	1
2	6
3	18
4	44
5	100
6	222

5. The establishment of numerous standards increases predictability and provides the basis for effective control, thereby resulting in a wider effective span.

6. Managers and employees who are highly skilled, experienced, and motivated generally can operate with wider spans of management and with less supervision.

7. Where high commitment to the organization is as important as technical efficiency, such commitment can be enhanced through wider spans of management.[9]

In addition, technology can have a significant impact on the span of management. Joan Woodward, a British researcher, conducted studies in a hundred English manufacturing firms. She discovered that the type of production technology used in business organizations affected span of management. Woodward classified production technology on the basis of the following categories:

- Unit or small-batch processing (for example, made-to-order goods such as custom-tailored clothing).

- Mass production (assembly-line operations).

- Process production with continuous long runs of a standardized product such as oil, chemicals, or pharmaceuticals.

She discovered that spans of management were widest in firms using mass-production technology. The jobs in a mass-production situation tend to be more routine and similar to one another, thereby leading to wider appropriate spans of management.[10] On the other hand, unit and process production were marked by narrower spans of management.

Centralization Versus Decentralization

Centralization

The degree to which authority is retained by higher-level managers in an organization rather than being delegated.

Decentralization

The condition that exists when a significant amount of authority is delegated to lower levels in the enterprise.

It is important that management determine the appropriate levels of responsibility and authority to be delegated. **Centralization** is *the degree to which authority is retained by higher-level managers in an organization rather than being delegated.* If a limited amount of authority is delegated, the organization is usually characterized as being centralized. **Decentralization** is *the condition that exists when a significant amount of authority is delegated to lower levels in the enterprise.* According to Wayland Hicks, a Xerox executive vice-president, the business world is headed toward more decentralization, with offices, factories, and suppliers spread throughout the world.[11] There are many degrees of centralization. IBM CEO John F. Akers moved around twenty thousand people to help solve IBM's many problems. According to Akers, "Nobody's ever decentralized IBM to the degree we did."[12] In the future, the real question will be not whether a company should decentralize but what degree of decentralization is appropriate.

In a highly centralized structure, individual managers and workers at lower levels in the organization have a rather narrow range of decisions or actions they can initiate. By contrast, the scope of authority to make decisions and take actions is rather broad for lower-level managers and employees in decentralized organizations. In a highly centralized organizational structure, upper management makes all decisions regarding the hiring or firing of personnel, the approval of equipment and supply purchases, and similar activities. In a decentralized structure, lower-level management may make these decisions.

Decentralization is advocated by many who believe that a greater share in management decision making should be given to lower organizational levels. Decentralization tends to create a climate for more rapid growth and development of personnel. If virtually all decisions and orders come from one central source, organization members tend to act like robots and unthinking executors of someone else's commands. On the other hand, there are exceptionally competent managers in high positions—for example, chief executive James W. Kinnear at Texaco—who are better able to make valid decisions than are their subordinates. When this is the case, a reasonable tendency is to lean toward centralization. In addition, many employees and lower-level managers do not wish to be involved at high levels in the organization.

In addition to the human behavior implications of decentralization and centralization, several other factors affect a manager's decision in this regard. Centralization

1. Produces uniformity of policy and action.
2. Results in few risks of errors by subordinates who lack either information or skill.
3. Utilizes the skills of central and specialized experts.
4. Allows close control of operations.

On the other hand, decentralization

1. Tends to make for speedier decisions and actions on the spot without the need to consult higher levels.
2. Results in decisions that are more likely to be adapted to local conditions.
3. Results in greater interest and enthusiasm on the part of the subordinate to whom the authority has been entrusted. (These expanded jobs provide excellent training experience for possible promotion to higher levels.)
4. Allows top management to use its time for more study and consideration of the basic objectives, plans, and policies of the enterprise.

The following sections discuss several factors that may account for differing decisions about the amount of centralization that is appropriate.

Size and Complexity of the Organization

The larger the enterprise, the more authority the central manager is forced to delegate. The globalization of business that will occur in the 1990s will definitely increase the size and complexity of organizations.[13] If a firm is engaged in many separate businesses, the limitations of expertise usually lead to decentralization. Authority is delegated to the heads of the various units. Each major product group is likely to have different product problems, customers, and marketing channels. If speed and adaptability to change are necessary for success, decentralization is a must.

Dispersion of the Organization

When the difficulties of size are compounded by geographic dispersion, it is evident that a greater degree of decentralization must occur. General Motors is a prime example of decentralization caused by size and geographic dispersion. Not every decision or every function must be decentralized, however. Control of operations may have to be pushed down to lower levels in the organization, even though control of financing may still be centralized. Because of the increasing complexity of federal and state legislation affecting employment practices and unionization, centralization of labor relations is often established for purposes of uniformity throughout the company.

Competence of Available Personnel

A major limiting factor in centralization is the degree of competence of personnel. If an enterprise has grown up under centralized decision making and control, subordinates are often poorly equipped to start making major decisions. They were hired and trained to be followers, not leaders and decision makers. In some convenience store chains, this has developed into a major problem. Store managers are promoted to supervisor, not because of their decision-making ability but because they are experienced in basic store functions and can ensure that the new store managers follow standard operating procedures. In such situations, people who eventually make it to the top may not be equipped to cope with all the necessary decision-making requirements that are not based on established practices and procedures. Those inclined toward more independent thought and action may be driven away from the centralized firm.

ETHICAL DILEMMA

You run the Medallion Construction Company, and your company is bidding on an estimated $2.5 million public housing project. A local electrical subcontractor submitted a bid that you know is 20 percent too low; it could put the subcontractor out of business. In fact, the bid was $30,000 below those of the other four subcontractors. But accepting it will improve your chance of winning the contract for the big housing project.

You are asking yourself the same question over and over again: Is it fair to allow someone to drive himself into possible bankruptcy when he doesn't know it but you do? You can either accept the low bid and almost assure that your company will get the $2.5 million contract, or you can throw out the bid and submit a realistic overall bid on the contract.[14]

What would you do?

Adequacy of the Communication System

Greater size, increased complexity, and geographic dispersion lead to the delegation of larger amounts of authority for decision making to lower levels in the organization. Unwanted decentralization can be avoided through the development of a communication system that will provide for the speed, accuracy, and sufficiency of information top management needs to exercise centralized control. In effect, although large size and geographic dispersion may preclude one's being on the spot, one can control subordinates by detailing standards of performance and by ensuring that information flows quickly and accurately to the person with central authority.

The lack of an effective communication channel caused problems for the joint venture between Chrysler and Maserati. Size, complexity, and geographic dispersion led to communication problems in the building of the Chrysler TC automobile. Making 770 trips to Italy—to resolve the problem of whether the car's top should be made of composite materials, steel, or aluminum—caused the final cost to be 14 percent over budget. There were also inventory problems. At one point, $23 million worth of Chrysler components were discovered piled up in a Milan warehouse. Because of the financial losses caused by these communication problems, Chrysler dropped the option to increase its stake in Maserati, modified TC production plans, and killed other joint projects.[15]

Computer Technology

The widespread use of computers in business gives managers more flexibility in deciding whether to decentralize. Today, computers or terminals are available at almost all sites, and information can be supplied to headquarters virtually instantaneously. In the past, an organization might have decided to decentralize because of the time delay involved in getting decision-making information to top-level managers. Today, this is less of a problem.

Even when it is not feasible to centralize all aspects of management, certain functions can be handled at headquarters. For example, the functions of accounting and finance have been centralized to some degree in most major companies. Other firms have formed data communications networks, which link computers and ter-

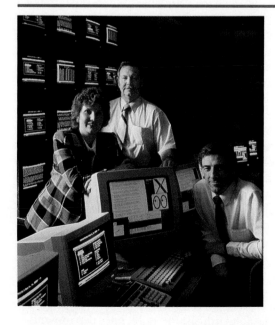

The widespread use of computers in business gives managers more flexibility in deciding whether to decentralize.

Source: Photograph courtesy of Lockheed Corporation

minals throughout the organization. It appears likely that widespread use of such networking may be the next major wave in the evolution of information technology.[16]

The next horizon in the computer field is "thinking machines." As decentralization occurs and spans of management are broadened, computers will become even more important in helping managers keep track of what is going on in the organization. According to Mike Maples, a longtime IBM veteran, machines of the future will be so easy to use that "managers will barely realize they're using them." The computer will teach managers everything they need to know about using the machines. Apple Computer's management believes that the basic technology that led to the development of the Macintosh will allow computers of the 1990s to think of creative ways of solving problems.[17]

Other technology that will be available includes such advancements as Xerox's document-processing center. This system will translate memos, contracts, books, and eventually videocassettes into foreign languages. Two executives, one in Tokyo and one in Houston, can both be working on the same report, shooting it back and forth from computer to computer, making changes each time. Management productivity could increase by at least 40 percent over the next decade with such innovative systems.[18] Computer and technological advancements are discussed in more detail in Chapter 20.

Types of Organizational Structures

Organizational structure

The formal relationships among groups and individuals in the organization.

The formal relationships among groups and individuals in the organization are the **organizational structure.** This structure provides guidelines essential for effective employee performance and overall organizational success. It should clarify and communicate the lines of responsibility and authority within the firm and assist management in coordinating the overall operation.

Although it is common to think only of large companies when organizational structures are discussed, every firm, large or small, has a structure of some kind. It may or may not have an organizational chart. Small businesses may have structures that are simple and easy to understand. In fact, the organizational structure may be informal and highly changeable in small, uncomplicated businesses. By contrast, large, diverse, and complex organizations usually have a highly formalized structure. But that should not mean the structure is so rigid that it does not change, perhaps even frequently. Determining the most appropriate organizational design or structure is not a simple matter if one must consider frequency of reorganization as a factor. Newly formed high-technology companies are most likely companies to restructure or reorganize frequently, but even some of the largest *Fortune* 500 industrial firms often experience major reorganization.

Many variations of organizational structures are used today. The most common types of structures, the ones from which variations are developed, are line, line and staff, functional authority, project, and matrix.

Line organizations

Organizations that have only direct, vertical relationships between different levels in the firm.

Line departments

Departments directly involved in accomplishing the primary purpose of the organization.

Line Organizational Structure

Organizations that have only direct, vertical relationships between different levels in the firm are **line organizations.** These organizations consist of only **line departments**—

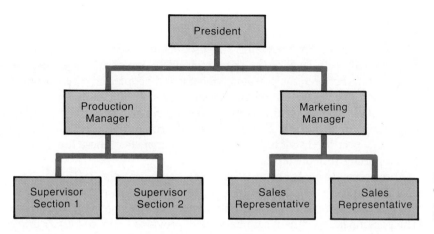

FIGURE 8–4

A Line Organizational
Structure

departments directly involved in accomplishing the primary purpose of the organization. In a typical company, line departments include production and marketing. In a line organization, authority follows the chain of command. Figure 8–4 is an illustration of a simple line organizational structure.

Several advantages are often associated with pure line organizational structure.

1. A line structure tends to simplify and clarify responsibility, authority, and accountability relationships in the organization. The levels of responsibility and authority in a line organization are likely to be precise and understandable.

2. A line structure promotes fast decision making and allows the organization to change direction rapidly, because there are few people to consult when problems arise.

3. Because pure line organizations are small, there is greater closeness of management and employees, and everyone usually has an opportunity to know what is going on in the firm.

There are also certain disadvantages to the line structure. The major disadvantage is that as the firm grows larger, there is an increasing lack of effectiveness. At some point, improved speed and flexibility do not offset the lack of specialized knowledge and skills. In other words, a line structure may reduce the effectiveness of managers by forcing them to be experts in too many fields. In a line organization, firms tend to become overly dependent on the few key people who can perform numerous jobs. If the organization is to remain purely line, management can create additional levels to share the managerial load. This, however, will result in a longer chain of command and consequent loss of some of the speed, flexibility, and centralized control. Therefore, there are few pure line organizations of any substantial size.

Line and staff organizations

Organizations that have direct vertical relationships between different levels and also specialists responsible for advising and assisting other managers.

Line and Staff Organizational Structure

Most large organizations are of the line and staff type. **Line and staff organizations** are *organizations that have direct, vertical relationships between different levels and also specialists responsible for advising and assisting other managers.* Such organizations have both line and staff departments. **Staff departments** are *departments that provide line people with advice and assistance in specialized areas.*

Staff departments

Departments that provide line people with advice and assistance in specialized areas.

As the line and staff organization chart in Figure 8–5 shows, staff functions under the president typically include personnel, quality control, research, and accounting. The line functions are marketing and production. Each staff manager is responsible to people at every level of the organization. For simplicity, however, only the staff relationships between the personnel director and people in the production department are shown. Notice the dotted lines from personnel to superintendents, supervisors, and workers. The personnel director, however, also has staff responsibilities to the other department heads. Personnel, quality control, research, and accounting are separate, specialized staff functions, but the managers of these functions have a direct line reporting relationship to the president.

Three separate types of specialized staffs can be identified: (1) advisory, (2) service, and (3) control. It is possible, though, for one unit to perform all three functions. For example, the personnel manager advises line managers on labor relations topics. The personnel department simultaneously provides a service by procuring and training needed production and sales personnel. A control orientation enters when the personnel manager audits people's salaries to ensure conformity to line-approved pay ranges. Some staffs perform only one function. For example, a staff economist advises on the establishment of long-range plans, and a quality control staff unit enforces authorized product standards. It is apparent that the potential for conflicts in coordination between line and staff tends to grow as one moves from advice to service to control. One can possibly ignore advice, but service is needed, and control is often unavoidable.

The line and staff organizational structure offers both advantages and disadvantages. The primary advantage is the organization's use of the expertise of staff specialists. Their concentrated and skillful analysis of business problems allows managers to be more scientific. In addition, managers' effective span of management can

FIGURE 8–5

Line and Staff Structure of a Typical Manufacturing Company

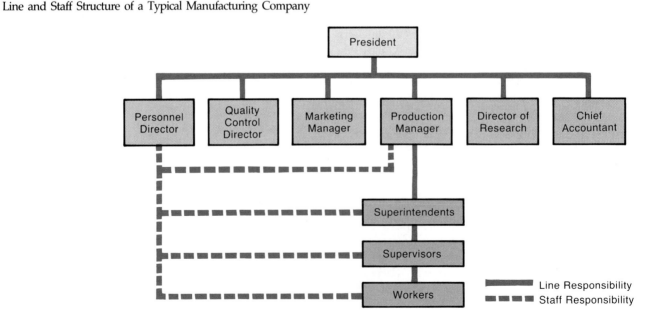

be lengthened; that is, once relieved of technical details, managers can supervise more people. Some staff people even operate as extensions of managers and assist in coordination and control.

Despite the fact that a line and staff structure allows for increased flexibility and specialization, it may create conflicts. When specialists are introduced into the organization, line managers may feel that they have lost authority over certain specialized functions. These managers do not want staff specialists telling them what to do or how to do it, even though they recognize the specialists' knowledge and expertise. It is important to use staff personnel without destroying unity of command. The authority of line managers should be preserved while their ability to produce is enhanced. Some staff people have difficulty adjusting to the role, especially if line managers are reluctant to accept advice. Staff people may also resent their lack of authority, and this may cause line and staff conflict.

There is a tendency for specialists to seek to enlarge personal influence by assuming line authority in their specialty. The tendency is compounded by the realization that the fundamental purpose of all staff is to produce greater economy and effectiveness of operation. This means that staff must attempt to introduce changes that result in more efficiency. These changes will not always be welcomed by line personnel. Thus, the introduction of specialists into what was once a fairly simple organizational structure often complicates relationships.

Functional Authority Organizational Structure

Organizations whose staff departments have authority over line personnel in narrow areas of specialization (a modification of line and staff organizations) are **functional authority organizations.** In a pure line organization, there is limited use of specialists by management. In the line and staff organization, specialization of particular functions characterizes the structure, but the specialists only advise and assist. In the functional authority organizational structure, however, specialists are given **functional authority**—*the right of staff specialists to issue orders in their own names in designated areas.*

The principle of unity of command (having one boss) is violated when functional authority exists. Even though few organizations give all of their staff managers functional authority, it is quite common for one or two specialists to have such authority. If a function is considered to be of crucial importance, it may be necessary for the specialist to exercise direct rather than advisory authority. The violation of unity of command is intentional. The possible losses resulting from confusion and conflicting orders from multiple sources may be more than offset by increased effectiveness.

Examples of specialists often given functional authority are the managers of quality control, safety, and labor relations. Figure 8–6 shows a functional authority organizational structure. Notice that this structure is quite similar to the line and staff organizational structure shown in Figure 8–5, except for the nature of the relationship between the staff specialist and other managers. Quality control is a very important function in most manufacturing firms, and its level of authority and status has increased over the years. A traditional staff department would merely advise. Because of the critical nature of its work, however, a quality control department often directs as well as advises.

Functional authority organizations

Organizations whose staff departments have authority over line personnel in narrow areas of specialization (a modification of line and staff organizations).

Functional authority

The right of staff specialists to issue orders in their own names in designated areas.

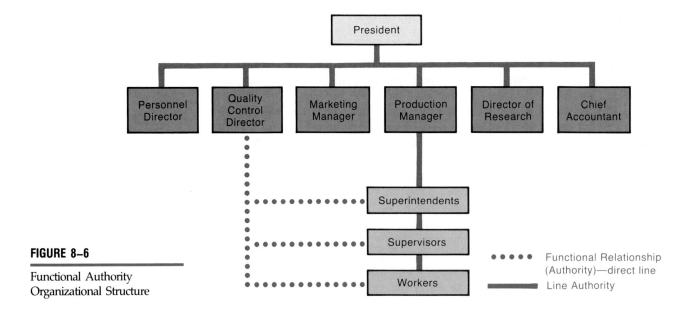

FIGURE 8–6

Functional Authority
Organizational Structure

Safety and labor relations specialists may exercise functional authority over personnel in other areas throughout the organization, but only in relation to their specific specialties. A safety manager may issue compliance guidelines and give direct interpretations of the Occupational Safety and Health Act throughout the organization. The labor relations specialist often will have complete authority in contract negotiations with the union.

In each of these illustrations—quality control, safety, and labor relations—the traditional chain of command has been split. As long as the splitting process is restricted, coordination and unity of action are not in excessive danger. Many organizations that utilize functional authority relationships attempt to confine the impact to managerial rather than operative levels. Thus, a department supervisor may have to account to more than one boss, but the supervisor's employees are protected from this possible confusion.

The major disadvantages of a functional authority organizational structure are (1) the potential conflicts resulting from the violation of the principle of unity of command and (2) the tendency to keep authority centralized at higher levels in the organization. If the functional authority organizational structure is used extensively, there may be a tendency for the line department supervisor to become little more than a figurehead. The structure can become very complicated when functional specialists exist at various levels of the organization.

Project and Matrix Organizational Structures

The line, line and staff, and functional authority organizational structures have been the traditional approaches to organization. The primary objective of these forms of organizing has been the establishment and distribution of authority to coordinate and control the firm by an emphasis on vertical, rather than horizontal, relationships. In major aerospace projects such as the Space Shuttle Project, however, work processes flowed horizontally, diagonally, up, or down. The direction of work flow depends

- Work is definable in terms of a specific objective and target date for completion.
- Work is unique and unfamiliar to the existing organization.
- Work is complex with respect to the interdependence of activities and specialized skills necessary for accomplishment.
- Work is critical in terms of possible gain or loss.
- Work is temporary with respect to the duration of need.

TABLE 8–5

When the Project Organizational Structure Is Most Valuable

on the distribution of talents and abilities in the organization and the need to apply them to the problem that exists. The organizations that have emerged to cope with this challenge have been referred to as project and matrix organizations.

Project Organizations   *A temporary organization designed to achieve specific results by using teams of specialists from different functional areas in the organization* is a **project organization.** The team focuses all of its energies and skills on the assigned project. Once the project has been completed, the team is broken up, and its members are reassigned to their regular positions in the organization or to other projects. Many business organizations and government agencies make use of project teams or task forces to concentrate efforts on specific project assignments, such as the development of a new product or technology or the construction of a new plant.

As Table 8–5 shows, there are times when the project organizational structure is the most valuable type of structure. Figure 8–7 illustrates a highly simplified project

Project organization

A temporary organization designed to achieve specific results by using teams of specialists from different functional areas in the organization.

FIGURE 8–7

Project Structure

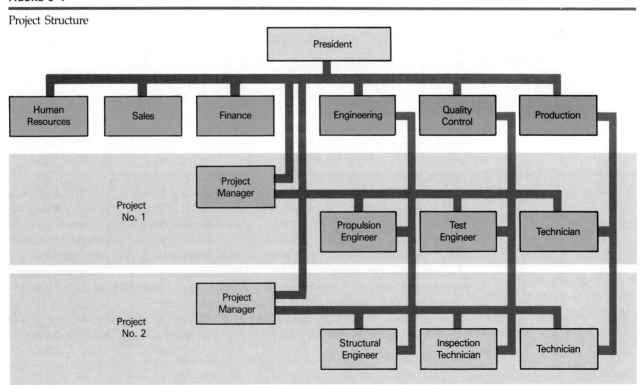

structure attached to an existing organization. Personnel are assigned to the project from the existing permanent organization and are under the direction and control of the project manager. The project manager specifies what effort is needed and when work will be performed, whereas the concerned department managers may decide who in their unit is to do the work and how it is to be accomplished. Home base for these project members is the existing department—human factors, engineering, quality control, and production.

The authority over each of the three project members is shared by the project manager and the respective function managers in the permanent organization. The four specialists are on loan on a temporary basis and spend only a portion of their time on the project assignment. It is apparent that authority is one of the crucial questions of the project structure. A deliberate conflict has been established between the project manager and the other managers in the organization. The authority relationships are overlapping, presumably in the interest of ensuring that all problems will be covered.

Project managers and department heads are often forced into using means other than formal authority to achieve results. Informal relationships become more important than formal prescriptions of authority. In the event of conflict and dispute, discussion and consensus are required, rather than the forcing of compliance by threat or punishment. Full and free communication, regardless of formal rank, is required among those working on the project. More attention is allocated to roles and competencies in relation to the project than to formal levels of authority. The National Aeronautics and Space Administration (NASA) provides the most widely known example of the use of the project organization.

The Benefits of Project Organization at NASA

"One small step for man, one giant leap for mankind." The words of Neil Armstrong as he stepped onto the surface of the moon are part of the American legend. His feat was the culmination of a determined ten-year effort initiated by President John F. Kennedy. It was one of the most highly organized and technically complex endeavors ever undertaken. It is a symbol of the effectiveness of the project organization.

The complexity was no less for the 1980s space shuttles *Columbia*, *Challenger*, and *Discovery*. Just to build the shuttle orbiter, external tank, and boosters for one shuttle required 6,027 contractor employees. NASA clearly had to be well organized to coordinate such complex activities. In addition, the participating corporations—for example, Lockheed, Rockwell International, and Martin Marietta—had to align their own organizations to accomplish the tasks at hand. For example, Lockheed established competing teams, each including a former astronaut. Each team formed an alliance with a major airline to take advantage of the airline's operational experience.

But progress was interrupted by the *Challenger* accident in 1986. A tragic explosion destroyed the vehicle and crew just over a minute after liftoff. NASA was plagued by the same problems that often plague large operations: a lack of communication between different segments of the organization and a failure to adequately supervise those responsible for the accomplishment of key activities. In addition, the project deadlines became overly important, with a seeming disregard for matters such as the safety of those affiliated with the mission. But despite the explosion and the problems associated with the project organization, NASA's successes probably would not have been possible without project organizations. Most of the aerospace industry remains committed to this form of organization, and successful missions in 1991 and 1991 attest to its continued success. In fact, many firmly believe no other type of organization can safely carry out such projects.

••

Matrix Organization *A permanent organization designed to achieve specific results by using teams of specialists from different functional areas in the organization* is a **matrix organization.** This type of organization is often used when it is essential for the firm to be highly responsive to a rapidly changing external environment. For example, an electronics firm might find that the matrix structure facilitates the company's quick response to its environment. Matrix organizational structures have been used successfully in such industries as banking, chemicals, computers, and electronics. However, they require an effective coordinating mechanism to offset the negative effect of dual authority.[19]

In matrix organizations, there are functional managers and product (or project) managers. Functional managers are in charge of specialized resources such as production, quality control, inventories, scheduling, and selling. Product managers are in charge of one or more products and are authorized to prepare product strategies and call on the various functional managers for the necessary resources. When a firm moves to a matrix structure, functional managers must realize that they will lose some of their authority and will have to take some direction from the product managers, who have the budgets to purchase internal resources. In fact, true matrix organizations imply that project and line managers will have roughly equivalent power.[20]

Despite their limitations, project and matrix management concepts demonstrate that people can work for two or more managers and that managers can effectively influence those over whom they have only partial authority. There is the possibility of conflict and frustration, but the opportunity for prompt, efficient accomplishment is great.

Matrix organization

A permanent organization designed to achieve specific results by using teams of specialists from different functional areas in the organization.

A Global Perspective

Global organizations often create problems for employees. The international movement of employees is a high-stakes game which can be a major stressor for host country nationals.[21] It is vitally important that management properly prepare employees to cope with the stress they will encounter because of global assignments. Expatriates are often stressed from the time they learn of global assignments until well after returning home.

Stress is evident in most any work environment, but is usually quite high in the global arena. Inappropriately addressing global stressors can result in failure of the assignment and a disinterested employee. Culture shock is the main stressor, resulting in maladies such as poor job performance, unhappy social lives, broken marriages, change in sex drives, eating binges, bouts with depression, nervousness, anger and aggression, substance abuse, homesickness, impatience with family members, and insomnia.[22]

Management should work to limit the impact of culture shock by properly preparing individuals for overseas assignments. Global assignments for those who are unprepared is costly to the individual involved, and is also quite costly to the organization. The Employee Relocation Council (ERC) reports that the average annual cost to send an employee overseas for a year or two is between $200,000 and $250,000. One executive estimates the cost of a failed expatriate assignment to the multinational firm is three times the individual's salary, not including the price of lost productivity.[23] Basically, management should help assure that these individuals have the personal skills, the people skills, and the perceptual skills needed to cope with the global environment they will encounter.

How Managers Can Become Better at Working with Committees

Committee

A group of people assigned to work together to do something not included in their regular jobs.

Committees have been the brunt of many harsh jokes. For example, it has been said that a camel is a horse designed by a committee. A **committee** is *a group of people assigned to work together to do something not included in their regular jobs.* Other names used to designate committees include *boards, councils,* and *task forces.* A permanent committee is referred to as a standing committee. Committees are necessary for several reasons. They can bring together experts from various areas to handle difficult problems. At least in theory, two heads are better than one. Even if the decisions that committees make are technically no better than those made by individuals, such decisions are often more readily accepted. In fact, it is common practice to make sure that people who are likely to oppose an expected decision are placed on the committee responsible for making it.

Committees also have weaknesses. Often, the decision process is slow. One person can make decisions faster than a group can. Committees are also costly. If five people are on a committee and the average cost of each is $25 an hour, it costs $250 to have a two-hour meeting. Another weakness of committees is that they encourage compromise, even though the best decision may be at one extreme or the other.

The shortcomings of committees can be minimized if a few simple rules are followed:

1. The purpose of the committee should be clearly stated in writing.
2. The size of the committee should be just adequate to obtain the representation and intellectual input required.
3. There should be an odd number of members so the committee will not deadlock on important issues.
4. Every committee meeting should have a specific written agenda.
5. The committee should be immediately disbanded when it has accomplished its purpose.

Self-Assessment
Exercise

Will You Be Good at
Dealing with
Organizing Concepts
and Developing
Organizational
Structure?

1. Are you willing to work to ensure that authority equals responsibility?
   ☐ Yes   ☐ No

2. Are you willing to place people where they fit best within the organization?
   ☐ Yes   ☐ No

3. Are you willing to delegate?
   ☐ Yes   ☐ No

4. Are you willing to consider the human element when organizing?
   ☐ Yes   ☐ No

5. Are you willing to be flexible?
   ☐ Yes   ☐ No

6. Are you willing to hold workers accountable for what they do?
   ☐ Yes   ☐ No

7. Are you willing to learn to determine what needs to be done?
   ☐ Yes   ☐ No

8. Are you willing to understand that most individuals work best when they have one immediate superior?
   ☐ Yes   ☐ No

9. Are you willing to learn that there is a maximum number of workers any manager can effectively supervise?
   ☐ Yes   ☐ No

10. Are you willing to work with the staff people in your organization?
    ☐ Yes   ☐ No

Summary

Responsibility is the obligation to perform work activities. Authority is the right to decide, to direct others, and to perform certain duties. Delegation is the process of assigning responsibility along with the needed authority. Accountability is any means of ensuring that the person who is supposed to perform a task actually performs it and does so correctly.

These concepts are basic to the organizing process. In addition, managers follow certain guidelines in performing the organizing function. The unity of command principle is the belief that each person should answer to only one immediate superior. Another important principle is that authority should equal responsibility. The scalar principle is the philosophy that authority and responsibility should flow from top management downward in a clear, unbroken line, called the chain of command. A clear chain of command clarifies relationships, avoids confusion, and tends to improve decision making. The number of subordinates reporting directly to any manager is referred to as the span of management (control).

Management must determine appropriate levels of responsibility and authority to be delegated. Centralization is the degree to which authority is retained by higher-level managers. If a significant amount of authority is delegated to lower levels, the enterprise is described as being decentralized.

The organizational structure is the formal relationships among groups and individuals in the organization. Line organizations have direct, vertical relationships between different levels in the firm. They include only line departments—the departments directly involved in accomplishing organizational objectives. Line and staff organizations also have direct, vertical relationships, but they also include specialists responsible for advising and assisting other managers. The functional authority organization is a modification of the line and staff organization. Staff departments have authority over line personnel in narrow areas of specialization. A project organization is a temporary organization designed to achieve specific results, using teams of specialists from different functional areas in the organization. A matrix organization is the same as a project organization, except that it is permanent rather than temporary.

Committees are groups of people working together to do something not included in their regular jobs. They bring together experts from various areas to handle difficult problems.

Review Questions

1. Distinguish by definition among the following terms:
   a. responsibility
   b. authority
   c. delegation
   d. accountability
2. Describe each of the following organizing principles:
   a. unity of command
   b. equal authority and responsibility
   c. scalar principle

3. Distinguish between centralization and decentralization. Briefly describe the primary factors to be considered in determining the degree of centralization that is appropriate for an organization.
4. What are the basic types of organizational structures? Briefly describe each type.
5. Under what circumstances are project and matrix structures the most appropriate?
6. Discuss the merits of this statement: A camel is a horse designed by a committee.

Key Terms

Responsibility
Authority
Delegation
Accountability
Unity of command
  principle
Scalar principle
Chain of command
Span of management
  (control)

Centralization
Decentralization
Organizational structure
Line organizations
Line departments
Line and staff
  organizations

Staff departments
Functional authority
  organizations
Functional authority
Project organization
Matrix organization
Committee

CASE 8.1   WHO HAS THE AUTHORITY?

Doughboy Snack Foods is a large bakery, with approximately five hundred employees, located in Atlanta, Georgia. The company is six years old and unionized. It features a wide line of products, including various cakes and snack foods and an extensive array of commercial and household bread items. Doughboy ships its products all over the Southeast. The bread distribution department is the smallest section of the company, consisting of one department head, one supervisor, one assistant supervisor, two leadmen, and eight full-time employees.

Jim Davis, the first-shift supervisor, has been with Doughboy since it opened. Before coming to the company, he owned and operated a cabinet shop. He is a no-nonsense, autocratic manager. Jim usually makes all of the decisions and gives them to his assistant, Sam Smith, the second-shift supervisor, who has been with Doughboy for five years. Before Jim leaves each day, he writes down all that needs to be done and leaves Sam in charge. Jim was responsible for Sam's getting the job at Doughboy. The two had worked together in the past, when Sam was an employee in Jim's cabinet

shop. Jim was also responsible for Sam's promotions to leadman and assistant. Jim's recommendations to his superiors were the reason the positions were approved and Sam was given them.

The employees in the bread distribution section are the highest paid in the company. Most of them are happy with the company and look forward to long employment. However, one employee of this section is currently experiencing some problems. Murphy Bowen is the second-shift leadman, but until two months ago he was the third-shift leadman, a position he had held for over three years. Murphy accepted the job on the new shift because Jim had assured him he could have Saturdays and Sundays off. However, from the first day on the new job, Murphy has been assigned weekend duty because he is the most experienced employee on the shift and the best to supervise new employees on the weekends.

Murphy spoke with Sam, his shift supervisor, asking for weekends off. Sam explained the need for the present schedule and gave Murphy the impression that if he wanted to continue with the company, the present schedule was his only choice. Company policy dictated that after an employee accepted a job, it was up to management to establish working hours. Also, nothing in the union contract stated that an employee's schedule couldn't be changed after he accepted a specific job. But Murphy can't help feeling betrayed by the undesirable schedule and angry with Sam for not giving him the hours he had expected when he joined this shift.

To complicate Murphy's position further, Murphy happened to see Jim one afternoon as he was returning home with some furniture in the back of his truck. Murphy stopped the truck and explained to Jim that he was moving the furniture to his home and asked if it would be all right not to work that evening. Jim agreed to let him off, and Murphy figured that since company policy stated that he had to give at least two hours' notice of personal business, he would have an excused absence. As Murphy came into the office the next day, he noticed that Sam was not in the office. Murphy knew that Sam was responsible for the attendance records for his shift, so he checked the records while waiting for Sam to return. He was surprised by the notation "unexcused" by his name for the previous evening and was angered because he believed he had followed company policy in requesting an excused absence two hours before shift time.

Because of these problems, Murphy began to feel Doughboy was not treating him fairly. Although he had always been a hard-working employee, he developed a sullen attitude and began to be inefficient in his work. As a matter of fact, the next shift had begun to suffer because of the lack of productivity of Murphy's group.

Questions

1. What problems relating to authority and responsibility relationships exist in this case?
2. What do you believe should be done to keep this type of problem from recurring?

| CASE 8.2 | MISCO PAPER CONVERTERS |

When Dick Valladao and George Smeltzer, owners of Misco Paper Converters, began their business, it was only a part-time operation. The operation involved buying rolls of brown kraft paper, such as that used for grocery bags, cutting the paper into various shapes and sizes, bundling the sheets together, and shipping the bundles to industrial customers. The pieces of paper were used for various purposes: as vapor barriers in electronic equipment, to place between glass or china plates and bowls prior to shipping, and as a protective wrapping for many small manufactured items.

As the business grew and became more profitable, Dick and George decided to leave their jobs and work at Misco full time. They had been doing the work in a small metal building behind George's house; but when they went into the business full time, they rented a 6,000-square-foot warehouse. They also purchased a shear press and a stripper in addition to the press and stripper they already owned, as well as a truck to pick up the raw paper at the paper mill and to make some deliveries. Usually, the bundles of paper were shipped by common carrier to customers, some of whom were as much as 600 miles away.

Dick and George found it necessary to hire six operators. The operation was simple. The paper was fed off the large rolls through a stripper, which cut it to the appropriate widths. The stripping machine was set to clip the paper off every 50 feet or so. Then the strips were stacked on top of one another on a set of rollers that allowed the paper to be fed back into one of the shear presses. When a stack of strips was fifty layers thick, it was fed into the shear press, which clipped it to the appropriate length. The resulting rectangular stacks of brown paper were tied with twine and stacked onto shipping pallets. When a pallet was full, it was set aside to wait for shipment.

At first, George and Dick worked with the operators as a team, each worker doing whatever needed to be done. Each person soon learned to operate the forklift, the strippers, and the shear presses and to tie bundles as well. Dick and George felt themselves to be relative equals, so neither attempted to exercise authority over the other. As time went on, however, Dick began to think that the whole operation could be accomplished more efficiently if some kind of structure were imposed.

Questions

1. Do you believe that anything is to be gained at Misco by establishing an organizational structure, including specialization and lines of authority and responsibility? Explain your answer.

2. Assuming that George and Dick decide to set up a typical kind of organization, how should they decide who is to be chief executive? Should they have to decide that at all? Explain.

Notes

1. This case is a composite of a number of published accounts, among them: Allanna Sullivan, "Texaco Alters Exploration and Production," *Wall Street Journal*, March 8, 1989, p. A4; Mark Ivey, "Jim Kinnear Is Pumping New Life into Texaco," *Business Week*, April 17, 1989, pp. 50–52; Randolph B. Smith and David B. Hilder, "Icahn Sells Stake in Texaco Inc. in Surprise Move," *Wall Street Journal*, June 2, 1989, p. A3; "He's Baaaack, with $2 Billion," *Time*, June 12, 1989, p. 51; Stratford P. Sherman, "Who's in Charge at Texaco Now?" *Fortune*, January 16, 1989, pp. 69–72; Todd Vogel and Brian Bremner, "Texaco: From Takeover Bait to Dynamo," *Business Week*, July 22, 1991, pp. 50–52; Alison L. Sprout, "America's Most Admired Corporations," *Fortune*, February 11, 1991, p. 60; and Standard & Poor's Corporation, "Texaco Inc.," *Standard NYSE Stock Reports* 56, no. 93 (May 15, 1989): sec. 20.

2. Vogel and Bremner, "Texaco: From Takeover Bait to Dynamo," pp. 50–52.

3. Andrew Kupfer, "Bob Allen Rattles the Cages at AT&T," *Fortune*, June 19, 1989, pp. 58–66.

4. J. D. Ford and W. H. Hegarty, "Decision Makers' Beliefs about the Causes and Effects of Structures: An Exploratory Study," *Academy of Management Journal*, June 1984, p. 281.

5. Brian Dumaine, "What the Leaders of Tomorrow See," *Fortune*, July 3, 1989, pp. 48–62.

6. Susan Caminiti, "Sears' Need: More Speed," *Fortune*, July 15, 1991, p. 89 and Wilton Woods, "Can John Akers Save IBM?" *Fortune*, July 15, 1991, p. 44.

7. "GM's Leaders Go on the Record," *Fortune*, March 9, 1992, pp. 51–52, 57.

8. V. A. Graicunas, "Relationships of Organizations," in L. Gulick and L. Urwick, eds., *Papers on the Science of Administration* (New York: Columbia University Press, 1947).

9. L. W. Fry and J. W. Slocum, Jr., "Technology, Structure, and Workgroup Effectiveness: A Test of a Contingency Model," *Academy of Management Journal*, June 1984, p. 236.

10. Joan Woodward, *Industrial Organization: Theory and Practice* (London: Oxford University Press, 1965), pp. 52–62.

11. Dumaine, "What the Leaders of Tomorrow See," pp. 48–62.

12. John A. Byrne. "The Changing Corporation," *Business Week*, February 15, 1988, p. 95.

13. Dumaine, "What the Leaders of Tomorrow See," pp. 48–62.

14. Adapted from a case presented in Karen Berney's article, "Finding the Ethical Edge," *Nation's Business*, August 1987, p. 24.

15. John Rossant and Wendy Zellner, "How Chrysler's $30,000 Sports Car Got Sideswiped," *Business Week*, January 23, 1989, p. 68.

16. Ronald M. Locklin, "Choosing a Data Communications Network," *Journal of Business Strategy* 6 (Winter 1986): 14.

17. Dumaine, "What the Leaders of Tomorrow See," pp. 48–62.

18. Ibid.

19. J. L. C. Cheng, "Interdependence and Coordination in Organizations: A Role-System Analysis," *Academy of Management Journal*, March 1983, pp. 160–161.

20. William F. Joyce, "Matrix Organization: A Social Experiment," *Academy of Management Journal* 29 (September 1986): 537.

21. Mike Fergus, "Employees on the Move," *HRMagazine* 36 (May 1990): 45.

22. Mark E. Mendenhall and Gary Oddon, "The Overseas Assignment: A Practical Look," *Business Horizons* 31 (September–October 1988): 78–79.

23. Fergus, "Employees on the Move," p. 45.

CHAPTER 9

Human Resource Management and the Staffing Function

LEARNING OBJECTIVES

After completing this chapter students should be able to

- Identify and briefly describe the basic human resource functions.

- Describe the predominant laws and executive orders that affect equal employment opportunity.

- Explain the staffing process, job analysis, human resource planning, and recruitment.

- Explain each phase of the selection process.

- Describe the factors involved in internal staffing administration.

- State some special considerations involved in selecting managerial personnel.

Among *Fortune* magazine's 1991 list of "Most Admired Corporations," PepsiCo was fifth overall and ranked first among beverage companies. Chief executive James Calloway explained Pepsi's success this way: "We have a great team spirit. Our people want to be the Marines. We hire eagles and teach them to fly in formation." Throughout the late 1980s, PepsiCo earned large profits in all its main businesses, soft drinks (Pepsi-Cola, Slice, Seven-Up, Mountain Dew), snack foods (Frito-Lay), and restaurants (Pizza Hut, Kentucky Fried Chicken, Taco Bell). PepsiCo is now one-third beverages, one-third snacks, and one-third restaurants. They are number 1 in the chicken category, number 1 in the Mexican category, and number 1 in the pizza category. They aren't in the hamburger business because they couldn't buy McDonald's, so they couldn't be number 1 in this category.

Calloway claims to spend 40 percent of his time on people issues. "People, people, people" are his "three P's" of good management. *Fortune* ranked PepsiCo first among beverage companies at attracting and developing good people. But toughness, not "touchy-feely" seems to be the watchword at Pepsi. One executive remarked, "We'll never be nor should we be a warm and cuddly environment." Managers usually work 60 hours a week. At annual performance reviews, bosses make subordinates justify themselves on the basis of meeting sales targets, making useful innovations, and other objective measures. According to the Frito-Lay chief, "Nothing is ever good enough." When goals are met one year, they are upped for the next. Failure to meet goals brings quick help, but if failure continues, it brings discharge.

There is a feedback program which involves confidential performance reports by each manager's subordinates. Each spring every manager's career is assessed. A personnel manager sits in on each performance interview. Calloway personally reviews the records of the top 550 managers, involving each manager's boss in the review.

Personnel managers, especially, get rotated. "We expect our personnel people to be in the business up to their eyeballs—to know sales, profits, and margins," said Calloway. A new personnel manager usually spends time in a line job right away, perhaps driving a delivery truck or selling. Since graduates of top business schools are seldom willing to start out in menial jobs, Pepsi often recruits from second-tier schools.

Obviously, there are benefits to being a manager at Pepsi. The winners get bonuses of up to 90 percent of annual salary, stock options, first-class air travel, fully-loaded company cars, and rapid promotions. And many like the challenge, variety, and excitement of their high-demand jobs, not to mention the security of knowing where they stand.

Workers see similar pressures and rewards. Calloway said, "It's been part of our whole culture to say 'you are important.'" The goals PepsiCo sets for workers are to build team spirit, increase identification with the company and its work, encourage longevity, and increase productivity. PepsiCo compensates its workers well and the company's SharePower program was the first major stock option plan for lower-level employees. PepsiCo appears to be innovative in many ways, but it is interesting to note that even though PepsiCo is ranked fifth and Coca-Cola is ranked sixth among the 1991 "Most Admired Corporations," Coke has had a higher total stockholder return over the last ten years.[1]

Human Resource Management (HRM) is *the wide range of organizational activities
involved in staffing, training and development, compensation, health and safety, employee and
labor relations, and human resource research.* The main HRM principles at Pepsi seem
to be hire good people; train them well; demand that they perform; evaluate them
thoughtfully; and reward those who make the grade. A company's human resource
management policies and practices must be integrated into a sound overall administrative system.

In Chapter 7, we said that organizations, large or small, have these three
characteristics:

1. They are composed of people.
2. They exist to achieve objectives.
3. They require some degree of limitation on member behavior.

Thus, a major focus of the organizing function is the people who work together in
pursuit of organizational objectives. In this chapter, we will first define the basic
human resource management functions. Then, we will describe the primary legislation affecting equal employment opportunity. We will devote the next, and largest,
part of the chapter to the elements of the staffing process: job analysis, human
resource planning, recruitment, and selection; then, internal staffing administration
will be discussed. In the concluding sections, we will discuss special considerations
involved in selecting managerial personnel and the global perspectives of human
resource management.

Human Resource Management Functions

As we discussed in Chapter 2, the labor force is constantly changing. In the midst
of these changes, every successful organization must attract, select, train, and retain
qualified people. Just having adequate numbers of people is not enough; they must

FIGURE 9–1

The Human Resource
Management System

*Source: Reprinted by permission from
R. Wayne Mondy and Robert M. Noe III,
Human Resource Management, 4th ed.
(Boston: Allyn and Bacon, 1990), p. 9.*

Training and development (T&D) programs are formal efforts to help employees learn new skills, improve existing skills, or otherwise improve their ability to perform in the organization. T&D is needed in part because people, jobs, and organizations are always changing. Amoco designed this mock tanker trailer to allow firefighting and emergency personnel from any community to gain actual training in a simulated accident.

Source: Photograph courtesy of Amoco

also be qualified or the organization will have problems attaining its objectives. This fact was brought home recently to the Boeing Company. Boeing had geared up at its main plant in Seattle to handle hundreds of new orders for its big commercial jets. Companywide employment jumped 83 percent in seven years. But the employees could not be assimilated and trained fast enough. For the first time in twenty years, Boeing had to push back delivery deadlines to which it had been firmly committed. Dean D. Thornton, president of Boeing's commercial airplane subsidiary, said, "We overcommitted."[2]

The six basic human resource management functions are illustrated in Figure 9–1. They are staffing, training and development, compensation, health and safety, employee and labor relations, and human resource research.[3]

Staffing

The formal process of ensuring that the organization has qualified workers available at all levels to meet its short- and long-term business objectives is **staffing.**[4] The staffing process involves job analysis, human resource planning, recruitment, selection, and internal staffing administration. These topics will be covered in greater detail later in the chapter.

Training and Development

Formal efforts to help employees learn new skills, improve existing skills, or otherwise improve their ability to perform in the organization are **training and development programs.** Training and development is needed in part because people, jobs, and organizations are always changing. Mr. Jerry Jasinowski, president of the National Association of Manufacturers, firmly believes that the key to being competitive is the quality of worker education and the proper training of employees. Training and development should begin when individuals join the firm and should continue throughout their careers. It often includes classroom instruction, on-the-job training, and various forms of counseling, such as career planning. Performance appraisal systems may be used to identify training and development needs and to measure progress in the area. PepsiCo is well known for using performance appraisal in this way. **Organizational development (OD),** a special kind of training and development, is *planned and systematic attempts to change the organization, typically to a more behavioral environment.*

Staffing

The formal process of ensuring that the organization has qualified workers available at all levels to meet its short- and long-term business objectives.

Training and development programs

Formal efforts to help employees learn new skills, improve existing skills, or otherwise improve their ability to perform in the organization.

Organizational development (OD)

Planned and systematic attempts to change the organization, typically to a more behavioral environment.

Compensation

The question of what constitutes a fair day's pay has been a major concern of managers for centuries. Employees must be provided with adequate and equitable rewards for their contributions to the achievement of organizational objectives. **Compensation** is *all rewards individuals receive as a result of their employment*. As such, it is more than monetary income. The rewards may include one or any combination of the following:

- *Pay*—the money a person receives for performing a job.
- *Benefits*—economic rewards other than pay, such as paid holidays, medical insurance, and retirement programs.
- *Nonfinancial rewards*—noneconomic rewards, such as job satisfaction and a pleasant working environment.

Senior executives often receive stock options—the right to purchase company stock at a set price during a specified period. The set price is usually near the market price of the company's stock at the time the option is granted. Holders of stock options can wait until the stock goes up and then purchase it at the lower, fixed price.

Health and Safety

Health is *the condition of being physically and emotionally able to perform vital functions normally or properly*. It includes general physical and mental well-being. **Safety** is *freedom from danger*. Most managers believe employees who enjoy good health and who work in a safe environment are more likely to be efficient. Beyond that, however, many companies believe it is their social responsibility to provide safe and healthful working conditions. Federal legislation, especially the Occupational Safety and Health Act (OSHA), has forced all organizations to be concerned with their employees' safety and health.

Employee and Labor Relations

In 1990, unions represented 16.4 percent of all nonfarm workers and the unionized share of the private work force had shrunk to only about 12 percent.[5] According to a study presented at a recent National Bureau of Economic Research conference, union membership in the private sector could drop below 5 percent by the year 2000, if present trends continue.[6] Even so, a business firm is required by law to recognize unions and to bargain with them in good faith if employees vote to be represented by them. According to a Conference Board survey, many managers believe that developing good employee relations systems that eliminate employees' need for a union is a better strategy than seeking sound collective bargaining results.[7]

ETHICAL DILEMMA

You are general superintendent for the Sunbelt Construction Company. You learned a few weeks ago that an attempt was under way to unionize Sunbelt's construction crews. A disgruntled carpenter, Harlan Duhon, was spearheading the organizing attempt. You recently saw Duhon talking to a known professional organizer.

You believe unionization will bring with it demands for higher wages and for costly work rules. And Sunbelt is already on the verge of bankruptcy. The company president, a hard-nosed businessman, has just told you to stop the unionizing attempt, even if you have to "invent a reason" to fire Duhon.

The problem is that you think you understand why Duhon has turned against the company, and you sympathize with him. A few months ago, you had a superintendent's job open and hired a friend for it, although Duhon had applied for the job and you knew he was better qualified. Your friend did not work out, and you had intended to offer the job to Duhon. But if you do so now, it will seem like a bribe to get his cooperation. Besides, he might tell you to "take the job and shove it."

What would you do?

Human Resource Research

Human resource research has become increasingly important, and the trend is likely to continue. The human resource researcher's laboratory is the entire work environment, and studies may involve every HRM function. For instance, a study of recruitment may suggest the types of workers who are most likely to succeed in a particular firm. Or research on job safety may identify the causes of certain work-related accidents.

The causes of problems such as excessive absenteeism and too many grievances may not be readily apparent. When such problems occur and the reasons are not evident, human resource research can fill the knowledge void. In Sweden, the labor force is highly educated and well trained. But the country's high income tax rates reduce the motivational power of pay, even incentive-type pay. Research at Sweden's Volvo auto factory during the 1980s revealed that the Swedes objected to the dinginess and grime of the typical automobile factory. Close supervision and machine pacing of work on the assembly lines were also sore points. So Volvo built more pleasant and colorful factories where teams of workers are allowed to largely manage themselves. Each team assembles a substantial portion of the car, which is moved from area to area. In the new Volvo plants, morale and productivity are better and absenteeism is lower than in the older factories.[8] Human resource research is clearly an important key to developing the most productive and satisfied work force possible.

MANAGEMENT IN PRACTICE: A Skill-Building Exercise

Allen Fender is personnel manager for ML Plastics, a small injection molding company near Wichita, Kansas. ML has been experiencing some worker unrest, and there have been hints of a unionizing attempt. As Allen rounded the corner in the mixing department one day, he heard Judy Morgan reprimanding one of her operators. Several other workers were watching the episode. Allen quickly figured out that the operator had spilled some oil near his machine and had failed to clean it up. The operator was obviously embarrassed and was trying to put oil absorbent on the spill.

But Judy continued to press the issue. She said, "When you risk other people's safety around here, you are risking *your* job."

What should Allen do?

Interrelationships of HRM Functions

The functional areas of HRM are not separate and distinct; they are highly interrelated.[9] Management must recognize that decisions in one area will have impacts on other areas—and they must predict what those impacts are likely to be. For instance, a firm that emphasizes recruiting and training of a sales force while neglecting to provide adequate compensation is wasting time, effort, and money. In addition, if management is truly concerned about employee welfare, it must ensure a safe and healthy work environment. An added benefit may be keeping the firm union-free. An understanding of the interrelationships among the six HRM functional areas is very important.

Laws and Executive Orders Affecting Equal Employment Opportunity

Numerous federal laws and executive orders are concerned with providing equal employment opportunity. In general, the regulations reflect changing public attitudes toward the employment practices of business. The most significant of these laws and one executive order are briefly described in the following sections.

Civil Rights Acts of 1866 and 1871

The Civil Rights Act of 1866 forbids racial discrimination in making and enforcing contracts, which has been taken to include hiring and promotion agreements. This act applies to private employers, unions, and employment agencies. The Civil Rights Act of 1871 invalidates state and local laws that violate civil rights protected by federal law. There is virtually no effective statute of limitations for either of these acts, so cases can be brought under them long after any alleged offense.[10]

Equal Pay Act of 1963

The Equal Pay Act of 1963 (an amendment to the Fair Labor Standards Act of 1938) prohibits discrimination in pay on the basis of sex for certain employees. A 1972 amendment expanded the act to cover employees in executive, administrative, professional, and outside sales force categories, as well as employees in most state and local governments, hospitals, and schools. As evidence that the act has teeth, women have received millions of dollars in compensation for past discrimination in pay policies and practices.

The Equal Pay Act requires equal pay for equal work, but advocates of comparable worth prefer a broader interpretation: equal pay for *comparable* work. **Comparable worth** is *the concept that requires the value for dissimilar jobs to be compared under some form of job evaluation and pay rates to be assigned according to their evaluated worth.* The basic premise behind comparable worth is that jobs traditionally held by women are paid less than those traditionally held by men even though both types may make equal contributions to the organization's objectives.[11]

Comparable worth
The concept that requires the value for dissimilar jobs to be compared under some form of job evaluation and pay rates to be assigned according to their evaluated worth.

Title VII of the Civil Rights Act of 1964— Amended 1972

One law that has had an extensive influence on human resource management is Title VII of the 1964 Civil Rights Act, as amended by the Equal Employment Opportunity Act of 1972. This legislation prohibits discrimination based on race, color, sex, religion, or national origin. Title VII covers employers in industries affecting interstate commerce that have fifteen or more employees for at least twenty calendar weeks in the year in which a charge is filed or the year preceding the filing of a charge. Included in the definition of employers are state and local governments, schools, colleges, unions, and employment agencies. The act created the Equal Employment Opportunity Commission (EEOC), which is responsible for its enforcement.

Age Discrimination in Employment Act of 1967— Amended in 1978 and 1986

As originally enacted, the Age Discrimination in Employment Act (ADEA) prohibited employers from discriminating against individuals who were at least forty but less than sixty-five years old. The 1978 amendment changed the upper age limit to seventy. On October 31, 1986, President Reagan signed into law an amendment to the ADEA making it illegal for employers to discriminate against anyone over the age of forty because of age. The latest amendment prohibits employers from firing anyone on the basis of age, with no maximum age limit.[12] The act pertains to employers that have twenty or more employees for twenty or more calendar weeks in either the current or the preceding calendar year. It also applies to unions of twenty-five or more members, employment agencies, and federal, state, and local government units. The EEOC is charged with administering the act.

Rehabilitation Act of 1973

The Rehabilitation Act of 1973 prohibits discrimination in employment on the basis of present or previous handicaps. The act applies to contractors, subcontractors, and other organizations that have a federal contract or grant in excess of $2,500. Individuals are considered handicapped if they have a physical or mental impairment that substantially limits one or more major life activities. An employer is required to have an affirmative action program if it has a contract, subcontract, or grant that exceeds $50,000 or if it has fifty or more employees. The employer must show it is making reasonable accommodations in hiring and promoting handicapped persons.

Pregnancy Discrimination Act of 1978

Passed as an amendment to Title VII of the Civil Rights Act, the Pregnancy Discrimination Act extends the protection of that law to pregnancy, childbirth, and related medical conditions. A woman is protected against such penalties as being fired or being refused a job or promotion merely because she is pregnant or has had an abortion. Also, she usually cannot be forced to take a leave of absence solely on the basis of her pregnancy. And after pregnancy-related leave, she must be allowed to return to work under the same rules that govern other employees who have been on disability leave.

The same principle applies in the benefits area, including disability benefits, sick leave, and health insurance. A woman unable to work for pregnancy-related reasons is entitled to disability benefits or sick leave on the same basis as employees unable to work for other medical reasons. Also, any health insurance must cover expenses for pregnancy-related conditions on the same basis as expenses for other medical conditions. However, health insurance for expenses arising from an abortion is not required, except where the life of the mother would be endangered if the fetus were carried to term or where medical complications have arisen from an abortion.

Immigration Reform and Control Act of 1986

The Immigration Reform and Control Act (IRCA) of 1986 establishes criminal and civil sanctions against employers who hire an unauthorized alien if they know of the person's status. It requires employers to verify employment authorization and identity. Violators are subject to fines of $250 to $2,000 per worker for the first offense, $2,000 to $5,000 for the second offense, and $3,000 to $10,000 for the third offense. In addition, employers that fail to comply with the recordkeeping provisions of the law are subject to penalties of $100 to $1,000 for each individual they fail to document, even if the individual is legally entitled to be employed. Further, IRCA lowers the threshold for coverage under the Civil Rights Act of 1964, as amended, to employers with four (from fifteen) employees if discrimination on the basis of national origin is involved.[13]

The Americans with Disabilities Act (ADA)

Passed in 1990, the ADA prohibits discrimination against "qualified individuals with disabilities." Persons discriminated against because they have a known association or relationship with a disabled individual also are protected. The ADA defines an "individual with a disability" as a person who has a physical or mental impairment that substantially limits one or more major life activities, a record of such an impairment, or is regarded as having such an impairment. The ADA prohibits discrimination in all employment practices, including job application procedures, hiring, firing, advancement, compensation, training, and other terms, conditions, and privileges of employment. It applies to recruitment, advertising, tenure, layoff, leave, fringe benefits, and all other employment-related activities.

Effective July 1992, the employment provisions apply to private employers, state and local governments, employment agencies, labor unions, and employers with 25 or more employees. Employers with 15 or more employees will be included beginning July 26, 1994.[14] The full impact of this new law is yet to be determined; some believe that obesity may emerge as a life-style that is protected under the act.[15]

Civil Rights Act (CRA) of 1991

The CRA of 1991 amended the Civil Rights Act of 1964 and had the following purposes:

1. To provide appropriate remedies for intentional discrimination and unlawful harassment in the workplace.
2. To codify the concepts of "business necessity" and "job related" pronounced by the Supreme Court in Griggs v. Duke Power Co., and in the other Supreme Court decisions prior to Wards Cove Packing Co. v. Atonio.
3. To confirm statutory authority and provide statutory guidelines for the adjudication of disparate impacts under Title VII of the Civil Rights Act of 1964.
4. To respond to recent decisions of the Supreme Court by expanding the scope of relevant civil rights statutes in order to provide adequate protection to victims of discrimination.

Under this Act, a complaining party may recover punitive damages if the complaining party demonstrates that the company engaged in a discriminatory practice with malice or with reckless indifference to the law. However, the following limits were placed on the amount of the award:

1. Between 15 and 100 employees—$50,000
2. Between 101 and 200 employees—$100,000
3. Between 201 and 500 employees—$200,000
4. Greater than 500 employees—$300,000

In each case, employees must be with the firm for 20 or more calendar weeks in the current or preceding calendar year.

With regard to burden of proof in disparate impact cases, an unlawful employment practice passed on disparate impact is established under this title only if a complaining party demonstrates that a respondent uses a particular employment practice that causes a disparate impact on the basis of race, color, religion, sex, or national origin and the company fails to demonstrate that the challenged practice is job related for the position in question and consistent with business necessity. The Act also extends the coverage of the Civil Rights Act of 1964 to extraterritorial employment. However, the Act does not apply to United States companies operating in another country if it would violate the law of the foreign country. Further, the Act reverses the following Supreme Court decisions: Patterson v. McLean Credit Union, Martin v. Wilks, and Wards Cove Packing Co. v. Atonio.

The Act mandates the establishment of the Equal Employment Opportunity Commission's Technical Assistance Training Institute (TATI) and enhances Title VII's provisions regarding education and outreach. The TATI provides technical assistance and training regarding the laws and regulations enforced by the Commission. The Commission is charged with carrying out educational and outreach activities (including dissemination of information in languages other than English) targeted to individuals who historically have been victims of discrimination and have not been equitably served by the Commission. The Act also extends the nondiscrimination principles to Congress and other government agencies such as the General Accounting Office and the Government Printing Office.

Also included in the CRA of 1991 is the Glass Ceiling Act of 1991. The purpose of this Act is to establish a Glass Ceiling Commission to study: the manner in which businesses fill management and decision-making positions, the developmental and skill-enhancing practices used to foster the necessary qualifications for advancement into such positions, and the compensation programs and reward structures currently utilized in the workplace. It also established an annual award for excellence in promoting a more diverse skilled work force at the management and decision-making levels in business.

Glass Ceiling

In a recent study, it was determined that the proportion of women managers has more than doubled since 1975 and is currently at 40 percent. However, the number of women who hold top management positions is less than three percent.[16] A phrase that has begun to be used in recent years is the "glass ceiling," meaning the invisible barrier in organizations which prevents many women from achieving top-level management positions. Companies are discovering that the courts are being forceful in eliminating such barriers. In one instance, a highly rated female supervisor was denied a promotion because her boss said it would be easier for employees to work with a man who was their "chum." The employer reasoned that when it came to working long hours, the staff would work better with the male worker who was promoted. The courts disagreed and called this action unlawful discrimination.[17] It is expected that this area will be vigorously pursued in the future.

Executive Order 11246, as Amended by Executive Order 11375

Executive Orders

Directives issued by the President that have the force and effect of laws enacted by Congress.

Affirmative action

Performance required to ensure that applicants are employed, and that employees are treated appropriately during employment, without regard to race, creed, color, or national origin.

Executive Orders are *directives issued by the President that have the force and effect of laws enacted by Congress.* On September 24, 1965, President Lyndon B. Johnson signed Executive Order 11246. This order made it the policy of the government of the United States to provide equal opportunity in federal employment for all qualified persons. It prohibits discrimination in employment because of race, creed, color, or national origin. It also requires promoting the full realization of equal employment opportunity through a positive, continuing program in each executive department and agency. The policy of equal opportunity applies to every aspect of federal employment policy and practice.

A major provision of Executive Order 11246 is that every executive department and agency that administers a program involving federal financial assistance will require adherence to a policy of nondiscrimination in employment as a condition for the approval of grants, contracts, loans, insurance, and guarantees. During the performance of a contract, contractors agree not to discriminate in employment because of race, creed, color, or national origin. **Affirmative action,** which is a major part of Executive Order 11246, is *performance required to ensure that applicants are employed,*

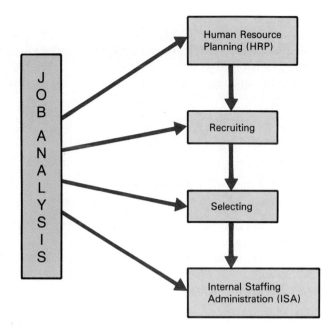

FIGURE 9–2

The Staffing Function

and that employees are treated appropriately during employment, without regard to race, creed, color, or national origin. The human resource practices covered relate to employment, upgrading, demotion, transfer, recruitment and recruitment advertising, layoffs and firings, rates of pay and other forms of compensation, and selection for training, including apprenticeships. In 1968, Executive Order 11246 was amended by Executive Order 11375, which changed the word *creed* to *religion* and added sexual discrimination to the other prohibited items.

The Staffing Process

Staffing, defined earlier in the chapter, is a major component of human resource management. Staffing is concerned not only with getting people but also with keeping them. There are several components of the staffing process, each closely linked to the others. Figure 9–2 illustrates these basic components.

Job Analysis

The systematic process of determining the skills and knowledge required for performing jobs in the organization is **job analysis.**[18] Facts about the job are gathered, recorded, and analyzed. Areas of interest here include job duties, working conditions, and relationships to other jobs. Referring again to Figure 9–2, notice that job analysis affects all of the components of staffing. It is also vital to the other human resource management functions, as Boeing Company discovered.

In order to help assure quality, Boeing carried out job analyses for its aircraft plant jobs. Using the information it obtained, the company modified its training program.

Job analysis

The systematic process of determining the skills and knowledge required for performing jobs in the organization.

For example, new assembly-line workers were required to take blueprint-reading classes and to practice riveting and drilling before starting work. Boeing also increased its emphasis on preemployment training for serious job candidates at local vocational-technical schools.[19]

Several techniques may be used in conducting job analyses. Among them are the following:

- Observing the work.
- Interviewing workers and supervisors.
- Having workers and their supervisors complete questionnaires.
- Having workers and their supervisors keep job diaries.
- Having job information evaluated by experts.

Job description

A document that describes the tasks and responsibilities of a job and its relationships to other jobs.

Information obtained through job analyses is used in developing job descriptions. The **job description** is *a document that describes the tasks and responsibilities of a job and its relationships to other jobs.* Job descriptions should be both relevant and accurate.[20] They should clearly answer the questions: What is to be done? When? Where? And how? Among the items often included in a job description are the following:

- Major duties.
- Percentage of time devoted to each duty.
- Performance standards.
- Working conditions.
- Possible hazards.
- Number of persons working on each job.
- Reporting relationships.
- Machines and equipment used.

Job specification

A statement of the minimum acceptable qualifications a person should possess to perform a particular job.

Another item often included in the job description is the **job specification**—*a statement of the minimum acceptable qualifications a person should possess to perform a particular job.* Job specifications may include standards for education, experience, physical abilities, and, sometimes, personality.

Human Resource Planning

Human resource planning (HRP)

The developing of strategies and tactics to ensure that the required numbers of employees with the required skills are on the job when they are needed.

The developing of strategies and tactics to ensure that the required numbers of employees with the required skills are on the job when they are needed is **human resource planning (HRP).** There is a growing mismatch between emerging jobs and the people available to fill them. The labor pool is shrinking and changing as American companies try to cope with rapid technological change and increasing globalization of the economy.[21]

There are two main aspects to human resource planning: requirements and availability. Forecasting human resource requirements involves determining the numbers of employees needed at each location and the qualifications they must have. Availability refers to both internal sources (current employees) and external sources (the labor market). If a mismatch between requirements and availability is projected, action should be taken right away. Any surplus may be eliminated through restricted hiring, reduced hours, early retirement, or layoffs. Shortages can be prevented through any combination of training and transferring present employees and hiring new ones.

Human resource planning should have the following objectives, among others:

- To avoid or correct human resource management problems before they become serious.

- To forecast recruitment needs, in terms of both the numbers of employees required and the skills they should have.

- To identify and evaluate sources of new employees and to focus recruitment efforts on the best sources.

- To identify replacements, from inside or outside the organization, for key managers and workers.

- To integrate personnel plans with financial plans and forecasts.

As mentioned earlier, employment at Boeing jumped 83 percent, to 155,000, in only seven years. The company's human resource planners were able to forecast the numbers of people Boeing would need with some accuracy. But many of the new recruits lacked needed skills, and plans either were inadequate or were not made early enough to correct this problem. So a shortage of qualified workers continued to plague Boeing as it faced an increasing backlog of orders extending to 1995.

Recruitment

The process of attracting individuals—in sufficient numbers and with appropriate qualifications—and encouraging them to apply for jobs with the organization is **recruitment.**[22] In most large organizations, this process begins with an employment requisition. An **employment requisition** is *a form issued to activate the recruitment process, typically including such information as the job title, starting date, and pay scale and a brief summary of principal duties.* Recruitment can range from locating qualified individuals within the firm to a sophisticated and extensive search for a new president.

The usual means of internal recruiting is through the use of a job bidding and posting system. The purpose of job posting is to communicate the fact that job openings exist. Job bidding permits individuals in the organization who believe they possess the required qualifications to apply (bid) for the job. At PepsiCo, for example, an attempt is made to fill every job above the entry level from within. So job posting and bidding is an integral part of PepsiCo's recruitment program. Internal recruitment, or promotion from within, is an important source of workers for positions above the entry level. Here are several potential advantages of promotion from within:

1. It may improve morale.

2. It may improve the quality of selection, since the strengths and weaknesses of internal applicants are usually better known than those of external ones.

3. It may motivate employees to prepare for more responsible positions.

Recruitment

The process of attracting individuals—in sufficient numbers and with appropriate qualifications—and encouraging them to apply for jobs with the organization.

Employment requisition

A form issued to activate the recruitment process, typically including such information as the job title, starting date, and pay scale and a brief summary of principal duties.

4. It may allow the attraction of better external applicants, since it ensures better promotion prospects.

5. It may assure that existing employees are more fully utilized.

A firm policy of promotion from within can also have its disadvantages. Here are two that are frequently mentioned:

1. An adequate supply of qualified applicants may not be available inside the organization.

2. Internal sources may lead to the inbreeding of ideas. (That is, current employees may lack new ideas on how to do a job more effectively.)

Some well-known companies that practice promotion from within are Delta Airlines, Lincoln Electric, IBM, and Hewlett-Packard.

Even if a company is committed to promotion from within, external recruitment is required just to maintain a stable work force. It is particularly necessary when organizations change and grow. Common sources of new employees include competitors, other business firms and government agencies, high schools, vocational schools, community colleges, other colleges and universities, and pools of applicants at state employment offices. Recruiting often involves ads in newspapers and other media, employment agencies, recruiters, and employee referrals. The recruiter must first determine where the right kind of applicants are likely to be found and then select the best method to get them to apply.

The Selection Process

Selection

Determining which individual to hire for a particular job.

Of course, recruitment at any company is designed to attract the individuals who are most capable of meeting the requirements of the job. **Selection** is *determining which individual to hire for a particular job.* Companies with guaranteed employment and promotion from within, such as Delta Airlines, must pay special attention to selecting good employees.

Human Resource Management at Delta

Delta Airlines has earned respect inside and outside its industry, especially in the area of human resource management. In the late eighties, Delta had the smallest number of passenger complaints to the Federal Aviation Administration of any major airline. As the nineties began, yearly pay at Delta averaged over $50,000 per employee, higher than for any competitor. At this time, Delta serves 132 domestic and 23 international cities with 392 planes.

The airline industry had been in a state of turmoil throughout the 1980s. A major recession early in the decade lasted for several years. The air traffic controllers' strike, which occurred in 1981, placed a great strain on the air traffic system. At the same time, the airline industry was deregulated, resulting in an intensification of competition. Braniff and Continental failed, throwing thousands out of work. Meanwhile, Delta's employees were optimistically buying the company its first Boeing 767 aircraft. They named the plane *Spirit of Delta.*

When other major airlines were selling off planes to survive, Delta was modernizing its fleet with new Boeing 737s, 757s, and 767s. Delta was hiring pilots, expanding its routes, and adding to its previous orders for 74 new planes.

A top-to-bottom open-door policy enables Delta employees to air any grievances. Flexibility in work assignments—a ticket agent willingly shifts to baggage handling, for example—helps increase productivity. For many years, nonunion Delta workers have selected their own lead mechanics and quality control supervisors. In general, Delta practices decentralized management, but the human resource function is tightly controlled from Atlanta. For example, firing someone requires central office approval. Guaranteed employment and a promotion from within policy are credited with giving employees a feeling of security. All of the company's top managers have been with the company for over two decades. [23]

• •

The selection process is shown in Figure 9–3. Its elements are discussed in the sections that follow.

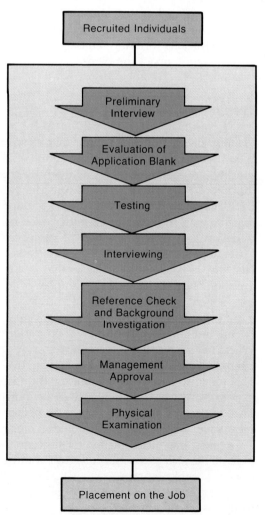

FIGURE 9–3

The Selection Process

Preliminary Interview

Preliminary interview

The type of interview used to eliminate any obviously unqualified job applicants.

The type of interview used to eliminate any obviously unqualified job applicants is the **preliminary interview.** This type of interview may be conducted before or after an application form is completed. Reasons for elimination may include excessive salary requirements, inadequate training or education, or lack of job-related experience.

Evaluation of Application Blank

The next step in the selection process is to evaluate each applicant on the basis of the completed application. The specific type of information requested in an application blank may vary from firm to firm and by positions within the organization. Separate sections of an application typically relate to education, work experience, and other job-related information.

An application blank must supply the firm's information needs while meeting legal requirements. Only questions that have job relevance should be included. Questions related to sex, national origin, religion, color, and race should not be asked. Questions regarding criminal convictions should be considered only if job-related. For jobs requiring licenses, such as pilot positions at Delta, the application blank may ask about the license.

Testing

Traditionally, testing was an integral component of the selection process. Tests have been used to screen applicants in terms of skills, abilities, aptitudes, interests, personality, and attitudes. The Civil Rights Act and various federal court rulings have discouraged the use of selection tests, however. For instance, in the 1973 *Griggs v. Duke Power Company* decision, the U.S. Supreme Court ruled that preemployment requirements, including tests, must be job-related. It has proved to be very difficult to design tests consisting totally of job-related items.

Certain conditions should be met if tests are to be used for employee selection. First, the tests should be reliable; that is, they should provide consistent results. If a person takes the same test a number of times, scores should be similar. Second, tests should be valid; they should measure what they are designed to measure. If a test is designed to predict job performance, prospective employees who score well on the test should prove to be good performers. Third, tests should be objective. When different scorers interpreting the results of the same test arrive at similar interpretations, the test is said to be objective. Finally, tests should be standardized. This requires them to be administered under standard conditions to a large group of persons who are representative of the individuals for whom the tests are intended. The purpose of standardization is to obtain norms, so specific test scores will be meaningful when compared to other scores in the group.

The most important criterion for selection tests is that they be valid. If a test cannot indicate the ability to perform the job, it must not be used. Validity has always been a proper concern of organizations that use tests. This concern is especially important today, for economic as well as social reasons. Increasing competition demands that all management activities be carried out efficiently and directed toward productivity enhancement. Testing, if it is done, should help achieve the most efficient matching of applicants with jobs. From a social standpoint, testing that is job-related serves the objective of equal employment opportunity, to which our society is increasingly committed. So it is vital that organizations have a thoughtful process for validating any selection tests they employ.

Drug Testing

A major survey recently found that 23 percent of the responding companies require some type of substance abuse testing as a condition of employment. In addition, 11 percent are considering requiring testing. Drug testing appears to be most common in utility, transportation, and communication firms, with 73 percent of these organizations requiring or considering tests. Overall, more than one-third of the organizations surveyed are in this category.[24]

In two cases, the U.S. Supreme Court upheld drug testing required by federal agencies. These cases stemmed from Fourth Amendment challenges.[25] Although these cases did not apply directly to private sector employers, the decisions are nevertheless important. First, it can be anticipated that drug testing conducted by private sector employers under similar circumstances will be upheld. If drug testing can pass rigorous Fourth Amendment scrutiny, it should also be defensible under normal invasion-of-privacy claims. In addition, federal rules, regulations, and programs tend to become models for private sector behavior.[26]

Interviewing

The interview is the most widely used method of assessing the qualifications of job applicants, and many interviewers consider it to be highly valid. The subjective judgments made during employment interviews, however, may reduce their reliability. And giving too much weight to interview results certainly risks discrimination against persons who are unlike the interviewers. However, interviews can accomplish the following purposes:

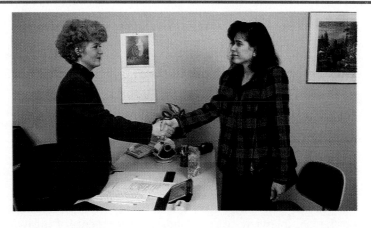

The interview is the most widely used method of assessing job applicants. But giving too much weight to subjective interview results risks discrimination against persons who are unlike the interviewer.

Source: © Frank Sitemann 1990

1. Allow interviewers to get information not included on the application forms and to clarify any questionable information.
2. Allow applicants to obtain additional information about the prospective employer and job.
3. Allow interviewers to transmit a favorable impression of the organization to applicants.
4. Allow applicants to "sell" themselves to the interviewer.

Interviews are often classified according to how structured they are. Probing, open-ended questions are asked in what are called *nondirective interviews*. Usually, the interviewers who use the nondirective technique are highly trained because it requires a subjective appraisal of the job candidate. The *patterned interview*, on the other hand, consists of standardized questions that are asked of all applicants for certain jobs. Standardization permits easy comparison of candidates. It also helps in achieving, and proving, validity. Of course, no interview can be completely nondirective, and it is hard to conceive of one that is totally patterned.

Interviews also differ according to how many interviewers and applicants are involved. Normally, job applicants meet with interviewers one-on-one. But in the *group interview*, several applicants are questioned together by one or more interviewers. For important jobs, especially those of a political nature, the *board interview* may be used. Here, one or more candidates are quizzed by several interviewers, often members of a government board or committee.

Most interviewers try to place interviewees at ease. But the opposite is true in the *stress interview*. Here, the applicant is intentionally placed on the defensive by being criticized or ridiculed. The purpose is to observe the interviewee's reaction to stress and tension. This type of interview may be used in hiring for intelligence-type positions (for example, with the Central Intelligence Agency or the Federal Bureau of Investigation) or, less commonly, for certain sales or management jobs.

As mentioned earlier, the interview is the most widely used element in the selection process. It is also an important part of promotion decisions. It is therefore important that interviewing be done in a sound way. Here are some guidelines for interviewers:

1. *Plan for the interview.* Review applications thoroughly, along with job specifications and descriptions. Make notes of areas to be discussed or write specific questions to be asked.
2. *Create a good climate for the interview.* Make sure the space is comfortable and private. Unless there are specific reasons to do otherwise, try to establish good rapport with the interviewee.
3. *Allow sufficient time.* Set aside an adequate block of time and arrange not to be interrupted by telephone calls or visits.
4. *Conduct an objective-oriented interview.* Seek the information needed to assist in the employment decision.
5. *Avoid certain types of questions.* Try not to ask leading questions or questions that may imply discrimination.
6. *Seek answers to all questions and check for inconsistencies.*
7. *Record the results of the interview immediately on completion.*[27]

Over the years, many have questioned whether interview results predict success on the job. Interviews can certainly be instruments of unlawful discrimination. For these reasons, among others, they have received close scrutiny by the EEOC in recent years. Such attention has led to an increase in the use of patterned interviews. It is easier to control the content of patterned interviews than of nondirective ones to prevent bias. Patterned interviews are also easier to defend when they are criticized, since their content can be objectively determined. Of course, this does not necessarily mean patterned interviews are better in predicting job success; they are just safer.

Reference Check and Background Investigation

Once applicants successfully clear the interview hurdle, reference checks and background investigations are often conducted. The reference check has a major weakness as a screening device: Job applicants normally provide their own references, often selected because they are likely to make favorable comments about the applicant. A provision of the Federal Privacy Act of 1974 further increases the likelihood of bias in comments by references. That act gives employees of the federal government the right to see those comments, although the right may be waived.

Background investigations may be similarly unreliable, unless done carefully and at great expense. For example, a prime source of background information is the applicant's previous employers. But the only information many organizations are willing to provide about former employees is dates of employment and salary ranges. Some require the former employees' written authorization to do even this. Further, if comments are provided, they may represent a "whitewash job," because negative remarks are often avoided, even for employees who were fired.[28]

Many companies dispense with reference checks because they are concerned that the practice might be discriminatory or be perceived as an invasion of privacy. A study conducted by the National Consumers League in 1990 found that about 80 percent of the job-seeker respondents stated that the firms they wanted to join intruded into their private lives by asking inappropriate questions.[29]

Sometimes, the expense of doing a thorough background investigation is justified. It has been found that between 7 and 10 percent of job applicants are not what they present themselves to be.[30] One area of particular concern is credentials fraud, which has increased in recent years. Professors, stockbrokers, and even doctors have claimed credentials they did not have in attempting to get a new position.[31]

The polygraph, or lie detector, test has often been used in efforts to verify background information. However, the validity of such tests is questionable. In 1988, the Employee Polygraph Protection Act was passed. This act makes it unlawful for any employer engaged in or affecting interstate commerce to test job applicants using the polygraph.

Negligent Hiring and Retention

Negligent hiring is one of the hottest issues in current HRM law. An employer can be held responsible for an employee's unlawful acts if it does not reasonably investigate an employee's background, and then assigns the person to a position where he or she can inflict harm. A firm can't go overboard with the investigation, however, since invasion of privacy is a possibility. Negligent retention involves keeping dangerous workers on the payroll.

In the last ten years, employers have begun to be held responsible for actions outside the scope of the employee's duties. For example, if an employer hired a manager of an apartment complex without investigating the person's background and the individual later assaulted a tenant, the employer could be held responsible for the action if it were discovered that the manager had a history of assault. Employers are required by law to provide employees a safe place to work. This duty has been extended to providing safe employees because the courts have reasoned that a dangerous worker is comparable to a defective machine.

Court award outcomes in negligent-hiring cases are in the hundreds of thousands of dollars. In addition, they are likely to be upheld on appeal. The primary consideration in negligent hiring is whether the risk of harm from a dangerous employee was reasonably foreseeable. The nature of the job also has a critical bearing on the employer's obligation. If the job gives employees access to homes or property, as in the case of meter readers, security guards, or exterminators, the hiring firm may be found to have an obligation to make a reasonable investigation into the person's background. Industries that have a greater responsibility for safe hiring include landlord-tenant relationships, common carriers, hospitals and other patient-care facilities, and taxi services.[32]

"A case in point is a Fort Worth cab company. One of its drivers picked up a young mother and her daughters at a bus station, took them to a deserted area where he raped and robbed the mother. The young woman sued the cab company and won a judgment of $4,500,000 for 'negligent hiring.'"[33] The Texas Supreme Court determined a reasonable background investigation would have made it quite clear that the cab driver should not have been hired. He had previously been convicted of robbery and forgery and, before that, had been arrested and charged with using a hammer to assault a woman. To avoid cases of this sort, employers should consider how employees are exposed to customers. They should also make reasonable background investigations and keep written records of them.[34]

Management Approval

In large organizations, the human resource, or personnel, department performs many of the selection functions. However, the final hiring decision is usually reserved for the person who will be the immediate superior of the new employee. This person normally reviews all the available information about the applicant and conducts a final interview. Sometimes, the decision is made on the spot and communicated to the applicant. At other times, the superior consults with the personnel department or with other managers before deciding.

Physical Examination

Typically, job offers are contingent on the applicant's passing a physical examination. Physicals screen out individuals who have contagious diseases. They may also help spot physical deficiencies that can limit the person's ability to do the work. An often ignored purpose of a physical examination is to develop a record of the employee's condition at the time of employment. This can protect the company and its insurer against claims for previously existing medical conditions.

Unwelcome sexual advances, requests for sexual favors, and other verbal or physical conduct of a sexual nature that occur under any of the following situations:

1. When submission to such contact is made either explicitly or implicitly a term or condition of an individual's employment.
2. When submission to or rejection of such conduct by an individual is used as the basis for employment decisions affecting such individual.
3. When such conduct has the purpose or effect of unreasonably interfering with an individual's work performance or creating an intimidating, hostile, or offensive working environment.

TABLE 9–1

EEOC Definition of Sexual Harassment

Sexual Harassment

In a recent survey, 42 percent of the women and 15 percent of the men reported that they had been sexually harassed on the job.[35] Today, one of the most fervently pursued civil rights issues relates to sexual harassment.[36] As we previously mentioned, Title VII of the Civil Rights Act generally prohibits discrimination on the basis of gender in employment. The EEOC has also issued interpretative guidelines which state that employers have an affirmative duty to maintain a workplace free from sexual harassment. The Office of Federal Contract Compliance Programs has similar guidelines. Managers in both for-profit and not-for-profit organizations should be particularly alert to the issue of sexual harassment, as the EEOC believes that sexual harassment continues to be a widespread problem. Table 9–1 contains the EEOC's definition of sexual harassment.

According to the guidelines, employers are totally liable for the acts of their supervisors, regardless of whether the employer is aware of the sexual harassment act. Where co-workers are concerned, the employer is responsible for such acts if the employer knew, or should have known, about them. The employer is not responsible if it can show that it took immediate and appropriate corrective action as soon as it learned of the problem.

Another important aspect of these guidelines is that employers may be liable for acts committed by nonemployees in the workplace if the employer knew, or should have known, of the conduct and failed to take appropriate action. Firms are responsible for developing programs to prevent sexual harassment in the workplace. They must also investigate all formal and informal complaints alleging sexual harassment. After investigating, a firm must take immediate and appropriate action to correct the situation.[37] Failure to do so constitutes a violation of Title VII, as interpreted by the EEOC.[38]

There have been numerous sexual harassment court cases. In *Miller v. Bank of America*, a U.S. Circuit Court of Appeals held an employer liable for the sexually harrassing acts of its supervisors, even though the company had a policy prohibiting such conduct and even though the victim did not formally notify the employer of the problem. Another U.S. Circuit Court of Appeals ruled that sexual harassment, in and of itself, is a violation of Title VII. The court ruled that the law does not require the victim to prove that she resisted harassment and was penalized for that resistance. The first sexual harassment case to reach the U.S. Supreme Court was the June 1986 case of *Meritor Savings Bank v. Vinson*. The Vinson decision was the first time the Supreme Court recognized that Title VII could be used for offensive environment claims.[39]

Internal Staffing Administration

Staffing encompasses much more than planning, recruitment, and selection. It is also concerned with employees after they are hired. Internal staffing administration (ISA) involves providing advice and assistance in the following areas:

- Employee orientation.
- Employee assistance programs.
- Performance appraisal.
- Employee status changes, such as promotions, transfers, demotions, resignations, discharges, outplacements, layoffs, and retirements.

Employee Orientation

Employee orientation

The formal process of helping new employees adjust to the organization, job, and work group.

New workers bring with them fears and anxieties about the job. They worry about their ability to handle the work or whether they will be accepted by their co-workers. They are also anxious to learn as much as possible about their employer. **Employee orientation** is *the formal process of helping new employees adjust to the organization, job, and work group.* It has three main purposes:

1. To provide specific information.
2. To ease the adjustment process.
3. To enhance new employees' impression of the organization.

The specific information an employee needs first usually relates to the job. How is the job to be done? What results are expected? How is the job related to others? It is important that the new hire become productive as rapidly as possible. And although being thrown into a job to sink or swim may build character, it probably does not build productivity. Therefore, job-related information should be provided early and in as specific terms as possible. In addition, reporting relationships need to be clear. Orientation also involves a great deal of information only indirectly related to the job. Where is the infirmary? How do benefit programs work? What are the rules and regulations of employment? Many such questions are often answered in an employee handbook.

The second concern in orientation is adjustment. The new hire's relationship to the formal organization can be easily and quickly spelled out. But relationships with the informal organization must be worked out over time. The first days on a new job are thus often lonely and anxious. To make matters worse, new employees are not always greeted with open arms. There may be a certain amount of hazing and kidding by "old hands." Such problems can hurt a new employee's productivity or even cause the person to quit. To reduce the anxiety new employees may have, attempts should be made to help them build informal relationships. A sympathetic and knowledgeable superior can speed this process. Perhaps a peer will accept responsibility for showing the new person the ropes. But above all, the need to integrate new employees into the social structure of the organization should be taken seriously.

The final purpose of orientation is to enhance the impression the new employee has of the organization and its work. The flow of information to job applicants is somewhat controlled during the hiring process. But as an insider, the employee is able to see the organization's bad points. It is important to continue the selling job that started with recruitment.

Effective orientation is particularly important for employees with disabilities. There is no reason to think these employees are less adaptable than others, but disabilities often make the adaptation process somewhat different. For example, a person with a hearing loss may not be able to understand all that is said in a group presentation. For this person especially, thorough written orientation material or individual briefings may be appropriate. In addition, other employees may not know how to act around a disabled person. Managers can lead the way here. No one should act as if the disability does not exist. Also, it is important to remember that most workers with disabilities want to be as independent as possible. Such a desire should be respected. A manager may have to stop other employees from "helping" the person. A good way to handle questions about whether to do this or that for a person with disabilities is just to ask the person. Insofar as possible, disabled people should be treated like everyone else. Employee assistance programs are an important way of dealing with special needs of disabled employees.[40]

Employee Assistance Programs

A coordinated effort by an organization to help employees deal with special problems and needs is an **employee assistance program.** The kinds of problems specifically covered by the program may include stress and burnout, alcohol and drug abuse, and depression. AIDS (acquired immune deficiency syndrome) is an increasingly serious problem for employers, and some assistance programs are being expanded to deal with this issue. Among the needs these programs often address are those for child care and for transportation to and from work. There are at least ten thousand employee assistance programs in the United States, and 80 percent of the *Fortune* 500 firms have them.[41]

Most programs focus on problems related to substance abuse, emotional problems, and personal situations that produce emotional stress. Such problems are a proper concern of employers because they may affect productivity as well as employee well-being.[42] A particular program may provide for in-house professional counselors or for the referral of employees to an appropriate outside agency or professional. Typically, most or all of the costs are borne by the employer, up to a predetermined amount. The trend is toward providing the same consideration for people with emotional problems as for those with physical illnesses.

Employee assistance programs should actively promote health improvement and disease prevention. Treatment only after a problem affects productivity is the common practice. But there is evidence that preventing alcohol and drug abuse, at least, may be more cost-effective than treatment.[43]

An executive of a national benefits consulting firm states that investments in employee assistance programs are repaid many times over, through increased productivity and decreased health-care claims. Others report benefits in the form of reduced absenteeism, fewer workers' compensation claims, and fewer accidents.[44]

Employee assistance program

A coordinated effort by an organization to help employees deal with special problems and needs.

Performance Appraisal

Performance appraisal

The formal and systematic measurement and evaluation of job performance.

The formal and systematic measurement and evaluation of job performance is **performance appraisal.** It involves observing workers' behavior and measuring that behavior in accordance with certain standards. Performance appraisal is central to the staffing function. It provides feedback needed to evaluate the effectiveness of recruitment and selection. It also identifies individuals who are trainable and those who already have the skills to meet current and future job requirements.

However, the main contribution of the performance appraisal process may be in helping to create work environments in which managers and subordinates set objectives, monitor results, and formally evaluate success against predetermined standards. A good performance appraisal process ensures improved communication throughout the organization; however, it is vital that managers realize employee evaluation is a continuous process rather than an event that happens once a year.[45]

MANAGEMENT IN PRACTICE: A Skill-Building Exercise

"There, at last it's finished," thought Tom Baker, as he laid aside the last of twelve performance appraisal forms. It had been a busy week for Tom, who supervised a road maintenance crew for the Georgia Department of Highways.

The governor, in passing through Tom's district a few days earlier, had complained to the area superintendent that repairs were needed on several of the highways. Because of this, the superintendent assigned Tom's crew an unusually heavy workload. In addition, Tom received a call from the personnel office that week telling him that the performance appraisals were late. Tom explained his predicament, but the personnel specialist insisted that the forms be completed right away.

Looking over the appraisals again, Tom thought about several of the workers. The performance appraisal form had places for marking quantity of work, quality of work, and cooperativeness. For each characteristic, the worker could be graded outstanding, good, average, below average, or unsatisfactory. Since Tom's crew had completed all of the extra work assigned for that week, he marked every worker outstanding in quantity of work. He marked Joe Blum average in cooperativeness because Joe had questioned one of his decisions that week. Tom had decided to patch a pothole in one of the roads, and Joe thought the small section of road surface ought to be broken out and replaced. Tom didn't include this in the remarks section of the form, though. As a matter of fact, he wrote no remarks on any of the forms.

Tom felt a twinge of guilt as he thought about Roger Short. He knew that Roger had been sloughing off and the other workers had been carrying him for quite some time. He also knew that Roger would be upset if he found that he had been marked lower than the other workers. So he marked Roger the same to avoid a confrontation. "Anyway," Tom thought, "these things are a pain in the neck, and I really shouldn't have to bother with them."

As Tom folded up the performance appraisals and put them in the envelope for mailing, he smiled. He was glad he would not have to think about performance appraisals for another six months.

What weaknesses do you see in Tom's performance appraisals?

Employee Status Changes

Few employees remain in the same job, with the same company, throughout a career. Most people experience one or more of the following types of status changes:

- *Promotion*—advancement to a more responsible job in the organization.
- *Lateral move*—transfer to another job at the same level of responsibility.
- *Demotion*—assignment within the organization to a job with less responsibility.
- *Resignation*—voluntary termination of employment initiated by the employee.
- *Discharge*—involuntary termination of employment initiated by the employer.
- *Outplacement*—placement of a person in another company with the active assistance of the former employer.
- *Layoff*—involuntary termination of employment that is viewed as temporary.
- *Retirement*—withdrawal from active employment with a certain organization, usually with some form of pension.
- *Reduction in force*—systematic process of reducing the size of the work force, initiated by the employer.

To ensure the highest level of productivity, better-managed firms strive to achieve a proper match between individuals and jobs. Careless or random selection of employees can seriously impair the ultimate ability of the company to survive. A series of court cases in the late 1980s showed that careless or random firing can also have its down side.

· ·

Recently, Jury Verdict Research, Inc., found that a person suing for physical or emotional injury caused by wrongful discharge by a private employer had an 86 percent chance of winning. Awards were averaging over $300,000. Rand Corporation, a Santa Monica think tank, found that judgments in California averaged $650,000. Such suits had been practically unheard of just a decade earlier; it was well established that employers could fire at will. But exceptions to the employment-at-will doctrine came to be recognized in forty states after 1980. Some believe that "Workplace litigation is causing unbelievable problems for employers. You fully expect that every time you discharge an employee, or don't promote an employee, or demote an employee, you're going to get a lawsuit."

There were signs the pendulum was reversing its swing as the decade drew to a close. The California Supreme Court decided to prohibit punitive damages and place other limitations on wrongful discharge cases. But employment lawyer Victor Schachter remained uncomfortable.[46]

Fire at Will, Carefully

· ·

Special Considerations in Selecting Managerial Personnel

The effect on the organization of a poor or excellent choice of a manager is typically greater than that of a worker. Also, more subjective judgment is commonly involved. Here are some of the characteristics managers might be expected to have:

- Good planner.
- Good communicator.
- Good decision maker.
- Good organizer.
- Good motivator.
- Good leader.
- Good conceptualizer.
- Adaptable to change.
- Self-confident.
- Aggressive.
- Empathic.

Of course, no one is outstanding in all these talents. And it is hard to say that any are more important than the rest. For this reason, among others, it is hard to say just who should be groomed for a management job.

There has been continuing interest in whether personal characteristics are accurate predictors of managerial success. AT&T, Sears, General Electric, and many other firms have researched the question. But answers have been elusive. The traits studied included college grades and such subjective variables as self-confidence, intelligence, nonverbal reasoning, personal values, and attitudes about several matters, such as pragmatism. Various studies have defined managerial success in terms of salary level, position in the organizational hierarchy, and ability as assessed by others at work. It seems logical that some relationship between present traits and future managerial success should exist. But only one clear relationship was found, and it involved college grades, not really a trait.

AT&T's study involved ten thousand managers in the Bell System. It was found that 51 percent of those in the top 10 percent of their college classes were in the top third of the company by salary level. No other significant relationships were discovered.

The *assessment center* provides one avenue for evaluating management potential. AT&T introduced the concept to American business in the mid-1950s. More than two hundred large companies now have assessment centers. The assessment center provides for the systematic evaluation of the potential of individuals for future management positions. In the typical assessment center, a series of activities are designed to test the potential manager's skills, abilities, attitudes, and judgment. The activities are similar to those the manager might be expected to do in an actual job. They include in-basket exercises, management games, leaderless group discussions, mock interviews, and tests. Assessors observe the participants and study written results of the exercises. Table 9–2 illustrates a three-day schedule of activities at a typical center.

A survey of thirty-three companies with assessment centers revealed that the three most widely used assessment techniques were in-basket exercises (thirty-one firms), business games (thirty firms), and leaderless group discussion (thirty-one firms).[47] In the in-basket exercise, the participant is asked to respond to a stack of notes, messages, telephone calls, letters, and reports. One or two hours is normally allowed to do this. The participant's decisions can be rated by assessors on such dimensions as decisiveness and ability to prioritize items properly.

Day 1	Orientation of a dozen candidates.
	Breaking up into groups of four to play a *management game* (observe and assess organizing ability, financial acumen, quickness of thinking, efficiency under stress, adaptability, leadership).
	Psychological testing (measure and assess verbal and numerical abilities, reasoning, interests, and attitudes) or *in-depth interviews* (assess motivation).
	Leaderless group discussion (observe and assess aggressiveness, persuasiveness, expository skill, energy, flexibility, self-confidence).
Day 2	*In-basket exercise* (observe and assess decision making under stress, organizing ability, memory and ability to interrelate events, preparation for decision making, ability to delegate, concern for others).
	Role-playing of employment or performance appraisal interview (observe and assess sensitivity to others, ability to probe for information, insight, empathy).
	Group roles in preparation of a budget (observe and assess collaboration abilities, financial knowledge, expository skill, leadership, drive).
Day 3	*Individual case analyses* (observe expository skill, awareness of problems, background information possessed about problems, typically involving marketing, personnel, accounting, operations, and financial elements).
	Obtaining *peer ratings* from all candidates.
	Staff assessors' meeting to discuss and rate all candidates.
Weeks later	Manager with assessor experience meeting with each candidate to discuss assessment and counsel about careers and areas to develop.

TABLE 9–2

Typical Assessment Center Schedule

A typical business game might involve computer simulation of several firms in an industry. Teams of participants, in competition with each other, are required to decide how much to expend each period on, for example, advertising, research and development, and maintenance. They also may be asked to establish target production and inventory levels. The computer program is usually designed to provide financial statements reflecting the results of all the decisions, as if the firms were real. Leaderless group discussions may be employed to see how effectively participants take the lead in discussion, influence others, mediate arguments, speak, and summarize or classify issues.

Various other assessment exercises may grow out of a particular firm's situation. For example, J. C. Penney uses the "irate customer phone call," made by an assessor, in order to rate the participant's emotional stability under duress, tactfulness, and ability to resolve complaints.[48] Psychological tests and in-depth interviews are used by some centers. But it has been hard to show whether these techniques really improve validity. It appears that personality test results are only weak predictors of management success.

AT&T began in the mid-1950s to try to determine the predictive accuracy of the assessment center approach. Assessor ratings were concealed from company management for eight years, so the ratings themselves could not influence participant success. The assessment center had correctly predicted success for 78 percent of the participants who became middle managers. It had predicted less than success for 95 percent of those who failed to progress beyond the first management level. AT&T has kept its assessment centers, which now process an average of ten thousand participants a year. A recent ten-year study shows that the centers continue to produce reliable predictions of management success.

A Global Perspective

In the global job market, human resource managers are facing a growing mismatch between new jobs requiring higher-level skills and the people available to fill them. In the case of American multinationals, human resource management is becoming an even greater challenge because, according to the Commission on Workforce Quality and Labor Market Efficiency, "unless government and business undertake a vast increase in their investment in human capital, U.S. companies will not be able to hire the types of workers they need to compete in international markets."[49] To compound the problem, managers affiliated with some companies—for example, General Motors—are learning the techniques for improving the quality of production but are not learning the management attitudes that make operations such as GM's joint venture with Toyota (NUMMI) successful.[50]

In Sweden, both labor and management support work reforms, labor cooperates with plant managers in training the work force, and everyone supports the team concept. The teams largely manage themselves by handling scheduling, quality control, hiring, and other duties normally performed by first-line supervisors. Human resource managers in Sweden must ensure that the environment remains conducive for this self-management. Volvo gives workers sixteen weeks of training before they are allowed to get close to a car and sixteen months more of on-the-job orientation.[51]

Coping with human resource problems in the global environment is very complex. American human resource managers must find a way to educate, or reeducate, much of the American labor force to give the United States a competitive labor force; they must carefully review the human resource situation in the host countries; and they must plan to cope with the limitations of the labor situation and take advantage of the strengths of the host countries' labor forces. Whether it will take more progressive attitudes toward managing the country's labor force, or the development of more pleasant factories, or some other approach, effective human resource management is essential for success in the global environment.

· ·

Self-Assessment Exercise

Will You Be Good at Dealing with Human Resource Management and the Staffing Function?

1. Are you willing to be selective in hiring employees?

☐ Yes   ☐ No

2. Are you willing to try not to be too gullible?

☐ Yes   ☐ No

3. Are you willing to devote time and effort to the selection process?

☐ Yes   ☐ No

(continued)

4. Are you willing to follow company policies and procedures in hiring?

☐ Yes ☐ No

5. Are you willing to learn the government regulations affecting selection?

☐ Yes ☐ No

6. Are you willing to stay on the lookout for good potential employees?

☐ Yes ☐ No

7. Are you willing to assume personal responsibility for orienting new workers on the job?

☐ Yes ☐ No

8. Are you willing to use the personnel department when needed?

☐ Yes ☐ No

9. Are you willing to learn to know what to look for in hiring workers?

☐ Yes ☐ No

10. Are you willing to evaluate workers on a timely basis?

☐ Yes ☐ No

Summary

If organizational objectives are to be accomplished, firms must attract, select, train, and retain qualified people. To meet the firm's human resource needs, six basic functions of human resource management must be accomplished: staffing, training and development, compensation, health and safety, employee and labor relations, and human resource research. The functional areas of HRM are not separate and distinct; they need to be highly interrelated.

Numerous national laws and executive orders are concerned with providing equal employment opportunity, thus signifying an attitude in the general population that changes should be made in employment practices. The most significant are the Civil Rights Acts of 1866 and 1871, the Equal Pay Act of 1963, Title VII of the 1964 Civil Rights Act and its 1972 amendment, the Age Discrimination in Employment Act of 1967 and its 1978 and 1986 amendments, the Rehabilitation Act of 1973, the Pregnancy Discrimination Act of 1978, the Immigration Reform and Control Act of 1986, the Americans with Disabilities Act of 1990, the Civil Rights Act of 1991 and Executive Order 11246, as amended by Executive Order 11375. A phrase that has begun to be used in recent years is the "glass ceiling," meaning the invisible barrier in organizations which prevents many women from achieving top level management positions. Negligent hiring is one of the hottest issues in current HRM law. An employer can be held responsible for an employee's unlawful acts if it does not reasonably investigate an employee's background, and then assigns the person to a position where he or she can inflict harm.

Staffing is an integral part of human resource management. The basic elements of the staffing process are job analysis, human resource planning, recruitment, and selection. Job analysis is the systematic process of determining the skills and knowledge required for performing jobs in the organization. Developing strategies and tactics to ensure that the required numbers of employees with the required skills are on the job when they are needed is human resource planning. The ultimate objective of recruitment is to attract the individuals who are most capable of meeting the requirements of the job. Selection is the process of identifying the recruited individuals who will best assist the firm in achieving organizational objectives. Steps in the selection process typically include the preliminary interview, evaluation of the application blank, testing, interviewing, reference checking and background investigation, management approval, and physical examinations. Today, one of the most fervently pursued civil rights issues relates to sexual harassment. Title VII of the Civil Rights Act generally prohibits discrimination on the basis of gender in employment. The EEOC has also issued interpretative guidelines, which state that employers have an affirmative duty to maintain a work place free from sexual harassment.

Internal staffing administration includes orientation, employee assistance programs, and performance appraisals, among other activities. In recruiting and selecting managerial personnel, more subjective than objective judgment is often required, focusing on an evaluation of skills, abilities, attitudes, and characteristics, many of which are intangible. In general, the activity involves determining the significant personal characteristics or behaviors that seem to predict managerial success and establishing assessment centers.

Review Questions

1. Briefly define each of the basic functions of human resource management.
2. Describe the major federal laws and executive orders affecting equal employment opportunity.
3. Distinguish between a job description and a job specification.
4. Describe the advantages and disadvantages of promotion from within.
5. What steps are involved in the personnel selection process?
6. Describe the two basic types of employment interviews.
7. List the various types of employee status changes.
8. Discuss the purpose of assessment centers.

Key Terms

Human resource management (HRM)	Organizational development (OD)	Comparable worth
		Glass ceiling
Staffing	Compensation	Executive Orders
Training and development programs	Health	Affirmative action
	Safety	Job analysis

Job description
Job specification
Human resource planning (HRP)

Recruitment
Employment requisition
Selection
Preliminary interview

Employee orientation
Employee assistance program
Performance appraisal

CASE 9.1   "SEND HIM ON DOWN"

Jack Stephens was production manager for Thompson Manufacturing Company, a Seattle, Washington, maker of electrical enclosures. Jack had to approve the hiring of any new supervisors in the plant. The personnel manager performed the initial screening.

One Friday afternoon, Jack got a call from Pete Schneider, Thompson's human resource director. "Jack," Pete said, "I've just spoken to a young man who may be just who you're looking for to fill that supervisor job you asked me about. He has some good work experience and it seems his head is screwed on straight." Jack replied, "Great, Pete, I look forward to seeing him." Pete continued, "He's here right now, Jack, if you could possibly talk with him." Jack hesitated a moment before answering. "Gee, Pete," he said, "I'm certainly busy today but I'll try to squeeze him in. Send him on down."

A moment later Allen Guthrie, the new applicant, arrived at Jack's office and introduced himself. "Come on in, Allen," said Jack. "I'll be right with you after I make a few phone calls." Fifteen minutes later, Jack finished the calls and began talking with Allen. Jack

was quite impressed. After a few minutes, Jack's door opened and a supervisor yelled, "We have a small problem on line number 1 and need your help."

"Sure," Jack replied. "Excuse me a minute, Allen." Ten minutes later, Jack returned and the conversation continued for at least ten more minutes before a series of phone calls again interrupted them.

The same pattern of interruptions continued for the next hour. Finally, Allen looked at his watch and said, "I'm sorry, Mr. Stephens, but I have to pick up my wife."

"Sure thing, Allen," Jack said as the phone rang again. "Call me later this week."

Questions

1. What specific policies might a company follow to avoid interviews like this one?
2. Explain why Jack, not Pete, should make the selection decision.

CASE 9.2   SOMETHING'S MISSING

John Case, accounting supervisor, was clearly annoyed as he approached his boss, Gerald Jones. He began, "Gerald, this note you sent me says I have to update descriptions for all ten of the jobs in my department within the next two weeks."

"Well," asked Gerald, "what's the problem with that?"

John explained, "This is a waste of time, especially since I have other deadlines. It will take at least thirty hours. We still have two weeks of work left on the internal audit reviews. You want me to push that back

and work on *job descriptions*? No way.

"We haven't looked at these job descriptions in years. They'll need a lot of revision. And as soon as they get into the hands of the employees, I'll get all kinds of flak."

"Why would you get flak for getting the job descriptions in order?" asked Gerald. John answered, "This whole thing is a can of worms. Just calling attention to the existence of job descriptions will give some people the idea they don't have to do things that aren't in the description. And if we write what the people in my division really do, some jobs will have to be upgraded and others downgraded, I'll bet. I just can't afford the morale problem and the confusion right now."

Gerald replied, "What do you suggest, John? I've been told just to get it done, and within two weeks." "I don't want to do it at all," said John, "and certainly not during the audit period. Can't you just go back up the line and get it put off until next month?"

Notes

1. This case is a composite of a number of published accounts, among them: Jolie Solomon, "Pepsi Offers Stock Options to All, Not Just Honchos," *Wall Street Journal,* June 28, 1989, p. B1; Michael J. McCarthy, "PepsiCo's Net Income in Second Quarter Rose 21% Due in Part to Special Gains," *Wall Street Journal,* July 27, 1989, p. A4; Carol Davenport, "America's Most Admired Corporations," *Fortune,* January 30, 1989, pp. 68–94; Walter Guzzardi, "Wisdom from the Giants of Business," *Fortune,* July 3, 1989, pp. 78–88; Alison L. Sprout, "America's Most Admired Corporations," *Fortune,* February 11, 1991, pp. 57–58; CNN Inside Business Program: PepsiCo CEO James Calloway; Standard and Poor's Corporation, "PepsiCo," *Standard NYSE Stock Reports* 56, no. 95 (May 17, 1989): sec. 18.

2. Maria Shao, Seth Payne, John Templeman, and Mark Maremont, "Trying Times at Boeing," *Business Week,* March 13, 1989, p. 35.

3. Based on the discussion in R. Wayne Mondy and Robert M. Noe III, *Personnel: The Management of Human Resources,* 3d ed. (Newton, MA: Allyn and Bacon, 1987), pp. 6–11.

4. R. Wayne Mondy, Robert M. Noe, and Robert E. Edwards, "What the Staffing Function Entails," *Personnel* 63 (April 1986): 55.

5. Gene Koretz and Celeste Whittaker, "More Picket Lines, Fewer Rank-And-Filers," *Business Week,* May 7, 1990, p. 24.

6. Ibid.

7. Alexander B. Trowbridge, "A Management Look at Labor Relations," in *Unions in Transition* (San Francisco: ICS Press, 1988), p. 414.

8. Jonathan Kapstein and John Hoerr, "Volvo's Radically New Plant: The Death of the Assembly Line?" *Business Week,* August 28, 1989, pp. 92–93.

9. Robert J. Sahl, "Get It Together! Integrating the HR Department," *Personnel* 66 (February 1989): 39.

10. Howard C. Lockwood, "Equal Employment Opportuni-

Questions

1. What have John and Gerald forgotten to do prior to the creation of job descriptions? Why is this step important?

2. Evaluate John's statement: "Just calling attention to the existence of job descriptions will give some people the idea they don't have to do things that aren't in the description."

ties," in Dale Yoder and Herbert G. Heneman, eds., *Staffing Policies and Strategies* (Washington, D.C.: Bureau of National Affairs, 1979), pp. 4–252.

11. Doug Grider and Mike Shurden, "The Gathering Storm of Comparable Worth," *Business Horizons* 30 (July–August 1987): 81–82.

12. Michael R. Carrell and Frank E. Kuzmits, "Amended ADEA's Effects on HR Strategies Remain Dubious," *Personnel Journal* 66 (May 1987): 112.

13. Art L. Bethke, "The IRCA: What's an Employer to Do?" *Wisconsin Small Business Forum* 6 (Fall 1987): 26.

14. *The Americans with Disabilities Act: Questions and Answers* (U.S. Government Printing Office, 1991), p. 1.

15. Christine D. Keen, "Lifestyle Disabilities Could Become a Civil Rights Frontier," *HRNews* 9 (October 1990): 7.

16. Gary N. Powell, "Upgrading Management Opportunities for Women," *HR Magazine* 35 (November 1990): 67.

17. Jack Raisner, "When Workplace Relationships Cause Discrimination," *HR Magazine* 36 (January 1991): 75.

18. Mondy and Noe, *Personnel: The Management of Human Resources,* p. 101.

19. Shao, Payne, Templeman, and Maremont, "Trying Times at Boeing," p. 35.

20. Donald C. Busi, "The Job Description: More than Bureaucratic Control," *Supervisory Management* 35 (October 1990): 5.

21. Walter Kiechel III, "Love, Don't Lose the Newly Hired," *Fortune,* June 6, 1988, pp. 271–274.

22. Mondy, Noe, and Edwards, "What the Staffing Function Entails," pp. 55–56.

23. This case is a composite of a number of published accounts, among them: "Delta Air Lines Boosts Output by Letting Mechanics Vote for Top Wrench," *Wall Street Journal,* January 24, 1989, p. A1; Howard Banks, "Is Delta Too Nice for Its Own Good?" *Forbes,* November 28, 1988, pp. 91–94; "A Bleak New Year for Airline Profits," *Busi-*

ness Week, January 10, 1983, p. 38; James Ott, "Delta Expanding Route System with 737-200s," *Aviation Week and Space Technology*, April 2, 1984, pp. 32–33; "Delta: The World's Most Profitable Airline," *Business Week*, August 31, 1981, pp. 68–71; James Ott, "Delta Anticipates Savings in Flight-Planning System," *Aviation Week and Space Technology*, April 30, 1984, pp. 34–39; Standard and Poor's Corporation, "Delta Air Lines," *Standard NYSE Stock Reports* 56, no. 132 (July 12, 1989): sec. 9; and numerous additional articles from the *Wall Street Journal*.

24. Joseph E. McKendrick, Jr., "Latest AMS Foundation Survey Finds: One-Third of Nation's Employers Have or Are Considering Drug Testing," *Management World* 19 (March–April 1990): 3.

25. The Fourth Amendment prohibits the government from conducting unreasonable searches or seizures.

26. Gerard P. Panaro, *Employment Law Manual* (Boston: Warren, Gorham & Lamont, 1990), pp. 4–28.

27. C. Harold Stone and Floyd L. Ruch, "Selection, Interviewing, and Testing," in Dale Yoder and Herbert Heneman, eds., *ASPA Handbook of Personnel and Industrial Relations* (Washington, D.C.: Bureau of National Affairs, 1974), pp. 152–154.

28. Bradford D. Smart, "Progressive Approaches for Hiring the Best People," *Training and Development Journal* 41 (September 1987): 51.

29. Arthur Bragg, "Checking References," *Sales and Marketing Management* 142 (November 1990): 68.

30. Scott T. Rickard, "Effective Staff Selection," *Personnel Journal* 60 (June 1981): 477.

31. Kenneth C. Cooper, "Those 'Qualified' Applicants and Their Phony Credentials," *Administrative Management* 38 (August 1977): 44.

32. James W. Fenton, Jr., "Negligent Hiring/Retention Adds to Human Resources Woes," *Personnel Journal* 69 (April 1990): 62; and Stephanie Overman, "A Delicate Balance Protects Everyone's Rights," *HR Magazine* 35 (November 1990): 36–39.

33. Caleb S. Atwood and James M. Neel, "New Lawsuits Expand Employer Liability," *HR Magazine* 35 (October 1990): 74.

34. Joseph W. Ambash, "Knowing Your Limits: How Far Can You Go when Checking an Applicant's Background?" *Management World* 19 (March–April 1990): 8–10.

35. Kely Flynn, "Preventive Medicine for Sexual Harassment," *Personnel* 68 (March 1991): 17.

36. Michele Galen, "Ending Sexual Harassment: Business Is Getting the Message," *Business Week*, March 18, 1991, p. 98.

37. Robert K. McCalla, "Stopping Sexual Harassment Before It Begins," *Management Review* 80 (April 1991): 44.

38. Ibid.

39. Stacey J. Garvin, "Employer Liability for Sexual Harassment," *HR Magazine* 36 (June 1991): 107.

40. Thomas R. Horton, "Drugs in the Workplace," *Management Review* 76 (February 1987): 5.

41. Patricia Galagan, "Here's the Situation," *Training and Development Journal* 41 (July 1987): 21.

42. Fred Dickman and William G. Emener, "Employee Assistance Programs: Basic Concepts, Attributes and an Evaluation," *Personnel Administrator* 27 (August 1982): 55.

43. Keith McClelland, "The Changing Nature of EAP Practice," *Personnel Administrator* 30 (August 1985): 34.

44. Kay Wyrtzen, "Employee Assistance Programs," *Supervision* 47 (May 1985): 6–7.

45. Peter M. Tafti, "Face to Face," *Training and Development Journal* 44 (November 1990): 68.

46. Donald C. Bacon, "See You in Court," *Nation's Business*, July 1989, pp. 17–28.

47. Joseph M. Bender, "What Is 'Typical' of Assessment Centers?" *Personnel* 50 (July–August 1973): 51.

48. William C. Byham, "Assessment Centers for Spotting Future Managers," *Harvard Business Review* 48 (July–August 1970): 158.

49. Stephen B. Wildstrom, "A Failing Grade for the American Workforce," *Business Week*, September 11, 1989, p. 22.

50. Dean Foust, "A Tough Look at General Motors," *Business Week*, September 18, 1989, p. 17.

51. Jonathan Kapstein and John Hoerr, "Volvo's Radical New Plant: The Death of the Assembly Line?" *Business Week*, August 28, 1989, pp. 92–93.

Management Skills

Since you will probably work for an organization one day, it is important for you to appreciate the differences between types of bureaucratic organizations. Some individuals prefer highly bureaucratic organizations, whereas others prefer less bureaucratic organizations. Since your happiness as an employee may be affected by the bureaucratic orientation of the firm you work for, you should evaluate your preference prior to selecting a firm. To assess your degree of bureaucratic orientation, take the self-assessment exercise "How Well Would You Fit in a Bureaucracy?" Then, turn to page 633 to evaluate yourself.

How Well Would You Fit in a Bureaucracy?

INSTRUCTIONS: Check either Mostly Agree or Mostly Disagree.

	MOSTLY AGREE	MOSTLY DISAGREE
1. I value stability in my job.	☐	☐
2. I like a predictable organization.	☐	☐
3. The best job for me would be one in which the future is uncertain.	☐	☐
4. The U.S. Army would be a nice place to work.	☐	☐
5. Rules, policies, and procedures tend to frustrate me.	☐	☐
6. I would enjoy working for a company that employed 85,000 people worldwide.	☐	☐
7. Being self-employed would involve more risk than I'm willing to take.	☐	☐
8. Before accepting a job, I would like to see an exact job description.	☐	☐
9. I would prefer a job as a free-lance house painter to one as a clerk for the Department of Motor Vehicles.	☐	☐
10. Seniority should be as important as performance in determining pay increases and promotion.	☐	☐

	MOSTLY AGREE	MOSTLY DISAGREE
11. It would give me a feeling of pride to work for the largest and most successful company in its field.	☐	☐
12. Given a choice, I would prefer to make $30,000 per year as a vice-president in a small company to $35,000 as a staff specialist in a large company.	☐	☐
13. I would regard wearing an employee badge with a number on it as a degrading experience.	☐	☐
14. Parking spaces in a company lot should be assigned on the basis of job level.	☐	☐
15. An accountant who works for a large organization cannot be a true professional.	☐	☐
16. Before accepting a job (given a choice), I would want to make sure that the company had a very fine program of employee benefits.	☐	☐
17. A company will probably not be successful unless it establishes a clear set of rules and procedures.	☐	☐
18. Regular working hours and vacations are more important to me than finding thrills on the job.	☐	☐
19. You should respect people according to their rank.	☐	☐
20. Rules are meant to be broken.	☐	☐

Source: Adapted from Andrew J. DuBrin, *Human Relations: A Job Oriented Approach*, © 1978, pp. 667–688. Reprinted with permission of Reston Publishing Co., a Prentice-Hall Co., 11480 Sunset Hills Road, Reston, VA 22090.

10

Motivation

LEARNING OBJECTIVES

After completing this chapter students should be able to

- Describe some philosophies of human nature.
- Describe needs theories, equity theory, and reinforcement theory.
- Explain expectancy theory and objective setting and motivation.
- Describe how managers can be better at motivating.
- Discuss job design, possible rewards a first-level manager can dispense, and recent trends in motivation.

As the decade of the 1990s began, Domino's Pizza was the world's largest pizza chain. Domino's main strategy: "fast service." Delivery was guaranteed in 30 minutes, but it averaged only 23 minutes. Drivers were motivated by getting to keep their tips and being paid so much for each delivery. Young restaurant workers sometimes jumped at the chance to deliver. But motivated driving has its downside. In 1989, Domino's admitted that primarily its younger drivers had been involved in 20 fatal accidents within the year. To rectify this situation, the company agreed to terminate or reassign drivers who were under 18.

Tom Monaghan, the former chief executive of privately owned Domino's, called his employees "Dominoids," and insisted they focus on customer satisfaction. "Mystery customers," ten thousand of them, were paid to sample pizzas throughout the year and report on service and quality; store managers' pay was adjusted based on the results. Each restaurant rated the service and ingredient quality provided by distribution employees, whose pay was determined in part by these scores. The district offices evaluated the headquarters staff. Mrs. Monaghan, who was payroll chief, considered those ratings in setting monthly bonus amounts for home office employees. It is fairly obvious that Monaghan viewed money as an extrinsic motivator that would enhance customer service and keep Domino's the world's largest pizza chain.

Seventy percent of Domino's five thousand units were owned by franchisees, entrepreneurs who adopted the standardized system and paid the franchisor part of their income. Domino's clay-animated "Noid" figure became popular through the company's ads and three million units of Noid merchandise were sold in two years. Overall, Monaghan said, his franchisees were "happy." Many of them had also gotten rich.

However, competitors were creeping up on Domino's fast delivery times. Monaghan welcomed the challenge, especially from industry giant Pizza Hut. "I think it's costing [Pizza Hut] a lot to do this, and it's probably proving a lot harder than they thought," he said, "They're a challenge, and I'm kind of glad they came along, because we didn't have a national challenge in the delivery business. It was almost getting boring."

But his viewpoint changed quickly. "I want people here in the company to think it's a war," said Monaghan, "because somebody's got to emerge on top in two or three years." The new national ad campaign said "Nobody delivers better." Shortly after the new ads began running, Monaghan announced he wanted to deliver Domino's itself into new hands. But within two years, Monaghan was back. Currently, Domino's sales are up 6 percent, to $2.65 billion, and Domino's share of the delivery market is still the largest.[1]

Motivation

The desire to put forth effort in pursuit of organizational goals.

Monaghan's people were well aware that their performance was directly tied to their earnings; the better they performed, the more money they earned. From Monaghan's perspective the better employees performed, the more everyone would gain. Some managers, like Monaghan, motivate employees through the use of rewards, while other managers use punishment and formal authority to motivate. **Motivation** is *the desire to put forth effort in pursuit of organizational goals.* Managers can improve their understanding of the forces that energize employees. There is enormous energy within every person, and managers certainly should not prevent its release.

In this chapter, we first discuss three philosophies of human nature. Then, we describe four major motivation theories: needs theories, equity theory, reinforcement theory, and expectancy theory. Next, we review objective setting as related to motivation and how it relates to the reward system. We follow this by consideration of how managers can be better at motivating and job design. In the final sections, we present ideas that relate to possible rewards a first-level manager can dispense, to recent trends in motivation, and to a global perspective of motivation.

Philosophies of Human Nature

A manager's philosophy of human nature helps determine the motivational techniques the manager will employ. Early in this century, Frederick Taylor and Elton Mayo proposed what many consider contrasting philosophies. Taylor was convinced that the scientific method, which provides a logical framework for the analysis of problems, could be applied to the management process. He believed that use of the scientific method would direct the manager to the most efficient way of doing work. Individuals were components of the process but had to be guided by rationality. When they performed most efficiently, Taylor said, both they and the organization would gain. The organization would have increased profits, and workers would make more money.

Elton Mayo and his associates conducted their famous Hawthorne studies in the 1920s and 1930s at Western Electric's Hawthorne facility, on Chicago's West Side. Their research demonstrated that the attitudes and feelings of workers significantly influence productivity. This "illogic of sentiments" turned out to be just as important as Taylor's "logic of efficiency." The studies also revealed the Hawthorne effect — the fact that the presence of researchers influences the behavior of the people being studied and, therefore, biases the results. Never again could human behavior be seen as determined by simple, or even completely discoverable, cause-and-effect rules.

Modern managers tend to take a balanced view, giving attention to both logical and sentimental aspects of behavior. For example, at Boeing, Ford, General Electric, Procter & Gamble, and many other U.S. companies, employees work in teams which are frequently self-managing, including responsibility for problem solving.[2]

McGregor's Theory X and Theory Y

Douglas McGregor stressed the importance of understanding the relationships between motivation and the manager's philosophy of human nature. He believed most managers of his day tended to make a certain set of assumptions about employees. He labeled this traditional view **Theory X**—*the assumption that people dislike work and responsibility, lack ambition and creative ability, and mainly want security and money.* McGregor pointed out that managers who hold such a view think they must coerce, control, and threaten employees in order to motivate them. McGregor proposed an alternate philosophy of human nature, which he considered more realistic. He called it **Theory Y**—*the assumption that expending physical and mental effort is natural, that people can be self-directed if achievement brings rewards, and that most can exercise imagination, ingenuity, and creativity and learn to seek responsibility.* Thus, McGregor believed employees do not require coercion or excessive control to perform effectively.[3]

The Theory X and Theory Y assumptions are shown in Table 10–1. The Theory Y assumptions suggest a high degree of faith in the capacity and potential of people. Here are some managerial practices Theory Y managers may follow: (1) abandonment of time clocks, (2) flexible work hours, (3) job enrichment, (4) management by objectives, and (5) participative decision making. All are based on the beliefs that abilities are widely, not narrowly, distributed in the population and that each person can be trusted to behave responsibly. If Theory Y is correct, management need only create an environment that permits workers to be motivated and realize their potential.

Theory Y does provide a basis for improved management and organizational performance. But it is not a panacea for all managerial problems. Simply assuming people are creative, responsible, and so forth may not always make them so. And McGregor himself said most managers made Theory X assumptions. Surely, some of those Theory X managers were effective.

William Ouchi offers a theory that, some say, goes beyond theories X and Y. His Theory Z is discussed later in the chapter.

Theory X

The assumption that people dislike work and responsibility, lack ambition and creative ability, and mainly want security and money.

Theory Y

The assumption that expending physical and mental effort is natural, that people can be self-directed if achievement brings rewards, and that most can exercise imagination, ingenuity, and creativity and learn to seek responsibility.

Theory X	Theory Y
The average person inherently dislikes work and will avoid it if possible.	The expenditure of physical and mental effort in work is as natural as play or rest.
Because of the dislike of work, most people must be coerced, controlled, directed, and threatened with punishment to get them to perform effectively.	People will exercise self-direction and self-control in the service of objectives to which they are committed.
The average person lacks ambition, avoids responsibility, and seeks security and economic rewards above all else.	Commitment to objectives is a function of the rewards associated with achievement.
Most people lack creative ability and are resistant to change.	The average person learns, under proper conditions, not only to accept but to seek responsibility.
Since most people are self-centered, they are not concerned with the objectives of the organization.	The capacity to exercise a relatively high degree of imagination, ingenuity, and creativity in the solution of organizational problems is widely, not narrowly, distributed in the population.

TABLE 10–1

A Comparison of McGregor's Theory X and Theory Y Assumptions

SOURCE: Based on material in Douglas McGregor, *The Human Side of Enterprise* (New York: McGraw-Hill, 1960).

Argyris's Maturity Theory

The research of Chris Argyris helped explain an important dimension of human behavior in organizations. Argyris believed healthy individuals develop along a continuum from immaturity to maturity. Mature people, he said, tend to be active, not passive; independent, not dependent; and self-aware and self-controlled, rather than unaware and controlled by others. Argyris saw fundamental conflict between the demands of a mature personality and those of typical organizations. He described the ways in which four attributes of formal structure inhibit maturation:

- Specialization of labor limits initiative and self-expression and allows few of one's abilities to be used.
- Chain of command limits self-control and makes individuals passive and dependent on the leader.
- Unity of direction (or unity of command) puts the path to the objective under the control of one leader, which creates problems when employees are not able to use a wide range of abilities and to define their own objectives on the basis of inner needs.
- Span of control (or span of management) decreases self-control and shortens the time perspective of lower-level employees.

In an organization where these characteristics are embedded in rigid rules and procedures, Argyris believed, employees cannot grow to maturity. He said this is true for the following reasons:

1. They have little control over their workaday world.
2. They are expected to be passive, dependent, and subordinate.
3. They are expected to have a short time perspective.
4. They are induced to perfect and value the frequent use of a few shallow abilities.
5. They are expected to produce under conditions leading to psychological failure.[4]

Argyris argued that when mature employees encounter such conditions, three reactions are possible:

1. *Escape.* An employee may escape by quitting, being absent, or attempting to climb to higher levels in the firm, where the structure is less rigid.
2. *Fight.* A person can fight the system by exerting pressure on the organization by means of informal groups or through formally organized labor unions.
3. *Adapt.* The most typical reaction of employees, Argyris found, is to adapt by developing an attitude of apathy or indifference. The employee plays the game, and pay becomes the compensation for the penalty of working.

Of the three responses, Argyris considered adaptation most contrary to good mental health. At many companies, the need for adaptation is diminished by letting workers participate in decisions that affect them.

Criticisms of McGregor and Argyris

Managers cannot assume that all employees are mature, as defined by Argyris, or Theory Y types, as described by McGregor. Security may mean more than a challenging job to some individuals. And some workers may thrive doing highly structured and repetitive tasks that may be boring to others.

Argyris argued that a highly structured environment will cause employees to act immaturely. One could argue as well that maturity involves the ability to adapt to any kind of environment, structured or not. Many people can and do adjust to tightly regimented work situations. One need only observe workers on a well-functioning assembly line to recognize this. Further, workers who prefer challenges can find them. In U.S. business, only a fraction of jobs are of the highly structured, totally controlled type. To the degree that an open job market operates efficiently, there will be a matching of various human needs and organizational demands.

The ideas of McGregor and Argyris have great relevance to the practice of management, of course. Managers probably have tended to make Theory X–type assumptions about their subordinates, and the modern organization does restrict behavior somewhat. However, to suggest that either McGregor or Argyris has provided an adequate guide for managers in all situations is erroneous.

The Self-Fulfilling Prophecy

The idea that the manager's positive or negative expectations will have a significant influence on employee motivation and performance is the **self-fulfilling prophecy**. This concept is very important in management. According to J. Sterling Livingston:

- A manager's expectations of employees and the way the manager treats employees largely determine their performance and career progress.
- A unique characteristic of superior managers is their ability to create high performance expectations that subordinates fulfill.
- Less effective managers fail to develop high performance expectations, and as a consequence, the productivity of their subordinates suffers.
- More often than not, subordinates appear to do what they believe they are expected to do.[5]

High performance expectations tend to be self-fulfilling prophecies. A manager communicates expectations through both verbal and nonverbal means. The manager's facial expressions, eye contact, body posture, or tone of voice can indicate high approval and high expectations or the reverse.

Numerous studies support the notion of the self-fulfilling prophecy. In one study, eighteen elementary school teachers were informed that certain of their students were "intellectual bloomers." The supposedly exceptional students had been chosen at random and so did not differ in intelligence or abilities from the rest of the students. During the school year, the chosen students actually did make significantly greater progress. Thus, the teachers' high expectations apparently became self-fulfilling prophecies.

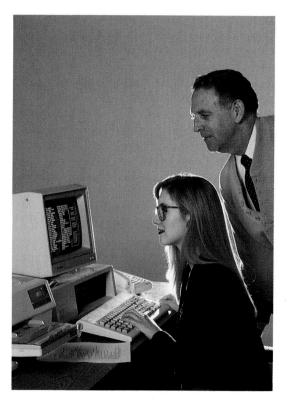

High performance expectations tend to be self-fulfilling prophecies. The manager's facial expressions, eye contact, body posture, or tone of voice can indicate high approval and high expectations, or the reverse. This manager seems to be communicating a sense of confidence in the computer operator, and vice versa.

Source: © Jim Pickerell

Similar results have been achieved by managers. More often than not, if managers communicate high expectations to their employees, the employees will perform well. To illustrate: David McNeill was the manager of the computer center at a state university in Louisiana. While McNeill was working late one night, George Johnson, who was employed as a janitor, talked with him about learning to operate computers. McNeill became convinced that Johnson had the necessary potential, although none of his experience or education seemed to qualify him. At McNeill's suggestion, Johnson enrolled in a training program. He became not only an operator but eventually a trainer as well.

The self-fulfilling prophecy can be an important element in developing managers internally. And no company has an excess of truly exceptional managers. The greatest impact of high expectations may be on younger employees, whose self-image may not be well formed. But anyone is likely to strive harder and develop faster if expected to do that. A superior's confidence in a subordinate can build the subordinate's self-confidence and spark efforts aimed at self-development and advancement.

Of course, a negative prophecy can be self-fulfilling as surely as can an affirmative one. So managers who wish their units to achieve excellence must guard against expecting too little. Managers who expect little of employees tend to create organizational cultures marked by low employee motivation and performance. Working in such cultures can damage employees' self-esteem or self-image, as well as their careers.[6]

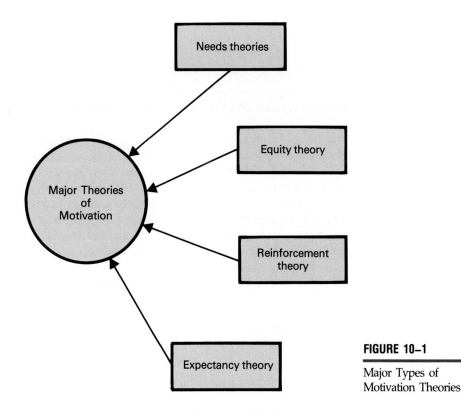

FIGURE 10–1

Major Types of
Motivation Theories

Needs Theories

Figure 10–1 illustrates four major types of motivation theories. The first is *needs theories*. As the name implies, such theories are based on the proposition that motivation can be best explained in terms of needs fulfillment. Four of the most popular needs theories are discussed in this section: (1) Maslow's hierarchy of needs theory, (2) Herzberg's motivator-hygiene (two-factor) theory, (3) Alderfer's ERG theory, and (4) McClelland's needs theory. As Table 10–2 indicates, the categories of needs associated with each differ somewhat. The theories also differ as to how unfulfilled needs influence motivation. (The other major types of motivation theories—equity

TABLE 10–2

Comparison of Needs in Four
Theories of Motivation

Maslow's	Herzberg's	Alderfer's	McClelland's
Physiological	Hygiene	Existence	
Safety and Security			
Belongingness and love		Relatedness	Need for affiliation
Self-esteem	Motivators	Growth	Need for achievement Need for power
Self-actualization			

theory, reinforcement theory, and expectancy theory—are discussed later in the chapter.)

One of your employees, Bob Edison, spends every free minute that he's off the job—and most of his earnings—on bowling. Bob belongs to three leagues and bowls in a tournament every weekend. He has won numerous trophies. His name constantly appears on the sports page of the local paper.

You have observed that Bob does only enough to keep his job. You made the following comments on Bob's latest performance report: "Gets along well with everyone. Does not disrupt anyone else's work. But seems to live for quitting time, his paycheck, and bowling." Upon reading this, Bob said it was true. He just shrugged when you told him you expected him to improve. It is three weeks later, and one of Bob's co-workers has just complained that she has been having to do most of Bob's work, because he keeps sloughing off.

What would you do?

Maslow's Hierarchy of Needs

Many psychologists believe there are certain patterns, or configurations, of human needs, although there obviously are individual differences. A common approach to establishing a pattern of needs is that of developing a universal needs hierarchy. Psychologist Abraham Maslow proposed one widely accepted pattern (see Figure 10–2). Examples of how an organization might help satisfy these basic needs are also presented here.

Maslow stated that individuals are motivated to satisfy certain unsatisfied needs. His theory of human motivation is based on the following assumptions:

- Unsatisfied needs motivate or influence behavior.
- Satisfied needs do not motivate behavior.
- Needs are arranged in a hierarchy.
- Needs at any level of the hierarchy emerge as a significant motivator only when the lower-level needs are reasonably well satisfied.[7]

According to Maslow, the needs hierarchy extends from physiological needs at the bottom to the need for self-actualization at the top. Until physiological needs are reasonably well satisfied, he believed, higher-level needs will not significantly influence behavior. Maslow acknowledged that a person is never completely satisfied on any need level. But he said a type of need can be prepotent (have exceptional power to influence behavior) only when those below it in the hierarchy are largely fulfilled.

Maslow's advice to managers was to focus motivational efforts on the lowest-level category of needs that is substantially unsatisfied. He said an average person might be 85 percent satisfied in physiological needs, 70 percent in safety and security needs,

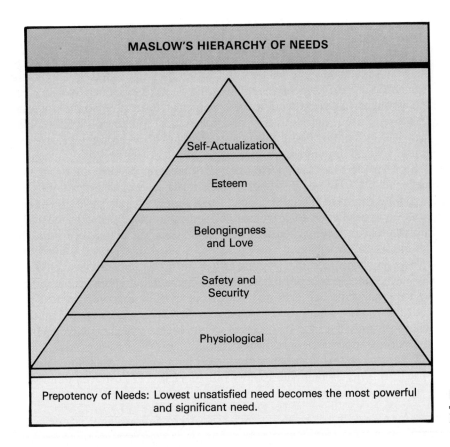

FIGURE 10–2

Maslow's Hierarchy of Needs

50 percent in belongingness and love needs, 40 percent in esteem needs, and 10 percent in self-actualization needs. Thus, Maslow's theory implies that the manager of the average person should pay attention to the belongingness and esteem needs. Physiological and safety needs are viewed as weak motivators in this instance because they are, respectively, 85 and 70 percent satisfied. And although self-actualization needs are only 10 percent satisfied, they are seen as weak motivators too. They cannot come into play, according to Maslow's theory, until something is done about the needs for belongingness and esteem.

There were early predictions that Nissan's U.S. plant would fail because of the firm's reliance on stable employment as a motivator. Job security fulfills a safety need. It was reasoned that U.S. workers were higher on the Maslow hierarchy than Japanese workers and thus were less concerned with the need for safety.

Maslow's theory is widely known and is used as a guide by many practicing managers. But researchers have called it into question.[8] Certain studies suggest needs fall into only two or three distinct categories, not five. In addition, some critics say the *order* of need fulfillment may not always be the same. These authorities admit that considerable importance should be placed on physiological needs if they have not been satisfied. A person has to eat, for example. But once physiological needs are satisfied, there appears to be no clear-cut order in which higher-level needs become prepotent.

Herzberg's Motivator-Hygiene Theory

In his classic study in the 1950s, Frederick Herzberg asked his research sample, a group of professionals, to tell of a time when they felt especially good or bad about their job. Such an approach is often called "critical incident" research, because respondents are expected to describe a particular event that seems important. From responses to the initial question and follow-ups, Herzberg identified two distinct classes of factors that he said were important to behavior on the job. He called these classes hygiene factors and motivators.[9]

Hygiene factors, he said, were capable of creating dissatisfaction but not positive motivation. As Figure 10–3 shows, they relate to the *job context*—the interrelated conditions in which the job is done. These factors include pay and benefits as well as working conditions, interpersonal relations, and other elements. When Herzberg's subjects told of times when they felt particularly bad about their jobs, these were the factors they mentioned.

Herzberg concluded that hygiene factors cannot promote motivation but can cause dissatisfaction. He believed hygiene factors maintain an employee, in the way dental hygiene maintains the teeth and gums. But hygiene can only prevent problems; it does not create a high level of well-being. Herzberg suggested that an organization that meets only the hygiene needs of its employees will eliminate dissatisfaction but will not get superior performance.

Motivators, on the other hand, produced high levels of satisfaction, which Herzberg treated as synonymous with motivation. As Figure 10–3 shows, motivators include

FIGURE 10–3

Hygiene and Motivator Factors

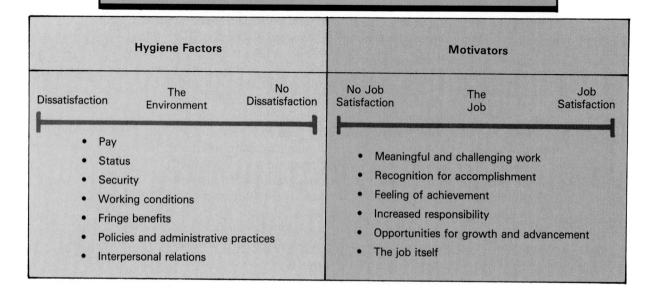

HERZBERG'S TWO-FACTOR THEORY

Hygiene Factors	Motivators
Dissatisfaction — The Environment — No Dissatisfaction	No Job Satisfaction — The Job — Job Satisfaction
• Pay • Status • Security • Working conditions • Fringe benefits • Policies and administrative practices • Interpersonal relations	• Meaningful and challenging work • Recognition for accomplishment • Feeling of achievement • Increased responsibility • Opportunities for growth and advancement • The job itself

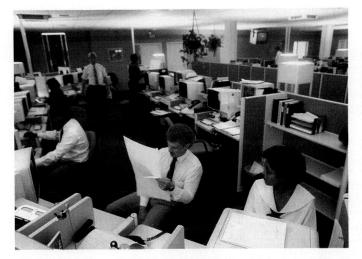

Hygiene factors relate to the job context, the interrelated conditions in which the job is done. Herzberg concluded that hygiene factors cannot promote motivation, but can cause dissatisfaction. Thus, a neat, well-organized office, such as the one shown here, may be vital to preventing worker dissatisfaction. But workers in such an office will not necessarily be highly motivated.
Source: © Jim Pickerell

challenging work, recognition for accomplishment, and the feeling of achievement. Herzberg's motivators are concerned mainly with the job content (whereas hygiene factors relate mostly to the job context). That is, motivators tend to be internal to the job. When Herzberg's subjects described times when they felt especially good about their jobs, these were the factors they mentioned.

Criticisms of Herzberg's theory include the following:

1. The analysis of critical incident–type responses is highly subjective.

2. The theory is most applicable to managers, engineers, accountants, and other professionals. Studies show less relevance to blue-collar workers.

3. Herzberg's study focused on level of satisfaction, not performance per se. Satisfaction and performance are not synonymous.

Herzberg's motivators are closely related to the esteem and self-actualization needs of Maslow's hierarchy. His hygiene factors closely correspond to Maslow's physiological, safety, and social needs. (See Figure 10–4.)

Herzberg contended that most managers give inadequate attention to the motivators, focusing instead on employee pay, benefits, and working conditions. We might add that collective bargaining also tends to concern the hygiene factors. This tendency, of both management and labor, is understandable. Hygiene factors tend to be tangible and measurable. Motivators, on the other hand, are intangible and generally unquantifiable.

But hygiene factors, Herzberg said, cannot produce positive motivation. To achieve excellence, he believed, organizations must satisfy the needs related to both hygiene factors and motivators. The obvious implication is that management should show relatively more concern for providing challenging work, increased responsibility, recognition, and other motivators. Avis chairman Joseph V. Vittoria found a way to involve all of his employees in management.

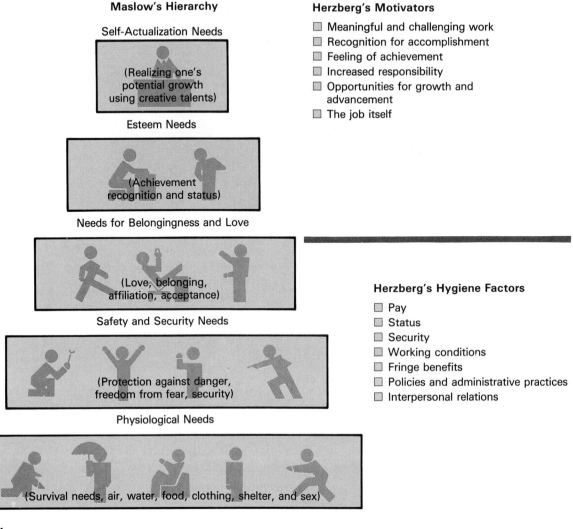

Maslow's Hierarchy

Self-Actualization Needs

(Realizing one's potential growth using creative talents)

Esteem Needs

(Achievement recognition and status)

Needs for Belongingness and Love

(Love, belonging, affiliation, acceptance)

Safety and Security Needs

(Protection against danger, freedom from fear, security)

Physiological Needs

(Survival needs, air, water, food, clothing, shelter, and sex)

Herzberg's Motivators

☐ Meaningful and challenging work
☐ Recognition for accomplishment
☐ Feeling of achievement
☐ Increased responsibility
☐ Opportunities for growth and advancement
☐ The job itself

Herzberg's Hygiene Factors

☐ Pay
☐ Status
☐ Security
☐ Working conditions
☐ Fringe benefits
☐ Policies and administrative practices
☐ Interpersonal relations

FIGURE 10–4

Maslow and Herzberg Related

Avis, Still Number 2 and Trying Even Harder with Employee-Owners

As the decade of the 1990s began, Avis, the big car rental company, was gaining on Hertz. Chairman Joseph V. Vittoria had formed an employee stock ownership plan (ESOP), which bought the company from Wesray Capital Corporation in 1987. Essentially, the employees then owned Avis. And Vittoria spent several days each month flying around the country to inform and get advice from the new owners, who were then his bosses as well as his subordinates.

Employee participation groups were formed, one in each city where Avis has an office. Each group has a variety of members, from rental agents to car washers. They suggest ways of improving customer service and efficiency. "The suggestions don't just lie there. They're actually worked on," said airport bus driver Herman Jones. Among the ideas proposed by group members that were adopted companywide are nonsmoker cars and briefings on local traffic laws for agents. Selected members meet at the zone and district levels to filter ideas and manage the participative system. A national meeting of Avis employee-owners is held annually to allow interaction with Vittoria and other managers. Management consultant Frederick M. Rumack sees employee ownership as a great motivator. "Employees with an equity stake will work harder and do better by the company," he said.[10]

• •

Alderfer's ERG Theory

Clayton Alderfer reorganized Maslow's needs hierarchy into three levels of needs: (1) *existence* needs, (2) *relatedness* needs, and (3) *growth* needs (ERG).[11] The Alderfer model is illustrated in Figure 10–5. *Existence needs* relate to physical well-being and roughly correspond to Maslow's physiological and safety needs. *Relatedness needs* relate to interpersonal relationships—Maslow's belongingness needs. Alderfer's *growth needs* incorporate both self-esteem and self-actualization, the higher-order needs in the Maslow hierarchy.

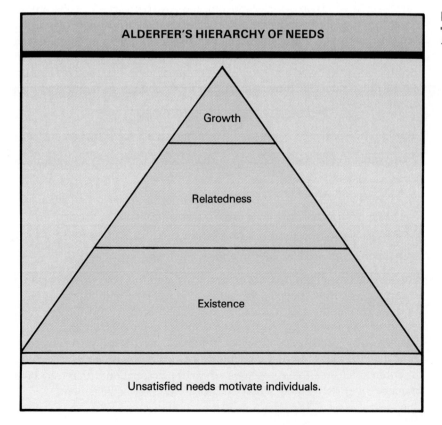

FIGURE 10–5

Alderfer's Hierarchy of Needs

The Mechanism of Needs Satisfaction   Alderfer agreed with Maslow that unsatisfied needs motivate individuals. For example, he believed workers with unsatisfied relatedness needs will be motivated to produce if peers and superiors affirm and encourage efforts to increase productivity. Alderfer also agreed that individuals, in satisfying their needs, generally move up the hierarchy; that is, they satisfy lower-order before higher-order needs. Like Maslow, he believed that as lower-order needs are satisfied, they become less important. But he also believed that as higher-order needs are satisfied, they become more important. Under some circumstances, however, individuals might return to a lower-level need. An employee frustrated in the effort to satisfy growth needs, for example, might be motivated to satisfy the lower-level relatedness needs.

Consider the employee who earns a good salary, has a reasonably high standard of living, and has made many friends at work. According to Maslow and Alderfer, this person is probably motivated to satisfy growth needs. However, what if the individual is continually frustrated in attempts to get more autonomy and responsibility—features of a job that generally encourage individual growth? When asked, the employee reports that having friends at work and getting together with them outside of work is most important. Frustration in satisfying a higher-level (growth) need has resulted in regression to a lower level of (relatedness) needs.

McClelland's Needs Theory

The research of David McClelland emphasizes that certain needs are learned and socially acquired as the individual interacts with the environment. McClelland's needs theory is concerned with how individual needs and environmental factors combine to form three basic human motives (needs): the need for achievement (*n Ach*), the need for power (*n Pow*), and the need for affiliation (*n Aff*). Motives explain behavior. McClelland conducted numerous studies in an attempt to define and measure basic human motives.

Need for Achievement   A person with a high need for achievement is one who

- Wants to take personal responsibility for finding solutions to problems.
- Is objective oriented.
- Seeks a challenge—and establishes moderate, realistic, and attainable objectives that involve risk but are not impossible to attain.
- Desires concrete feedback on performance.
- Has a high level of energy and is willing to work hard.

People exhibiting a high need for achievement find this pattern of behavior personally rewarding. For these people, the value of objective accomplishment is enhanced if the objectives are at least moderately difficult to achieve and if there is a significant degree of risk involved.[12] McClelland's research has shown that a high need for achievement is probably a strong or dominant need in only 10 percent of the U.S. population. Persons high in the need for achievement tend to gravitate toward entrepreneurial and sales positions. In these occupations, they are better able to "manage" themselves and satisfy the basic drive for achievement.

Need for Power   A high need for power means that an individual seeks to influence or control others. Such an individual tends to be one who

- Is concerned with acquiring, exercising, or retaining power or influence over others.
- Likes to compete with others in situations that allow him or her to be dominant.
- Enjoys confrontations with others.

McClelland says power can be positive or negative. Positive use of power is essential if a manager is to accomplish objectives through the efforts of others. The negative side of power is seen in an individual who seeks power for personal benefit, which may prove detrimental to the organization.[13]

Need for Affiliation   A high need for affiliation is related to the desire for affection and for establishing friendly relationships. A person with a high need for affiliation tends to be one who

- Seeks to establish and maintain friendships and close emotional relationships with others.
- Wants to be liked by others.
- Enjoys parties and social activities.
- Seeks a sense of belonging by joining groups or organizations.

To varying degrees, each person possesses all three needs; however, one of the needs tends to be more characteristic of the individual than the other two.[14] People in a given culture may have the same needs, but the relative strength of those needs differs. For example, the strength of Japanese workers' need for affiliation may be stronger than that of U.S. workers.

Each of McClelland's three motives evokes a different type of satisfaction. For example, the achievement motive tends to evoke a sense of accomplishment. A manager whose prevalent motive is power may experience satisfaction by being in control or influencing others.

According to McClelland's theory, the probability that an individual will perform a job effectively and efficiently depends on a combination of

- The strength of the motive, or need, relative to other needs.
- The possibility of success in performing the task.
- The strength value of the incentive or reward for performance.

The most effective mixture of these three motives depends on the situation. In a study of over five hundred managers, it was concluded that the most effective managers have a high need for power, a moderate need for achievement, and a low need for affiliation. These managers tend to use their power in a participative manner for the good of the organization. The best managers have a moderate need for achievement, one not strong enough to interfere with the management process. Persons with high needs for both power and achievement have high managerial motivation, but they may not make the best managers.[15] After all, managing means getting work done through the efforts of others, not overpowering them.

Outstanding salespeople tend to be high in the need for achievement and moderately high in the need for power. Entrepreneurs who develop ideas and promote specific enterprises tend to be high in achievement motivation. They delight in personally solving problems and getting immediate feedback on the degree of success. Entrepreneurs sometimes are unable to make the transition to top-level management positions. Their need for personal achievement gets in the way of the requirements for effectively influencing the organization's employees.

Equity Theory

The second major type of motivation theory—equity theory—is generally credited to J. Stacy Adams.[16] It evolved from social comparison theory—the theory that individuals must assess and know their degree of performance and the "correctness" of their attitudes in a situation. Lacking objective measures of performance or correct attitudes, they compare their performance and attitudes to those of others. **Equity theory** is *the motivation theory that people assess their performance and attitudes by comparing both their contribution to work and the benefits they derive from it to the contributions and benefits of "comparison others" whom they select—and who in reality may be like or unlike them.*

Determination of Equity

Equity theory further states that a person is motivated in proportion to the perceived fairness of the rewards received for a certain amount of effort as compared to what others receive.[17] Someone might say, "I'm going to stop working so hard—I work harder than Susan and she gets all the bonuses." This individual has compared his effort and the rewards he received to the effort exerted and the rewards received by Susan. In fact, no actual inequity may exist, but the perception of inequity influences subsequent actions.

According to equity theory, individuals are motivated to reduce any perceived inequity. They strive to make the ratios of outcomes to inputs equal.[18] When inequity exists, the person making the comparison strives to make the ratios equal by changing either the outcomes or the inputs.

Determining Equity in the Workplace

When inequity exists in an organization, individuals react in a variety of ways, some of which have been described earlier. Some people adjust their inputs; for example, they exert less effort or spend more time at work. Others change the outcomes; they request pay increases or more vacation time. Still others adjust their perception of their own or others' inputs and outcomes; they might revalue their own or others' effort, experience, or education. Some workers leave the situation entirely. The remaining people choose a different comparison person.[19] Table 10–3 illustrates the conditions under which these alternatives occur. It can be used to diagnose potentially inequitable situations and the likely consequences.

Condition*	Responses of Perceiver
$\dfrac{O_A}{I_A} > \dfrac{O_B}{I_B}$	A increases inputs. A asks for reduced outcomes. A changes the comparison person. A leaves the situation.
$\dfrac{O_A}{I_A} < \dfrac{O_B}{I_B}$	A reduces inputs. A asks for increased outcomes. A changes the comparison person. A leaves the situation.

TABLE 10–3

* O_A is the outcome for the perceiver (person A). I_A is the input of the perceiver (person A). O_B is the outcome for the comparison person (person B). I_B is the input of the comparison person (person B).

Conditions of Perceived Inequity

Thus, when high absenteeism, low productivity, high turnover, or other such symptoms exist, the following questions can be asked for each person to determine whether inequity exists:

1. What contributions, or inputs, does the person make to the situation? What is the person's level of education, effort, or experience?

2. What benefits, or outcomes, does the person receive? What is the level of job complexity, pay, or status of that person?

3. What is the ratio of inputs to outcomes? (Some quantification of both inputs and outcomes should occur. The results can then be compared in ratio form. If the inputs or outcomes cannot be quantified, the ratio must be determined qualitatively.)

4. Is the ratio the same as, greater than, or less than the ratio of comparison others?

Answers to the first three questions must also be obtained for the relevant others. The resulting ratios can then be compared.

Equity theory does not negate needs theory. Rather, it provides another perspective for analyzing motivational problems and predicting individuals' behaviors and attitudes.

ETHICAL DILEMMA

Your company is a leading producer of advanced microchips. You are the chief researcher in your firm's "think tank," which consists of eight people with various specialties. Your group has generated most of the ideas and product innovations that have kept the company an industry leader for ten years.

In fact, the think tank has been so successful that another one has been organized to support the company's newest manufacturing operation on the Gulf coast. The individuals to be included in the new think tank have already been selected, but your boss has just assigned you the task of deciding who from your group of thinkers will head the new think tank.

The person best qualified for the job is Tim Matherson. Tim is a Massachusetts Institute of Technology graduate, the informal team leader, and the individual who personally spearheaded three of the team's five most successful product advancements. However, if Tim is given the promotion, the void created by his leaving will be difficult to fill. On the other hand, the boss's niece, Marthanne Bello, was forced on the group by the boss. She is a sharp graduate of the local state university, but she is not a team player and she is always trying to push you around. You can either recommend Tim, illustrating how those who produce the most, benefit the most, or you can recommend Marthanne, making the boss happy and getting rid of her.

What would you do?

Reinforcement Theory

Reinforcement theory

The idea that human behavior can be explained in terms of the previous positive or negative outcomes of that behavior.

Reinforcement theory, which has been increasingly applied in business situations, is based primarily on the research of psychologist B. F. Skinner. **Reinforcement theory** is *the idea that human behavior can be explained in terms of the previous positive or negative outcomes of that behavior.* People tend to repeat behaviors that they have learned will produce pleasant outcomes. Behavior that is reinforced will be repeated; behavior that is not reinforced will not be repeated.

Skinner contends that people's behavior can be controlled and shaped by rewarding (reinforcing) desired behavior while ignoring undesirable actions. Over time, the reinforced behavior will tend to be repeated, whereas the unrewarded behavior will tend to be extinguished and disappear. Punishment of undesired behavior is to be avoided, since it may contribute to a feeling of restraint and actions of rebellion. Over a period of years, one can control the behavior of another without that person being aware of it. In his book *Beyond Freedom and Dignity*, Skinner says people can be controlled and shaped while at the same time feeling free.[20] Skinner's theory of shaping behavior is useful to managers, although one should not assume that human behavior is simple to understand or to modify. The primary technique suggested by Skinner is organizational behavior modification.

Organizational behavior modification

The application of B. F. Skinner's reinforcement theory to organizational change efforts.

Organizational behavior modification is *the application of Skinner's reinforcement theory to organizational change efforts.* It is based on two fundamental concepts: (1) people act in ways they find most rewarding personally, and (2) behavior can be shaped and determined by controlling the rewards. The rewards are termed *reinforcers* because the objective is to stimulate the continuation of the rewarded behavior. Which reinforcers work in motivating people is determined by trial and error and experience. What is successful with one employee may not work with another because needs and wants differ. Praise is used most frequently because it is most readily available. It becomes less effective whenever it becomes predictable or is continuously applied. Often, however, managers do not understand the importance of praise and recognition as motivators.[21] Money is also used, as are public or private letters of commendation, time off, and increased status.

Punishment is rejected as a reinforcer because although it suppresses the undesired behavior, it stimulates anger, hostility, aggression, and rebellion. And at times it is difficult to identify the punishment. In one instance, placing prisoners in solitary confinement on bread and water turned out to be a status symbol and led to the repetition of offenses. When the bread and water were changed to baby food, the status symbol disappeared, leading to a significant reduction in the number of undesirable acts. When undesired behavior is not rewarded, it tends to disappear over time.

In reinforcing desired behavior in a positive fashion, it is important to allocate the rewards soon after the behavior occurs so the person perceives a clear and immediate linkage. Fast and accurate feedback of information to the performer in itself constitutes reinforcement.

Organizational behavior modification has been used successfully in a number of organizations to improve performance. In one firm, positive reinforcement was used to reduce absenteeism. Each day an employee came to work on time, the person received a playing card. At the end of the week, the person with the highest poker hand received $20. Over a three-month period, the absenteeism rate of the experimental group decreased 18 percent, whereas that of a control group increased.[22] In its use of organizational behavior modification, Michigan Bell Telephone identified specific desired behaviors such as the following: (1) service promptness in answering calls, (2) shortness of time taken to give information, (3) use of proper references in handling the call, and (4) improvement in attendance.[23] Praise and recognition were the dominant reinforcers. The results were a 50 percent improvement in attendance and above-standard productivity and efficiency levels.

For the manager who desires to use organizational behavior modification, the following actions are necessary:

- Identifying the desired performance in specific terms—for example, improved attendance rates or answering questions within one hour.
- Identifying the rewards that will reinforce the desired behavior—for example, praise, money, and time off.
- Making the reward a direct consequence of the behavior.
- Selecting the optimum reinforcement schedule.

Despite the successes achieved by behavior modification, it has been criticized as being a manipulative and autocratic approach to the management of people. People are conditioned to change their behavior in the direction required by management and the organization. Some critics argue that organizational behavior modification is not consistent with the theories of such behavioral scientists as Maslow, Argyris, and McGregor. The assumption underlying these theories is that people are motivated by their own internal needs and are capable of a degree of self-control. On the other hand, behavior modification assumes that the causes of human behavior are in the environment and therefore are external to the individual.

Expectancy Theories of Motivation

In recent years, one of the more popular theories of motivation has been expectancy theory.[24] The approaches to motivation developed by Maslow, Herzberg, and McClelland do not adequately account for differences in individual employees or explain why people behave in certain ways. Victor Vroom developed **expectancy theory**—*the approach to motivation that attempts to explain behavior in terms of an individual's goals and choices and the expectations of achieving the objectives.*[25] The theory assumes that

Expectancy theory

The approach to motivation that attempts to explain behavior in terms of an individual's goals and choices and the expectations of achieving the objectives.

people can determine which outcomes they prefer and can make realistic estimates of their chances of obtaining them. Expectancy theory offers a comprehensive view of motivation and integrates many of the elements of the needs, equity, and reinforcement theories.

Vroom popularized expectancy theory in the 1960s. His model states that motivation is a function of expectancy, valence, and instrumentality.[26] In other words:

$$\text{Motivation} = E \times V \times I$$

Expectancy (E) refers to a person's perception of the probability that effort will lead to performance. For example, a person who perceives that he or she will produce more by working harder has a high expectancy that hard work leads to productivity. A person who perceives that he or she will be ostracized by other workers by working harder has a high expectancy that effort leads to exclusion. A person who sees no link between effort and performance will have zero expectancy about this relationship. If expectancy is zero, then motivation will be lower than if expectancy is positive.

Valence (V) refers to a person's perception of the value of the projected outcomes—that is, how much the person likes or dislikes receiving those outcomes. An individual with high esteem needs generally will attach a high valence to a new job title or a promotion. An individual with strong security needs will value pension and retirement programs or the awarding of tenure. An individual with growth or self-actualization needs will view challenging jobs or increased responsibility as motivating because of their high valence. When valence is high, motivation is likely to be higher than when valence is low or negative.

Instrumentality (I) refers to a person's perception of the probability that certain outcomes, positive or negative, will be attached to performance. For example, a person who perceives that he or she will receive greater pay or benefits for producing well has high instrumentality. A person who sees no link between performance and pay has zero instrumentality. Motivation is a function of the value of instrumentality.

Barry Staw, among others, introduced a revised expectancy theory in the late 1970s.[27] Rather than limiting his model to **extrinsic motivation** (*motivation by factors outside the job, such as pay, job title, and tenure*),[28] Staw also considers **intrinsic motivation** (*motivation by factors within the job, such as creativity, autonomy, and responsibility*).[29] In short, performing a task has intrinsic and extrinsic valence, both of which enter into the calculation of motivation.

In this model, motivation is reduced if an individual does not value either the intrinsic or the extrinsic outcomes or if the person perceives that the intrinsic or extrinsic performance-to-outcome expectancies (rewards) are low. For example, a worker's motivation will be reduced if (1) the person does not like doing certain tasks or (2) the person does not receive the rewards desired for performing them. A manager can increase extrinsic motivation either by depriving a worker of a valued outcome or by giving the worker the extrinsic rewards valued most; the manager can also ensure that rewards accompany task performance. Managers can increase intrinsic motivation by changing the characteristics of work activities—for example, by redesigning jobs.[30]

Expectancy theory has dominated research on motivation since the early 1970s, principally because it has provided three factors useful to managers in their efforts to increase employee motivation: expectancy, valence, and instrumentality. Its emphasis on the individual and its ability to highlight individual differences can also

Extrinsic motivation

Motivation by factors outside the job, such as pay, job title, and tenure.

Intrinsic motivation

Motivation by factors within the job, such as creativity, autonomy, and responsibility.

be useful to the practicing manager. Expectancy theory, more than any other presented so far, offers a comprehensive guide for understanding motivation.

Objective Setting and Motivation

Objective setting is a common technique used in applying the motivation theories presented so far. Setting objectives can help individuals identify ways of meeting their needs. Accomplishing objectives can be reinforcing in itself. In these ways, objective setting encourages individuals to exert effort, and objective accomplishment motivates them to perform. Employees at every Domino's restaurant know how they stack up against the companywide average of twenty-three-minute delivery.

Objectives, which any member of an organization can set, describe desired future states. Once established, objectives can focus behavior and motivate individuals to achieve the desired end state. Examples in organizations are cutting costs, reducing absenteeism, increasing employee satisfaction, and changing the work climate. In 90 percent of the reported studies, objective setting has shown a positive effect on performance.[31]

Research suggests that objectives that are specific, moderately difficult, and yet accepted by a worker are more likely to be motivating than those that are not. Further, research has indicated that objective-setting programs improve performance at both managerial and nonmanagerial levels over an extended period of time in a variety of organizations.[32] In very complex jobs, however, objective setting may not be feasible. In fact, it may lead to bureaucratic behavior, where setting objectives becomes an end in itself. Feedback through performance reviews and pay can enhance performance, but only when these incentives lead individuals to set higher objectives.[33] Thus, objective setting provides a link between motivational perspectives and issues of interpersonal communication, since a clear statement and sharing of objectives is a prerequisite to resolving motivational dilemmas.

Motivation and the Reward System

Money is undoubtedly a motivator to many, and fear may well alter behavior; but more long-term motivators, such as a comprehensive and applicable reward system, should be sought. Thus, pay based on performance is one of the best means for motivating people and encouraging increased productivity, but more money is simply a short term motivator.[34]

Edward Lawler has concluded that five factors influence the degree of satisfaction gained from rewards. First, satisfaction depends on the amount received and the amount the individual thinks should be received. Typically, the larger the reward, whether extrinsic (such as pay) or intrinsic (such as job challenge), the more satisfied people feel. However, this feeling is moderated somewhat by the perception of whether the reward is justified. Some people feel uneasy if they receive a disproportionately large reward, particularly for the amount of effort they exert or in comparison to the rewards of co-workers whom they perceive as similar.

Second, comparison to what happens to others influences people's feelings of satisfaction. If an employee believes she is being over- or underrewarded in comparison to other employees whom she views as similar to herself, she probably feels less satisfied than if she believes she is being treated equitably.

Third, an employee's satisfaction with both the intrinsic and extrinsic rewards received affects overall job satisfaction.

Fourth, people differ widely in the rewards they desire and in the value they attach to each. For instance, some individuals are willing to trade off flexible working hours for increased compensation. Others choose benefits (sick leave, medical insurance, pension contributions) over salary increases.

And fifth, many extrinsic rewards satisfy only because they lead to other rewards. For example, increased pay may satisfy because it results in more recreational opportunities or increased status for an employee.[35]

These observations suggest the need for a diverse reward system. Lawler's observations also suggest that a comprehensive reward system demands a complete analysis of the organization's members and their work situation before rewards are chosen and allocated. They emphasize the nature and consistency of rewards while not ignoring the individual members and their specific needs.

An effective reward system ties rewards to performance. Individuals who work harder, produce more, or produce better-quality outputs should receive greater rewards than poorer performers. Reward systems should also offer a sufficient number and diversity of rewards.

The criteria for the allocation of rewards must be clear and complete. Individual members of the organization should know whether they will receive rewards for level or quality of performance, attendance, innovativeness, or effort, for example. The criteria for achieving specific wages, benefits, and incentives must be clearly defined. But different individuals should be treated differently when appropriate. Workers who perform at different levels or who have different needs often should not receive the same rewards. At the same time, management must ensure that workers perceive the distribution of rewards as equitable. Finally, organizational rewards should compare favorably with rewards in similar organizations. For organizations to attract, motivate, and retain qualified and competent employees, they must offer rewards comparable to their competitors'.

How Managers Can Be Better at Motivating

One of the primary objectives of managers is to achieve higher worker productivity. A prime means of accomplishing this task is through creation of a motivated work force. For a worker to achieve higher productivity, the following three elements must be correctly isolated and combined into a package tailored to motivate each individual worker: specific employee desires, the probability of satisfying these desires, and the time frame for satisfying the desires.[36]

Specific Employee Desires

A worker must have a personal desire for something in order to be motivated. Factors that motivate one person may have no effect on another. One worker may strongly desire additional money, whereas another may want a promotion. Some workers prefer status symbols to money; others hope for praise. It is likely that many of the drivers for Domino's Pizza are motivated by the money they receive from the company and in tips for each delivery.

For some workers, nothing related to the job or the job environment serves to motivate. Work is merely a means to pay the bills and put food on the table — something unpleasant that must be endured. Perhaps the only factor that could possibly increase productivity among these individuals is the fear of being fired.

Understandably, workers want to know: What's in it for me? Managers must first attempt to determine the specific desires of each worker and then, where possible, create an environment in which the worker can satisfy personal needs through increased performance.

Probability of Satisfying Employee Desires

The identification of personal needs is but one factor in increasing productivity. Workers want to know their chances of getting what they want if they produce more. Therefore, employee rewards must be directly tied to the desired result — increased productivity—so workers can connect their efforts with the possible rewards. When the drivers with Domino's Pizza make more deliveries, they receive extra money in the form of both tips and company payment for the deliveries. Although the tips are not guaranteed, there is a high probability they will be provided. More deliveries mean more money.

An employee's perception of the manager's past actions significantly influences motivation. Suppose a manager frequently says, "If you don't get moving, I'm going to fire you!" but he never does. Workers probably will attach a low probability to the enforcement of his threats. If the manager always follows through on oral statements, workers are likely to respond.

Motivation requires a relatively high likelihood that the worker's needs will be fulfilled—that the offer of money will yield a raise or that the threat of disciplinary action will result in that action. At times, however, the manager may be able to identify a need but have no control over fulfilling it. For example, some managers cannot grant pay raises or promotions themselves but can still use these rewards as motivators if they have a reputation of getting their recommendations approved. Realistically, a manager who cannot satisfy a strong need may not be able to obtain higher productivity.

Time Frame Involved in Satisfying Desires

The closer the reward is to the expenditure of effort, the greater the likelihood that the worker will put forth that effort. And the degree of effort will increase when the reward and the expenditure of effort occur within a limited time frame. The worker who desires more money may be highly motivated if the money is to be received in the next paycheck, but enthusiasm may wane if the possible pay increase is a year away. Drivers for Domino's Pizza receive tips immediately on delivery and a weekly paycheck based on the number of deliveries.

How the Factors are Related

In practice, employee desires, probability, and timing all combine to produce motivation. All three factors must be correctly isolated and combined into a package so each worker will be motivated. Incorrectly identifying or misrepresenting any of these three factors could substantially reduce a manager's motivation efforts. The better the manager is at identifying employee desires, the greater the likelihood of inducing increased performance. But identification of a specific desire is not enough; the manager must be able to satisfy that desire or it is useless as a motivator. Then the time frame must be structured so the reward is forthcoming soon after the expenditure of effort. The glue that holds this entire relationship together is the credibility of the manager. The manager's behavior must be related directly to the promises or threats made. There are managers, though, who seem to violate many of the rules and still succeed. NCNB's Hugh McColl, Jr., is one such manager.

Hugh McColl, Jr., Commando Banker

In four years of aggressive acquisitions, Hugh McColl built NCNB Corp., formerly North Carolina National Bank, into the nation's tenth largest non-money center bank. At one point, McColl was one of *Fortune* magazine's 10 "Toughest Bosses." Obviously, McColl had been a winner.

McColl eschewed individuality. "There's no place for the lone wolf here," he said, "We're team driven." A *Fortune* reporter observed, "The company's executives are almost hyperspirited, rather like members of a cult." An NCNB executive said the company looks for people who are "malleable." Piped another, "Hugh's always breathing down your neck. He's such a forceful person that it's hard to be who you are."

Terror was a common theme at NCNB. For a while, McColl kept a dummy hand grenade on his desk. He once pulled the pin during a meeting, it was said, "to see who would flinch." Asked about McColl's management style, subordinates said, "We sit on the edge of our chairs. . . . He manages with aggressiveness and perfectionism, and he expects us to cope with the tension." McColl did not disagree. "I expect the Herculean," he said. "There's no golf in the middle of the day, no coasting to retirement. If you're not leading, you're out of here. . . . You've got to feed the tiger, and what the tiger demands is victory. That's what galvanizes the company." He once considered adopting the slogan, "Crush the sons of bitches and have a nice day." McColl's personnel chief observed, "That slogan shows that warmth and sensitivity are paramount—we want to win, but we don't want to ruin anyone's day." [37]

MANAGEMENT IN PRACTICE: A Skill-Building Exercise

Mary Martin was assistant for planning at Diamond Technologies Corporation in Dallas, Texas. She had just completed a report, and she smiled as she handed it to the boss, administrative vice-president Jim Newberg. Mary knew she had done an excellent job on the report and that he would be impressed. "I have all my work caught up," Mary said. "Would you like me to do that budget workup on the new copy machine you mentioned last week?"

"It has to be in by the middle of next week if we're going to get the machine," Jim said with a smile. "Do you think you can do it that fast?"

"Yes, sir," Mary replied. "I may have to work a few extra hours, but it'll be on your desk Tuesday."

Mary had a pleasant feeling as she left Jim's office. Everyone knew that he was being promoted to executive vice-president within a couple of months and that he would select his own replacement. Mary believed she was definitely in the running. Doing a good job on this project might clinch it. As she walked eagerly back to her desk, she thought, "I'd better call Harry and let him know that I'll be working late tonight."

Is Mary a motivated employee? Explain.

Job Design

When a problem occurs, the usual trend is to blame the worker when the real obstacle was job design. Many believe that the manner in which the job is accomplished is fixed. This is often not the case, but the boss looks to the worker first—not the design of the job—as the cause of the problem. Many times jobs can be redesigned with a substantial improvement in productivity.[38] The challenge is to increase worker productivity by finding ways to "unlock the potential that exists in the overwhelming majority of our workforce."[39] J. Richard Hackman and Greg R. Oldham contend that it is possible to achieve an improvement in the quality of work life and also to increase or maximize worker productivity. They challenge several traditionally held assumptions, such as these:

- The basic nature of work is fixed and cannot be changed.
- Technology and work processes determine job design.
- All management can do is properly select and train personnel.

Job design is *the process of determining the specific tasks to be performed, the methods used in performing these tasks, and how the job relates to other work in the organization.* Hackman and Oldham offer additional insight regarding job design. In their book *Work Redesign*, Hackman and Oldham assert that if managers wish to create a climate for a high level of motivation, they must provide reliable feedback on performance. There must be a sense that the worker is accountable for specific results and a feeling that the job has meaning beyond pay.[40] Workers get more satisfaction from completing a whole and identifiable piece of work than from producing indistinguishable pieces. Because of this, job design becomes an important concept in creating a motivational climate for today's work force.

Technology constraints on job design include the type of equipment and tools, as well as the work layout and methods used in producing the goods or services. These constraints may make job redesign difficult, perhaps expensive, and at times impossible. For example, adapting or redesigning the assembly-line production of automobiles or electronic components may not be technically or economically feasible.[41]

Job design

The process of determining the specific tasks to be performed, the methods used in performing these tasks, and how the job relates to other work in the organization.

Economic factors affect job design. The question must be asked: Are sufficient resources available to the organization if it wants to redesign some or all of its jobs? Although one can suggest ways to redesign jobs to improve output and the level of worker satisfaction, the cost may be prohibitive. A manager must continually balance the benefits of job design with the costs.

Job design is also affected by government requirements and regulations. Management might want to design a job in a way that would increase worker performance, but the new design might violate safety standards covered by the Occupational Safety and Health Act.

If a company has a union, job design can be affected by the union's philosophy, policies, and strategies. Typically, the contract between the company and the union specifies and defines the types of jobs and the duties and responsibilities of workers. Unions traditionally have been opposed to many work redesign experiments. They perceive them to be attempts by management to squeeze more work out of the worker without increasing wages. Also, unions may view job redesign as a threat to their power and position with workers.

Important considerations for job design are employees' abilities, attitudes, skills, and motivation. Obviously, the design of particular jobs depends on the ability or training of present or potential employees. It would be ridiculous to design a job that would be considerably more complex than could be handled by employees available for the positions. The ability and willingness of employees to be trained can limit job redesign.

Finally, management philosophy, objectives, and strategies may determine the degree of job redesign possible. Top management must be committed to the concept of job redesign. Job redesign may allow employees to gain greater authority in determining how their jobs are performed and how they themselves are managed. Thus, managers who tend to possess Theory X assumptions would likely have difficulty with job redesign.

Job Enrichment and Job Enlargement

Job enrichment

Basic changes in the content and level of responsibility of a job so as to provide greater challenge to the worker.

In the past two decades, there has been considerable interest in and application of job enrichment in a wide variety of organizations. Strongly advocated by Frederick Herzberg, **job enrichment** is *basic changes in the content and level of responsibility of a job so as to provide greater challenge to the worker.* Job enrichment provides a vertical expansion of responsibilities. The worker has the opportunity to derive a feeling of achievement, recognition, responsibility, and personal growth in performing the job. Although job enrichment programs do not always achieve positive results, they have often brought about improvements in job performance and in the level of satisfaction of workers in many organizations.

AT&T, Polaroid, Texas Instruments, Monsanto, Weyerhaeuser, General Motors, and Corning Glass, among many other firms, have achieved excellent results after implementing job enrichment programs. In most instances, productivity and job satisfaction increased, and employee turnover and absenteeism were reduced.[42]

According to Herzberg, five principles should be followed in implementing job enrichment:

1. *Increasing job demands.* The job should be changed in such a way as to increase its level of difficulty and responsibility.

2. *Increasing the worker's accountability.* More individual control and authority over the work should be allowed, while the manager retains ultimate accountability.

3. *Providing work scheduling freedom.* Within limits, the individual workers should be allowed to schedule their own work.

4. *Providing feedback.* Timely periodic reports on performance should be made directly to the workers rather than to their supervisors.

5. *Providing new learning experiences.* Work situations should encourage opportunities for new experiences and personal growth.[43]

Many people have attempted to differentiate between job enrichment and job enlargement. **Job enlargement** is *changes in the scope of a job so as to provide greater variety for the worker.* Job enlargement is said to provide a horizontal expansion of duties. For example, instead of being taught how to operate only one machine, a person may be taught how to operate two or even three; but no higher level of responsibility is provided. Job enrichment, on the other hand, provides a person with additional responsibilities along with the additional tasks. For instance, the worker who is taught how to operate three machines may be given the responsibility of scheduling the machines as well. Increasing a worker's responsibility means providing the worker with increased freedom to do the job—to make decisions about and to exercise more self-control over the work.

Employee-Centered Work Redesign[44]

An innovative concept designed to link the mission of the company with the job satisfaction needs of employees is **employee-centered work redesign.** Here, employees are encouraged to become involved in redesigning their work to benefit both the organization and themselves. Workers can be innovative in proposing changes in their job design to make the job more satisfying. But at the same time, they must show how these changes better accomplish the goals of the unit as a whole—for example, improved quality and productivity. With this approach, the contribution of each employee is recognized, while at the same time, the focus remains on effective accomplishment of the organizational mission.

Flextime

The practice of permitting employees to choose, with certain limitations, their own working hours is **flextime.** In a survey involving companies of all sizes, from all industries, and from every region of the United States and Canada, flextime was being used by 30 percent of the responding firms.[45]

In a flextime system, employees work the same number of hours per day as they do on a standard schedule. However, they are permitted to work these hours within what is called a *band width,* which is the maximum length of the workday. The part of the day when all employees must be present is the *core time.* The time period within which employees may vary their schedules is the *flexible time.*[46] A typical schedule permits employees to begin work between 6:00 A.M. and 9:00 A.M. and to complete the workday between 3:00 P.M. and 6:00 P.M. Perhaps flextime's most important feature is that it allows employees to schedule their time to minimize

Job enlargement
Changes in the scope of a job so as to provide greater variety for the worker.

Employee-centered work redesign
An innovative concept designed to link the mission of the company with the job satisfaction needs of employees.

Flextime
The practice of permitting employees to choose, with certain limitations, their own working hours.

conflicts between personal needs and job requirements. Flextime also permits employees to work the hours during which they believe they function best.

Compressed Workweek

Any arrangement of work hours that permits employees to fulfill their work obligation in fewer days than the typical five-day workweek is the **compressed workweek.** The most common approach to the compressed workweek is four ten-hour days. Working under this arrangement, some employees have reported an increase in job satisfaction. In addition, the compressed workweek offers them the potential for better use of leisure time for family life, personal business, and recreation.[47] Some employers have cited advantages such as increased productivity and reduced turnover and absenteeism.

On the other hand, problems have been encountered in the areas of work scheduling and employee fatigue. In some cases, these problems have resulted in lower-quality products and reduced customer service. Some firms have therefore reverted to the conventional five-day week. It seems clear that, overall, acceptance of the compressed workweek is not as clear-cut as acceptance of flextime.

Job Sharing

A relatively new approach to work—job sharing—is attractive to people who wish to work fewer than forty hours per week. **Job sharing** is *two part-time people splitting the duties of one job in some agreed-on manner and being paid according to their contributions.* From the employer's viewpoint, compensation is paid for only one job, but creativity is obtained from two employees. Job sharing may be especially attractive to individuals who have substantial family responsibilities and to older workers who wish to move gradually into retirement.

The Globalization of Job Design

Redesigning the way jobs are done is a strategy to increase global quality and productivity. One example of the positive impact of job redesign is the General Motors–Toyota NUMMI joint venture in Fremont, California. Before the NUMMI joint venture, General Motors' Fremont plant had one of the worst records in the company for poor labor relations and defective production. The plant was a typical assembly-line operation in which workers and supervisors were encouraged to push as many parts as possible down the line and to let quality control inspectors ferret out defects at the end of the line.[48]

Four years after the joint venture started, its productivity and quality levels rivaled Japan's best and exceeded anything in the American automobile industry. The question arises: What caused these changes? It couldn't be the workers, since they are still members of the United Auto Workers (UAW), being paid union-scale wages and benefits. Nor did the change spring from the introduction of advanced robotics. It occurred because of a revolutionary team-production system run by the workers themselves. Each worker is responsible for quality control and for ensuring that no car moves on to the next station unless every job already done on it is perfect. The

---

Compressed workweek

Any arrangement of work hours that permits employees to fulfill their work obligation in fewer days than the typical five-day workweek.

Job sharing

Two part-time people splitting the duties of one job in some agreed-on manner and being paid according to their contributions.

system was worked out jointly with the plant's Japanese and American managers, and by the third partner in the joint venture, the UAW rank and file on the assembly line.[49]

Conflict is common in international alliances, especially in partnerships between high-technology companies filled with big egos. NUMMI's lessons for these alliances are simple ones: Involve all parties in the effort to redesign jobs. Be willing to listen, and be receptive to new ideas. Learn from each other's strengths and weaknesses.[50]

How First-Level Managers Can Dispense Rewards

It has already been said that different individuals are motivated by different things. The effective first-level manager attempts to satisfy needs in order to increase productivity. Some of the rewards the manager might control are

- Formal recognition, such as letters of appreciation.
- Invitations to coffee or lunch.
- Recommendations for pay increases and promotions.
- Time off.
- Desirable work assignments.

Lower-level managers may be able to recommend only certain rewards, such as pay and promotion. But these rewards can still be motivators, particularly for managers who have a reputation for getting their recommendations approved.

Theory Z

William Ouchi, in his book *Theory Z: How American Business Can Meet the Japanese Challenge*, and Anthony Athos and Richard Pascale, in *The Art of Japanese Management*, describe management practices in a number of progressive U.S. companies that are similar to those used by successful Japanese firms for years.[51] Ouchi identifies Hewlett-Packard, IBM, Procter & Gamble, and Eastman Kodak as Theory Z organizations. **Theory Z** is *the belief that a high degree of mutual responsibility, loyalty, and consideration between companies and their employees will result in higher productivity and improved employee welfare.* Theory Z companies tend to practice a system of lifetime employment and to avoid layoffs. The companies usually enjoy low employee turnover, low absenteeism, and high employee morale. The workers are more involved in their jobs with the company, a factor that leads to increased productivity and performance.

Theory Z companies tend to develop their own traditions, ideals, and culture and to foster something of a family environment. This family, or culture, within the organization tends to bond its members—employees and managers—thereby facilitating decision making and communications in the company. All of this has much in common with Japanese patterns and practices. Companies in the United States have not necessarily imitated Japanese practices but have developed their own management style through recognition of the types of employees who make up today's U.S. work force.

Theory Z
The belief that a high degree of mutual responsibility, loyalty, and consideration between companies and their employees will result in higher productivity and improved employee welfare.

While U.S. managers obviously can learn a great deal from the Japanese, the support for Theory Z has not been unanimous. A study of managers in five developed countries found that successful managers favor an achievement orientation, interaction, and risk taking. Less successful managers emphasize the family type of culture, which is central to Theory Z. It was also found that Japanese managers emphasize ordinary motivational ideas, such as the use of advancement, money, and challenging assignments to motivate workers.[52]

A Global Perspective

In order to create an environment conducive to a high level of employee motivation, global managers must understand some basic philosophies of human nature in the host country. They must have a thorough appreciation of the characteristics of the work force and of any cultural or social elements that could affect motivation. Multinational managers must encourage the development of subordinates in ways that contribute to their performance, career development, and personal satisfaction. They must also realize that motivating employees globally is a complex job. Individuals in different countries are often motivated differently, and managers must realize the various differences.

At the American NUMMI automobile plant, team members are motivated by a formal agreement between management and employees that assures the workers that if the team concept works, and productivity increases, no one will lose a job.[53] The overwhelming motivation for these employees is job security.

Motivational factors in other countries may vary from those in the United States. In Sweden, the labor force is highly educated and well trained, but people do not like to work in factories. Further, because of the high tax rates on overtime earnings, more money typically cannot be used to motivate them. So Swedish auto maker Volvo has built more pleasant factories and allows teams to largely manage themselves as a means of keeping workers on the job and productive. In this case, people work best in environments that are pleasant, and they appear to be very concerned with having better factories for their children to work in. Morale seems high in the new plants, productivity is up, and absenteeism is lower.[54] In Sweden, as in all countries, the environment surrounding the work force is extremely important. Basically, motivating in the global environment requires that managers develop a system that will cause employees to desire to put forth effort in the pursuit of organizational objectives.

• •

Self-Assessment Exercise

Will You Be Good at Dealing with Motivation?

1. Are you willing to not assume that everyone is motivated by the same thing?

    ☐ Yes   ☐ No

2. Are you willing to get to know workers as individuals?

    ☐ Yes   ☐ No

(continued)

3. Are you willing to learn the difference between high morale and motivation?

   ☐ Yes   ☐ No

4. Are you willing to learn to develop predictability in the workplace?

   ☐ Yes   ☐ No

5. Are you willing to let the rewards and penalties be applied as soon as possible after they are earned?

   ☐ Yes   ☐ No

6. Are you willing to reinforce desired behavior?

   ☐ Yes   ☐ No

7. Are you willing to learn to not issue idle threats?

   ☐ Yes   ☐ No

8. Are you willing to attempt to make the work interesting for employees?

   ☐ Yes   ☐ No

9. Are you willing to listen to workers?

   ☐ Yes   ☐ No

10. Are you willing to learn that the manager's positive or negative expectations will have a significant influence on employee motivation and performance?

    ☐ Yes   ☐ No

Summary

Motivation is the willingness to put forth effort in the pursuit of organizational objectives. To create an environment conducive to a high level of motivation, managers must understand some philosophies of human nature, such as McGregor's Theory X and Theory Y, Argyris's maturity theory, and the self-fulfilling prophecy.

Four popular needs theories are (1) Maslow's hierarchy of needs theory, (2) Herzberg's motivator-hygiene (two-factor) theory, (3) Alderfer's ERG theory, and (4) McClelland's needs theory. Maslow stated that individuals have a hierarchy of five needs, from the most basic level of physiological needs to the highest level of self-actualization needs. Herzberg suggested that motivators—features of a job's content, such as responsibility—satisfy higher-order needs, motivate a person to exert more effort, and encourage better performance. Hygiene factors, which meet physiological, security, or social needs, satisfy lower-order needs and prevent dissatisfaction. Alderfer reorganized Maslow's needs hierarchy into three needs levels: (1) existence, (2) relatedness, and (3) growth. McClelland focused on needs similar to the higher-order needs identified by Maslow—needs for achievement (*n Ach*), affiliation (*n Aff*), and power (*n Pow*).

Equity theory is the theory that people assess their performance and attitudes by comparing their contribution to work and the benefits they derive from it to those of "comparison others." In reinforcement theory, human behavior is explained in terms of the previous positive or negative outcomes of that behavior. Vroom's expectancy theory states that motivation is a function of expectancy, valence, and instrumentality.

Objective setting is a common technique used in applying the motivation theories. Setting objectives helps individuals identify ways of meeting their needs, and accomplishing objectives can be reinforcing in itself. Objective setting thus encourages individuals to exert effort, and objective accomplishment tends to motivate individuals.

Research suggests that rewards now cause performance and satisfaction later. A complete analysis of the members of an organization and their work situation is a prerequisite to choosing and allocating rewards.

For a worker to achieve higher productivity, the following three elements must be isolated and combined into a package tailored to motivate each individual worker: specific employee desires, the probability of satisfying these desires, and the time frame for satisfying the desires.

Job design is concerned with the specific tasks to be performed in a job, the methods used in performing them, and the relationship of each job to other work in the organization. Job enrichment is basic changes in the content and level of responsibility of a job so as to provide greater challenge to the worker. An innovative concept designed to link the mission of the company with the job satisfaction needs of employees is employee-centered work redesign. Here, employees are encouraged to become involved in redesigning their work to benefit both the organization and themselves. Job enlargement is changes in the scope of a job so as to provide greater variety for the worker. The practice of permitting employees to choose, with certain limitations, their own working hours is flextime. Any arrangement of work hours that permits employees to fulfill their work obligation in fewer days than the typical five-day workweek is the compressed workweek. In job sharing, two part-time people split the duties of one job in some agreed-on manner and are paid according to their contributions.

The effective first-level manager attempts to satisfy needs in order to increase productivity. Lower-level managers may be able to recommend only certain rewards, such as pay and promotion. But these rewards can still be motivators.

Theory Z is the belief that a high degree of mutual responsibility, loyalty, and consideration between companies and their employees will result in higher productivity and improved employee welfare. Type Z companies tend to practice a system of lifetime employment and avoid layoffs. The companies usually enjoy low employee turnover, low absenteeism, and high employee morale.

Review Questions

1. Define *motivation*.

2. Compare and contrast McGregor's Theory X and Theory Y. What are some examples of managerial practices that are consistent with a Theory Y philosophy

of human nature?

3. What is Argyris's maturity theory?

4. Relate Herzberg's theory of motivation to the needs theory developed by Maslow.

5. Describe McClelland's theory of human motives. How does it relate to motivation, and what are the basic characteristics of individuals described by the theory?

6. Define *equity theory* and describe it as it relates to motivation.

7. Briefly describe reinforcement theory.

8. What is expectancy theory?

9. How can objective setting act as a common technique in the application of motivation theories?

10. What are the factors that Edward Lawler has concluded influence satisfaction with a reward?

11. Explain how managers can be better at motivating.

12. Define the following terms:
    a. job enrichment
    b. job enlargement
    c. flextime
    d. compressed workweek
    e. job sharing

Key Terms

Motivation

Theory X

Theory Y

Self-fulfilling prophecy

Equity theory

Reinforcement theory

Organizational behavior
  modification

Expectancy theory

Extrinsic motivation

Intrinsic motivation

Job design

Job enrichment

Job enlargement

Employee-centered
  work redesign

Flextime

Compressed workweek

Job sharing

Theory Z

Bob Rosen could hardly wait to get back to work Monday morning. He was excited about his chance of getting a large bonus. Bob was a machine operator with Ram Manufacturing Company, a Wichita, Kansas, maker of electric motors. He operated an armature-winding machine. The machine wound copper wire onto metal cores to make the rotating elements for electric motors.

Ram paid machine operators on a graduated piece-rate basis; operators got a certain amount for each part made, plus a bonus for producing above standard. A worker who produced 10 percent above standard for a certain month received a 10 percent bonus. For 20 percent above standard, the bonus was 20 percent. Bob realized that he had a good chance of earning a 20 percent bonus that month. That would be $287.

Bob had a special use for the extra money. His wife's birthday was just three weeks away. He was hoping to get her a new Chevrolet Citation. He had already saved $450, but the down payment on the Citation was $700. The bonus would enable him to buy the car.

Bob arrived at work at seven o'clock that morning, although his shift did not begin until eight. He went to his work station and checked the supply of blank cores and copper wire. Finding that only one spool of wire was on hand, he asked the fork truck driver to bring another. Then he asked the operator who was working the graveyard shift, "Sam, do you mind if I grease the machine while you work?"

"No," Sam said, "that won't bother me a bit."

After greasing the machine, Bob stood and watched Sam. He thought of ways to simplify the motions involved in loading, winding, and unloading the armatures. As Bob took over the machine after the eight o'clock whistle, he thought: "I hope I can pull this off. I know the car will make Kathy happy. She won't be stuck at home while I'm at work."

Questions

1. What are the advantages and disadvantages of a graduated piece-rate pay system such as that at Ram?
2. Explain Bob's high level of motivation in terms of needs theory, reinforcement theory, and expectancy theory.

Harry Neal had been employed with Trimark Data Systems, Inc., for five years. During that time, he progressed from programmer to senior programmer analyst. He was generally pleased with the company and thoroughly enjoyed the creative demands of his job.

One Saturday afternoon during a golf game with his friend and co-worker Randy Dean, Harry discovered that his department had hired a recent state university graduate as a programmer analyst. Although Harry was good-natured, he got upset when he learned that the new man's starting salary was only $30 a month lower than his own. Harry was bewildered. He felt that he was being treated unfairly.

The following Monday morning, Harry confronted Dave Edwards, the personnel director, and asked if what he had heard was true. Dave apologetically admitted that it was and attempted to explain the company's situation: "Harry, the market for programmer analysts is very tight. In order for the company to attract qualified prospects, we have to offer a premium starting salary. We desperately needed another analyst, and this was the only way we could get one."

Harry asked Dave if his salary would be adjusted accordingly. Dave answered: "Your salary will be re-evaluated at the regular performance appraisal time. You're doing a great job, though, and I'm sure the boss will recommend a raise." Harry thanked Dave for his time but left the office shaking his head and wondering about his future with the company.

Questions

1. Do you believe Dave's explanation was satisfactory? Discuss.
2. What is likely to be the impact of this incident on Harry's motivation to work?
3. What action do you think the company should have taken with regard to Harry? Explain.

Notes

1. This case is a composite of a number of published accounts, among them: Patricia Sellers, "Getting Customers to Love You," *Fortune*, March 13, 1989, pp. 38–49; Raymond Serafin, "Domino's Kneads Pan Pie," *Advertising Age*, September 19, 1988, p. 36; Philip E. Ross, "President Is Chosen for Domino's Pizza," *New York Times*, June 13, 1989, p. D5; Raymond Serafin, "Making Domino's Deliver," *Advertising Age*, November 28, 1988, pp. 10, 56; "Policy on Drivers at Domino's Pizza," *New York Times*, June 23, 1989, p. D4; "Domino's," *New Yorker*, March 27, 1989, p. 37; Elenor Blau, "Domino's Pulls 'Saturday Night' Ads," *New York Times*, April 11, 1989, p. D25; Jerry Buckley, "The Pizza Man Chooses God," *U.S. News & World Report*, July 29, 1991, pp. 43–44; Lisa Driscoll and David Woodruff, "With Tom Monaghan Back, Can Domino's Deliver?" *Business Week*, October 28, 1991, pp. 136–137.

2. John Hoerr, "The Payoff from Teamwork," *Business Week*, July 10, 1989, pp. 56–62.

3. Douglas McGregor, *The Human Side of Enterprise* (New York: McGraw-Hill, 1960), pp. 15–60.

4. Chris Argyris, *Personality and Organization* (New York: Harper & Row, 1957), pp. 31–42.

5. John L. Single, "The Power of Expectations: Productivity and the Self-Fulfilling Prophecy," *Management World*, November 1980, pp. 19, 37–38.

6. Ibid.

7. Abraham Maslow, *The Human Side of Enterprise* (New York: Harper, 1954), pp. 16–23.

8. Clayton P. Alderfer, "A Critique of Salancik and Pfeffer's Examination of Need-Satisfaction Theories," *Administrative Science Quarterly* 22 (December 1977): 658–672.

9. Frederick Herzberg, *Work and the Nature of Man* (Cleveland: World, 1966), pp. 91–106.

10. Harris Collingwood, "With Its ESOP, Avis Tries Even Harder," *Business Week*, May 15, 1989, p. 122; and Christopher Farrel and John Hoerr, "ESOPs: Are They Good for You?" *Business Week*, May 15, 1989, pp. 116–123.

11. Clayton P. Alderfer, *Existence, Relatedness, and Growth: Human Needs in Organizational Settings* (New York: Free Press, 1972), pp. 29–51.

12. S. M. Klein and R. R. Ritti, *Understanding Organizational Behavior* (Boston: Kent Publishing, 1984), p. 257.

13. David C. McClelland and David H. Burnham, "Power Is the Great Motivator," *Harvard Business Review* 54 (March–April 1976): 103.

14. David R. Hampton, Charles E. Summer, and Ross A. Webber, *Organizational Behavior and the Practice of Management* (Glenview, IL: Scott, Foresman, 1978), pp. 11–15.

15. M. J. Stahl, "Achievement, Power and Managerial Motivation: Selecting Managerial Talent with the Job Choice Exercise," *Personnel Psychology*, Winter 1983, p. 786.

16. J. S. Adams, "Toward an Understanding of Inequity," *Journal of Abnormal and Social Psychology* 67 (November 1963): 422–436.

17. J. S. Adams, "Inequity in Social Exchange," *Advances in Experimental Social Psychology*, ed. Leonard Berkowitz (Washington, D.C.: Academic Press, 1965), 2: 267–300; see also E. Walster, W. Walster, and E. Berscheid, *Equity: Theory and Research* (Boston: Allyn and Bacon, 1978), pp. 131–141.

18. R. P. Vecchio, "Predicting Worker Performance in Inequitable Settings," *Academy of Management Review* 7 (1982): 103–110, presents four mathematical models of equity theory.

19. Adams, "Inequality in Social Exchange"; Walster et al., *Equity: Theory and Research*, pp. 131–141.

20. B. F. Skinner, *Beyond Freedom and Dignity* (New York: Knopf, 1971), pp. 60–100.

21. J. Solomon, "Managing," *Wall Street Journal*, April 18, 1989, p. B1.

22. Ed Pedalino and Victor U. Gamboa, "Behavior Modification and Absenteeism," *Journal of Applied Psychology* 59 (December 1974): 694–698.

23. W. Clay Hamner and Ellen P. Hamner, "Behavior Modification on the Bottom Line," *Organizational Dynamics* 4 (Spring 1976): 12.

24. Adrian Harrell and Michael Stahl, "Additive Information Processing and the Relationship between Expectancy of Success and Motivational Force," *Academy of Management Journal* 29 (June 1986): 424–425.

25. Victor Vroom, *Work and Motivation* (New York: Wiley, 1964), pp. 38–62.

26. Ibid.

27. B. M. Staw, *Intrinsic and Extrinsic Motivation* (Morristown, N.J.: General Learning Press, 1976), pp. 13–29.

28. See S. Koch, "Behavior as 'Intrinsically' Regulated: Work Notes towards a Pretheory of Phenomena Called Motivation," in M. R. Jones, ed., *Nebraska Symposium on Motivation* (Lincoln: University of Nebraska Press, 1956), pp. 68–81.

29. K. C. Montgomery, "The Role of the Exploratory Drive in Learning," *Journal of Comparative Physiological Psychology* 47 (February 1954): 60–64.

30. Staw, *Intrinsic and Extrinsic Motivation*, pp. 13–29.

31. E. A. Locke, K. N. Shaw, L. M. Saari, and G. P. Latham, "Goal Setting and Task Performance," *Psychological Bulletin* 90 (August 1981): 125–152.

32. G. P. Latham and G. A. Yukl, "A Review of Research on the Application of Goal Setting in Organizations," *Academy of Management Journal* 18 (August 1975): 824–845.

33. G. P. Latham and E. A. Locke, "Goal-Setting—A Motivational Technique that Works," *Organizational Dynamics* 7 (1979): 68–80.

34. *Pay for Performance* (Chicago: Commerce Clearing House, 1990), p. 7.

35. E. E. Lawler, III, "Reward Systems," in J. R. Hackman and J. L. Suttle, eds., *Improving Life at Work* (Santa Monica, CA: Goodyear, 1977).

36. Portions of this section were adapted from R. Wayne Mondy, Shane R. Premeaux, and Arthur Sharplin, "Motivation in Practice," *Manage* 39 (Second Quarter, 1986): 13, 22–23.

37. Peter Nulty, "America's Toughest Bosses," *Fortune* 119 (February 27, 1989): 50, 54.

38. Michael A. Campion, "How Do You Design a Job?" *Personnel Journal* 68 (January 1989): 43.

39. Robert H. Guest, "Review of Work Redesign," *Harvard Business Review* 24 (January–February 1981): 46–47, 52.

40. J. Richard Hackman and Greg R. Oldham, *Work Redesign* (Reading, MA: Addison-Wesley, 1980), pp. 130–158.

41. John F. Runcie, "By Days I Make the Cars," *Harvard Business Review* 58 (May–June 1980): 106–115.

42. See "Case Studies in the Humanization of Work," in *Work in America: Report of Special Task Force to the Secretary of Health, Education, and Welfare* (Cambridge, MA: MIT Press, 1973), appendix, pp. 188–200.

43. Frederick Herzberg, "One More Time: How Do You Motivate Employees?" *Harvard Business Review* 65 (Sept–Oct 1987): 109–120.

44. Stephen L. Perlman, "Employees Redesign Their Jobs," *Personnel Journal* 69 (November 1990): 37–40.

45. Joseph E. McKendrick, Jr., "Stretching Time in '89," *Management World* 18 (July–August 1989): 10.

46. James E. Bailey, "Personnel Scheduling with Flexshift: A Win/Win Scenario," *Personnel* 63 (September 1986): 62.

47. Simcha Ronen and Sophia B. Primps, "The Compressed Work Week as Organizational Change: Behavioral and Attitudinal Outcomes," *Academy of Management Review* 6 (January 1981): 61.

48. Wayne F. Cascio and Manuel G. Serapio, Jr., "Human Resources Systems in an International Alliance: The Undoing of a Done Deal?" *Organizational Dynamics* 19 (Winter 1991): 68.

49. Ibid., pp. 68–69.

50. Ibid., p. 69.

51. William Ouchi, *Theory Z: How American Business Can Meet the Japanese Challenge* (Reading, MA: Addison-Wesley, 1981), pp. 97–131; and Anthony Athos and Richard Pascale, *The Art of Japanese Management: Applications for American Executives* (New York: Simon and Schuster, 1981), pp. 48–91.

52. A. Howard et al., "Motivation and Values among Japanese and American Managers," *Personnel Psychology* Winter 1983): 883, 897.

53. Dean Foust, "A Tough Look at General Motors," *Business Week*, September 18, 1989, p. 17.

54. Jonathan Kapstein and John Hoerr, "Volvo's Radical New Plant: 'The Death of the Assembly Line?'" *Business Week*, August 28, 1989, pp. 92–93.

CHAPTER 11

Leadership

LEARNING OBJECTIVES

After completing this chapter students should be able to

- Define *leadership*.
- Describe the trait approach to the study of leadership.
- Identify and describe the major behavioral leadership theories.
- Describe the major situational leadership theories.
- Explain how managers become better leaders and the importance of leading through example.

For seventy-five years, IBM has had one extraordinary boss after another. Founder Thomas J. Watson turned the reins over to his son, Thomas, Jr., who was followed by T. Vincent Learson, Frank Cary, John Opel, and then John Akers. More than any other factor, the leadership of these men is credited with keeping IBM number 1 in the computer business.

Thomas Watson, Jr., became chief executive of IBM in 1955. Watson described himself as "perhaps innovative, certainly highly motivated, and not cautious at all." Basically he was willing to risk the possibility of "getting hit by a rock." He felt leaders should place toughness ahead of friendship. Watson said, "I never hesitated to promote someone I didn't like. The comfortable assistant—the nice guy you like to go on fishing trips with—is a great pitfall. Instead I looked for those sharp, scratchy, harsh, almost unpleasant guys who see and tell you about things as they really are."

Watson was also a "conceptualist." He told a Harvard Business School professor what he wanted IBM leaders to learn—"We are going to educate them in IBM management: communications, supreme sales and service efforts, frequent meetings, going to a guy's house if his wife is ill and seeing if you can help out, making post-death calls." Watson kept his door open to employees who had tried to settle gripes with their managers but could not. He tried to blur the distinction between white-collar and blue-collar workers. All employees were shifted to salary, eliminating what Watson called "the last difference between factory and office work." He often fired managers for unethical behavior, saying, "You cannot treat management differently from the employees." In his time, Thomas Watson, Jr., was exactly what IBM needed to become the strong giant it is now, but in the decade of the nineties, a different type leader is needed. Possibly a leader like John Akers.

When current IBM CEO John Akers took over, he had his work cut out for him. He set about changing his company's entrenched corporate culture, which in large measure was a legacy of Thomas Watson, Jr. According to consultant Bob Djurdjevic, "This is the most radical cultural change in IBM's history." Akers shook up the company. When IBM began to stumble, Akers marshalled the strengths of Big Blue, and struck back.

Under Akers's leadership, the company launched an all-out offensive to retain current markets and recapture lost turf. IBM announced new products virtually nonstop, the company kicked off a $40 million campaign to rescue the struggling software system, and it beefed up its sagging mainframe business. Akers determined that the next step was to become price competitive, so he cut prices. Cutting prices means cutting costs, and in a six-year war on expenses, Akers has reduced them by $1.8 billion. Advertising spending is down, perks and benefits have been scaled back, the work force has been reduced through attrition and early retirement, and the sale of its typewriter and printer business has allowed the company to better focus its efforts. Akers is determined to reshape IBM to fit the times, to keep IBM huge, powerful, and full of talent.

How is IBM doing under Akers's leadership? Well, IBM remains very strong with increased revenues and rising earnings making IBM an extremely profitable industrial company. Even though IBM is "under siege at every rampart of its empire" Akers's leadership has allowed IBM to fend off competitors and remain a fearsome force. An ever-increasing worry of IBM watchers is the scheduled retirement of Akers in 1995. The question uppermost in the minds of those in the IBM organization is: Which of Akers's successors has the "expertise and insight needed to carry the company into the next century?" One reason IBM is such a fearsome force is the string of effective leaders who have headed IBM. This leadership legacy is virtually unmatched by any other corporation, and hopefully IBM will find another leader the likes of John Akers.[1]

kers is recognized worldwide as an effective leader. Because of his leadership, IBM remains a major force in the industry. Akers is enthusiastic, knowledgeable, and willing to do whatever is needed to maintain IBM's position as a very profitable industrial company. Akers has managed to accomplish this and position IBM for the future without negatively impacting employees.

What does it take to be a good leader? And what is the most effective leadership style? These questions have perplexed and challenged managers for generations. Literally thousands of research studies have focused on them. But the research has not identified any set of traits or qualities that are consistently related to effective leadership. The main conclusion that can be drawn from this is that there is no single most effective leadership style.

We do know that effective leadership is essential to the survival and growth of every organization. Despite high salaries and excellent opportunities in large corporations, there continues to be a shortage of competent managers. The shortage is not confined to business but also exists in government, churches, schools, and all other types of organizations. The problem is not a lack of people who would like to be leaders or managers but rather a scarcity of people who have developed the ability to lead effectively.

The primary challenge of leadership and management is to guide an organization toward the accomplishment of objectives. The leader does so by influencing and encouraging employees to attain high levels of performance within the limitations of available resources, skills, and technology. Although we do not have all the answers, a more complete understanding of the skills, attitudes, and values related to effective leadership should greatly improve our ability to select, train, and develop effective managers.

In this chapter, we first define *leadership* and distinguish it from the related term *management*. Then we discuss three perspectives that have been used to develop leadership theories: (1) trait, (2) behavioral, and (3) situational perspectives. Next, we address the difficult question of how managers become better leaders. We end the chapter with a discussion of leading through example and the global perspectives of leadership.

Leadership Defined

Leadership (leading)

Influencing others to do what the leader wants them to do.

Influencing others to do what the leader wants them to do is **leadership,** or **leading.** It is only one of the many things that a manager does. Highly regarded companies often have a history of excellent leadership. For example, for seventy-five years, IBM has had one extraordinary leader after another. More than any other factor, this leadership is credited with keeping IBM number 1 in the computer business. Currently, John Akers is the individual leading IBM into the future.[2]

In Chapter 1, we defined *management* as the process of getting things done through the efforts of other people. Obviously, this definition overlaps with that of *leadership*. Managers get all sorts of things done through the efforts of other people, so they must lead. The main distinction between the two terms is one of focus. *Leadership* focuses on human interactions—influencing others. *Management* is more concerned with procedure and results—the process of getting things done. Also, *management* suggests more formality. *Manager* often refers to a position in an organization. On

Autocratic Style	Participative Style	Democratic Style	Laissez-Faire Style
Leader tells workers what to do.	Leader allows and expects worker participation.	Leader seeks majority rule from workers.	Leader lets group members make all decisions.
McGregor's Theory X workers	McGregor's Theory Y workers		Expert-specialist workers

TABLE 11–1

Leadership Styles as Related to Types of Workers

the other hand, a leader may have no formal title at all and may rely on personal traits and style to influence followers. These shades of meaning will grow clearer as we discuss leadership style.

Four basic leadership styles have been identified: autocratic, participative, democratic, and laissez-faire (see Table 11–1). An **autocratic leader** is *a leader who tells subordinates what to do and expects to be obeyed without question.* This style is typical of a person who accepts McGregor's Theory X assumptions, described in Chapter 10. Research suggests that autocratic leadership is most effective where the task is simple and fairly repetitive and where the leader has only short-term relationships with subordinates. For example, some construction managers hire a new crew of laborers for each project and treat them autocratically. But this approach begins to break down as the task becomes more involved and requires more talented and experienced employees. And it fails where building long-term relationships is important to success. Patrick Bennett proudly classifies himself as an autocratic leader, and his experience with the approach confirms much of what has been said here.

Autocratic leader

A leader who tells subordinates what to do and expects to be obeyed without question.

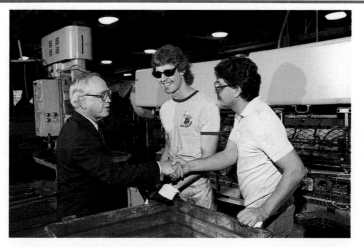

Autocratic leadership is not recommended where building long-term relationships is important to success. Here, Deere & Company Chairman, Robert A. Hanson, visits with employees at the company's Welland Works as part of Deere's 150th anniversary observance.

Source: Photo courtesy of Deere & Company.

Patrick Bennett runs a small automotive machine shop in Lake Charles, Louisiana. His twelve machinists are all paid on a piece-rate basis, so they have no financial incentive to stop and clean up. Pat had tried several ways to get the workers to keep the shop clean, at one point ordering each person to clean "just one little area." "Nothing worked," said Pat, "so one morning I just pulled the main breaker. When everything shut down and the men came to see why, I told them I would restore the power when the shop was clean." Pat said two of the "main culprits" came in to punch in on the time clock, expecting to be paid for doing the cleaning. Pat objected to paying them "for cleaning up a mess they had a big part in creating," and they both quit. Asked how he replaced the men, Pat replied, "They weren't worth replacing."

The shop was cleaner for a while afterwards. But Pat was disappointed in other aspects of his subordinates' performance. A few weeks later, he said: "Everybody screwed up. Jack [the foreman] has trouble ordering anybody to do anything. Someday he's got to learn he isn't 'one of the gang' anymore. Dale loaded the wrong engine on a customer's truck. Lance spent the whole day chasing his tail, pretending to go get parts. One of my good customers asked for his car at 1:00—and it wasn't out until 4:00."

Pat continued his tirade. "Know what I'm going to do?" he asked. "I'm moving my desk right out to the middle of the shop, right by the boring bars. They'll be nervous with me watching every move. But I'm going to get this mess under control." Pat had a 6 foot by 8 foot office built in the center of the shop near the assembly area. It has one-way windows so Pat can observe the machinists but cannot be seen by them.[3]

Participative leader

A leader who involves subordinates in decision making but may retain the final authority.

Democratic leader

A leader who tries to do what the majority of subordinates desire.

Laissez-faire leader

A leader who is uninvolved in the work of the unit.

A **participative leader** is *a leader who involves subordinates in decision making but may retain the final authority.* Prior to his death in 1992 Sam Walton, the flamboyant founder of Wal-Mart stores, established a management team that kept employees closely informed about company plans and practices, and he includes employees in corporate decision making.[4] Walton prided himself on being a participative leader.

A **democratic leader** is *a person who tries to do what the majority of subordinates desire.* Participative and democratic leaders tend to be those who make Theory Y assumptions. Democratic leaders are becoming more and more important as the use of the team approach to management increases.

Russell A. Nagel, general manager of Westinghouse Furniture Systems, evidently is a democratic leader. He has supported the existence of an elaborate system of committees and ad hoc task forces to discuss issues ranging from business strategy to the constant redesign of work areas for product innovation. This high degree of worker participation has been accompanied by a 74 percent increase in productivity.[5]

The **laissez-faire leader** is *a leader who is uninvolved in the work of the unit.* It is difficult to defend this leadership style unless the leader's subordinates are expert and well-motivated specialists, such as scientists. In fact, practically every leader who has attained recognition for effectiveness—from Mahatma Gandhi in India to John Akers at IBM—has done so by being deeply involved and active.

With this understanding of the definition of leadership and the four basic leadership styles, let us now turn to the trait, behavioral, and situational theories of leadership.

Democratic leaders are becoming more and more important as the use of the team approach to management increases. Nowhere is this more prevalent than in the computer industry. In this photograph, a research team at Atari Corporation discusses new software developments.

Source: Photo courtesy of Atari Corporation.

The Trait Approach to Leadership

The leader has always occupied a central role in management theory. Most of the early research on leadership attempted to either compare the traits of people who became leaders with those who did not or identify characteristics and traits possessed by effective leaders. The **trait approach to leadership** is *the evaluation and selection of leaders on the basis of their physical, mental, social, and psychological characteristics.* Research studies comparing the traits of leaders and nonleaders have found that leaders tend to be somewhat taller, more outgoing, more self-confident, and more intelligent than nonleaders. Even within an organization, leaders often have far different traits, depending in part on the type of work they supervise.[6] But a specific combination of traits that can differentiate leaders or potential leaders from followers has not been found.[7] Clearly, it is difficult to identify a leader from an initial impression. Still, some leaders seem to be readily identifiable even at a young age. National eminent consultant Frederick W. Gluck was described by a close longtime personal friend as "one little kid who was obviously running the whole show."[8]

Trait approach to leadership
The evaluation and selection of leaders on the basis of their physical, mental, social, and psychological characteristics.

MANAGEMENT IN PRACTICE: A Skill-Building Exercise

Marian Lillie, general project manager at Prodyne Corporation's Los Alamos, New Mexico, plant, was studying progress reports when she heard a tap at her door. "Got a minute, Marian?" asked Scotty Needham, a project director.

"Sure, come on in," said Marian. "What've you got?"

"You know that new manager the boss sent over, Brit Salvo?"

"Yes," answered Marian. "I approved hiring him."

"Well," Scotty continued, "you know he's a retired military officer. Wanted to start a second career. I thought it was a good idea, because we have that tank fire control project. But Brit sure is creating problems."

"What kind of problems?" asked Marian.

Scotty was obviously trying hard to stay calm. He spoke slowly. "I put him on the team with Chuck Talley. But Chuck claims Brit acts like he's the team leader, and Chuck is. I talked to Brit about it, but he bristled and said something about working with a bunch of wimps. I told him two of the team members are Ph.D.'s. I remember his exact words: 'Any organization needs strong leadership, no matter who's in it.' I didn't know what to say, so I just ended the conversation."

How would you respond if you were Marian?

Aggressiveness, ambition, decisiveness, dominance, initiative, intelligence, physical characteristics (looks, height, and weight), self-assurance, and other factors have been studied to determine if they were related to effective leadership. The major question is: Could traits differentiate effective from ineffective leaders? Perhaps the underlying assumption of some trait research has been that leaders are born, not made. Some people still believe there are certain inborn or acquired traits that make a person a good leader. Clearly, physical traits have not been shown to distinguish effective from ineffective leaders.[9]

The trait approach to the study of leadership is not dead, however. Edwin Ghiselli has tried to identify personality and motivational traits related to effective leadership. Ghiselli has identified thirteen traits, the six most significant of which are as follows:

1. *Supervisory ability*—the performance of the basic functions of management, including planning, organizing, influencing, and controlling the work of others.

2. *Need for occupational achievement*—the seeking of responsibility and the desire for success.

3. *Intelligence*—creative and verbal ability, including judgment, reasoning, and thinking capacity.

4. *Decisiveness*—the ability to make decisions and solve problems capably and competently.

5. *Self-assurance*—the extent to which the individual views himself or herself as capable of coping with problems.

6. *Initiative*—the ability to act independently and to develop courses of action not readily apparent to other people; to self-start and find new, innovative ways of doing things.[10]

Most of the "traits" Ghiselli has defined are subsets of a broader trait we might call "leadership ability" and are, of course, related to it. For example, supervisory ability, intelligence, and decisiveness surely makes one a better leader.

In this same vein, though without the use of the word *trait*, Warren Bennis offers the following "protocol" for effective leadership:

1. Leaders must develop the vision and strength to call the shots.

2. Leaders must be conceptualists (not just tinkering with the nuts and bolts).

3. Leaders must have a sense of continuity and significance in order to see the present in the past and the future in the present.

4. Leaders must get their heads above the grass and risk the possibility of getting hit by a rock.

5. Leaders must get at the truth and learn how to filter the unwieldy flow of information into coherent patterns.

6. Leaders must be social architects who study and shape what is called "the culture of work."

7. To lead others, leaders must first know themselves.[11]

Individuals can cultivate these qualities as the basis for building leadership effectiveness. And, of course, people differ from birth in their capacity for learning, including learning related to leading. Still, there are few shortcomings that cannot be overcome through effort—and there are few strengths that cannot be frittered away or misdirected.

A recent revival of trait theory emphasizes the importance of charisma. Robert House has proposed a "theory of charismatic leadership" that suggests great leaders employ four personal characteristics—dominance, self-confidence, a need for influence, and conviction of moral righteousness—to increase their effectiveness. The terms House has used imply that leaders with these traits are more charismatic than others.[12]

Leadership is never more vital than during periods of sweeping organizational change, such as turnarounds and Chapter 11 bankruptcy reorganizations. *A person who has the special ability to lead an organization through major strategic change* is a **transformational leader.** Such a leader can modify the mission, structure, and human resource management system and continue to guide the organization toward its objectives. Often marked by charisma, this type of leader must inspire followers. Followers are told how essential their performance is, how confident the leader is in them, how exceptional they are, and how the leader expects their group's performance to break records.[13]

Transformational leader
A person who has the special ability to lead an organization through major strategic change.

Lee Iacocca, former chairman of Chrysler Corporation, assumed a transformational leadership role when he took over Chrysler and brought it back from the brink of financial ruin in the early 1980s. He shared his vision of success with employees—and, through television advertisements in which he starred, with America at large. He was able to mobilize thousands of workers to enact their respective visions, which resulted in record profits and high levels of employee morale and productivity.[14] Recall the discussion of motivation in Chapter 10. It was noted there that individuals work to satisfy certain needs and to achieve desired outcomes. A manager who is a transformational leader often motivates subordinates to do better than they expected—in three ways. The leader (1) raises employee consciousness about the importance of certain outcomes, such as high productivity or efficiency; (2) shows the value of concentrating on team success rather than on individual interests; and (3) rearranges the workers' need structure to increase the value given to challenges, responsibility, and growth.[15]

Many leaders find it useful to assume a developmental role in relation to subordinates. According to behaviorist Judith Gordon, such a role involves elevating employee potential, setting examples, assigning tasks on an individual basis, increasing subordinate responsibilities, delegating challenging work, serving as a role model, keeping subordinates informed, providing intellectual stimulation, seeking ways of acting, and being proactive (acting in anticipation of change).[16]

The trait approach leaves many unanswered questions about what is required for effective leadership. A major limitation of trait theory is that traits associated with leadership success in one situation may not relate to achievement in another.[17] This has led to a continuing search for an appropriate leadership style.

Behavioral Leadership Theories

Dissatisfaction with the trait approach led most leadership researchers to focus on how leaders should behave rather than on traits or characteristics they might possess. In general, the behavioral theories discussed in this section provide greater insight into appropriate leadership principles than does trait theory.

Ohio State Leadership Studies

Beginning in 1945, researchers in the Bureau of Business Research at Ohio State University made a series of in-depth studies of the behavior of leaders in a wide variety of organizations. The key concern of the Ohio State leadership studies was the leader's behavior in directing the efforts of others toward group objectives. After a considerable number of studies had been completed, two important dimensions of leader behavior were identified: initiating structure and consideration. **Initiating structure** is *the extent to which leaders establish objectives and structure their roles and the roles of subordinates toward the attainment of the objectives.* **Consideration** is *the extent to which leaders' relationships with subordinates are characterized by mutual trust and respect for employees' ideas and feelings.* H. Ross Perot, founder of Electronic Data Systems, has great consideration for his employees' ideas and feelings, as well as for their physical welfare. He once put together a commando team and sent them across the Turkish-Iranian border to rescue two of his employees who had been trapped by political turmoil in Iran.[18]

Initiating structure and consideration are separate and distinct dimensions of leadership behavior. Figure 11–1 illustrates four leadership styles representing different combinations of the two dimensions. A manager can be high in both consideration and initiating structure, low in both, or high in one and low in the other. The Ohio State researchers did not suggest a single most effective combination of initiating structure and consideration. Rather, they found that the right combination depended on the demands of the situation.

Initiating structure

The extent to which leaders establish objectives and structure their roles and the roles of subordinates toward the attainment of the objectives.

Consideration

The extent to which leaders' relationships with subordinates are characterized by mutual trust and respect for employees' ideas and feelings.

FIGURE 11–1

Ohio State Leadership Model

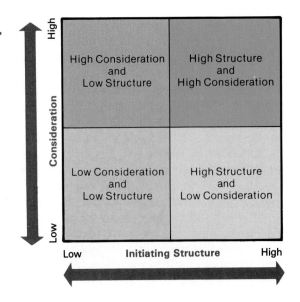

University of Michigan Studies

Rensis Likert and his colleagues at the University of Michigan Institute for Social Research were conducting leadership studies at about the time of the Ohio State research. The Michigan researchers chose two leadership orientations as the focal point for their experiments: the employee orientation and the production orientation. These orientations are similar to the dimensions used at Ohio State. The results were also similar.[19] Productivity differences among work groups were checked against differences in supervisor behavior. It was found that supervisors of highly productive groups spent more time planning departmental work and supervising employees and spent less time working alongside subordinates and performing the same task. They also tended to be employee oriented.[20]

Managerial Grid®

One of the most widely known leadership theories is that based on the Managerial Grid.[21] The **Managerial Grid**—or as it is labeled in its latest form, the Leadership Grid (Blake & McCanse, 1991)—is *the two-dimensional matrix developed by Robert Blake and Jane Mouton that shows concern for people on the vertical axis and concern for production on the horizontal axis.* The Managerial Grid is illustrated in Figure 11–2. Five leadership styles are depicted, representing varying degrees of concern for people and production:

- 1,1 *Impoverished management.* The manager has little concern for either people or production.

- 9,1 *Authority-compliance.* The manager stresses operating efficiently through controls in situations where human elements cannot interfere.

- 1,9 *Country club management.* The manager is thoughtful, comfortable, and friendly and has little concern for output.

- 5,5 *Middle of the road management.* The manager attempts to balance and trade off concern for work in exchange for a satisfactory level of morale—a compromiser.

- 9,9 *Team management.* The manager seeks high output through committed people, achieved through mutual trust, respect, and a realization of interdependence.[22]

According to Blake and Mouton, the first four styles listed are not the most effective. They suggest that the 9,9 team management style, maximum concern for both output and people, is the most effective style. Blake and Mouton say their studies prove this approach will result in improved performance, lower employee turnover and absenteeism, and greater employee satisfaction. Managerial Grid consultants attempt to use job enrichment and participative decision making to create a situation where both the organization and its members are accorded maximum and equal concern. The Managerial Grid concept has been introduced to thousands of practicing managers since its development in the early 1960s. Blake and Mouton and their adherents have conducted Grid training seminars around the world.

Now let us turn from the Managerial Grid, which promotes one leadership style, to a group of theories that assume there is no single best way to lead.

Managerial Grid

The two-dimensional matrix developed by Robert Blake and Jane Mouton that shows concern for people on the vertical axis and concern for production on the horizontal axis.

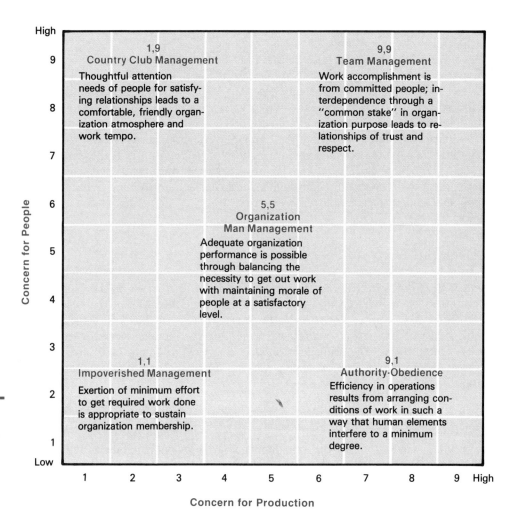

FIGURE 11–2

The Managerial Grid

SOURCE: *The Managerial Grid figure is from* The Managerial Grid III: The Key to Leadership Excellence, *by Robert R. Blake and Jane Srygley Mouton. Houston: Gulf Publishing Company, Copyright © 1985, page 12. Reproduced by permission.*

The grid figure contains the following labels and text:

High / 9 — 1,9 Country Club Management
Thoughtful attention needs of people for satisfying relationships leads to a comfortable, friendly organization atmosphere and work tempo.

9,9 Team Management
Work accomplishment is from committed people; interdependence through a "common stake" in organization purpose leads to relationships of trust and respect.

5,5 Organization Man Management
Adequate organization performance is possible through balancing the necessity to get out work with maintaining morale of people at a satisfactory level.

1,1 Impoverished Management
Exertion of minimum effort to get required work done is appropriate to sustain organization membership.

9,1 Authority-Obedience
Efficiency in operations results from arranging conditions of work in such a way that human elements interfere to a minimum degree.

Vertical axis: Concern for People (Low to High, 1–9)
Horizontal axis: Concern for Production (1–9, High)

Situational Leadership Theories

Situational, or contingency, leadership theories start out with the assumption that appropriate behavior depends on the circumstances at a given time. The more prominent of these theories are House's path-goal theory, Tannenbaum and Schmidt's leadership continuum, Fiedler's contingency leadership theory, Vroom and Yetton's normative theory, and Hersey and Blanchard's situational leadership theory.

Path-goal theory

The proposition that managers can facilitate job performance by showing employees how their performance directly affects their receiving desired rewards.

Robert House developed what he termed the path-goal theory of leadership,[23] which is closely related to the expectancy theory of motivation discussed in Chapter 10. **Path-goal theory** is *the proposition that managers can facilitate job performance by showing employees how their performance directly affects their receiving desired rewards.* In other words, a manager's behavior causes or contributes to employee satisfaction and acceptance of the manager if it increases goal attainment by employees. According to the path-goal approach, effective job performance results if the manager clearly defines the job, provides training for the employee, assists the employee in performing the job effectively, and rewards the employee for effective performance.

Leadership style facilitates accomplishing a particular objective by clarifying the path to that objective in subordinates' minds. The following four distinct leadership behaviors are associated with the path-goal approach:

- *Directive.* The manager tells the subordinate what to do and when to do it (no employee participation in decision making). Some historians view Henry Ford, founder of the Ford Motor Company, as a directive manager, because he tended to view his employees as factors of production, like raw materials and capital. Such individuals tend to chart their own course and go ahead regardless of the obstacles. It may be appropriate for CEOs to practice directive leadership under certain circumstances.

- *Supportive.* The manager is friendly with employees and shows interest in them. Ross Perot, founder of Electronic Data Systems, seems to be a supportive leader.

- *Participative.* The manager seeks suggestions and involves employees in decision making. The late Sam Walton, founder of the Wal-Mart and Sam's stores, always got his employees involved in decision making. During his tenure, employee suggestions were forwarded to the Wal-Mart main office, where they were rewarded by management.

- *Achievement oriented.* The manager establishes challenging goals and demonstrates confidence that employees can achieve them. Robert Kavner, AT&T's chief financial officer, was brought in to run AT&T's computer division. He initiated achievement-oriented leadership in his group, focusing on the capabilities of his "very able team."[24]

Following the path-goal theory, a manager may use all four of the behaviors in different situations. For instance, a manager may use directive behavior toward a

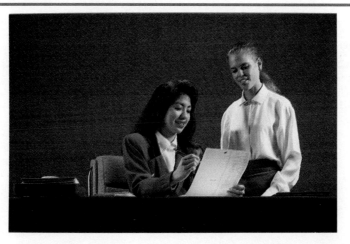

A supportive manager is friendly with employees and shows interest in them. Young workers, like the woman in this photograph, especially need support from their superiors. But we never outgrow the need for supportive leadership.
Source: © Jim Pickerell

new employee and supportive behavior toward an experienced one who is aware of the goals to be attained.

Two sets of contingency factors influence the nature of the leadership situation, according to path-goal theory. The first set, subordinates' characteristics, includes such factors as authoritarianism of the subordinate, locus of control (an individual's perception of how much control she or he has), and ability. The second set is environmental factors, which include the nature of the task, the formal authority system, and the primary work group. The characteristics of subordinates influence job satisfaction and the subordinates' acceptance of the leader. Environmental factors affect the motivational behavior of subordinates. Utilizing the appropriate leadership style and properly accounting for the two groups of contingency factors can increase employee motivation and job satisfaction by clarifying performance objectives and the path to achieve them.[25]

Leadership continuum

The graphical representation, developed by Robert Tannenbaum and Warren H. Schmidt, of the trade-off between a manager's use of authority and the freedom that subordinates experience as the leadership style varies from boss-centered to subordinate-centered.

Tannenbaum and Schmidt's Leadership Continuum

The **leadership continuum** is *the graphical representation, developed by Robert Tannenbaum and Warren H. Schmidt, of the trade-off between a manager's use of authority and the freedom that subordinates experience as the leadership style varies from boss-centered to subordinate-centered.* Tannenbaum and Schmidt described several factors they thought should influence a manager's choice of leadership style. They advocated a continuum of leadership behavior, based on the notion that the choice of an effective leadership style depends on the demands of the situation. The Tannenbaum and Schmidt model is illustrated in Figure 11–3.

FIGURE 11–3

Continuum of Leadership Behavior

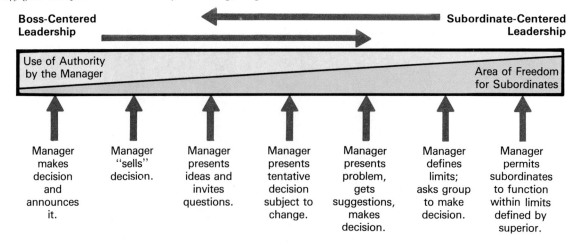

The boss-centered and employee-centered dimensions are similar to initiating structure and consideration, discussed earlier. Here are the factors Tannenbaum and Schmidt believed should determine the appropriate leadership style:

- *Characteristics of the manager*—background, education, experience, values, knowledge, objectives, and expectations.
- *Characteristics of the employees*—background, education, experience, values, knowledge, objectives, and expectations.
- *Requirements of the situation*—size, complexity, objectives, structure, and climate of the organization, as well as technology, time pressure, and nature of the work.

According to the Tannenbaum and Schmidt leadership continuum, a manager may engage in a more participative leadership style when subordinates

- Seek independence and freedom of action.
- Are well educated and experienced in performing the jobs.
- Seek responsibility for decision making.
- Expect a participative style of leadership.
- Understand and are committed to the objectives of the organization.

If these conditions do not exist, the manager may need to adopt a more autocratic, or "boss-centered," leadership style. Thus, in essence, managers must be able to diagnose the situations confronting them and then choose a leadership style that will improve their chances of effectiveness. The most effective leaders are flexible enough to select a leadership style that fits their needs as well as the needs of their subordinates and the situation.

Fiedler's Contingency Leadership Theory

The contingency theory of leadership developed by Fred E. Fiedler has received considerable acceptance.[26] Like all situational theorists, Fiedler believes there is no single most effective style that is appropriate to every situation. The Fiedler framework, illustrated in Table 11–2, involves eight situations and two basic leadership orientations. Three major elements are said to determine whether a given situation is favorable to a leader:

- *Leader-member relations*—the degree to which the leader feels accepted by subordinates. The atmosphere may be friendly or unfriendly, relaxed or tense, and threatening or supportive.
- *Task structure*—clearly defined objectives, decisions, and solutions to problems.
- *Position power of the leader*—the degree of influence over rewards and punishments, determined mainly by the official authority the leader has.

The eight situations in Table 11–2 vary in degree of favorableness for the leader — which determines the leader's influence and control over the group. A leader has maximum influence in situation 1 and minimum influence in situation 8. Fiedler's

TABLE 11–2

Situation	Degree of Favorableness of Situation to Leader	Leader-Member Relations	Task Structure	Position Power of Leader
1	Favorable	Good	Structured	High
2	Favorable	Good	Structured	Low
3	Favorable	Good	Unstructured	High
4	Moderately favorable	Good	Unstructured	Low
5	Moderately favorable	Poor	Structured	High
6	Moderately favorable	Poor	Structured	Low
7	Moderately favorable	Poor	Unstructured	High
8	Unfavorable	Poor	Unstructured	Low

TABLE 11–2

Framework of Fiedler's Contingency Leadership Model

Source: Reprinted by permission from Edwin B. Flippo and Gary M. Munsinger, *Management*, 5th ed. (Boston: Allyn and Bacon, 1982), p. 342.

research indicates that a task-oriented, controlling leader will be most effective when the situations are either very favorable or very unfavorable to the leader.[27] According to Fiedler, the more permissive, considerate leader performs best in intermediate situations, those moderately favorable to the leader.

Figure 11–4 illustrates Fiedler's framework in another way. The task-oriented leader is considered more effective in situations 1, 2, 3, and 8, whereas the relations-oriented leader is more effective in situations 4, 5, 6, and 7. Akers's situation at IBM should probably be placed in category 1, suggesting a task-oriented style. Leader-member relations were good because of Akers's established reputation. The task structure was clearly defined in terms of their goal (to maintain their number 1 position in computer sales). As chairman of the board and chief executive officer, Akers had extremely high positive power.

Vroom and Yetton's Normative Theory

Victor Vroom and Philip Yetton finalized their normative theory of leadership and decision making in 1973.[28] It attempts to show to what extent leaders should involve

FIGURE 11–4

Appropriateness of Leadership Styles to Situation

Source: Adapted by permission from Edwin B. Flippo and Gary M. Munsinger, Management, *5th ed. (Boston: Allyn and Bacon, 1982), p. 342.*

Task-Oriented Style	Relations-Oriented Style	Task-Oriented Style
Situations 1,2,3	4,5,6,7	8
Situations that are highly favorable to the leader	(Intermediate) Moderate degree of favorableness of leadership situation	Situations that are highly unfavorable

subordinates in decision making. Managers always have some freedom to make decisions that affect subordinates. According to the Vroom-Yetton model, managers can choose one of five processes for involving subordinates in decision making (see Table 11–3). The processes are on a continuum—from solving the problem alone, using available information, to delegating the problem-solving responsibility. A similar set of choices exists for group problems: The leader can make the decision alone, using available information; solve the problem with information or ideas from subordinates; or solve the problem together with subordinates.

Selecting the appropriate decision process involves assessing the characteristics of the particular problem. The aim of using the correct one is to improve one or more of the following elements:

1. "The quality or rationality of the decision."

TABLE 11–3

Decision-Making Processes

For Individual Problems	For Group Problems
AI You solve the problem or make the decision yourself, using information available to you at that time.	**AI** You solve the problem or make the decision yourself, using information available to you at that time.
AII You obtain any necessary information from the subordinate, then decide on the solution to the problem yourself. You may or may not tell the subordinate what the problem is, in getting the information from him. The role played by your subordinate in making the decision is clearly one of providing specific information which you request, rather than generating or evaluating alternative solutions.	**AII** You obtain any necessary information from subordinates, then decide on the solution to the problem yourself. You may or may not tell subordinates what the problem is, in getting the information from them. The role played by your subordinates in making the decision is clearly one of providing specific information which you request, rather than generating or evaluating solutions.
CI You share the problem with the relevant subordinate, getting his ideas and suggestions. Then *you* make the decision. This decision may or may not reflect your subordinate's influence.	**CI** You share the problem with the relevant subordinates individually, getting their ideas and suggestions without bringing them together as a group. Then *you* make the decision. This decision may or may not reflect your subordinates' influence.
GI You share the problem with one of your subordinates and together you analyze the problem and arrive at a mutually satisfactory solution in an atmosphere of free and open exchange of information and ideas. You both contribute to the resolution of the problem with the relative contribution of each being dependent on knowledge rather than formal authority.	**CII** You share the problem with your subordinates in a group meeting. In this meeting you obtain their ideas and suggestions. Then, *you* make the decision, which may or may not reflect your subordinates' influence.
DI You delegate the problem to one of your subordinates, providing him with any relevant information that you possess, but giving him responsibility for solving the problem by himself. Any solution which the person reaches will receive your support.	**GII** You share the problem with your subordinates as a group. Together you generate and evaluate alternatives and attempt to reach agreement (consensus) on a solution. Your role is much like that of chairman, coordinating the discussion, keeping it focused on the problem, and making sure that the critical issues are discussed. You do not try to influence the group to adopt "your" solution and are willing to accept and implement any solution which has the support of the entire group.

SOURCE: Victor H. Vroom and Arthur J. Jago, "Decision-Making as a Social Process: Normative and Descriptive Models of Leader Behavior," *Decision Sciences* 5 (October 1974): 745. Reprinted with permission of the Decision Sciences Institute, Georgia State University.

2. "The acceptance or commitment of the subordinates to execute the decision effectively."

3. "The amount of time required to make the decision."[29]

For example, assume you must decide which of three subordinates to promote next week. You would prefer to approach this problem in a way that ensures (1) a high-quality decision and (2) one that subordinates will accept and to which they will be committed. But (3) you would not like to waste time making the decision.

A manager's view of a situation as a crisis, a challenging problem, or a minor issue may affect the choice of a decision process. The degree of urgency may also determine the appropriate leader-subordinate interaction.[30]

ETHICAL DILEMMA

You are a recently appointed supervisor for the St. Louis branch of your company. Your ex-boss, an old friend, recommended that you get the promotion, over the objections of your current boss. You got the job primarily because your overall ratings for the last five years were better than all of the competitors', and your ex-boss has pull with the company president. Your new boss just told you that she is going to keep an eye on you and that she expects you to increase employee productivity by at least 10 percent, as your ex-boss had promised the president.

After you get settled, the foreman comes over to you and begins to brief you on how things are done here. According to the foreman, there are seven key people in the work area. These individuals normally split the gifts provided by the various departmental suppliers, and they are always assigned double-time work assignments so they can make more money and so they will not take a job with one of the many regional competitors.

Then, a representative of the five newer, less experienced workers approaches you and asks you for fairness. According to him, the boss looks the other way in order to keep the more experienced employees happy.

You can either maintain the status quo, or you can lead on the basis of fairness and equity, realizing that losing even one of these experienced workers could hurt short-run departmental productivity.

What would you do?

Hersey and Blanchard's Situational Leadership Theory

Paul Hersey and Kenneth Blanchard have developed a situational leadership theory that has attracted considerable attention from managers.[31] Hersey and Blanchard's theory is based on the notion that the most effective leadership style varies according to the level of readiness of the followers and the demands of the situation. Their model uses two dimensions—task behavior and relationship behavior. These dimensions are similar to the classifications used in the leadership models developed by the Ohio State researchers and in the Managerial Grid. Hersey and Blanchard argue that an effective leader is one who can diagnose the demands of the situation and the level of readiness of the followers and use a leadership style that is appropriate. Their theory is based on the relationship of these factors:

1. The amount of task behavior the leader exhibits (providing direction and emphasis on getting the job done).
2. The amount of relationship behavior the leader provides (consideration of people and emotional support for them).
3. The level of task-relevant readiness followers exhibit toward the specific objective, task, or function that the leader wants accomplished.

The key concept of Hersey and Blanchard's leadership theory is the level of task-relevant readiness of the followers. Readiness is defined not as age or psychological stability but as the following:

- A desire for achievement—a level of achievement motivation based on the need to set high but attainable objectives.
- The willingness and ability to accept responsibility.
- Education or experience and skills relevant to the particular task.

A leader should consider the level of readiness of followers only in relation to the work to be performed. Certainly, employees are "ready" on some tasks when they have the experience and skills as well as the desire to achieve and the capability of assuming responsibility. For example, Dianne Crawford, an accountant, is "ready" to prepare accurate quarterly IRS tax reports but not to prepare written audits of the company's operations. She needs little task-related direction from her manager in preparing the tax reports but may require considerably closer supervision and more direction in preparing and writing audits. Dianne may not currently have the skills or motivation to prepare audits; but with proper training, direction, and encouragement from her manager, she can assume greater responsibility in this area.

As Figure 11–5 illustrates, the appropriate leadership style used by a manager varies according to the readiness level (represented by R1 through R4) of the followers. Four leadership styles are appropriate, given different levels of readiness. As the task-relevant readiness level of followers increases, the manager should reduce task behavior and increase relationship behavior. The four styles can be classified as follows:

S1—Telling	High-task, low-relationship behavior
S2—Selling	High-task, high-relationship behavior
S3—Participating	High-relationship, low-task behavior
S4—Delegating	Low-relationship, low-task behavior

With the S1 (telling) high-task, low-relationship leadership style, the leader uses one-way communication, defining the objectives and roles of employees and telling employees what, how, when, and where to do the work. This style is appropriate for managers dealing with subordinates who lack task-relevant readiness—for example, those who are relatively new and inexperienced.

As employees learn their jobs, a manager can begin to use an S2 (selling) leadership style. There still is a need for a high level of task behavior, since the employees do not yet have the experience or skills to assume more responsibility. But the manager also provides a high level of emotional support—high-relationship behavior—to encourage the employees and demonstrate trust and confidence in them.

FIGURE 11–5

Hersey and Blanchard's Situational Leadership® Theory

SOURCE: *Paul Hersey and Kenneth Blanchard, Center for Leadership Studies, 1989. Used with permission of Leadership Studies, Inc.*

As employees exhibit an increase in task-relevant readiness—as they become more experienced and skilled, as well as more achievement-motivated and more willing to assume responsibility—the leader should reduce the amount of task behavior but continue the high level of emotional support and consideration. Continuing a high level of relationship behavior is the manager's way of reinforcing the employees' responsible performance. Thus, the S3 (participating) high-relationship and low-task behavior becomes the appropriate leadership style.

The S4 (delegating) low-relationship, low-task leadership style goes with the highest level of follower readiness. In this stage, the employees are at a high level of task-relevant readiness. They are skilled and experienced, possess a high level of achievement motivation, and are capable of exercising self-control. At this point, they no longer need or expect a high level of task behavior from their leader.

We should not conclude from this discussion that Hersey and Blanchard consider it simple to determine the appropriate leadership style. The ability to diagnose the readiness level of followers, as well as the specific needs of the situation, is complex. The leader must have insight into the abilities, needs, demands, and expectations of followers and must be aware that these elements can and do change over time.

Also, managers must recognize that they need to adapt or change their style of leadership whenever there is a change in the level of readiness of followers, for whatever reason—a change in jobs, personal or family problems, or a change in the complexity of the job caused by new technology. For example, Bill Woodall, a sales manager, has been using an S4 leadership style in supervising John Chriswell, who normally is a highly productive sales representative. John's pending divorce, however, has recently been adversely affecting his performance. In this situation, Bill might increase the level of both task and relationship behavior in order to provide John with the direction, support, and confidence he may need to cope with his problems and improve his performance.

Hersey and Blanchard's theory provides a useful and understandable framework for situational leadership. In essence, it suggests that there is no single best leadership style to meet the needs of all situations. Rather, a manager's leadership style must be adaptable and flexible enough to meet the changing needs of employees and situations. Evidence indicates that a given individual might respond differently to a certain leadership strategy at different times.[32] The effective manager is one who can change styles as employees develop and change, or as required by the situation.

How Managers Become Better Leaders

The discussion of leadership theories may seem to imply that managers merely decide which leadership style to use, sometimes changing styles to adapt to different situations. Even when the situation the leader must cope with is known, the appropriate leadership style may not be obvious. But three important factors should be considered in determining a leadership style: those related to the manager, to the worker, and to the situation.

Factors Related to the Manager

Self-knowledge is important to effective leadership. Leaders have different abilities and objectives. They also have had different experiences. Through those experiences, they develop basic beliefs about people. Some think people must be threatened to make them work. Others believe in encouraging workers and rewarding them for performance. Although managers should be flexible in the choice of a leadership style, they usually perform better if they use a style consistent with their personal beliefs.

The manager's professional and technical competence also affects leadership style. Not only are competent managers more confident, but workers are less likely to challenge or question them. This would seem to allow the manager to be more autocratic. Actually, though, it gives the manager more flexibility in leadership styles. Thus, a particular manager can be gentle and supportive in certain situations and a stern disciplinarian in others.

Factors Related to the Workers

Characteristics of subordinates should also be taken into account in deciding on a leadership style. One important consideration is the work ethic of subordinates. Some workers feel that work is, in and of itself, satisfying, pleasurable, and fulfilling. Such workers are easy to lead. Others see work as an unpleasant way to get money. Perhaps rewards and punishments are the only effective motivators for these workers.

Workers' attitudes toward authority must also be considered. Some believe that the job of the manager is to tell them what to do. They do not want to help make decisions. Others wish to make all the decisions; they resist any exercise of authority by the leader.

The maturity level of the subordinates is another influence on leadership style. Some workers are mature in the way they approach their work. They exercise initiative not only in doing their job but also in self-development. Others may have to be watched quite closely if even minimum performance is to be obtained. Workers may handle one aspect of their job maturely yet be quite immature in other aspects.

Another factor is the experience level and skill of subordinates. The leadership style used with a trainee will be different from that used with an experienced craftsperson. A more directive style may prove best for the trainee, while the craftsperson may need no direction at all.

For some employees, an autocratic style will work best. This may be particularly true in extremely favorable or extremely unfavorable situations. Studies have shown, however, that workers with a very wide range of characteristics generally respond more favorably to a participative approach.[33] Even at companies with a strong authority structure, such as IBM, workers tend to be more highly motivated if they take part in the decision-making process.

Factors Related to the Situation

Many situational factors affect the manager's leadership style. Following are some of the major ones:

1. *Number of people in the work group.* Managers can give more individualized attention in smaller work groups. As group size increases, management by exception may tend to be used.

2. *Kinds of tasks.* Jobs involving simple repetition may permit the manager to be more autocratic. Workers with creative or complex jobs require more freedom.

3. *Situational stress.* Managers often shift to a more autocratic style when the going gets tough. If a firm is in financial difficulties, a manager may be experiencing unusual pressure to increase output. However, the manager should be careful in changing leadership styles and should not do so purely as a reflex action.

4. *Objectives of the unit.* The specific objectives the manager is expected to accomplish affect leadership style. If the only objective is to get the job done immediately, the use of strong authority may be justified, even though it may make workers unhappy. When there is an important rush project, subordinates are more likely to accept simply being told what to do.

5. *Leadership style of the manager's boss.* Managers tend to lead as they are led. If the manager's boss is autocratic, the manager may lean toward this leadership style.

6. *Relationship of the manager with subordinates.* If the manager-subordinate relationship is one of mutual respect, the manager will usually let workers take

part in managing themselves. Workers, too, are likely to contribute more when they are respected and liked by their supervisor.

This list does not, unfortunately, answer the question: What leadership style should be used? In fact, there is no absolute answer. In the 1990s, organizations are moving toward flatter, more decentralized structures. This has increased, not decreased, the need for interdependence, collaboration, and communication—for flexibility in leadership style.[34] A recent critical review of contingency leadership theories noted that for situational leadership to be effective, (1) the leader must be flexible in behavior (patterns of habit must be broken), and (2) the leader must recognize the subordinate as a major situational determinant. This recognition involves not only careful observation of subordinates' behavior but the ability to interpret that behavior in a meaningful way.[35]

The best we can suggest is that managers thoroughly evaluate themselves, their subordinates, and the situation and then choose an appropriate style. The style may change as the manager deals with various members of the work group and at various times.

MANAGEMENT IN PRACTICE: A Skill-Building Exercise

"Phil is a great leader," said Jim Hollis, the plant manager, as he looked out over the factory floor from the production manager's office.

"Yes," said the production manager, "I believe those carpenters would follow him off the end of the Earth."

Phil Granger is the carpentry supervisor in the shipping department at Jacobs Castings Company. Phil and his crew of six make wooden boxes for packaging the several hundred custom-made castings that Jacobs ships every day. The work requires little skill, but it is vital to the plant.

Jim has said that before Phil took over, the carpentry division was a bottleneck. Shipments were often delayed for days because the carpentry work just did not get done. Turnover in the department had been high. And Jim has noted that the carpenters had more personal problems than other workers in the plant.

According to Jim, everything changed almost immediately after Phil took over. The work was caught up within a few days, and castings no longer have to wait for more than a day to be shipped. The carpenters are happier because Phil leads by example and does not expect more from his people than he is willing to do. During the first two months that Phil was in charge, there was not a single complaint, and only one day was lost because of absenteeism.

One day, Jim came by as Phil was determining how the boxes were to be made the next morning. "Phil," he said, "I thought you would be home with the kids by now." "I sure would like to go home a little early today," Phil replied, "but I want the others to know I'm trying as hard as they are. Anyway, I need to finish these sketches so I'll have time to help with the boxes in the morning. I also want to check with Brad before he leaves today. Since I took him around and showed him how our work affected the rest of the plant, he sure has done a great job."

Would you consider Phil a good leader? Explain.

Leading Through Example

Workers often look to their managers for examples of what to do and what not to do. Managers who want their people to be on time should come to work a little early and stay a few minutes late. The way managers behave in the community will also be noticed by workers. If they see managers drinking and carousing, they will assume that this is acceptable conduct.

All managers can set an example by showing enthusiasm for and seriousness about the work. Another aspect of leading by example is the way managers deal with superiors. Lower-level managers who are not honest with upper management cannot expect workers to be honest with them. Managers who want their subordinates to trust them must be seen by the workers as being trustworthy. Many managers try to stay in clear view of their subordinates. Bill Marriott, of the Marriott hotel chain, is one of them.

Bill Marriott of Marriott Corporation

"They see how hard I work and I think they ask themselves if it's worth it," said Bill Marriott, chairman of Marriott Corporation. Marriott was referring to his two sons and a son-in-law, who were his heirs apparent. But he could have been talking about any of his subordinates, at any level. During his frequent visits to Marriott hotels, he noticed everything—chipped paint, gum on a rug, food that was not perfect. He often picked up scraps of paper himself. He remained constantly on the move, with a hug for a housekeeper and a ready smile for everyone he met.

Marriott is a devout Mormon, according to *Fortune* magazine, "absorbed in work, family and the Mormon church." He said setting an example was what he did best as a manager: "Maybe setting an example of hard work and concern for both the customer and the employee, while also driving hard to make money. People say you can't balance the two, but my father believed you could, and I do too."[36]

A Global Perspective

Although leading is only one of the many things a manager does, it is one of the most distinguishing factors separating effective managers from ineffective ones. The most appropriate leadership style depends on many factors, and a style that is appropriate in one firm or country may be inappropriate in others. This makes the concept of effective global leadership quite complex.

Some individuals have already surfaced as effective multinational leaders. American businessman H. Ross Perot, for example, has distinguished himself as a global business leader. As mentioned earlier, Perot is the founder of Electronic Data Systems. He is said to lead his employees by instilling in them mutual trust and respect. Perot believes companies must properly balance the human component with technology and take measured risks to achieve objectives that are beyond those of the competition. He is also a firm believer in the entrepreneurial spirit, which allowed him to create his own very successful company.

Japanese businessman Akio Morita, co-founder of the Sony Corporation, is also a successful leader in the multinational environment. His company has gained more and more market share by setting new standards for quality and by developing innovative new products. He is imaginative, and so are his company's products. He believes in being straight and direct with his trading partners and in offering high-quality products at salable prices. He appears to understand what motivates people to be productive and competitive. Under Morita's direction, Sony has become a world leader at devising innovative ways of creating new products from basic technologies, thereby capturing new markets.[37]

1. Are you willing to learn how to gather influence?

   ☐ Yes   ☐ No

2. Are you willing to learn to lead through example?

   ☐ Yes   ☐ No

3. Are you willing to learn how to be specific?

   ☐ Yes   ☐ No

4. Are you willing to learn how to be competent, then confident?

   ☐ Yes   ☐ No

5. Are you willing to learn to look like a leader?

   ☐ Yes   ☐ No

6. Are you willing to learn to sound like a leader?

   ☐ Yes   ☐ No

7. Are you willing to learn to be goal oriented?

   ☐ Yes   ☐ No

8. Are you willing to not pass on a directive from upper management with an apology?

   ☐ Yes   ☐ No

9. Are you willing to not blindly follow directives that you know to be incorrect?

   ☐ Yes   ☐ No

10. Are you willing to accept that the most effective leadership style varies according to the level of maturity of the followers and demands of the situation?

    ☐ Yes   ☐ No

Summary

Leadership (or *leading*) is influencing others to do what the leader wants them to do. Four basic leadership styles have been identified. Autocratic leaders tell subordinates what to do and expect to be obeyed without question. Participative leaders involve subordinates in decision making but may retain final authority. Democratic leaders try to do what the majority of subordinates desire. And laissez-faire leaders are uninvolved in the work of the unit.

The trait approach to leadership is the evaluation and selection of leaders on the basis of their physical, mental, social, and psychological characteristics. Dissatisfaction with the trait approach has caused most leadership researchers to focus attention instead on how leaders should behave. In studies conducted by researchers at Ohio State University, the key concern was the leader's behavior in directing the efforts of others toward group objectives. These studies identified two important dimensions of behavior: initiating structure and consideration. A series of leadership studies at the University of Michigan related differences in high-productivity and low-productivity work groups to differences in supervisors' behavior. The Managerial Grid, a two-dimensional matrix developed by Robert Blake and Jane Mouton, depicts five leadership styles, each representing a different degree of concern for people and for production.

Contingency, or situational, leadership theories assert that no single way of behaving works in all situations. Robert House's path-goal theory proposes that managers can facilitate job performance by showing employees how their performance directly affects their receiving desired rewards. The leadership continuum, developed by Robert Tannenbaum and Warren Schmidt, shows the trade-off between a manager's use of authority and the freedom that subordinates experience as the leadership style varies from boss-centered to subordinate-centered. Fred Fiedler developed the contingency leadership theory that states that the most effective leadership style depends on the nature of the situation.

Victor Vroom and Philip Yetton introduced a normative theory of leadership and decision making. In their theory, managers determine the extent to which they should involve subordinates in the decision-making process. In Paul Hersey and Kenneth Blanchard's situational leadership theory, effective leadership depends on the level of readiness of the followers and the demands of the situation.

There are certain practical aspects of choosing a leadership style. Self-knowledge is important to effective leadership. Leaders have different abilities and objectives; they also have had different experiences. Through those experiences, they develop basic beliefs about people. Characteristics of subordinates should also be taken into account in deciding on a leadership style. Many situational factors, too, affect the manager's leadership style. Finally, workers often look to their managers as examples of what to do, and what not to do.

Review Questions

1. Define *leadership*. What are the basic leadership styles?
2. Distinguish between leadership and management.
3. Discuss the trait approach to leadership.

4. List and briefly describe the various behavioral leadership theories.
5. Describe each of the following situational leadership theories:
   a. House's path-goal theory of leadership
   b. Tannenbaum and Schmidt's leadership continuum
   c. Fiedler's contingency theory of leadership
   d. Vroom and Yetton's normative theory of leadership and decision making
   e. Hersey and Blanchard's situational leadership theory
6. What are the ways that managers can become better leaders?
7. Why is it important to lead by example?

Key Terms

Leadership (leading)	Trait approach to	Consideration
Autocratic leader	leadership	Managerial Grid
Participative leader	Transformational leader	Path-goal theory
Democratic leader	Initiating structure	Leadership continuum
Laissez-faire leader		

CASE 11.1   **"YOU KNOW THE POLICY"**

Dwayne Alexander was the Dallas-area supervisor for Quik-Stop, a chain of convenience stores. There were seven Quik-Stop stores in Dallas, and Dwayne had full responsibility for managing them. Each store operated with only one person on duty at a time. Although several of the stores stayed open all night, every night, the Center Street store was open all night Monday through Thursday but only from 6:00 A.M. to 10:00 P.M. Friday through Sunday. Because the store was open fewer hours during the weekend, money from sales was kept in the store safe until Monday. Therefore, the time it took to complete a money count on Monday was greater than normal.

The company had a policy that when the safe was being emptied, the manager had to be with the employee on duty, and the employee had to place each $1,000 in a brown bag, mark the bag, and leave the bag on the floor next to the safe until the manager verified the amount in each bag.

Bill Catron worked the Sunday night shift at the Center Street store and was trying to save the manager time by counting the money prior to his arrival. The store got very busy, and, while bagging a customer's groceries, Bill mistook one of the money bags for a bag containing three sandwiches and put the money bag in with the groceries. Twenty minutes later, the manager arrived, and both men began to search for the money. While they were searching, the customer came back with the bag of money. The company had a policy that anyone violating the money-counting procedure must be fired immediately.

Bill was very upset. "I really need this job," Bill exclaimed. "With the new baby and all the medical expenses we've had, I sure can't stand to be out of a job."

"You knew about the policy, Bill," said Dwayne.

"Yes, I did, Dwayne," said Bill, "and I really don't have any excuse. If you don't fire me, though, I promise you that I'll be the best store manager you've got."

While Bill waited on a customer, Dwayne called his boss at the home office in Houston. With the boss's approval, Dwayne decided not to fire Bill.

Questions

1. Discuss Dwayne's leadership style in terms of the Managerial Grid.
2. Evaluate the action Dwayne took. Take particular note of how the events in the case might affect other store managers.

Allen Russell was chosen in mid-1990 to supervise the research and development department of Western Engineering Company, near Denver. Bob Pursnell, the senior vice-president who made the decision, explained that the R&D department needed a "production man" in charge. Allen had been a line foreman and had an excellent reputation for getting the job done. According to Bob, Allen was well organized and was known for solving problems before they reached upper management. Allen was aware, though, that none of the researchers had been willing to take the supervisor's job, and a production person had been second choice.

Allen was surprised at how "unorganized" the researchers were. He learned they might come to work at 10:00 A.M. and leave at 3:00 P.M., although they often carried papers home. Allen decided to insist that everyone follow a regular schedule. He held a meeting the next day and informed the researchers that he expected them to work regular hours—at the facility.

One of the researchers complained it was impossible to be creative on a regular schedule, but Allen said, "Well, you'll just have to learn to do it." He went on to say he would be checking with each person to see what projects were under way and to help in any way he could. He made it clear he would take an active part in assuring the efficiency and timeliness of each project.

The next day, Bob Pursnell came by to see Allen. After the niceties were exchanged, Bob said, "Allen, you've got the researchers up in arms. What's wrong?" "Well," Allen replied, "they're used to being allowed to come and go as they please. There's a lot of goofing off around here. I suppose they know I'm about to tear up their playhouse."

Questions

1. Was Allen a reasonable choice for R&D supervisor? Explain.
2. How would you describe Allen's leadership style? How appropriate was this style to the management of the R&D department?
3. What should Bob Pursnell do now?

Notes

1. This case is a composite of a number of published accounts, among them: Joel Dreyfuss, "Reinventing IBM," *Fortune*, August 14, 1989, pp. 31–39; "The Greatest Capitalist in History," *Fortune*, August 31, 1987, pp. 24–35; Joanne Lipman, "Wells Rich's New IBM Campaign Presents Firm as User-Friendly," *Wall Street Journal*, April 13, 1989, p. B6; Paul B. Carroll, "IBM Names Jack Kuehler President, Recognizing His Role in Technology," *Wall Street Journal*, May 31, 1989, p. A3; John W. Verity, "A Bold Move in Mainframes," *Business Week*, May 29, 1989, pp. 72–78; Geoff Lewis, Anne R. Field, John J. Keller, and John W. Verity, "Big Changes at Big Blue," *Business Week*, February 15, 1988, p. 92; Rick Whiting and Hugh Willett, " IBM at the Crossroads," *Electronic Business*, September 9, 1991, pp. 36–46; and Thomas McCarroll, "The Humbling of a Computer Colossus," *Time*, May 20, 1991, pp. 41–44.

2. Lewis, Field, Keller, and Verity, "Big Changes at Big Blue," p. 92.

3. Arthur Sharplin, "Bennett's Machine Shop, Inc.," in Lawrence R. Jauch and James Townsend, *Cases in Strategic Management*, 2d ed. (McGraw-Hill, 1989), pp. 337–351.

4. Thomas J. Murry, "Wal-Mart Stores Penny Wise," *Business Month*, December 1988, p. 42.

5. John Hoerr, "Getting Man and Machine to Live Happily Ever After," *Business Week*, April 20, 1987, p. 61.

6. Paul C. Nystrom, "Comparing Beliefs of Line and Technostructure Managers," *Academy of Management Journal* 26 (December 1986): 816.

7. Howard M. Weiss and Seymour Adler, "Personality and Organizational Behavior," *Research in Organizational Behavior* 6 (1984): 1–50.

8. John A. Byrne, "What's a Guy like This Doing at McKinsey's Helm?" *Business Week*, June 13, 1988, pp. 82–84.

9. Dorwin Cartwright and Alvin Zander, eds., *Group Dynamics*, 3d ed. (New York: Harper & Row, 1968).

10. Edwin Ghiselli, *Explorations in Managerial Talent* (Pacific Palisades, CA: Goodyear, 1971).

11. W. Bennis, "Leadership: A Beleaguered Species?" *Organizational Dynamics* 5 (1976): 13–14.

12. R. J. House, "A 1976 Theory of Charismatic Leadership," in *Leadership: The Cutting Edge*, ed. J. G. Hunt and L. L. Larson (Carbondale: Southern Illinois University Press, 1977), pp. 205, 207.

13. B. M. Bass, "Leadership: Good, Better, Best," *Organizational Dynamics* 13 (Winter 1985): 26–40.

14. Judith R. Gordon, *A Diagnostic Approach to Organizational Behavior*, 2d ed. (Boston: Allyn and Bacon, 1987), pp. 425–426.

15. Ibid.

16. Ibid.

17. R. M. Stogdill, "Personal Factors Associated with Leadership: A Survey of the Literature," *Journal of Psychology* 25 (1948): 35–71.

18. Walter Guzzardi, "Wisdoms from the Giants of Business," *Fortune*, July 3, 1989, pp. 78–88.

19. E. Fleishman, E. F. Harris, and R. D. Burtt, *Leadership and Supervision in Industry* (Columbus: Ohio State University Press, 1955); and E. Fleishman and E. F. Harris, "Patterns of Leadership Behavior Related to Employee Grievances and Turnover," *Personnel Psychology* 1 (1959): 45–53.

20. R. L. Kahn and D. Katz, "Leadership Practices in Relation to Productivity and Morale," in D. Cartwright and A. Zander, eds., *Group Dynamics* (Evanston, IL: Row, Peterson, 1953), pp. 585–611.

21. Robert R. Blake and Anne Adams McCanse. *Leadership Dilemmas—Grid Solutions* (Houston: Gulf Publishing Company, 1991).

22. Robert R. Blake and Jane Srygley Mouton, *The Managerial Grid III: The Key to Leadership Excellence*, 3d ed. (Houston: Gulf Publishing Company, 1985).

23. Robert House, "A Path-Goal Theory of Leadership Effectiveness," *Administrative Science Quarterly* 16 (September 1971): 321–338.

24. John J. Keller, "Has the AT&T–Olivetti Romance Lost Its Magic?" *Business Week*, May 9, 1988, p. 46.

25. Alan C. Filley, Robert House, and Steven Kerr, *Managerial Process and Organizational Behavior* (Glenview, IL: Scott, Foresman, 1976), pp. 256–260.

26. Fred E. Fiedler, *A Theory of Leadership Effectiveness* (New York: McGraw-Hill, 1967).

27. Ibid.

28. V. H. Vroom and P. W. Yetton, *Leadership and Decision-Making* (Pittsburgh, PA: University of Pittsburgh Press, 1973).

29. V. H. Vroom and A. J. Jago, "Decision-Making as a Social Process: Normative and Descriptive Models of Leader Behavior," *Decision Sciences* 5 (October 1974): 743–769.

30. D. Tjosvold, "Effects of Crisis Orientation on Managers' Approach to Controversy in Decision-Making," *Academy of Management Journal* 27 (1984): 130–138.

31. See Paul Hersey and Kenneth Blanchard, "So You Want to Know Your Leadership Style?" *Training and Development Journal*, February 1974, pp. 22–32. This article contains the Leader Adaptability and Style Inventory (LASI), an instrument that can be used to examine leadership behavior, style adaptability, and effectiveness. Since this article, the LASI has been renamed as the Leader Effectiveness and Adaptability Description (LEAD). Information, LEAD inventories, and training materials may be obtained from the Center for Leadership Studies, 17253 Caminito Canasto, Rancho Bernardo, San Diego, CA 92127.

32. S. D. Malik and Kenneth N. Wexley, "Improving the Owner/Manager's Handling of Subordinate Resistance to Unpopular Decisions," *Journal of Small Business Management* 24 (July 1986): 27.

33. M. E. Heilman, H. A. Hornstein, J. H. Cage, and J. K. Herschdag, "Reactions to Prescribed Leader Behavior as a Function of Role Perspective: The Case of the Vroom-Yetton Model," *Journal of Applied Psychology* 69 (February 1984): 50.

34. R. Lippitt, "The Changing Leader-Follower Relationships of the 1980s," *Journal of Applied Behavioral Science* 18 (March 1982): 396.

35. C. L. Graeff, "The Situational Leadership Theory: A Critical View," *Academy of Management Review* 8 (April 1983): 290.

36. Carol J. Loomis, "Stars of the Service 500," *Fortune*, June 5, 1989, pp. 54–62; and Judith H. Dobrzynski, "The CEO on the Move," *Business Week*, October 21, 1988, pp. 49–53.

37. Gene Bylinsky, "A Japanese View: Why America Has Fallen Behind," *Fortune*, September 25, 1989, p. 52.

12

Communication

LEARNING OBJECTIVES

After completing this chapter students should be able to

- Describe the basic components of the communication process and state what should be communicated to workers.

- Explain the two basic forms of communication channels.

- Describe communication networks and their characteristics.

- Identify the barriers to individual communication and discuss the barriers to effective group behavior.

- Describe how managers can become better communicators and explain the concept of directing.

PPG Industries, the Pittsburgh glass, paint, and chemical maker, was always considered to be dull and bureaucratic until Vincent A. Sarni took over in 1984. Sarni has shattered the old company's culture and helped remold PPG into a model of modern management. The company that he inherited was reasonably successful and technically competent, but it suffered through each economic downturn and sleepily responded to recoveries. Sarni changed all that with his *Blueprint for the Decade,* an eight-page pamphlet he developed in 1984 that contains PPG's mission statement, corporate objectives, and performance goals. Sarni trudged from plant to plant communicating the virtues of his blueprint.

To effectively implement the *Blueprint for the Decade,* the PPG organization was revised to assure that everyone was pulling in the same direction, and to afford everyone an opportunity to grow. Under the organizational section of the pamphlet is an explanation of how PPG's strategy will be carried out and how their goals of making PPG more profitable and as recession proof as possible will be achieved. Management, staffing, and information for decision making are the elements of the PPG organization essential for goal attainment. As the focal point of the PPG organization, effective communication is vital to corporate success.

According to PPG's *Blueprint for the Decade,* it is mandated that "management communicate openly and challenge people to be creative and entrepreneurial, with the aim of deepening understanding of each other's point of view and rallying everyone to the pursuit of excellence." In relation to staffing, PPG employees must have the appropriate technical skills, but it is also imperative that they have effective communication skills. Finally, PPG's blueprint specifies that information for decision making must "provide information across the company so that people can communicate more fully with each other, and provide and maintain state-of-the-art systems for information handling." A recent action by PPG underscored their concern for effective communication in their plants. Quality action teams called "Mythbusters" were assembled for the purpose of recommending to management effective ways of communicating timely information to employees.

Through effective communication and by following the essence of Sarni's blueprint, PPG earned record sales and earnings. The company's return on investment also increased to a modern high. The combination of effective communication and Sarni's blueprint has PPG ready for just about anything.[1]

Perhaps the worst criticism that managers can receive from their peers, superiors, and subordinates is that they cannot communicate effectively. PPG is acutely aware of the importance of effective communication. Communication could be a costly, productivity-affecting component of any organization, but at PPG it is cost effective, enhances productivity, and has a positive effect on the company's bottom line.

In Chapter 1, *management* was defined as the process of getting things done through the efforts of other people. In order for employees to achieve the objectives identified by the manager, they must have a clear understanding of those objectives. The statement by a frustrated manager—"You did what you thought I meant very effectively; unfortunately, that was not what I wanted you to do"—reveals that effective communication did not take place. Effective communication should be considered not an end in itself but a means of achieving company objectives. The most encouraging feature of communication is that it is learned. Individuals who desire to improve their ability to communicate can do so by giving proper attention to the task.

This chapter begins with a discussion of the communication process and of what should be communicated. Next, it presents the various channels of communication, which are followed by a discussion of communication networks and their characteristics. Then, the chapter reviews the barriers to both individual and group communication. Finally, it discusses the means by which managers can become better communicators and explains the concept of directing.

The Communication Process

Communication

The transfer of information, ideas, understanding, or feelings among people.

Communication is such a complex concept that one researcher uncovered over ninety-five definitions, none of which were widely accepted.[2] We define **communication** as *the transfer of information, ideas, understanding, or feelings among people*. It is hard to conceive of an organizational objective that could be accomplished without communication. Effective communication is fundamental to success in every organization.

When *Fortune* magazine identified America's most successful managers, it noted that one of the prime contributors to their success was excellent communication skills.[3] The manner in which plans are to be implemented and actions coordinated to achieve a particular objective must be communicated to the individuals who must accomplish the task. In fact, managers spend a considerable portion of their time communicating. Communication provides the means by which members of the firm may be stimulated to implement organizational plans willingly and enthusiastically.

Communication must have a recipient. Shouting for help on a desert island is not communication. Similarly, if a professor lectures and no one listens or understands, there is no communication. The basic elements of the communication process are shown in Figure 12–1. Each step in the sequence is critical to success. The **source** (or **sender**) is *the person who has an idea or message to communicate to another person or persons*. A problem that often affects the communication process is that people have different backgrounds, experiences, and objectives. As the first step in the communication process, the sender must *encode* the message or idea—put it into a set of symbols that the receiver will understand. Words on this page are symbols to

Source (sender)

The person who has an idea or message to communicate to another person or persons.

the reader. The sound of a car's horn on a busy freeway often means the likelihood of an accident. Thus, the blast of a horn becomes a symbol of danger.

When communication is attempted, messages are transmitted through such means as speaking, writing, acting, and drawing. A number of communication channels may be used to transmit any message. **Communication channels** are *the means by which information is transmitted in organizations*. Words can be communicated orally through such methods as face-to-face conversations, telephone conversations, radio, and television. Books, articles, and letters can serve as written channels. The senses of touch, smell, and taste are nonverbal channels (although for a blind person reading braille, touch is a verbal channel). Much meaningful communication takes place without a word being spoken.

Continuing to the lower part of Figure 12–1, the receiver must *decode* the message—convert the symbols into meaning. Like senders, receivers have diverse backgrounds,

Communication channels
The means by which information is transmitted in organizations.

FIGURE 12–1

The Communication Process

SOURCE: *Adapted from H. Joseph Reitz,* Behavior in Organizations *(Homewood, IL: Richard D. Irwin, 1981), p. 310. Copyright © 1981 by Richard D. Irwin, Inc. Used with permission.*

Effective communication should not be considered an end in itself, but a means of achieving company objectives. At Fleming Companies the main objective of the employee shown here is communication with her customer.

Source: *Photo courtesy of Fleming Companies*

experiences, and aspirations. When the receiver's decoding matches the sender's encoding, communication is likely to be effective. The receiver acts in response to the communication. This action can be to ignore the message, to perform some task, to store the information for future use, or something else. The receiver also usually provides feedback so the sender will know if the message was accurately received and the proper action was taken. An unavoidable part of communication is *noise*— any interference that occurs during the communication process.

In business, communication is vital to success. If communication breakdowns occur, costly mistakes may result. At PPG, the establishment of the quality action teams called "Mythbusters" illustrated that the company wanted to communicate effectively with all employees.

MANAGEMENT IN PRACTICE: A Skill-Building Exercise

One of your oldest and most trusted employees has just taken you aside and said: "It's all over the plant about you and the boss's secretary. I always thought you were a fine, respectable person. Your wife and I have been friends since grade school. Everyone around here admired you in the past. I am really disappointed. I just can't believe you'd do such a thing!" You are stunned because you do not know what she is talking about.

How would you respond?

What Should Be Communicated?

Henry Mintzberg and others have estimated that individual managers spend about 80 percent of their time communicating.[4] Some managers limit their communication with subordinates to the issuance of orders. But communication should take on a much larger scope. Communication with employees is a critical requirement of good management and of the performance of various managerial roles.

Mintzberg has described the manager's job in terms of three types of roles— interpersonal, informational, and decision-making—and communication is vital to the performance of each role. In their *interpersonal roles*, managers act as figureheads and leaders of their organizations. Mintzberg indicates that managers spend 45 percent of their time with peers, about 45 percent with people outside their company, and 10 percent with superiors. In their *informational roles*, managers exchange information about jobs and responsibilities with peers, subordinates, and other personal contacts. They also provide information to others, such as suppliers, peers outside the organization, and other outside groups. Finally, in their *decision-making roles*, managers implement new projects, handle problems, and allocate resources. Even private decisions that managers make will be based on information provided to the managers by others. The managers will then communicate their decisions to others for implementation.[5] Accomplishing all of these roles is not easy, but without effective communication it is virtually impossible.

Today's managers face a complex environment. The acceleration of technology both expedites and complicates communication. When a corporation is in a state of flux, an even greater burden is placed on the communication process, as is the case with Xerox Corporation.

· ·

Xerox Corporation

David Kearns, chairman of Xerox Corporation, has been sparking radical change inside Xerox since May 1982, when he stepped in as the company's third chief executive officer in a year. Xerox had been growing more and more bureaucratized for decades. Success, according to industry experts, had made Xerox "fat and slow."

Kearns is credited by Wall Street analysts with putting the company back on the revolutionary road it embarked on in 1959, with its first copier machine. Kearns believes the best way to facilitate good management is to take out layers of executives so that the communication route from the people who actually do the work to top management is shorter. According to Kearns, "The key to simplifying the bureaucracy is an efficient communication system."[6]

· ·

Behavioral scientists have demonstrated that worker motivation is impossible without effective communication. Research has also underscored the need for subordinates to be heard and understood by their supervisors. The globalization of the business environment complicates the communication process and acts as a barrier to effective communication. The need for an effective communication system to advance the objectives of the organization is obvious. The responsibility to maintain a good communication climate clearly falls to management.[7]

- *How their jobs should be performed.* Most workers want to do a good job. In order to be effective, they must be told the proper way to do it.

- *How effectively they are performing their jobs.* Workers need and want to know how their superiors view their performance. Problems cannot be corrected if workers do not know what needs to be changed.

- *How much they will be paid.* Pay is a sensitive subject. Workers need to have a clear understanding of how much they will receive and how their pay is calculated.

- *Changes in conditions within the firm that might affect them.* Workers want to know what is going on. If management does not tell them the real story, they may get inaccurate information through informal sources.

- *Company policies and rules that directly affect their jobs.*

TABLE 12–1

Information Employees Want to Know

Determining the specific topics to be communicated is often difficult. The manager who believes that everything is suitable for transmission will not only clog the channels with insignificant trivia but may harm operations by releasing wrong information. To sustain employee cooperation in the pursuit of organizational objectives, the manager must consider employee needs and must communicate how those needs will be addressed. As Table 12–1 indicates, employees want to know certain types of things.

Channels of Communication

Formal communication channels

The communication channels that are officially recognized by the organization.

As Figure 12–2 shows, organizations provide many communication channels. The channels can be formal or informal. **Formal communication channels** are *the communication channels that are officially recognized by the organization.* Instructions and information are passed downward along these channels, and information flows

FIGURE 12–2

Communication Channels in an Organization

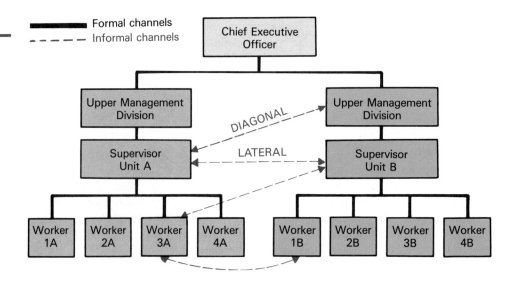

upward. Information also travels through informal channels. **Informal communication channels** are *ways of transmitting information within an organization that bypass formal channels.* (The informal channels shown in Figure 12–2 will be discussed later in the chapter.)

Formal Downward Channels

Many managers emphasize the importance of downward channels of communication. They are aware of the need to convey upper-level management's orders and viewpoints to subordinates, although they may be unaware of how subordinates will perceive the communicated information. The managers believe that the logic of the orders will stimulate desired action. Some of the formal channels available to carry the information downward are the chain of command, posters and bulletin boards, the house organ, letters and pay inserts, employee handbooks and pamphlets, annual reports, and loudspeaker systems.

Chain of Command   Orders and information can be given personally or in writing and can be transmitted from one level to another through the chain of command (the line along which authority flows from the top of the organization to any individual). This is the most frequently used formal channel and is appropriate on either an individual or a group basis. The most common way in which communication flows downward is face-to-face interaction. Therefore, the subordinate, whether manager or worker, should become a good listener. The junior person can usually ask questions to clarify the message.

Written documents also provide a major means of downward communication. Letters and memorandums should be written with consideration for how they will be understood. Incorrect interpretations are frequent, however. Lower- and middle-level managers may not have originated the confusing communication, but they can help subordinates understand any from upper management. The directive may require some translation into the language of subordinates.

Written communications should be used for matters that are extremely important to either the manager or the company. Relatively permanent information such as policies, procedures, and rules should also be written. Additionally, managers should write communications that they suspect might otherwise be misunderstood.

Posters and Bulletin Boards   Information of concern to company employees is often communicated on posters and bulletin boards. Some workers may not read them, however. This is especially true when the information is not kept current. Materials often remain long after their usefulness has passed. Thus, this channel may be considered only a supplementary device.

The House Organ   Many firms have company newsletters or newspapers, often referred to as house organs. A great deal of information regarding the organization can be communicated this way. Newsletters often contain information about new products, about how well the company is doing, and even about policies. Readership is increased if some space is allocated to items of personal interest to employees. For instance, scores of the company bowling team or an award to a long-term employee might be mentioned.

Letters and Pay Inserts   Direct mail may be used when top management wants to communicate matters of importance. Since letters are sent directly to employees from the company, there is a reasonable chance they will be read. Inserting a note with the paycheck may also encourage readership. It at least ensures that each worker will receive a copy. Also, workers may be in a mood to read the insert because it is payday. Letters also help stimulate interest in company matters by spouses of employees.

Employee Handbooks and Pamphlets   Handbooks frequently are used during the hiring and orientation process as an introduction to the organization. Too often, however, they are unread, even when the firm demands a signed statement that the employee is acquainted with their contents. When a special system is being introduced, such as a pension plan or a job evaluation system, a concise, well-illustrated pamphlet about the subject may facilitate understanding and stimulate acceptance.

Annual Reports   Annual reports are increasingly being written not only for stockholders but also for employees. A worker may be able to obtain information about the firm in this way. Information about new plants, new products, and company finances is often included.

Loudspeaker Systems   The loudspeaker system is used not only for paging but also to make announcements while they are "hot." Such systems can also be misused, as in the case of a vacationing company president who thoughtlessly sent greetings from his cool mountain retreat to the hot, sweaty workers on the production floor. State Farm Mutual Automobile Insurance Company uses loudspeakers and a number of other means to get the message out.

Getting the Message Out at State Farm

Headquartered in Bloomington, Illinois, State Farm Mutual Automobile Insurance Company has been the country's largest automobile insurer since 1942. The company has about 40 million policyholders and employs over 30,000 people. It sells life, health, and fire coverage, in addition to automobile insurance.

State Farm executives have said their first concern is their policyholders. That makes sense. A mutual company's customers are its owners. In keeping with this concern, State Farm was a leader in promoting "plain talk," a trend toward writing legal documents such as insurance policies in understandable language. Profits declared to be in excess of the company's financial needs were paid out to policyholders in the form of dividends. Vice-president Leon C. Maxwell said: "What does State Farm advertise to the consumer? Not insurance policies. We advertise the 'good neighbor around the corner,' the one who cares, who is available, who is professional." How to get that message out? In addition to national advertising, there are product brochures for specific markets. Agents print personalized sales proposals on their computers, which are tied in to regional offices. Then there are glossy coffee-table booklets to tell prospective customers about the company, its agents, and even the local office staff.

State Farm also pays a good bit of attention to informing its internal work force. Aside from tight financial controls and constant pressure to live up to the "good neighbor" slogan, the company tries to promote a family feeling among its employees. There is a firm open-door policy. And each employee can expect a birthday card and a rose. "It sounds hokey," said one programmer, "but the family feeling does exist."

The company provides excellent working conditions, informal management, and open communications. For example, when the work area became crowded at State Farm's largest regional office, in Jacksonville, Florida, more space was added. Workers and managers alike, for the most part, work in large, open areas with partitions separating only the various divisions. An ample number of strategically located loudspeakers permit officewide announcements. In the entrance area is a rack containing cards describing the benefits available to State Farm workers and answering most of the common questions they might have about their company.[8]

Formal Upward Channels

Advocates of participative management emphasize the establishment of upward channels of communication. These channels are necessary not only to determine if subordinates have understood the information sent downward but also to satisfy the need of subordinates to be involved. A communication effectiveness survey of thousands of employees showed that only half believed that significant upward communication was present. Most saw little chance of discussion or dialogue with upper management.[9] An upward flow of information is also necessary if management is to coordinate the various activities of the organization. Among the many channels from which to choose for the upward flow of information are an open-door policy, suggestion systems, questionnaires, the grievance procedure, an ombudsperson, and special meetings.

Open-Door Policy *An established guideline that allows workers to bypass immediate supervisors in regard to substantive matters without fear of reprisal* is an **open-door policy.** This communication channel can go a long way toward reducing tension among subordinates and improving trust. It is important that employees know of the open-door policy and believe management is sincere about it. At Rubbermaid Inc., the former chairman and chief executive officer, Stanley C. Gault, took the open-door policy one step further by strolling through the factories and talking directly with workers.[10]

The advantages of an open-door policy are well known, but the disadvantages should also be recognized. Managers often feel insecure when they know that subordinates can take complaints directly to upper-level managers. At times, a supervisor first finds out a problem exists when an upset upper-level manager calls. Also, an open-door policy may cost management time. Feeling obligated to stop work any time a worker shows up at the door may make it hard to complete administrative tasks.

Suggestion Systems Many companies have formal suggestion systems. Some have suggestion boxes; others have suggestion forms that workers are encouraged to complete. When a suggestion system is used, every suggestion should receive careful

Open-door policy

An established guideline that allows workers to by-pass immediate supervisors in regard to substantive matters without fear of reprisal.

consideration. Workers should be promptly informed of the results of the decision on each suggestion.

Questionnaires Anonymous questionnaires sometimes are given to workers in an attempt to identify problem areas in the organization. When a large number of workers rate the firm low in a given area, management should search for solutions. For instance, if a significant number of workers indicate dissatisfaction with pay, an investigation is certainly warranted. Pay may actually be too low, or the workers may just be unaware of what other firms are paying. Whatever the case, the company should take some action, or workers' faith in the use of the questionnaires may be lost.

Grievance procedure

A systematic process through which employees complain about matters affecting them.

The Grievance Procedure *A systematic process through which employees complain about matters affecting them* is a **grievance procedure.** This procedure is a mechanism that gives subordinates the opportunity of settling disputes within the organization. Most unions have negotiated formal grievance procedures. When employees do not have avenues to voice their complaints, even small gripes may grow into major problems. Some managers believe a formal grievance procedure weakens their authority. Others see the grievance procedure as a way of keeping minor problems from becoming serious.

Ombudsperson

A complaint officer with access to top management who hears employee complaints, investigates, and recommends appropriate action.

Ombudsperson In nonunion organizations, the ombudsperson provides a means of resolving grievances. An **ombudsperson** is *a complaint officer with access to top management who hears employee complaints, investigates, and recommends appropriate action.* This form of grievance resolution has been used for some time in Europe, and the practice is becoming more popular in the United States. Ombudspersons act as top management's eyes and ears. Because of their access to top management, ombudspersons can often resolve problems swiftly. In many cases, they simply help employees find people who can solve their problems. Sometimes they recommend specific action to managers.

In recent years, ombudspersons have assumed the additional duty of helping management uncover scandals in their organizations. Workers for large defense contractors, such as McDonnell Douglas and General Electric, who believe that a company problem exists can now bypass their supervisors and gain an audience with the ombudsperson.[11]

Special Meetings Special employee meetings to discuss particular policies or procedures are sometimes scheduled by management to obtain employee feedback. The keystone of teamwork in the Pitney Bowes Company, for example, is monthly departmental meetings of all employees. In addition, a central employee council of thirteen employee representatives meets monthly with top executives. Employees on the council are elected for two-year terms and devote time to investigating company problems and improving communication processes.

Informal Communication Channels

The formal organization structure does not include informal communication channels. If a manager has a problem that is affected by another department, the two managers

Informal communication may be either lateral or diagonal. Managers involved may get together over coffee or lunch and discuss problems of mutual interest. The relaxed atmosphere of this informal meeting undoubtedly contributes to openness in communication.

Source: © Jim Pickerell

involved may get together informally over coffee. Informal communication may be either lateral or diagonal (see Figure 12–2). Communication by managers at the same organizational level is **lateral communication.** This form of communication benefits from established personal relationships and mutual trust. The development of lateral communication often takes time; but if it is effective, it can improve the productivity of both departments.

Diagonal communication also bypasses the formal chain of command. **Diagonal communication** is the exchange of information with people who are higher or lower in the organization but who are not directly in the formal chain of command. Again, this is not an automatic process; trust must first develop. Care must be taken in using diagonal communication because immediate supervisors might take offense. Used effectively, diagonal communication can be an important source of information for managers.

As discussed in Chapter 7, the grapevine is the organization's informal communication system. It exists within the organization, but it may also extend beyond it (see Figure 12–3). The grapevine does not respect formal lines of authority. It reaches into every unit and level of an organization. However, most of the information it transmits is derived from the formal organization. The grapevine usually transmits information more rapidly than the formal system does, although sometimes not as accurately. Employees generally consider the grapevine one of the primary sources of current information.[12]

The grapevine has four basic characteristics:

1. It transmits information throughout the organization in every direction. Information on the grapevine can go down, up, laterally, and diagonally, all at the same time. The grapevine can connect organizational units that have only indirect formal relationships.

2. The grapevine transmits information rapidly. It is not restricted by formal policies and procedures. The chain of command does not have to be followed. Once a message gets into the grapevine, it can move almost instantaneously to any point in the organization.

Lateral communication

Communication by managers at the same organizational level.

Diagonal communication

The exchange of information with people who are higher or lower in the organization but who are not directly in the formal chain of command.

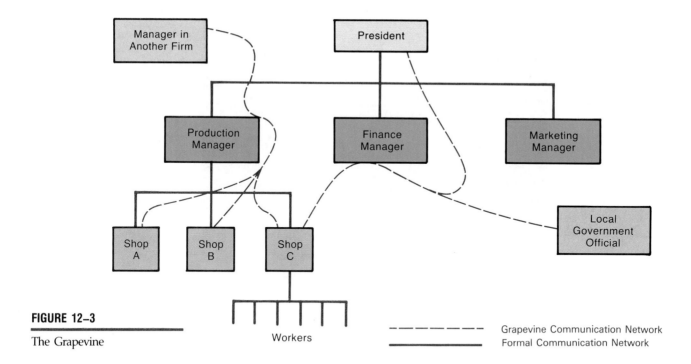

FIGURE 12–3

The Grapevine

Workers

– – – – – – – – – Grapevine Communication Network
———————— Formal Communication Network

3. The grapevine is selective in regard to who receives the information. Some people are tuned in to it and others are not. There are certain people to whom even gossips do not talk. Consequently, some managers are not even aware of the grapevine.

4. The grapevine extends beyond the formal organization. Considerable communication about the firm occurs off the job. Workers at a party may pass on or receive information about the company. Figure 12–3 shows the grapevine connecting to a manager in another company as well as to a government official. There are usually hundreds or even thousands of such connections.

Managers should not ignore the grapevine, because it cannot be eliminated. Wise managers attempt to remain tuned in to the grapevine. Not only will they obtain useful information, but they will be able to replace incorrect messages with accurate ones. The grapevine is an important part of the communication process, even for enlightened companies that try to make the formal communication system as effective as possible.

Communication Networks

Communication networks

The pathways through which messages between and among people in organizations flow.

Organizations are made up of individuals in certain positions or roles. The relatively permanent role arrangements in a group describe in part the group's structural configuration, or group structure. Group structure may also be described by the enduring patterns of communication among the role holders. *The pathways through which messages between and among people in organizations flow* are **communication networks.** Figure 12–4 illustrates five such networks.

The wheel network consists of a single person who communicates with all the others in the work group. The Y network (particularly if it is inverted) and the chain network resemble the chain of command in a formal communication channel. Communication flows up and down a hierarchy, with little skipping of levels of communication outside the hierarchy. The circle resembles the chain except that the communication loop is closed. For example, the lowest-level member of a group may have a top manager as a mentor and may communicate with that person. In the completely connected network, all group members regularly communicate with all other members.

Of course, a single network does not precisely describe the communication in any one group. Rather, a group's communication may be typified by one network, or the group may use variants of one or more networks. Identifying the predominant structural configuration, however, helps explain or predict the performance and satisfaction of the group and its members.

In the wheel configuration, information is exchanged relatively quickly between the center position and peripheral ones. Information flows somewhat slower between two spoke positions because it must pass through a third position, the center, which acts as an intermediary. Compare this speed of information exchange with the speed between two positions in the chain. Obviously, passing information through two positions requires less time than moving it through three.

In the wheel, accuracy of information is high, because little filtering occurs; only one person, the central person, can pass information on to others. Contrast this to the chain or Y network, where distortions increase as information passes through several positions. The links of the wheel, chain, and Y receive less information than the links of the circle and the completely connected network.

In the circle and completely connected network, the greater opportunity for feedback seems to be associated with greater member satisfaction. This satisfaction may

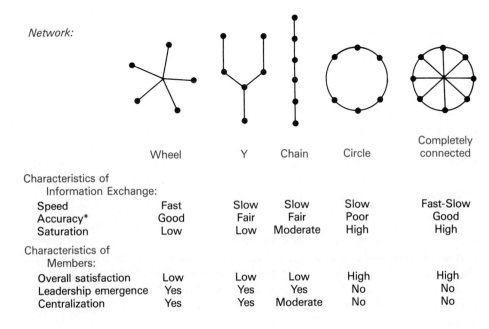

FIGURE 12–4

Characteristics of Five Communication Networks

SOURCE: *Based on A. Bavelas, "Communication Patterns in Task-Oriented Groups," Journal of the Acoustical Society of America 22 (1950): 725–730.*

Network:

	Wheel	Y	Chain	Circle	Completely connected
Characteristics of Information Exchange:					
Speed	Fast	Slow	Slow	Slow	Fast-Slow
Accuracy*	Good	Fair	Fair	Poor	Good
Saturation	Low	Low	Moderate	High	High
Characteristics of Members:					
Overall satisfaction	Low	Low	Low	High	High
Leadership emergence	Yes	Yes	Yes	No	No
Centralization	Yes	Yes	Moderate	No	No

also be due to sharing of the leadership responsibility and decentralization of decision making.

The effectiveness of the structural configuration selected will vary among groups and at different times within the same group. For example, when a group is newly formed, a wheel configuration may be best, so a large quantity of information can be conveyed as rapidly as possible to the new members. But in an established group whose members must identify and evaluate alternatives, discussion is more essential than information conveyance; and a completely connected network may therefore be more appropriate. Effectiveness exists when the network, the group members, and the task characteristics fit together well.

Barriers to Communication

For communication to be effective, the receiver must correctly interpret the sender's message. Often, however, communication is ineffective because of breakdowns that can occur at any stage in the communication process. A survey of 32,000 employees in twenty-six organizations showed that only half of the employees thought the organization's communications were accurate and candid, and two-thirds believed them to be incomplete.[13] If a manager tells an employee to "produce a few more parts," and the employee makes two but the manager wanted two hundred, a breakdown in communication certainly took place. If managers are to develop their ability to communicate, they must understand the ways in which communication breakdowns occur.

As Figure 12–5 shows, successful management decisions must pass through the barriers to communication if organizational objectives are to be achieved. If the barriers are excessive, communication may be reduced to the point where the firm's objectives simply cannot be met. Barriers are classified as technical, language, and psychological.

Technical Barriers

Environmental barriers to communication are referred to as technical barriers. Timing, information overload, and cultural differences are three such barriers.

Timing
The determination of when a message should be communicated.

Timing   *The determination of when a message should be communicated* is **timing.** It is often important for a manager to determine the most appropriate time to transmit a message. For instance, a manager who must reprimand a worker for excessive tardiness will want to speak to the worker as soon as possible after the event. If, say, six months passes before the reprimand is made, the worker will likely have forgotten the event.

Information overload
The condition that exists when an individual is presented with too much information in too short a time.

Information Overload   *The condition that exists when an individual is presented with too much information in too short a time* is **information overload.** With the many channels and media available, as well as the desire of organizations to share more information than in the past, it is little wonder that information overload occurs. A person can absorb only so many facts and figures at any one time. When excessive information is provided, a major breakdown in communication can occur.

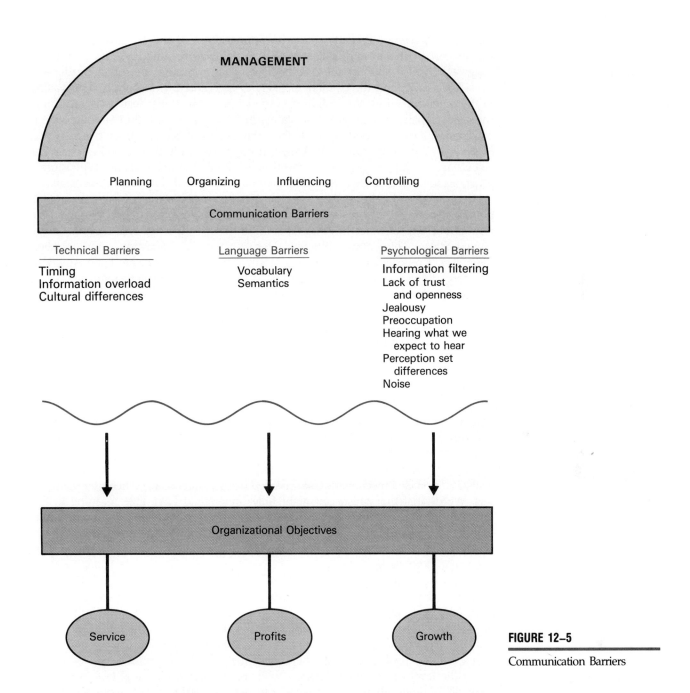

FIGURE 12–5

Communication Barriers

As a professor, one of the authors contributed to information overload in a class-room. The course was a statistics class that met one day a week for four hours. In the first hour, students were eager to take notes. By the fourth hour, few students could repeat what the instructor had said. Information overload had occurred. Some students have discovered that their grades suffer when they attempt to take all of their classes on Monday, Wednesday, and Friday or on Tuesday and Thursday. By the end of the last class, many of the students have no idea what the instructor said.

Cultural Differences   Breakdowns in communication can also be caused by cultural differences. In the United States, time is a valuable commodity, and a deadline suggests urgency. But in the Middle East, giving another person a deadline is considered rude, and the deadline is likely to be ignored. If a client is kept waiting in the outer office for thirty minutes in the United States, the delay may mean that the client is perceived to have low status. In Latin America, a thirty-minute wait is common. If a contract offer in the United States has not been acted on over a period of several months or a year, an American might conclude that the other party has lost interest. In Japan, long delays mean no slackening of interest, and delay is often a negotiation tactic, known to be effective in dealing with impatient Americans.

Americans conduct most business at an interpersonal distance of five to eight feet; a distance of one to three feet suggests more personal or intimate undertakings. The normal business distance in Latin America is closer to the personal distance in the United States. This cultural difference results in some interesting communication difficulties. Consider the backpedaling North American as his or her Latin American counterpart presses ever closer. Regarding status symbols, consider a manager's office in the United States. Spacious, well furnished, and located on the top floor, it conveys an aura of prestige. In the Middle East, size and decor of office mean little or nothing; and in France, managers are likely to be located in the midst of their subordinates in order to control them.

Language Barriers

Language problems can result from the vocabulary used and from different meanings applied to the same word (semantics).

Vocabulary   A manager must understand the type of audience being addressed. Statisticians, skilled mechanics, and unskilled laborers likely have different vocabulary sets. Words that the statistician might fully understand have little meaning to the unskilled laborer, and vice versa. Breakdowns in communication often occur when the sender does not tailor the message to match the knowledge base of the receiver. This problem is most severe when someone deliberately uses fancy words just to seem more knowledgeable.

Certain words are part of practically every person's vocabulary. Figure 12–6 calls them the common vocabulary base. Arbitrarily selected difficulty levels from 0 to 4 on a scale of 10 are used to determine the level of difficulty of a vocabulary. If a speaker uses words of level 4 or less, both the statistician and the unskilled laborer will understand. As the speaker progresses above this base level, more and more people will be unable to comprehend the message. If the statistician uses words above the level of 6, communication with the skilled mechanic is lost. Naturally, there will be times when higher-level words must be used to communicate a technical concept, but if managers can concentrate their messages in the common vocabulary base, they have a much better chance of being understood.

Semantics   When a sender transmits words to which a receiver attaches meanings different from those intended, a semantic (relating to the meaning of words) communication breakdown will likely occur. A major difficulty with the English language is that multiple meanings may be attached to a single word. Take, for instance, the

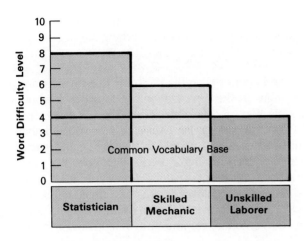

FIGURE 12–6

Common Vocabulary Base

word *charge.* A manager may place an employee *in charge of* a section. A company *charges* for its services. A person gets a *charge* out of a humorous story.

Jargon also creates barriers to communication. **Jargon** is *a special language that group members use in their daily interaction.* Virtually every industry develops a jargon that is used in everyday business. So do groups within an industry. The statistician, computer programmer, word processor, and unskilled laborer are likely to use the jargon associated with their jobs. When one person in a trade speaks to another not associated with the trade—and therefore unfamiliar with the jargon—a breakdown in communication may occur. For this reason, many firms provide new employees with a list of definitions of terms associated with the particular industry.

Jargon

The special language that group members use in their daily interaction.

Psychological Barriers

Technical factors and semantic differences cause many breakdowns in communication, but psychological barriers tend to be the major cause of miscommunication. These barriers include various forms of distortion and problems involving interpersonal relations.

Information Filtering *The process by which a message is altered through the elimination of certain data as the communication moves from person to person in the organization* is **information filtering.** As subordinates and superiors communicate, they know the information will be used for at least two purposes: (1) to help management control and direct the firm (and therefore the worker), and (2) to evaluate the worth of their performance. Managers often discover that information that has been provided to them by subordinates has been filtered. Managers at all levels are also tempted to filter information as it progresses through the chain of command. Even the president may filter information before it goes to the board of directors or is communicated to subordinates.

Information filtering

The process by which a message is altered through the elimination of certain data as the communication moves from person to person in the organization.

There have been many managerial attempts to reduce the levels of authority that clog organizational communication channels. Decentralization is one means of reducing the number of levels of authority in the organization. One organization reduced the number of managerial levels from eight to four, with a consequent speeding up of the communication process. Such reorganizations are drastic and require considerable efforts in the areas of retraining and establishing realistic control standards.

Lack of Trust and Openness Trust and openness on the part of both managers and employees must exist if orderly changes in the organization are to occur. Without these elements, barriers to communication are likely to occur. There are no such barriers at PPG. According to PPG's *Blueprint for the Decade*, it is mandated that "management communicate openly and challenge people to be creative and entrepreneurial, with the aim of deepening understanding of each other's point of view and rallying everyone to the pursuit of excellence."

Managers who are open and receptive to employees' ideas encourage employee feedback. Managers need this feedback to do their job. If managers give the impression that their orders should never be questioned, communication tends to be stifled.

A major factor in the success of Japanese business is that Japanese managers trust their peers and superiors as well as their workers. This attitude results in a simpler organization structure. Japanese firms assume that people at all levels of the company are trustworthy, and they do not have to employ highly paid executives to review the work of other highly paid executives.[14]

Jealousy Not everyone may be pleased by a manager's successful performance. In fact, a manager's competence may actually be viewed by peers and superiors as a threat to their security. They may even try to minimize the manager's accomplishments in the eyes of upper management. Because of the jealousy of peers, the effectiveness of communication between the manager and upper management may be severely reduced.

Preoccupation Some people are so preoccupied with themselves that they do not hear the message they are listening to. Preoccupation causes people to respond in certain predictable though inappropriate ways. A columnist tells the story of attending a party at the home of a socialite. The socialite was famous for being so preoccupied with making a favorable impression on his guests that he did not listen to what the guests said. The columnist decided to play a trick on the person. He deliberately

Openness and trust must exist if orderly changes in the organization are to occur. When employees feel that openness and trust do not exist, barriers to communication are present. Honeywell, long a leader in communication technology, pays attention to the need for open communication within the company.

Source: Photograph courtesy of Honeywell, Inc.

arrived late. As he entered, he gave this explanation: "I'm sorry to be late, but I killed my wife this evening and had a difficult time stuffing her body into the trunk of my car." The host responded, "Well, the important thing is that you've arrived; now the party can really begin."

Hearing What We Expect to Hear   Most of us are conditioned to hear what we expect to hear, not what is actually said. Because of past experiences, we develop preconceptions of what is being said. Sometimes, we hear what we want to hear. An employee who has been reprimanded quite a few times by a certain supervisor may even interpret a compliment by that supervisor as a negative statement.

Perception Set Differences   *A fixed tendency to interpret information in a certain way* is a **perception set.** Differences in past experiences, educational background, emotions, values, beliefs, and many other factors affect each person's perception of a message or of words. The word *management,* for example, may provoke an entirely different image in the minds of two persons. The parents of one may have been business managers, while the parents of the other may have been labor union organizers. Perception set differences even affect the meanings of words such as *chair, pencil,* and *hat,* which represent tangible objects. The impact is clearly much greater for such intangibles as *liberal* and *conservative.*

Perception set
A fixed tendency to interpret information in a certain way.

ETHICAL DILEMMA

You are the public relations manager for the J. L. Shiely Company, a St. Paul mining concern. Your company has always coexisted harmoniously with the community in which it is located. Suddenly, however, the town turns against your company. A new town board views digging for profit as immoral, and in order to punish your company the new board passes an ordinance to take fifteen acres of your property without payment. In 1955, Shiely had given the town permission to use the park, with a provision that the firm could eventually reclaim it for mining. You could probably win a lawsuit against the town, but that would sour the relationship even further. You can either take the town to court, or you can lobby residents to intervene to make the town start treating your company fairly.[15]

What would you do?

Noise   *Anything that interferes with the accurate transmission or reception of messages* is **noise.** Noise, which can occur at several or all points in the communication process, is the principal source of error in communications. Although it cannot be completely eliminated from the communication process, its negative impacts can be lessened.

Noise
Anything that interferes with the accurate transmission or reception of messages.

Barriers to Effective Group Communication

Barriers to communication also affect groups. Additionally, group attitudes toward collaboration and competition can create barriers. Parties with a competitive attitude

- Define conflict as win-lose.

- Pursue only their own objectives.
- Understand their own needs but publicly disguise them.
- Aggrandize their power.
- Use threats to get submission.
- Overemphasize their own needs, objectives, and position.
- Adopt an attitude of exploiting the other party whenever possible.
- Emphasize only differences in positions and the superiority of their own position.
- Isolate the other person or group.[16]

This "we-they" perspective is a major barrier to intergroup communication. It polarizes the interacting groups, and it causes communications to take on an aura of bargaining, rather than of transmitting facts or solving problems. Unions and management are especially prone to this type of interaction.

How Managers Can Become Better Communicators

When breakdowns in communication occur, the result is often lowered productivity. Sometimes managers believe they have told a worker to do one thing, and the worker perceives the message as a directive to do something else. In this case, the manager not only may lose the worker's time but also may discover that harm was done when the worker performed the wrong task. Thus, learning how to communicate effectively can significantly improve productivity. The main thing to remember is that communication skills can be learned. Empathy, listening, reading skills, observation, word choice, body language, and actions are all involved in improving communication.

Empathy

Empathy

The ability to identify with the feelings and thoughts of another person.

The ability to identify with the feelings and thoughts of another person is **empathy.** It does not mean you necessarily agree with the other person, but you understand why that person speaks and acts in a certain way. If someone is bitter, an empathic person is able to "feel" the bitterness. Managers should take the time to understand as much as possible about the people they work with daily. By being empathic, they can more easily get to the heart of many workers' problems.

Listening

To facilitate communication, one of the most effective tools managers have at their disposal is the ability to listen. Constant talking interferes with listening and learning. Listening skills help managers discover problems and determine solutions.

Communication cannot take place unless messages are received and understood. It has been observed that the average speaking speed is about 120 words per minute.

The speed at which most people are able to comprehend words is more than four times the speed at which the words are spoken. The question therefore arises, What does the listener do with the free time that results from this difference in speeds?

As Figure 12–7 shows, at least three types of listening have been identified: marginal, evaluative, and projective. The slower speed of the speaker provides the listener with an opportunity for marginal listening—letting the mind stray while someone is talking. This can lead to misunderstanding and even insult. Most of us have experienced the situation in which, when speaking to someone, we realize that the person's mind is "a million miles away." The person may have heard a few words, but most of the message was not understood.

Evaluative listening occurs when any free time is devoted to evaluating the speaker's remarks. As soon as the sender says something that is not accepted, communication ceases, as the receiver begins to develop a response. Instead of one idea being transmitted and held by two people, two ideas develop, neither of which is really communicated. If the listener allocates too much time to disapproving or approving of what is heard, there may not be time to understand it fully. This is particularly true when the remarks are loaded with emotion or threats to the security or status of the receiver.

Projective listening holds the greatest potential for effective communication. To fully utilize their time, listeners attempt to project themselves into the position of the speaker and to understand what is being said from the speaker's viewpoint. Effective listening should precede evaluation. After understanding what has been said, individuals are better able to evaluate it. Carl Rogers has suggested a rule to

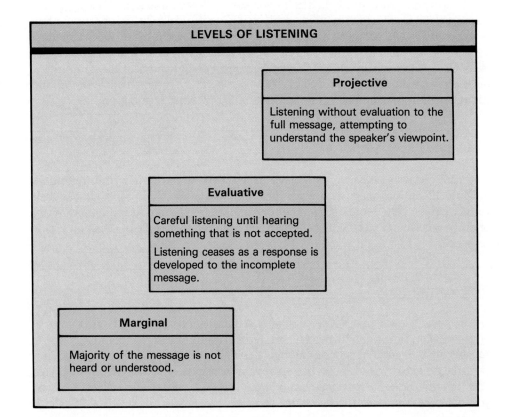

FIGURE 12–7

Levels of Listening

follow to ensure some degree of projective listening: "Each person can speak for himself only *after* he has related the ideas and feelings of the previous speaker accurately and to that speaker's satisfaction."[17] There is no need to agree with the statements, but there is a need to understand them as the speaker intended. Only in this way is it possible to frame a reply that will actually respond to the speaker's remarks. Effective listening is empathic listening. It requires an ability to listen for feeling as well as for words. The listener attempts to "stand in the shoes" of the other person.

Reading Skills

The amount of written material managers must cover has increased significantly in recent years, and some attempt should be made to consolidate and reduce it. Particularly in larger organizations, the ability to read rapidly and with understanding is an essential communication skill. It has been found that, through training, reading speeds can be doubled and tripled with little or no loss in comprehension.

Observation

Most people have heard of police reports of traffic accidents where there were many witnesses. When the witnesses are questioned by the police, they come up with many different versions of what occurred. "The blue car went through the stop light," says one witness. "No, that is not correct," says another. "The light was green." Most people miss a great deal by failing to carefully observe important elements in the environment. We mentioned earlier that some managers are adept at assessing the atmosphere of an organization merely by strolling through its workplace. Observation of furnishings, housekeeping, clothing, and activities can provide much information. Using our powers of observation to supplement listening and reading adds immeasurably to our understanding of what is going on.

Word Choice

There is a certain base of words that virtually everyone can understand (refer back to Figure 12–6). Managers who want to communicate effectively must choose their words carefully. The words transmitted by the sender should be in the vocabulary set of the receiver. Generally, for effective communication, simple or common words are best.

Body Language

Body language

The nonverbal method of communication in which physical actions such as motions, gestures, and facial expressions convey thoughts and emotions.

Research has shown that 90 percent of first impressions are based on nonverbal communication and only 10 percent on verbal communication.[18] Because it is the manager's job to get things done through the efforts of other people, it is important for managers to be aware of how they are communicating nonverbally. **Body language** is *the nonverbal method of communication in which physical actions such as motions, gestures, and facial expressions convey thoughts and emotions.*

An infinite variety of body positions are available to the receiver at any one moment. The manager will find it useful to know the language of body position and to use it correctly. Although body language is highly individualized, some generalizations, used cautiously, may be helpful. Crossed legs or ankles and folded arms may indicate a defensive posture or a dislike of the situation. A more open position may indicate the opposite, as may leaning forward or backward in a relaxed manner. A worker facing away from the manager, or putting hands in pockets, may be adopting a negative posture.

Many people almost literally talk with their hands. Usually, the meaning of hand gestures is readily understandable. As part of the total message, the importance of these gestures should not be ignored by the manager. Free use of hand gesturing is likely to indicate one of two contrasting psychic states—highly emotional and animated or relaxed and relatively carefree. If the emotional zeal of the first state develops into stress, gesturing becomes more restricted. The really tense individual is likely to hold the body rigid and use limited hand movement.

While free use of hand gestures generally reflects a positive attitude toward the other person, it sometimes can indicate other states. Nervousness, discomfort, or an unfavorable attitude may be reflected by such things as clenching the fists, drumming the fingers, twiddling the thumbs, and tugging at the nose, ear, or chin. The more neutral stance of thinking or evaluating may be indicated by stroking or rubbing of the chin or forehead.

Facial expressions are usually readily understood. By observing a person's face, we can often distinguish among such emotions as anger, interest, happiness, disgust, contempt, surprise, fear, and love. Facial expressions may indicate true feelings more reliably than verbal messages. In fact, when these two types of messages are contradictory, the receiver is more likely to believe the facial expression. For most people, it is more difficult to communicate false information through facial expression than through any speaking or writing.

Effective managers appreciate the importance of body language in the communication process. All people give off physical signals in attempting to communicate. These signals provide significant insight into the exact meaning of the message. Managers, particularly, must be aware of the signals they are presenting. Employees grasp at these small signals to determine what "the boss" really means. A frown may cause words that are positive in nature to be perceived as negative. A sarcastic smile along with the words "you did a good job" will likely be interpreted to mean that the worker actually did not do a good job. A blank stare may mean to the employee that the manager is not interested.

A manager must also be aware of the signals that a subordinate may be giving off. Sweaty hands or nail biting may mean that the worker feels ill at ease. Managers need to recognize these signs and be prepared to adjust their actions. Most nonverbal signals are given subconsciously. Hence, it may take great effort to change them.[19]

Actions

The manager must also recognize that one communicates by what one does or does not do. If a man comes to work one day and finds his desk moved from a location in a private office to one in an open area, communication of a sort has taken place. If no verbal explanation accompanies the action, people will interpret it their own way; the missing symbol or signal will be supplied by the observers. And despite any verbal statement to the contrary, such a move will likely be interpreted as a demotion.

In one company, management had introduced a change in procedure for a small crew of employees. The new method was timed, and standards were established. The workers all produced less than half the standard, and they all filed grievances protesting the unfairness of the standard. Management tried everything it could think of to correct the problem, from all-day time studies to providing each employee with a private instructor in the new method. A check on similar jobs in other companies revealed that the standard was in line. Thus, management concluded that the workers were deliberately restricting their output.

The next move was one of communication by action. An engineer was sent to the production department, and he proceeded to measure various angles and spaces on the floor. He volunteered no information to the group. Finally, one man's curiosity got the best of him, and he asked the engineer what he was doing. The engineer indicated that management wanted to see if there was sufficient room to locate certain machinery that could do the work of this crew. He continued about his business of measuring. The next day, all work crew members were producing amounts well above the established standard.

Directing

The process of telling a person what to do is **directing.** Naturally, much of a manager's work is associated with directing. After giving a directive, the manager should ensure that the subordinate knows:

- What to do.
- How to do it.
- When to do it.
- Why to do it.
- That it is a directive.

It is not being suggested that a manager should tell a worker each of these items every time an order is given. The manager should consider whether the worker already knows the elements. If not, the worker should be told. Difficulties often arise because the manager assumes the worker has the information. A good rule of thumb is to provide the information when you're unsure.

When a directive or order is particularly important, do not simply ask the worker, "Do you understand?" Instead, ask the worker to describe the action to be taken.

A Global Perspective

In the global environment, communication problems are intensified by language barriers. Faced with the ongoing globalization of business, an increasing number of U.S. executives are learning a second language. For instance, du Pont chief executive Edgar S. Woolard, Jr., learned Japanese. Other du Pont managers are cramming second languages as well. Their counterparts at Eastman Kodak, Citicorp, General Electric's Medical Systems division, and other corporations are doing the same thing.[20]

Most big companies sign up with 111-year-old Berlitz International to teach executives to speak another language. Berlitz is the leading language school worldwide, operating 267 centers in 25 countries and teaching 50 languages. Recently there has been a steady increase in corporate clients. Enrollment in the company's corporate-oriented total language emersion program and other classes has increased more than 50 percent. French and German are among the most popular languages for Americans attending Berlitz classes, with Japanese picking up fast.[21]

Because many international companies have declared English as their official language, English classes account for 64 percent of Berlitz's business internationally. Since language proficiency tends to make employees more effective communicators, the trend toward learning a second language is likely to continue.[22]

MANAGEMENT IN PRACTICE: A Skill-Building Exercise

As accounting supervisor Dave Roberts started walking toward accounting clerk Brad Stewart to give him some paperwork on an order, he saw that Brad was on the phone. When he got within earshot, he heard Brad say, "I really need twenty-four months on this because I don't want the monthly payments to take too much of my paycheck." Not wanting to seem too nosy about Brad's personal business, Dave went back to his office.

Thirty minutes later, Dave returned with the same papers, only to find Brad away from his desk and involved in a conversation with two of the other accounting clerks. Dave decided to interrupt what seemed to be a social conversation and give Brad the papers. As they walked back to Brad's desk together, Dave explained, "This is that Osborn order that the boss was so excited about." At about that time, Brad's phone rang. He answered it and said, "My supervisor is here right now. Can I call you back in a few minutes?" Dave said, "That's okay. Just come to my office when you have time to talk."

As Dave returned to his office, he thought about how Brad had changed. He had been an excellent worker. But now he was spending a lot of his time visiting and chatting with the other workers in the office. He also seemed to have "telephonitis." Brad's work was still satisfactory, but Dave didn't like the idea of his spending so much time on nonproductive activities. "I don't know what I can do," thought Dave. "Brad does have a good record here, and as long as he does his job I suppose I can't really say much about it."

What action should Dave take to return Brad to his former level of productivity?

• •

1. Are you willing to learn to have a plan for effective communication?

   ☐ Yes ☐ No

2. Are you willing to get organized for effective communication?

   ☐ Yes ☐ No

   (continued)

Summary

Communication is the transfer of information, ideas, understanding, or feelings among people. Through communication, organizational objectives may be accomplished. The manner in which plans are to be implemented and actions coordinated is communicated to those who must accomplish the task. Each step in the communication process is critical to success.

In the communication process, a sender encodes a message into a set of symbols that the receiver will understand. Messages are transmitted through such means as speaking, writing, acting, and drawing. The receiver decodes the message by converting the symbols into meaning. Communication is effective to the extent that the receiver's decoding matches the sender's encoding. The receiver can ignore the message, perform some task, store the information, or do something else. Through feedback, the sender knows if the message was accurately received and if the proper action was taken.

Communication channels, the means by which information is transmitted in organizations, may be formal or informal. Formal channels are those that are officially recognized by the organization. Instructions and information are passed downward, and information flows upward. Information also travels through informal channels, which bypass formal channels. The grapevine is an informal communication system that extends in every direction throughout an organization and even beyond it.

Messages flow along communication networks, such as the wheel and chain configurations. In a group, communication may be through one type of network, or the group may use variants of one or more networks. Identifying the predominant structural configuration, however, helps explain or predict the performance and satisfaction of the group and its members.

Communication breakdowns often occur when messages are not interpreted correctly. Barriers to communication may be technical, language, or psychological. Environmental barriers such as timing, information overload, and cultural differences are referred to as technical breakdowns.

Language problems can result from vocabulary and semantics. A manager must understand the type of audience being addressed. When a sender sends words to which a receiver attaches different meanings than those intended by the sender, a semantic (relating to the meaning of words) communication breakdown has occurred.

Psychological barriers tend to be the major cause of miscommunication. These barriers include various forms of distortion and problems involving interpersonal relations. With information filtering, for example, messages are altered through the elimination of certain data as the communication moves from person to person in the organization. Openness and trust must exist if orderly changes are to occur. Jealousy is often a barrier to communication, as is self-preoccupation and the tendency to interpret information in a certain way. Differences in past experiences, emotions, and beliefs affect each person's perception of a message.

When groups take a competitive stance, a "we-they" attitude is projected. This attitude polarizes the interacting groups and thus establishes a communication barrier between them. Communications take on an aura of bargaining, rather than of transmitting facts or solving problems.

Empathy, listening, reading, observation, word choice, body language, and actions all facilitate communication. And all are skills that can be learned. Body language is a nonverbal method of communication. Physical actions such as motions, gestures, and facial expressions convey thoughts and emotions. An infinite variety of body positions are available to the receiver at any one moment. The manager will find it useful to know the language of body position and to use it correctly.

The process of telling a person what to do is directing. Naturally, much of a manager's work is associated with directing. After giving a directive, the manager should ensure that the subordinate knows what to do, how to do it, when to do it, why to do it, and that it is a directive.

Review Questions

1. Define *communication*. Describe the basic communication process.
2. Distinguish by definition between formal and informal channels of communication. Provide examples of both types of channels.
3. Distinguish among technical, language, and psychological barriers to communication.
4. Describe barriers to effective group communication.
5. List the factors that have the ability to improve communication.
6. Define *empathy*. Explain why empathy is important to a manager.

Key Terms

Communication
Source (sender)
Communication
  channels
Formal communication
  channels
Informal communication
  channels
Open-door policy

Grievance procedure
Ombudsperson
Lateral communication
Diagonal communication
Communication
  networks
Timing
Information overload

Jargon
Information filtering
Perception set
Noise
Empathy
Body language
Directing

CASE 12.1   MOVING OUT TO MOVE UP

"Could you come to my office for a minute, Bob?" asked Terry Geech, the plant manager. "Sure, be right there," said Bob Gore. Bob was the plant's quality control director. He had been with the company for four years. After completing his degree in mechanical engineering, he had worked as a production supervisor and then as maintenance manager, prior to being promoted to his present job. Bob thought he knew what the call was about.

"Your letter of resignation catches me by surprise," began Terry. "I know that Wilson Products will be getting a good man, but we sure need you here, too." "I thought about it a lot," said Bob, "but there just doesn't seem to be a future for me here." "Why do you say that?" asked Terry. "Well," replied Bob, "the next position above mine is yours. With you only thirty-nine, I don't think it's likely that you'll be leaving soon."

"The fact is that I am leaving soon," said Terry. "That's why it's even more of a shock to know that you're resigning. I think I'll be moving to the corporate offices in June of next year. Besides, the company has

several plants that are larger than this one. We need good people in those plants from time to time, both in quality control and in general management."

"Well, I heard about an opening in the Cincinnati plant last year," said Bob, "but by the time I checked, the job had already been filled. We never know about job opportunities in the other plants until we read about them in the company paper."

"All this is beside the point now. What would it take to get you to change your mind?" asked Terry. "I don't think I can change my mind now," replied Bob. "I've already signed a contract with Wilson."

Questions

1. Evaluate the communication system at this company.
2. What actions might have prevented Bob's resignation?

CASE 12.2   OPEN THE DOOR!

Barney Cline, the new human resource manager for Ampex Utilities, was just getting settled in his office. He had recently moved from another firm to take over his new job. Barney had been selected over several in-house candidates and numerous other applicants because of his record for getting things done. He had a good reputation for working with people to get the job accomplished.

Just then his phone rang. The person on the other end of the line said, "Mr. Cline, could I set up an appointment to talk with you?" "Certainly," Barney said. "When do you want to get together?" "How about after work? It might be bad if certain people saw me speaking to anyone in management."

Barney was a bit puzzled, but he set up an appointment for 5:30 P.M., when nearly everyone would be gone. At the designated time, there was a knock on his door. It was Mark Johnson, a senior maintenance worker who had been with the firm for more than ten years.

After the initial welcome, Mark began talking, "Mr. Cline, several of the workers asked me to talk to you. The grapevine has it that you're a fair person. The company says it has an open-door policy. We're afraid to use it. Roy Edwards, one of the best maintenance men in our section, tried it several months ago. They hassled him so much that he quit only last week. We just don't know what to do to get any problems settled. There has been talk of organizing a union. We really don't want that, but something has to give."

Barney thanked Mark for his honesty and promised not to reveal the conversation. In the weeks following the conversation with Mark, Barney was able to verify that the situation was just as Mark had described it. There was considerable mistrust between managers and workers.

Questions

1. What types of communication breakdowns had occurred in the company?
2. Discuss the impact of the grapevine on the resolution of this problem.

Notes

1. This case is a composite of a number of published accounts, among them: Bill Saporito, "PPG: Shiny, Not Dull," *Fortune*, July 17, 1989, p. 107; Jack Keough and Christine Forbes, "Welcome to Vendor City," *Industrial Distribution*, May 1991, p. 32; Jack Keough and Christine Forbes, "Selling Innovation," *Industrial Distribution*, May 1991, pp. 38–40; Vincent A. Sarni, *Blueprint for the Decade* (Pittsburgh, 1984), pp. 1–8; and William J. Storck, "PPG Industries Works on Ways to Dampen Business Cycle Effects," *Chemical and Engineering News*, May 29, 1989, pp. 9–10.

2. F. E. X. Dance, "The 'Concept' of Communication," *Journal of Communication* 20 (June 1970): 201–210.

3. Roy Rowan, "America's Most Wanted Managers," *Fortune*, February 3, 1986, pp. 18–25.

4. Henry Mintzberg, *The Nature of Managerial Work* (New York: Harper & Row, 1973).

5. Henry Mintzberg, "The Manager's Job: Folklore and Fact," *Harvard Business Review* 53 (July–August 1975): 49–61.

6. **PINNACLE:** CNN correspondent Tom Cassidy discusses these and other issues with David Kearns.

7. M. L. Fahs, "Communication Strategies for Anticipating and Managing Conflict," *Personnel Administrator* 27 (October 1982): 28–34.

8. This case is a composite of a number of published accounts, among them: Sylvia Nasar, "Hard Road Ahead for Auto Insurers," *Fortune*, May 8, 1989, pp. 99–103; Ronald Grover, "California Insurers Won't Roll Over," *Business Week*, February 27, 1989, p. 38; Lisa Grose, "The Hook," *Forbes*, November 9, 1982, pp. 110–111; John R. Dorfman, "Insurance," *Forbes*, January 3, 1983, pp. 80–82; State Farm Mutual Automobile Insurance Company, "*Report to Policyholders*," 1989; "A Matter of Culture," *Manager's Magazine*, October 1987, pp. 26–27.

9. R. Foltz and R. D'Aprix, "Survey Shows Communication Problems," *Personnel Administrator* 28 (February 1983): 8.

10. Christy Marshall, "Rubbermaid Yes, Plastic," *Business Week*, December 1988, p. 37.

11. Michael Brody, "Listen to Your Whistleblower," *Fortune*, November 24, 1986, pp. 77–78.

12. Foltz and D'Aprix, "Survey Shows Communication Problems."

13. Ibid.

14. Claudia H. Deutsch, "Trust: The New Ingredient in Management," *Business Week*, July 6, 1981, p. 104.

15. Adapted from a case presented in Karen Berney's article, "Finding the Ethical Edge," *Nation's Business*, August 1987, p. 24.

16. D. W. Johnson and F. P. Johnson, *Joining Together: Group Theory and Group Skills* (Englewood Cliffs, NJ: Prentice-Hall, 1975).

17. Carl R. Rogers and F. J. Roethlisberger, "Barriers and Gateways to Communication," *Harvard Business Review* 30 (July–August 1952): 48.

18. Murray Mizock, "What You Aren't Saying May Be Everything," *Data Management*, September 1986, p. 33.

19. L. R. Cohen, "Minimizing Communication Breakdown between Male and Female Managers," *Personnel Administrator* 27 (October 1982): 57–58.

20. Richard S. Teitelbaum, "Language: One Way to Think Globally," *Fortune*, December 4, 1989, p. 11.

21. Ibid.

22. Ibid., p. 12.

13

Group Performance, Intergroup Behavior, and Conflict

LEARNING OBJECTIVES

After completing this chapter students should be able to

- Describe groups, group formation, and group development.
- Explain the factors influencing group effectiveness and the means of increasing group effectiveness.
- State ways of improving work team effectiveness.
- Define *conflict* and explain its potential causes.
- Explain how conflict becomes apparent.
- Describe how managers can become better at managing interpersonal and structural conflict.

At Volvo's two radically innovative factories, a fixed rather than moving assembly line is the norm. Gone are the days of the moving assembly line introduced by Henry Ford three-quarters of a century ago. In Sweden, the close supervision and machine-pacing of work on the assembly lines were major sore points with employees. At Volvo's newer plants, "work teams build cars much like doctors operate on a patient. Each car frame sits on its individual rotating holder while assembly crews attach the pieces. Instead of foreman and engineers, ordinary workers manage the shop floor." This radical change was brought about because Sweden's highly educated and well-trained labor force does not like to work in conventional factories.

This factory environment is conducive to so-called self-management. Volvo gives workers 16 weeks' training before they are allowed to get close to a car, and 16 months more of on-the-job orientation. In Sweden, at two Volvo plants, functional work groups assemble entire cars and assist in certain management activities. The work groups at these two innovative Volvo automobile plants assemble large units of a car without much supervision from managers. At the Kalmar plant, 15 or 20 people are grouped into teams that build cars without a moving assembly line. Each team builds a large section of a car, with a work cycle of 30 minutes.

According to Volvo management, productivity is higher at Kalmar than at the large, conventional assembly plant at Gothenburg. Uddevalla goes much further with functional work teams. The Uddevalla facility is divided into six assembly plants, each of which has eight teams. The teams basically manage themselves, handling scheduling, quality control, hiring, and other duties normally performed by supervisors. There are no first-line supervisors and only two tiers of management. Each group has a spokesperson who reports to one of the six plant managers. These six individuals report directly to the company president.

In Sweden, as in many countries, the move toward utilization of functional work groups is increasing. Basically, in Sweden the "old way" of running automakers and other large industrial companies is outmoded. However, this radical approach to automobile manufacturing is not perfect. Problems have occurred with some assembly teams. Workers have reported "friction" and disagreements among team members that has created a certain degree of conflict. Still, few wish to go back to the old way, with supervisors making all the decisions. In Sweden, as in all countries, the environment surrounding the work force is extremely important and must be designed to encourage employees to put forth effort in the pursuit of organizational goals.[1]

Group behavior, intergroup behavior, and conflict are part of the realities of today's business world, and the problems associated with these factors are often intensified by the movement toward teamwork. At Volvo, individuals are brought together for the purpose of transforming certain inputs into a Volvo automobile. Functional group members interact with one another on a daily basis to facilitate accomplishment of Volvo's organizational objectives. Conflict has resulted at times but most employees agree that this approach is better than the alternative.

In this chapter, we first define the term *group* and describe the various types of groups. Next, we review the significant aspects of group formation and development. Then, we address the factors influencing group effectiveness, the variables involved in increasing group effectiveness, and the aspects involved in work team effectiveness. Next, we discuss conflict in organizations, including potential causes of conflict and the need for conflict to become apparent. We devote the final portion of the chapter to how managers can become better at managing interpersonal and structural conflict.

Groups

Group

Two or more people having a unifying relationship, such as common objectives or physical proximity.

A **group** is *two or more people having a unifying relationship, such as common objectives or physical proximity*. Although group members generally share certain similarities with one another, each member may have personal reasons for joining the group. People join groups for many reasons, including security, affiliation, esteem, power, and goal accomplishment. Basically, individuals choose group membership to achieve an outcome that requires their association with other people. In the future, group membership will be required of more and more employees in many organizations. Companies such as Boeing, Caterpillar, Digital Equipment, Ford, and General Electric are already making groups part of their push toward greater productivity.[2]

Everyone belongs to many groups—at work, in the community, and even at home (the family is a group). There are formal work groups, of course, made up of managers

Everyone belongs to many groups, at work, in the community, and even at home (the family is a group). Business teams throughout Honeywell help make the company more competitive, according to a company official. Kathryn Ybarra (center) is shown with part of her 30-person engineering team at Honeywell's Air Transport Systems Division in Phoenix.

Source: Photo courtesy of Honeywell, Inc.

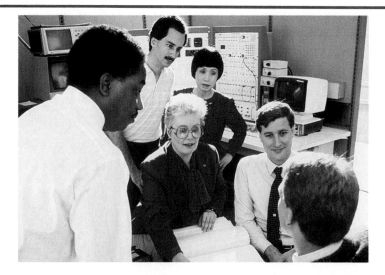

and subordinates. To a certain degree the line between managers and subordinates is becoming blurred at some companies. To increase individual and group job performance, managers need to understand the kinds of groups that exist both within and outside the organization. Remember that at the Volvo's Kalmar plant, 15 or 20 people are grouped into teams that build cars without a moving assembly line.

Groups are categorized in a number of ways. Understanding the characteristics of each type of group can affect a manager's expectations of relationships among group members. Initially, managers need to appreciate the difference between primary and secondary groups. **Primary groups** are *small groups characterized by relatively close associations among members.* As might be expected, the closeness of these associations directly influences the behaviors of individuals in the group. In contrast, **secondary groups** are *groups that are larger and less intimate than primary groups.* Relationships tend to be more impersonal and frequently are formalized.

Everyone participates in both types of groups. Primary groups exert a greater influence on individuals' day-to-day activities through the presence of other group members and their ability to reinforce member behavior. Secondary groups rely instead on sanctions imposed through control systems (rules, regulations, policies) or exercised by designated individuals, such as group leaders. Groups also can be classified according to their function or the circumstances under which they are formed. Three types of groups commonly encountered in organizations are task (or functional) groups, project groups, and informal groups.

Primary groups
Small groups characterized by relatively close associations among members.

Secondary groups
Groups that are larger and less intimate than primary groups.

Task (Functional) Groups

Groups determined by prescribed job requirements are **task,** or **functional groups.** The workers at the Kalmar plant who are grouped into teams would be considered a task group. They are brought together for the purpose of transforming certain inputs (raw materials, ideas, objects) into a distinguishable output, such as a physical product or a decision. Functional group members usually interact with one another on a daily basis, and they are often organized into departments or work teams to facilitate the accomplishment of organizational objectives.

Task (functional) groups
Groups determined by prescribed job requirements

Project Groups

As discussed in Chapter 7, project groups include formal, but temporary, assignments to groups, committees, and special projects. All organizations have some activities requiring group cooperation across functional lines—for example, a committee made up of members from several departments. After a project has been completed, project group members return to their routine work activities or go to another temporary project group. Examples of project groups include research and development teams and internal consultant groups.

Informal Groups

Two or more persons associated with one another in ways not prescribed by the formal organization are an **informal group.** Such groups are very common. In some cases,

Informal group
Two or more persons associated with one another in ways not prescribed by the formal organization.

they arise because people find themselves in a common location. They can also result from the need to solve organizational problems or achieve formal objectives. Thus, similarities or differences within formal groups can lead to informal activities in organizations. Informal groups can also take the form of two or three people who belong to the same church or baseball team or who play racquetball or have parties together.

Group Formation

People join groups for a multitude of reasons. As mentioned, they may spontaneously form informal groups in an organization or within a formal group, such as a network of professionals. They may also join *formal groups*—those officially sanctioned and organized by managerial or other authority to accomplish organizational objectives, such as organizational departments or task forces.

As Figure 13–1 shows, groups form when individuals exhibit one or more of the following:

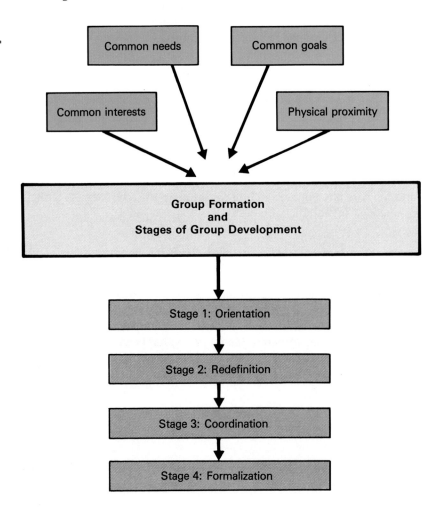

1. **Common interests.** Engineers employed by different companies often join the same professional groups.
2. **Common needs.** Food cooperatives may be formed because individuals want to satisfy their basic needs for food at a low cost.
3. **Common objectives.** A board of directors of a company is formed to help the company reach its objectives.
4. **Physical proximity.** Employees in the same work area often join together as a social group.[3]

The reason for forming a group influences the nature and quality of the group's functioning. Studying the causes of group formation, then, helps predict and anticipate the ways a group is likely to act. The group must evolve into an effective collective unit through the process of group development.

ETHICAL DILEMMA

You are an up-and-coming manager who has been employed by a major tobacco company for six years. Managers in the company have a fairly consistent path up the corporate ladder to senior-level management positions. Most managers work in a department, making use of their general expertise, for four to six years. Then they work as a member of a special committee for five to seven years. Ultimately, they reach a senior management position.

You are placed on the committee that handles suits by clients who claim that they or their loved ones have gotten cancer from smoking cigarettes. The committee is composed of you, one R&D manager, one marketing manager, and four attorneys. Initially, this committee reviews the merits of each case and takes action to limit the financial and public relations impact on the company.

You have finished reviewing documents used in a case against the Liggett Group, Inc. A Liggett scientist duplicated the experiments that suggested that the tar in cigarettes caused cancerous tumors to grow in mice. You also have read memos used as evidence against R. J. Reynolds. RJR lawyers had written management several warnings to the effect that marketing a *safer* cigarette could increase the company's vulnerability to charges that it knew conventional tobacco products were less safe than the company had maintained.

You have just found several memos from a research scientist at your company that indicate cigarettes do actually cause cancer in humans and do increase the likelihood of heart disease. The memos state further that the research department has come up with a new, safer cigarette. Follow-up memos from company executives, however, show that the project was killed, out of fear of severe legal action. When you review these documents you get a sick feeling.

You confront the chairman of the committee with the memos and express your disgust at company executives choosing not to market a safer cigarette. You are told to forget what you have seen and to fall in line or to forget your career. You can either fall in line and protect the profitability and reputation of the company, and your career, or you can blow the whistle.

What would you do?

Group Development

Once a group forms, it must resolve a variety of issues before it can function effectively. Tracing the development of groups provides one perspective for assessing a group's performance. There are essentially four stages of development—orientation, redefinition, coordination, and formalization (see Figure 13–1)—and they focus on two dimensions of group behavior: (1) task activity and (2) group structure process. **Task activity** is *the steps used to perform a task, not including the procedures and materials required to accomplish it.*[4] **Group structure process** is *the interpersonal interactions needed to accompany and accomplish task activities.*[5]

Task activity

The steps used to perform a task, not including the procedures and materials required to accomplish it.

Group structure process

The interpersonal interactions needed to accompany and accomplish task activities.

Orientation

The orientation stage occurs when the group views the task and determines acceptable interpersonal behaviors. At this stage, the group members gather information about the nature of the group's task. They also discover acceptable behaviors.

Redefinition

The redefinition stage occurs when the group redefines the task, tries to agree on its objectives and strategy, and develops group structure. Conflict may result at this stage as the group members determine whether they like the task and their degree of commitment to it. Differences in members' reactions to the demands of the task often lead to conflict. Members may differ in the amount of time they are willing to devote to a particular task, the priority they assign to the task, or the means they believe will best accomplish it. The sharper the differences, the greater the intragroup (within the group) conflict.

Coordination

During the coordination stage, which is often the longest one, the group collects information and interprets it in order to facilitate the accomplishment of group objectives. Arguments over interpretation frequently occur. Here, discussions about the nature of the task, different emotional responses to it, alternatives, and possible action take place. A group's discussions about the types and quality of existing programs, as well as its members' participation in the process of developing a new program, illustrate the activities of this stage. The members resolve their differences after an open exchange of relevant interpretations and opinions and begin to act as a group. Often, groups do not reach this stage and therefore disintegrate.

Formalization

The group specifies the final version of the decision in the formalization stage. It is at this stage that the choice and implementation of task activities occur. At this time, too, roles that match the group's needs for leadership and expertise, as well as the members' abilities and attitudes, are assigned.

Moving Through the Developmental Stages

A group may recycle through the four stages of development, particularly as changes in its membership, its task, or the environment occur. For example, if a new member is added to the group, the group begins its development anew. Of course, movement through the stages may occur more rapidly the second time. For example, orientation of a new member may require ten minutes rather than two hours. Instead of receiving new members, a group may change its objectives. The extent and uniqueness of the membership, task, or environmental changes will influence the speed with which the group moves through stages after the first time.

Some groups remain at one stage by failing to resolve the issues associated with it. In normally functioning groups, the orientation stage is the shortest, followed in length by the redefinition and formalization stages; the coordination stage is longest. Groups experiencing difficulties tend to have an elongated formation stage.[6] Failure to move beyond redefinition signals a group's lack of conflict resolution mechanisms. Occasionally, groups remain stuck at other stages. Remaining at the orientation stage suggests that the group lacks the skill to screen out irrelevant information and behavior. Inability to move beyond coordination often reflects a group with poor information, which hinders effective interpretation. Frequently, such dilemmas can remain unresolved when a group lacks clear objectives or when individual members have incompatible objectives.

Factors Influencing Group Effectiveness

An effective group can attain, or make acceptable progress toward, its objectives or the objectives of its members. In an organization, this may mean getting a job done, providing group members with a sense of belonging, or successfully competing with another group. As Figure 13–2 suggests, many factors influence group effectiveness. Among them are individual roles, group norms, conformity, leadership, group cohesiveness, group size, and synergism.

Individual Roles

The concept of role is broader than that of its counterpart in the formal organization— the job. A **role** is *the total pattern of expected behavior of an individual.* It includes the official content of the job description but goes beyond it. If a person is officially designated a supervisor, the person may be pressured to dress, talk, and act like other managers in the organization. If managers in a particular firm typically dress formally, the manager who fails to do so may not be fulfilling the expected role.

Role
Total pattern of expected behavior of an individual.

Individuals who are members of an informal group also are presented with roles to act out. Whether or not the informal group is supportive of management has a major impact on the roles of the group members. If the group decides not to support a decision made by top management, the pattern of members' behavior (role) may reflect indifference or slowing down on the job. Failure to conform to the expected role may result in a member's being cast out of the informal group. This may harm the formal organization as well as the individual. On the other hand, managers can usually work through informal group leaders to maximize productivity.[7]

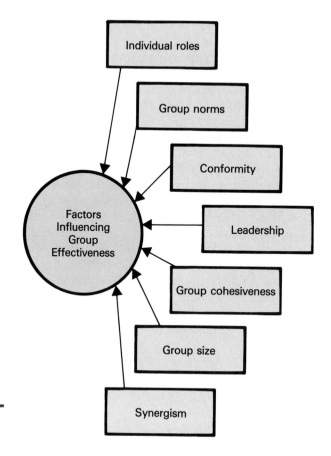

FIGURE 13–2

Factors Influencing Group
Effectiveness

A person may have many roles to play. For instance, when working toward a doctorate, one of the authors was a student, a teacher, a consultant, and a military officer in the reserves. The failure to change roles immediately at the proper time often resulted in difficulties. Being a military officer with considerable authority on the weekend and a humble doctoral student on Monday morning was sometimes not easy. Students who go back to school part time while working as supervisors often encounter the same difficulties.

Group Norms

Norm

A standard of behavior expected of informal group members.

Underlying group development and implicit in group functioning are expectations that guide behavior. A **norm** is *a standard of behavior expected of informal group members.* A student, for example, is expected to attend classes, prepare homework, and take examinations. A worker is expected to be at work on time, miss work only in case of illness, and put in a good day's work for a good day's pay. These unwritten expectations develop through the interaction of group members and the reinforcement of behaviors by the group. Generally, the expectations are in line with group objectives, which in turn are helpful in accomplishing organizational objectives. In some cases, however, the group's expectations do not fit with the organization's objectives.

Some work groups, for example, insist that their members maintain a suboptimal production level. In other organizations, certain management-level employees are expected to arrive late.

Group members may act to encourage certain behaviors—for example, by reinforcing a specific level of production. Members may also discourage certain behaviors by responding negatively to their occurrence. A group may, for example, reject very low or very high performance.

Norms generally develop for behaviors that group members view as important. Most norms develop in one of four ways:

1. Supervisors or co-workers may explicitly state certain expectations.
2. Critical events in the group's history may establish norms.
3. The initial pattern of behavior may become a norm.
4. Group members may carry over behavior from other situations.[8]

There are norms about attendance, performance, interpersonal interactions, and dress. But not all norms apply to everyone.[9] Different norms exist for managers and nonmanagerial employees, for professionals and nonprofessionals, for men and women. They might differ in the extent to which people are expected to be innovative on the job, follow organizational rules and regulations, or demonstrate loyalty to a specific department or supervisor. Members who are expected to demonstrate loyalty to their department might try to provide a larger role for that department than would individuals with more organizational loyalty.

Furthermore, norms are established and enforced only for selected behaviors.[10] A group enforces norms that facilitate its survival, help predict the behavior of group members, prevent embarrassing interpersonal problems from arising, express the group's central values, and clarify the group's identity.[11]

Conformity

Once norms are established, the issue of conformity necessarily becomes a matter of concern. The anticipation of acceptance or rejection by the group for following or violating norms is usually enough to ensure that members conform to the group's expectations.[12] Conformity offers the advantage of maintaining a predictable pattern of work, nurturing teamwork, and defending individual and group interests. When an individual does not conform to group norms, other group members will, at least initially, try to persuade the deviant to conform.[13] In some groups, the nonconformist may even be physically harassed. For example, the pilots who returned to fly for Eastern Airlines during the employee 1989 strike against the company were often treated badly by their striking counterparts. Some pilots even gave up their seniority at ill-fated Eastern Airlines and took jobs with other airlines rather than violate group norms.[14]

Conformity clearly has its negative side. It can stifle innovation and initiative, reduce performance, and even encourage undesirable actions. Solomon Asch demonstrated the power of small groups to pressure individuals into yielding to the majority opinion, even when that opinion is clearly false. Asch showed a group of people a card with lines of varying lengths and asked each person to determine which line was the same length as the line on a comparison card. Asch planted all but one of the people in the group, and the plants deliberately gave the wrong answers. About 35 percent of the subjects also gave the wrong answer. Asch found, however, that if just one of the individuals planted in the group gave the right answer, violating the unanimous judgment of the group, the tendency of the subject to conform was lessened considerably. Just one ally was often enough to encourage independent judgment on the subject's part.[15]

Leadership

In the formal organization, leaders are managers; they are placed in their positions of authority by top management. An entirely different process occurs in selecting a leader for the informal organization. The informal leader is usually chosen in one of two ways. First, people may appoint themselves informal leaders. A leadership vacuum may exist, and the first person who takes charge may be automatically followed. Second, the informal leader may be chosen through consensus. In this case, the person whose behavior is closest to the norms of the group often becomes the leader.

Although the informal leader may have no formal title, this person is the one who is looked to for guidance in achieving the group's objectives. If the leader begins to deviate from group norms, a group member whose behavior is closer to the norms may take the leader's place.

Group Cohesiveness

Cohesiveness

The degree of attraction the group has for each of its members.

The degree of attraction the group has for each of its members is **cohesiveness.** Important to both the formal and the informal organization, cohesiveness is identified by attitudes such as loyalty to the group, friendliness and congeniality, a feeling of responsibility for group efforts, and a willingness to defend the group against outside attack. Cohesive informal work groups are powerful instruments; they can work for or against the formal organization. For instance, a highly cohesive group whose goals are in agreement with organizational objectives can use its strength to help the firm increase productivity. On the other hand, a highly cohesive group whose goals are not in agreement with organizational objectives can have an extremely negative effect on the accomplishment of the firm's objectives. Because of this potential problem, some managers attempt to reduce cohesiveness in order to maintain control.

Several factors affect the degree of cohesiveness group members have for each other (see Figure 13–3). First, a group that is exposed to danger or to threats often develops great cohesiveness. For example, a manager who is seen as a threat to workers can cause the workers to band together in opposition. Second, frequency of contact has an effect. Groups whose members seldom see each other are not likely to be cohesive. Third, homogeneous groups are likely to be more cohesive than heterogeneous groups. For example, workers of one sex, race, or age are usually more cohesive than are mixed groups. That is one of the reasons women and minorities may not be readily accepted into a work group that consists of white males. Fourth, if being a member of the group satisfies members' needs, they will have a stronger desire to stay with the group. Finally, smaller groups tend to be

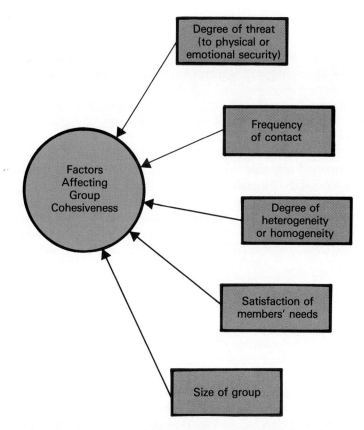

FIGURE 13–3

Factors Affecting Group
Cohesiveness

more cohesive. Large groups have so many different relationships that cohesiveness is reduced.

Some managers oppose the existence of cohesive informal groups because they know they will have to implement unpopular decisions sooner or later. However, even for small companies—perhaps especially for them—a clear understanding of informal group characteristics such as cohesiveness can make implementing unpopular decisions easier.[16]

Group Size

The informal group tends to be small so its members can interact frequently. But when groups get too small, difficulties arise. The *dyad*, or two-person group, provides a perfect example. When a decision is required and there is no consensus, one group member must lose.

Considerable research has been devoted to determining the most effective group size. This research has led to the following conclusions:

- When the quality of a complex group decision is important, the use of seven to twelve members under a formal leader is most appropriate.

- When consensus in a conflict situation is important, the use of three to five members with no formal leader will ensure that each member's view will be discussed.

- When both quality and consensus are important, five to seven members seems most appropriate.[17]

There tends to be greater group conflict in even-sized groups, and there is more conflict in groups of two and four members than there is in groups of six members. In seating arrangements, members who sit across from each other tend to engage in more frequent, and often more argumentative, communication. If consensus is the objective, members with any conflict potential should be seated alongside each other.

Thus, managers dealing with the subject of effective work groups should be concerned primarily that they be small ones. Obviously, many organizations consist of thousands of members. The initial approach to organizing must therefore be formal in nature, resulting in the design of official units, jobs, and formal relationships of authority, responsibility, and accountability. Within the formal organization, a limitless number of small, informal work groups will be spontaneously established. It is hoped, of course, that they will be aligned with overall organizational objectives.

Synergism

Synergism

The cooperative action of two or more persons working together to accomplish more than they could working separately.

The cooperative action of two or more persons working together to accomplish more than they could working separately is **synergism.** Managers need to recognize that greater effect may be achieved when two workers are placed together.

Synergism may also allow the organization to attain a special advantage with regard to cost, market power, technology, or management skill. One of the prime reasons for acquiring certain organizations is the synergistic advantages the right pairing of organizations can provide. R. J. Reynolds Industries Inc. (RJR) gained synergistic effects when it acquired Nabisco Brands Inc. Since the product lines of the two firms were complementary, they provided the new company, RJR Nabisco, with greater clout for supermarket shelf space and a more powerful distribution system in both domestic and global markets.[18] Additional synergism can be gained by integrating computer-driven technology and employees who are multiskilled, highly skilled, and highly motivated.[19]

The concept of synergism has implications for both formal and informal groups. However, through the synergistic effect, the informal group may become more powerful. People in groups often have much more influence than the same number of individuals working alone. In addition, group members themselves can significantly influence group effectiveness. The mammoth 3M Corporation has found ways to promote synergism in large organizations.

Groups, Teams, and Innovation at 3M

3M Corporation makes about fifty thousand products, from Scotch tape and Post-It notes to bioelectronic ear implants and heavy industrial abrasives. But despite its size and diversity, 3M is apparently not very bureaucratic. It was number 3 on *Fortune*'s 1989 list of America's most admired corporations, mainly because of its innovativeness. Famed management author Thomas J. Peters said, "It is far more entrepreneurial than any $10 billion company I've come across, and probably more entrepreneurial than a majority of those one-tenth its size."

The rules at 3M are few and simple: Keep divisions small, tolerate failure, motivate the champions, stay close to the customer, share the wealth, and don't kill a project. These rules translate into small, entrepreneurial divisions where the boss knows every staffer's first name. Each employee is allowed to spend 15 percent of each workweek on any product-related activity. And dozens of $50,000 "Genesis grants" are awarded to provide seed money each year. Anyone who comes up with a product idea can recruit an "action team" to develop it. If it works, the inventor has a chance to form and run the division that will take the product to market.

Recently, a decision was made to decentralize the human resource management function "in a big way." Study groups were formed, with members from every organizational level. Each group met for several days to help create the new structure. Most activities—for example, training—were spun off into the group being served. Manufacturing, sales and marketing, and research and development, for example, each got their own training group.

Groups of workers were asked to improve the work flow through the Aberdeen, South Dakota, plant. Their solution: Scrap the old manufacturing system entirely and rearrange the machinery into "work cells." Then, the entire product, in this case respirator masks, could be made in one small area.

Within each product team at 3M, there is constant peer review and feedback. And the reviews affect pay. A *Business Week* reporter wrote, "Informal information-sharing sessions spring up willy-nilly at 3M—in the scores of laboratories and small meeting rooms or in the hallways." The "share the wealth" rule encourages such meetings, because technology, once developed at 3M, belongs to any division that can use it.

A former worker who returned to visit wrote: "The workers with whom I talked appreciate the new responsibilities. I had hated feeling like an automaton when I worked in the 3M plant, but it's an entirely different story for my former colleagues."[20]

Increasing Group Effectiveness

J. Richard Hackman and Charles Morris note that group members can enhance the effectiveness of their group by increasing the following three variables:

1. The level of effort the group applies to carrying out its task.

2. The adequacy of the task performance strategies used by the group carrying out the task.

3. The level and appropriateness of the knowledge and skills brought to bear on the task by group members.

Organizational members can then manipulate (1) behavioral norms, (2) task design, or (3) group composition as ways of increasing these three variables.[21]

Changing existing norms is the most promising way of increasing the effort of group members. The group or its leader can require regular attendance at meetings, extensive time—three to five hours, say—preparing for them, or extension of the length of meetings until a particular objective is reached.

Redesigning the task is the most promising way to improve task performance strategies. The group might introduce greater specialization of responsibilities or increase the amount of job enrichment. Each group member could be given responsibility for a single, integral part of the task, the part that best fits the person's expertise or experience.

Changing the composition of the group can affect the knowledge and skills brought to bear on the task. The group might be changed to include volunteers rather than appointed employees, representatives of different departments, or only experienced workers.

Work Team Effectiveness

Teams are collections of people who must rely on group collaboration if each member is to experience the optimum of success and objective achievement.[22] They generally have specific projects of specified (short- or long-term) duration. Management groups, committees, task forces, and other work units strive to act as teams, because they recognize the importance of concerted effort in accomplishing group objectives.

Characteristics of Effective Teams

Table 13–1 summarizes one view of the characteristics of an effective work team. A team-building program can begin when a new team is formed or when an existing team stops functioning effectively. In forming a new team, members should ideally follow four steps:

1. Each member must determine the priority she or he attaches to participating in the team's activities and must assess the personal importance of these activities.

2. The members must share their expectations about working on the team.

3. The members must clarify the team's objectives.

Teams are collections of people who must rely on group collaboration for objective achievement. Here, Lockheed team leader Kathy A. Shockey (third from right), is shown with some of her Milstar team members. Lockheed is prime contractor on Milstar, the multibillion-dollar, next-generation military communication satellite network.

Source: Photo courtesy of Lockheed Corporation

Objectives are clear to all and shared by all, and all care about and feel involved in the goals.

All members participate and are listened to.

Members freely express themselves and receive empathic responses.

When problems arise, the situation is carefully diagnosed before action is proposed; remedies attack basic causes.

As needs for leadership arise, various members meet them; anyone feels free to volunteer as he or she sees a group need.

Consensus is sought and tested; decisions, when made, are fully supported.

Members trust one another; they reveal to the group what they would be reluctant to expose to others; they respect and use the responses they get; they can freely express negative reactions without fearing reprisal.

The group is flexible and seeks new and better ways of acting; individuals change and grow; they are creative.

SOURCE: Adapted from Edgar Schein, *Process Consultation* (Reading, MA: Addison-Wesley Publishing Co., Inc., 1969), pp. 42–43. Reprinted with permission.

TABLE 13–1

Characteristics of an Effective Work Team

4. The team must formulate operating guidelines about the process of decision making, basic work methods, the extent and nature of member participation in discussion, ways of resolving differences, ways of ensuring that work is completed, and ways of changing nonproductive activities.[23]

To ensure the effectiveness and productivity of a task force, managers must carefully form the task force, define and allocate resources, and manage day-to-day activities.[24] To do this, a manager might choose individuals whose job performance will be affected by the objectives of the task force. Generally, the person who organizes the task force selects a leader or requests that task force members participate in selecting one. Once the selection has been made, the leader should set agendas for group meetings, help reduce members' hidden agendas, and build members' commitment to the task and to other group members. The individual who forms a task force must select members who have a vested interest in its mission, will be challenged by its task, and have complementary skills. Some operations can become much more effective through the use of teamwork, as AFG Industries discovered.

. . . .

In the everyday business of making glass, group effectiveness is often enhanced when group members are provided with a sense of belonging, through teamwork. Teamwork contributes to the successful completion of the job of glass making and helps maintain profits in an extremely competitive business.

AFG Industries

AFG's "team" concept involves everybody in the plant learning every job in the plant. Pay is based on the number of jobs employees know and can successfully perform. The competitive situation in the glass business is even more intense because Japanese firms are now building some automotive glass plants in the United States. To remain competitive, AFG has combined strong leadership and the team approach which has also helped AFG increase its revenues dramatically and greatly increase its stock price.[25]

. . . .

Strategies for Team Building

To improve the performance of work teams, managers (or outside consultants) may prescribe a variety of team-building activities. Data collection is one essential activity. Managers, group members, or outside parties may use group process observation as one means of data collection.[26] The observer collects data about the communication, decision making, and leadership in a team. The observer acquires information about group norms and roles by tabulating who talks to whom, how frequently, and about what topics, then feeds this information back to team members. A group process consultant may also be called in to help set agendas, coach the group or its individual members in effective interpersonal processes, and offer recommendations for more effective performance.

For effective team building to occur:

1. The primary objective of a team development meeting must be explicit and well articulated.

2. This objective must be held by the leader of the group and must be understood (and, one hopes, agreed to) by the work group members.

3. The objective should be the condition under which third parties (consultants) work. That is, the primary purpose is defined by the leader, who sets the agenda and activities of the meeting.

4. If consultants are working with the team directly, they should help the leader explicitly define and share the primary purpose with team members.[27]

Even though every effort may be made to foster effective team building, conflict may still exist.

A Global Perspective

Competitors globally are aware of the so called Japanese marvels. Two of these so-called marvels are the top-quality products Japanese companies make and their loyal and dedicated work forces. However, even more amazing is that the Japanese can export their methods and create such products and work forces wherever they choose to do so. It is no simple matter to import the Japanese system to the United States and put it in place with the effectiveness that such systems enjoy in Japan. Whatever arrives on the shores of the United States must be "Americanized" to some degree, especially those aspects of work that require group cooperation, tolerance, and understanding. Like most Japanese companies, Mazda, the Japanese automaker, uses work teams in its assembly plants. Mazda management tailored their work process plan and created a work group system they believed would be effective in America. This work group system involves a work group for each department at the plant as well as a central work group that monitors, controls, and coordinates the activities of the departmental work groups.

To make their first U.S. assembly plant in Flat Rock, Michigan, successful, Mazda recognized that such a work group system would require employees to be carefully selected and developed. They went to unprecedented lengths to find just the right kinds of people and then properly trained them. Mazda management realized that not everyone is suited for such a work environment, so it was essential that the staffing and development process be effective.

Each and every applicant was thoroughly assessed in significant factors such as interpersonal skills, motivation, and aptitude for learning and re-learning. They were also evaluated to determine their interest in teamwork and participation. Employees who were hired completed three weeks of training that focused on helping them understand how to function better as individuals, and more importantly, as group members. Finally, employees received another ten weeks of technical training before they were put to work as members of the Mazda team. Mazda invested $40 million, $13,000 per employee, to hire and properly develop this highly select group of workers. Mazda's Joe Galusha stressed that the job of this work group system has only begun, and that it will never end. He views the proper functioning of Mazda's work group system as a continuing developmental effort.

Mazda is a global competitor that appreciates the importance of tailoring the process to the characteristics of the work to be accomplished, and to further take into account the characteristics of those who will accomplish the work. The desire to tailor their methods will surely pay off in big dividends in America, as it has in Japan, and will certainly serve Mazda well in other countries around the globe. Other global players may well benefit from the Mazda example. Basically, tailoring the process often translates into success regardless of where in the world the company is doing business.[28]

Conflict in Organizations

When individuals and groups interact, there is always the potential for conflict. **Conflict** is *antagonism or opposition between or among persons*. It occurs when there is competition or mutual interference among people. Whenever individuals are brought together in a highly structured environment, the potential for conflict exists. As more companies implement the team approach, the occurrence of conflict may also increase.

Conflict

Antagonism or opposition between or among persons.

U.S. companies use an approach to teamwork that is more encompassing than the Japanese approach. American teamwork not only involves workers in decision making but extends that involvement into the management arena. American managers see this extended involvement as an important way to compete with foreign firms based in and outside the United States. Militant unionists, however, believe that management has a "hidden agenda to erode the collective bargaining system, to lessen resistance to changes that are more favorable to the company than they are to the employees."[29] These two divergent views are an excellent breeding ground for conflict between labor and management. Conflict is also a reality of social situations, such as team member interactions, and its costly repercussions cannot be ignored.

Conflict usually follows a pattern, as Figure 13–4 shows. First, conflict does not just happen; there must be causes. Second, even though the potential for conflict exists, it cannot be managed until it becomes apparent. Third, the results of conflict must be determined, since they may help or hurt the organization. Finally, the conflict is eventually resolved, sometimes to the benefit of the participants and the organization. At other times, the resolution of conflict harms one or more of the conflicting parties or the organization.

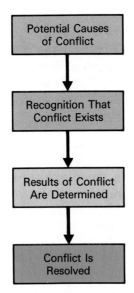

FIGURE 13–4

Conflict Resolution Sequence

Potential Causes
of Conflict

↓

Recognition That
Conflict Exists

↓

Results of Conflict
Are Determined

↓

Conflict Is
Resolved

Potential Causes of Conflict

Since conflict results from the normal interactions of people, no organization is completely without it. Although conflict is not necessarily harmful, its potential cost is so great that it cannot be ignored. It is imperative that managers be familiar with the following categories of causes: objective interference, competition for scarce resources, personality differences, perception set differences, change, and failure to communicate.

Objective Interference

In many situations, the achievement of one person's objectives blocks the achievement of another's objectives. Both people may have the same objective, but only one may attain it. Suppose, for instance, a new office becomes available. Two supervisors want the office, but only one can get it. Another example of objective interference might be the manager who wants to produce as much as possible without worrying about quality versus the quality control person who concentrates primarily on quality. This kind of conflict can also result from a worker who wants to make as much as possible while the boss wants to maintain a balance in the pay structure.

Competition for Scarce Resources

No matter how much of a resource there is, there never seems to be quite enough to go around. For example, at budget time, managers seldom get all they want. There is only so much money available. Giving one manager more money usually means giving someone else less.

Logic seldom prevails when people compete for resources. It is human nature to want more. Sometimes, this competition becomes a way of keeping score as to status. A substantial budget increase implies influence with upper management. Telling people that your department received a budget cut may not be as pleasant.

Personality Differences

We all have different personalities, and each of us thinks and acts differently. It would be a boring world if this were not so. But personality differences among workers create the potential for conflict. An extrovert may find it difficult to work with an introvert, and vice versa. A highly disciplined person may find it impossible to work with a free spirit. Some people care about social relationships, and others do not. All of these instances hold the possibility of conflict.

Differences in Perception Sets

A **perception set** is *a fixed tendency to interpret information in a certain way.* Life experiences and objectives strongly influence the way things are seen. Differences in perception sets are a major source of conflict. For instance, a person who grew up in a racially segregated environment might be unfavorably disposed toward blacks, particularly black managers. Men who grew up in an environment where women rarely worked outside the home might experience conflict with a woman supervisor. A worker who grew up in a strong union community might be antagonistic toward anyone in management. The list could go on and on. Many potential conflict situations are caused by differences in perception sets.

Perception set
A fixed tendency to interpret information in a certain way.

MANAGEMENT IN PRACTICE: A Skill-Building Exercise

You are the supervisor of a great group of people, but today you would rather be doing anything else. Today is the day you must antagonize your friend Fred, who is the most successful dock foreman you have. You realize Fred will not understand when you tell him he must accept some foreigners, minorities, and women in his work group. He believes that he best understands what is needed to make his group effective. Fred has stated, many times, that "on the docks we don't shuffle paper, we do real work, and it takes real men to do the work." According to Fred, his "men are the best dock workers on the pier. They have always exceeded the tonnage moved by any other group, and that is because they work so well together. Change the makeup of the work group and the productivity of the group will be severely damaged."

What would you do?

Jerry Sharplin eagerly drove his new company pickup onto the construction site. He had just been assigned by his employer, Lurgi-Knost Construction Company, to supervise a crew of sixteen equipment operators, oilers, and mechanics. This was the first unionized crew Jerry had supervised. As he approached his work area, he noticed one of the "cherry pickers" (a type of mobile crane with an extendable boom) standing idle with the operator beside it. Jerry pulled up beside the operator and said, "What's going on here?"

"Out of gas," the operator said.

"Well, go and get some," Jerry said.

The operator reached to get his thermos jug out of the tool box on the side of the crane and said, "The oiler's on break right now, but he'll be back in a few minutes."

Jerry remembered that he had a five-gallon can of gasoline in the back of his pickup. So he quickly got the gasoline, climbed onto the cherry picker, and started to pour the gas into the tank. As he did, he heard the other machines shutting down in unison. He looked around and saw all the other operators climbing down from their equipment and standing to watch him pour the gasoline. A moment later, he saw the union steward approaching.

How might this conflict be resolved?

Change

Change

Moving from a known to an unknown.

Moving from a known to an unknown is **change.** We live in a world where change is occurring at an ever-faster pace. When we are confronted with change, most of us feel insecure, even if the change is good for us. This insecurity often causes us to resist change, thereby creating conflict between us and whoever is imposing the change.

Organizations are usually in a constant state of change. Some changes are minor and others are major. It is human nature to enjoy doing things the way they have always been done. But change will occur, and the resulting conflict must be resolved.

In most instances, if a change is justified, people will accept it even if they do not like it. However, what might appear to be completely reasonable to the company might not appear so to the workers. Suppose, for instance, that a group of machine operators has to be moved to a new work area with new machines. A study by the company has shown that this is necessary to maintain efficiency and protect jobs. The new work area is also cleaner and safer than the old one. Still, workers may tend to resist the change unless management carefully presents the reason for it.

Failure to Communicate

Communication was defined earlier as the transfer of information, ideas, understanding, or feelings among people. In many instances, communication is not complete because it does not result in understanding. The words are heard, but the meaning is not transmitted. For instance, a supervisor might say, "Turn off the word processor!" One worker might interpret the message to mean he did something wrong and might therefore become defensive, creating the potential for conflict. Another worker might hear the message as a simple order to turn the word processor off. In this case, no conflict is likely.

Even when a manager communicates clearly, failure to communicate to everyone involved can cause conflict. For example, a supervisor might tell several workers that it will be necessary to work overtime for two days next week. Conflict could arise when workers who were not told are suddenly required to work overtime.

Communication also breaks down when the supervisor fails to obtain accurate information from the workers. Perhaps the workers fail to communicate honestly and openly or the supervisor fails to listen. For example, a worker may be dissatisfied with a certain machine assignment. He may be experiencing trouble, although the boss is not aware of it. The conflict may surface when the worker talks back to the boss about something completely unrelated to machine assignments. The classic case of inaccurate worker communication can be found in the reasons people give for leaving their jobs. Workers often mention higher pay in the new job as the reason for leaving, when, in actuality, conflict in the old job is the real cause. A worker may not have been able to get along with the boss or with a co-worker, for example. But the real reason may never be known.

Conflict Becomes Apparent

Until a conflict becomes apparent, nothing can be done about it. One or both parties must recognize that conflict exists in order to resolve it. Conflict exists to the extent that it is felt, or perceived.

The degree of conflict perceived may be different for each of the involved parties, as Figure 13–5 illustrates. Conflict is high for Joe but virtually nonexistent for Bill. The conflict might have arisen when Bill told Joe how to accomplish a task in a better way. To Bill, there was nothing negative about his training efforts. But Joe apparently saw them as a reprimand. He was heard saying to other co-workers: "Who does Bill think he is? He just walks around looking for chances to get on to someone."

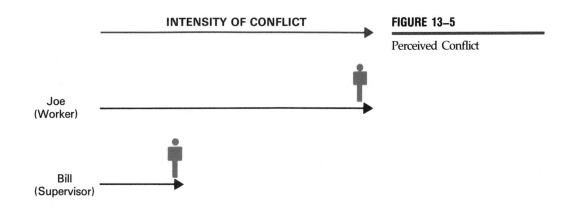

FIGURE 13–5

Perceived Conflict

At some point, conflict becomes noticeable. It is out in the open, and at least one party knows it exists. When conflict becomes apparent, a key point to consider is its impact on productivity. Conflict can sometimes be beneficial, leading to even higher productivity. But when productivity is lowered, the conflict must be resolved. It cannot be permitted to continue when it hurts the overall effectiveness of the organization.

Once it is recognized that conflict exists, how can it be dealt with most constructively? In the next section, ways of managing conflict in organizations are examined.

Interpersonal Conflict Management

There are numerous techniques for dealing with conflict between two or more individuals. They range from the use of force to a problem-solving approach. Among the techniques are overpowering the other party, using outside force, planning a delay, ignoring the conflict, giving in, withdrawing, smoothing, compromising, using mediation and arbitration, having superordinate objectives, and problem solving.

Overpowering the Other Party

At times, one of the parties to a conflict will simply overpower the other one in order to resolve the conflict. Confrontation occurs, and the result is that one party clearly wins and the other clearly loses. At times, this form of conflict resolution is used to settle once and for all who is "boss." Some have compared this form of conflict resolution to the ways cowboys used to "break" horses. The wild horse and the cowboy were certainly in conflict when the cowboy got into the saddle. Conflict ended when the horse realized he could not get rid of the rider.

As humans, we are not horses to be broken. The person who has lost will often experience increased, though hidden, conflict. Grudges may be held. The losing party may find some way to sabotage the winner in the future. For this reason, overpowering the other party is not recommended as a usual practice for resolving conflict.

Using Outside Force

At times, a person in authority will step in to resolve conflict. For instance, two supervisors may be in conflict over who will be assigned a terrific new worker. Arguments may break out about it. Their boss may impose a decision on the supervisors. Since neither supervisor was forced to give in to the other, the loss of ego was slight. Resolution of conflict by an outside force may sometimes be best. It provides a face-saving means for the conflicting parties.

Planning a Delay

The planned delay creates a cooling-off period for conflicting parties. Although few managers readily confess to using this approach, practically all have used it at some time. For example, an angry worker comes to the supervisor about something that has just happened. The supervisor might say: "I know this is really important. But right now I have to go to a meeting. Let's get together the first thing tomorrow and talk about it." This allows time for the worker to think through the matter and to settle down. As a result, the discussion is often less emotional than it would have been earlier.

Ignoring the Conflict

Another technique is for the manager to pretend the conflict does not exist. A supervisor may sense that someone is angry and may even know the cause of the anger. Rather than bring it out into the open, however, and create a confrontation, the supervisor may choose to ignore it. Such a reaction may be appropriate if the cause of the conflict is beyond the supervisor's control, particularly if the supervisor has confidence in the general goodwill of the angry party. However, management must monitor the condition of the angry party to assure that the anger doesn't become destructive to either the individual or the organization. .

Giving In

When one of the conflicting parties is clearly in error, that person should give in. Giving in also may be a useful tactic in at least two other circumstances. First, when the matter that is causing the conflict is a minor one, winning may not be as important as maintaining the goodwill of the other party. Sometimes, winning the conflict can cause major problems in the future, whereas giving in might be viewed as a favor. Second, it is often best to give in when the issue at conflict is a lost cause. It is better to lose gracefully than to pursue a lost cause doggedly. Others, including the boss, will appreciate the person who has the common sense to know when to quit and the maturity to do it.

A supervisor should not give in simply to avoid conflict, however. If the supervisor is right about an important matter and there is a reasonable chance of winning, the supervisor should stand firm. Giving in may not resolve the conflict. In fact, conflict could be even greater, although hidden. In addition, the winner may see the supervisor as weak and as a person who can be taken advantage of. Giving in when one is right can diminish future influence.

Withdrawing

Although withdrawal may appear to be similar to giving in, it is different. This approach involves pulling back from a previously announced position. A problem often has several equally good solutions. However, one might create more conflict than another. The manager may tentatively decide to take one approach and see that considerable conflict is developing. The manager may then withdraw and decide to tackle the problem from another position. The situation that caused the conflict may never be mentioned again. This is the reason administrators, especially government officials, often send up "trial balloons." If the trial balloon raises too much conflict, it is allowed to float away.

Smoothing

A manager who uses the smoothing approach is attempting to provide a semblance of peaceful cooperation by presenting an image such as "we're one big happy family." With this approach, problems are rarely permitted to come to the surface, but the potential for conflict remains.

Compromising

Neither party gets all it wants in a compromise. This is the most typical way of dealing with labor-management conflict. For example, management may offer to increase wages by 4 percent, while the union may be seeking 8 percent. A compromise figure of 6 percent may result in a reasonable settlement of the conflict.

Using Arbitration and Mediation

Arbitration

The process in which a dispute between two parties is submitted to a third party to make a binding decision.

Mediation

The process in which a third party enters a dispute between two parties for the purpose of assisting them in reaching an agreement.

Both arbitration and mediation call for outside neutral parties to enter the situation to assist in resolving the conflict. **Arbitration** is *the process in which a dispute between two parties is submitted to a third party to make a binding decision.* Arbitration is frequently used in union-management grievance conflicts. The arbitrator is given the authority to act as a judge. The decision rendered is usually final because both union and management agree in advance that it will be.

   Mediation is *the process in which a third party enters a dispute between two parties for the purpose of assisting them in reaching an agreement.* A mediator can only suggest, recommend, and attempt to keep the two parties talking in hopes of reaching a solution.

Having Superordinate Objectives

At times, the opposing factions may encounter an objective that overshadows their own interests. For example, if a firm is in danger of going out of business, both

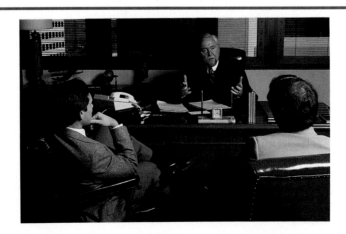

Both arbitration and mediation call for outside neutral parties to enter the situation to assist in resolving the conflict. When arbitration is used to settle formal employee grievances, as in the situation shown here, the arbitrator's decision is usually final because both parties have agreed in advance that it will be.

Source: © Jim Pickerell

union and management have been known to put aside minor conflicts and work toward the common objective of survival. There have been instances where union members have taken a decrease in pay and benefits in order to assist in the survival of the firm. Union members and management at Chrysler, General Motors, and other large firms have cooperatively worked together to ensure the survival of their firms. Responding to major financial crises, such firms experienced significant reductions in their management ranks as well as reductions in the work force, wages, and benefits.

Problem Solving

A recommended approach to conflict management is problem solving. Ideally, problem solving is characterized by an open and trusting exchange of views. Building trust is vital to resolving conflict. Managers who have established an environment of mutual trust are better able than others to resolve conflict situations. With the problem-solving approach, both parties realize that conflict is caused by relationships among people and is not within one person. An individual can disagree with your ideas and still remain your friend. Problem solving is a healthy approach in that it recognizes that usually neither person is completely right or wrong. Granting a concession is not seen as a sign of weakness. Neither party feels that it has to win every battle to maintain self-respect.

A certain amount of conflict is healthy when the problem-solving approach is taken. If a difference of opinion exists between two individuals and they openly discuss their difficulties, a superior solution often results. With problem solving, a person is encouraged to bring difficulties into the open without fear of reprisal. When this occurs, a situation that initially appeared to be a major problem may become only a minor one, which is easily resolved.

Structural Conflict Management

Conflict can often be managed by a change in procedures, organizational structure, or physical layout.

Procedural Changes

Conflict can occur because a procedure is illogically sequenced. When a credit manager and a sales manager were both about to be fired because of an irreconcilable personality conflict, it was discovered that the processing of credit applications too late in the credit procedure was the cause of their difficulty. The credit manager was being forced to cancel too many deals already made. When the credit check was placed earlier in the procedure, most of the conflict disappeared. In another instance, the personnel director and the production manager were in continuous disagreement. At times, the conflict almost caused them to come to blows. Then it was discovered that the production manager was not being permitted to review applications at an early stage of the hiring sequence and to make comments. When the procedure was changed, many of the difficulties were resolved.

Organizational Structure Changes

Some degree of conflict is often desirable. This is the case, for example, where the quality control department must inspect the work of the production department. Conflict between quality control and production could probably be minimized if the quality control director reported to the production manager. However, the quality control department would then lose its independence. This is why the quality control director typically reports to someone at a high level in the organization. The potential conflict is justified by the quality improvement that results from such a structure.

In other cases, conflict between departments is unplanned and undesirable. In some firms, sales and distribution are in separate departments, each reporting to a senior manager. This division often creates conflict. Individuals in sales expect quick delivery in response to customer requests. But the distribution department, in an effort to keep costs down, wants to make deliveries in full trucks and at scheduled intervals. To resolve this kind of conflict, it may be desirable to combine the two departments under a marketing manager who has experience in both sales and distribution. A marketing manager is likely to ensure that the organization's needs take priority over the preferences of sales and distribution personnel.

Physical Layout Changes

Changes in the design of the physical workplace have been used effectively to reduce or eliminate conflict. Office space can be designed either to force interaction or to make it difficult. People can use desks as barriers and buffers. Some offices have dividers to separate workers. However, if a manager wants to stimulate a problem-solving atmosphere, a more open office arrangement may be permitted. When known antagonists are seated in conference directly across from each other, the amount of conflict increases. When they are seated side by side, the conflict tends to decrease. These principles can be applied in arranging work spaces.

A detrimental conflict involving physical layout existed between two groups of workers in a truck assembly plant. Working at different phases of production on the assembly line, the two groups came into conflict because both had to obtain parts from the same shelving unit. Each group believed the other was deliberately rearranging its supply of parts, which sometimes resulted in fights. The conflict was resolved by moving the shelving unit between the two groups so as to set up a barrier between them. Thus, each group had its own supply area. As a result of this change, mistakes were reduced by 50 percent within two days.[30]

· ·

Self-Assessment Exercise

How Well Will You Deal with Group Performance, Intergroup Behavior, and Conflict?

1. Are you willing to recognize that the objectives of the informal group may not always be in line with those of management?

   ☐ Yes   ☐ No

2. Are you willing to not expect absolute conformity?

   ☐ Yes   ☐ No

   (continued)

3. Are you willing to not fight upper managers?

   ☐ Yes ☐ No

4. Are you willing to understand that if conflict exists, you should try to use it to accomplish objectives?

   ☐ Yes ☐ No

5. Are you willing to try to not let conflict get out of hand?

   ☐ Yes ☐ No

6. Are you willing to try to determine the real causes of conflict?

   ☐ Yes ☐ No

7. Are you willing to give in if you are wrong?

   ☐ Yes ☐ No

8. Are you willing to accept a certain amount of conflict as natural?

   ☐ Yes ☐ No

9. Are you willing to learn that when you impose change, even change for the better, you should expect a certain amount of conflict?

   ☐ Yes ☐ No

10. Are you willing to understand that people join groups for a multitude of reasons?

    ☐ Yes ☐ No

Summary

Groups—two or more people having a unifying relationship—are often categorized by size, function, or other criteria. Task (functional) groups are determined by job requirements, and project groups include formal, but temporary, assignments to groups, committees, and special projects. An informal group is two or more persons associated in ways not prescribed by the formal organization. Groups form when individuals exhibit common interests, common needs, common objectives, or physical proximity, which influence the nature and quality of the group's functioning. Individual roles, group norms, conformity, leadership, group cohesiveness, group size, and synergism all influence group effectiveness.

Group members can enhance the effectiveness of their group by increasing the following three variables: (1) the level of effort the group applies to carrying out its task, (2) the adequacy of the task performance strategies used by the group carrying out the task, and (3) the level and appropriateness of the knowledge and skills brought to bear on the task by group members. Organizational members can then manipulate behavioral norms, task design, or group composition as ways of increasing these three variables.

Teams are collections of people who must rely on group collaboration if each member is to experience the optimum of success and objective achievement. They generally have specific projects of specified duration. Management groups, committees, task forces, and other work units strive to act as teams, because they recognize the importance of concerted effort in accomplishing group objectives.

When individuals and groups interact, there is always the potential for conflict— antagonism or opposition between or among persons. Conflict occurs when there is competition or mutual interference among people. Whenever individuals are brought together in a highly structured environment the potential for conflict exists.

Conflict usually follows a pattern. First, it does not just happen; there must be causes. Second, even though the potential for conflict exists, it cannot be managed until it becomes apparent. Third, the results of conflict must be determined, since they may help or hurt the organization. Finally, the conflict is eventually resolved, sometimes to the benefit of the participants and the organization.

Potential causes of conflict include objective interference, competition for scarce resources, personality differences, perception set differences, change, and failure to communicate. There are numerous techniques for dealing with conflict between two or more individuals. They range from the use of force to a problem-solving approach.

Review Questions

1. Define *group* and describe the various types of groups.
2. What are the reasons that groups form?
3. Describe the typical developmental progression of a group.
4. Define the following terms:
    a. role
    b. norm
    c. cohesiveness
    d. synergism
5. List ways of increasing group effectiveness.
6. Define *conflict*. What are the potential causes of conflict?
7. How may managers become better at managing interpersonal conflict?
8. What are the means by which managers can overcome structural conflict?

Key Terms

Group	Group structure process	Conflict
Primary groups	Role	Perception set
Secondary groups	Norm	Change
Task (functional) groups	Cohesiveness	Arbitration
Informal group	Synergism	Mediation
Task activity		

As James Mitchell approached the table where Betty Fuller was seated, he asked, "Mind if I sit here?"

"Of course not," said Betty. "I've been wanting to talk to you anyway." James placed his tray on the table and sat down.

"James," Betty said, "you heard that Dave is being transferred?"

"Yes," said James. "I think he'll be leaving next month and going to the Jackson plant."

"Well," said Betty, "I've decided to apply for the job. I don't really have much hope, though. A woman doesn't have much chance for promotion, no matter how hard she works. Even if a woman did get promoted, she would probably be paid less."

"You have the same chance that everyone else does," James said. "I'm going to apply for that job myself."

"Well, that pretty well settles it," said Betty. "I don't really have a chance. But I am still going to apply."

"Don't you think that's a little unfair, Betty? Now, if you don't get promoted, you're going to think that it's because you're a woman."

"Well," said Betty, "don't you think it will be?"

"Of course not," James said. "I don't think you're so obviously superior to me. Of course, if you make a big issue of this sex thing, they might promote you just to show how open-minded they are."

"Look, James," said Betty, "I've earned everything I've gotten. Not only have I worked hard here and made a real effort to get along with everybody, I also went to night school and got my degree."

"Having a degree in management doesn't make you a manager, Betty. Anyway, I think I'm about to lose my temper. I'd just as soon not talk about this anymore." James took his half-eaten lunch and moved across the lunchroom to another table.

Questions

1. What is the cause of this conflict situation? Discuss.
2. What means of resolving the conflict would you recommend? Explain.

Springfield Products Company in Springfield, Missouri, is a medium-sized manufacturer of small outboard motors. The motors are supplied to major retailing chains, which sell them under their own brand names. For the past few years, sales at Springfield Products had been falling. The decline was industrywide. In fact, Springfield was faring better than its competitors and had actually been able to increase its share of the market slightly. Although forecasts indicated that the demand for the company's outboards would improve in the future, Anne Goddard, the company's president, believed that something needed to be done immediately to help the company maintain its financial health through this temporary slump. As a first step, she employed a consulting firm to determine if a reorganization might be helpful.

A team of three consultants arrived at the firm. They told Goddard that they had to gain a thorough understanding of the current situation before making any recommendations for action. After informing them that the company was open to them, Goddard told the company's supervisors to not inform anyone of the purpose of the investigation because this might cause employees to act differently.

The grapevine was full of rumors from the day the consulting group arrived. Some employees heard that the company might be shut down, others heard that massive transfers were possible, and still others heard that forced retirements were probable. The work groups at Springfield Products Company were very close-knit, and the rumors upset virtually everyone. Matters were made even worse when workers received no explanation from their supervisors. The climate quickly changed from one of concern to one of fear. Rather than being concerned about their daily work, employees worried about what was going to happen to the company and their jobs. Productivity dropped drastically as a result.

Three weeks after the consultants left, a memorandum was circulated through the company. It stated that the consultants had recommended a slight modification in the top levels of the organization. No one would be fired, and any reductions in staff would be the result of normal attrition. However, by this time, some of the best workers had already found other jobs, and company operations were severely disrupted for several months.

Questions

1. What part did the informal group play in what happened at Springfield Products?
2. Describe in terms of cohesiveness the conditions that existed before the consultants arrived and after they left.

Notes

1. This case is a composite of a number of accounts, among them: Jonathan Kapstein and John Hoerr, "Volvo's Radical New Plant: The Death of the Assembly Line?" *Business Week*, August 28, 1989, pp. 92–93; David Bartal, "Volvo's Back-to-the-Future Factory," *U.S. News & World Report*, August 21, 1989, p. 42; and Leigh Bruce and Jack Burton, "Strained Alliances," *International Management*, May 1990, p. 29.

2. Work in America Institute, in John Hoerr, "The Payoff from Teamwork," *Business Week*, July 10, 1989, pp. 56–62.

3. R. W. Napier and M. K. Gershenfeld, *Groups: Theory and Experience*, 2d ed. (Boston: Houghton Mifflin, 1981).

4. V. W. Tuchman, "Developmental Sequences in Small Groups," *Psychological Bulletin* 63 (May 1965): 384–399; N. R. F. Maier, *Problem Solving and Creativity in Individuals and Groups* (Belmont, CA: Brooks/Cole, 1970); R. F. Bales and F. L. Strodtbeck, "Phases in Group Problem Solving," *Journal of Abnormal and Social Psychology* 46 (October 1951): 485–495.

5. A. C. Kowitz and T. J. Knutson, *Decision-Making in Small Groups: The Search for Alternatives* (Boston: Allyn and Bacon, 1980); and Tuchman, "Developmental Sequences in Small Groups."

6. Ibid.

7. P. J. Nicholson, Jr., and S. C. Goh, "The Relationship of Organization Structure and Interpersonal Attitudes to Role Conflict and Ambiguity in Different Work Environments," *Academy of Management Journal* 26 (March 1983): 148.

8. D. C. Feldman, "The Development and Enforcement of Group Norms," *Academy of Management Review* 9 (January 1984): 47–53.

9. J. W. Thibaut and H. H. Kelley, *The Social Psychology of Groups* (New York: Wiley, 1959).

10. M. E. Shaw, *Group Dynamics*, 3d ed. (New York: Harper, 1980).

11. Feldman, "The Development and Enforcement of Group Norms."

12. Kenneth Bettenhausen and J. Keith Murninghan, "The Emergence of Norms in Competitive Decision-Making Groups," *Administrative Science Quarterly* 30 (September 1985): 350–372.

13. Feldman, "The Development and Enforcement of Group Norms."

14. Gail DeGeorge, Seth Payne, and Mark Ivey, "Advantage, Lorenzo," *Business Week*, July 10, 1989, pp. 24–26.

15. Solomon E. Asch, "Effects of Group Pressure on the Modification and Distortion of Judgments," in *Groups, Leaders, and Men*, ed. H. Guetzkow (Pittsburgh: Carnegie Press, 1951).

16. S. D. Malik and Kenneth N. Wexley, "Improving the Owner/Manager's Handling of Subordinate Resistance to Unpopular Decisions," *Journal of Small Business Management* 24 (July 1986): 22–28.

17. L. L. Commings, George P. Huber, and Eugene Arendt, "Effects of Size and Spatial Arrangements in Group Decision Making," *Academy of Management Journal* 17 (September 1974): 473.

18. "Why Nabisco and Reynolds Were Made for Each Other," *Business Week*, June 17, 1985, pp. 34–35.

19. John Hoerr, "Getting Man and Machine to Live Happily Ever After," *Business Week*, April 20, 1987, p. 61.

20. Russell Mitchell, "Masters of Innovation," *Business Week*, April 10, 1989, pp. 58–63; Stephanie Lawrence, "Voices of Experience," *Personnel Journal* 68 (April 1989): 71–73; Paul Kemezis, "3M's High-Flying R&D Program," *Chemical Week*, February 1, 1989, p. 25; Russell Mitchell, "Mining the Work Force for Ideas," *Business Week Innovation*, June 16, 1989, p. 121; Standard and Poor's Corporation, "Minnesota Mining," *Standard NYSE Stock Reports* 56, no. 114 (June 14, 1989): sec. 9.

21. J. R. Hackman and C. G. Morris, "Improving Group Performance Effectiveness," in *Advances in Experimental Social Psychology*, ed. L. Berkowitz (New York: Academic Press, 1975), 8:345.

22. W. G. Dyer, *Team Building: Issues and Alternatives* (Reading, MA: Addison-Wesley, 1979).

23. Ibid.

24. S. D. Van Raalte, "Preparing the Task Force to Get Good Results," *Advanced Management Journal* 47 (Winter 1982): 11–19.

25. **INSIDE BUSINESS:** In the interview with Myron Kandel, CNN financial editor; Stuart Varney, CNN senior correspondent; and Jan Hopkins, CNN correspondent, R. D. Hubbard describes his management philosophy and the need for teamwork in the glass business.

26. E. H. Schein, *Process Consultation* (Reading, MA: Addison-Wesley, 1969).

27. R. Beckhard, "Optimizing Team Building Effort," *Journal of Contemporary Business* 1 (Summer 1972): 23–32.

28. "How Does Japan Pick Its American Workers," *Business Week*, October 3, 1988, pp. 84–88; Louis Kraar, "Japan's Gung-Ho U.S. Car Plants," *Business Week*, January 30, 1989, pp. 98–108.

29. John Hoerr, "The Payoff from Teamwork," *Business Week*, July 10, 1989, pp. 56–62.

30. H. Kenneth Bobele and Peter J. Buchanan, "Building a More Productive Environment," *Management World* 8 (January 1979): 8.

14

Power, Organizational Politics, and Stress

LEARNING OBJECTIVES

After completing this chapter students should be able to

- Define *power* and give reasons for exerting power.
- Describe the sources of power, how managers can increase their power, power configurations, and power differences.
- Explain the strategies for obtaining power, the significance of power to the manager, and means of resisting intimidation.
- Describe political action in organizations.
- Describe stress in organizations.
- Explain the concept of burnout.

Ross Perot: America's Most Famous Billionaire and an Effective Power Broker

Ross Perot is a self-made billionaire who is a power broker extraordinaire. However, for many it is somewhat difficult to separate myth from reality. The mythical Perot is a person who as a boy delivered newspapers in a Texarkana, Texas, ghetto and who as a young salesman for IBM met his annual sales quota in January. He definitely is the man who started Electonic Data Systems, Inc. (EDS), the most anti-bureaucratic company in American history, after reading Thoreau's famous line, "The mass of men lead lives of quiet desperation." Perot is often portrayed as a "David bedeviling Goliath," and he is definitely a man who would relish the challenge of exerting his power over such a force.

Perot's power-centered personality is probably best illustrated by a remark he often quotes from Winston Churchill, which has become his credo. "Never give in. Never give in. Never. Never. Never." According to Doron P. Levin, author of *Irreconcilable Differences: Ross Perot versus General Motors*, Perot's motives are money, attention, and power. Power can be a highly effective instrument for good, or it can be an instrument of evil. Perot's power is so intimidating because, "When right, he is an incomparable ally; when wrong, he is a fearsome foe." However, whatever course Perot selects, he is always utterly convinced that he is right, and those who disagree with him become the enemy. Being Perot's enemy is not a comfortable position to be in, because Perot will never give in; he will always exert the maximum power needed to win.

Perot definitely has the ability to influence behavior. The instances of Perot wielding his power are many.

When a competitor outbid EDS for a $2 billion Texas data-processing contract, Perot declared a "scorched earth" campaign to discredit the competitor. After his campaign and some political arm-twisting, EDS regained the contract.

When Perot was in the midst of a conflict with General Motors, the unions hailed him as a hero. But in the 1960s, Perot waged open war on organized labor. When one EDS facility in California voted to organize, Perot shut the facility down rather than tolerate a union at EDS.

When Perot took on General Motors, he was uncompromising, slow to change, and he refused to budge, threatening to declare "World War III." Perot's power was so intimidating that GM management decided to buy his stock for a premium price of $742 million. After the buy-out was complete, Perot publicly denounced GM for the outrageous expenditure at a time when GM was closing plants. Then Perot raided EDS ranks to launch a competing data-processing company. By 1989, he had Perot Systems up and running.

Ross Perot has immense power, and he is willing to exercise it to get his way. For Perot, power is indispensable. The exercise of power and the utilization of political alliances are inherent in his life. Perot is a master at influencing the behavior of others, always perceiving his actions as righteous.[1] This is perhaps best illustrated by his recent bid for a presidential nomination. Even after Perot officially withdrew from the race, many of his supporters fervently believed in his message and continued to campaign on his behalf.

Many effective managers work within the political system of the organization. Others confront "the system" at every opportunity. It is natural for people to struggle for power and to exercise it to accomplish objectives. It is also natural to fear, and sometimes admire, people like Ross Perot who possess extraordinary personal power.

Much of a manager's power can come from political alliances. Managers who play politics well are often able to gain the cooperation and assistance of their peers and superiors. The more powerful a manager's political alliances, the more able that person is to "work" the system. Also, developing political connections may help the manager achieve personal goals. Perot plays all angles to assure that he has enough power to exert his will.

In this chapter, we will first define *power* and give reasons for exerting power. Then, we will discuss sources of power, how managers can increase their power, power configurations, and power differences. We will follow the discussion with sections on strategies for obtaining power, the significance of power to the manager, resisting intimidation, and political actions in organizations. In the final portions of the chapter, we will deal with a global perspective of politics, stress in organizations, and burnout.

Power Defined

Power

The ability to influence behavior.

Power is *the ability to influence behavior*. Power covers a wide range, from outright domination to the gentlest persuasion. But the popular concept of power leans toward the harsh side. Whether exercised compassionately or ruthlessly, power is necessary to get things done the way a manager wants them done. Ross Perot is certainly a person who knows how to use power. Remember that when a competitor outbid EDS for a $2 billion Texas data-processing contract, Perot declared a "scorched earth" campaign to discredit the competitor. After his campaign and some political arm-twisting, EDS regained the contract.

MANAGEMENT IN PRACTICE: A Skill-Building Exercise

Fredda Flint, the vice-president of Just-in-Time Manufacturing, called Barney Rubble in human resources to ask a favor. "Barney, I have a friend whose daughter needs a job. I'd like you to consider her for the new human resource position. I would really like to help out my friend and would appreciate anything you could do."

"Tell me about the person," said Barney.

"Well, she just graduated from the state university with a degree in history. She has no work experience, but I'm sure she'll learn quickly. Like I said before, her mother is a real good friend of mind, and I sure would like to help her out.

How would you respond?

Power is an emotion-laden term, particularly in cultures that emphasize individuality and equality. To call a manager a power seeker is to cast doubt on that manager's motives and actions. Some of these negative views are from older analyses that suggest power is evil and corrupts people, that it is composed largely of naked force, and that the amount of it available is fixed. Certainly, modern corporations constitute major concentrations of economic power. These concentrations have materially improved the standard of living of millions of people; but when they lead to abuse, control rather than elimination would appear to be the more desirable course of action.

Power can be a highly effective instrument for good, or it can be an instrument of evil. Frequently, there is disagreement regarding the exact nature of power. Ross Perot, founder of Electronic Data Systems (EDS), had loyal followers at EDS who respected the man and his actions; and from their high regard for him came his power over them. Organizational researchers increasingly cite the value of identifying and using power to improve individual and organizational performance.[2] Theorists and practitioners have translated an early view of power—that it was evil and stemmed mainly from coercion[3]—into a model of viable political action in organizations. Yet, although aggressive power behavior is functional and advantageous in many situations, it can also create conflict that is harmful to the organization.

Different individuals and groups within and outside the organization can exert power. Top and middle managers, technical analysts and specialists, support staff, and other workers can influence the actions an organization takes to reach its objectives. Formal groups of employees—including departments, work teams, management councils, and task forces, as well as informal groups of people with offices near one another or people who see one another socially—can similarly exercise power. In addition to individuals or groups within the organization, nonemployees may try to influence the behavior of an organization and its members. Owners, suppliers, clients, competitors, employee associations (including unions and professional associations), the general public, and directors of the organization may all exert power.[4] Power is an inescapable part of a well-functioning organization and a definite result of human interaction. Therefore, it must be carefully managed to benefit everyone involved.

Reasons for Exerting Power

Why do individuals in organizations initiate acts of power? The reasons for developing a power base and then applying that power vary. In the case of job-related dependence—how dependent a person's position is on other positions—an individual's exercise of power may be a job-related necessity. In other cases, the basic needs of individuals may motivate them to exert power. Power and dependence relationships and individual needs for power are two of the more common reasons for exerting power.

Power and Dependence

Power has often been described as a property of social relationships. It usually involves exchange processes, through which a person who commands services needed by others exchanges them for compliance or obedience.[5] A supervisor may exchange time off for high-quality performance by workers. In such a relationship, power has also been viewed as a function of the ties of dependence.[6] For example, supervisors often have power because subordinates depend on them for rewards. In the same way, subordinates may have power if their supervisor's performance is linked to their own.

According to marketing researcher John Kotter, individuals engage in power-oriented behavior to reduce their dependence on others.[7] In such situations, individuals may seek to increase the size of their power bases in order to decrease their dependence on current power holders. A technician who must rely on the supervisor for pay increases may reduce dependence by acquiring expertise in an area that no one else in the firm has. As the number of job-related dependencies increases, the manager or other employee increases the time and energy devoted to power-oriented behavior as a way of coping with the dependencies.[8] Alternatively, a manager generates power over others by creating in them a sense of obligation, building their belief in the manager's expertise, encouraging others to identify with the manager, and making others feel—or in fact be—dependent on the manager for resources.[9] By creating such a dependence situation, managers can weave a web of control that will result in an enhanced degree of power.

Diagnosing dependence is a first step in properly understanding and using power. The diagnosis can be made through a power/dependence analysis, which involves asking the following questions:

1. On whom does the incumbent really depend? How important is each dependency? What is the basis of each dependency?

2. Are any of these dependencies obviously inappropriate or dysfunctional? If so, what has created that pattern of dependence?

3. In how much effective power-oriented behavior does the incumbent engage? Is it enough to cope well with the dependencies in the job?

4. Does the manner in which the incumbent generates or uses power have any negative consequences for the organization? If so, exactly what are they?[10]

Consider other people to whom power is typically attributed: the President of the United States, for example, or the head of a large corporation. The President of the United States is viewed as extremely powerful, but he can be severely stifled by uncooperative individuals in Congress. In order to limit such occurrences, the President often builds a power base of support, first among people in his own party, then among those who share his views in the other party, and finally among those who need his support to accomplish their political agendas. This type of dependence analysis essentially derives from the association of power with mutual dependence in social relationships.

Individual Needs for Power

As was noted in Chapter 10, David McClelland and his associates have identified the *need for power* as a motivator that causes a person to wield power.[11] Individuals with a high need for power try to influence and control others, seek leadership positions in groups, enjoy persuading others, and are perceived by others as outspoken, forceful, and demanding.[12] Often, politicians, top managers, and informal leaders are perceived as having a high need for power. Most observers would probably assume that Ross Perot is an individual who has a high need for power.

McClelland identified two types of men who demonstrate this need (although the research did not include women, realistically either sex could be either type):

1. The first type strives for dominance. He is the impulsive tough guy. He may be rude, fight with others, boast of sexual conquest, and try to exploit women. Such men tend to reject institutional responsibility and hate to join organizations.[13] These individuals influence subordinates to be responsible to them personally.

2. The second type, in contrast, is more successful at creating a good climate for regular work. His subordinates have both a sense of responsibility and a clear knowledge of the organization. Loyal to the organization, they are less defensive and more willing to seek expert advice in personal matters when they need it. They collect fewer status symbols.[14] This kind of maturity improves their performance from the organization's viewpoint.

Studying the specific types of individuals in an organization may allow a manager to predict their power behavior and its consequences for organizational performance. Such preparation could be beneficial for the person who must manage subordinates with different needs for power. The manager could predict, for example, that individuals high in the need for power would be more likely to look for opportunities to exert power than would individuals high in other needs. For example, one study of first-line supervisors showed that the need for affiliation, not power, related to favorable job performance and favorable attitudes of subordinates.[15]

Power is not limited to individuals, of course. Organizational units, such as departments or work teams, can also exercise power. The power of these units can be analyzed the same way as the power of individuals. For both, the sources of power are also the same.

Sources of Power

The sources of power are many and varied, and not all of them are under the control of management. A listing of the sources of power, popularized by John French and Bertram Raven, is presented in Figure 14–1.[16] Legitimate, reward, and coercive power can be given to a person by a company, but expert and referent power must be earned.

Marge Schott, owner of the Cincinnati Reds, is a powerful businesswoman. Whether she is checking in at her car dealerships or checking the team's lineup, she is in charge; and she knows how to use her power. The Reds were down and almost out when she bought the team, and the new Reds owner was faced with a challenge. But that is nothing new for this tenacious woman. Marge Schott loves to win and appears to have the power to help her win, regardless of the nature of the challenge.[17]

Legitimate Power

The power that results from a person's being placed in a formal position of authority is **legitimate power.** Subordinates feel obligated to do as their legitimate superior says;

Legitimate power

The power that results from a person's being placed in a formal position of authority.

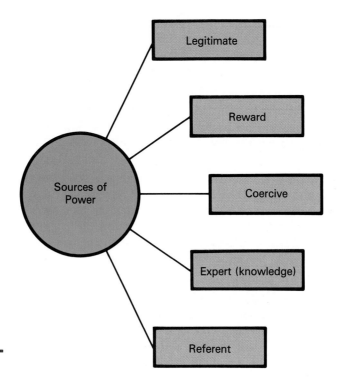

FIGURE 14–1

Sources of Power

they obey the superior's rules or orders because they view them as coming legitimately from the position the superior holds. Legitimate power exists regardless of the performance level of the person holding the position. For example, because Ross Perot is the man who started Electronic Data Systems, Inc., he had legitimate power over all of his employees.

Reward Power

Reward power

The power that is derived from a person's ability to reward another individual.

The power that is derived from a person's ability to reward another individual is **reward power.** It may be formal or informal. An individual who has control over organizational rewards, including pay raises, status, desirable work assignments, as well as praise, recognition, or group sanctions, may use them to encourage others' compliance with desired behaviors or goals. A manager can use this power effectively if subordinates believe that complying with the manager's request will result in their receiving some type of reward. Rewards are best used to reinforce the desired actions of subordinates, rather than as bribes for carrying out assigned tasks.[18]

Ross Perot has the power to reward or deny rewards to any of his employees. However, even individuals without legitimate power may possess reward power. For example, a worker who has influence with upper management might informally put in a good word regarding a co-worker who has been cooperative. Or a worker with information desired by other workers may reward another worker by sharing this information when a favor is granted.

Marge Schott, owner of the Cincinnati Reds, is often viewed as a powerful businesswoman who loves to win and knows how to use her power.

Source: Photograph courtesy of Marge Schott

Coercive Power

The power that is derived from the ability to punish or to recommend punishment is **coercive power.** A manager can exert this type of power over workers who fear punishment for violation of a rule or policy. The manager can force individuals to behave in certain ways by demoting or dismissing them or by increasing the direction provided to them. Olin King, the founder and chairman of SCI Systems Inc., used coercive power in dealing with union members. He referred to union members as criminals and outlaws from the North, and he did everything in his power to demoralize and cause problems for them. As was previously mentioned, Ross Perot also has the ability to use coercive power.

Coercive power must be used with extreme caution. Misapplied, it can negate the manager's effectiveness. However, as with reward power, individuals do not have to possess legitimate power to possess coercive power. One worker might punish another, for example, by withholding information from an uncooperative co-worker.

Coercive power

The power that is derived from the ability to punish or to recommend punishment.

Expert Power

The power that comes from a person's possessing special knowledge or skills is **expert,** or **knowledge, power.** It is considered by some to be the most effective type of power. Even if an individual has limited formal authority, expertise in a particular area will give that person considerable influence. "Red" Adair, the famed oil well fire-fighting

Expert (knowledge) power

The power that comes from a person's possessing special knowledge or skills.

expert, is well known by roughnecks (oil field workers) the world over for his knowledge of how to put out oil well fires. This expertise gives him the ability to go aboard an oil-drilling platform anywhere in the world and immediately issue orders that will be obeyed without question.

Expert power possessed by subordinates is often difficult for managers to accept. For example, if a computer programmer becomes so knowledgeable and competent as to be considered indispensable to the organization, the manager may feel unable to even reprimand the programmer for fear that person will quit or sabotage the manager.

This brings to light a potential problem with line and staff organizations: The line has the legitimate power, whereas the staff depends on expert power. The formal right to manage a firm remains with line managers, but the capacity to manage it is spread among a number of experts.

Access to information or resources provides a source of influence by helping individuals or organizational units cope with uncertainty. An employee who has obtained information that others do not possess, but do desire, has a certain degree of power. For example, the first individual to learn how to operate a new software package has the power to share or not share the information. If other workers also have to learn how to use the software, this individual has the power to reduce their uncertainty.

Referent Power

Referent power

The power that is based on a liking for, or a desire to be liked by, the power holder.

The power that is based on a liking for, or a desire to be liked by, the power holder is **referent power.** In the opinion of some, referent power is frequently stronger than expert power because the referent base is helped by perceived or imagined expertise on the part of those being influenced. The personality and characteristics of an individual affect the degree to which other people wish to identify and be associated with that person. President John F. Kennedy possessed referent power to a remarkable degree. His admonition "Ask not what your country can do for you but what you can do for your country" resulted in thousands of volunteers for the Peace Corps.

How Managers Can Increase Their Power

The concept of power extends far beyond the legitimate power normally associated with managers. A person's total power can be represented by the formula in Table 14–1, which shows that total power is the sum of all five types of power. The main power given by the manager's position in the organization is legitimate power. The formula shows that total power can be strengthened or weakened by reward, coercive, expert, and referent power. That is the reason for the plus or minus signs. For instance, a supervisor with little legitimate power might still be quite powerful by

TABLE 14–1

Determining a Person's Total Power

$$\frac{\text{Total}}{\text{power}} = \frac{\text{Legitimate}}{\text{power}} \pm \frac{\text{Reward}}{\text{power}} \pm \frac{\text{Coercive}}{\text{power}} \pm \frac{\text{Expert}}{\text{power}} \pm \frac{\text{Referent}}{\text{power}}$$

virtue of being an expert in the field. On the other hand, a manager with considerable legitimate power might be almost powerless because of a lack of job knowledge.[19]

Before President Bush appointed Clarence Thomas as a justice of the Supreme Court, Thomas probably already had great expert and referent power. After his appointment, this power was supplemented by legitimate power, based on the respect people have for his position, and reward and coercive power, resulting from his ability to determine benefits and penalties in important cases.

Power Configurations

Until now, we have addressed the concept of power as if it were absolute. However, there are various configurations of power. Henry Mintzberg has identified eight configurations based on the nature of influence either inside or outside the organization.[20] He has described the external influencers as *dominated*, where one individual or group has the most power; *divided*, where a few competing groups or individuals share power; and *passive*, where no one outside the organization tries to exert power. The influence of those inside the organization is of five types: *personalized*, where the leader relies on personal control; *bureaucratic*, where formal standards are key; *ideologic*, where the norms created by the organization's ideology dominate; *professional*, where technical skills and knowledge are used; and *politicized*, where the political system is the key system.

By appreciating the nature of the power configurations, managers are better able to understand and appreciate the nature of organizational power. It is also important that managers know about the impact of power differences on organizational effectiveness. When interacting groups experience performance difficulties, power differences are frequently the source of the problem.

Power Differences

Performance difficulties occur when interacting groups differ in the power they have. These power differences can create managerial problems, and managers must be prepared to deal with the differences effectively. Three major causes of power differences are perceptions of substitutability, the ability to cope with uncertainty, and the control of resources.

Perceptions of Substitutability

If the activities of a group are viewed as replaceable or if another group can perform the same work, the group is considered substitutable. The less a group performs substitutable tasks, the more power it possesses. Top managers often have unique knowledge and experience, which reduces their substitutability and results in greater power. Those with technical knowledge in companies that have a computerized operation may be perceived by the less technically knowledgeable as essential to the organization's functioning, and therefore they may have greater power than the less technically able employees. Basically, as the degree of substitutability increases, the degree of power a group possesses decreases, and vice versa.

Ability to Cope with Uncertainty

How well a group can deal with, and compensate for, a rapidly changing environment influences its power.[21] Typically, engineers can cope with uncertainty better than technicians can because of their broader professional training and more diverse experiences; hence, they have greater power. It might be hypothesized that physicians can cope with a changing, complex environment and its demands better than nurses because physicians have a wider range of knowledge and experience to draw on. As nurses increase their professional training, however, this power difference is reduced. Essentially, as the ability to cope with uncertainty increases, so does the degree of power a group possesses, and vice versa.

Control of Resources

The amount of money, people, and time a group controls influences its power. The greater the amount of these resources the group controls, the more power the group has. Managers who control budgets often have greater power than those who do not. Similarly, managers of line functions may have greater power than managers of staff functions. Further, when two groups must divide resources, disagreements often arise about their optimal allocation, creating conflict between them. Communication between groups can increase or reduce these differences. Basically, however, as a group's control of resources increases, so does the degree of power the group possesses, and vice versa.

Strategies for Obtaining Power

Power is an inescapable element of management. When properly used, it enhances a manager's ability to attain organizational objectives. Because of the usefulness of power, individuals and groups constantly seek more favorable power positions in organizations. There are numerous means by which a manager may secure power. Among the most common are networking, coalescing, co-opting, and accepting the right projects.

Networking

Networking

The cultivating of relationships with the right people for the purpose of obtaining power.

Anyone who has worked in an organization for any length of time has likely heard the expression, "It's not what you know but who you know." At times, there is more than a smattering of truth to this statement. **Networking** is *the cultivating of relationships with the right people for the purpose of obtaining power*. As an example, a lower-level manager may meet an upper-level manager at the golf course. A friendship may develop as they build a social relationship at the golf club. This friendship

Networking is the cultivating of relationships with the right people for the purpose of obtaining power. A lower-level manager may build social relationships with upper-level managers through participation in sports, such as golf or racquetball.

Source: © Jim Pickerell

may enhance the lower-level manager's personal power at the company. Networking relationships, however, do not necessarily involve upper-level management. They may also involve powerful peers and even subordinates. Influential peers and competent subordinates can enhance an individual's personal power, thereby facilitating the person's ability to perform.

Research has shown that informal influence among peers in a work unit and formal influence up the chain of command correlate positively with positional and personal bases of power.[22] For example, the informal network may result in the transfer of legitimate authority from a supervisor to an influential subordinate. Thus, the informal network can be used to build a power base.

Coalescing

The process of individuals or groups combining their resources to pursue common objectives is **coalescing.** The purpose of individuals or groups creating such alliances is to increase the ability to influence others and to secure greater control over resources. Labor union leaders and members have long recognized the value of coalescing. "If I don't get a raise, I'll quit" will provoke little or no action on the part of management unless all the workers issue the same statement in unison. By coalescing, the groups have considerably more influence with management. Even competing companies may coalesce to lobby for or against proposed legislation. Normally, the greater the influence of the individuals or groups combining their resources to pursue common objectives, the more significant the coalescing effort.

Coalescing
The process of individuals or groups combining their resources to pursue common objectives.

Co-Opting

The method of increasing power and creating alliances in which individuals or groups whose support is needed are absorbed into another group is **co-opting.** Its purpose is to eliminate or reduce threats and opposition to the individual's or group's power base. Suppose,

Co-opting
The method of increasing power and creating alliances in which individuals or groups whose support is needed are absorbed into another group.

for instance, that a manager wants to implement a particular project but another manager of similar status has reservations about the project. The manager with the reservations may be invited to participate on the team responsible for implementing the project. If the invitation is accepted, it is likely that the resistance will be neutralized.

Accepting the Right Projects

Individuals can obtain power in organizations by engaging in activities that are highly visible, extraordinary, and related to accomplishing organizational objectives.[23] For example, a faculty member may request and obtain the task of developing an important accreditation report. In obtaining data for the report, the person must work with the president, vice-presidents, deans, department heads, and other administrators across campus. If the faculty member accomplishes the task in an exceptional manner, and accreditation results, then the person has obtained significant power. As might be expected, of course, risk is involved. If the project fails, everyone on campus will know who was in charge, and the faculty member may be left with less power than before.

Since power is an inescapable element of management, those with substantial power often have an edge in accomplishing organizational objectives. In fact, only those with a reasonable degree of power may be able to operate effectively. To maximize their effectiveness, therefore, managers should first obtain a reasonable power base. Donald Trump is well known for his ability to acquire and exercise power.

. . . .

Deal Maker
Donald Trump

Before his bankruptcy problems symbols of Trump's unbroken chain of successes were everywhere. His big, black French helicopter proclaimed "TRUMP" in bright red. Trump Tower, next to Tiffany's on Fifth Avenue, was a premier address for businesses and fancy condo homes. There were Trump Plaza and Trump Castle in Atlantic City—sparkling casino hotels that took most of the gambling money on the East Coast.

But beyond the glamour, wealth, and ego, according to *Fortune* writer Monci Jo Williams, was "an investor with a keen eye for cash flow and asset value, a smart marketer, and a cunning wheeler-dealer given to tough-guy tactics." From a wealthy family, Trump attended the Wharton School of Finance and earned an economics degree. He had $200,000 set aside when he graduated and parlayed it into $200 million by the time he was thirty. That grew to billions later, mostly thanks to deals Trump personally engineered and closed.

Negotiating opponents have often heard him say, "You need me more than I need you." Explaining why he would not meet with a community group opposing his plan to build the world's tallest building, Trump said: "What they think doesn't matter. They have no power." These comments by Trump may suggest his image of himself: "I'm only interested in Old Masters; contemporary art is a con." "I love great equipment; boats or helicopters—it's art, in a different form." "I tend to thrive on solving problems, on doing what's not supposed to be able to be done." "I like playing real-life Monopoly." "And then you folks come up to me and say, 'You're very litigious.' The truth is, I'm not. I just don't settle."

Even though several reverses are changing the tendency to accept Trump's extraordinary self-promotion, it remains to be seen if Trump can deal himself another winning hand in his real-world game of monopoly.[24]

●●

Significance of Power to the Manager

Donald Trump seems to enjoy being powerful. Research has indicated that most managers want to acquire and use power. The famous power researcher David McClelland found that over 70 percent of the managers he studied had a higher need for power than did the general population.[25] Among better managers, McClelland said, the need for power was stronger than the need to be liked by others. The need for power is not normally a desire to be dictatorial, nor is it necessarily a drive for personal enhancement. Rather, it may simply reflect a manager's concern for influencing others on behalf of the organization.

Better managers probably have a need for power to get the job done rather than personal power. Managers who feel a greater need to be liked than to influence others tend to be less effective. Deal makers such as Trump generally place being liked second to cutting a good bargain.

The control of situational factors, both inside and outside the organization, is of significant concern to modern managers. It has been noted that when organizations grow so large and complex that no single individual has the capacity to manage all of the interdependencies, a dominant managing group will develop. This coalition is sometimes formalized into a presidential or executive office. Normally, however, it is not actually so recorded on a formal organizational chart. If the president of the firm depends heavily on the vice-president of finance to develop crucial programs, that vice-president will likely be a member of the dominant coalition and therefore will have power in excess of what the official chart suggests. Within the organization, smaller and sometimes more temporary coalitions are formed to execute tasks involving significant interdependencies.

Resisting Intimidation

One reason power is often viewed negatively is that we feel intimidated when we deal with powerful people. Certainly, any average person would feel intimidated in a confrontation with Donald Trump and Ross Perot. **Intimidation** is *the compelling of action or inaction through fear or awe.* Many who might not be fearful of Donald Trump might be awed by him and therefore intimidated. Supervisors may be intimidated by subordinates, peers, or other managers. A new or young supervisor who is managing more senior or older workers may be afraid of them. Often, a supervisor fails to discipline a worker because the supervisor thinks the worker knows a powerful person in the firm. Or the supervisor may fear that disciplining one worker will cause others to rebel.

Fear of peers can also intimidate. Perhaps a supervisor in another department is sending a supervisor too many defective parts and the receiver is afraid to reject

Intimidation

The compelling of action or inaction through fear or awe.

them. If the sender is older or gives the impression of being mean and tough, that could be intimidating.

Intimidation by one's superior can cause major problems. Supervisors intimidated by their superiors cannot represent subordinates well or perform other aspects of their jobs well. When faulty instructions are passed down, the supervisor may be afraid to question them. This hurts both the subordinates and the organization. It is also likely that the workers will recognize such errors and the reason for them. Their future performance and their opinion of the supervisor may suffer.

At one time or another, everyone has been intimidated. But supervisors can take steps to keep intimidation from affecting their job performance. First, they can make themselves indispensable by being good at their job. It is difficult to intimidate a competent person. Second, they can view powerful people as simply other human beings. Most upper-level managers do not want supervisors to fear them. Third, they can show confidence. It is difficult to intimidate a confident person. A confident manager knows what action to take and is decisive in taking it. Finally, they can directly confront anyone who attempts intimidation.

Political Action in Organizations

Government-level politicians often receive low marks of approval from the general public. Political scandals regularly hit the front pages of daily newspapers. But politics and politicians exist in all forms of organized society, not just government. And political action can be positive when it promotes cooperation among individuals and groups with different interests and objectives.

Politics

A network of interactions by which power is acquired, transferred, and exercised on others.

Politics is a *"network of interactions by which power is acquired, transferred, and exercised on others."* [26] Individuals and organizational units use power to take political action. Politicians work with and through many people (hence the term *networking*). Thus, politics transcends traditional organizational boundaries. Power is the medium of exchange in politics, just as the dollar is a medium of exchange in economics. Shrewd politicians acquire power and transfer it to others when it can purchase something of value. Just like a banker, a politician can keep a balance sheet. When power is transferred, something is expected in return. To the politician, a favor given now is often power to be extracted in the future.

Managers must at least recognize the political forces in their organizations. Some may choose to behave essentially as politicians. In fact, some management theorists apply political science techniques to their analysis of organizations. [27]

The degree of politicking a manager does is limited not only by formal organizational restrictions but also by the manager's personal code of ethics and conscience. The fact that at times politics may be unethical should not preclude studying the subject. And politicking cannot be condemned per se. Some politically based accommodations are constructive; others perhaps are destructive, both of organized activity and of individual morals.

It is apparent that some degree of politicking is a fact of organized life, regardless of the caliber of people involved or the degree of formalization of organizational rules and regulations. No doubt, some political maneuvering can make contributions toward an organization's effectiveness. Where there is head-on conflict, and where interdependencies make some degree of cooperation essential, concessions worked out between parties often involve some bending or reinterpretation of rules. On many occasions, the conflicting interests are all legitimate and rest on solid ground. In the late 1980s, USX Corporation used politics to begin solving its productivity problems.

● ●

USX Corporation held a worker-management fling at an amusement park. This was part of a USX effort to promote cooperation beyond that envisioned by the company's contract with the United Steel Workers union (USW). A USX insider said, "We want worker cooperation, but we don't want to broker it through the union."

Bypassing the Union at USX

In its steel division, USX had achieved massive cost reductions through layoffs and give-backs by the union. The company had a reputation for toughness with its workers. "In the past, it was unheard of for USX managers and workers to do anything together," said a union official. The company even refused to join other steel makers in the early 1980s in "co-management" plans. USX endured a six-month strike in 1986 and eventually won pay concessions that reduced costs $100 million a year. The USW cooperated in forming rank-and-file "All Product Excellence" (APEX) teams to get worker help in improving efficiency. A USW local president said, "USX finally realizes that quality takes a team effort by the union and the company." A steel buyer for General Electric's appliance division said: "USX has made exceptional progress. You don't get quality like Irvin's [a USX plant] without good worker involvement programs."

But the new moves, aimed at winning the workers' hearts as well as their heads, were objectionable to many hard-line union officials. One USW official said the move would not succeed because it was "a management-controlled process where the company does just what suits them." "USX hasn't changed a bit," said another local president. "They slap you on the back and ask for cooperation with one hand and then stab you in the back with the other by violating the contract." [28]

● ●

For the basic work of the organization to continue, some degree of reconciliation is required, necessitating informal accommodation, compromise, or exchange. In the next section, we will consider means of influence and means of improving political action.

ETHICAL DILEMMA

You are a successful salesperson who has just been rewarded by being appointed the regional sales manager for the company's most successful region. This operation is in a mid-sized city, whose close-knit community places a high value on local basketball. In fact, you soon realize that to most people local basketball is much more important than the Super Bowl.

While watching a local game with a buyer who purchases almost 40 percent of your yearly volume, you learn that the star on the team may be leaving town because his father was laid off. The buyer has heard that you have an opening for a sales manager, and he asks you to hire the boy's father. You tell him that you will be glad to review the man's résumé, but you have already found an extremely qualified person. The next day, the woman you are replacing explains that in this town people do each other favors, and that is how they build trust. She also tells you that if the boy's father is not hired, you may lose all of the buyer's business.

You receive the individual's résumé and soon realize that the man has no sales experience. You can either hire the extremely qualified person or capitulate to the demand of your primary buyer.

What would you do?

Means of Influence

As discussed in the section on power configurations, individuals can exert influence in a variety of ways. The influence may be regular or irregular, general or focused, detached or personal, supportive or obstructive, formal or informal. Society or individuals outside the organization attempt to influence organizational behavior by using existing or developing social norms, imposing formal constraints on the organization, conducting pressure campaigns, instituting direct controls on the organization, or obtaining membership on the board of directors. Those inside the organization, in contrast, use authority, ideology, expertise, or politics, among others, to influence.[29] The legitimacy of each type of influence might be argued, but each can affect decision making.

Most attempts at influencing in an organization are oriented downward. Managers, for example, can give direct orders to subordinates, establish guidelines for their decision making, approve or reject their decisions, and allocate resources to them.[30]

Individuals in an organization can also exert upward influence, typically to promote or protect their self-interest.[31] They can control the type of information passed to superiors, and they may consciously withhold information they think is detrimental to themselves. Occasionally, workers punish or reward their superiors—by withholding or providing a quality work effort, for example. Managing the boss effectively requires understanding and responding to the boss's needs.[32]

People who identify and use resources implement their political influence along one of three dimensions: (1) internal-external, (2) vertical-lateral, or (3) legitimate-illegitimate.[33] On the internal-external dimension, they may rely on resources internal to the organization, exchanging favors or forming networks with other employees. When internal resources fail or become inadequate, they may turn to outside resources by joining professional organizations or forming alliances elsewhere. On the vertical-lateral dimension, individuals exert influence by relating either to superiors and subordinates or to peers. Mentor-protégé activities occur vertically; coalition formation occurs laterally. On the legitimate-illegitimate dimension, normal and extreme behavior are contrasted. For example, most organizational members view forming coalitions as legitimate and sabotaging production as illegitimate.

Means of Improving Political Action

Exchange theories discuss power in terms of bargaining and negotiations, rather than in terms of social networks.[34] Labor negotiations, in particular, often involve acts of power that significantly influence bargaining outcomes.[35] Coalitions often are formed as a way of increasing an individual's or group's power in a bargaining situation; that is, members of coalitions frequently muster sufficient resources to resolve a negotiating problem.

In the political arena, bargaining and negotiations are particularly important. Interest groups and political parties use power to influence authorities to give them what they want.[36] A party will choose among the strategies of inaction, problem solving, yielding, and contending, depending on its level of concern for its own and another party's outcomes. A party with low concern for both its own and the other's outcome will not act (the inaction strategy). A party with high concern for both parties' outcomes will take a problem-solving approach. A party with low concern for its own outcomes and high concern for the other's will yield to the other party. It will not yield (but will contend) if concern for its own outcomes is high and concern for the other's is low.[37] An effective negotiator is aware of negotiation tightropes, avoids the need to impress others, develops interpersonal sensitivity, helps induce the other party's sense of negotiating competence, avoids commitments to irreconcilable positions, and is sensitive to conflict intensity and necessary coping strategies.[38]

Conflict is often created by the exercise of political power. To reduce conflict, formal leaders of both private and public organizations frequently seek ways to exert power without generating conflict, to limit power, and to restore an organization to equilibrium after the exercise of power.[39]

A Global Perspective

Global managers must recognize and be prepared to deal with the political forces affecting their organizations. The degree of politicking a global manager does is limited not only by formal organizational restrictions and the manager's personal code of ethics and conscience, but also by the global environment the manager is operating in.

At times, politics in a multinational environment may appear unethical from the American perspective. For example, many multinationals attempting to enter the Mexican market simply pay *mordita* (a "little bite"), a bribe of sorts. But when Empire Southwest, a distributor of Caterpillar equipment in Phoenix, wanted to enter the Mexican market, it did not pay. The company did, however, build good relations with Mexican mining companies, farmers, and contractors and eventually got to do business in Mexico.[40]

Some politically based accommodations are constructive, and others are destructive. But either way, politics is a reality of operating in the global environment. Managers used to internal politics should be prepared to deal with global politics, since some political maneuvering can make a significant contribution toward an organization's effectiveness.

Stress in Organizations

Hans Selye first used the term *stress* to apply to humans (rather than to animals) in the 1930s.[41] **Stress** is *the body's reaction to any demand made on it*. It is a psychological and physiological state that results when certain features of an individual's environ-

Stress

The body's reaction to any demand made on it.

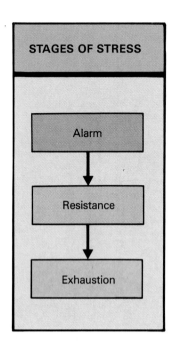

FIGURE 14–2

Stages of Stress

ment—including noise, pressures, job promotions, monotony, or the general climate—impinge on that person. Both positive and negative occurrences can give rise to stress.

As Figure 14–2 shows, individuals in stressful situations generally go through three stages: (1) alarm, (2) resistance, and (3) exhaustion.[42] In the alarm stage, they experience a stressor that causes a rise in adrenaline and anxiety. If the stressor persists, they respond to it during the resistance stage. They may attack the stressor directly, adopt a previously successful coping behavior, deny the stressor, withdraw physically or psychologically from the situation, or persist in responding whether or not the response is effective.[43] When a stressor persists to the point of physiological or psychological damage, exhaustion has occurred.

Some respond to stress by becoming more productive and creative. Have you ever heard a friend or co-worker say, "I work best when I have a deadline in sight; I can't do anything productive unless I feel some pressure"? This person likely uses the stress resulting from the time pressure to increase productivity. Others respond to stress by experiencing gastrointestinal, glandular, or cardiovascular disorders or by overeating, drinking excessively, or taking tranquilizers.[44] Still others become impatient, detached, or despairing. Such physiological and psychological reactions can decrease creativity and productivity, which in turn often increases the level of stress, thereby causing a further decrease in effectiveness. Stress causes American workers to miss an average of sixteen days on the job each year.[45]

Causes of Stress

Stress has become increasingly common in organizations, largely because of greater job complexity and economic pressure on individuals. People at the beginning of their career who are trying to establish themselves often experience stress. The midcareer crisis is virtually synonymous with stress. And facing the changes of retirement creates significant stress. Table 14–2 lists the major life stress events and provides a way of calculating the probability of experiencing stress-related illness.

Stress is a psychological and physiological state that results when certain features of an individual's environment, including noise and job pressures, impinge on that person. The telephone, computers, and other tools of the information age may increase productivity, but can also create stress.

Source: Frank Siteman

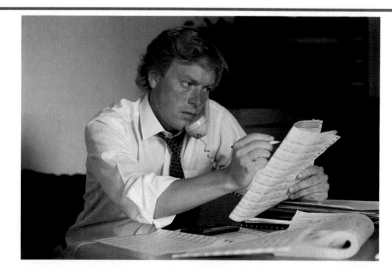

TABLE 14–2

Life Stress Events

Complete the scale by circling the mean value figure to the right of each item if it has occurred to you during the past year. To figure your total score, add all the mean values circled (if an event occurred more than once, increase the value by the number of times). Life stress event totals of 150 or less indicate generally good health, scores of 150 to 300 indicate a 35–50 percent probability of stress-related illness, and scores of 300+ indicate an 80 percent probability.

Life Event	Mean Value	Life Event	Mean Value
1. Death of spouse	100	24. In-law troubles	29
2. Divorce	73	25. Outstanding personal achievement	28
3. Marital separation from mate	65	26. Spouse beginning or ceasing work outside the home	26
4. Detention in jail or other institution	63	27. Beginning or ceasing formal schooling	26
5. Death of a close family member	63	28. Major change in living conditions	25
6. Major personal injury or illness	53	29. Revision of personal habits	24
7. Marriage	50	30. Troubles with the boss	23
8. Being fired at work	47	31. Major change in working hours or conditions	20
9. Marital reconciliation with mate	45	32. Change in residence	20
10. Retirement from work	45	33. Changing to a new school	20
11. Major change in the health or behavior of a family member	44	34. Major change in usual type and/or amount of recreation	19
12. Pregnancy	40	35. Major change in church activities	19
13. Sexual difficulties	39	36. Major change in social activities	18
14. Gaining a new family member	39	37. Taking out a mortgage or loan for a lesser purchase	17
15. Major business readjustment	39	38. Major change in sleeping habits	16
16. Major change in financial state	38	39. Major change in number of family get-togethers	15
17. Death of a close friend	37	40. Major change in eating habits	15
18. Changing to a different line of work	36	41. Vacation	13
19. Major change in the number of arguments with spouse	35	42. Christmas	12
20. Taking out a mortgage or loan for a major purchase	31	43. Minor violations of the law	11
21. Foreclosure on a mortgage or loan	30		
22. Major change in responsibilities at work	29		
23. Son or daughter leaving home	29		

SOURCE: Thomas H. Holmes, "Social Readjustment Rating Scale," *Journal of Psychosomatic Research 11*, Pergamon Press, pp. 213–218. Copyright 1967. Reprinted with permission.

Interpersonal variables such as leadership style and extent of group cohesiveness and participation also contribute to stress both in and outside the workplace. Where the personalities of leaders and followers conflict, such as when an extroverted employee is supervised by an introverted manager, stress often occurs. Thus, the relationship between stressors and stress may be affected by personality, culture, or the nonwork environment. Professional women at times experience unique stressors: discrimination, stereotyping, conflicting demands of work and family, and feelings of isolation—all of which can dramatically affect performance and health.[46]

TABLE 14–3

Twelve Jobs with the Most Stress

1. Laborer	5. Office manager	9. Machine operator
2. Secretary	6. Foreman	10. Farm owner
3. Inspector	7. Manager/administrator	11. Miner
4. Clinical lab technician	8. Waitress/waiter	12. Painter

Other High-Stress Jobs (in Alphabetical Order)

■ Bank teller	■ Machinist	■ Railroad switchperson
■ Clergy	■ Meatcutter	■ Registered nurse
■ Computer programmer	■ Mechanic	■ Sales manager
■ Dental assistant	■ Musician	■ Sales representative
■ Electrician	■ Nurse's aide	■ Social worker
■ Firefighter	■ Plumber	■ Structural-metal worker
■ Guard/watchperson	■ Policeperson	■ Teacher's aide
■ Hairdresser	■ Practical nurse	■ Telephone operator
■ Health aide	■ Public relations person	■ Warehouse worker
■ Health technician		

TABLE 14–3

Stressful Jobs

SOURCE: From a ranking of 130 occupations by the National Institute for Occupational Safety and Health.

The Federal government's National Institute for Occupational Safety and Health (NIOSH) has studied stress as it relates to work. Its research indicates that some jobs are inherently more stressful than others. The twelve most stressful jobs are listed in Table 14–3.

The Stress Audit

In many organizations today, managers find that they must be sensitive to potential stressors in order to maintain the productivity and involvement of employees. At the same time, employees often opt for minimizing stress, sometimes at the expense of promotions or significant pay increases. Managers and employees should recognize, however, that a certain amount of stress may be necessary for creative and productive work. Very little stress in the workplace can result in complacency.

Yet predicting the level of stress in situations can be difficult, largely because stress is often person-specific. Often, job features intuitively rated as stressful—such as the mental demands on and responsibilities of air traffic controllers or the life-and-death situations faced by the police—are neither disliked nor experienced as stressful by the job holders.[47] Alternatively, simple requests for overtime or revisions of completed work may cause stress.

The extent of dysfunctional stress in the work situation can be evaluated with a **stress audit,** *a review that helps identify the symptoms and causes of stress.* An audit includes managers' questions, such as the following:

Stress audit

A review that helps identify the symptoms and causes of stress.

1. Do any individuals demonstrate cardiovascular, gastrointestinal, allergy-respiratory, or emotional distress irregularities?

2. Is job satisfaction low? Is job tension, turnover, absenteeism, strikes, or accident proneness high?

3. Does the organization's design contribute to the symptoms?

4. Do interpersonal relations contribute to the symptoms?

5. Do career development variables contribute to the symptoms?

6. What effects do personality, sociocultural influences, and the nonwork environment have on the relationship between stressors—individual careers, interpersonal relations, and organizational design—and stress?[48]

To answer questions 1 and 2 completely and accurately requires a thorough description of the situation. To answer questions 3 through 6 requires an understanding of issues discussed in various chapters of this book.

Burnout

The state of fatigue or frustration that stems from devotion to a cause, a way of life, or a relationship that does not provide the expected reward is **burnout**.[49] In essence, burnout is the perception that an individual is giving more than he or she is receiving—whether it is money, satisfaction or praise.[50] It is often associated with a midlife or midcareer crisis, but it can happen at different times to different people.[51] Individuals in the helping professions, such as teachers and counselors, seem to be susceptible to burnout because of their jobs, whereas others may be vulnerable because of their upbringing, expectations, or personalities.[52] Burnout is frequently associated with people whose jobs require close relationships with others under stressful and tension-filled conditions.[53] While any employee may experience this condition, perhaps 10 percent of managers and executives are so affected.[54]

The dangerous part of burnout is that it is contagious. A highly cynical and pessimistic burnout victim can quickly transform an entire group into burnouts. Therefore, it is important that the problem be dealt with quickly. Once it has begun, it is difficult to stop.[55] Some of the symptoms of burnout are (1) chronic fatigue; (2) anger at those making demands; (3) self-criticism for putting up with demands; (4) cynicism, negativism, and irritability; (5) a sense of being besieged; and (6) hair-trigger displays of emotion.[56] The burnout victim is often unable to maintain an even keel emotionally; for example, unwarranted hostility may occur in totally inappropriate situations. Another possible symptom is recurring health problems, such as ulcers, back pain, or frequent headaches. Burnout is harmful to the individual's mental and physical health and results in performance problems for both the individual and the organization.

Burnout

The state of fatigue or frustration that stems from devotion to a cause, a way of life, or a relationship that does not provide the expected reward.

Self-Assessment Exercise
How Well Will You Deal with Power, Organizational Politics, and Stress?

1. Are you willing to use alliances, obligations, and debts?

   ☐ Yes   ☐ No

2. Are you willing to use your influence to get the job done?

   ☐ Yes   ☐ No

   (continued)

3. Are you willing to know your job well to gain more power?

   ☐ Yes   ☐ No

4. Are you willing to save up chips (power) and use them when they count the most?

   ☐ Yes   ☐ No

5. Are you willing to tolerate individual differences?

   ☐ Yes   ☐ No

6. Are you willing to put stressful activities in perspective?

   ☐ Yes   ☐ No

7. Are you willing to stay physically active?

   ☐ Yes   ☐ No

8. Are you willing to have at least one person you can confide in?

   ☐ Yes   ☐ No

9. Are you willing to recognize that power may be both formal and informal?

   ☐ Yes   ☐ No

10. Are you willing to resist intimidation?

    ☐ Yes   ☐ No

Summary

Power is the ability to influence behavior. Why do individuals initiate an act of power? The reasons vary. In the case of job-related dependence, an individual's exercise of power may be a job-related necessity. In other cases, the basic needs of individuals may motivate them to exert power. Power and dependence relationships and individual needs for power are two of the more common reasons for exerting power.

The sources of power are many and varied, and not all are under the control of management. Legitimate power results from a person's being placed in a formal position of authority. Reward power is derived from a person's ability to reward another individual. Coercive power is derived from the ability to punish or to recommend punishment. Expert (knowledge) power comes from a person's possessing special knowledge or skills. Referent power is based on a liking for, or a desire to be liked by, the power holder. A person's total power is the sum of all of these forms of power.

Three major causes of power differences are perceptions of substitutability, the ability to cope with uncertainty, and the control of resources. If the activities of a group are replaceable or if another group can perform the same work, the group is considered substitutable. The less a group performs substitutable tasks, the more power it possesses. How well a group can deal with, and compensate for, a rapidly changing environment (coping with uncertainty) influences its power. The amount of money, people, and time a group controls (the control of resources) also influences its power. The greater its amount of these resources, the more power the group has. There are numerous means by which a manager may secure power. Among the most common are networking, coalescing, co-opting, and accepting the right projects. Research has indicated that most managers want to acquire and use power.

One reason power is often viewed negatively is that we feel intimidated when we deal with powerful people. Intimidation is the compelling of action or inaction through fear or awe. At one time or another, everyone·has been intimidated. But supervisors can take steps to keep intimidation from affecting their job performance.

Politics is a network of interactions by which power is acquired, transferred, and exercised on others. Individuals and organizational units use power to take political action. Individuals can exert influence in a variety of ways. Exchange theories discuss power in terms of bargaining and negotiations, rather than in terms of social networks.

Stress is the body's reaction to any demand made on it. It is a psychological and physiological state that results when certain features of an individual's environment—including noise, pressures, job promotions, monotony, or the general climate—impinge on that person. Both positive and negative occurrences can give rise to stress. The stages of stress are alarm, resistance, and exhaustion. A stress audit can help identify the symptoms and causes of stress.

Burnout is the state of fatigue or frustration that stems from devotion to a cause, a way of life, or a relationship that does not provide the expected reward. Burnout is frequently associated with people whose jobs require close relationships with others under stressful and tension-filled conditions.

Review Questions

1. Define *power*.
2. Briefly describe each of the sources of power.
3. How can managers increase their power?
4. Briefly discuss each of the major causes of power differences.
5. What are the most common strategies for obtaining power?
6. What is the significance of power to a manager?
7. Define *politics*. What is the importance of an understanding of politics to a manager?
8. Define *burnout*. What are some symptoms of burnout?

Key Terms

Power

Legitimate power

Reward power

Coercive power

Expert (knowledge)
  power

Referent power

Networking

Coalescing

Co-opting

Intimidation

Politics

Stress

Stress audit

Burnout

CASE 14.1 — THREATENED BY A SUPERSTAR

When Doug Self came to work in the accounting department at Ritger Paper Products Company, James Norris considered it a personal victory. Doug had been the top business school graduate at nearby Wichita State College the previous year. For two years, he had been president of the Student Government Association, and he had been active in every aspect of campus life.

James was the comptroller at Ritger. He supervised nine accountants and clerks. He was pleased to have attracted such an outstanding young man, and he made sure his superiors knew of the excellent recruiting job he had done.

Within a short while, it became clear to everyone in the department that Doug was not only friendly, outgoing, and easy to talk to but also well informed about accounting. Before long, Doug had made friends with everyone in the office, and James noticed that a number of the accountants began to take their questions and problems to Doug. He always seemed to have the right answer and to enjoy taking time to help. He also did an excellent job on all his own work.

Doug's presence in the accounting department made James's job easier. Only when a decision was required from outside the department would James be consulted. In a way, James was pleased with the way things were turning out. But two things bothered him. First, the accountants and clerks began to consult with Doug even about personal matters. James was twenty years older than Doug, and he felt more qualified in that regard. Second, Doug had developed a number of friendships outside the department, especially with two of the company's senior officials. James felt very insecure about this. He thought it was only a matter of time until Doug began to bypass him on official matters.

James decided to take action. Although he was not really sure how to handle the situation, he began to look for chances to criticize Doug in front of his peers. Anyone who took a problem or question to Doug was reminded that James was their direct superior, and he looked for ways to change or disparage the advice Doug had given. It was not long before the other employees got the signal. Ultimately, James's strategy worked; Doug quit. But within a week, three others of James's best accountants turned in their resignations, and the department was thrown into confusion.

Questions

1. What sources of power did Doug possess? What sources of power did James possess?
2. To what extent was Doug a threat to James? Explain your answer in relation to power differences.

CASE 14.2 — POWER, ANYONE?

Jim Perry was the director of special projects at the Main Street Bank and Trust Company, reporting directly to the bank president. Jim was assigned responsibility to initiate partnership banking at Main Street. This had become the "hot product" in the banking industry. In partnership banking, each customer is assigned a "partner" at the bank. The partner coordinates services and acts as an advocate for that customer.

Jim was assigned a "partnership task force" of five people, each selected by a different department head. The five were (1) Paul Goodman, an administrative assistant to the vice-president of operations; (2) Jenny Jackson, a newly appointed senior loan officer; (3) Michael Tracy, a recently promoted branch manager of a suburban branch; (4) Anne Richards, a marketing staff member; and (5) Jeffrey Wilson, a management trainee working for the president. The task force was to meet weekly with Jim to help him plan and implement the partnership program.

At the first meeting, Jim outlined his objectives for the project and set a tentative timetable. There was little discussion, and the meeting was quickly adjourned. At the second meeting, Anne presented a list of ideas she had garnered from an article in the *Journal of Commercial Bank Lending.* Michael offered several biting remarks about Anne's suggestions, to which Anne responded in kind. Otherwise, there was little interest in any particular suggestion.

Subsequent meetings followed a similar pattern. Either Jim offered suggestions, ideas, and comments,

with little discussion, or discussions were reduced to verbal battles between Michael and Anne. Occasionally, task force members seemed to agree that they had identified some viable components of the new program. However, no one worked on the project outside the group meeting time; and at the start of each meeting, previous progress was ignored.

Jim expressed considerable frustration over the slow progress. He believed the task force members were not working as a team and that individual agendas were surfacing too frequently. After two months of weekly meetings, Jim told the president he thought the group should be reconstituted if partnership banking were ever to be successful at Main Street Bank and Trust.

Questions

1. From this case, identify any power positions that have developed or are developing.
2. Could politics be used to assist in this situation? Discuss.

Notes

1. This case is a composite of a number of published accounts, among them: Steven Emerson, "Perot and the Politics of Power," *U.S. News & World Report,* June 20, 1988, p. 28; Keith F. Girard, "Profiles in Power," *Business Month,* May 1989, pp. 28–37; Peter Elkind, "Perot and Con," *The Washington Monthly,* November 1990, pp. 51–53; Todd Mason, "Will the Real Ross Perot Please Stand Up?" *Business Week,* May 21, 1990, pp. 22–23, 26; and Mark M. Colodny, "Ross Perot on His Good Luck," *Fortune,* June 3, 1991, p. 211.

2. R. M. Kanter, "Power Failures in Management Circuits," *Harvard Business Review* 57 (July 1979): 65–75.

3. A. Kaplan, "Power in Perspective," in R. L. Kahn and E. Boulding, eds., *Power and Conflict in Organizations* (London: Tavistock, 1964); M. Weber, *The Theory of Social and Economic Organization* (Glencoe, IL: Free Press, 1947).

4. H. Mintzberg, *Power in and around Organizations* (Englewood Cliffs, NJ: Prentice-Hall, 1983).

5. P. M. Balu, *Exchange and Power in Social Life* (New York: Wiley, 1964).

6. R. M. Emerson, "Power-Dependence Relations," *American Sociological Review* 27 (February 1962): 31–41.

7. J. P. Kotter, "Power, Dependence, and Effective Management," *Harvard Business Review* 55 (July 1977): 125–136.

8. Ibid.

9. J. P. Kotter, "Power, Success, and Organizational Effectiveness," *Organizational Dynamics* 6 (Winter 1978): 27–40.

10. Ibid.

11. D. McClelland and D. H. Burnham, "Power Driven Managers: Good Guys Make Bum Bosses," *Psychology Today,* December 1975, pp. 69–71.

12. R. M. Steers and L. W. Porter, *Motivation and Work Behavior* (New York: McGraw-Hill, 1979).

13. McClelland and Burnham, "Power Driven Managers: Good Guys Make Bum Bosses."

14. Ibid.

15. E. T. Cornelius III and F. B. Lane, "The Power Motive and Managerial Success in a Professionally Oriented Service Industry Organization," *Journal of Applied Psychology* 69 (February 1984): 32–39.

16. John French and Bertram Raven, "The Basis of Social Power," in *Studies in Social Power*, ed. Dorwin Cartwright (Ann Arbor: University of Michigan Press, 1959), pp. 150–167.

17. PINNACLE: Marge Schott discusses her latest challenge, turning the Reds around, and other aspects of her business career, with CNN correspondent, Jan Hopkins.

18. Gary Yukl and Tom Taber, "The Effective Use of Managerial Power," *Personnel* 60 (March–April 1983): 37–44.

19. R. Wayne Mondy and Shane R. Premeaux, "Power, Politics, and the First-Line Supervisor," *Supervisory Management* 31 (January 1986): 36–39.

20. H. Mintzberg, "Power and Organization Life Cycles," *Academy of Management Review* 9 (April 1984): 207–224; Mintzberg, *Power in and around Organizations*.

21. D. Hickson, C. Hinings, C. Lee, "A Strategic Contingencies Theory of Intraorganizational Power," *Administrative Science Quarterly* 23 (March 1978): 65–90.

22. A. Cobb, "Informal Influence in the Formal Organization: Perceived Sources of Power Among Work Unit Peers," *Academy of Management Journal* 23 (March 1980): 155–161.

23. R.M. Kanter, *Men and Women of the Corporation* (New York: Basic Books, 1977).

24. This case is a composite of a number of published accounts, among them: Gregory Jaynes, "Tycoons," *Life*, January 1989, pp. 45–53; Terence P. Pare, "Pepsi's Trump," *Fortune*, July 18, 1988, p. 99; "Trader Don's," *Fortune*, March 13, 1989, p. 140; Agis Salpukas, "Trump Takes Control of Eastern Shuttle," *New York Times*, June 8, 1989, p. D6; Monci Jo Williams, "Will Donald Trump Own the World?" *Fortune*, November 21, 1988, pp. 145–162; Daniel Seligman, "Man in Motion," *Fortune*, January 16, 1989, p. 135; Robert T. Grieves, "The Brains behind Trump," *Forbes*, October 3, 1988, p. 193.

25. David C. McClelland and David H. Burnham, "Power Is the Great Motivator," *Harvard Business Review* 54 (March–April 1976): 102.

26. John M. Pfiffner and Frank P. Sherwood, *Administrative Organization* (Englewood Cliffs, NJ: Prentice-Hall, 1960), p. 311.

27. Rob Lucas, "Political-Cultural Analysis of Organizations," *Academy of Management Journal* 12 (January 1987): 144–156.

28. Gregory L. Miles, "Suddenly, USX Is Playing Mr. Nice Guy," *Business Week*, June 26, 1989, pp. 151–152.

29. Mintzberg, "Power and Organization Life Cycles."

30. Ibid.

31. R. Allen, D. Madison, L. Porter, "Organizational Politics: Tactics and Characteristics of Its Actors," *California Management Review* 22 (Fall 1979): 77–83.

32. J. Gabarro and J. Kotter, "Managing Your Boss," *Harvard Business Review* 58 (January–February 1980): 92–100.

33. D. Farrell and J. C. Petersen, "Patterns of Political Behavior in Organizations," *Academy of Management Review* 7 (July 1982): 403–412.

34. D. Kipnis, *The Powerholders* (Chicago: University of Chicago Press, 1976).

35. R. E. Walton and R. B. McKersie, *A Behavioral Theory of Labor Negotiations* (New York: McGraw-Hill, 1965).

36. W. A. Gamson, *Power and Discontent* (Homewood, IL: Dorsey Press, 1968).

37. D. G. Pruitt, "Strategic Choice in Negotiation," *American Behavioral Scientist* 27 (November–December 1983): 167–194.

38. J. Z. Rubin, "Negotiation," *American Behavioral Scientist* 27 (November–December 1983): 136–148.

39. R. L. Kahn and E. Boulding, *Power and Conflict in Organizations* (New York: Basic Books, 1964).

40. Karen Berney, "Finding the Ethical Edge," *Nation's Business*, August 1987, p. 22.

41. H. Selye, *The Stress of Life* (New York: McGraw-Hill, 1956).

42. H. Selye, *The Stress of Life*, 2d ed. (New York: McGraw-Hill, 1976).

43. C. N. Cofer and M. H. Appley, *Motivation: Theory and Research* (New York: Wiley, 1964).

44. D. R. Frew, *Management of Stress* (Chicago: Nelson Hall, 1977), p. xix; see also A. P. Brief, R. S. Schuler, and M. Van Sell, *Managing Job Stress* (Boston: Little, Brown, 1981).

45. Janice Somerville, "Stress Treatment Costing Billions," *American Medical News* 32 (November 1989): 17.

46. D. L. Nelson and J. C. Quick, "Professional Women: Are Distress and Disease Inevitable?" *Academy of Management Review* 10 (January 1985): 206–218; G. L. Cooper and M. J. Davidson, "The High Cost of Stress on Women Managers," *Organizational Dynamics* 10 (Winter 1982): 44–53.

47. S. V. Kasl, "Epidemiological Contributions to the Study of Work Stress," in *Stress at Work*, ed. G. L. Cooper and R. Payne (New York: Wiley, 1978).

48. M. Kets de Vries, "Organizational Stress: A Call for Management Action," *Sloan Management Review* 21 (Fall 1979): 3–14.

49. Herbert J. Freudenberger, *Burnout: The High Cost of High Achievement* (Garden City, NY: Anchor Press, Doubleday and Company, 1980), p. 13.

50. Hugh F. Stallworth, "Realistic Goals Help Avoid Burnout," *HR Magazine* 35 (June 1990): 1.

51. John G. Nelson, "Burn-Out—Business's Most Costly Expense," *Personnel Administrator* 25 (August 1980): 82.

52. Dick Friedman, "Job Burnout," *Working Woman* 5 (July 1980): 34.

53. Christina Meslack and Susan E. Jackson, "Burned-Out Cops and Their Families," *Psychology Today* 12 (May 1979): 59.

54. Beverly Norman, "Career Burnout," *Black Enterprise* 12 (July 1981): 45.

55. Cary Cherniss, "Job Burnout: Growing Worry for Workers, Bosses," *U.S. News & World Report*, February 1980, p. 72.

56. Harry Levinson, "When Executives Burnout," *Harvard Business Review* 59 (May–June 1981): 76.

15

Corporate Culture, Change, and Development

After completing this chapter students should be able to

- Define *corporate culture,* describe the factors that influence it, and explain the evidence of culture.

- Distinguish between a participative and a nonparticipative culture.

- Describe the change sequence and technological change.

- Identify sources of resistance to change and the approaches that can be used in reducing resistance to change.

- Describe the organizational development techniques that are available to implement change.

Apple Computer's Second Comeback Could Clash with Their Corporate Culture

According to Apple Computer, Inc. chairman John Sculley, the company has always been full of creative and intuitive people who "flitted from idea to idea." However, Sculley's plan for the 1990s involves making Apple more logical and predictable. Product introductions would be evolutionary, not revolutionary, Sculley said. And the organizational structure would be less loose and free. Apple's "California mystique," an industry analyst said, was gone.

Apple was founded by Steve Jobs and Steve Wozniak in 1976, after they built a few personal computers in Jobs's garage and sold them to friends. Through the mid-1980s the company was known for its counter-culture-type organization, as well as its innovative product offerings and marketing savvy. Blue jeans, long hair, and yogurt were common at the informal gatherings that passed for management meetings in those days. A coat and tie, a Cadillac, a clear, direct order, or an organization chart would have seemed out of place. Wozniak left after a few years and Jobs led Apple through nearly a decade of rapid growth. Until about 1983 Apple was the market-share leader in personal computers. Then it dropped to number 2, behind IBM.

Sculley took over from Jobs in 1985. Under Sculley, the company nearly tripled in sales, to $5.3 billion a year. Each year saw new highs in both sales and profits. Apple computers had evolved during those years toward compatibility with other brands.

As part of the 1989 reorganization, Sculley promoted a conservative authoritarian, Allan Z. Loren, to run Apple USA, the company's main division. Several executives quit. A former manager complained, "No company I know of has such chaos in the executive suite." Initially Sculley was pleased with the kind of chaos Loren had fostered. "Allan scared the hell out of people, and I'm thrilled," he remarked. "I knew a tough guy from the East Coast demanding implementation would be unpopular." Loren said, "The role of leadership is not to make all the popular decisions. It's making sure the company prospers." Apple employees indeed found Loren to be abrasive and quickly closed ranks against him.

Sculley's solution was to name Michael H. Spindler CEO of the Apple USA division. Spindler made himself a hero by nearly tripling Apple's European sales to $1.2 billion in two years. Spindler is emphasizing teamwork. His changes will dramatically alter the corporate culture of the Apple corporation. According to Spindler, "There will be no more prima donnas at Apple." Insiders say that this may be the most important change of all. However, some of the other changes will also affect the culture at Apple. Apple no longer depends on a few brilliant key people, but rather on more of an organized research methodology. Apple now assigns product-development teams the challenge of "finding value in the inevitable mistakes, half steps and dead ends." Planning is now more of a discipline than a fantasy. Changes such as eliminating lavish spending is marshalling in a new way of life at Apple. Will the second comeback of Apple under the direction of Spindler be successful or will the current corporate culture win again? [1]

The "loose and free" corporate culture at Apple was a reflection of the philosophies of Steve Jobs and his California friends. The emerging culture will surely show the influence of Sculley and Spindler. Every organization has a distinct culture, though, whether or not it has an influential chief executive.

Business scholars often treat the corporate culture as a constraint within which the management job is accomplished. However, recent research has shown that it is desirable—and to some degree possible—to modify the corporate culture to help accomplish company objectives. Sculley was doing that at Apple. Culture can foster commitment to the organization and provide an identity for organization members. Managers need to understand the cultures that exist in their firms, whether or not they seek to change them. This is all the more important as Western countries try to match the Japanese devotion to quality and output.[2]

In this chapter, we first define *corporate culture* and discuss the factors that influence it. Then, we offer evidence of culture and discuss participative versus nonparticipative cultures. Next, we present a model of the change sequence and address technological change. Then we explore the sources of resistance to change and ways to overcome it. In the final section of the chapter, we address organizational development.

Corporate Culture Defined

Corporate culture

The system of shared values, beliefs, and habits within an organization that interacts with the formal structure to produce behavioral norms.

The system of shared values, beliefs, and habits within an organization that interacts with the formal structure to produce behavioral norms is **corporate culture.**[3] Corporate culture embodies the values and standards that guide people's behavior. It determines the organization's overall direction. Culture governs what the company stands for, how it allocates resources, its organizational structure, the systems it uses, the people it hires, the fit between jobs and people, the results it recognizes and rewards, what it defines as problems and opportunities, and how it deals with them.[4]

Writing in 1967, Anthony Jay stated: "It has been known for some time that corporations are social institutions with customs and taboos, status groups and pecking orders, and many sociologists and social scientists have studied and written about them as such. But they are also political institutions, autocratic and democratic, peaceful and warlike, liberal and paternalistic."[5] What Jay was writing about, although the term had not then achieved broad usage, was corporate culture.

Culture gives people a sense of how to behave and what they ought to be doing.[6] It is similar in concept to meteorological climate. Just as the weather is described by such variables as temperature, humidity, and precipitation, corporate culture is described by such variables as friendliness, supportiveness, and risk taking. For instance, the weather of the southwestern United States may be described as "warm and pleasant," and the employees of an organization may characterize their organization as being "open and supportive." Such perceptions are gradually formed by each individual over a period of time as the person performs assigned activities under the general guidance of a superior and a set of organizational policies.

The culture existing within a firm influences the employees' degree of satisfaction with the job as well as the level and quality of their performance. For example, if an employee is seeking an environment where employee input is important, Wal-Mart may be just the place. Employee suggestions for improvements and changes are collected every week and are taken very seriously at Wal-Mart headquarters.[7] The assessment of how desirable the organization's culture is may differ for each

Just as physical climate is described by such variables as temperature, humidity, and precipitation, corporate culture is composed of such factors as friendliness, supportiveness, and risk taking. The culture existing within a firm influences the employee's degree of satisfaction with the job as well as the level and quality of their performance. The late Sam Walton said the "Customer is the Boss" at Wal-Mart. At each store, customers are met at the door by "People Greeters."

Source: Photograph of Wal-Mart, Inc.

employee. One person may perceive the environment as bad, and another may see the same environment as good. An employee may actually leave an organization in the hope of finding a more compatible culture.

The late Ray Kroc, founder of McDonald's Corporation, was straightforward in what he expected in his corporate culture. He created a direct, people-oriented corporate culture. According to Kroc, "If you got time to lean, you got time to clean." In relation to company expansion, "When you're green, you grow; when you're ripe, you rot."[8] When Mike Quinlan became McDonald's new CEO, he pledged that McDonald's culture would remain unchanged under his leadership. McDonald's has no formal staff hierarchy. The annual report lists the company officers alphabetically instead of by rank, and no employee has an office door.[9] Corporate culture is an integral part of the organization and has important implications for managerial action.

If a corporate culture is productive, it probably should be continued. In the case of McDonald's, the culture appears to be appropriate to successfully take the organization well into the future. At Apple Computer, John Sculley believes the culture must change to be competitive, which is why he hired Michael H. Spindler to run Apple USA. Playboy Enterprises has already changed its culture dramatically to survive in the 1990s.

The original corporate culture of Playboy Enterprises was the product of Hugh Hefner's dream. That dream was of bunny ears, centerfolds, sexual imaging, hotel casinos, clubs, a Playboy mansion, and a black painted DC-9 with the Playboy logo. The image, values, beliefs, and habits of Hugh Hefner interacted to develop a unique

Changing Hugh Hefner's Dream

corporate culture of an organization that was quite successful throughout the 1960s and 1970s. Because of major social and business changes that occurred in the 1980s, however, the Playboy empire began to lose money. In 1986, for example, Playboy Enterprises lost $60 million, and the existing corporate culture was a prime contributor.

Christie Hefner inherited control of the troubled Playboy empire and turned it around. The corporate culture she developed was one of a business organization that could no longer make a profit on bunny ears and centerfolds alone. Christie Hefner, a woman who is only a year older than the company she runs, is now one of the most influential women in American publishing. Her father's living symbolism no longer permeates the organization.

Her strategy for revival has meant venturing into new territory. For example, she spearheaded home videocassettes and the Playboy channel. Christie Hefner is a Phi Beta Kappa college graduate who describes herself as an accessible and informal manager. She holds meetings at her Chicago apartment near Lake Michigan. The management style has changed, the Playboy image has changed, and so has the corporate culture.[10]

MANAGEMENT IN PRACTICE: A Skill-Building Exercise

You are general manager of Clean-Care Janitorial Service, which was recently acquired by Super-Clean of North America (SCNA). SCNA is a nationwide commercial cleaning service, specializing in large office buildings. Its price schedules are fixed, and its cleaning and maintenance procedures are standardized. You have met some of the company's crew leaders, and you were surprised to find they were aggressive and well-spoken young management types.

Clean-Care does mainly residences, although the company accepts some commercial subcontracts. Clean-Care accepts residential calls on short notice. Much of its business is overflow from larger cleaning firms that have mostly commercial clients. Your work force is basically unskilled and uneducated, and your supervisors are people who consistently did a good job as workers.

SCNA has just informed you that it will impose its participative management approach on Clean-Care. You are to establish formal procedures to make sure employees really help in solving problems and participate in decisions that affect them.

What would you do?

ETHICAL DILEMMA

Your company has recently adopted the Mead Corporation approach to ethics. Your recently appointed CEO worked at Mead for several years and is determined to make your company the ethical leader in the industry. Mead Corporation has incorporated ethics into the total corporate culture as an effective and enforceable control for workplace behavior. Mead encourages line managers and other workers to spot potential problem areas and initiate appropriate responsible policies. One of the key aspects of this program is Project Hotline, a telephone hotline maintained by the company's corporate security department. Employees who believe they have observed unethical behavior in a fellow employee or supervisor can use the hotline to report the details of the behavior.[11]

You are aware that the company that disposes of the waste your plant generates is not following Environmental Protection Agency guidelines. The less toxic waste is being dumped at night in a closed landfill six miles from the plant. To make matters worse, the waste disposal company is operated by your brother-in-law. You have already warned him once, and you have just learned that he is still illegally dumping. You confront him, telling him that you are going to use the hotline to report him if he illegally dumps waste one more time. Your brother-in-law threatens to implicate you if you ever blow the whistle. You are now sure he will continue to dump illegally. You can either call and report your brother-in-law, or you can let him continue to dump illegally.

What would you do?

Factors that Influence Corporate Culture

The purpose of transforming corporate culture is simple: "to increase productivity by converting worker apathy into corporate allegiance."[12] Basically, this statement means that an organization should change its personality unless it is supporting the accomplishment of organizational objectives. Firms such as IBM and AT&T have been successful with the same corporate cultures for many decades, but their cultures no longer allow the firms to be as successful as they could be in the current global business climate.

To change or maintain a corporate culture, managers should understand the factors that influence it. Among those factors are work groups, managers' and supervisors' leadership style, organizational characteristics, and administrative processes (see Figure 15–1).[13] As in most management situations, the external environment also influences corporate culture.

Work Group

The character of the immediate work group will affect one's perception of the nature of corporate culture. For example, commitment to the mission of the work group directly influences cultural perceptions. Commitment refers to whether or not the group is really working. If people in the work group are just going through the motions of work, it is difficult for an individual member to obtain high levels of output and satisfaction. Hindrance may also occur when individuals work together as a group. Hindrance is concerned with the degree of busywork (work of doubtful value) given to the group. Morale and friendliness within the group also affect the environment of the work group and the perceived nature of the corporate culture.

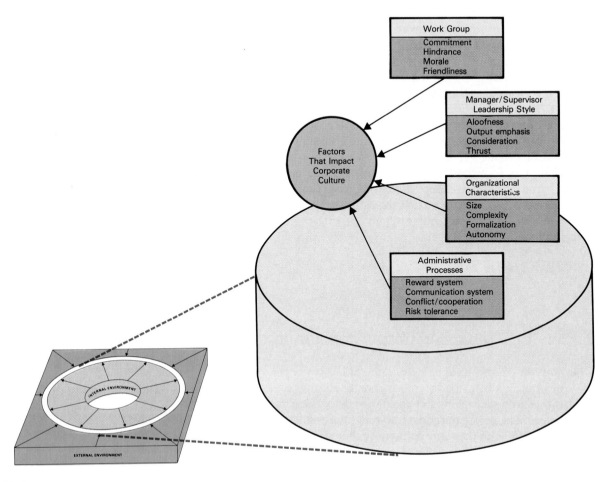

FIGURE 15–1

Factors that Influence
Corporate Culture

Manager/Supervisor Leadership Style

The leadership style of the immediate supervisor will have a considerable effect on the culture of the group, and vice versa. If the manager is aloof and distant in dealing with subordinates, this attitude could have a negative influence on the organization. If the supervisor is always pushing for output, this too alters the environment. Consideration is a desirable leadership characteristic that can positively influence group effectiveness. Thrust—supervisory behavior characterized by hard work and example setting—is also a positive influence on the group.

Organizational Characteristics

The type of culture that develops can also be affected by organizational characteristics. Organizations vary on such attributes as size and complexity, for example. Large organizations tend toward higher degrees of specialization and impersonalization. Labor unions often find that large firms are easier to organize than smaller ones because smaller firms tend to be closer and have more informal relationships among employees and management. Complex organizations tend to employ a greater number of professionals and specialists, which alters the general approach to solving problems. Organizations also vary in the degree to which they write things down and attempt to program behavior through rules, procedures, and regulations. They can be distinguished, too, on the basis of the degree of decentralization of decision-making authority, which affects the degree of autonomy and employee freedom.

Administrative Processes

Corporate culture may be affected by administrative processes. Firms that can develop direct links between performance and rewards tend to create cultures conducive to achievement. Communication systems that are open and free flowing tend to promote participation and creative atmospheres. The general attitudes that exist toward the tolerance of conflict and the handling of risk have considerable influence on teamwork. They also affect the amount of innovation and creativity.

From these and other factors, organization members develop a subjective impression of what kind of place the organization is to work in. This impression will affect performance, satisfaction, creativity, and commitment to the organization.

Classification of Cultures

Within most large organizations, both a dominant culture and many subcultures exist.[14] The **dominant culture** is *the corporate culture that expresses the shared views of the majority of the organization's members.* **Subcultures** are *corporate cultures characteristic of various units in an organization.* For instance, the marketing department may have a culture that is different from that of the production department. Although members from both departments share the dominant culture, they may also develop other cultural aspects unique to their particular unit.

Cultures are also classified as strong or weak.[15] *The dominant corporate culture that is widely and ardently adhered to by members of the organization* is a **strong corporate culture.** Many Japanese firms appear to have strong corporate cultures. Apple USA has a strong corporate culture, but it appears to be hindering needed changes.

The dominant culture at PPG Industries, the Pittsburgh glass, paint, and chemical maker, was dull and bureaucratic until Vincent A. Sarni took over in 1984. Called "an Iron City behemoth" (Pittsburgh is known as the Iron City), the company suffered through each economic downturn and sleepily responded to recoveries. But Sarni changed all that.

Dominant culture
The corporate culture that expresses the shared views of the majority of the organization's members.

Subcultures
Corporate cultures characteristic of various units in an organization.

Strong corporate culture
The dominant corporate culture that is widely and ardently adhered to by members of the organization.

· ·

As was mentioned in an earlier chapter, PPG Industries chief executive Vincent A. Sarni shook up PPG by publishing his "Blueprint for the Decade." The eight-page pamphlet included a mission statement along with corporate objectives regarding the desired return on equity (ROE) and the desired percentage growth in sales. The "blueprint" called for major emphasis on quality and productivity as well as for

PPG'S Blueprint for the Decade

globalization of the company. Sarni jawboned everyone—employees, customers, suppliers—about his plan for PPG. Soon it became the company's plan. "My first two or three years I always started with a discussion of the Blueprint," said Sarni, "I don't have to do that anymore. The Blueprint's on the shop floor, and it has meaning."

PPG's "Blueprint for Performance" bonus, directly tied to ROE, was initiated. In addition, the company adds money to each employee's profit sharing account each year and calculates contributions above that on ROE performance. "This is a program which rewards teamwork," said human resources chief Russell L. Crane, "and we're all part of a team." Several other awards focus on goals in the blueprint. The Achievement of Excellence Award, for a major contribution corporatewide, involves $2,500 in PPG stock. Special Achievement Awards ($500) and Product Champion Awards ($1,000) are given for "Anything employees do to increase customer satisfaction, cut costs, or increase revenues." PPG's sales and earnings went up again. Sarni's blueprint is working.[16]

Evidence of Culture

Determining exactly what type of culture exists in an organization can be difficult, but there are means available. The evidence of an organization's culture can be found in many places, particularly in status symbols, traditions, history, rituals, jargon, and the physical environment (see Figure 15–2).

Status Symbols

Status symbol

A visible, external sign of one's social position.

A visible, external sign of one's social position is a **status symbol.** A stranger who is aware of status hierarchies can enter an organization and obtain a social fix quickly by reading the various symbols. Status symbols vary from firm to firm. For example, one would usually expect higher-status positions to be accompanied by newer office furnishings. In one organization, however, the high-status managers were given antique roll-top desks, and the lower-level managers received new, shiny, modern furniture. Some typical status symbols in business are the following:

- Title.
- Pay.
- Bonus and stock plans.
- Size and location of desk or office.
- Location of parking space or reserved parking.
- Type of company car assigned.
- Secretaries.
- Privacy.
- Use of executive clubs.
- Cocktail party invitations.

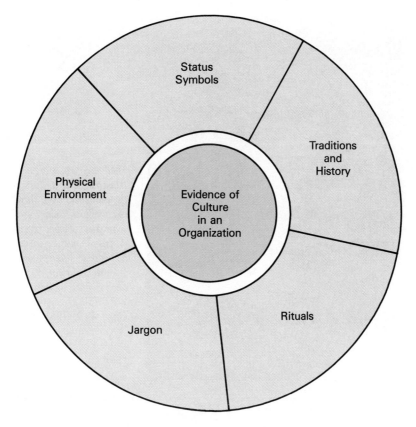

FIGURE 15–2

Evidence of an Organization's
Culture

- Furnishings, including rugs, pictures, and tables.
- Posted certificates.
- Privileges, including the freedom to move about, to not punch a time clock, to set one's own working hours, and to regulate one's own coffee breaks.
- Number of windows in office.

In addition, status symbols tend to be different for different professionals. For example, research scientists and engineers often regard the importance or size of their projects as a status symbol.

Many status symbols are not controlled by management and may be the basis of unwarranted preoccupation. Executives have gotten down on their hands and knees to measure the comparative size of their offices. Windows are counted, steps from the president's office are paced off, secretaries who can use a word processor are sought, parking space is fought for, and company cars are wangled. In some organizations, having an office with windows is a major status symbol.

Traditions and History

Organizational traditions tend to distinguish one firm from another. Even firms that produce essentially the same product will be somewhat different because of certain traditions. Workers act and react on a daily basis because of past events that have

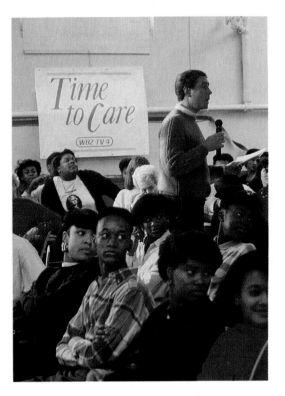

There are certain organizational traditions that tend to distinguish one firm from another. Even firms that produce essentially the same product will be somewhat different because of certain traditions. Public service programming is a hallmark of Westinghouse Broadcasting Company (Group W). Shown here conducting an interview is Bob Lobel of WBZ-TV. This program is part of Group W's "Time to Care" campaign, a program to highlight concern for social issues such as AIDS, homelessness, and inner city decay.

Source: Photograph courtesy of Westinghouse

become traditional. Typically, their actions are unconscious. They just know what is expected of them in certain situations. IBM has a tradition of conservative dress, incentive-type compensation, internal competition among employees, and a push for new ideas. Apple USA's traditions are much different.

Rituals

Closely related to traditions and history are company rituals. Many Japanese firms have their employees begin the day by doing exercises. The Mary Kay Cosmetics Company provides high-profile and embellished meetings, during which saleswomen are awarded gold and diamond pins, fur stoles, and the use of pink Cadillacs. These awards are presented in an environment easily reminiscent of a Miss America pageant. There is a cheering audience in a large auditorium, and all the participants are dressed in glamorous evening clothes.

Jargon

Jargon

The special language that group members use in their daily interactions.

The special language that group members use in their daily interactions is **jargon.** The jargon used in one firm is often quite different from another's. Sales representatives are keenly aware of this, and they train themselves to recognize the sales jargon of competing firms. Then, when they call on a new prospect, they can recognize which other sales representatives have already visited the prospect through the terminology the prospect uses when asking questions. Even in a single firm, jargon separates one group or unit from another. Accountants may use one jargon and sales workers another.

The Physical Environment

The firm's physical environment often makes a statement about its type of culture. Office areas with few common locations for organization members to meet creates an image of a closed form of culture. An office building with open offices and considerable common areas for employee interaction indicates a different culture. Whether office doors are consistently open or closed is a clue to the level of formality that exists in an organization. Even the type of furniture used can tell much about an organization's culture. For instance, round tables suggest more equality than do long ones.

Participative Versus Nonparticipative Cultures

Culture is often viewed in terms of the level of participation within the organization. On a continuum, involvement may range from highly participative to completely nonparticipative, with many degrees in between. An open and participative culture is characterized by such attributes as the following:

- Trust in subordinates.
- Openness in communications.
- Considerate and supportive leadership.
- Group problem solving.
- Worker autonomy.
- Information sharing.
- High-output objectives.

Some behaviorists contend that this type of culture is the only viable one for all situations.

The opposite of the open and participative culture is the closed and autocratic one. Both may be characterized by high-output objectives; but in a closed culture, such objectives are more likely to be declared and imposed on the organization by autocratic and threatening leaders. There is greater rigidity in this culture, resulting from strict adherence to the formal chain of command, short spans of management, and strict individual accountability. The emphasis is on the individual rather than on teamwork. Workers often simply go through the motions of work, doing as they are told.

Despite behaviorists' criticism of traditional corporate cultures, a more participative philosophy may not always work. In an instance involving the packaging of low-priced china, low productivity of the work group was caused by excessive and unnecessary interaction between employees during working hours. Management found that the threat of dismissal did not solve the problem. Management finally solved it by redesigning the space allocated to the china-packaging process. A cubicle constructed of soundproofing material was built for each worker. The cubicles virtually eliminated the unproductive conversation between workers. As a result, productivity increased substantially. The total cost of building the cubicles was $3,200, which was recovered during the first three weeks of their use.[17] IBM has become a leaner and more open-minded and fast-moving company in recent years. These changes have altered its corporate culture, which now places greater emphasis on an entrepreneurial spirit.[18]

MANAGEMENT IN PRACTICE: A Skill-Building Exercise

Jack Williams is the hydraulic motor assembly supervisor for Dyer Manufacturing Company, a Columbus, Ohio, producer of specialized hydraulic systems. Jack was preoccupied about a rush order as he approached the assembly area. At one of the assembly tables, he noticed Alice Baxter and another worker casually chatting across the table. They stopped talking and busied themselves as Jack approached. They looked up again only when Jack spoke. "Alice," Jack said, "this Norris order has been put on rush. We really need a little extra effort today. How about it?"

"We'll give it our best," Alice said. As soon as Jack was out of earshot, however, Alice turned to the other worker and said, "He saw us goofing off, and that 'rush' business is just an excuse. I'll bet if we really did rush, they would increase our workload just like last time."

What type of culture likely exists in this company?

Developing a Participative Culture

The managerial approach in most organizations has been characterized as highly structured. Consequently, most attempts to alter organizational culture have been directed toward creating a more open and participative culture. As Chapter 10 indicated, the theme of participation developed by Douglas McGregor, Frederick Herzberg, and Abraham Maslow, among others, relates primarily to self-actualization, motivator factors, consultative and democratic leadership, job enrichment, and management by objectives.

Benefits of Participation

The possible benefits of involving more people in the decision-making process relate primarily to morale. The Grand Rapids, Michigan, manufacturing plant of Westinghouse Furniture Systems, a unit of Westinghouse Electric Corporation, is successful because of a high degree of worker involvement in decision making.[19] Increases in the levels of morale and job satisfaction when cultures are made more open and participative result in the following:

- Increased acceptability of management's ideas.

- Increased cooperation between managers and staff.
- Reduced turnover.
- Reduced absenteeism.
- Fewer complaints and grievances.
- Greater acceptance of changes.
- Improved attitudes toward the job and the organization.

The development of greater employee participation may have a direct and immediate effect on employee morale. Employees are likely to take a greater interest in the job and the organization. They will tend to accept, and sometimes initiate, change, not only because they understand the necessity for change but also because knowing more about the change reduces their insecurity.

Though there is some question about the relationship between degree of participation and productivity, most experience and research indicate a positive relationship between employee participation and measures of morale, turnover, and absenteeism—which are all related to job satisfaction. However, there has been little evidence of a positive relationship between job satisfaction and productivity. Still, if productivity is not harmed by participation, these benefits should make participative management worthwhile. If management finds that productivity is actually decreased in a particular situation, then serious decisions will have to be made concerning the trade-off between organizational needs and human needs.

Limitations of Participation

Despite the value of a participative approach to management, there are some limitations. The requirements for greater participation in decision making are (1) sufficient time, (2) adequate ability and interest on the part of the participants, and (3) freedom to do the job.

If immediate decisions are required, time may not be available for group participation. The manager frequently decides what to do and issues orders accordingly. Also, if management decides to switch from a practice of autocracy to one of increased participation, some time for adjustment on the part of both managers and subordinates will be required. Participation calls for the ability to govern oneself and may therefore require the time for subordinates to learn how to handle this newfound freedom—and for supervisors to learn to trust their subordinates.

Whether or not greater involvement in decision making can be developed depends largely on the ability and interest of the participants, both subordinates and managers. This is not an easy concept to implement. Obviously, if a subordinate has neither knowledge of nor interest in a subject, there is little need to consult that person. As organizations and technologies become increasingly complex, and as management becomes more professionalized, it is likely that employee participation will be characterized more by cooperation seeking or information gathering than by full participation. Also, not all employees are desirous of participation. Managers should face the fact that some workers do not want more responsibility and involvement in their job.

Finally, as Figure 15–3 indicates, the area of job freedom left to the individual may be quite restricted, but it can be expanded. An individual's task may be governed

FIGURE 15–3

Limits to
Participative Freedom

SOURCE: Adapted by permission from Edwin B. Flippo and Gary M. Munsinger, Management, *5th ed. (Boston: Allyn and Bacon, 1982), p. 360.*

by management directives, organizational policies and procedures, the union contract, staff specialists, and colleague and subordinate power. The greater the area in the "Freedom to Do Job" section of the figure, the greater the degree of participative freedom. In the figure, employee A would have more freedom to accomplish the job than would employee B. Upper-level management may permit substantial latitude in decision making for employee A and less for employee B.

Measuring the Participation Level: Likert's Systems of Management

Rensis Likert, former director of the Institute for Social Research at the University of Michigan, developed a management systems theory that keyed in on a continuum of management styles ranging from autocratic to participative. Likert's theory calls for four systems of management: System I, exploitative autocratic; System II, benevolent autocratic; System III, consultative; and System IV, participative team. According to Likert, the last style is the best in the long run for all situations.[20]

System I—Exploitative Autocratic   Managers make all decisions in the exploitative autocratic system. They decide what is to be done, who will do it, and how and when it is to be accomplished. Failure to complete work as assigned results in threats or punishment. Under this system, management exhibits little confidence or trust in employees. A typical managerial statement is: "You do it my way or you're fired." According to Likert, there is a low level of trust and confidence between management and employees.

System II—Benevolent Autocratic   Managers who are benevolent autocrats make the decisions, but their employees have some degree of freedom and flexibility in performing their jobs so long as they conform to specific procedures. Under the benevolent autocratic system, managers take a paternalistic attitude—"I'll take care of you if you perform well." This system offers a fairly low level of trust between management and employees, which causes employees to use caution when dealing with management.

System III—Consultative   Managers in the consultative system consult with employees prior to establishing objectives and making decisions about work. This system is used by Wal-Mart Stores, whose employees are encouraged to make suggestions for improvements and changes, which are forwarded to Wal-Mart headquarters weekly. Wal-Mart management also includes employees in corporate decision making.[21] In the consultative system, employees have a considerable degree of freedom in deciding how to do their work. A manager using this system might say to an employee, "I'd like your opinion on this before I make the decision." Management also tends to rely on rewards rather than punishments to motivate employees. And the level of trust between employees and management is fairly high. This creates a culture in which employees feel relatively free to openly discuss work-related matters with management.

System IV—Participative Team   Likert's recommended system is the participative team. The emphasis of this system is on group participation, with full involvement of the employees in the process of establishing objectives and making job-related decisions. In the Grand Rapids plant of Westinghouse Furniture Systems, employees are involved in decision making in all areas, including objective setting, hiring, scheduling of work and hours, and operations planning, resulting in an increase in the plant's productivity.[22]

Employees involved in a participative team system feel free to discuss matters with their manager, who is supportive rather than condescending or threatening. Likert contends that entire organizations should be designed along the lines of participative teams, with work being performed by a series of overlapping groups. The leader provides a link between the group and other units at higher levels in the organization. (This concept is often referred to as the *linking-pin theory*.) Decision making is widespread throughout the enterprise, with the power of knowledge usually taking precedence over the power of authority.

Measurement of the type of style in the Likert framework is usually accomplished by having the employees assess the organizational culture and management system on a Likert scale (see Figure 15–4). For example, when the statement "Extent to which superior willingly shares information with subordinates" is made, the employee can respond on the continuum from "Provides minimum of information" all the way to "Seeks to give subordinates all relevant information and all information they want" (see item 3.*c*.2 in Figure 15–4). It has been found that the positions on these scales can be significantly altered through organizational and management development programs.

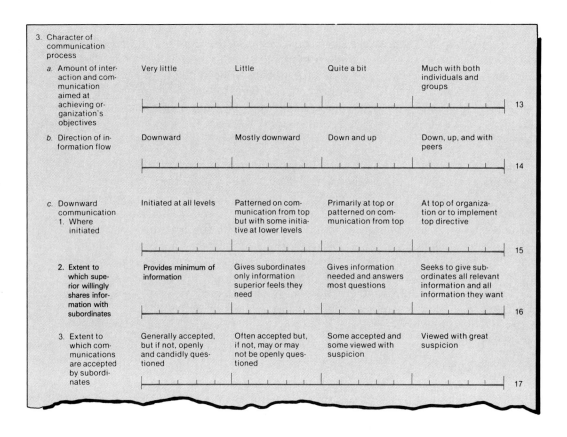

FIGURE 15–4

Sample Statements on the Likert Scale Relating to Communications within the Organization

SOURCE: *Rensis Likert,* The Human Organization *(New York: McGraw-Hill, 1967). Copyright by McGraw-Hill Book Company. Used with permission.*

Global Blending of Cultures and Management Styles

Often when a U.S. corporation goes global, it forms an alliance with a company in the host country. Once an alliance is formed, it is essential that the cultures and management styles of the partners blend together as quickly as possible.[23] Alliances are useful for all partners because they make it possible to share the cost and risks of doing business; collaboration enables companies to share financial resources, technology, production facilities, marketing know-how, and human resources.

The AT&T alliance with Olivetti was plagued with problems because of a "failure to blend its partners' divergent cultures and management styles." AT&T senior executive Robert Kravner blames the problems on differences in these areas. According to a *Wall Street Journal* article, Kravner said, "I don't think we or Olivetti spent enough time understanding the behavior of the other partner. We knew that culture was different but we never really penetrated. We would get angry and they would get upset." [24] Problems will occur in international alliances, where people from different organizational and national cultures work together. Such problems can often be traced to cultural differences. Overcoming such problems requires both parties to invest considerable time and effort in understanding each other's culture, on team-building efforts, and on continually improving two-way communication.[25]

For instance, when General Motors (GM) and the Fanuc Company of Japan formed the joint venture GMF Robotics Corporation, their management styles were quite different. Fanuc's managers operated with more autonomy than did GM managers. Yet despite this and other differences, GM and Fanuc were able to arrange a workable alliance. During the negotiation stage and the early years of the venture, both parent companies focused their efforts on building trust and on understanding each other's operations. To build trust, both avoided conflict and acceded to each other's demands. Today, GMF Robotics Corporation holds the dominant share of the heavy robotics market in the U.S.[26]

The Change Sequence

Change may affect individuals, groups, or even an entire organization. All organizations will experience change at one time or another. Among the most prominent changes occurring today in business are:

- Changes in organizational structure caused by mergers, acquisitions, rapid growth and downsizing.
- Changes in technology and the way people work, resulting largely from computerization.
- Changes in employees—a diverse work force consisting of:
  Older workers
  More women
  More minorities
  Highly educated employees
  Illiterate people
  Many different ethnic groups[27]

Change will require a sequence of events to occur in the organization. *The sequence of events that is needed to bring about change in an organization* is the **change sequence.** Whether the intended change is from a less participative to a more participative corporate culture or along some other dimension, the process tends to follow a certain pattern. The sequence of events, which was identified by social psychologist Kurt Lewin, is as follows (see also Figure 15–5): Management should first recognize a need for change. Then, the specific change method should be identified. Finally, the following steps should be carried out: (1) unfreezing the status quo, (2) moving to a new condition, and (3) refreezing to create a new status quo. Feedback is provided to determine if the change has occurred or if further change is needed.

Change sequence
The sequence of events that is needed to bring about change in an organization.

Recognizing the Need for Change

Perhaps the most important question to ask about change is: Is this change necessary? Some people unwisely believe that changes should be made merely for the sake of change. Managers who make a change merely to satisfy a desire for change may disrupt their section. Organizations and people want some degree of stability in

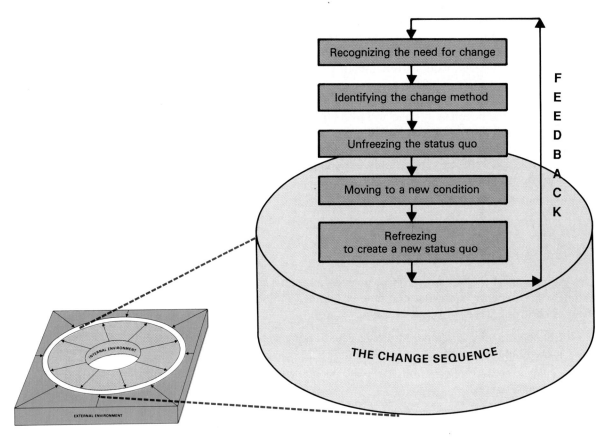

Recognizing the need for change

Identifying the change method

Unfreezing the status quo

Moving to a new condition

Refreezing
to create a new status quo

FEEDBACK

THE CHANGE SEQUENCE

INTERNAL ENVIRONMENT

EXTERNAL ENVIRONMENT

FIGURE 15–5

The Change Sequence

order to accomplish their assigned tasks. Yet there are times when changes are necessary, and the failure to be quick and decisive can have disastrous effects.

A number of major companies, particularly in the fast-moving computer industry, have found that cultural change is not only feasible but necessary. One expert writes about Apple Computer, "Things have changed since its salad days before IBM entered the market in August 1981 [when IBM became an Apple competitor by introducing its personal computer, a time when Apple was seen as a kind of playground for ambitious and idealistic computer wizards]."[28] Apple used to be noted for a corporate culture that emphasized blue jeans and tennis shoes, video games outside the executive offices, free thinking, and a flexible organization structure. IBM, on the other hand, traditionally emphasized white shirts, gray suits, and conservative thinking. But IBM is changing too. Its new strategy appears to be aimed at making the company more like Apple—whereas Apple is becoming more like IBM. Some other companies that have accomplished large-scale cultural change are AT&T, PepsiCo, Chase Manhattan Bank, and Twentieth Century Fox.[29]

Gordon Donaldson and Jay Lorsch argue that, at times, companies may need to change their culture or go out of business.[30] There are five possible reasons for imposing rapid cultural change:

1. If your company has strong values that don't fit a changing environment.
2. If the industry is very competitive and moves with lightning speed.

3. If your company is mediocre or worse.

4. If your company is about to join the ranks of the very largest companies.

5. If your company is small but growing rapidly.[31]

Identifying the Change Method

Management has at its disposal numerous methods and techniques for organizational change and development. Some specific techniques (which will be discussed later in the chapter) are survey feedback, team building, sensitivity training, management by objectives, job enrichment, and the Managerial Grid approach. The technique a firm chooses should meet its needs in reacting to the external environment and identifying the type of culture that will provide the greatest productivity.

Unfreezing the Status Quo

If individuals are to change their present attitudes, their current beliefs need to be altered, or unfrozen.[32] Resistance to change needs to be eliminated or reduced if a change is to be effective. Reducing resistance to change may be accomplished by building trust and confidence, developing open communication, and encouraging employee participation. Once resistance is reduced, the manager is in a position to implement the desired change. Sources of resistance to change and some approaches to reducing resistance are discussed later in the chapter.

Unfreezing often generates self-doubt, but it also provides a means of overcoming it. Employees should be made to feel that ineffectiveness is undesirable but that it can be remedied. If organization members are to be receptive to change, they should feel that they can change.

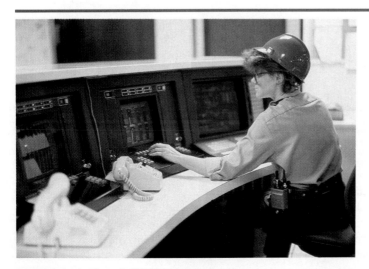

This information revolution has forced change even in formerly staid agribusiness firms. Here, a state of the art computer system at Archer Daniels Midland Company's vegetable oil refinery in Des Moines controls the highly automated facility. Gages at individual pieces of equipment have been replaced with sensors tied in to the computer system and many hand-operated valves have been replaced with automatic ones. This has reduced cost as well as improved product consistency.

Source: Photograph courtesy of Archer Daniels Midland Company

Moving to a New Condition

The initiation of a change can come from an order, a recommendation, or a self-directed impetus. A manager with authority can command that a change be made and can enforce its implementation by threats, punishments, and close supervision. If this path of implementing change is taken, the manager will likely find that the change has to be constantly monitored. Change is more permanent and substantial if people truly want and feel a need to change.

The most effective approach to initiating change is developing a two-way relationship between the person who is attempting to implement the change and those who will be changed. The person implementing the change should make suggestions, and those who will be changed should be encouraged to contribute and participate. The initiators should respond to suggestions, either by reformulating the change or by explaining why the suggestions cannot be incorporated.

Refreezing to Create a New Status Quo

If a person changes to a new set of work habits for a week and then reverts to former practices, the change has not been effective. Too often, changes that are introduced do not stick. If the change is to be permanent, people need to be convinced that the change is in their own and the organization's best interest. One of the best ways to accomplish this is to collect objective evidence of the success of the change. A manager who sees production increase because of a change in leadership style has excellent evidence of the success of the change.

People should feel competent about and take pleasure in using the new behavior. But the change will be completely accepted only if the reward system of the organization is geared to the new form of behavior. If the administrators of a university state that all faculty should publish, and there is no reward attached to publishing, it is likely that few faculty members will be motivated to make this change. An employee's job may be substantially enriched in terms of content and self-supervision, but if the change is not accomplished by properly enriched pay and status symbols, dissatisfaction is likely to result. People tend to repeat behavior that they find rewarding.

Technological Change

The tremendous impact of technological change on business was discussed in Chapter 2. It was pointed out that, as a result of technological advances, more than half of all existing jobs will be changed in the nineties and an estimated 30 percent will be eliminated.[33] High technology is one of the most important causes of organizational change today. United Parcel Service (UPS), for example, was forced into the high-tech era by competitors. UPS employees are now using on-board computers to assure the quickest pickup and delivery service possible.[34]

Factories too have been changed dramatically through the infusion of new technology. Rapidly moving into oblivion is the once-familiar scene of the blue-collar worker with grease-stained hands in front of a drill or stamping machine. Now there is an almost antiseptic atmosphere. Robots and other computer-controlled machines manufacture items while technicians stand by computer controls monitoring activities.

The General Electric diesel locomotive factory in Erie, Pennsylvania, provides an ideal example of high-tech changes in manufacturing. Its system machines ten different locomotive components, ranging from a small gearbox weighing only 150 pounds to large castings of more than a ton and containing as many as 140 machined surfaces. When a casting or welded frame enters the machining process, it is turned over to the central computer. This "executive computer" then orders the automatic transporter to take the piece to its first machining station and loads the proper program into the individual machine's computer. The various parts being manufactured are shuffled among the machines to make sure each machine is used efficiently. Not a single nonrobotic hand works on the parts until the computer summons a human to take them away.[35] Events such as these are occurring virtually daily in organizations around the world.

Sources of Resistance to Change

A change may cause some loss to the person or organization affected by it. Attachments to old and familiar habits, places, and people need to be given up. In major and unexpected changes, employees, groups, and even divisions often experience daze, shock, recoil, and turmoil.[36] Some of the many sources of resistance to change are shown in Figure 15–6 and discussed in the next several sections.

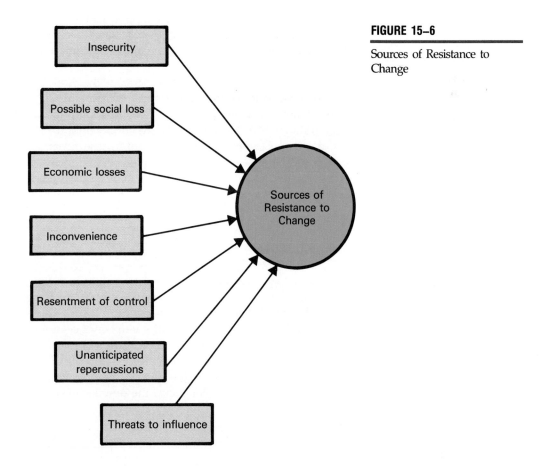

FIGURE 15–6

Sources of Resistance to Change

Insecurity

Once people have operated in a particular environment for a long time, they begin to feel comfortable. A change of environment often brings about uncertainty; people no longer know exactly what to expect. Almost everyone feels insecure during the transition from high school to college. The same sense of insecurity continues as the move is made from undergraduate to graduate work or from one job to another or to a new city.

Possible Social Loss

Change has the potential to bring about social loss. The informal work group may be extremely powerful. But if change causes individuals in the group to be transferred, the power of the group is likely to be diminished. A change may also cause established status symbols to be destroyed or low-status individuals to be awarded high-status symbols.

The effect a change can have on the social environment was vividly illustrated when one of the authors was doing a consulting job for a regional medical center. The hospital had been a small, local hundred-bed hospital. But because industry was moving rapidly into the area, the board of directors decided to expand the hospital to three hundred beds. In one department, all the employees reported directly to the department head, and a close rapport had developed among the department members. Staff members on rotating shifts sometimes had to work the evening and night shift, but they could still maintain close contact with the other department members.

Because of the great increase in workload, the work force was expanded, and a decision was made to have three shifts with a shift supervisor for each. The department head now had only three people reporting directly to him, and it was believed that the work could be performed much more efficiently. But the social loss was drastic. Subordinates no longer had a close relationship with the department head. Some, because they were on a different shift, rarely even saw him. This created a tremendous social loss and resulted in several workers quitting in a six-month period.

Economic Losses

New technology may enable a company to produce the same amount of output with fewer workers. While most companies make an honest attempt to transfer or retain employees affected by the change, the fear of being laid off remains. When the computer was first introduced, the number of clerical workers needed was often drastically reduced. Firms attempted to lessen employees' fear of losing their jobs by claiming that the number of jobs needed had actually increased through the use of the computer. This explanation did not help employees who were capable only of handling clerical work. For them, the new technology caused a major economic loss.

Inconvenience

Even when a change is not associated with a social or economic loss, new procedures and techniques may have to be learned. Physical and mental energy need to be expended, and for some people this is not enjoyable. When a new telephone system was installed at a university, there were many complaints. Time and effort had to be expended in learning how to use the system. It took approximately a year for the system to be accepted by a majority of the faculty and staff.

Resentment of Control

When employees are told that a change is to take place, they are made to realize that they do not have control over their destiny. Although the change may be for the better, a certain amount of resentment may develop. IBM's founder, Thomas J. Watson, was convinced that conservative dress would help sustain the company's image and, indirectly, increase profitability. Some within the company, however, resented being told how to dress. This might be true even for people who normally dress conservatively.

Unanticipated Repercussions

Because the organization is a system, a change in one part is likely to have unforeseen repercussions in another. For example, a newly enriched job is likely to demand a change in supervisory behavior. Supervisors may resist this change even if they initially supported the concept of job enrichment.

Threats to Influence

At times, a change will reduce the power base of a group, department, or division. Even when the change is best for the organization as a whole, resistance may persist. This scene has often been enacted as state boards of education attempt to reduce the duplication of programs. If a university gives up a program, its personal influence in the total system is diminished. Calls are made to alumni and supporters throughout the state to keep this event from occurring, even though a reduction in program duplication would improve the overall quality of the state's educational program.

Approaches for Reducing Resistance to Change

Change is often necessary, despite the resistance that might arise. During downsizing, companies can minimize resistance by communicating the need for new strategies, using pep talks, treating people who are let go with respect and kindness, letting key people know that the company, and the people, will be around for a long time.

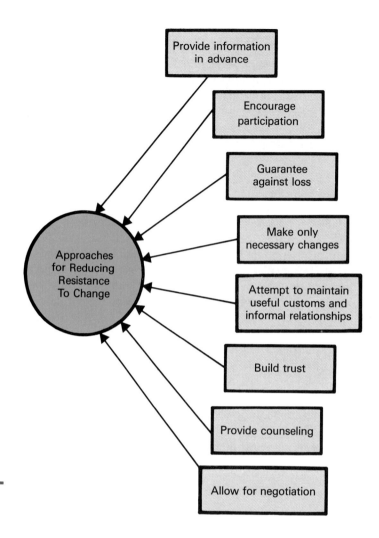

FIGURE 15–7

Approaches for Reducing
Resistance to Change

Then, a grieving process will be needed to get the change behind everyone who remains with the organization.[37] Some of the approaches designed to reduce resistance to change are shown in Figure 15–7 and discussed in the following sections.

Provide Information in Advance

Whenever possible, managers should provide the reasons for the upcoming change, its nature, its planned timing, and its possible effects on the organization and its personnel. Managers should avoid, if possible, withholding information that could seriously affect the lives and futures of particular individuals. A firm that is secretive about a change will have difficulty making future changes. There are, however, occasions when competitive survival requires that information be closely held until shortly before the change is to occur. In these cases, the information should be provided on an "as required" basis.

Encourage Participation

When possible, subordinates should be encouraged to participate in establishing the change. A person who is involved in implementing change procedures will likely be more supportive of the change. As mentioned in Chapter 10, Theory Y assumes that abilities are widespread in the population. Thus, many valuable ideas may be gained by permitting employees to participate in implementing the change. A company that has gained a reputation for participative management is Xerox Corporation. David Kearns, president, said to his employees, "I pledge to you that management of this company at all levels will listen to you and put your ideas to work."[38]

Guarantee against Loss

To promote acceptance of technological changes, some organizations guarantee that there will be no layoffs as a result of such changes. In cases of changes in methods and output standards, employees are often guaranteed retention of their present level of earnings during the learning period.

Make Only Necessary Changes

Changes should be made only when the situation demands them, not because of a whim on the part of a manager. A manager who gains a reputation for making changes for the sake of change will discover that any change, beneficial or not, will receive only minimal acceptance.

Attempt to Maintain Useful Customs and Informal Norms

The informal work group has real value from the standpoint of interpersonal understanding and cooperation. When possible, changes should be made to coincide with the culture and informal norms of the organization. When safety shoes were introduced, few would wear them willingly because of their unusual appearance. When they were redesigned to resemble normal shoes, resistance faded. Civilian consultants who are to work with military personnel are granted fictional rank to make their integration into ongoing operations more understandable and acceptable. A staff expert who wants a change introduced may find it advisable to have the announcement made by a line executive, with some sharing of the credit. Changes that go against established customs and informal norms will likely create resistance and have little chance of being readily accepted.

Build Trust

If a manager has a reputation for providing reliable and timely information to employees, the person's explanation as to why a change is to be made will likely be believed. The change may still be resisted; but if the manager is trusted by the employees, problems will be minimized. On the other hand, managers who have gained a reputation for providing incomplete or inaccurate information will often have difficulty convincing employees that a proposed change is good for them.

Provide Counseling

At times, some form of nonthreatening discussion and counseling not only may prevent rebellion but may stimulate voluntary adoption of a change. Nondirective counseling has been used effectively in many change situations. The approach rests on the belief that people have the ability to solve their own problems with the aid of a sympathetic listener. The role of the counselor is one of understanding and perhaps advising rather than passing judgment. This requires a somewhat permissive, friendly atmosphere, with actions and statements that exhibit continuing interest but not judgment. In most instances, managers with authority are unable to establish this type of atmosphere.

To be successful, nondirective counseling usually should be undertaken by staff psychologists. What the manager can do is to permit subordinates to ventilate some of their feelings, particularly those of frustration and anger. Just talking about the "good old days" will assist in the transition process. Discovering that others have similar feelings and doubts will often make the transition less painful.

Allow for Negotiation

Resistance to change can be reduced by the process of negotiation. Negotiation is the primary method used by labor unions to effect modification of proposed managerial changes.

Organizational Development

Organizational development (OD)

Planned and systematic attempts to change the organization, typically to a more behavioral environment.

Change efforts that affect the entire organization involve techniques of organizational development. **Organizational development (OD)** is *planned and systematic attempts to change the organization, typically to a more behavioral environment.* OD education and training strategies are designed to develop a more open, productive, and compatible workplace despite differences in personalities, culture, or technologies.[39] The organizational development movement has been strongly advocated by such researchers as Chris Argyris and Warren Bennis.

Change Agents

Change agent

The person or group responsible for ensuring that the planned change in organizational development is properly implemented.

The person or group responsible for ensuring that the planned change in organizational development is properly implemented is the **change agent.** This individual or group may be either an external or an internal consultant. Change agents have knowledge in the OD techniques described in the following sections. They use this knowledge to assist in organizational change.

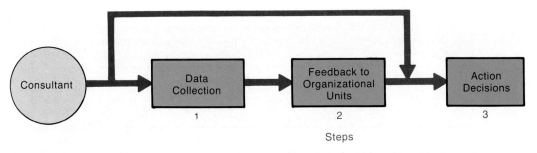

FIGURE 15–8

The Survey Feedback Method

SOURCE: *Reprinted, by permission of the publisher, from* Organization Development for Operating Managers, *by Michael E. McGill, p. 66.*
© 1977 AMACOM, a division of American Management Association, New York. All rights reserved.

When an organization first attempts to change, outside consultants are often used. They may bring objectivity to the situation and be better able than insiders to obtain the acceptance and trust of the organization's members. With time, internal consultants may move into the role of change agent. It is important to understand and appreciate the following techniques for implementing change: the survey feedback method, team building, sensitivity training, management by objectives, job enrichment, the Grid approach to OD, and management development programs.

The Survey Feedback Method

The organizational development method of basing change efforts on the systematic collection and measurement of subordinate's attitudes through anonymous questionnaires is the **survey feedback method.** The three basic steps in the process are shown in Figure 15–8. First, a consultant collects data from members of the organization. Survey questions typically require either objective multiple-choice responses (see Table 15–1) or scaled

Survey feedback method

The organizational development method of basing change efforts on the systematic collection and measurement of subordinates' attitudes through anonymous questionnaires.

Why did you decide to do what you are now doing?

    a. Desire to aid or assist others.
    b. Influenced by another person or situation.
    c. Always wanted to be in this vocation.
    d. Lack of opportunity or interest in other vocational fields.
    e. Opportunities provided by this vocation.
    f. Personal satisfaction from doing this work.

What do you like least about your job?

    a. Nothing.
    b. Pay.
    c. Supervisor relations.
    d. Problems with fellow workers.
    e. Facilities.
    f. Paperwork and reports.

TABLE 15–1

Examples of Multiple-Choice Responses to Survey Questions

SOURCE: Reprinted by permission from R. Wayne Mondy and Robert M. Noe III, *Human Resource Management,* 4th ed. (Boston: Allyn and Bacon, 1990), p. 711.

Considering all aspects of your job, evaluate your compensation with regard to your contributions to the needs of the organization. Circle the number that best describes how you feel.					
Pay Too Low	Pay Low	Pay Average	Pay above Average	Pay Too High
1 2	3 4	5 6	7 8	9 10

FIGURE 15–9

Examples of Scaled Responses to Survey Questions

SOURCE: *Reprinted, by permission from R. Wayne Mondy and Robert M. Noe III, Human Resource Management, 4th ed. (Boston: Allyn and Bacon, 1990), p. 711.*

What are your feelings about overtime work requirements? Circle the number that best indicates how you feel.		
Unnecessary	Necessary on Occasion	Necessary
1 2 3	4 5 6 7	8 9 10

responses that suggest agreement or disagreement with a particular question (see Figure 15–9). If truthful information about attitudes is to be obtained, employees should feel comfortable, secure, and confident in responding. Hence the need for anonymity.

In the second step, the results of the study are presented to concerned organizational units. In the final step, the data are analyzed and decisions are made. The means by which the data may be compared and analyzed include the following:

- Scores for the entire organization now and in the past.
- Scores for each department now and in the past.
- Scores by organizational level.
- Scores by seniority.
- Relative scores on each question.
- Scores for each question for each category of personnel cited above.

The decisions are directed at improving relationships in the organization. This is accomplished by revealing problem areas and dealing with them through straightforward discussion.

Team Building

Team building

A conscious effort by management to develop effective work groups throughout the organization.

One of the major techniques in the arsenal of the organizational development consultant is **team building**—*a conscious effort by management to develop effective work groups throughout the organization.*[40] Team building utilizes self-directed teams composed of a small group of employees responsible for an entire work process or segment. Team members work together to improve their operation or product, plan and control their work, and handle day-to-day problems. They may even become involved in broader companywide issues such as vendor quality, safety or business planning.[41] Team building is one of the more popular approaches to OD.[42]

Frequently work groups focus on solving actual problems to build efficient management teams. The team-building process begins when the team leader defines a problem that requires organizational change. Next, the group analyzes the problem to determine its underlying causes. These causes may be in such areas as communication, role clarification, leadership style, organization structure, and interpersonal relations. The next step is to propose several solutions and then to select the most appropriate one. Through this process, the participants are likely to be committed to the solution, and interpersonal support and trust are developed. The support and trust of group members enhance the implementation of the change. The concept of the quality circle, imported from Japan, is a modern example of team building. Quality circles are discussed in Chapter 17.

The American Society for Training and Development (ASTD) recently conducted a survey which asked for the areas most improved through the use of trained self-directed teams. The factors that had either improved or significantly improved were:

- Productivity (77 percent of responding firms).
- Quality (72 percent).
- Job satisfaction (65 percent).
- Customer service (57 percent).
- Waste reduction (55 percent).[43]

Sensitivity Training

The organizational development technique that uses leaderless discussion groups to develop awareness of and sensitivity to oneself and others is **sensitivity training** (also called T-group training and laboratory training).[44] The objectives of sensitivity training include the following:

- Increased openness with others.
- Greater concern for the needs of others.
- Increased tolerance for individual differences.
- Less ethnic prejudice.
- Awareness and understanding of group processes.
- Enhanced listening skills.
- Greater appreciation of the complexities of behaving competently.
- Establishment of more realistic personal standards of behavior.

Sensitivity training
The organizational development technique that uses leaderless discussion groups to develop awareness of and sensitivity to oneself and others. (Also called T-group training and laboratory training).

Sensitivity training is not widely used today as an organizational development technique. It has been labeled psychotherapy rather than proper business training, and leaders of T-groups have been criticized for having an insufficient background in psychology. Detractors also suggest that individuals' defense mechanisms—built up to preserve the personality over a period of years—may be destroyed, with little help provided in replacing them with more satisfactory behavioral patterns. It is contended that one cannot exist without ego defense mechanisms.

Management by Objectives

As described in Chapter 5, management by objectives (MBO) is the philosophy of management that emphasizes the setting of agreed-on objectives by managers and their subordinates and the use of those objectives as the primary bases of motivation, evaluation, and control efforts. It is a systematic approach to change that facilitates the achievement of results by directing efforts toward attainable objectives. MBO encourages managers to plan for the future. It is considered a philosophy of management because it emphasizes participative management. In this context, MBO is an important method of organizational development. The participation of individuals in setting objectives and the emphasis on self-control promote not only individual development but also the development of the entire organization.

Job Enrichment

Job enrichment

Basic changes in the content and level of responsibility of a job so as to provide greater challenge to the worker.

In the past two decades, there has been considerable interest in, and application of, job enrichment in a wide variety of organizations. As discussed in Chapter 10, **job enrichment** is *basic changes in the content and level of responsibility of a job so as to provide greater challenge to the worker.* These changes expand the worker's responsibilities, providing the worker with an opportunity to derive a feeling of achievement, recognition, responsibility, and personal growth in performing the job. Although job enrichment programs have not always achieved positive results, they have improved job performance and level of job satisfaction in many organizations.

AT&T, Polaroid, Texas Instruments, Monsanto, Weyerhaeuser, General Motors, Corning Glass, and many other firms have achieved excellent results after implementing job enrichment programs. In most instances, productivity and job satisfaction were increased, and employee turnover and absenteeism were reduced.[45]

According to Herzberg, a number of principles are applicable for implementing job enrichment programs:

1. *Increasing job demands*—changing the job in such a way that the level of difficulty and responsibility of the job is increased.

2. *Increasing a worker's accountability*—allowing more individual control and authority over the work while retaining the manager's accountability.

3. *Providing work scheduling freedom*—within limits, allowing individual workers to schedule their own work.

4. *Providing feedback*—making timely periodic reports on performance to employees (directly to the workers rather than to the supervisor).

5. *Providing new learning experiences*—having work situations that encourage opportunities for new experiences and personal growth.[46]

Job enrichment was discussed in greater detail in Chapter 10.

The Grid Approach to OD

One of the best-known organizational development programs is the Managerial Grid® developed by Robert Blake and Jane Mouton. As Chapter 11 noted, Blake and Mouton suggest that the most effective leadership style is the one that stresses maximum concern for both output and people. The Grid approach provides a systematic approach for analyzing managerial styles and helping the organization move to the best style.

Management Development Programs

Organizational development techniques are designed to change the entire organization. **Management development programs** are *formal efforts to improve the skills and attitudes of present and prospective managers.* In these programs, managers learn effective approaches to managing people and other resources. Specific areas identified as possible organizational weaknesses are included. These areas might include, among others, leadership style, motivation approaches, and communication effectiveness.

The programs are administered either in-house or by outside consultants. A management development program of a major independent telephone company is outlined in Table 15–2. The intent of such programs is not only to teach new methods and techniques but to develop an inquisitive thought process. Too often, employees become so accustomed to performing the same task day after day that they forget how to think. A properly designed management development program puts people in a frame of mind to analyze problems. It is often used to provide the foundation for a change.

Management development programs

Formal efforts to improve the skills and attitudes of present and prospective managers.

I. **Management Development Program Title:**
   "Improving Group Effectiveness and Team Building"

II. **Objectives:**
   1. To identify the reasons for group formation.
   2. To understand the types of groups and their attributes.
   3. To discover the implications of research on group dynamics.
   4. To acquire an understanding as to forces in intra- and intergroup processes.
   5. To learn the characteristics of teamwork and ways to achieve it.
   6. To provide experience in analyzing and diagnosing work group dimensions.
   7. To acquire an appreciation for various team-building techniques.

III. **Description and Evaluation:**
   The course is designed to provide greater understanding of, and ability to work with and through, groups. Special emphasis is given to understanding the various need levels of groups and what can be done to appeal more effectively to those levels. Actual practice in team-building techniques is given, as well as experience in analyzing work groups. Evaluation is made of the major contingencies affecting groups. Observing group behavior through various media is a portion of the course content.

IV. **Size of Class:**
   The class should have a maximum enrollment of twenty participants so as to be large enough to allow the group process to be seen in action in the group itself and small enough to allow for active participation.

V. **Assignment of Instructor:**
   The instructor allocates an equal amount of time to lecture and active class discussion, with approximately one-third of the time devoted to various media presentations and group involvement. The course is designed for a two- or three-day session.

VI. **Enrollment Requirements:**
   Middle- and upper-level managerial experience desired.

TABLE 15–2

Course Content for a Management Development Program

Self-Assessment
Exercise

*How Well Will You
Deal with Corporate
Culture, Change, and
Development?*

1. Are you willing to realize that organizations continually evolve?

   ☐ Yes   ☐ No

2. Are you willing to understand that change may be resisted?

   ☐ Yes   ☐ No

3. Are you willing to maintain open and effective lines of communication?

   ☐ Yes   ☐ No

4. Are you willing to be honest and straightforward regarding the need for change?

   ☐ Yes   ☐ No

5. Are you willing to let your people know how the change will influence them?

   ☐ Yes   ☐ No

6. Are you willing to work to establish trust?

   ☐ Yes   ☐ No

7. Are you willing to recognize the status symbols at work in your organization?

   ☐ Yes   ☐ No

8. Are you willing to learn that when possible, subordinate participation should be encouraged in establishing the change?

   ☐ Yes   ☐ No

9. Are you willing to not make changes for the sake of change?

   ☐ Yes   ☐ No

10. Are you willing to learn organizational traditions in your firm?

    ☐ Yes   ☐ No

Summary

Corporate culture, the system of shared values, beliefs, and habits within an organization that interacts with the formal structure to produce behavioral norms, influences employees' degree of job satisfaction and the level and quality of their performance. The assessment of how good or poor the corporate culture is may differ for each employee. Work groups, managers' and supervisors' leadership style, organizational characteristics, and administrative processes affect corporate culture.

Within most large organizations, both a dominant culture and many subcultures exist. Dominant cultures are those that express the shared views of the majority of the organization's members. Subcultures are cultures characteristic of various units of an organization.

Most attempts to change organizations have been directed toward creating a more open and participative culture. Involving more people in the decision-making process improves productivity and morale. Still, there are some limitations.

Rensis Likert developed a management systems theory that uses a continuum of management styles ranging from autocratic to participative. System IV, participative team, was deemed best in the long run for all situations.

No matter what the intended change, the change process tends to follow a pattern. Management first recognizes a need for change and then identifies a specific change method. Finally, the following steps are carried out: (1) unfreezing the status quo, (2) moving to a new condition, and (3) refreezing to create a new status quo. A change may cause a social or economic loss to the person affected by it. Despite the resistance that might arise, change is often necessary.

A change may cause some loss to the person or organization affected by it. Attachments to old and familiar habits, places, and people need to be given up. In major and unexpected changes, employees, groups, and even divisions often experience daze, shock, recoil, and turmoil. Some of the many sources of resistance to change include insecurity, possible social loss, economic losses, inconvenience, resentment of control, unanticipated repercussions, and threats to influence.

Organizational development (OD) is planned and systematic attempts to change the organization, typically to a more behavioral environment. The person responsible for ensuring that the planned change is properly implemented is the change agent. Change efforts may be based on the survey feedback method. A major technique in the arsenal of the organizational development consultant is team building, a conscious effort to develop effective work groups throughout the organization. Other OD techniques include sensitivity training, management by objectives, job enrichment, and the Grid approach to OD. Management development programs are formal efforts to improve the skills and attitudes of present and prospective managers. In these programs, managers learn effective approaches to managing people and other resources.

Review Questions

1. Define *corporate culture.* What are the factors that influence it?

2. Identify the benefits and limitations of a participative culture.

3. List and describe the elements of the change sequence.

4. What are the sources of resistance to change?

5. Describe the approaches that may be used in reducing resistance to change.

6. Define each of the following terms:

   a. organizational development

   b. team building

   c. sensitivity training

Key Terms

Corporate culture

Dominant culture

Subcultures

Strong corporate culture

Status symbol

Jargon

Change sequence

Organizational development (OD)

Change agent

Survey feedback method

Team building

Sensitivity training

Job enrichment

Management development programs

CASE 15.1   **BREAKING UP THE TEAM**

Wayne, Don, and Robert were supervisors with a small chain of fifteen convenience stores in north Dallas. Each had nominal responsibility for five stores and reported directly to the company president. But actually they all just worked as a team. Wayne coordinated the scheduling of clerks at all fifteen stores, Don took care of inventory control and purchasing, and Robert took responsibility for recruiting and hiring. Otherwise, they each just did whatever needed to be done.

Things changed markedly within just a year. The president, wishing to relieve himself of daily details, promoted Robert to vice-president. Another supervisor, Phillip, was hired to manage Robert's five stores. At first, everything went well. But soon Robert, who was much more involved in store management than the president had been, told the three supervisors he wanted each of them to take care of his own five stores.

Wayne, Don, and Phillip initially resisted Robert's

frequent orders and demands. After a few "chewing outs," though, the men decided to do as Robert wanted. They rarely saw one another, and each took care of all aspects of store operations, as well as filling in for clerks who were late or sick. There were frequent problems however. Robert accused the three supervisors of working against him and threatened them with dismissal if operations did not get better. Wayne, Don, and Phillip saved him the trouble; they quit within days of one another. The president fired Robert a few days later.

Questions

1. What different organizational environment was created as a result of Robert's promotion to vice-president?
2. How do you think this situation could have been avoided? Discuss the use of the participative approach in this instance.

CASE 15.2	FEAR OF LAYOFFS AT DUNCAN ELECTRIC

Donna Garcia was a supervisor for Duncan Electric Corporation, a manufacturer of high-quality electrical parts. Donna had been with the firm for five years and had one of the best teams in the plant. Donna had picked the majority of these employees and was proud of the reputation they had earned. But a problem was brewing that she felt could destroy her team.

For weeks, there had been rumors of a reduction in force at Duncan. Donna heard her workers talking about it, she heard it from other supervisors, and a local newspaper story even mentioned the possibility. The corporate office had said nothing about it, but the rumors persisted. The only basis for the fears that Donna could identify was a temporary cutback in production, which had soon been restored. Donna was able to refute the rumors for a while, because her people trusted her. But soon she began to have doubts herself. Donna checked with her superior, who claimed he knew nothing of any possible reduction. She asked one of her most trusted workers why he thought there might be a layoff, but he said, "I just hear it around the plant."

On Friday, Bob Phillips and Henry Barham, two of Donna's best workers, told her they had taken jobs with a competitor. This was what she had feared. The most qualified workers were leaving, and it was due to rumors. Instead of having one of the best crews at Duncan Electric, she might end up with the worst.

Questions

1. To what extent did the rumors of the anticipated change in the work force affect the morale of the employees?
2. What should management do to reduce the fear of the anticipated change?
3. What should Donna do in this situation?

Notes

1. This case is a composite of a number of published accounts, among them: Brian O'Reilly, "Apple Computer's Risky Revolution," *Fortune*, May 8, 1989, pp. 75–83; "Apple Reshuffles Its Corps," *Business Week*, September 5, 1988, p. 34; Maria Shao, "Allan Loren," *1989 Business Week Top 1,000*, 1989, p. 158; Maria Shao, "Apple Turns

from Revolution to Evolution," *Business Week*, January 23, 1989, pp. 90–92; Lawrence M. Fisher, "Apple's Stock Falls $3; Estimates of Profit Cut," *New York Times*, June 17, 1989, p. 33; Pascal Zachary, "Apple Computer Net Rose by 5.3% in Its 3rd Quarter," *Wall Street Journal*, July 19, 1989, p. B4; Stephen Kindel, "Water Into Wine," *Financial World*, May 30, 1989, pp. 32–35; Richard Brandt, Thane Peterson, and Deidre A. Depke, "The Toughest Job in the Computer Business," *Business Week*, March 19, 1990, pp. 118–122; and Barbara Buell, Jonathan B. Levine, and Neil Gross, "Apple Cover Story," *Business Week*, October 15, 1990, pp. 87–96; and other articles from the *Wall Street Journal*.

2. David A. Garvin, "Quality Problems, Policies, and Attitudes in the United States and Japan: An Exploratory Study," *Academy of Management Journal* 29 (December 1986): 653.

3. Arthur Sharplin, *Strategic Management* (New York: McGraw-Hill, 1985), p. 102.

4. Frank Petrock, "Corporate Culture Enhances Profits," *HR Magazine* 35 (November 1990): 64–66.

5. Anthony Jay, *Management and Machiavelli* (New York: Holt, Rinehart and Winston, 1967).

6. "Corporate Culture: The Hard-to-Change Values that Spell Success or Failure," *Business Week*, October 27, 1980, pp. 148–160.

7. Thomas J. Murry, "Wal-Mart Penny Wise," *Business Month*, December 1988, p. 42.

8. Robert Johnson, "McDonald's Combines a Dead Man's Advice with Lively Strategy," *Wall Street Journal*, December 18, 1987, p. 1.

9. John J. Keller, "Has the AT&T-Olivetti Romance Lost Its Magic?" *Business Week*, May 9, 1988, p. 97.

10. On Pinnacle: Bill Hartley, CNN business news correspondent, interviews Playboy CEO Christie Hefner.

11. Barbara Jean Gray, "Taking a Stand on Ethics," *Human Resource Executive* 2 (May 1988): 34–35.

12. Peter Waldman, "Motivate or Alienate? Firms Hire Gurus to Change Their 'Cultures,'" *Wall Street Journal*, July 24, 1987, p. 19.

13. Many of the factors were taken from the Organizational Climate Description Questionnaire generated by Halpin and Croft as described in Andrew W. Halpin, *Theory and Research in Administration* (New York: Macmillan, 1966), chap. 4. Another widely used measure is that of Litwin and Stringer, found in G. Litwin and R. Stringer, *Motivation and Organizational Climate* (Cambridge, MA: Harvard University Press, 1968).

14. K. L. Gregory, "Native-View Paradigms: Multiple Cultures and Culture Conflicts in Organizations," *Administrative Science Quarterly* 28 (September 1983): 359–376.

15. T. E. Deal and A. A. Kennedy, *Corporate Cultures: The Rites and Rituals of Corporate Life* (Reading, MA: Addison-Wesley, 1982), pp. 65–66.

16. Bill Saporito, "PPG: Shiny, Not Dull," *Fortune*, July 17, 1989, p. 107; Anne Ritter and William H. Wagel, "Special Awards for Special Achievers," *Personnel* 66 (May 1989): 17–23; Langdon Brockinton, "PPG's Rompala: A Dramatic Flair," *Chemical Week*, March 15, 1989, pp. 53–54.

17. H. Kenneth Bobele and Peter J. Buchanan, "Building a More Productive Environment," *Management World* 1 (January 1979): 8.

18. Geoff Lewis, Anne R. Field, John J. Keller, and John W. Verity, "Big Changes at Big Blue," *Business Week*, February 15, 1988, p. 92.

19. John Hoerr, "Getting Man and Machine to Live Happily Ever After," *Business Week*, April 20, 1987, p. 61.

20. Rensis Likert, *The Human Organization* (New York: McGraw-Hill, 1967).

21. Murry, "Wal-Mart Penny Wise," p. 42.

22. Hoerr, "Getting Man and Machine to Live Happily Ever After," p. 61.

23. Wayne F. Cascio and Manuel G. Serapio, Jr., "Human Resources Systems in an International Alliance: The Undoing of a Done Deal?" *Organizational Dynamics* 19 (Winter 1991): 65.

24. Ibid., pp. 67–68.

25. Ibid., p. 68.

26. Ibid.

27. Marcia Kleiman, "Ease the Stress of Change," *Personnel Journal* 68 (September 1989): 107.

28. Peter D. Petre, "Meet the Lean, Mean New IBM," *Fortune*, June 13, 1983, pp. 69–82.

29. "Corporate Culture," pp. 148–160.

30. Gordon Donaldson and Jay Lorsch, *Decision Making at the Top* (New York: Basic Books, 1983).

31. Bro Uttal, "The Corporate Culture Vultures," *Fortune*, October 17, 1983, pp. 66–72.

32. Kurt Lewin, *Field Theory and Social Science* (New York: Harper & Row, 1964), chaps. 9, 10.

33. Eric G. Flanholtz, Yvonne Randle, and Sonja Sackmann, "Personnel Management: The Tenor of Today," *Personnel Journal* 66 (June 1987):. 64.

34. "High Tech Takes Off," *Fortune*, January 16, 1989, pp. 56–64.

35. John Holusha, "The New Allure of Manufacturing," *New York Times*, December 18, 1983, sec. 3, p. 1; and "Here Are GE's Latest Advances in Robotic Welding Systems," *Purchasing*, December 19, 1985, p. 18.

36. Ralph G. Huschowitz, "The Human Aspects of Managing Transition," *Personnel* 51 (May–June 1974): 13.

37. Anne B. Fisher, "The Downside of Downsizing," *Fortune*, May 23, 1988, pp. 42–52.

38. Ibid.

39. Portions of the following discussion were adapted from R. Wayne Mondy and Robert M. Noe III, *Personnel: The Management of Human Resources*, 2d ed. (Newton, MA: Allyn and Bacon, 1984), pp. 224–240.

40. Edgar F. Huse, *Organization Development and Change* (St. Paul, MN: West Publishing, 1975), p. 230.

41. Richard Wellins and Jill George, "The Key to Self-Directed Teams," *Training and Development Journal* 45 (April 1991): 27.

42. Bert A. Spector, "From Bogged down to Fired up: Inspiring Organizational Change," *Sloan Management Review* 30 (Summer 1989): 31.

43. Wellins and George, "The Key to Self-Directed Teams," p. 27.

44. For a detailed review of one hundred research studies on sensitivity training, see P. B. Smith, "Control Studies on the Outcome of Sensitivity Training," *Psychological Bulletin*, July 1975, pp. 597–622.

45. See "Case Studies in the Humanization of Work," in *Work in America: Report of Special Task Force to the Secretary of Health, Education, and Welfare* (Cambridge, MA: MIT Press, 1973), appendix, pp. 188–200.

46. Frederick Herzberg, "One More Time: How Do You Motivate Employees?" *Harvard Business Review* 65 (Sept–Oct 1987): 109–120.

Management Skills

Although there is no single best leadership style, it is important for you to appreciate the nature of your leadership style. Since an appropriate leadership style is crucial to the effectiveness of managers, you should assess your leadership style by taking the self-assessment exercise "What Is Your Leadership Style?" Then, turn to page 633 to evaluate yourself.

What Kind of Leader Are You?

INSTRUCTIONS: Circle whether you would be likely to behave in the described way:

Always	=	**A**			Seldom	=	**S**
Frequently	=	**F**	Occasionally	= **O**	Never	=	**N**

IF I WERE THE LEADER OF A WORK GROUP . . .	ALWAYS				NEVER
1. I would most likely act as the spokesperson of the group.	A	F	O	S	N
2. I would encourage overtime work.	A	F	O	S	N
3. I would allow members complete freedom in their work.	A	F	O	S	N
4. I would encourage the use of uniform procedures.	A	F	O	S	N
5. I would permit the members to use their own judgment in solving problems.	A	F	O	S	N
6. I would stress being ahead of competing groups.	A	F	O	S	N
7. I would speak as a representative of the group.	A	F	O	S	N
8. I would needle members for greater effort.	A	F	O	S	N
9. I would try out my ideas in the group.	A	F	O	S	N
10. I would let the members do their work the way they think is best.	A	F	O	S	N
11. I would be working hard for a promotion.	A	F	O	S	N
12. I would be able to tolerate postponement and uncertainty.	A	F	O	S	N
13. I would speak for the group when visitors were present.	A	F	O	S	N
14. I would keep the work moving at a rapid pace.	A	F	O	S	N
15. I would turn the members loose on a job and let them go to it.	A	F	O	S	N

IF I WERE THE LEADER OF A WORK GROUP . . .	ALWAYS				NEVER
16. I would settle conflicts when they occur in the group.	A	F	O	S	N
17. I would get swamped by details.	A	F	O	S	N
18. I would represent the group at outside meetings.	A	F	O	S	N
19. I would be reluctant to allow the members any freedom of action.	A	F	O	S	N
20. I would decide what shall be done and how it shall be done.	A	F	O	S	N
21. I would push for increased production.	A	F	O	S	N
22. I would let some members have authority which I could keep.	A	F	O	S	N
23. Things would usually turn out as I predict.	A	F	O	S	N
24. I would allow the group a high degree of initiative.	A	F	O	S	N
25. I would assign group members to particular tasks.	A	F	O	S	N
26. I would be willing to make changes.	A	F	O	S	N
27. I would ask the members to work harder.	A	F	O	S	N
28. I would trust the group members to exercise good judgment.	A	F	O	S	N
29. I would schedule the work to be done.	A	F	O	S	N
30. I would refuse to explain my actions.	A	F	O	S	N
31. I would persuade others that my ideas are to their advantage.	A	F	O	S	N
32. I would permit the group to set its own pace.	A	F	O	S	N
33. I would urge the group to beat its previous record.	A	F	O	S	N
34. I would act without consulting the group.	A	F	O	S	N
35. I would ask that group members follow standard rules and regulations.	A	F	O	S	N

P (Participative) Score: _____

A (Autocratic) Score: _____

Source: Reprinted from J. William Pfeiffer and John E. Jones, eds., *A Handbook of Structured Experiences for Human Relations Training*, vol. 1 (San Diego, CA.: University Associates, 1974). Used with permission. Originally from *American Educational Research Journal* 6 (January 1969): 62–79. Copyright 1969 by the American Educational Research Association. Reprinted by permission of the publisher.

CHAPTER 16

The Controlling Processes and Techniques

LEARNING OBJECTIVES

After completing this chapter students should be able to

▪ Explain why controlling is necessary and describe the controlling process.

▪ Describe controlling and the business system and the importance of establishing strategic control points.

▪ Describe ways of overcoming negative reactions to controls.

▪ Explain the importance of disciplinary action and describe approaches to such action.

▪ Describe the various types of budgetary controls.

▪ Explain quality control and state the usefulness of control charts.

▪ Describe the importance of inventory control and explain various methods of inventory control.

▪ Explain network models and describe how PERT can assist in both planning and control.

McDonald's decisively won the "Great Burger War" of the 1980s, in which Burger King and Wendy's vied with it for leadership. By the beginning of the nineties, McDonald's operated over 11,000 restaurants in 52 countries, with $17 billion in sales, far ahead of the competition. The average domestic McDonald's had far greater annual sales than did Burger King and Wendy's. For 24 years—96 quarters—McDonald's had never failed to show an increase in quarterly profits. Yearly sales expanded at a double-digit percentage clip. And each sales dollar consistently produced more than a dime in net profit, twice the average for U.S. companies. McDonald's chief executive Michael R. Quinlan said, "We're putting the pedal to the metal."

McDonald's secret? Creative merchandising helps, of course. Beyond that, analysts believe consistency, speed, and quality are paramount. *Business Week* asserted, "McDonald's best weapon against upstart rivals remains the consistency of its operations." Such consistency grows out of a system of control which matches that of the best Japanese factories. Most McDonald's are franchised, so control of speed and quality starts with selection and training of franchisees. Of the 2,000 or so applicants a year, fewer than 10 percent get franchises.

McDonald's wants owner-operators who will work from before daybreak into the night seven days a week. According to one expert, successful franchisees must "conform, become part of the system and do what they're told." Aspirant franchisees who survive the initial barrage of applications, credit checks, and interviews spend most of the first two years working 20 hours a week at an existing McDonald's, for no pay. They must do it all—counter, kitchen, bathrooms, book work—and usually keep their regular jobs. In addition, trainees attend classes at regional offices, studying a four-volume guide and cramming for periodic tests. A two-week stint at Hamburger University, in Oakbrook, Illinois, winds up the training. But it still is often a year or more before a franchise is approved.

The administrative system at McDonald's is designed to tightly monitor the quality of food and service as well as the safety, cleanliness, and appearance of each restaurant. Precisely uniform raw materials—pre-cut potatoes, breaded chicken nuggets, hamburger patties, paper goods—are supplied through a sophisticated system that provides just-in-time delivery. McDonald's quality engineers inspect supplier factories and specify, for example, the average, minimum, and maximum lengths of french fry cuts. Every new product involves new training, for managers and workers. Company auditors sometimes pose as customers before announcing themselves and checking out the operation. A system of contract inspectors, college professors, and consultants hired to sample McDonald's fare and submit reports provides a cross-check.

The "manufacturing system" at a McDonald's restaurant—the grills, deep fryers, toasters, drink dispensers, coffee makers, and coolers—are designed to minimize errors. Temperature and speed controls are automatic. Buzzers indicate when critical actions, such as taking up fried items, are required. All system components, from the juice dispensers to the belt-mounted radios, are standardized, supplied, and maintained under carefully administered contracts.

The system is tough. And some franchise owners refuse to tolerate its rigor. But many wealthy and successful McDonald's franchisees agree with Geraldo Perez, a recent Sacramento, California, franchisee. Perez said, "I couldn't have fallen into taller clover." However, the clover may not be so comforting as it once was. In the early nineties, burger consumption dropped to 17 percent of all restaurant orders, from 19 percent in 1982. With just 20 percent of McDonald's sales occurring after 4 P.M., Quinlan had to take action. Quinlan's "Pedal to the metal" philosophy was definitely in jeopardy. His current message is: "Do whatever it takes to make a customer happy." This has led McDonald's to experiment with their food and decor. McDonald's is trying out 150 new menu items, but if the menu grows, so will the challenges of quality and speed.

489

Because McDonald's has well over 2,000 franchisees, they are determined to ensure that domestic sales keep improving. Quinlan is looking to new technology to make the operating system more flexible, while assuring speed, quality, and consistency. Quinlan is quite aware of what made McDonald's the king of the fast-food business and he will probably proceed with great caution to maintain the tradition of McDonald's excellence.[1]

At McDonald's the control function is a vital part of the management process. A properly designed control system has allowed McDonald's to cut cost and enhance customer service. The effective control system that is presently in place at McDonald's is constantly being refined.

This chapter first describes why controlling is necessary. Next, the controlling process is described followed by a discussion of controlling and the business system. Then, procedures for establishing strategic control points are described. This is followed by a discussion of how negative reactions to controls may be overcome, and a section on disciplinary action. Budgetary control, quality control, and the usefulness of control charts will then be discussed. Next, the importance of inventory control and the various methods of inventory control will be addressed. The final section is devoted to a discussion of network models.

Why Is Controlling Necessary?

Controlling

The process of comparing actual performance with standards and taking any necessary corrective action.

Controlling is *the process of comparing actual performance with standards and taking any necessary corrective action.* A good control system is designed to keep things from going wrong, not just to correct them afterwards. Most managers are aware of the

---

Controlling is the process of comparing actual performance with standards and taking any necessary corrective action. A good control system is designed to keep things from going wrong, not just to correct them afterward. Honeywell installed its TDC 3000 System to control digester operations at a bleach plant at the James River Corporation, a paper producer.

Source: *Photograph courtesy of Honeywell, Inc.*

need for control. Some are farsighted enough to avoid many problem situations. For example, in selecting an appropriate location for a factory, there are many issues to consider, such as the quality of the work force, the overall quality of life for managers and employees, and the availability of good schools and city services.

Managers often control activities too strictly, which can hurt morale and productivity. However, mistakes are more often made in the other direction. Among the symptoms that might indicate that the control process is not working are the following:

- Declining output or declining levels of service.
- Excessive machine breakdowns.
- An increase in absenteeism or tardiness.
- Increasing employee turnover.
- Declining product quality.
- Increasing customer complaints.
- Declining morale.
- Excessive labor, material, or energy costs.
- Too many accidents.
- Failure to meet objectives.
- Disorderliness.

Managers can use this list to help identify the critical symptoms in their units. However, the symptoms may be somewhat different for every department and organization. And if the symptoms of a problem are ignored, the problem is likely to worsen. It is vital that managers maintain control, in part because the price of regaining control may be high.

The Controlling Process

The controlling process has three steps: (1) establish standards, (2) evaluate performance, and (3) take corrective action. Figure 16–1 illustrates these steps. Notice that like the other management functions, the controlling function is subject to environmental influences.

Establish Standards

Workers must know what is expected before the control process can be implemented. **Standards** are *established levels of quality or quantity used to guide performance*. For example, a shaft might have a standard diameter, and the machinist must try to cut the shaft to that size. Standards are sometimes viewed as objectives. American standards, often rigidly stated, are frequently ignored to get the products out the door. Foreign manufacturers keep setting new, far tougher standards of performance, reliability, and durability, which American manufacturers, in the past could not meet. For the first time in twenty years, maintaining quality standards has been a problem for Boeing. Most notably, miswired fire control systems have gotten Boeing a lot of unwanted attention and publicity.[2]

Standards
Established levels of quality or quantity used to guide performance.

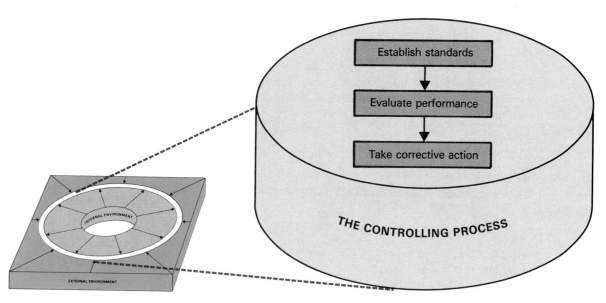

FIGURE 16–1

The Controlling Process

Wherever possible, standards should be expressed numerically to reduce subjectivity. Following are the most frequently used types of standards:

1. *Time standards.* Time standards state the length of time it should take to make a certain good or perform a certain service. An airline pilot has a standard time span in which to make a certain trip. Most organizations have a standard lunch time.

2. *Productivity standards.* Standards of productivity are based on the output of goods or services during a set time period. For instance, a productivity standard might be to complete ten units or to serve 150 customers per hour. Keying in on productivity standards and deemphasizing quality have caused problems for American manufacturers.

3. *Cost standards.* Cost standards are based on the cost associated with producing the goods or services. For example, the material cost might be $10 per unit. Cost standards are usually set in the expense budget for the supervisor's unit.

4. *Quality standards.* Standards of quality are based on the level of perfection desired. For instance, no more than a certain percentage of impurities may be allowed in a chemical, or a valve may have to hold pressure for ten minutes in order to pass inspection. American quality has been estimated to be below Japanese quality. For example, as many as one-quarter of American factory workers do not produce anything; they simply fix other workers' mistakes.[3] Fortunately, this trend is being reversed.

5. *Behavioral standards.* Standards of behavior are based on the type of behavior desired of workers in the organization. Expressing these standards precisely is difficult.

Control tolerances

Specifications of how much deviation will be permitted before corrective action is taken.

Although standards may be clear, control tolerances also need to be established. **Control tolerances** are *specifications of how much deviation will be permitted before corrective action is taken.* For instance, a standard size for a particular part may be 3.1 inches, but a tolerance of ±0.05 inch may be permitted. If a part is produced within the range of 3.05 to 3.15 inches, it is accepted. If it falls outside this range, it is rejected. As another example, a company might allow only two unexcused absences per month. A standard workday might be eight hours, but most managers have a certain control tolerance of lateness, perhaps five minutes. Whether the standard relates to a good, a service, or behavior, it is important to communicate both the standard and the control tolerances to workers. If this is done, many workers will control themselves.

Evaluate Performance

Evaluating performance consists of checking for deviations from standards and determining if the deviations exceed control tolerances. Basically, this evaluation process involves observing and measuring performance. Evaluation requires accurate measurement of what is taking place and an effective means of comparison with standards. Managers must realize that both problems and opportunities can be discovered during this phase.

When the process being controlled is a mechanical one, measurement and comparison may be quite simple. For example, a quality control inspector may use a micrometer or other instrument to measure a part. Other processes, especially behavioral ones, are more difficult to measure. When Art Sharplin was a young navy personnel officer, he reprimanded a clerk for working too slowly. The leading chief petty officer showed the young officer that, although the clerk appeared to be working slowly, he was actually doing more than his share. Managers should be careful to measure accurately before taking corrective action. They should also keep in mind that the evaluation of performance must be taken into account in developing future standards.

Take Corrective Action

The manager must consider what action to take to correct performance when deviations occur. Often, the cause of the deviation must be found before corrective

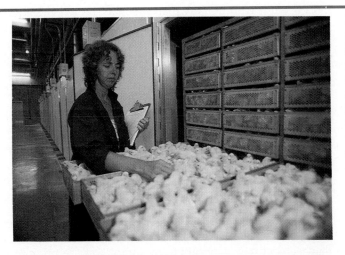

Evaluating performance consists of checking for deviation from standard and determining if those deviations exceed control tolerances. When the process being controlled is a mechanical one measurement and comparison may be quite simple. But the job is more complex for nonmechanical processes, as in the chicken hatchery shown here.

Source: © Jim Pickerell

action can be taken. Assume that the number of allowable defects produced by a certain machine exceeds standard. The cause may be a faulty machine, or it may be a careless operator. Clearly, proper corrective action depends on which one is the cause.

Problems associated with taking corrective action may also be compounded by various top managers trying to protect their own turf at the expense of the entire organization. For example, AT&T was turned around when the upper management group of twenty-seven executives, who were intent on controlling their own departments, met at a Cape Cod golf resort and agreed to compromise for the common good of the company, thereby allowing overall controls to be placed on the company, even to the point where they violated the traditional turf of different departments.[4]

Not all deviations from standard justify corrective action; and in some cases, personal judgment is necessary. Suppose that a worker is fifteen minutes late for work (a deviation from the standard of being on time), but you realize the lateness was unavoidable. As manager, you may decide to take no action, even though a deviation has occurred.

Corrective action may be either immediate or permanent. Immediate corrective action is often aimed at correcting *symptoms*. Permanent corrective action is aimed at correcting the *cause* of the symptoms or problem. Most frequently, corrective action is of the immediate type; it is done right away to correct the situation. For example, a particular project is a week behind schedule. If the delay is not corrected, other projects will be seriously affected. The first thing to do is to get the project back on schedule rather than worrying about who or what caused the difficulty. Depending on the authority of the manager, the following immediate corrective actions may be ordered: (1) overtime hours may be authorized; (2) additional workers and equipment may be assigned; (3) a full-time director may be assigned to push the project through; (4) extra effort may be asked from all employees; or (5) if all these fail, the schedule may have to be readjusted, requiring changes all along the line.

After the degree of urgency has diminished, attention can be devoted to more permanent corrective action. Just how and why did events stray from their planned course? What can be done to prevent a recurrence of this type of difficulty? It is at this phase that many managers fail. Too often, they find themselves "putting out fires," and they never discover the actual cause of the problem. For instance, managers may find themselves constantly having to interview and hire new people to replace those who quit. A manager may be working twelve hours a day locating new employees. But the high turnover problem is not solved merely by this type of immediate corrective action. Some type of permanent corrective action must be taken once the manager determines what is causing the high turnover. A supervisor may be extremely difficult to work with, or the pay scale may not be competitive for the area. Whatever the problem, it must be identified and corrected, or high turnover will likely continue. Permanent corrective action must be taken for the sake of economical and effective operations in the future.

Controlling and the Business System

Recall from Chapter 2 that, in the business system, inputs are converted to outputs through a transformation process. As Figure 16–2 shows, the controlling efforts by management may concentrate on inputs, on the process itself, or on outputs.

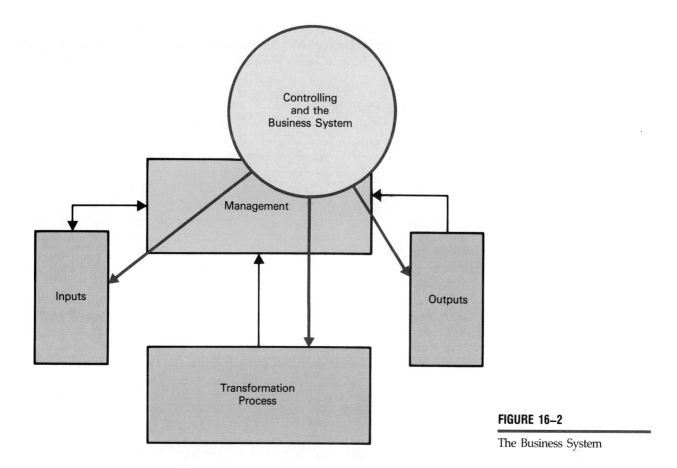

The figure shows "Controlling and the Business System" with Management, Inputs, Transformation Process, and Outputs.

FIGURE 16–2

The Business System

Controlling Inputs

With input controls, managers attempt to monitor the resources—materials and personnel—that come into the organization to ensure that they can be used effectively to achieve organizational objectives.

Material Controls   The material resources an organization requires must meet specified quality standards and must be available when needed by the firm. If Ethan Allen, a major furniture manufacturer, purchased low-quality wood with which to manufacture furniture, the company would not maintain its reputation for producing excellent furniture. Statistical sampling is often used to assist in material control. With statistical sampling, a portion of the items received by the firm are checked to estimate the quality of the entire lot. For instance, Ethan Allen might examine 5 percent of the lumber it receives. In many cases, the failure of even a small percentage of the incoming items could create difficulty. Components for commercial aircraft engines are an example. Statistical sampling is not typically used in such situations. Rather, each item is inspected individually.

Personnel Selection Controls   If a firm is to remain stable or grow, it continually needs new workers, because of factors such as death, retirement, and loss of employees to other organizations. In order to obtain new workers capable of sustaining the organization, certain controls must be established regarding their selection. The skill requirements of each job must be determined, and new employees should meet or exceed these requirements before they are employed.

Controlling the Process

Overseeing the process of producing goods and services offers an opportunity to correct problems before outputs have been affected. Most of the time of a typical lower-level manager is spent overseeing the process. Effective lower-level managers usually become familiar with the sights and sounds of the workplace and can often tell when something unusual is occurring. A wide range of possible signals is available to the manager. A noisy bearing on a bolt machine might warn the manager that the machine will begin to make defective bolts. Before a single faulty bolt has been produced, the bearing can be replaced.

Perhaps the most important aspect of this kind of control is observation and correction of employee behavior. An observant supervisor may notice a worker looking around or behaving carelessly and will take action before output has been affected. Observing workers, managers, and machines in the process of doing the organization's work is a tool of management at every level. A senior manager might observe a junior one cursing or otherwise behaving inappropriately and stop the misbehavior before it affects morale or productivity.

Controlling Outputs

The ultimate purpose of controlling focuses on the quality and quantity of output produced. In fact, most people think of controlling as simply checking what has occurred and taking corrective action. In the business system, controlling output consists of quality and quantity controls, financial controls, and evaluation of employee performance on the basis of output.

Quality and Quantity Controls   The purpose of quality control is to ensure that a certain level of excellence is attained. Quality has received renewed emphasis as Americans have become convinced that foreign manufacturers typically produce better automobiles, stereos, bicycles, and other products. Quality control must also be concerned with the costs of increasing quality. Therefore, it is important that the quality necessary to meet company objectives be determined in the planning stage. Trade-offs are necessary between the quality level one might prefer and the cost of achieving that level.

A common approach to evaluating quality is to seek comparison with other organizations or units. Figure 16–3 shows how three shift crews compare in terms of the acceptable parts they produce. The supervisor for Shift III should see that the third shift is deficient in comparison to the other two and should take corrective action.

Productivity is normally thought of in terms of quantity of output. Most companies also expect a certain amount of production from each individual or organizational unit, often expressed in terms of a quota. Sales quotas specify the amount of sales an individual, district, or region is expected to meet. Production quotas specify the

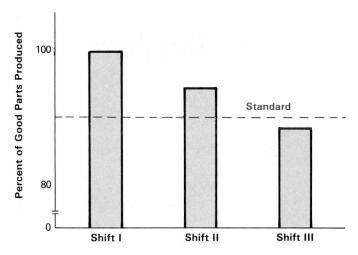

FIGURE 16–3

Monthly Quality Comparison Report, by Shifts

amount or number of an item that needs to be produced. Control of quotas at every level is important if the organization is to achieve its objectives.

Financial Controls   The ultimate output that most companies desire is profit. The quality and quantity of goods and services is often seen as a means to this end. Financial statements provide valuable information about whether a company, department, or unit is effectively using its financial resources. Intelligent interpretation of financial data provides an excellent means by which management can control its financial welfare.

Budgetary controls (discussed in the next section) also offer a way of ensuring that the company is performing well financially. Plans are made for certain levels of revenues and expenses. If at any time the company is not on track toward achieving those levels, a good budgeting system will initiate corrective action.

Evaluation of Employee Performance   As described in Chapter 9, performance appraisal is the formal and systematic measurement and evaluation of job performance.[5] An effective performance appraisal system is a means of control through which individuals learn of their strengths and weaknesses and are told what they should do to overcome deficiencies. The overall objective of such systems is to improve the organization's effectiveness by developing and communicating vital information about the firm's human resources. This requires providing feedback to employees about their performance. When the manager evaluates employees against established standards on the appraisal form, the manager is involved in controlling.

Establishing Strategic Control Points

Management is centrally concerned with controlling the business system, which consists of inputs, processes, and outputs. A frequent problem is determining what part of the system to monitor. Ideally, every resource, processing activity, and output should be measured, reported on, and compared to a standard. This can be extremely

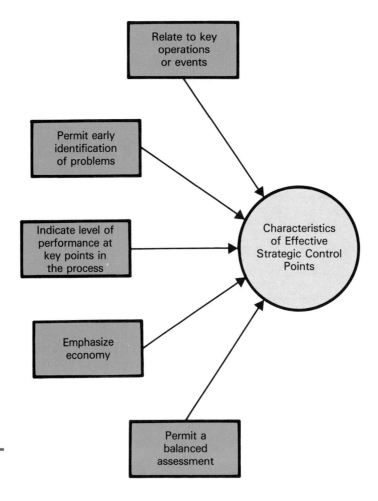

FIGURE 16–4

Characteristics of Effective
Strategic Control Points

Strategic control points

The critical points selected
for monitoring in the process of producing goods or
services.

costly and time-consuming. A manager must determine what activity to measure
and when to measure it.

The *critical points selected for monitoring in the process of producing goods or services* are
strategic control points. These points should have a number of basic characteristics
(see Figure 16–4).

First, strategic control points should relate to key operations or events. If a difficulty
occurs at a vital point, the entire operation may grind to a halt. The problem created
by poor-quality equipment may have a detrimental impact on the company's sales
even if the production personnel and sales force are of exceptional quality.

A second important characteristic of strategic control points is that they must be
set up so that problems can be identified before serious damage occurs. If the control
point is properly located, action can be taken to stop or alter a defective process
before major harm is done. Testing for defects early in the process typically cuts
costs and improves both production and quality.[6] It does little good to discover that
a million defective parts have been produced. The control point should be located
in such a way that deviations can be quickly identified and corrected.

One of the authors, in the early days of his career, had the opportunity to observe
how the improper selection of strategic control points almost caused a major tire

manufacturer to be forced to cease operations. In the manufacture of a tire, four basic phases are required: mixing, tread shaping, tire building, and tire molding (see Figure 16–5). The mixing department obtains the proper blend of rubber for the type of tire that is being produced. The tread is then shaped, with attention being given to length, width, and thickness. The next phase, building, entails placing the various components—such as the tread, steel belting, and white walls—together. In the molding department, the tires are heated and shaped into final form.

A major problem forced the tire company to reevaluate its entire control procedure. In the old system of control, a tire was inspected only after it had been molded. At that stage, there was already a large investment in the tire, and it would have to have a major defect before it would be rejected. The deficiency in the control process was recognized when the tire manufacturing firm delivered a several-million-dollar order to a company that purchased tires and sold them at retail outlets under its own brand name. The retail chain, after careful inspection of the tires, rejected the order and demanded that the entire batch be redone. The tire manufacturing firm nearly went out of business because of the large investment tied up in rejected inventory. The firm had to go heavily into debt to remake the order.

After this experience, major changes were made in the control process. A separate quality control department, reporting directly to the president, was established. Quality control inspectors were hired and given authority to stop operations, even over the advice of the production superintendent. Strategic control points were located in the four major departments (see Figure 16–5). If a problem occurred in the mixing department, it would be discovered before the tire progressed to the other stages. Because of this intensive effort to improve quality, the firm was able to survive and prosper.

A third consideration in selecting strategic control points is that together they should indicate the level of performance for a broad spectrum of key events. At times, comprehensiveness conflicts with the need for proper timing. Profit, for example, is a comprehensive strategic control point, indicating the progress of the entire

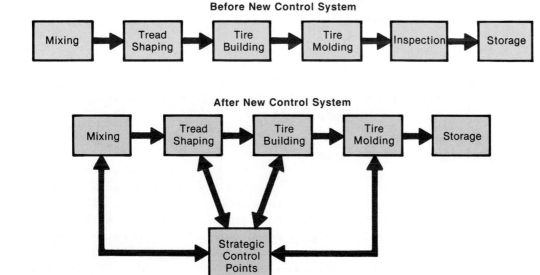

FIGURE 16–5

Example of Placement of Strategic Control Points

enterprise. Yet, if one waits until the end of the regular accounting period to obtain this figure, one loses control of the immediate future. It does little good to recognize that the firm is now bankrupt; managers need to have accounting figures ahead of time so corrective action may be taken.

Economy is the fourth consideration in the choice of proper control points. With computers and management information systems (discussed in Chapter 20) readily available, there is a strong temptation to demand every conceivable bit of information. But an executive can effectively use only a limited amount of information. With so much available, critical information may be lost in the masses of data. Simply stated, you can't see the forest for the trees.

Finally, the selection of strategic control points should be balanced. If only credit losses are watched and controlled, for example, sales may suffer because of an overly stringent policy in accepting credit risks. If sales are emphasized too strongly, credit losses will mount. There is a tendency to place tight control over tangible functions, such as production and sales, while maintaining limited control over intangible functions, such as employee development and other staff services. This often leads to a state of imbalance where production executives are held to exact standards and staff executives are seemingly given blank checks.

How Managers Overcome Negative Reactions to Controls

Although people may be inclined to resist controls, there are means that managers can use to reduce negative reactions. Some of the solutions may appear obvious, but the ineffectiveness of some control systems makes it clear that they are not always employed.

Justifiable Controls

A control system will have higher acceptability if the reason for the control appears justifiable to those who must comply with it. For instance, the firm may have to increase the quality of its product in order to obtain future contracts. These contracts may mean not only profit for the firm but job stability for the employees.

Understandable Expectations

Employees who know exactly what is expected of them with regard to a control system tend to exhibit less resistance. For instance, a statement by a manager that quality should increase does not clearly convey what is expected. A requirement that the percentage of defective parts should decrease by 10 percent is precise and understandable. When workers do not understand what is expected of them, frustration and resentment can result. The control system at Compaq Computer Corporation, headquartered in Houston, Texas, is legendary for the high level of employee acceptance it receives.

On the factory floor at Compaq, flashing lights and sirens mean a worker has spotted a flaw and pulled the red cable to call attention to it. The efforts made to keep employees informed at Compaq are just as extreme as this response to a defect. At quarterly meetings, held in three shifts in a nearby church, Compaq chief executive Rod Canion informs and challenges employees. He said, "Everyone's job is critical, and so is a spirit of teamwork." According to the vice-president of manufacturing, "Whatever the objective, we talk it through so everybody understands why it's important."

At the start of each shift, workers are updated on company news. This updating was begun after a worker misunderstood a conversation he overheard about labor-saving machinery and started a rumor that layoffs were imminent. Basically, Compaq didn't realize the amount of change they had on a daily basis. Shifts end with time for worker suggestions for improvements. Information sharing has become more difficult as the company has grown, but Canion and his teams keep it up. And the resulting quality led two *Wall Street Journal* reporters to call the Compaq machine "the BMW of PCs."[7]

Flashing Lights and Sirens at Compaq

Realistic Standards

A realistic control system involves standards that are attainable by the employees who work within the control system. At times, it may appear that controls are established merely to harass the worker. Standards that are higher than needed to accomplish the purpose of the organization not only are expensive but may well be resisted by company employees. Although Chase Manhattan Bank, for example, may desire to have zero loan losses, such an expectation is unrealistic. Banks typically have to decide what degree of risk is acceptable.

Timely Communication of Findings

For a control system to be effective, information about deviations should be communicated to employees as quickly as is practical. It does little good to tell workers that their performance was below standard three weeks ago. If a problem is to be corrected, it must receive timely attention. At Chase Manhattan Bank, many managers were fired during the 1980s for making bad loans years earlier.[8] They would probably have appreciated knowing what the standards were before they made the loans.

Accurate Findings

Nothing could be worse than to have a control system that provides inaccurate information. If information feedback has proved incorrect in the past, employees may not trust the control system. If workers consistently find errors made by supervisors, all management input may be questioned. In such a case, for example, an employee who receives a low performance evaluation may have reason to suspect the evaluation is inaccurate even if it is not.

Disciplinary Action

Discipline

The state of employee self-control and orderly conduct present in an organization.

Disciplinary action

Action taken to correct unacceptable behavior.

The state of employee self-control and orderly conduct present in an organization is **discipline**. A necessary, but often trying, aspect of control is taking disciplinary action.[9] **Disciplinary action** is *action taken to correct unacceptable behavior*. In spite of a firm's desire to solve its employee problems in a positive way, at times this is not possible. A major purpose of disciplinary action is to ensure that employee behavior is consistent with the firm's objectives. Rules are established to assist the organization in accomplishing these objectives. When a rule is violated, the effectiveness of the organization is diminished to some degree, depending on the severity of the infraction. For instance, if a worker reports late to work, the loss to the firm may be minimal. However, if a worker fails to use the safety guard on a machine and is severely injured, the loss may be substantial. Managers must realize that disciplinary action can be a positive force for the company. The firm benefits from developing and implementing effective disciplinary action policies. Without a healthy state of discipline, or the threat of disciplinary action, the firm's effectiveness may be severely limited.

The Disciplinary Action Process

The disciplinary action process is dynamic and ongoing. One person's actions can affect others in the group. For instance, if a worker receives disciplinary action, it is likely that this action will influence other workers when they learn that such mistakes will not be tolerated.

The disciplinary action process is shown in Figure 16–6. The external environment affects the process, as it does with all management activities. Laws that affect company policies are constantly changing. For instance, the Occupational Safety and Health Administration has caused many firms to establish new safety rules. Unions are another external factor. Specific punishments for rule violations are subject to negotiation. For instance, a union may negotiate three written warnings for tardiness instead of the two warnings the present contract might require.

Changes in the internal environment of the firm can also alter the disciplinary action process. Through organizational development, the firm may alter its culture. This change may result in first-line supervisors handling disciplinary action in a more positive manner. Organization policies can also have an impact on the disciplinary action process. Seeing employees as mature adults rather than as irresponsible children could significantly affect the process.

The disciplinary action process deals largely with infractions of rules. Rules—specific and detailed guides to action—are created to facilitate the accomplishment of organizational objectives. The do's and don't's associated with accomplishing tasks are highly inflexible. A company rule may prohibit smoking or require the wearing of hard hats in hazardous areas. And, of course, after rules have been established, they must be communicated to the affected employees. Individuals cannot obey a rule if they do not know it exists. As long as employee behavior does not vary from acceptable practices, there will be no need for disciplinary action. But when an employee's behavior violates a rule, corrective action may be taken. The purpose of this action is to alter behaviors that can have a negative impact on the achievement of organizational objectives.

Note that Figure 16–6 shows a feedback loop from "take appropriate disciplinary action" to "communicate rules to employees." Some employees find out that a rule is being enforced only when a peer receives disciplinary action. Employees will then conform to the rule to avoid similar disciplinary action.

FIGURE 16–6

The Disciplinary
Action Process

SOURCE: *Reprinted by permission from R. Wayne Mondy and Robert M. Noe III, Human Resource Management, 5th ed. (Boston: Allyn and Bacon, 1993), p. 672.*

Approaches to Disciplinary Action

Several concepts regarding the administration of disciplinary action have been developed. Two of these concepts are progressive discipline and discipline without punishment.

Progressive discipline is *the disciplinary action approach designed to ensure that the minimum penalty appropriate to the offense is imposed.* It involves answering a series of questions about the severity of the offense (see Figure 16–7). If the improper behavior is minor and has not previously occurred, perhaps an oral warning will be sufficient. Or an individual may receive several written warnings before a violation warrants more than another written warning. The manager does not consider termination until each lower-level question has been answered yes. However, major violations, such as hitting a supervisor, may justify the immediate dismissal of the employee.

Discipline without punishment *gives a worker time off with pay to think about whether he or she really wants to follow the rules and continue working for the company.*[10] When an employee violates a rule, the manager issues an "oral reminder." Repetition brings

Progressive discipline

The disciplinary action approach designed to ensure that the minimum penalty appropriate to the offense is imposed.

Discipline without punishment

A process whereby a worker is given time off with pay to think about whether he or she really wants to follow the rules and continue working for the company.

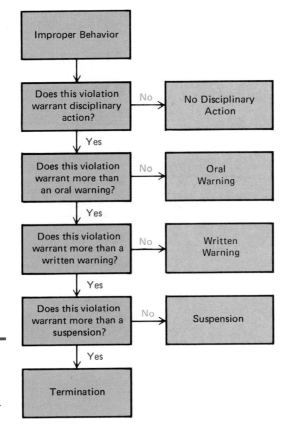

FIGURE 16–7

The Progressive
Discipline Approach

SOURCE: *Reprinted by permission from R. Wayne Mondy and Robert M. Noe III,* Human Resource Management, *5th ed. (Boston: Allyn and Bacon, 1993), p. 675.*

a "written reminder." The third violation results in the worker having to take one, two, or three days off (with pay) to think about the situation. During the first two steps, the manager tries to encourage the employee to solve the problem.[11] If the third step is taken, after the time-off period, the worker and supervisor meet to agree that the employee will not violate the rule again or that the employee will

TABLE 16–1

Guidelines for
Disciplinary Action

- The manager should assume that all employees desire to conform to reasonable organizational requirements.
- The act, rather than the person, should be condemned.
- Future desired behavior should be described.
- Reasonable promptness is important, so the employee can connect the penalty to the violation.
- A managerial listening role is highly essential to effect greater understanding of the reasons for the act and to prevent hasty decisions that may lead to unjustified penalties.
- Negative disciplinary action should normally be administered in private.
- Definite, but tactful, follow-up should occur to determine the degree of success of the disciplinary action.
- Consistency and flexibility, though apparently contradictory, are both desirable elements of a good program of disciplinary action.

leave the firm. When discipline without punishment is used, it is especially important that all rules be explicitly stated in writing. At the time of orientation, new workers should be told that repeated violations of different rules will be viewed as several violations of the same rule. This keeps workers from taking undue advantage of the process.

The main purpose of disciplinary action is not to punish or fire employees but to improve their contribution to the organization. Rehabilitation achieves this objective more often than termination. Table 16–1 lists guidelines for handling disciplinary action cases, whether or not managers explicitly practice the progressive disciplinary action approach.

MANAGEMENT IN PRACTICE: A Skill-Building Exercise

"I think I might have messed up this morning," said the maintenance supervisor, Carl Martin, to Doug Williams, the industrial relations manager. "One of the workers in my section wasn't doing the job exactly to specs and I told him rather forcefully how to do it correctly. He told me, rather sarcastically, to 'take it easy.' Then, he said, 'Don't worry, be happy.' I blew up and fired him. Five minutes later, the union steward was in the office reading me the riot act. She said situations such as this one are covered in our contract and that I was violating it. I had never spoken to the worker before about that particular offense, and the steward said the contract called for both oral and written warnings before dismissal. Also, several of the worker's friends were around when I fired him. What are we going to do?"

How would you respond?

Budgetary Control

The most basic and widely used quantitative controlling technique is the budget. A **budget** is *a statement of planned allocation of resources expressed in financial or numerical terms.* Budgetary control is concerned with the comparison of actual and planned expenditures. Most areas of operation in a business enterprise—marketing, production, materials, labor, manufacturing expense, capital expenditures, and cash— have budgets. The operating budget for a McDonald's restaurant includes a specific allowance for every major activity.

In order to make a profit, a corporation must keep all of its operations within budgetary guidelines. If an operation cannot control its expenses through appropriate budgetary controls, then profit objectives may be difficult, or impossible, to achieve.

Budget

A statement of planned allocation of resources expressed in financial or numerical terms.

Types of Budgets

Often, the budget is the most important document a manager uses in planning and controlling operations. There are basically two broad categories of budgets: capital budgets and operating budgets. A **capital budget** is *a statement of planned expenditures of funds for facilities and equipment.* It therefore typically extends over several years.

Capital budget

A statement of planned expenditures of funds for facilities and equipment.

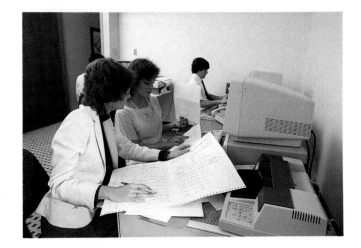

The most basic and widely used quantitative controlling technique is the budget. Budgetary control is concerned with the comparison of actual to planned expenditures. Variances are individually noted and usually must be justified.

Source: © Jim Pickerell

Operating budget

A statement of the planned income and expenses of a business or unit.

When it is first known that a new or replacement machine will be needed, the capital budget is modified to include the expected expenditure.

An **operating budget** is *a statement of the planned income and expenses of a business or unit*. It includes allowances for utilities, maintenance, and all other recurring expense items. For a unit of a large organization, the planned "income" is the allocation of funds from headquarters.

Benefits of the Budgeting Process

Most organizations—profit or nonprofit—operate within the framework of budgets. Budgeting is a significant part of both the planning and the controlling processes. Budgets are widely used by managers to plan, monitor, and control various activities and operations at every level of an organization. Some of the benefits of the budgeting process are as follows:

1. *Provides standards against which actual performance can be measured.* Budgets are quantified plans that allow management to measure and control performance objectively. If, for instance, a department manager knows that the budgeted expenditure for supplies is $1,000 per month, the manager is in a position to monitor and control the expenses for supplies.

2. *Provides managers with additional insight into organizational objectives.* The allocation of funds more often than not is the true test of a firm's dedication to a particular objective. For instance, suppose that two firms of relatively equal size have a stated policy of being innovative with regard to research and development. Firm A allocates $1 million a year to R&D programs, and Firm B budgets only $100,000. We can conclude that Firm A has a much stronger commitment to R&D than Firm B.

3. *Tends to be a positive influence on the motivation of workers.* People typically like to know what is expected of them, and budgets often clarify specific performance standards.

4. *Causes managers to divert some of their attention from current to future operations.* To some extent, a budget encourages managers to anticipate and forecast changes in the external environment. For example, an increase in transportation costs created by higher-priced petroleum might force a firm to seek an alternate transportation or distribution system.

5. *Improves top management's ability to coordinate the overall operation of the organization.* Budgets are blueprints of the company's plans for the coming year. They greatly aid top management in coordinating the operations of each division or department.

6. *Enables management to recognize or anticipate problems in time to take the necessary corrective action.* For example, production costs substantially higher than the budgeted amount will alert management to make changes to realign actual costs with the budget. Not only are overall departmental costs monitored, but the costs of individual activities are isolated and controlled. Long before departmental expenditures can get out of control, corrective action can begin.

7. *Facilitates communication throughout the organization.* The budget significantly improves management's ability to communicate the objectives, plans, and standards of performance important to the organization. Budgets are especially helpful to lower-level managers. They let them know how their operations relate to other units or departments in the organization. Also, budgets tend to pinpoint managers' responsibility and improve their understanding of the organization's objectives. This usually results in increased morale and commitment on the part of managers.

8. *Helps managers recognize when change is needed.* The budgeting process requires managers to review the company's operations carefully and critically to determine if resources are being allocated to the right activities and programs. The process causes management to focus on such questions as: Which products appear to have the greatest demand? Which markets appear to offer the best potential? What business are we in? Which businesses should we be in?[12]

Limitations of the Budgeting Process

Although numerous benefits can be attributed to the use of budgets, problems may arise. If the budgetary process is to achieve maximum effectiveness, these problems must be recognized, and attempts must be made to solve them. Some of the major problems are as follows:

- *Some managers believe that all funds allocated in a budget must be spent.* This attitude may work against the intent of the budgeting process. Often, managers learn from experience that if they do not spend the funds that have been budgeted, their budget will be reduced the following year. They have found that such conscientious cost-effectiveness can hurt their departments. A manager who operates in this type of environment may make an extraordinary effort to spend extra funds for reasons that may be marginal at best.

- *A budget may be so restrictive that supervisors are permitted little discretion in managing their resources.* Actual amounts that can be spent for items may be specified, and funds may not be transferable from one account to another. This sometimes results in seemingly ludicrous situations. For example, there may be funds to purchase personal computers but no money for printer ribbons.

- *In evaluating a manager, the main criterion may be conformity to the budget, rather than what the manager has actually accomplished.* If this philosophy is prevalent in a firm, poor managers may be viewed as superior because they met the budget and good managers may be reprimanded for failing to follow exact budgetary guidelines. This state of affairs can severely reduce the amount of risk a manager will be willing to take. Managers may spend a majority of their time ensuring that they are in compliance with the budget, when their time might be better spent developing new ideas.

Zero Base Budgeting

Zero base budgeting

The system of budgeting that requires management to take a fresh look at all programs and activities each year, rather than merely building on last year's budget.

Originally developed by Texas Instruments, **zero base budgeting (ZBB)** is *the system of budgeting that requires management to take a fresh look at all programs and activities each year, rather than merely building on last year's budget.* In other words, last year's budget allocations are not considered a basis for this year's budget. Each program, or "decision package," must be justified on the basis of cost-benefit analysis. The three main features of zero base budgeting are as follows.

1. The activities of individual departments are divided into decision packages, which provide information to management so that management can compare the costs and benefits of each program or activity.

2. Each decision package is first evaluated and then ranked in order of decreasing importance to the organization. Thus, priorities are established for each program and activity. Each of these is evaluated by top management, which arrives at a final ranking.

3. Resources are allocated according to top management's final ranking of the programs and activities. As a rule, decisions to allocate resources for high-priority items are made quickly. Closer scrutiny is given lower-priority programs or activities.[13]

Zero base budgeting is not a panacea for all the problems associated with the budgeting process. Organizations may experience problems in implementing the system. Most managers are reluctant to admit that not all of their activities are of the highest priority and don't like submitting their programs to close scrutiny.

Nonetheless, under ZBB, a system is established whereby an organization's resources can be allocated to higher-priority programs, and programs of lower priority can be reduced or eliminated. Thus, the benefits of zero base budgeting appear to outweigh the costs.

Quality Control

Quality

The degree of excellence of a good or service.

Quality is a concern of most Americans. But what exactly is meant by the term? **Quality** is *the degree of excellence of a good or service.* Quality control is the means by which a firm makes sure that its goods or services will serve the purposes for which

When the human element is made part of the quality control environment, it is inevitable that mistakes will occasionally be made. Some good items may be rejected, and some bad items may be accepted. If even occasional mistakes are unacceptable, as in the Fluor Corporation operation, 100-percent monitoring is used.

Source: Photograph courtesy of Fluor Daniel

they are intended. Alcoa, Inc., is fully aware of the importance of quality. In the early 1980s, Japanese producers of aluminum cans began to cut into Alcoa's market. The Japanese firms were exporting to the United States higher-quality aluminum sheets that worked better in high-speed can-making machines. In order to fight off the Japanese competitors, Alcoa built a state-of-the-art facility and launched a quality improvement program. Alcoa not only regained lost market share but also exports aluminum sheets to Japan.[14]

Quality standards are determined by the company's objectives. McDonald's Corporation CEO Mike Quinlan seems dedicated to maintaining the standard of excellence instilled in the company by its founder, Ray Kroc. Kroc said: "Don't compromise. Use the best ingredients, the best equipment."[15] If a company wishes to gain a reputation for high-quality products, standards will have to be high, and the company must have a rigid quality control program to help it meet those high standards. Although increased quality generally results in higher costs, it also allows for higher prices. On the other hand, some firms may sell to market segments that desire lower prices and will accept lower quality. Certain standards remain, but they are not as high as those of quality-oriented firms.

There are numerous ways to maintain product quality. A company could decide on 100 percent inspection of all items manufactured. Even so, some defects might not be discovered. When the human element is made part of the quality control environment, it is inevitable that mistakes will occasionally be made. Some good items may be rejected, and some bad items may be accepted.

In most instances, it is not feasible or desirable to have 100 percent inspection. For instance, if the standard for the life of a light bulb were two hundred hours, the bulb would have to be burned for that many hours to determine if it met the standard. Naturally, there would be no product to sell after the inspection. Tire manufacturing provides a similar example. Companies set standards for their tires that specify the number of miles they can be safely driven. If each tire were placed on a machine to run the assigned number of miles, there would be no product to market. In still other instances, the costs involved in 100 percent inspection would be prohibitive. If each nail in a keg were inspected separately, for example, the cost of inspection might be higher than the price of the nails.

The technique used to overcome these deficiencies is statistical quality control. In *statistical quality control,* a portion of the total number of items is checked. For instance, inspectors might select five items out of one hundred and estimate the characteristics of the other ninety-five. Some degree of error exists, of course. For instance, if only five out of a hundred items are defective (this amount of error may be perfectly acceptable), it is conceivable that all five defective samples might be selected for testing and the entire lot might therefore be rejected. On the other hand, there might be only five good parts. These five good parts might be the ones drawn. Then the entire batch would be accepted. Statistical quality control involves risk, but in many instances the benefits justify the risk.

Acceptance Sampling

The inspection of a portion of the output or input of a process to determine acceptability is **acceptance sampling.** Assume that it has been statistically determined that taking a sample of fifteen items from each batch of one hundred and limiting allowable defective units to one will result in the desired quality. In this case, if two or more items are defective, the entire lot will be rejected. When an entire lot is rejected, every item in it may have to be inspected. Or the lot may have to be returned to the supplier, who must evaluate the problem.

There are two basic approaches to acceptance sampling: sampling by variables and sampling by attributes. Each method is used under different circumstances.

Sampling by Variables A plan developed for sampling by variables consists of determining how closely an item conforms to an established standard. In essence, degrees of goodness and degrees of badness are permitted. For instance, a stereo speaker is designed to project a certain tone quality. But not all speakers will behave the same way. Some speakers will perform above the standard and some below it. The variance does not necessarily mean that the speaker will be rejected. It will be rejected only when the quality is outside a certain range.

Sampling by Attributes With sampling by variables, degrees of conformity are considered. With sampling by attributes, the item is either acceptable or unacceptable. The product is either good or bad; there are no degrees of conformity to consider. For example, if an engine block has a hole in the side of any cylinder, it is rejected.

Control Charts

The graphic record of how closely samples of a good or service conform to standards over time is the **control chart.** An example is shown in Figure 16–8. The chart is used with both variable and attribute sampling, although the statistical procedures for devel-

FIGURE 16–8

An Example of a
Control Chart

oping the chart are different for each type of sampling. In both instances, though, the standard is first determined. A variable sampling plan in the manufacture of tire treads might have standards that test thickness, weight, length, and width. If the average thickness of a certain tire tread is expected to be .87 inch, this becomes the standard.

Once the standard has been established, the acceptable amount of deviation must be determined. The maximum level that will be allowed is referred to as the upper control limit (UCL), and the minimum level is called the lower control limit (LCL). In the tire tread example, the UCL might be .89 inch and the LCL might be .85 inch. If the thickness of a tread being evaluated falls within the two extremes, it will be accepted. If it falls outside the limits, it will be rejected.

Another benefit of control charts is that potential problems may be recognized prior to their actual occurrence. Figure 16–8 shows that from day 10 until day 17, the quality of the product progressively worsened. The item is still within the limits of acceptability, but if the problem is not corrected, the deviation may soon go above the upper control limit. When managers see this pattern developing, they are in a position to take corrective action.

Inventory Control

Inventory is *the goods or materials available for use by a business.* Concern with inventory is almost continuous. A car dealer with excessive inventory will offer a special deal to sell a car. A furniture dealer provides a similar offer. Although there may be a bit of sales promotion in these offerings, inventory does represent a cost that must be controlled. A product in inventory constitutes a valuable, although idle, resource. Much of the resources of many major companies is inventory, so failure to control inventory can mean the difference between profit and loss.

Inventory

The goods or materials available for use by a business.

ETHICAL DILEMMA

Your firm received a large contract last summer to manufacture transaxles to be used in a new line of front-wheel-drive cars, which a major auto manufacturer plans to introduce in the near future. The contract is very important to your firm. As you began examining test reports, you discovered that the transaxle tended to fail when it was loaded at more than 20 percent over rated capacity (120 percent) and subjected to strong torsion forces. Such a condition could occur with a heavily loaded car braking hard for a curve down a mountain road. The results would be disastrous. The manufacturer's specifications call for the transaxle to carry 130 percent of its rated capacity without failing.

The likelihood of a disastrous occurrence is fairly low. And the fact that there is no time or money to redesign the assembly makes your options seem limited. You can either not deliver the transaxles that are rated at 120 percent over capacity and possibly ruin the company financially, or you can deliver the transaxles, which will probably never fail.

What would you do?

Purposes of Inventory

Inventory permits the relative independence of operations between two activities. For instance, if machine A makes a product that will be used by machine B, and machine A breaks down, machine B will have to cease operations unless an inventory of the product has been built up.

Inventory also provides for continuous operations when demand for the product is not consistent. Electric razors are sold primarily during the Christmas holiday season, but a manufacturer of electric razors typically keeps production going through the entire year. That way, a skilled work force can be maintained and equipment usage can be kept at an optimal level.

Another purpose of inventory is to allow the filling of orders quickly, thereby maintaining customer satisfaction. If orders come in at a constant rate, there may be no need to maintain inventory. But if five orders come in this month and a

FIGURE 16–9

An Example of Economic Order Quantity

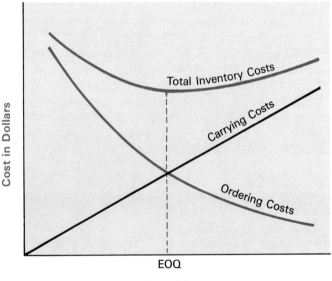

TABLE 16-2

Basic Equation for EOQ

$$EQQ = \sqrt{\frac{2\left(\begin{array}{c}\text{ordering}\\\text{cost}\end{array}\right)\left(\begin{array}{c}\text{annual}\\\text{demand}\end{array}\right)}{\text{carrying costs}}} = \sqrt{\frac{2(O) \times (D)}{C}}$$

hundred next month, a company without product inventory might be hard pressed to fill the hundred requests. Apple Computer must ensure that it has inventories on hand to ship to retailers. It also has to be concerned with the inventories retailers carry. Distribution contracts between Apple and computer stores require the stores to keep a minimum quantity of products on hand.

Economic Order Quantity Method of Inventory Control

The **economic order quantity (EOQ) inventory control method** is the *procedure for balancing ordering costs and carrying costs so as to minimize total inventory costs.* The *economic order quantity (EOQ)* is the amount of an inventory item that should be purchased to minimize total inventory cost. **Ordering costs** are *administrative, clerical, and other expenses incurred in obtaining inventory items and placing them in storage.* **Carrying costs** are *the expenses associated with maintaining and storing products before they are sold or used.* Taxes, insurance, interest on capital invested, storage, electricity, and spoilage are some of the carrying costs. The total inventory costs associated with a particular order are represented by the following general formula:

Total inventory costs = Ordering costs + Carrying costs

If orders are made less frequently, ordering costs go down but carrying costs go up. If frequent orders are submitted, ordering costs go up but carrying costs are reduced. This is graphically illustrated in Figure 16-9. The optimal number of items to order at any one time—the economic order quantity—is represented by the lowest point on the total cost curve. This is where the carrying cost and ordering cost lines intersect.

Managers need to identify the two primary costs: carrying costs (C) and ordering costs (O). The EOQ formula is determined from the total cost equation. The basic equation for EOQ is presented in Table 16-2.

If the assumption is made that ordering costs are $4, annual demand is 1,000 units, and carrying costs are $2 per unit, the economic order quantity is as follows:

$$EOQ = \sqrt{\frac{2(\$4 \times 1,000)}{\$2}} = \sqrt{\frac{\$8,000}{\$2}} = \sqrt{\$4,000} = 63.25$$

which is rounded to 63. No other order quantity would lower the total cost. This model is one of the simplest to develop. The sophistication level of the model a manager will use depends on the needs of the company.

ABC Inventory Method

Sometimes, it is impractical to monitor every item in inventory with the same degree of intensity. In such cases, it is useful to categorize the items in inventory according

Economic order quantity (EOQ) inventory control method

The procedure for balancing ordering costs and carrying costs so as to minimize total inventory costs.

Ordering costs

Administrative, clerical, and other expenses incurred in obtaining inventory items and placing them in storage.

Carrying costs

The expenses associated with maintaining and storing products before they are sold or used.

ABC inventory method

The classification of inventory items, for control purposes, into three categories, according to unit costs and number of items kept on hand.

to the degree of control needed. The **ABC inventory method** is *the classification of inventory items, for control purposes, into three categories, according to unit costs and number of items kept on hand*. The usual categories are as follows:

- *Category A.* Items in this group account for 70 percent of the dollar value of the inventory used. They represent a small number of items but high unit cost. They receive frequent, even daily, attention.

- *Category B.* Items in this group represent the next 20 percent of the dollar value of the inventory used. These items are not as important as category A items, but they do represent a substantial investment and should receive moderate attention.

- *Category C.* Items in this group are less expensive and may be used less often and therefore require less frequent attention.

To determine an item's classification, multiply the cost of the item by how often the item is used in a specific period. Then, list all items in order of total dollar amounts. Items representing 70 percent of the total dollars constitute the A group, items constituting the next 20 percent are the B group, and the remainder are the C group.[16]

A manager using the ABC method should carefully monitor A items. This category might include automobiles, machinery, and tractors. B items, such as tables and chairs, require less vigorous control. C items might not even be formally controlled, especially if the cost associated with monitoring them is prohibitive, as may be the case for pencils and paper.

Just-In-Time Inventory Method

Just-in-time (JIT) inventory method

The practice of having inputs to the production process delivered precisely when they are needed, thereby assigning to suppliers the responsibility for keeping inventories to a minimum.

The success of Japanese companies in cutting manufacturing costs is attributed in part to their use of the **just-in-time (JIT) inventory method**—*the practice of having inputs to the production process delivered precisely when they are needed, thereby assigning to suppliers the responsibility for keeping inventories to a minimum*. McDonald's uses a system of just-in-time delivery for its raw materials, such as hamburger patties and paper goods. Traditionally, U.S. factories attempted to manage inventories internally. More and more, however, they are using the just-in-time method. One expert suggests that the use of this method can even result in "zero" inventory.[17] Zero inventory may seem unrealistic. Nevertheless, JIT can reduce inventory considerably. In the United States, automobile manufacturers have led the way in adopting this method.

JIT at Buick and Chrysler

At General Motors' Buick plant in Flint, Michigan, a number of suppliers were encouraged to place their facilities within walking distance of the assembly line. Buick gave them complete responsibility for quality, inventory, and delivery of the items they supplied.[18]

An important factor in the near failure of Chrysler in 1980 was the high cost of inventory. To keep its production lines running, the company had produced cars and stored them on lots in the Detroit area. Other automakers produced vehicles only after dealers ordered them. In Chrysler factories, large stocks of components had to be kept on hand in case of strikes and other work stoppages in the plants of suppliers. Attempting to spring back from its near collapse in 1980, Chrysler quit producing cars for inventory. It also adopted JIT. "In the past," said Chrysler's production control chief, "suppliers paid very little attention to inventory. Now they have to because inventory costs so much. Automakers may not be able to afford suppliers who do not control inventory."[19]

• •

Automobile makers are not alone in efforts to improve inventory control. Paragon Industries, a six-store home center chain headquartered in Fresno, California, has a similar system in effect.[20] To win back customers in the apparel market, America's textile companies are mounting a just-in-time delivery campaign. Each morning, Swift Textiles Inc. ships just enough denim for a day's production at the nearby Levi Strauss plant in Valdosta, Georgia. With Swift certifying the quality of the denim, Levi closed its warehouse and quality testing lab and gained a competitive advantage.[21]

Evidence suggests that just-in-time purchasing has produced substantial benefits for U.S. companies.[22] One survey showed that when companies moved to JIT purchasing, inventory turnover increased by an average of 97 percent, delivery promises kept increased from 67 percent to 83 percent, and scrap cost declined 40 percent. However, some problems exist in just-in-time systems. For example, a number of managers are concerned about how dependent they should be on their suppliers.[23] The level of trust between firms and their suppliers may be higher in Japan than it is in the United States.

Network Models

The many complex tasks involved in building a skyscraper or a dam are almost impossible for the average person to comprehend. When a one-time project is large and complex and involves multiple organizations, two primary tools are available for coordinating the complicated network of interdependencies.

The two tools are the program evaluation and review technique (PERT) and the critical path method (CPM). PERT was developed under the Navy Special Projects Office to assist in the rapid development of the Polaris submarine program. During approximately the same time period (1957–1958), researchers for E. I. du Pont de Nemours and Company and computer specialists from Remington Rand's Univac division combined their talents to develop CPM. The initial purpose of CPM was to schedule and control all activities involved in constructing chemical plants.

Both PERT and CPM have received widespread acceptance. One major advantage of these techniques is the ease with which they can be computerized. PERT and CPM are used primarily for construction projects. But some firms, such as 3M Corporation, use the techniques to assist in the development of new products. Firms that do major construction work for the government are often required by their contracts to use PERT. Because of the similarity of PERT and CPM, only PERT will be discussed in detail. The primary difference between the two is that, in CPM, time and cost are known factors. In PERT, time must be estimated and costs determined.

Program evaluation and review technique (PERT)

The planning and control technique that involves the display of a complex project as a network of events and activities with three time estimates used to calculate the expected time for each activity.

The planning and control technique that involves the display of a complex project as a network of events and activities, with three time estimates used to calculate the expected time for each activity, is the **program evaluation and review technique (PERT).** An event is the beginning or completion of a step. It does not consume time or resources. It is represented by a circle, or node, in the network. An activity is a time-consuming element of the program. It is represented by an arrow.

PERT may serve as both a planning and a control tool. In planning, it forces the manager to think through the project and identify the tasks that must be accomplished and how they interrelate. PERT facilitates control mainly by highlighting the critical path.

Improvements in information-processing capabilities have expanded the inclusion of cost considerations in PERT analysis referred to as the PERT/Cost analysis. The purpose of PERT/Cost is to reduce the entire project completion time by a certain amount at the least cost. Reducing completion time might be especially important to a company that faces costly penalties for being late with a project. Also, there may be very high fixed costs for every day of the project.

Critical path method (CPM)

The planning and control technique that involves the display of a complex project as a network, with one time estimate used for each step in the project.

The planning and control technique that involves the display of a complex project as a network, with one time estimate used for each step in the project is the **critical path method (CPM).** The developers of CPM were dealing with projects for which the times and costs of tasks (activities) required to complete the project were known. In CPM, the points, or nodes, of the network represent activities, rather than the events represented in PERT. In PERT, three time estimates are used. In CPM, there is only one time estimate, because CPM was designed to accommodate situations in which sets of standardized activities are required for the completion of a complex project. Time for completion of a task is relatively easy to determine accurately. Because there is only one time estimate, probabilities for completing the project on time cannot be computed. With these exceptions, PERT and CPM are very similar.

A Global Perspective

Multinational managers must be concerned with the controlling techniques that should be applied globally. According to W. Edwards Deming, the man who is given credit for much of Japan's manufacturing preeminence, certain controlling techniques for improving quality can be effective globally. Deming recommends (1) that managers not rely on mass inspection; (2) that they drive out fear by encouraging open, two-way communication; (3) that they teach statistical techniques; and (4) that they make maximum use of the statistical knowledge and talent in their companies. In addition, the control systems that are imposed must support and encourage employees, not constrain them. Deming also claims that a company can improve quality by controlling its purchasing system. He recommends that management work with fewer vendors—by finding one good supplier, then looking for more. He also recommends that management insist on evidence of quality through control charts from every vendor.

Just as the Deming system worked in Japan, it is working in America at Pontiac's Plant 18. James Harbour, an auto industry consultant, writes, "The Pontiac engine plants are superb examples of what can be accomplished when you decide that quality and productivity go hand in hand."[24] American firms will have to maintain a competitive level of quality, at an appropriate price, to be successful globally.

1. Are you willing to make controls objective oriented?

   ☐ Yes   ☐ No

2. Are you willing to state controls as simply as possible?

   ☐ Yes   ☐ No

3. Are you willing to be practical when establishing controls?

   ☐ Yes   ☐ No

4. Are you willing to use controls to improve performance, not to punish?

   ☐ Yes   ☐ No

5. Are you willing to be as accurate as possible when measuring performance?

   ☐ Yes   ☐ No

6. Are you willing to not procrastinate when corrective action is necessary?

   ☐ Yes   ☐ No

7. Are you willing to quantify standards?

   ☐ Yes   ☐ No

8. Are you willing to set a good example?

   ☐ Yes   ☐ No

9. Are you willing to consider the human element in establishing controls?

   ☐ Yes   ☐ No

10. Are you willing to not over-control?

   ☐ Yes   ☐ No

Summary

Controlling is the process of comparing actual performance with standards and taking any necessary corrective action. The controlling process has three steps: (1) establish standards, (2) evaluate performance, and (3) take corrective action. Standards are established levels of quality or quantity used to guide performance. Although standards may be clear, control tolerances may also need to be established. Control tolerances are specifications of how much deviation will be permitted before corrective action is taken. Evaluating performance consists of checking for deviations from standards and determining if the deviations exceed control tolerances. The manager must consider what action to take to correct performance when deviations occur. Immediate corrective action corrects symptoms. Permanent corrective action corrects the cause of the symptoms or problem.

With input controls, attempts are made to monitor the resources—materials and personnel—that come into the organization to ensure that they can be used effectively to achieve organizational objectives. Overseeing the process of producing goods and services offers an opportunity to correct problems before outputs have been affected. The ultimate purpose of controlling focuses on the quality and quantity of output produced. In monitoring the process of producing goods or services, critical points called strategic control points are selected. Despite the importance of controls to effective management, employees often view them in a negative way because controls take away a certain amount of individual freedom. However, there are means that managers can use to assist in reducing negative reactions.

Discipline is the state of employee self-control and orderly conduct present in an organization. It indicates the potential for genuine teamwork. Disciplinary action is action taken to correct unacceptable behavior.

Progressive discipline ensures that the minimum penalty appropriate to the offense is imposed. In discipline without punishment, workers are given time off with pay to determine if they really want to follow the rules and continue working for the company.

A budget is a statement of planned allocation of resources expressed in financial or numerical terms. Budgetary control is concerned with the comparison of actual and planned expenditures. There are basically two broad categories of budgets: capital budgets and operating budgets. A capital budget is a statement of planned expenditures of funds for facilities and equipment. An operating budget is a statement of the planned income and expenses of a business or unit. Although there are numerous benefits in the use of budgets, problems may arise. They must be recognized, and attempts must be made to solve them. Zero base budgeting is the system of budgeting that requires management to take a fresh look at all programs and activities each year, rather than merely building on last year's budget.

Quality control, the means by which firms make sure their goods or services will serve the purposes for which they are intended, involves quality standards derived from company objectives. Inspection may be by acceptance sampling, either sampling by variables or sampling by attributes. Control charts show how closely samples conform to standards over time.

Inventory is the goods or materials available for use by a business. It permits independence of operations between two activities, provides for continuous operations when demand is not consistent, and allows orders to be filled quickly. One method of inventory control is the economic order quantity (EOQ) method, which balances ordering costs and carrying costs to minimize total inventory costs. The ABC inventory control method classifies items into three categories, according to unit costs and number of items kept on hand. The success of Japanese companies in cutting manufacturing costs is attributed in part to their use of the just-in-time (JIT) method of inventory control. Inputs to the production process are delivered precisely when they are needed, thereby assigning to suppliers the responsibility for keeping inventories to a minimum.

Network models are used in planning and controlling large, complex projects, usually construction projects. The program evaluation and review technique (PERT) involves the display of a complex project as a network of events and activities, with three time estimates used to calculate the expected time for each activity. The purpose of PERT/Cost is to reduce the entire project completion time by a certain amount at the least cost. The critical path method (CPM) also involves the display of a complex project as a network, but with one time estimate used for each step in the project.

Review Questions

1. Define *controlling*. What are the steps in the controlling process?
2. What are the most frequently used types of standards? Briefly discuss each.
3. What are specific means of controlling inputs and outputs? Briefly describe each.
4. What factors should a manager consider in establishing strategic control points?
5. List and describe the reasons for negative reactions to controls. What are the ways of overcoming these reactions?
6. Define *disciplinary action* and *progressive discipline*. What guidelines should a manager follow when disciplinary action must be taken?
7. Define *budget*. What are the two broad categories of budgets?
8. What are the benefits and limitations of the budgeting process?
9. What is zero base budgeting?
10. Define *quality control*.
11. Describe the two basic approaches to acceptance sampling. How are control charts used?
12. Explain the purposes of inventory. What is the economic order quantity (EOQ) method of inventory control?
13. Distinguish between PERT and CPM.

Key Terms

Controlling
Standards
Control tolerances
Strategic control points
Discipline
Disciplinary action
Progressive discipline
Discipline without
  punishment
Budget

Capital budget
Operating budget
Zero base budgeting
Quality
Acceptance sampling
Control chart
Inventory
Economic order quantity
  (EOQ) inventory con-
  trol method

Ordering costs
Carrying costs
ABC inventory method
Just-in-time (JIT) inven-
  tory method
Program evaluation and
  review technique
  (PERT)
Critical path method
  (CPM)

TOTAL CONTROL ON THE NISSAN PAINT LINE

The automated painting plant at Nissan's Smyrna, Tennessee, factory was painting nearly a thousand vehicles a day in the late 1980s. And just two technicians ran a system which monitored three thousand information points in the half-million square foot facility every two to five seconds. The system was called NEMAC, for Nissan Energy Management Monitoring and Communication Control. It was tied together with a fiber-optics communications network with duplicate paths throughout the plant. When a cable was damaged, the system automatically bypassed that segment and continued working.

Nissan's chief engineer explained why continuous monitoring was so important: "Typically, what kills you in a paint plant is that when a defect shows up on the line, even if you catch it right away, there are probably 60 to 90 units behind it with the exact same defect. Those are 60 to 90 units that have to be taken off the line, sanded down and repainted." When a NEMAC

monitor spotted a variation from specification—in paint color, texture, or thickness, for example—an alarm sounded in the control room and a 16-digit alphanumeric code signaled the location and nature of the problem. In most cases it was up to the technicians to actually adjust equipment to get quality back within specifications. But an increasing number of valves and other devices were being placed under automatic control of NEMAC. This system more than paid for itself in the first two years of operation.[25]

Questions

1. What controlling techniques are used at Nissan's Smyrna, Tennessee, factory?
2. To what do you attribute the success at Nissan's Smyrna, Tennessee, factory?

A PROBLEM OF SHRINKAGE

Martha Young is the supervisor of ten stores in a convenience store chain. Each of these small stores has a day manager and two assistant managers who work the evening and midnight shifts. These "managers" are mistitled; they have no subordinates reporting directly to them. The day manager is typically the senior person, and thus has chosen the day shift.

Mark McCall is the day manager of one of the stores. He has worked at the store for three months, and sales have been increasing steadily. Mark maintains his store in good order, and the first two monthly inventory checks have been satisfactory. But as Martha reads the inventory report for this month, she becomes quite disturbed. Inventory is $1,000 short over the previous month (anything over $200 is considered out of the ordinary). Such a discrepancy is called shrinkage.

Martha realizes that this report is extremely serious. Other managers have been dismissed for inventory shortages of this amount. She likes Mark, but something must be done to keep this situation from occurring

in the future. Martha sits down and reviews the store's situation. The following points come to mind:

- The store is located close to a school. When Mark took control of the store, school was not in session. There might be some shoplifting occurring.

- One of the assistant managers has been with the store only a month. There is a possibility of internal theft.

- The other assistant manager broke up with his girlfriend last month. It is possible that he has not been paying close attention to his job.

Questions

1. What type of controls, if any, should Martha initiate?
2. If the inventory is short next month, what do you think Martha should do?

Notes

1. This case is a composite of a number of published accounts, among them: Barbara Marsh, "Going for the Golden Arches," *Wall Street Journal*, May 1, 1989, p. B1; Leon E. Wynter, "How Two Black Franchisees Owe Success to McDonald's," *Wall Street Journal*, July 25, 1989, pp. B1, B2; Brian Bremner, "Two Big Macs, Large Fries—and a Pepperoni Pizza, Please," *Business Week*, August 7, 1989, p. 33; Brian Bremner, "The Burger Wars Were Just a Warmup for McDonald's," *Business Week*, May 8, 1989, pp. 67–70; Peter Pae, "Salad Bar Is Poised to Make Fast Exit from Fast Food," *Wall Street Journal*, March 24, 1989, pp. B1, B3; John A. Byrne, "Is Your Company Too Big?" *Business Week*, March 27, 1989, pp. 84–94; Debi Sue Edmund, "The Secret Behind the Big Mac? It's Simple!" *Managment Review*, May 1990, pp. 32–33; and Lois Therrien, "McRisky," *Business Week*, October 21, 1991, pp. 114–122, and Standard and Poor's Corp., "McDonald's Corp.," *Standard NYSE Stock Reports* 56 (May 10, 1989); sec. 22.

2. Anthony Ramirez, "Boeing's Happy, Harrowing Times," *Fortune*, July 17, 1989, p. 40.

3. Karen Berney Pennar, "America's Quest Can't Be Half-Hearted," *Business Week* June 8, 1989, p. 136.

4. Aaron Bernstein, "AT&T: The Making of a Comeback," *Business Week*, January 18, 1988, pp. 56–62.

5. R. Wayne Mondy, Robert M. Noe III, and Robert E. Edwards, "What the Staffing Function Entails," *Personnel* 63 (April 1986): 55.

6. Jon Turino, "Test Strategies that Cut Manufacturing Costs," *SAM Advanced Management Journal* 49 (Winter 1984): 53.

7. Karen Blumenthal and Robert Tomsho, "Breaking Away: An IBM Tagalong Sets Independent Course, with Plenty of Risks," *Wall Street Journal*, April 21, 1989, pp. A1, A8; Karen Blumenthal, "Compaq's Profit Increased 78% in First Quarter," *Wall Street Journal*, April 27, 1989, p. B4; F. Lisa Beebe, "Rod Canion: Charting the Compaq Course," *American Way*, January 1, 1987, pp. 19–23.

8. Frederic A. Miller, "The Giants Retrench," *Business Week*, April 3, 1989, pp. 94–95.

9. Portions of the discussion regarding disciplinary action were adapted from R. Wayne Mondy and Robert M. Noe

III, *Personnel: The Management of Human Resources*, 3d ed. (Newton, MA: Allyn and Bacon, 1987), pp. 626–630.

10. Laurie Baum, "Punishing Workers with a Day Off," *Business Week*, June 16, 1986, p. 80.

11. David N. Campbell, R. L. Fleming, and Richard C. Grote, "Discipline without Punishment—at Last," *Harvard Business Review* 63 (July–August 1985): 168.

12. Robert N. Anthony and Regina E. Herzlinger, *Management Control in Nonprofit Organizations* (Homewood, IL: Irwin, 1975), pp. 222–226.

13. Gordon Shillinglaw, *Managerial Cost Accounting: Analysis and Control*, 4th ed. (Homewood, IL: Irwin, 1977), pp. 142–143.

14. Kenneth H. Bacon, "Higher Quality Helps Boost U.S. Products," *Wall Street Journal*, January 11, 1988, p. 1.

15. Penny Moser, "The McDonald's Mystique," *Fortune*, July 4, 1988, pp. 112–116.

16. Peter E. Alcide, "The ABCs of Inventory Management," *Practical Accountant* 19 (August 1986): 36.

17. Dollar, "Zero Inventory Concept," p. 43.

18. "Buick City Places Suppliers in Backyard," *Purchasing* 10 (November 1983): 15.

19. "U.S. Auto-Makers," p. 15.

20. "Paragon Tracks Inventory with Customized System," *Chain Store Age*, April 1984, p. 59.

21. Otis Port, "The Push for Quality," *Business Week*, June 8, 1989, p. 134.

22. A. Ansari and Batoul Modarress, "Just-in-time Purchasing: Problems and Solutions," *Journal of Purchasing and Materials Management* 22 (Summer 1986): 11–12.

23. Milt Ellenbogen, "Face of Purchasing," *Industrial Distribution* 75 (September 1986): 40.

24. This story is a composite from a number of sources, including: "Dr. Deming Shows Pontiac the Way," *Fortune* 18 (April 18, 1983): 19–36; and Daniel W. Gottlieb, "Purchasing's Part in the Push for Quality," *Purchasing* 10 (September 1981): 75–78.

25. Lindsay Chappel, "Paint by Alphanumerics," *Automotive News*, September 5, 1989, pp. E2, E6.

CHAPTER 17

Total Quality Management

LEARNING OBJECTIVES

After completing this chapter students should be able to

- Explain the history of Total Quality Management (TQM).
- Describe the objectives of TQM.
- Explain the concept of quality.
- Describe the approaches to implementing TQM.
- Discuss the components of TQM.

Total Quality Management: The Real Competitive Advantage

In the 1970s, many American companies tried to increase their competitiveness by imitating the Japanese, but that effort fell short. In the eighties, many companies organized workers into quality circles "as a kind of magic solution." According to Earl C. Conway, corporate director of quality improvement at Procter & Gamble, this concept was ineffective because "companies didn't recognize that such concepts are simply one methodology within a much larger concept of quality." Today most American companies have "total quality" programs that integrate every department from manufacturing to marketing and research in the effort to improve. This so-called system of Total Quality Management (TQM) has thus far been remarkably effective at allowing companies to gain a "Quality Edge."

In recognition of the quest for quality, two trophies stand out: America's Baldrige award and the Deming prize from Japan. To win either award, companies must sweat through long hours of mind-numbing paperwork to prove that they are more thorough, more profitable, and simply better companies, whose watchword is "Quality." Four winners of America's Baldrige award are 3M, IBM, Xerox, and Motorola. Besides being winners of the Baldrige National Quality Award for excellence in the area of Total Quality Management, these companies have two other things in common. They all are leaders in their respective industries. According to a recent *Fortune* rating, 3M is the highest-ranked company in the scientific and photo equipment category, with Xerox also placing in the top 10 in this category; IBM is the number 1 company in the computers and office equipment category; and Motorola is number 2, behind General Electric, in the electronics category. Secondly, they all have a strong sense that TQM is the best competitive tool available.

Winners of the Baldrige award have a clear commitment to ultimate quality. These companies embrace the idea of Total Quality Management because they want a competitive advantage; 3M turned to TQM in their quest to remain the leader in their field. The system at 3M has the objective of steadily moving toward its goal of achieving "uniform quality across the whole system." 3M's approach to TQM is so successful that it is being marketed to other corporations.

IBM mainframe factory manager Louis A. Guadagno learned a few months ago that TQM is effective. At a critical point in the launching of IBM's new mainframe computer, he had to fix and test the design of several dozen large processors in less than a week. TQM was in place and functioning, but Guadagno was very anxious about letting the system work. Nevertheless, he went ahead. He met with those involved and told them, "You own the project, see you next Tuesday." Then, he went home and worried. To his surprise and amazement, the project team fixed all the problems on time.

Xerox has been inundated with competition in the last several years. Their manufacturing costs were too high, their overhead was too large, and the organization was too complicated. According to David Kearns, "We lacked a real understanding of what our customers really needed, not just wanted from us." Xerox turned to a full commitment to TQM and thereby regained their competitive edge.

George M. C. Fisher, chairman of Motorola Inc., is one of the biggest fans of TQM. In the eighties, Motorola was trailing the Japanese. To be competitive, they turned to TQM. Today few U.S. companies can match Motorola's devotion to quality. The results of their commitment to TQM have been overwhelming. Overall product defects have been slashed from nearly 3,000 per million in 1983 to under 200, and their global sales rose 13 percent. In 1991, Motorola went one step further with its commitment to "Six Sigma" quality—statistical jargon for defect-free manufacturing—and the company appears intent to do whatever it takes to accomplish this goal. Under the current leadership, Motorola has increased its quality 100 fold and industry experts expect a statistical margin of 3.4 defects per million parts produced—99.9997 percent perfection—by 1994. Examples of the acceptance of TQM in the United States abound, but what remains to be seen is whether a company can really survive in the nineties without embracing the concepts of TQM.[1]

What has occurred at 3M, IBM, Xerox, and Motorola is happening in organizations throughout the United States, and indeed the world. It is quite possible that organizations that fail to pick up the baton and run with it are certain to become second-class players in our rapidly changing global environment.

In this chapter, we will first cover the essense of Total Quality Management. Then, the history of TQM will be addressed, followed by a discussion of the objectives of TQM. Next, the focal point of TQM, quality, will be reviewed. Approaches to implementing TQM will be explored, followed by a discussion of the components of TQM. Finally, an example of TQM is provided to help explain the concept in practice.

Total Quality Management (TQM) is *a commitment to excellence by everyone in an organization that emphasizes excellence achieved by teamwork and a process of continuous improvement.* According to Earl C. Conway in the opening vignette, "Now most companies have 'total quality' programs that integrate every department from manufacturing to marketing and research in the effort to improve." Implied in the concept is a commitment to be the best and provide the highest quality products and services which meet or exceed the hopes of the customer. Businesses are being forced to make many changes merely to stay competitive. They must find ways to improve quality, increase speed of operations, and adopt a customer orientation. These changes are so fundamental that they must take root in a company's very essence, which means in its culture.[2]

TQM often involves major cultural change. It requires a new way of thinking and strong leadership at all levels. Individuals throughout the organization must be inspired to do things differently. They must understand what needs to be done and why, and this takes strong leadership. As noted in the opening vignette, Motorola management increased quality with the implementation of a TQM system, which paid off for them in a big way.

Total quality management

A commitment to excellence by everyone in an organization which emphasizes excellence achieved by teamwork and a process of continuous improvement.

History of Total Quality Management

TQM had its beginning in the 1930s with the pioneering work of Walter A. Shewart, who acted as a mentor to W. Edwards Deming. The concept really got a lift in World War II when the Allied cause was suffering. Shewart's method made quality a science. It also replaced traditional end-line inspection with an "on-line" awareness of variation. This process proved key to the war effort—so much so that at one point the techniques became military secrets. Basically, America's defense needs gave birth to a highly guarded and valuable "body of knowledge." When the war ended, the files were opened to the public, but by that time the interest in quality was fading in the United States. However, the country it had just defeated would soon embrace the concept of quality.[3]

Deming took his message to Japan in the 1950s and is credited with being instrumental in turning Japanese industry into an economic world power. He said, "Improve quality and you automatically improve productivity. You capture the market with lower prices and better quality. You stay in business and you produce jobs. It's so simple."[4] Deming applied Shewart's principles of statistical process control in Japan and convinced the Japanese to do more than merely monitor the quality level of their manufacturing systems. He worked with their scientists, engineers, and managers to identify and remove the causes of variation. As we know, the Japanese were able to improve quality and productivity, capture world market share, add jobs, and improve the standard of living in their country. In a matter of 40 years, the Japanese rose from the ashes of World War II and became a powerful economic force throughout the world. As you might expect, Deming is a hero in Japan. Today Deming, who is over 90 years of age, remains the dean of Total Quality Management.[5]

J. M. Juran arrived in Japan shortly after Deming and built an equally impressive record around quality planning, quality control, and quality improvement. Although Juran and Deming appear to have mutual respect for one another, Juran believes that Deming is basically a statistician "a bit out of place talking about management."[6] However, both leaders in TQM have had a major influence in championing quality. The basic message of both is essentially the same:

- Commit to quality improvement throughout your organization.
- Attack the processes, not the employees.
- Strip down the process to find and eliminate problems that diminish quality.
- Identify your customers and satisfy their requirements.
- Instill teamwork and create an atmosphere for innovation and permanent quality improvement.[7]

Both Deming and Juran had been promoting TQM for many years before Philip B. Crosby entered the field in 1979. Since that time, Crosby has had amazing success in the United States, Europe, and even Japan. His approach is based on four concepts:

- Quality means conformance to requirements.
- Defect prevention—not inspection—is the way to achieve quality.
- The only acceptable quality standard is one that tolerates zero defects.
- The cost of poor quality—in warranty payments, excess inventory, engineering errors, and other money eaters—can amount to 25 percent of sales at manufacturing companies and up to 40 percent of operating costs at service companies.[8]

Although highly successful, some have criticized Crosby for lacking substance, being more inspirational than practical and more of a public relations person than a quality control advocate.[9]

The Objectives of TQM[10]

As world market share shifted away from U.S. producers, forward-thinking American managers recognized the necessity for change. Since 1960, more than half of the world market share had been lost to other international producers in a number of product lines. These lines included athletic equipment, automobiles, cameras, computer chips, industrial robots, medical equipment, optical equipment, radial tires, stereos, and television sets. Something had to be done, so TQM was employed.

The ultimate goal of TQM is to alter the process by improving customer satisfaction. Instead of being content with the status quo, employees at all levels continually seek alternative methods or technologies which will improve existing processes. TQM provides a strategy for reducing the causes of poor quality and thereby increase productivity. This was the case with Baldor Electric.

Baldor Electric

Like many traditional companies, Baldor Electric, a Fort Smith, Arkansas, maker of electric motors, was under extreme cost pressure in the late 1980s. Rather than shift its production overseas, though, Baldor evaluated its operation in terms of customer needs and made big changes. Costly features that did not relate to customer requirements were eliminated and operations were trimmed to cut costs. Baldor kept its production facilities in the United States and increased its profit margin to 4.5 percent from 3.3 percent two years earlier. Return on equity jumped from 7.3 percent to 10.6 percent, and Baldor stock zoomed 13 percent above its previous high. Baldor even began exporting to Japan.[11]

TQM is a process of continuously improving quality over the long run. In the short run, once each of the linked processes within a firm is operating at or above a desired level of quality, reliance on costly inspection practices can be reduced or eliminated altogether. Attention can then be turned to monitoring the overall process to determine the sources of variation still present. If these sources are also eliminated, then the process can be more precise and fewer defects or errors produced. In the customer's view, quality will have exceeded the expected level. The customer, more than satisfied, will probably remain a customer. Motorola has been so successful with TQM in Japan that they are taking market share from the Japanese.

The increased employee participation required by TQM creates a new role for all organizational members. Top management, middle managers, and first-level supervisors must embrace the philosophy and work to ensure its acceptance throughout the organization. According to Japan's quality guru Kaoru Ishikawa, "Quality literally becomes every top manager's business."[12] Operative employees are consulted for assistance in determining and analyzing sources of process variation, and they are relied on to develop proposals for reducing or eliminating them.

Cultural change must precede or accompany the introduction of any new management approach. "Total quality is not a cookbook thing," says David K. Snekiker, a vice-president who runs the quality program at Battelle Memorial Institute in Columbus, Ohio. "It's a culture-transforming approach."[13] And the organizational culture required to support the concepts of TQM is not likely to be changed quickly. Five to ten years is generally needed for such changes in the top management value system to permeate the organization. TQM is not a body of regulations and cannot be forced on employees. Since a company's culture is largely a product of positively reinforced behavior, the route to change is almost always through education and training.[14] In addition to training and development activities, employee selection practices will be a central component in implementing the TQM philosophy.

Several factors favor the growth of TQM in the United States. First, and perhaps most important, is the success of companies who embrace TQM. They are capturing world market share from traditionally managed organizations. Second, consumers are no longer satisfied with lower quality levels even if the products or services are labeled "Made in America." Third, national trade policy is decidedly against imposing trade restrictions of any kind to protect U.S. producers from international competitors, so American companies must actually compete.

The increased employee participation required by TQM creates a new role for all organizational members.

A fourth, and a fairly new factor, is the support and encouragement of the U.S. government for the TQM movement. Much as the Japanese created a national-level award for highest quality firms, the Deming award, so too has the Department of Commerce. In 1987, Congress created the Malcomb Baldrige National Quality Award. These awards recognize outstanding firms in both the manufacturing and service sectors for their quality management programs. In addition, the federal government is now requiring contractors bidding on federal jobs to provide evidence of the statistical control of their processes. These contractors are requiring similar evidence from their subcontractors.

The TQM movement began just over a decade ago in this country. However, many firms, including 3M, IBM, Xerox, Motorola, Ford Motor Company, Florida Power and Light, and Federal Express, have demonstrated a long history of commitment toward improving quality. These firms have been recognized here and abroad for their efforts. The decade of the 1990s may well be remembered as the time American industry reversed its general decline in world markets. This dream can become reality if managers and employees join together to become world-class competitors by continuously improving the processes which produce goods and services. As Robert Costello, former undersecretary of defense for acquisition, stated, "The ultimate goal is to ingrain basic cultural change to a depth where the slogan TQM will fade and, in its wake, the principles and practices of TQM will remain as a permanent, normal way of conducting business in the United States."[15] A summary of the differences between TQM and traditional management may be seen in Table 17–1.

TQM	Traditional Management
Customer focus	Management focus
Quality first	Profits first
Multiple quality dimensions	Single quality dimension
Management and worker involvement	No worker involvement
Process-oriented	Results-oriented

TABLE 17–1

The Differences Between TQM and Traditional Managment

SOURCE: Laurence M. Tobin, "The New Quality Landscape: Total Quality Management," *Journal of Systems Management* 41 (November 1990): 13.

What Is Quality?

The concept of quality is based on the customer being served to the maximum degree possible. "Quality means the product meets all requirements."[16] As discussed in the beginning of the chapter, Xerox lacked an understanding of what their customers really needed, not just wanted. To best satisfy consumers, Xerox turned to a full commitment to TQM and thereby regained their competitive advantage.

Adherence to the concepts of TQM means that before any product is produced, the producer must first know precisely the requirements the product must meet. Only those products that meet all of the conditions are produced and delivered to the customer. A product that meets 99 out of 100 requirements is defective and should not be shipped to the customer. According to Armand V. Feigenbaum of General Systems Co., "Done right quality becomes a competitive weapon."[17] Companies that embrace quality have an edge of up to $.10 on every sales dollar over rivals. That's because fewer defects mean less rework and wasted management time, lower costs, and higher customer-retention rates.

The concept of quality differs with the type of company involved. For example, the definition of quality would be different at McDonald's than it would be at the Ritz in Paris. The seller must understand the customer. Even a perfect product cannot do more than it was designed to do. A Chevy should not outperform a Rolls even if both are perfect. However, the customer should be able to get what he or she is willing to pay for, and maybe a little more.

With TQM, how a process is implemented is as important as what the process includes. Many organizations still work under a departmentalized approach in which some employees plan improvements, others carry out the work, and still others inspect to see if procedures and results are correct. With TQM, all employees are committed to improving the quality of their product or service so that customers' needs are not only met but exceeded. Under Motorola's "Six Sigma" quality program, everyone in the company is working for defect-free manufacturing that would lead to an unheard-of degree of consumer satisfaction.[18]

The concept of quality, as applied to services, has also become a major concern at MasterCard.

• •

MasterCard International, Inc.

When Alex W. Hart became president of MasterCard International, Inc. in 1989, he took charge of an organization one analyst called "a shambles." There had been a large amount of management turnover. Higher costs had forced a hike in service fees. Competitors American Express and Visa continued to generate new products, such as microchip-containing "smart cards" and travel vouchers, forcing innovation by MasterCard. MasterCard had perennially lagged behind Visa in number of cardholders and annual charge volume. Hart quickly changed the focus.

"If we become perceived as the best, the numbers will take care of themselves," Hart said, adding he wanted MasterCard to be "flat-out, world-wide, the brand of preference." Hart's focus was not just on name recognition, but on service quality. That would involve the same kind of corrective measures which might be needed in a troubled manufacturing firm. The variety of product offerings had required employees to learn new procedures before they were familiar with old ones. Hart felt it was better to provide just a few services efficiently and well. Costs had to be cut. And a consistent gospel of quality would have to be preached in the MasterCard "plants"—the New York back offices and the far-flung agencies which disseminated the "product" to customers.[19]

● ●

Until recently, many efforts to improve and gain a competitive advantage were delayed by the mistaken belief that better quality costs more.[20] The historical approach was to add more inspection steps. In an inspection-oriented plant, more than half of all workers are somehow involved in finding and reworking rejects.[21] The Japanese inspect a product in the design phase. They engineer the manufacturing process to be stable and reliable. As Genichi Taguchi, one of Japan's masters said, "To improve quality, you need to look upstream in the design stage. At the customer level, it's too late."[22]

ETHICAL DILEMMA

For years, Baxter Corporation was considered a likely takeover candidate. Baxter chief executive Wayne Sanders came up with this idea: Use the threat of desertion by managers to thwart any takeover attempt. After months of design work by dozens of lawyers from four firms, Baxter unveils their new employment contracts for senior managers. All top executives are asked to sign the three-year contracts that provide all would resign en masse if a new owner were to fire any of them or change their responsibilities. That would prevent any raider from restructuring the firm after a takeover, usually considered necessary to make a takeover profitable. The contracts also require severance pay of $10 million to $30 million, each, if the managers resign. Finally, the employment contracts do not contain the usual noncompetition provisions. So the executives could go to work for competitors immediately or start their own firms in the same business.

You are one of the executives. Will you sign?

TQM accomplishes just what Taguchi suggested. Under a system of TQM, managers are looking upstream to improve quality by focusing on the design stage, before the product reaches the customer level. When TQM is used, firms design quality into the product. Less emphasis is given to inspection and more emphasis is given to "front-end" planning and design. Certainly TQM does not advocate elimination of all inspection. Eliminating the cause of a defect is more important than continuing to reject defective parts. Josh Hammond, president of the American Quality Foundation, responded to a study in which more than half the U.S. companies reported that executive pay will soon be pegged in part to quality. "If that happens," Hammond stated, "the U.S. should eventually become far and away the leaders. In the U.S., what gets rewarded gets done."[23] At Texaco, salaries are already pegged to performance; the result has been a resurgence of the company. In fact recently Texaco was named by *Fortune* magazine as the most-improved company in their category for the second year in a row.[24]

Approaches to Implementing TQM

There are several approaches to implementing TQM and all have been successfully. The approaches to TQM that are discussed here include the TQM Element Approach, the Guru Approach, the Industrial Company Model Approach, and Next Generation.

The TQM Element Approach

This approach was used primarily in the early 1980s and employs elements of quality improvement programs such as quality circles and statistical process control, rather than full implementation of TQM.

Quality circles

Small groups of employees who get together on company time to develop ways to improve the quality and quantity of work.

Quality Circles **Quality circles (QCs)** are *small groups of employees who get together on company time to develop ways to improve the quality and quantity of work.*[25] Many current business-related periodicals tell numerous success stories about employees who are encouraged to work together to improve the quality and quantity of the company. Quality circles encourage workers' energy and creativity to solve the company's—and the workers'—problems. The concept of quality circles is as relevant today as it was in the early 1980s. Even with the effectiveness of this approach, it has yet to be accepted by those in the service industries, which account for more than 70 percent of the employees in the United States.[26]

Statistical process control

A process which gauges the performance of the manufacturing process by carefully monitoring changes in whatever is being produced.

Statistical Process Control (SPC) One technique for meeting manufacturing standards is called statistical process control, or SPC. Basically, **statistical process control** *gauges the performance of the manufacturing process by carefully monitoring changes in whatever is being produced.* The goal is to detect potential defects before they result in off-quality products, then pinpoint the reason for the deviation and adjust the process to make it more stable. The Japanese, who have been honing statistical quality

Quality circles are small groups of employees who get together on company time to develop ways to improve the quality and quantity of work. This quality circle at a Nissan plant in the United States is larger than most. The technique has been adopted to varying degrees by all U.S. automakers, oth foreign and domestic.

methods for over 30 years, picked up on SPC quickly. Few U.S. companies have had a tradition of quality-consciousness, but the majority of these quality-consciousness companies applied SPC as vigorously as the Japanese. AT&T, Corning Glass, du Pont, Ford, Hewlett-Packard, IBM, Kodak, and Westinghouse are frequently cited as leaders in management by quality.[27]

While statistical process control is not new in the United States, its focus had been to monitor rather than improve manufacturing systems. It had become normal to expect and even accept a certain percentage of defective products. This attitude necessitated conducting extensive inspection testing in order to identify the defects and either remove or rework them. All of this added to manufacturing costs, did little to improve quality, and lessened America's competitive position in world markets. Managers incorrectly perceived that the quality was satisfactory if products were not being returned, if complaints were not received, and if the price/performance ratio for the customer was improved.[28]

MANAGEMENT IN PRACTICE: A Skill-Building Exercise

"Our fully integrated operations ensure exacting control over every phase of engineering, testing, and production—everything right down to final inspection," read the annual report of Stratton Corporation. Stratton had been continuously profitable for decades. Declared vice president Lonnie Phelps, "We will consider automation wherever possible, practical, and economical; but if you are talking about one of those unmanned factories, you'll never see our operation all automated like that."

Stratton made small gasoline engines, up to 18 horsepower. Almost all parts—engine castings, starters, alternators, ignition coils, and carburetors—were made in the Stratton factory. Unlike manufacturers who use components supplied by subcontractors, Stratton had to absorb the impact of any sales decline in-house. Far from throwing in the towel, Stratton quadrupled the advertising budget. Phelps promised, "We are not going to let the Japanese take this market from us."

What would be your response?

The Guru Approach

This approach uses the writings of a guru such as Deming, Juran, or Crosby as a benchmark to determine what the organization lacks, then uses the guru's system to make changes. Deming's 14-point model is one example of a guru's approach that has been widely embraced in America as well as in Japan.

1. Create constancy of purpose for improvement of product and service.
2. Adopt the new philosophy.
3. Cease dependence on mass inspection.
4. End the practice of awarding business on price tag alone.
5. Improve constantly and forever the system of production and service.
6. Institute training.

7. Institute leadership.
8. Drive out fear.
9. Break down barriers between staff areas.
10. Eliminate slogans, exhortations, and targets for the work force.
11. Eliminate numerical quotas.
12. Remove barriers to pride of workmanship.
13. Institute a vigorous program of education and retraining.
14. Take action to accomplish the transformation.[29]

Organizations using this method focus on the Japanese Deming prize winners as a way to develop an implementation master plan. Japan's Deming prize symbolizes the excellence of Japanese quality. The prize, named after W. Edwards Deming, was established when Deming started donating lecture fees to the Union of Japanese Scientists and Engineers (JUSE) in 1951. They decided to use the funds to establish the prize. JUSE offered its first seminar in English in 1988 to such companies as Motorola, Volvo, Rolls-Royce, Dow Chemical, and Xerox.

With this approach, corporations try to duplicate the basics of Japanese quality management, popularly known as total quality control. Total quality control was first mentioned in an article published by Armand Feigenbaum entitled "Total Quality Control." Feigenbaum echoes the essence of TQM: "Quality is everybody's job." This approach focuses on fine-tuning an entire firm to make it as adaptable to changes in customer demands and market conditions as possible. Management must continually analyze strengths and weaknesses of their firms to allow improvement in processes. Although the prize is popular in nature, some companies have decided not to pursue it because of its strict guidelines. The Deming prize has been won by such firms as Toyota, Nippon Electric, Fuji Xerox, Yokogawa Hewlett-Packard, and Rhythm Watch Company.[30]

Other lesser-known quality gurus who contributed in various ways to TQM and have been briefly mentioned are Armand Feigenbaum, Kaoru Ishikawa, and Genichi Taguchi. Armand Feigenbaum recognized that statistics provided a "body of knowledge" for quality. As mentioned previously, he is responsible for adding a new concept to the idea of quality, in his article entitled "Total Quality Control." Feigenbaum also believed that design and material control departments had a responsibility to see what was producible on the shop floor. He also pointed out that quality is a technology that can be systemized and taught.

Kaoru Ishikawa strongly believed that every top manager's business is quality. He simplified the statistical methods of Deming into "Seven Tools," charts that any factory worker could use. These tools, such as Pareto charts, histograms, and scatter diagrams, are now part of America's TQM resources. According to Ishikawa, 95 percent of the problems that surface can be solved by utilizing these resources.

Genichi Taguchi focused mainly on the design stage of the process. Taguchi referred to his practice as "quality engineering." He was primarily concerned with the "losses" a product imparts to society from the time it is shipped to the consumer. To limit losses, quality must be designed into each product.

It is very important to remember that the concepts of these quality gurus cannot be reduced to a set of techniques. Regardless of the techniques utilized, the success of TQM is dependent upon a commitment to excellence by everyone in an organization. TQM also requires teamwork and a process of continuous improvement.[31]

Winners of the Baldrige Award have a clear commitment to ultimate quality. These companies embrace the idea of total quality management because they want a competitive advantage.

The Industrial Company Model Approach

This approach requires individuals to visit a U.S. industrial company that uses TQM, identify its successes, and integrate this information with their own ideas to create a customized approach. This method was used in the late 1980s by many of the Baldrige National Quality Award winners.

With the Baldrige approach, an organization uses criteria for the Malcomb Baldrige National Quality Award to identify areas of improvement. To apply for the award, a company must document, in no more than 75 data-filled pages, general statements such as the following:

- Top executives incorporate quality values into day-to-day management.
- The company is working with suppliers to improve the quality of their products or services.
- The company trains workers in quality techniques and has systems in place to ensure that products are high quality.
- Their products are as good as or better than those of their competitors.
- Customer needs and wants are being met—and customer satisfaction ratings are as good as or better than competitors'.
- The quality system yields concrete results, such as gains in market share and reduction in product-cycle time.

Once an application is submitted, examiners award points for accomplishments in the award criteria. Top scorers receive site visits by senior examiners, who then make recommendations to a panel of judges. As many as two winners each may be picked from the categories of manufacturing, services, and small business.

The Next Generation

The question has been asked, "What is after TQM?" Apparently a new plateau is presently being conceived and both Japan and the United States are involved. The concept involves a production function where defects and errors disappear completely. For example, using computerized controls, if one part in a sequence is slightly out of tolerance, the other part will be adjusted automatically to compensate for the deviation. Work on such a system is already under way at the National Center for Manufacturing Sciences in Ann Arbor, Michigan, and at Lehigh University.

Components of TQM[32]

Previously we discussed such concepts as strategic planning, management by objectives, and quality circles. TQM builds on the successful components of many of these concepts and does not use the failures. TQM is a structural system for creating organization-wide participation in planning and implementing a continuous improvement process that *exceeds* the expectations of the customer or client. It is built on the assumption that 90 percent of our problems are process problems, not employee problems. However, it is important that the 10 percent related to human problems is not ignored because this could have a negative impact on the components of TQM. For example, Ferrer-Westrop, Abshire, and Sower found that the human elements had a direct impact on the degree of consumer orientation and subsequently the degree of consumer satisfaction provided by service companies. Basically, they discovered that by emphasizing a human just-in-time (HJIT) approach a degree of customer orientation occurred that is a conduit to consumer satisfaction.[33] The three major components of TQM which address process problems are breakthrough planning, daily management, and cross-functional management.

Breakthrough Planning

Breakthrough planning is an extension of strategic planning (see Figure 17–1). It has the following purposes:

- Clarify a vision of where the organization wants to go in the next five or ten years.
- Identify objectives that move the organization toward its vision.
- Identify critical processes that must deliver the product or services provided to clients in a way that exceeds their expectations.
- Select a few (no more than four) breakthrough items that can help the organization reach its vision quickly.
- Communicate this vision and the methods by which it will be met to all employees.
- Provide a structure for monitoring progress toward the vision.

FIGURE 17–1

Breakthrough Planning

SOURCE: L. Edwin Coate, *Implementing Total Quality Management in a University Setting (Oregon State University Press, July 1990), p. 5. Used with permission.*

Daily Management

This system shows people what they personally must do, and what they must measure and control, to keep the organization running smoothly. It helps them define and understand the processes they use in producing goods and services to meet customers' needs and expectations. Once these processes are understood, individuals and departments can continuously improve them, then standardize the improvements to ensure that gains are maintained.

This continuous improvement is achieved by problem-solving teams who engage in identifying customer problems, finding solutions, and then providing ongoing control of the improved process. Use of several basic quality control tests and statistical methods helps people manage with facts, not opinions, and solve the real problems, not just the symptoms. Problem solving requires the collective efforts of everyone in the organization.

Daily management is the most revolutionary of the three components of TQM. It empowers employees at all levels of the organization and focuses management improvement efforts on process problems.

Cross-Functional Management

This is the integration of team activities across divisions or departments to achieve organizational objectives. It is the vehicle for breaking down departmental and divisional barriers. Through cross-functional management, top-level managers can ensure that all groups in the organization are working together for the good of the institution. This system leads the organization to listen to the "voice of the customer," identify customer needs, and incorporate those needs into every phase of the firm's operation.

TQM: An Example[34]

Early in 1990, Oregon State University set out to find its own answer to a question being asked by a growing number of colleges and universities across the United States: How adaptable are the quality management methods of W. Edwards Deming, J. M. Juran, and Philip Crosby to higher education?

It is obvious that manufacturing processes are far more predictable and controllable than the learning process. As OSU's top management explored Total Quality Management, they realized that TQM principles should not be applied without a period of research, adaptation, training, and pilot testing in the actual university setting. It was decided that testing could best be conducted in OSU's service areas, many of which have counterparts in industry. Administrative units such as physical plant, business affairs, and printing and mailing could more readily adapt techniques of quality improvement to their processes. What they learned from their experience could be applied to the more complex issues of adapting TQM to the university's academic side.

The Pilot Program

During breakthrough planning, an initial step in implementing TQM, OSU's top management identified the 12 critical processes basic to carrying out the university's mission. The vice-president and the division directors for finance and administration followed the same method to identify critical processes for their unit and for each division. These processes became the basis for the work of the pilot TQM study teams (see Figure 17–2).

Pilot TQM Teams   OSU's early exploration of TQM had convinced management that teams are the very heart of TQM.[35] Better solutions emerge, are implemented faster, and last longer when the people affected help develop them.

About TQM Study Teams   Study teams are composed of people who normally work together on the process being reviewed. They are led by someone from the natural work group, typically the supervisor, and are assisted by a facilitator.

Teams usually work with processes that can be improved with resources they control. Teams are kept small (no more than ten), and each has a sponsor, usually the group's division director. The sponsor ensures that the team's work is linked to the university's critical process and moves the university toward its vision.

Ten Teams Formed   The divisions of finance and administration formed ten pilot TQM teams (see Figure 17–3). Each sponsor assigned the team a study issue or problem related to one of his or her division's critical processes.

OSU Critical Processes: Finance and Administration Detail

Vice President for Finance & Administration: Critical Processes								
Fiscal Services	Information Services	Workforce Hiring & Development	Long-Range Planning	Budgeting	Community Relations	Facilities Management	Law Enforcement	Safety

Business Affairs
*Accounting
Property Control
Travel & Transport
*Fiscal Services
Telecommunications
Purchasing
Contracting
Risk Management
	Computing Service
	Maintaining Hardware
	Computer Purchasing
	*Networking
	Training
	Developing Standards
		Printing & Mailing
		Accounting
		*Printing
		Quick Copy
		U.S. Mailing Services
		Blank Paper Sales
			Human Resources
			Hiring
			Labor Relations
			Staff Development
			Position Classification
			Personnel Reporting
			*Benefits
			Administration
			Workers' Comp.
			   Claims Management
				Radiation Center
				Teaching
				Research
				*Technical Services
					Budget & Planning
					Long-Range Planning
					Archiving/Records
					   Managment
					Data Analysis
					Budgeting
					Policy Communication

| Facilities
*Maintenance
& Repair
*Remodeling
& Construction
Delivery Service | Facilities Planning
Campus Planning
Facilities Allocation
Capital Construction | University Police
Criminal Law
Enforcement
Traffic Law
Enforcement | Security
*Security
Parking | Environmental
Health & Safey
Information
   Dissemination
Compliance
Monitoring
Technical Services | Institutional Research
and Planning
Information Gathering
Information
   Dissemination
Long-Range Planning |

*Denotes Pilot Team

FIGURE 17–2

OSU Critical Processes: Finance and Administration Detail

* Denotes pilot team

Source: L. Edwin Coate, An Analysis of Oregon State University's Total Quality Management Pilot Program (Oregon State University Press, November 1990), p. 3. Used with permission.

Pilot TQM Teams in Finance and Administration

Team, Division		Critical Process	Issue Statement
1A	Physical Plant	Facilities Management	Reduce the amount of time it takes to copmlete the remodeling process.
1B	Physical Plant	Facilities Management	Improve servicing of fixed equipment
2	Printing	Information Services	Reduce the amount of time in the prepress stage of the printing process.
3	Budgets and Planning	Budgeting	Increase the timeliness of the Budget-Status-at-a-Glance report development process.
4	Computing Services	Information Services	Increase the timeliness and consistent delivery of network information.
5A	Business Affairs	Fiscal Services	Increase the availability of information provided by Business Affairs for the monitoring of 050 income and expense projections.
5B	Business Affairs	Fiscal Services	Reduce the time expended in processing grant and contract documents within Business Affairs.
6	Public Safety	Safety	Decrease response time for requests for service.
7	Radiation Center	(President's critical processes: teaching, research, service delivery)	Increase customer demand for the Center's products and streamline response process.
8	Human Resources	Workforce Hiring & Development	Increase the speed of initial response in the information dissemination process.

FIGURE 17–3

Pilot TQM Teams in Finance and Administration

SOURCE: *L. Edwin Coate,* An Analysis of Oregon State University's Total Quality Management Pilot Program *(Oregon State University Press, November 1990), p. 4. Used with permission.*

Leaders and facilitators of the teams received about 18 hours' training in TQM from a consultant. The consultant and the university's staff development officer then served as "coaches," providing "just-in-time" training to team members as they moved through TQM problem-solving steps.

Ten-Step Problem-Solving Process

OSU teams used a ten-step TQM problem-solving model to guide their study (see Figure 17–4). The process begins with the customer, focuses on root causes of problems, and ensures that decisions and actions are based on real data.

> **Step One.** **At the sponsor level,** opportunities for improvement that relate to the team's critical process are identified and team members who have ownership in that process are selected.

> **Step Two.** **Key customers** are surveyed to find out which services provided by the process are not meeting their expectations.

> **Step Three.** **The most important** customer issue or problem is selected and a clear issue statement is prepared.

FIGURE 17-4

Ten-Step Problem-Solving Process

SOURCE: *L. Edwin Coate, An Analysis of Oregon State University's Total Quality Management Pilot Program (Oregon State University Press, November 1990), p. 5. Used with permission.*

Step Four. **A flow diagram** is prepared, showing the process as it is now.

Step Five. **A process performance measure** is established to track progress in meeting or exceeding customer expectations.

Step Six. **Probable causes** of the problem are identified.

Step Seven. **Real-time data** on the probable causes are gathered to establish a benchmark against which to measure future progress.

Step Eight. The data are analyzed and shown in "pictures"—charts and graphs.

Step Nine. **Solutions to problems** are developed through brainstorming. Each solution is measured against criteria that reflect customer needs. The best solutions are then implemented, their performance monitored, and they are adopted if they are successful.

Step Ten. **If the problem is solved,** improvements are standardized as normal operating procedures.

Case Example: The Business Affairs Team

The following section analyzes one of the ten TQM teams at OSU—the Business Affairs Team.

The Problem   The number of erroneous journal vouchers returned to departments must be decreased.

Causes   When the team began measuring journal voucher errors, they found a one-month total of 200 errors out of 7,971 vouchers processed, a rate of 3 percent. Of these, more than half, 103, were returned to the originating department for correction, a time-wasting process loop.

Solutions   The team tested two solutions:

- Based on a better understanding of what customers wanted, the journal vouchers specialist called departments and corrected most errors over the phone.

- To help departments complete their journal vouchers correctly at the outset, the specialist prepared a checklist based on data about common customer errors and sent it to all departments. The team helped with suggestions and reviews.

Results   The journal vouchers error rate dropped from 3 percent to 2 percent and the number of journal vouchers returned to departments dropped dramatically from 103 to 4 (see Figure 17-5).

A Global Perspective

The global outlook for Total Quality Management (TQM) appears promising. First, the United States used it to help win World War II. Then, the United States abandoned it to "enjoy the war's legacy of consumer prosperity" without an interest in

Before Solutions

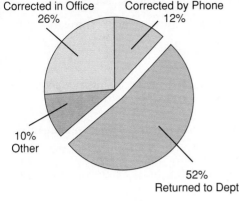

Corrected in Office
26%

Corrected by Phone
12%

10%
Other

52%
Returned to Dept

June 1990
Error Rate 3%

After Solutions

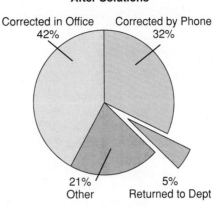

Corrected in Office
42%

Corrected by Phone
32%

21%
Other

5%
Returned to Dept

September 1990
Error Rate 2%

FIGURE 17–5

Before and After

SOURCE: *L. Edwin Coate, An Analysis of Oregon State University's Total Quality Management Pilot Program (Oregon State University Press, November 1990), p. 12. Used with permission.*

quality. On the road to recovery, Japan embraced the concept of TQM. On July 13, 1950, W. Edwards Deming addressed the presidents of Japan's leading companies, telling them that quality was essential to their survival. "They saw quality as percepts and practices permeating every level of the enterprise, from the board room to the factory floor. The effort toward quality was, in a word, 'total'."[36] From their humble beginnings, Japanese manufacturers have become the envy of the world. This level of success has come about primarily because of the conviction and discipline with which Japanese managers, over the last 40 years, have embraced various concepts of TQM.[37]

When faced with the competitive superiority of the Japanese, America began a "quiet" revolution toward TQM. William H. Oliver of TRW Corporation believes that this quiet revolution toward TQM is essential for American success in global markets.[38] Because of the importance of an emphasis on quality, the Baldrige National Quality Award for excellence in the area of Total Quality Management was created by the U.S. Department of Commerce in 1987.[39] This award is similar to Japan's Deming prize for excellence. Now, most major American companies have "total quality" programs that integrate every department from manufacturing to marketing and research in the effort to improve quality and allow companies to gain a "Quality Edge." Baldrige award winners like 3M, IBM, Xerox, and Motorola have embraced TQM and have become leaders in their respective industries. TQM is spreading throughout the United States, Europe, and indeed the world. It is quite possible that organizations that fail to embrace TQM may well become second-class players in our rapidly changing global environment. Started in the United States, first embraced by Japanese companies after World War II, reintroduced and currently accepted by U.S. companies, Total Quality Management may well progress next to the rest of the world.

Self Assessment
Exercise
How Well Will You
Work in a Total
Quality Management
Environment?

1. Are you willing to commit to quality improvement through your organization?

   ☐ Yes   ☐ No

2. Are you willing to find and eliminate problems that diminish quality?

   ☐ Yes   ☐ No

3. Are you willing to identify your customers and satisfy their requirements?

   ☐ Yes   ☐ No

4. Are you willing to instill teamwork and create an atmosphere for innovation and permanent quality improvement?

   ☐ Yes   ☐ No

5. Are you willing to recognize that defect prevention—not inspection—is the way to achieve quality?

   ☐ Yes   ☐ No

6. Are you willing to work to develop strategies for reducing the causes of poor quality and thereby increase productivity?

   ☐ Yes   ☐ No

7. Are you willing to accept the fact that the concept of quality differs with the type of company involved?

   ☐ Yes   ☐ No

8. Are you willing to focus on quality over the long run?

   ☐ Yes   ☐ No

9. Are you willing to commit to improving the quality of your product or service so that customers' needs are not only met but exceeded?

   ☐ Yes   ☐ No

10. Are you willing to continually seek alternative methods or technologies that will improve existing processes?

    ☐ Yes   ☐ No

Summary

Total Quality Management (TQM) is a commitment to excellence by everyone in an organization that emphasizes excellence achieved by teamwork and a process of continuous improvement. The ultimate goal of TQM is to alter the process by improving customer satisfaction. Instead of being content with the status quo, employees at all levels continually seek alternative methods or technologies which will improve existing processes. The concept of quality is based on the customer being served to the maximum degree possible.

The approaches to TQM which are discussed include the TQM element approach, the guru approach, the industrial company model approach and next generation.

The TQM element approach was used primarily in the early 1980s and employs elements of quality improvement programs such as quality circles and statistical process control, rather than full implementation of TQM. The Guru Approach uses the writings of a guru such as Deming, Juran, Feigenbaum, Ishikawa, Taguchi, or Crosby as a benchmark to determine what the organization lacks, then uses the guru's system to make changes. The Industrial Company Model Approach requires individuals to visit a U.S. industrial company that uses TQM, identify its successes, and integrate this information with their own ideas to create a customized approach. Next Generation involves a production function where defects and errors disappear completely.

TQM builds on successful components of many concepts such as strategic planning, management by objectives, and quality circles, but does not use the failures. TQM is a structural system for creating organization-wide participation in planning and implementing a continuous improvement process that exceeds the expectations of the customer or client. It is built on the assumption that 90 percent of our problems are process problems, not employee problems. The three major components of TQM are breakthrough planning, daily management, and cross-functional management. Breakthrough planning is an extension of strategic planning. Daily management shows people what they personally must do, and what they must measure and control, to keep the organization running smoothly. Finally, cross-functional management is the integration of team activities across divisions or departments to achieve organizational objectives. The last part of the chapter presents a real-world TQM example.

Review Questions

1. Define *Total Quality Management.*
2. What is the history of Total Quality Management?
3. Explain the basic message of both Deming and Juran.
4. What factors favor the growth of TQM in the United States?
5. In relation to TQM, what is quality?
6. Describe the approaches to implementing TQM.
7. What are the components of TQM? Describe each.

Key Terms

Total quality
  management

Quality circles

Statistical process
  control

CASE 17.1	STAFFING THE NEW STORES

As the personnel director for KBH Stores in St. Louis, Missouri, Virginia Knickerbocker knew that she had her work cut out for her. Company management had just announced a goal of opening 10 new stores during the next 12 months. KBH employed 480 people in the 35 stores already in operation. Virginia knew that staffing the new stores would require hiring and training about 150 people. She felt that her own small office was inadequately funded and staffed to handle such an increase in operations.

Virginia learned of the expansion plans from a friend who knew the president's secretary. Although she didn't like being kept in the dark, Virginia was not surprised that she had not been told. Glenn Sullivan, the president of KBH, was noted for his autocratic leadership style. He tended to tell subordinates only what he wanted them to know. He expected everyone who worked for him to follow orders without question. He wasn't an unkind person, though, and Virginia had always gotten along with him pretty well. She had never confronted Mr. Sullivan about anything, so it was with some concern that she approached his office that day.

"Mr. Sullivan," she began, "I hear that we are going to be opening ten new stores next year."

"That's right, Virginia," said Mr. Sullivan. "We've already arranged the credit lines and have picked out

several of the sites."

"What about staffing?" asked Virginia.

"Well, I presume that you will take care of that, Virginia, when we get to that point," replied Mr. Sullivan.

"What about my own staff?" asked Virginia. "I think I am going to need at least three or four more people. And we are already crowded, so I hope you're planning to expand the personnel office."

"Not really," said Mr. Sullivan. "You will have to get by with what you have for at least a year or so. It's going to be hard enough to afford the new stores and the people we need to staff them."

Questions

1. Do you believe TQM could work successfully in this environment? Explain.
2. What would Mr. Sullivan need to do to make TQM successful in his organization? Discuss.

CASE 17.2   THE FAULTY CUES

"This is the third batch of sticks we've gotten back from Brunswick this quarter," said Jerry Hodges, "and it's been different problems each time." Along with the returned pool sticks, Brunswick had provided a checklist of defects, and Jerry and his shop manager, John Kenner, were looking it over. The sticks had been made by Jerry's company, Hodges Woodworks. Brunswick is a major distributor of recreation equipment of all kinds, and Hodges had contracted to provide the company with five thousand pool sticks per month during 1992.

There were two hundred defective sticks in the returned batch. Defects ranged from misaligned leather tips, to thread defects where the sticks screwed together in the middle, to an incomplete covering of varnish. Altogether, sixteen types of defects were noted in the batch.

"The costs are just too high to inspect every piece of every stick," said Jerry.

"Yeah, I know," replied John, "but it's not as expensive as having to rework an entire batch. Anyway, Brunswick uses 100 percent inspection. Why shouldn't we?"

Jerry replied, "We may have to do that. But if the number of defects is below 2 percent, Brunswick will

accept the batch. Let's see if we can figure out a cheaper way to accomplish that."

The manufacturing process for pool sticks is complex. The wood parts are cut from solid maple and machined to shape on numerically controlled lathes. Then they are drilled and shaped on other machines to fit plastic, metal, and rubber parts purchased from other manufacturers. After being assembled, the pool cues are varnished in batches of twenty with a spray gun. Because of the small volume, most of the assembly work is done by hand.

After some discussion, John and Jerry determined that, except for the varnish problem, all of the defects in the present batch resulted from parts purchased from others. "Obviously," said Jerry, "we should do the same thing to our suppliers that Brunswick is doing to us: Check the parts when we get them, and return them if they are defective."

Question

1. Could TQM assist in this situation? Explain.

Notes

1. This case is a composite of a number of published accounts, among them: Robert Neff, "Going for the Glory," *Business Week*, October 25, 1991, p. 60; Mary T. Koska, "Case Study: Quality Improvement in a Diversified Health Center," *Hospitals*, December 5, 1990, pp. 19–20; David Kearns, "Quality in Copiers, Computers, and Floor Cleaning," *Management Review*, February 1989, pp. 61–63; Curt W. Reimann, "Winning Strategies for Quality Improvement," *Business America*, March 25, 1991, p. 8; Thane Peterson, Kevin Kelly, Joseph Weber, and Neil Gross, "Top Products for Less than Top Dollar," *Business Week*, October 25, 1991, p. 66; Kevin Kelly, "Motorola Wants to Light up Another Market," *Business Week*, October 14, 1991, p. 50; Alison L. Sprout, "America's Most Admired Corporations," *Fortune*, February 11, 1991, pp. 57–58.

2. Brian Dumaine, "Creating a New Company Culture," *Fortune* 121 (January 15, 1990): p. 127.

3. Ellis Pines, "The Gurus of TQM," *Aviation Week and Space Technology* 121 (May 21, 1990): S34.

4. W. Edwards Deming, *Out of the Crisis* (Cambridge, MA: Massachusetts Institute of Technology Center for Advanced Engineering Study, 1986), chap. 2.

5. Pines, "The Gurus of TQM," p. S29.

6. Jeremy Main, "Under the Spell of the Quality Gurus," *Fortune*, (August 18, 1986), p. 30.

7. Joseph Oberle, "Quality Gurus, the Men and Their Message," *Training*, January 1990, p. 47.

8. Jaclyn Fierman, "Why Enrollment Is Up at Quality College," *Fortune*, (April 29, 1985), p. 170.

9. Main, "Under the Spell of the Quality Gurus," p. 30.

10. The section on Total Quality Management was written by Robert M. Seay, Department of Marketing and Management, East Texas State University.

11. Alan Farnham, "Baldor's Success: Made in the U.S.A.," *Fortune*, July 17, 1989, pp. 101–105.

12. Pines, "The Gurus of TQM," p. S34.

13. Otis Port and John Carey, "Questing for the Best," *Business Week Bonus Issue, The Quality Imperative*, October 11, 1991, p. 11.

14. Ellis Pines, "TQM Training: A New Culture Sparks Change at Every Level," *Aviation Week and Space Technology* 132 (May 21, 1990): S38.

15. Ellis Pines, "From Top Secret to Top Priority: The Story of TQM," *Aviation Week and Space Technology* 132 (May 21, 1990): S24.

16. Benjamin D. Burge, "Producing a Quality Product," *Journal of Systems Management* 41 (November 1990): 7.

17. Pines, "The Gurus of TQM," p. S34.

18. B. G. Yovovich, "Motorola's Quest for Quality," *Business Marketing*, September 1991, pp. 14–29.

19. Frederic A. Miller, "Is MasterCard Mastering the Possi-bilities?" *Business Week*, October 10, 1988, p. 123; and Yvette D. Kantrow and Jeffrey Kutler, "MasterCard Defers Quest for No. 1 Spot," *American Banker*, March 20, 1989, p. 1.

20. Otis Port and John Carey, "Questing for the Best," *Business Week Bonus Issue, The Quality Imperative*, October 11, 1991, p. 10.

21. Ibid.

22. Karen Lowry Miller and David Woodruff, "A Design Master's End Run around Trial and Error," *Business Week Bonus Issue, The Quality Imperative*, October 25, 1991, p. 24; Pines, "The Gurus of TQM," p. S36.

23. Port and Carey, "Questing for the Best," p. 14.

24. Mark Ivey, "Jim Kinnear Is Pumping New Life into Texaco," *Business Week*, April 17, 1989, pp. 50–52; Todd Vogel and Brian Bremner, "Texaco: From Takeover Bait to Dynamo," *Business Week*, July 22, 1991, pp. 50–52; and Sprout, "America's Most Admired Corporations," p. 60.

25. "The New Industrial Revolution," *Business Week*, May 11, 1981, pp. 85–98.

26. John Hoerr, "The Payoff from Teamwork," *Business Week*, July 10, 1989, pp. 56–62.

27. Otis Port, "The Push for Quality," *Business Week*, June 8, 1989, p. 132.

28. Fred G. Steingraber, "Total Quality Management," *Vital Speeches of the Day* 57 (April 15, 1991): 415.

29. Mary Walton, *The Deming Management Method* (New York: Putnam's, 1986).

30. Ibid., p. 122.

31. Pines, "The Gurus of TQM," p. S34.

32. This section is based on the work of L. Edwin Coate, *Implementing Total Quality Management in a University Setting* (Corvallis, OR: Oregon State University Press 1990), pp. 5–6. Used with permission.

33. Sterling Ferrer-Westrop, Roger D. Abshire, and Victor E. Sower, "The Relationship between the Human Elements of JIT and Service Sector Professionals' Customer Orientation and Job Satisfaction," *1991 Proceedings Decision Sciences Institute*, Volume 3, pp. 1692–1694.

34. This example was adapted from L. Edwin Coate, *An Analysis of Oregon State University's Total Quality Management Pilot Program* (Corvallis, OR: Oregon State University Press, 1990), pp. 4–24.

35. Coate, *Implementing Total Quality Management in a University Setting*, p. 2.

36. Pines, "The Gurus of TQM," pp. S5–S8.

37. William H. Oliver, "The Quality Revolution," *Vital Speeches of the Day*, August, 1990, pp. 625–628.

38. Ibid.

39. Steingraber, "Total Quality Management," pp. 415–416.

Management Skills

Since effective managers must properly control their time, it is essential that you develop solid time management skills before entering management. To assess how well you currently manage your time, take the self-assessment exercise "Do You Manage Time Effectively?" Then, turn to page 634 to evaluate yourself.

Do You Manage Time Effectively?

INSTRUCTIONS: Check the box or boxes that are most appropriate to your usual behavior.

• •

1. I am a hard worker, and as such, try to do every job with total commitment. Even though I am frequently tired at the end of a day, I feel a great sense of accomplishment. ☐

2. If asked to take on an extra assignment, I will consent. Even if this new responsibility makes it nearly impossible for me to finish current projects on schedule, it is hard for me to refuse. ☐

3. Most people consider me a workaholic. I am usually involved in several projects at once. No one can make an appointment to see me without having to wait at least two weeks. I'd like to exercise more, but cannot seem to fit such a program into my heavy schedule. ☐

4. I pride myself on the ability to anticipate most problems before they occur. To me, the work schedule is sacred. Therefore, I rarely deviate from it. Interruptions must be discouraged. As much as possible, I limit phone calls and prolonged conversations. ☐

• •

5. The top and inside of my desk are covered with papers. A collector, I save telephone messages, reports, relevant newspaper articles, schedules, and letters. In fact, my filing system is so well organized that I can pull out a year-old memo at a moment's notice. Colleagues kid me about my tendency to store so many items, but I am sure that this is an asset. ☐

6. I tend to pay considerable attention to small details. I am an expert at catching even the tiniest mistake, whether in typing, grammar, or figures. Although most assignments take me hours to complete, I am known for my thoroughness and dedication. If necessary, I will take work home, to ensure that a job is finished on schedule. ☐

7. Large projects are not my forte. I find them too overwhelming and confusing. I much prefer to be given more routine tasks. It is generally difficult for me to focus on too many details at once. I enjoy the involvement and sense of accomplishment that results from a small job brought to completion. ☐

Source: Dorri Jacobs, "Your Time Management Profile," *Manage* 36 (May 1983): 4. With permission.

18

Management in the Multinational Enterprise

LEARNING OBJECTIVES

After completing this chapter students should be able to

- Explain the history and development of multinationals.
- Describe the multinational environment.
- Explain management in a multinational environment.
- Describe human resources in a multinational environment.

With sales of over $17 billion, Dow Chemical was the world's second largest chemical company, behind du Pont. Over half its sales, and even more of its operating income, came from foreign operations. Sales had increased at a compound rate of 6.8 percent over the past ten years, without an increase in shares outstanding. Dow's division president said, "We set strategies globally, R&D priorities globally—all the things that drive the business long-term we do in a global context." Dow's worldwide business was run through six "commercial" divisions (e.g., pharmaceuticals, chemicals) overlaying five geographic units (e.g., Dow Europe). According to CEO Frank Popoff, "Dow is one of the most balanced companies in the world. We've got a balance between our overseas and domestic markets." Even with this balance, Dow's foreign operations were more profitable than its domestic ones.

Industrial chemicals, the mainstay of Dow's international business, were subject to unpredictable swings. Events such as the turmoil in China, the economic crisis in Argentina, and the Persian Gulf War caused world chemical prices to tend downward. Dow's overseas ventures, such as the joint venture Dow entered into with China's Zhejiang Pacific Chemical Corporation near the East China Sea, was an example of Dow's global aggressiveness. Still, industry experts agreed that the region of the world with the best growth potential was Europe. For Dow, business in Europe remained strong and chief executive Frank Popoff predicted "another record year."

Dow's executive team was mostly American, although the trend in the nineties is toward internationalizing it. Dow's human resources vice president said, "We consider each overseas move to be unique because each situation is different." Prospective expatriates, and those moving from one overseas assignment to another, are briefed and given an information packet on their destination. "An adviser—normally the spouse of a recently returned expatriate—will visit the transferee and his or her spouse to explain what sort of emotional issues they are likely to face in the early stages of the move."

A "godfather" was also assigned to each expatriate manager at Dow. "It is a relationship of mutual trust and interest. The expatriate keeps the godfather up to date on his or her activities, and the godfather keeps track of the expatriate's career while he or she is overseas." Expatriate managers were guaranteed they could come back to jobs at the same level as the ones they left. The "godfather" was expected to arrange this. Upon repatriation, managers are encouraged to form support groups to discuss common experiences.

Dow's division president is proud of Dow's ability to "'execute geographically.' There are those who've said that, using astronomical terms, there's a 'red shift,' a 'big bang,' with things getting further apart and Dow Chemical becoming a big holding company. I don't think that's Frank Popoff's vision of Dow. I believe we'll be interlinked, intertwined, rather than continuing with the big bang." However accurate this assessment, the system at Dow clearly is not broken, so it might not require fixing. Dow is number 2 in the chemicals category, behind du Pont, among *Fortune*'s 1991 list of "America's Most Admired Corporations," but their goal appears to be number 1.[1]

A company such as Dow engages in international business typically because of significant opportunities beyond the home country's borders. These opportunities are usually partly offset by the well-known problems of international business: cultural differences, legal restrictions, language barriers, monetary effects, and the distances over which information and materials must travel.

In the 1980s, the need for adapting business practices to different national environments was not fully appreciated. Today, multinational corporations affect the lives of many U.S. citizens. Twenty percent of our work force depends on international trade for employment. One-third of U.S. farmland produces food for export. At some MBA-granting universities, approximately one-third of the graduating class accepts jobs with international responsibilities. By the year 1993, the United States will no longer be the world's largest industrialized market, being replaced by the united European Community.[2]

This chapter begins by describing the history and development of multinational enterprises. Then, environmental factors confronting multinationals are described. Next, management in a multinational environment is addressed. The final section of the chapter focuses on human resources in the multinational environment.

History and Development of Multinationals

Multinational company (MNC)

A firm that is based in one country (the parent, or home country) and produces goods or provides services in one or more foreign countries (host countries).

Parent country

The country where the headquarters of a multinational company is located.

Host country

The country where the operational unit of a multinational company resides.

A **multinational company (MNC)** is *a firm that is based in one country (the parent, or home country) and produces goods or provides services in one or more foreign countries (host countries).* The **parent country** is *the country where the headquarters of the multinational corporation is located.* The **host country** is *the country where the operational unit of the multinational corporation resides.*

The first MNC established with a global orientation grew out of a merger in 1929 between Margarine Unie, a Dutch firm, and Lever Brothers, a British company. The company became Unilever, and it has since become one of the largest companies in the world, with approximately 500 subsidiaries operating in about 60 nations. Unilever has two headquarters units, one located in Rotterdam and the other in London. Today, it is important for many companies to enter the multinational market if they are to survive. With operations in many countries, Dow is clearly an MNC.

The economic output of MNCs is a significant portion of the total economic output of the world. Some economists have estimated that by the year 2000, about 200 to 300 multinationals will account for one-half of the world's total output of goods and services. In recent years, there has been a rapid growth of direct investment by multinational firms. And this trend is expected to continue as majority-owned foreign affiliates of U.S. companies plan to increase capital expenditures to $61.2 billion, a 6 percent increase.[3]

U.S. companies must also have a global presence, if they are to expand. For example, the 100 largest U.S.-based multinationals experienced a decline in domestic sales of 1.6 percent after adjusting for inflation. But, foreign sales increased 15 percent. Of the total revenue of these firms, approximately 40 percent comes from foreign sales.[4] Recently, the top 10 exporters from the U.S. included Exxon, IBM, General Motors, Ford Motor, Mobil, Citicorp, Texaco, E. I. du Pont de Nemours, ITT, and Philip Morris. A firm had to generate foreign revenue in excess of $1.8 billion to rank in the 100 largest U.S. multinationals.[5] The worldwide impact of these companies

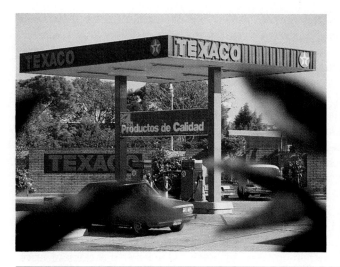

In recent years, there has been a rapid growth of direct investment by multinational firms averaging about ten percent per year. MNCs based in the United States account for more than half of this worldwide investment. This Texaco retail outlet is located in Guatemala.

Source: Photograph courtesy of Texaco, Inc.

is significant. Their operations create interrelationships between countries and cultures as well as between economic and political systems.

Other companies not among the top 10 exporters saw hefty gains in foreign revenues. Compaq Computer doubled its exports. Ethyl Corporation saw a 48 percent jump, mainly on the strength of sales of bromine as a flame retardant. And Alcoa's sales of aluminum products to foreigners shot up 75 percent. All together, export sales for the top 50 exporters grew 22 percent, to $97 billion.

One of the most aggressive countries, with multinationals quickly expanding into more and more countries, is Japan. Recently, Japanese manufacturers have been fighting to establish a solid presence in Europe, and their entry point appears to be Britain. Japanese companies fear they will face increased protectionism if they are not entrenched in Europe as the European Community reduces its barriers to international trade.[6]

In recent years many internationalists have distinguished between multinational companies and evolving transnational companies. A **transnational company** is *a firm that views the world as one market, conducts operations in many countries, and makes decisions as if national boundaries did not exist.* Thus a transnational manufacturing firm buys supplies, raises capital, conducts research and development, and manufactures its products wherever in the world it can do so most effectively and efficiently. It does not distinguish between its home and host countries; its headquarters can be in any country. It seeks to develop and maintain a single worldwide identity. Its executives are of various nationalities, and they are global managers. We will use international companies in the rest of the chapter when there is no need to distinguish between multinational and transnational firms.

Transnational company

A firm that views the world as one market, conducts operations in many countries, and makes decisions as if national boundaries do not exist.

The Multinational Environment

Global competition, air travel, and satellite communication technology have made doing business abroad both necessary and feasible, and companies have responded by establishing operations overseas. A survey by McKinsey and Company of mid-sized companies doing business abroad shows that companies expect their international sales to jump 15 to 20 percent a year for at least the next five years.[7] In addition, 95 percent of the world's population lies outside the U.S. and it's growing 70 percent faster.[8] Clearly, the majority of business opportunities in the future will be outside the U.S.

Unfortunately, historically, some American managers have tended to fall back on their own limited experiences, treating an assignment in Hong Kong, Sydney, or Paris much like a stint in Dallas or Atlanta. One person constantly dealing with the complexities involved in operating in the multinational environment is Cornelius Van Der Klugt, president and chairman of the Dutch electronics giant, Philips NV. According to Van Der Klugt, when operating overseas, domestic managers must be adaptive and appreciate the nature of the environment in which they are operating.[9]

American managers have recognized that the challenge of engaging in multinational operations is not easily met. This is especially true with regard to the challenges of management. In Chapter 2, the discussion was primarily focused on environmental factors of organizations located in the United States. However, the external environment that confronts multinational enterprises is even more diverse and complex than that confronted by domestic firms.

As is illustrated in Figure 18–1, working in a multinational climate adds another layer to the external environment (described in Chapter 2) that management must contend with. Although the basic tasks associated with management remain essentially the same, the manner in which the tasks are accomplished may be altered substantially by the multinational's external environment. As Figure 19–1 suggests, the MNC must deal with the environment not only of the parent country, but of the host country as well.

FIGURE 18–1

The External Environment of a Multinational Corporation

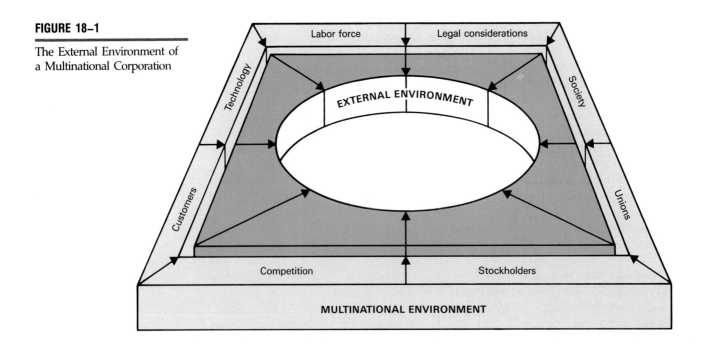

Legal Considerations

Multinational Corporations must obey the laws of the host country. In addition, some multinationals are under pressure to adhere to federal, state, and even local legislation of the parent country. However, there is no comprehensive system of international law or courts. Therefore, a multinational organization needs to understand in detail the laws of each host country. The United States, England, Canada, Australia, and New Zealand have developed their legal requirements by means of English common law. Under English common law, judges and courts are extremely important, for they are guided by principles declared in previous cases. In most of continental Europe, Asia, and Africa, the approach is one of civil law. Judges play a lesser role because the legal requirements are codified. The civil servant or bureaucrat has greater power under civil law than under the common law.

Although the United States is a highly legalistic country, and American MNCs tend to carry U.S. law with them, managers must realize that the legal systems of other countries can differ considerably. For instance, the Japanese dislike laws, lawyers, and litigation. Consider this example: "A Japanese contract is so vague it's unenforceable in U.S. courts. It says, well, the two of us will get together, and we think we're going to do this product, but if that doesn't work for us, then we'll have to change the terms of the agreement, because why would we want to go ahead with it and do it if it was killing us."[10] In France, lawyers are prohibited from serving on boards of directors by codes of the legal profession. The vastness and sheer complexity of various legal systems throughout the world demonstrate clearly the intricate and demanding legal environment of the MNCs. In order to function in a manner consistent with the host country, managers should become familiar with its legal considerations. Failure to carefully consider legal considerations could have a drastic effect on multinational success.

Multinational corporations headquartered in the United States must obey the laws of the host country. When operating in the multinational environment, U.S.-based firms often find their human resource policies to be in conflict with the laws and accepted norms of the host country. For instance, the influence of Title VII of the Civil Rights Act of 1964, as amended, has been felt by virtually all firms operating in the United States. But most countries in the world do not have such laws prohibiting discrimination. In fact, some countries practice overt discrimination against certain groups that would be protected if they were employed in the United States. The Civil Rights Act of 1991 extended the coverage of the Civil Rights Act of 1964 to extraterritorial employment. However, the Act does not apply to United States companies operating in another country if it would violate the law of the foreign country.

ETHICAL DILEMMA

Your company, Empire Southwest, a distributor of Caterpillar equipment in Phoenix, wants to trade in the Mexican market where cash under the table—*mordita* (a "little bite")—is part of doing business. This payoff practice is so ingrained in the Mexican culture that a business virtually cannot open a Mexican operation without going along. You have observed many companies that did not pay and that failed to enter the Mexican market, as well as those that paid and tended to enter the market and, overall, did fairly well. You can continue to raise your stature with mining companies, farmers, and contractors, and encourage them to lobby the government to freely open the market, or you can pay the bribe.[11]

What would you do?

Labor Force

In filling key managerial, technical, or professional positions abroad, multinationals can choose among three basic types of employees: (1) parent country nationals (PCN), (2) host country nationals (HCN), and (3) third country nationals (TCN). Initially, it was common for MNCs to fill foreign key posts with trusted and experienced employees from the parent company (PCNs). Using workers from the parent nation of the multinational ensures a greater degree of consistency and control in the firm's operations around the world. However, this approach is not without its costs, because these workers may experience considerable difficulty in understanding cultural differences and adapting to life in the host country. In addition, the common practice of frequent rotation of key employees intensifies the problem of understanding and adapting to local cultures. However, using PCNs facilitates communications with headquarters because both parties are of the same culture.

Utilizing workers from the host country in key positions will usually improve the MNC's relations with the host country government. It will also enable a quicker and

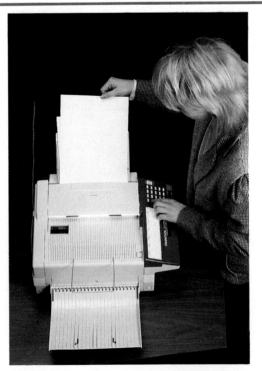

Using workers from the parent nation of the multinational company ensures a greater degree of consistency and control in the firm's operations around the world. However, this approach is not without its costs, because these workers may experience considerable difficulty in understanding cultural differences and adapting to life in the host country. Here, a worker in Sweden transmits a facsimile message to her employer's U.S. headquarters.

Source: © Jim Pickerell

more accurate adaptation to the requirements of the host country. Disadvantages include a lessened degree of centralized control and increased communication problems with headquarters. In addition, if the HCNs perceive that the opportunity for higher-level positions is blocked for ethnic reasons, they will use the MNC to gain experience and then transfer to higher positions in local national firms. Properly balancing the type of key employees stationed in the host country is often a complex and difficult task, but one that is critical to the success of the MNC.

The trend toward using large numbers of parent country nationals appears to be changing. In 1991, Resources Counselors, Inc. discovered that the number of U.S. parent country nationals per company is decreasing.[12] Recently, more and more firms are employing host country nationals and third country nationals. For example, in 1991, multinational firms were employing more TCNs for overseas posts. Apparently nationality is not as important a factor as the number of global managers. In the United States, the average number of third country nationals in an MNC rose from 33 in 1988 to 46 in 1990.[13]

MANAGEMENT IN PRACTICE: A Skill-Building Exercise

You have been managing in Japan for over 17 years. The new general manager of marketing has been transferred from an 8-year assignment in Britain. He came in and had to select four new marketing representatives. These individuals deal directly with the executives of major Japanese corporations. They are the company liaisons who make sure that the customer is satisfied with the products and services offered by the company. This position also requires the representative to frequently socialize with the client. The new general manager has decided that there aren't enough women in responsible positions in the Japanese operation, so he has decided to promote women to fill all four marketing representative positions. He has told you to notify them of their promotions. You quickly realize that he is making a mistake, so you inform him that the promotions would not be a good move. He tells you he is running the show now and will have a representative portion of management positions filled by women.

What would you do or say?

Society

It is apparent that the significant societal considerations of one nation will differ to some extent from those of other countries. Customs, beliefs, values, and habits of each society will vary. If the multinational corporation is to operate in many nations, it will be required to adapt some of its managerial practices to the specific and unique expectations and situations of each nation. Attitudes will differ concerning such subjects as work, risk taking, change introduction, time authority, and material gain. It is dangerous for managers to assume that the attitudes within the parent country will be similar in all other countries. However, it is sometimes possible for successful multinationals to change the way those in the parent countries do business. According to Barry Wilkinson, lecturer at Cardiff Business School and co-author of *The Japanization of British Industry*, the British are looking at the Japanese organization as the model for success.[14]

Lack of cultural sensitivity has limited the transfer of successful U.S. management practices to European countries and to Asia. For example, when Dow builds plants in foreign countries, they have to adapt somewhat to that culture. The same is true for some foreign MNCs doing business in the United States. A matter of concern to many Western managers is the demand for bribes in developing countries, especially those along the Pacific Rim. This is a cultural matter which is better illustrated than explained.

Paying Officials along the Pacific Rim

A U.S. business executive expressed shock that his European friend was opening an office in Thailand. "Are you crazy?" he asked, "Don't you know all the payoffs that'll be required?"

The European answered, "I know. They work."

Even more payoffs of public officials are said to be required to do business in Indonesia. Official corruption in China has resulted in public protests. From police to customs officials to local bureaucrats, payoffs are a way of life in most of the Pacific Rim countries.

Malaysian companies were copying the product and the logo of a major U.S. firm. But the offended manufacturer was hesitant to ask for help from the Malaysian government. Why? The law officers would not really try to help without being paid bribes. And the company believed U.S. law made such bribes illegal.

Such bribes are often accepted as a matter of course by Asians. A certain Western businessman was asked to deliver a briefcase full of cash to an Indonesian official. The Westerner bashfully carried the briefcase through an outer office to the private office of the official. But the Indonesian brought the money back to the outer office and openly gave a share to each person who had helped "earn" the money.[15]

In certain societies, authority is viewed as a natural right and is not questioned by subordinates. In other cultures, authority must be earned and is provided to those who have demonstrated their ability to lead. In some cultures, work is good and moral; in others it is to be avoided. David McClelland discovered that the fundamental attitude toward achievement is somewhat correlated with rates of economic development. If a nation's citizens are willing to commit themselves to the accomplishment of tasks deemed worthwhile and difficult, a country will benefit economically. McClelland contends that one's sense of ability to influence his or her future will have a definite impact on the behavior of a country's work force.[16] If the basic belief is one of fatalism—what will be, will be—then the importance of planning and organizing for the future is downgraded.

Societies also vary as to interclass mobility and sources of status. If there is little hope of moving up to higher classes in a society, then fatalism and absence of a drive for achievement are likely. In many instances, the MNC will have to adapt and conform to the societal requirements of the host country in order to successfully operate as a multinational corporation. Obviously, management is directly impacted by societal concerns; therefore, such concerns must be carefully considered by MNC managers.

Unions

Surprisingly, the future of unionism abroad seems much brighter than domestic unionism. According to economist Richard Freeman, unionism fell in some countries in the 1980s, but no country suffered the consistent abrupt drop experienced by U.S. unions. While unionism has waned in the U.S., it is maintaining its strength abroad. Unions in all countries have been under increasing pressure in recent decades because of slowing productivity and economic growth, rapid technological change, and a shift toward a free market system, but unionism in the U.S. has suffered the most.[17]

Freeman and fellow economist David Blanchflower believe that the critical difference between U.S. unions and their overseas counterparts is that U.S. unions have managed to win much higher wages than those received by nonunion workers. That gap is 20 to 25 percent in the U.S. compared with 10 percent or less abroad. This pronounced gap gives U.S. employers a major incentive to oppose unions and establish nonunion operations. In addition, foreign unions are generally less adversarial with management and are also less focused on wage gains, keying instead on worker councils and participative decision making. Freeman and Blanchflower warn that domestic unions must change their direction from pursuing their "monopoly wage advantage," or their influence in the U.S. economy may be reduced even more.[18]

Before doing business in another country or entering into an international alliance, companies must understand the characteristics of the industrial relations system in the other country and in each partner firm. For example, contrast the following two situations: In the first situation, a German firm (where roughly 40 percent of the work force is represented by unions domestically) forms an alliance with a Swedish firm (where roughly 93 percent of the work force is represented by a union domestically).[19] Both partners are quite sympathetic to the desires of the workers to be represented collectively, in association with national or international unions. In the second situation, a Japanese firm (whose U.S. plant is nonunionized) forms an alliance with a U.S. company whose workers are members of a union. When asked for their most important concern about the partnership, the plant managers cited the fact that their alliance called for two companies with different industrial relations systems to work together.[20]

Obviously, the industrial relations issues that managers must address in these two situations are quite different. Understanding the implications of, and agreeing to abide by, a particular type of industrial relations system before consummating an international alliance are critically important. Regardless of the union or nonunion status of the country or alliance, it is imperative that the industrial relations issues that could decrease the productivity of the work force be addressed prior to entering a country or forming an international alliance.[21]

Stockholders

Stockholders must be satisfied with their return on investment or they will seek other investment opportunities. An MNC seeks to produce and distribute products and services throughout the world in return for a satisfactory return on its invested capital. A multinational corporation survives, grows, and remains attractive to stockholders by maintaining its technological advantages and minimizing risks.

Competition

Competition impacting firms operating in a multinational environment typically comes from many directions. In the past, U.S. firms had the luxury of viewing the competition as primarily American. This is no longer true, however. Now these same firms find themselves competing with corporations in many countries. Furthermore, companies may now find themselves competing with other multinationals and host country firms for the same personnel. This situation compounds the problems associated with management and creates a need for greater emphasis on the importance of managers in multinational corporations.

Customers

In this new environment, customers may exist in any country in the world. Cultivating these potential customers often requires new, and sometimes innovative, management approaches. For example, fundamental selling skills transcend cultural barriers. However, the perception of the salesperson differs from country to country, and the manner in which the sale is culminated often differs.[22] Subsequently, it is the proper preparation of the sales force that could mean the difference between success and failure. Therefore, managers must make every attempt to ensure that critical personnel who directly influence customers are properly prepared to represent the MNC.

Technology

In the multinational arena, countries are quick to transfer changes in production machinery and technology across national borders.[23] Technology is borrowed and stolen constantly. Often the receiving country even improves on the product. For example, Toyota in Japan took the assembly line and made it radically better with the just-in-time parts delivery system.[24] Since copyright laws usually do not cross national boundaries, it is often easy to purchase a product with a given technology and then improve on it. Taizo Yakushiji, a professor of international relations at Saitama University, said, "U.S. manufacturers are not studying their overseas competitors carefully enough."[25] Many U.S. companies are developing international joint ventures to get access to new technology. For instance, Boeing joined with Kawasaki and Fuji to obtain help in manufacturing the 767 airplanes, which seat as many as 260 passengers and can fly 7,000 miles nonstop.[26]

The Economy

The economy of the world and of various countries of the world is a major environmental factor affecting a manager's job in the global environment. Further complicating this is the fact that one country may be experiencing a downturn, another a slow recovery, and another a boom.

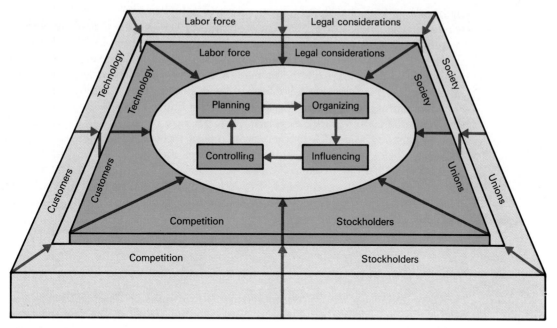

FIGURE 18–2

Management in a Multinational Environment

Management in a Multinational Environment

Each of the management functions is quite important in the multinational environment. In order to effectively manage a multinational firm, proper utilization of each of the management functions is essential. However, some differences should be recognized when planning, organizing, influencing, and controlling in the multinational environment (see Figure 18–2).

Planning

At first glance, the objectives of MNCs may not appear to be any different from the objectives of businesses operating exclusively within the United States. The typical MNC objectives of survival, profit, and growth are indeed similar to those of companies operating in the United States. However, there is a major difference: The objectives of the MNC may clash with the objectives of the economic and political systems of the various countries within which they operate. Some of the objectives of countries may coincide with those of the MNC, and some may not. Most countries want improved standards of living for their people, and such objectives as a trained labor force, full employment, reasonable price stability, a favorable balance of payments, and steady economic growth are fairly common.

In achieving some of these objectives, therefore, there is an overlapping of interests between the MNC and the host country. For example, a new MNC in a country will usually create jobs, thereby contributing to a higher level of employment, increased income, and economic growth. By doing so, MNCs often reduce the pressure on those political leaders who have high unemployment rates in their countries. Although the MNC usually contributes to the accomplishment of such objectives, it may not do so at the rate expected by the host country, and this can create problems.

One method for achieving a strategy of swift globalization is through the development of partnerships. Roland Smith, chairman of British Aerospace—which joined with counterparts from France, Germany, and Spain to form the aircraft manufacturer, Airbus Industries—said, "A partnership is one of the quickest and cheapest ways to develop a global strategy. " Recent partnerships include Texas Instruments and Japan's Kobe Steel (for a semiconductor plant in Japan) and du Pont and Korea's Han Yang Chemical (for a chemical plant in Korea).[27] Even firms such as AT&T and IBM that have a history of going it alone are forming partnerships in order to achieve their strategic plans.[28]

Organizing

The organizational structure of a multinational firm must be designed to meet the needs of the international environment. Typically, the first effort of a firm to become a multinational is the creation of an export unit in the domestic marketing department. At some point, the firm may perceive a need to locate manufacturing units abroad, and after a time, these various foreign units are grouped into an international division.

The international division becomes a centralized profit center, equal in status to other major domestic divisions. It is typically headed by a vice-president and operates on a fairly autonomous basis, independent of domestic operations. The reasons for this approach are (1) the necessity of obtaining managerial and technical expertise in the diverse environments of many countries and (2) the reduction of control from the often larger domestic divisions. The disadvantage is the decreased coordination and cohesion of the international division with the rest of the company.

As the international division grows, it usually becomes organized on either a geographical or product base of specialization. In giant MNCs, the international division is often a transitional stage in moving toward a worldwide structure that discounts the importance of national boundaries. Any such global structure requires a careful balance of three types of specialization: functional, area (geographical), and product. When the primary base is any one of the three, the other two must be present in the form of specialized staff experts or coordinators. A clear-cut decision heavily in favor of any one base is usually inappropriate.

In a global functional organizational structure for a multinational, the executive in charge of the production function has worldwide responsibility. Together with the presidents and executives in charge of sales and finance, a small group of managers enables worldwide centralized control of the MNC to be maintained.

MNCs with widely diversified lines of products requiring a high level of technology to produce and distribute tend to use the area base in their global structures. General Electric moved from the international division form to the global area structure. Primary responsibility for worldwide operations was assigned to the fifty to sixty general managers in charge of product divisions. International specialists, formerly in the international division, were reassigned to the various product divisions, to aid them in adapting to a multitude of national environments. To ensure that the product orientation did not dominate to the exclusion of area emphasis, four regional managers were established in Europe, Canada, Latin America, and the rest of the world. These executives were General Electric's eyes and ears in the countries to which they were assigned.

They advised product executives on the most suitable approach in each country, identified potential partners, and aided in establishing locally oriented personnel programs. The area executive might be given line authority when a product division had not yet gained sufficient skill in the region or when a subsidiary unit reported to many product divisions. Though the basic emphasis was on product, the addition of the geographical concept produced a type of matrix organizational structure.

Finally, when the range of products is somewhat limited, or when the product is highly standardized, MNCs tend to use the global product structure. Executives with true line authority are placed over major regions throughout the world. This type of structure is used by international oil companies (with a limited variety of products) and soft-drink producers (with a highly standardized product). As in other instances, some supporting staff is necessary in the product and functional areas.

In all forms of MNC structures, one makes sure (1) that the product is properly managed and coordinated throughout the world, (2) that the functional processes of production, sales, and finance are executed efficiently, and (3) that proper and efficient adaptations are made in response to the environments in the host country.

Influencing

Many aspects of the influencing function may be altered in a multinational environment. Of particular significance in the operation of a multinational firm are the topics of leadership, motivation, and communication.

Leadership Successful management of an MNC requires that the manager understand the needs, values, and problems of employees in the countries where the company operates. The requirements for effective leadership of personnel in the United States, Canada, Great Britain, Australia, or many of the Western European countries differ significantly from such countries as Turkey, Mexico, Malaysia, Taiwan, Thailand, or certain African, Asian, or South American countries. The needs and values of people vary from nation to nation, often the result of differences in economic living standards or cultural or religious influences.

In selecting individuals for overseas assignments, management must recognize that no one style of leadership will be equally effective in all countries. People in various countries have widely divergent backgrounds, education, cultures, and religions and live within a variety of social conditions and economic and political systems. Managers must consider all of these factors, because they all can have a rather dramatic effect on the working environment.

Much that is said concerning the appropriate management approach for international businesses must be based on common sense and informed conjecture. It seems reasonable that a successful international manager should possess the following qualities, among others:

- A knowledge of basic history, particularly in countries of old and homogenous cultures.

- A social background in basic economics and sociological concepts as they differ from country to country.
- An interest in the host country and a willingness to learn and practice the language.
- A genuine respect for different philosophical approaches.

Basically, individuals transferred overseas should have a desire to function, as well as possible, in the host country environment.

Motivation Unsatisfied needs tend to motivate behavior. In the United States and other highly developed countries, people's basic needs—physiological, and security—are fairly well satisfied. Research on the application of Maslow's hierarchy of needs theory of human behavior has shown considerable differences concerning the dominant needs of people in different countries. Thus, in some advanced countries, managers must try to satisfy the needs for esteem and self-actualization. In developing countries with lower standards of living, appeals to basic human needs may prove to be not only appropriate, but the primary means for motivating desired behavior.

Communication Communication is the transfer of information, ideas, understanding, or feelings among people. In a multinational environment, a difficulty one often encounters is ineffective communication. Certainly, working in a host country where the language differs from that of the parent country creates the possibility of communication breakdowns. An American working in an Asian country may experience this difficulty. Even when the same language is used, problems may occur. The meanings of words may be understood as defined. However, their intepretation may elicit other meanings. Even a tone of voice may be misinterpreted when two different cultures attempt to communicate.

The changing global environment has forced the need for global communication networks to the forefront. It has been estimated that global telecommunication networks may be more important to coordinate global operations than they are to the coordination of the parent country environment. Through such a system, electronic messages may be exchanged by people throughout the world who are tied into the network. The vast time-zone differences can be overcome through such a system.[29]

Controlling

Controlling has been defined as the process of comparing actual performance with standards and taking any necessary corrective action. The more multinational a firm becomes, the more important its control system. The need to effectively control inputs, processes, and outputs is certainly applicable in the multinational environment. However, certain aspects of controlling may not be the same as in the United States. For example, as a control mechanism, disciplinary action may take different forms in some countries.

Standards are established levels of quality or quantity used to guide performance. In establishing standards in the multinational environment, both corporate objectives and the local environment must be taken into consideration. Often host country managers need to be consulted with regard to the feasibility of a particular standard.

Evaluating performance is a critical but often more difficult task to accomplish when operating in a multinational environment. Often an extensive management information system is needed to provide managers in the parent country with the knowledge they need to make timely and proper decisions. At times, too much or too little information is fed into the system. This factor, combined with the distance factor, places increased pressure on evaluating the performance of a multinational organization. But, by almost any measure, Reebok has been a success.

• •

With five-year average sales growth of 254 percent a year, Reebok International Ltd. topped *Forbes* magazine's list of "Who's Where in Growth." In six years, sales had zoomed from $1.5 million to $1.4 *billion*. The company had earned a phenomenal 200 percent average return on equity during the same period. Most of Reebok's income was from shoes, made by Asian contract manufacturers. Reebok gained a remarkable 37 percent of the athletic shoe market. But the company also marketed a wide array of sportswear under the brands Reebok, Weebok, Metaphors, Avia, Ellessee, and Donner. The international division was headquartered in the UK, with subsidiaries in France, West Germany, Holland, and Austria. Reebok sold its products through distributors in 50 countries. Reebok rivaled Pepsi and Coke in name recognition and was in the top 5 on that basis worldwide. Recently, the company sponsored seven U.S. aerobic champions on a tour of the Soviet Union, viewed as an opening market for everything from peanut butter to locomotives. Of course, the team was decked out in Reebok shoes and active wear.

Reebok

By early 1990, the company was preparing to expand beyond its footwear and apparel product lines. Reebok agreed to buy Boston Whaler, an internationally prominent builder of premium powerboats. Chief financial officer Paul Duncan said the Whaler purchase was "certainly a little far afield of exactly where we were." But Duncan said such acquisitions would continue, adding, "We consider ourselves a marketing-type company." The purchase gave Reebok its first significant manufacturing operation. And it added unfamiliar distribution channels. There was some concern among analysts that the high-flying company might be overreaching.[30]

• •

Human Resources in the Multinational Environment

By and large, the success of a multinational corporation hinges on the human component of the organization. Recruitment and selection, orientation, and training and development needs are often quite different in the multinational climate. Career development of individuals may also be helped or hindered, depending on the internal and external factors affecting the multinational. Compensation, performance appraisal, and employee relations should reflect the unique culture of the host country as well as the needs of the multinational firm.

Recruitment and Selection

One of the most difficult management problems for the multinational organization is that of recruiting and selecting suitable people to be sent on foreign assignments. Inappropriate selections are often made, negatively impacting the multinational operation. As the globalization of the world economy intensifies, U.S. corporations have found it more difficult to assure the uninhibited flow of adequate human capital to the multinational organization. Recruiting individuals with appropriate qualifications and encouraging them to apply are essential for global success.[31] The essence of global business success is finding and employing the best people. Once the global business strategy is outlined, management must develop a corresponding recruiting strategy. The sooner human resource professionals are consulted about recruitment and selection, the better. In fact, establishing the global business strategy and the recruiting and staffing strategies concurrently will often result in a more effective overall strategy.

Poor selection, coupled with the stress of living and working overseas, has been documented as contributing to mental breakdown, alcoholism, or divorce. There are three common reasons why U.S. workers sent overseas fail: (1) Their family is misjudged as being adaptive to a multinational assignment or is not considered at the time of selection; (2) managers are selected solely on the basis of their domestic track records; or (3) they lack adequate cross-cultural training.[32] Other factors such as the following are also needed:

- A real desire to work in a foreign country.
- Spouses and families who have actively encouraged the person to work overseas.
- Cultural sensitivity and flexibility.
- A sense for politics.

Several surveys of overseas managers have revealed that the spouse's opinion and attitude should be considered the most important screening factor. Cultural sensitivity is also essential, to avoid antagonizing host country nationals unnecessarily.

The selection process for the expatriate should focus on measurement and evaluation of the candidate's current levels of expertise. Psychological tests, stress tests, evaluations by the candidate's superiors, subordinates, peers, and acquaintances, and professional evaluations from licensed psychologists can all aid in ascertaining the candidate's current level of ability in interpersonal and cross-cultural skills. The candidate's spouse and children should undergo modified versions of the selection process, since family members confront slightly different challenges overseas than do employees.[33]

Orientation

Orientation for new employees to the company, the job, and the work group varies in its degree of complexity, but global orientation will almost certainly be more complex than any domestic program. Because of the extreme cost of global staffing and the staggering cost of failed expatriate assignments, global orientation takes on increased importance;[34] orientation for new global employees is critical. It must incorporate an introduction to the organizational (and perhaps national) cultures of all parties that the individual is likely to encounter. Such an introduction should also include an overview of the history, traditions, and corporate values of any partners. Then, it should include a description of the new venture, its organization, and its management structure, followed by an introduction of the employee to the manager, department, and co-workers.[35]

Orientation cannot be a sketchy overview of the basics. It should be an in-depth process, thoroughly planned in advance, taking a long-term approach with provisions for follow-ups and evaluation. The benefits of such programs are just now beginning to become evident. Two years after developing such a system, Corning, Inc. showed a 69 percent reduction in voluntary turnover among new hires, an 8:1 benefit-to-cost ratio in the first year, and a 14:1 ratio annually thereafter.[36]

Both the General Motors–Toyota NUMMI joint venture and the Chrysler-Mitsubishi Diamond Star alliance made new employee orientation one of their first priorities. Each joint venture spent millions of dollars on orientation and training long before they formally started their manufacturing operations in the U.S. The success of these companies suggests that international alliances should be at least as concerned with preparing new employees to deal with the social context of their jobs and to cope with the insecurities and frustrations of a new learning situation as they are with developing the technical skills that employees need to perform effectively.[37]

Training and Development

Only a few multinational corporations offer formal training programs to prepare people to live and work overseas. People regarded as superior employees in the parent country often fail overseas because they are ill equipped to cope with the

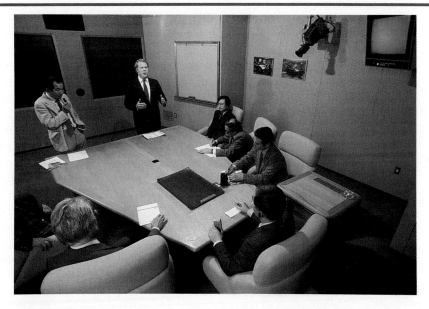

Only a few multinational corporations offer formal training programs to prepare people to live and work overseas. Employees often fail because they are ill-equipped to cope with the complexities and dangers of intercultural management. Imagine yourself as the American shown here making a presentation to his Japanese colleagues in a Tokyo affiliate company.

Source: © Jim Pickerell

complexities and dangers of intercultural management.[38] A review of the placement decisions of some American multinational companies found that the companies reported 30 percent of their placements to be mistakes—primarily due to the employees' failure to adjust properly to a new culture.[39] Some companies do offer training to expatriate employees, but the training is generally not comprehensive in nature.[40] The duration of cross-cultural training programs tends to be relatively short, considering the amount of knowledge and skills that need to be taught. Also, spouses tend to be left out of whatever training is offered by the company. However, multinational corporations are beginning to study culture to determine how different cultures communicate and work with each other.[41]

A major objective of intercultural training is to help people cope with unexpected events in a new culture. Once an expatriate is selected, it is essential to ensure that the person chosen is suitable for cross-cultural work. Needed skills may not be present in the most senior person—or in the person with the most technical competence.[42] An individual overwhelmed by a new culture will be unable to perform required work duties effectively. Further, an ill-prepared individual may inadvertently offend or alienate a foreign host and perhaps jeopardize the MNC's existing long-term relations with the host country.[43] Training should be sufficient to permit the manager (and spouse) to understand the new culture and adapt to their anticipated roles.[44]

Career Development

Foreign assignments have often been thought to provide career advancement opportunities. However, the relationship between expatriation and career development or advancement is often not clear. With varying results in terms of advancement, it appears there is no standard interpretation of the importance of an overseas assignment. The impetus for overseas staffing seems to be more to meet immediate human resource needs than to create an integrated career development strategy for future corporate executives.[45]

Whatever the case, without generous support during the overseas assignment, employees can become demoralized, frustrated, and anxious.[46] Despite a company's intention to provide career advancement opportunities, there is still some danger that skilled managers assigned to foreign operations will ultimately perceive that their career progress has suffered. Some managers have returned from foreign assignments to find no job available, or they are given jobs that do not utilize skills obtained overseas. To solve this problem, a godfather system is often set up. Before the person leaves on assignment, a specific executive is appointed as the "godfather" to look after the person's interests while he or she is in a foreign country and to assist the executive in achieving a smooth transition when returning home. A repatriation plan is worked out, including the duration of the assignment and to what job the appointee will return. Ordinarily, the godfather becomes the person's boss when the expatriate returns to the parent country. During the overseas assignment, the individual is kept informed of major events occurring in the unit to which this person will be assigned in the future. In this way, not only is there a logical career plan worked out, but there is no feeling of being lost in the vast international shuffle of the company.

Some repatriated managers report that the overseas assignment is a haphazard, ill-planned affair that is usually accompanied by vertical advancement. Upon return, many have difficulty in readjusting to domestic operations, experience lowered self-confidence in their domestic position, and on occasion find themselves without a job. Managers may be unaware of the challenges facing the repatriated employee; thus, career obstacles persist for the expatriate.

There is a need to assist the expatriate manager in career development. By putting in place policies and procedures toward that end, an organization can more efficiently manage human resources globally and encourage more employees to accept foreign assignments. The fundamental nature of such a system must be comprehensive; that is, the emphasis should not be solely on predeparture activities. The ideal international career management program should assess (and give preparation and feedback on) career and skill issues prior to departure, during the assignment, and subsequent to repatriation.[47]

Performance Appraisal

A performance appraisal system mandates a formal periodic review and evaluation of an employee's job performance. The development of an appropriate global performance appraisal system will undoubtedly be a complex process, but an effective global system is essential for credible employee evaluations.[48] Valid performance appraisal is difficult enough to achieve in the U.S., whereas valid evaluations for overseas employees make a normally complex problem nearly impossible. What normally works in one culture might not work in another. What is a strength in one culture might be considered a weakness in another.[49] When performance appraisals are done overseas, the issue of what performance standards to use comes into question. Differences in performance appraisal practices are almost always necessary. An improper performance appraisal system can create a great deal of misunderstanding and personal offense.[50]

Such problems can be partially avoided by taking the following actions. First, determine the purpose of the appraisal, whether it is to enhance administrative decision making or to enhance the personal development of the employee. Second, whenever possible, develop performance objectives for job assignments or tasks. Third, allow more time to achieve results in an overseas assignment. Finally, keep the objectives of the appraisal system flexible and responsive to potential markets and environmental contingencies. As with a domestic performance appraisal system, a global one should result in a realistic review and evaluation of the employee's job performance.[51]

Financial Compensation

The issue of global compensation is extremely important for a successful international business venture. Compensation must be a motivator and must encourage employees to perform. The ideal compensation system will help assure that the best performers receive the greatest level of compensation. Several additional questions arise when considering compensation levels for global employees. In the case of alliances, should the compensation systems of the partners be linked or will they be synthesized into a common system? Will compensation rates be pegged to local markets or tied to similar jobs in the partner's home country? Often each partner in a venture has an established pay policy but policies differ among partners. At the very least, partners in such ventures should reach an agreement on the broad objectives of a compensation program for employees.[52]

Global compensation programs should be designed to establish and maintain a consistent relationship between the compensation of employees in all international alliances and to maintain compensation levels that are reasonable in relation to leading competitors'. Failure to establish a uniform compensation policy can result in predictable adverse effects, especially for employees doing the same jobs. Such compensation systems will inevitably lead to low morale, motivational problems, and less productive employees.[53]

Employee benefits often vary drastically from country to country or from industry to industry. In Europe, for instance, it is common for employees to receive added compensation in proportion to their number of family members or the degree of unpleasantness in their working conditions. In Japan, a supervisor whose weekly salary is only $500 may also receive benefits that include family income allowances, housing or housing loans, subsidized vacations, year-end bonuses that can equal three months' pay, and profit sharing.[54]

Employee Relations

Crisis will occur regardless of whether the employee works in the domestic or global arena. "For an expatriate employee thousands of miles away from home the company is the family"; therefore, the company must provide support in times of crisis. According to Jay Hornsby, Dow Chemical Company's vice-president of human resources, "Whenever something goes wrong, and it will, he or she will naturally turn to the company for help." The key to maintaining good employee relations is for the company to be there when an expatriate employee needs help. Global human resource professionals have been called on to assist employees based abroad with a wide and often difficult range of problems. Some of these include medical emergencies, natural disasters, wars, revolutions, and other international crises.[55]

Medical emergencies occur fairly frequently. Ralph W. Stevens, vice-president of personnel and employee relations for Hamilton Oil Corp., recalls the case of a high-ranking technical manager who suffered a stroke while on business in Korea, where the company maintains no office. Stevens managed to find a first-rate physician, set the employee up in a well-regarded hospital, and transfer sufficient funds to cover his medical bills, while comforting the manager's frantic family.[56]

Because of its extensive operations in Latin America, Ferro, a $1 billion international manufacturer, has long had contingency plans in place for another kind of emergency: terrorist kidnapping. Nothing adverse has ever happened, but the company still strives to maintain a politically neutral and noncontroversial image when it operates in potential international trouble spots. Various contingency plans, including means and methods to evacuate workers if necessary, are in place for most U.S. companies currently operating in the Persian Gulf. CPC International Inc., for example, has a food-processing plant in Saudi Arabia. "Naturally we have contingency procedures approved and ready, although we would rather not discuss them," according to Richard P. Bergeman, the company's vice-president of human resources.[57]

During its more than 100-year history, Fluor Daniel has had to deal with almost every kind of international crisis. "Earthquakes, hurricanes, uprisings, we've probably had employees caught in all of them," says Tom Blackburn, the company's director of international administration. To Blackburn, more difficult and wrenching than politically induced crises are instances when an expatriate employee dies abroad. He once had to coordinate the transport of a worker's coffin from an international site back to the U.S., giving what solace he could to the man's grieving widow.[58] The ultimate test of the company's concern about positive employee relations comes in times of global crisis.

• •

Self-Assessment
Exercise
How Well Will You
Function in a
Multinational
Enterprise?

1. Are you willing to recognize that managing in a multinational environment provides different challenges?

   ☐ Yes   ☐ No

2. Are you willing to understand that managing in a multinational corporation is usually complex?

   ☐ Yes   ☐ No

3. Are you willing to recognize that the laws of the host country may be quite different from those in the United States?

   ☐ Yes   ☐ No

4. Are you willing to recognize that the significant societal considerations of one nation will differ to some extent from those of other countries?

   ☐ Yes   ☐ No

5. Are you willing to recognize that the organizational structure of a multinational firm must be designed to meet the needs of the international environment?

   ☐ Yes   ☐ No

(continued)

6. Are you willing to learn that successful management of an MNC requires that the manager understand the needs, values, and problems of employees in the countries where the company operates?

   ☐ Yes   ☐ No

7. Are you willing to learn that in selecting individuals for overseas assignments, you should realize that no one style of leadership will be equally effective in all countries?

   ☐ Yes   ☐ No

8. Are you willing to recognize the potential for communication breakdowns when operating in a multinational environment?

   ☐ Yes   ☐ No

9. Are you willing to remember that certain aspects of controlling may not be the same as in the United States?

   ☐ Yes   ☐ No

10. Are you willing to select individuals who can be effective in a multinational environment?

    ☐ Yes   ☐ No

Summary

Multinational corporations, organizations with extensive international operations in two or more countries simultaneously, usually operate through subsidiary companies abroad. Their operations create interrelationships between countries and cultures as well as between economic and political systems.

The external environment is extremely diverse and complex, and the manner in which managers' tasks are accomplished may be altered substantially. Additionally, organizational behavior considerations are much more complex. The MNC must deal with the environment of the parent country, in which the headquarters is located, and the host country, in which the operational unit resides.

The same management functions are important in the multinational environment. However, there are some differences. The MNC objectives differ from those of domestic firms because of their potential clash with the objectives of the economic and political systems of the host countries. Strategic plans tend to originate in the home office. Tactical plans tend to be delegated to the individual international branches. Further, the organizational structure of a multinational firm must be designed to meet the needs of the international environment.

Many aspects of the influencing function may be altered when operating in a multinational environment. Successful management of an MNC requires that managers understand the needs, values, and problems of employees in the host countries. In selecting individuals for overseas assignments, management must recognize that no one style of leadership will be equally effective in all countries. People's basic needs may differ and there may be problems in communication. A firm's control system is extremely important the more the company expands multinationally.

By and large, the success of a multinational corporation hinges on the human component. Selection and training and development needs are often quite different. Career development may be helped or hindered, depending on internal and external factors. The process of performance appraisal should reflect the unique culture of the host country as well as the needs of the multinational firm.

Review Questions

1. What is a multinational corporation?

2. Briefly describe the major environmental factors affecting the management of multinationals.

3. How are the management functions influenced by the multinational environment?

4. What types of organizational structures are used for multinational firms?

5. How are human resource needs different for multinational firms?

Key Terms

Multinational company (MNC)

Parent country
Host country

Transnational company

Throughout the eighties, the U.S. trade deficit with Japan grew worse. Especially in automobiles and electronics, the Japanese share of American markets steadily increased. The steadily growing stock of U.S. dollars in Japanese hands was used to buy up increasing shares of U.S. companies. Labor unions and politicians complained about the loss of American jobs. Citizens expressed fear that the Japanese would come to own too much of American industry. And corporations griped that they were shut out of potentially profitable foreign markets.

U.S. managers accused the Japanese of "dumping" products in the States (that is, selling items in the United States for less than the costs of production). Another frequent complaint was that the Japanese government erected every conceivable trade barrier to keep U.S. products out of Japan. At the same time, it was argued, U.S. markets were essentially open to Japanese companies.

But George Tanaka, senior vice-president of Toyonoka Electronics, said the problems were the Americans' own fault. Tanaka described what he saw as the "real" source of U.S. trade balance problems:

"In a nutshell, in Japan we treat customers as God and you only say, 'The customer is king.' Let me explain. Toyonoka sells microwave ovens in the United States. I have been trying for over a year to find an American company to make some of the parts we need. We want to have the parts shipped to Japan for installation in United States–bound ovens. That would improve your trade balance. It would also allow us to take advantage of present favorable exchange rates.

"But I cannot find anyone who will produce the quality we need to stay competitive. American managers tell me, 'This is as good as we can do. You will have to change your operation to make the parts work.' In Japan, of course, suppliers value contracts like this and do all they can to meet our specifications. I am under a great deal of pressure to buy American. But American firms just do not seem to care about our needs.

"The same kind of attitude surfaces when I ask about shipping schedules. In our factories, we practice 'just-in-time' inventory control. Japanese suppliers deliver the parts we need just when we need them—and in small quantities. I know United States companies have to ship long distances. So we are willing to accept larger shipments and be somewhat flexible about delivery dates. But no American firm I have talked to will guarantee even the *week* of delivery. They say there are too many variables involved—strikes, raw material shortages, shipping problems. In Japan, a supplier would not ask *me* to worry about those things. I am the customer.

"The language also presents a problem. United States firms will not bother to use Japanese. They refuse to even print installation instructions and invoices in any language but English. This is especially grating since we take the time to learn even the American dialect of English. Can any American imagine buying a Toyonoka stereo or a Mazda automobile with the owner's manual written in Japanese? We take care of those problems because Americans are our valued customers."

Mr. Tanaka went on to reemphasize that American companies could sell as much in Japan as Japan sells in the United States if they gave Japanese customers proper regard.

Questions

1. Does Mr. Tanaka's "ugly American" argument have some validity?

2. What are the cultural factors that may account for the difference in perspectives on the balance of trade issue?

At Memphis State University, Mark Brinson majored in industrial management and minored in French. He graduated cum laude. After graduation, Mark took a management trainee job with Tuborg International. Tuborg manufactured sporting equipment and had offices and factories in 30 countries. Mark's first assignment was to a plant in New York.

Mark did well and in three years advanced to the position of assistant plant superintendent. Just a few months later, he was offered a transfer to a similar position at a Tuborg plant in a rural area near Nice, France. Mark immediately accepted. During the three weeks before his departure, he refreshed himself on the French language. He expected problems adapting to the French culture but saw no way to prepare himself for that.

When he arrived at the factory, Mark learned the natives did not speak the "pure" French he was accustomed to. He also heard many slang expressions which were unfamiliar to him. For example, one of the workers said something to Mark that he interpreted as very uncomplimentary. Mark returned the "insult," to the consternation of all those present. Actually, the employee had greeted Mark with an expression which was often used locally as a friendly greeting, but which was rather risque. Such misunderstandings occurred frequently and Mark seriously considered asking for a transfer back to the United States.

Questions

1. What problems had Mark not anticipated when he took the assignment?

2. How could the company have assisted Mark to reduce the difficulty that he confronted.

3. Do you believe the situation that Mark confronted is typical of an American going to a foreign assignment? Discuss.

Notes

1. This case is a composite of a number of published accounts, among them: Peter R. Savage and Peter Coombes, "Sustaining Growth at Dow," *Chemical Week*, April 5, 1989, pp. 25–27; Paul L. Blocklyn, "Developing the International Executive," *Personnel* (March 1989): 44–47; "Dow Chemical Profit Forecast," *Wall Street Journal*, May 12, 1989, p. B4; Catherine Brady, "Plastics Recycling Moves Ahead," *Chemical Week*, March 29, 1989, pp. 20–21; Gregory Stricharchuk, "Dow Chemical Gets a Victory on Sarabond," *Wall Street Journal*, May 10, 1989, p. A4; Joseph B. White, "Dow Chemical Says Earnings May Disappoint," *Wall Street Journal*, June 16, 1989, p. B5; "Dow in China Deal," *New York Times*, April 5, 1989, p. D4; Douglas A. McIntyre, "Companies I'm Glad They Didn't LBO," *Financial World*, January 24, 1989, p. 76; David Hunter, "Atochem Bets on CFC in 1990s," *Chemical Week*, January 18, 1989, pp. 20–21; Ellen Goldbaum, "An Ag Venture is Born," *Chemical Week*, April 26, 1989, p. 9; "The Fortune 500 Largest U.S. Industrial Corporations," *Fortune*, April 24, 1989, pp. 354–399; Patricia L. Layman, "Chemical Company Execs Chart Progress toward Global Industry," *Chemical & Engineering News*, October 16, 1989, pp. 15–17; Alison L. Sprout, "America's Most Admired Corporations," *Fortune*, February 11, 1991,

pp. 68–69; Albert Richards, "Is BASF the Next Company to Watch in Europe?" *Chemical Week*, August 1, 1990, p. 11; and Standard and Poor's Corporation, "Dow Chemical," *Standard NYSE Stock Reports* 56, no. 125 (June 29, 1989): sec. 9.

2. Patricia Digh Howard, "World Shrink," *HR Magazine* 36 (January 1991): 43.

3. Raymond J. Mataloni, Jr., "Capital Expenditures by Majority-Owned Foreign Affiliates of U.S. Companies, Latest Plans for 1991," *Survey of Current Business* 71 (March 1991): 26.

4. "U.S. Corporations with the Biggest Foreign Revenues," *Forbes* 148 (July 2, 1991): 286.

5. Ibid.

6. Richard A. Melcher, Mark Maremont, Amy Borrus, and Thane Peterson, "The Japanese Are Coming—And Thatcher Is All Smiles," *Business Week*, February 20, 1989, p. 46.

7. Walter Kiechel, "Love, Don't Lose, the Newly Hired," *Fortune*, June 6, 1988, p. 87.

8. Ibid.

9. INSIDE BUSINESS: Cornelius Van Der Klugt shares his perspectives regarding certain realities of operating in the multinational environment with the CNN business news team of Kandel, Hartley, and Young.

10. Leonard Greenhalgh, "I Would Abandon Business Contracts," *Fortune* 121 (March 26, 1990): 49.

11. Adapted from a case presented in Karen Berney's article, "Finding the Ethical Edge," *Nation's Business*, August 1987, p. 22.

12. Calvin Reynolds, "U.S. Expatriates' Numbers Continue to Decline," *HR News International HR*, March 1991, sec. C, p. 2.

13. "Firms Woo Executives from 'Third Countries,'" *Wall Street Journal*, September 16, 1991, p. B1.

14. Melcher, Maremont, Borrus, and Peterson, "The Japanese Are Coming—And Thatcher Is All Smiles," p. 46.

15. Ford S. Worthy, "When Somebody Wants a Payoff," *Fortune*, Fall 1989 special issue, pp. 117–122.

16. Peter Wright, David Townsend, Jerry Kinard, Joe Iverstine, "The Developing World to 1990: Trends and Implications for Multinational Business," *Long Range Planning* 15 (1982): 122.

17. Gene Koretz, "Why Unions Thrive Abroad—But Wither in the U.S." *Business Week*, September 10, 1990, p. 26.

18. Ibid.

19. Wayne F. Cascio and Manuel G. Serapio, Jr., "Human Resources Systems in an International Alliance: The Un-

doing of a Done Deal?" *Organizational Dynamics* 19 (Winter 1991): 72–73.

20. Ibid.

21. Ibid., p. 73.

22. Brian H. Flynn, "The Challenge of Multinational Sales Training," *Training and Development Journal*, November 1987, p. 54.

23. Jay Jaikumar, "The Boundaries of Business: The Impact of Technology," *Harvard Business Review* 69 (September–October 1991): 100.

24. Susan Moffat, "To Be a Leader in Technology, You Must Share It," *Fortune* 124 (January 14, 1991): 34.

25. Ibid.

26. Ruth Simon and Graham Button, "What I Learned in the Eighties," *Forbes* 145 (January 8, 1990): 101.

27. Patricia A. Langan, "The New Look of Globalization," *Fortune* 121 (April 23, 1990): 18, 20.

28. Jeremy Main, "Making Global Alliances Work," *Fortune*, December 17, 1990, p. 121.

29. Steven M. Zeltmann, "Communications Networks for Managing Global Operations," *Business Perspectives* 14 (Fall 1990): 20–21.

30. This case is a composite of a number of published accounts, among them: Christopher J. Chipello, "Reebok to Buy CML Unit for $42 Million, Signaling Expansion of Product Line," *Wall Street Journal*, August 8, 1989, p. A7; Robert Hartlein, "Reebok Exporting Aerobics to Untapped Soviet Market," *Women's Wear Daily*, May 17, 1989, p. 13; Anthony Ramirez, "Meet One Big Bonus Baby," *Fortune*, December 19, 1988, p. 66; Gale Eisenstodt, "Apparel, Shoes and Textiles," *Forbes*, January 9, 1989, pp. 86–88; Standard and Poor's Corp. "Reebok International," *Standard NYSE Stock Reports* 56 (May 17, 1989), Sec. 20; John Sedgwick, "Treading on Air," *Business Month*, January 1989, pp. 29–34; Steve Kichen, "Who's Where in Growth," *Forbes*, January 9, 1989, p. 198; Pat Sloan, "'U.B.U.' Appears D.O.A. as Reebok Readies New Ads," *Advertising Age*, February 6, 1989, p. 3.

31. John P. Senko, "Dollar-Wise, Pound-Foolish Controlling Expatriate Execs' Costs," *Management Review* 80 (March 1991): 38.

32. Allen L. Hixon, "Why Corporations Make Haphazard Overseas Staffing Decisions," *Personnel Administrator* 31 (March 1986): 91.

33. Mark E. Mendenhall, Edward Dunbar, and Gary R. Oddou, "Expatriate Selection, Training and Career-Pathing: A Review and Critique, "*Human Resource Management* 26 (Fall 1987): 331–345.

34. Mike Fergus, "Employees on the Move," *HR Magazine* 36 (May 1990): 45.

35. Cascio and Serapio, Jr., "Human Resources Systems in an International Alliance: The Undoing of a Done Deal?" p. 68.

36. Ibid.

37. Ibid., p. 69.

38. Michael Berger, "Building Bridges over the Cultural Rivers," *International Management*, July–August 1987, p. 61.

39. Christopher Earley, "Intercultural Training for Managers: A Comparison of Documentary and Interpersonal Methods," *Academy of Management Journal* 30 (December 1987): 685.

40. Mendenhall, Dunbar, and Oddou, "Expatriate Selection, Training and Career-Pathing: A Review and Critique," pp. 331–345.

41. Berger, "Building Bridges over the Cultural Rivers," p. 61.

42. Prabhu Guptara, "Searching the Organization for the Cross-Cultural Operators," *International Management*, August 1986, p. 40.

43. Earley, "Intercultural Training for Managers: A Comparison of Documentary and Interpersonal Methods," p. 685.

44. Ibid.

45. Mendenhall, "Expatriate Selection, Training and Career-Pathing: A Review and Critique," p. 331.

46. Philip R. Harris, "Employees Abroad: Maintain the Corporate Connection," *Personnel Journal*, August 1986, p. 108.

47. Mendenhall, "Expatriate Selection, Training and Career-Pathing: A Review and Critique," p. 331.

48. Cascio and Serapio, Jr., "Human Resources Systems in an International Alliance: The Undoing of a Done Deal?" p. 70.

49. Mark E. Mendenhall and Gary Oddou, "The Overseas Assignment: A Practical Look," *Business Horizons* 31 (September–October 1988): 81.

50. Ibid., p. 70.

51. Ibid.

52. Cascio and Serapio, Jr., "Human Resources Systems in an International Alliance: The Undoing of a Done Deal?" 70.

53. Ibid., p. 71.

54. Ibid.

55. Ellen Brandt, "Global HR," *Personnel Journal* 70 (March 1991): 43.

56. Ibid.

57. Ibid.

58. Ibid.

19

Production and Operations Management

LEARNING OBJECTIVES

After completing this chapter students should be able to

- Explain the evolution of production and operations management.

- Identify and describe some of the graphic methods used in production and operations methods analysis.

- Explain the primary labor measurement methods and describe site selection.

- State the basic approaches to physical facility layout and explain the concepts of maintenance control and learning curves.

- Describe the major trends regarding factories of the future.

- Explain some of the basic financial models that are especially useful in production and operations management.

- Describe simulation and explain how it can be used in business.

Motorola Focuses on "Six Sigma" Quality: Defect-Free Manufacturing

Originally founded as Galvin Manufacturing Corporation in 1928, Motorola, Inc. adopted its present name in 1947. Motorola is a leading manufacturer of electronic equipment and components. A global corporation, Motorola has facilities on every continent. Its principal products are: two-way land mobile communications systems; paging systems; semiconductors, including integrated circuits and microprocessor units; modems, multiplexers, and network processors; electronic equipment for military and aerospace use; cellular phones; and computers. Domestic high-tech companies, including Motorola, face fierce competition from abroad, particularly from the Japanese. However, in all of these high-tech arenas, Motorola has successfully met Japanese competition.

Twelve years ago, then chairman Robert Galvin decided that Motorola would go toe to toe with the Japanese. To accomplish this, Galvin elevated the company's quest for quality, and Motorola began plowing massive funds into research and development and capital improvements. In 1991, it spent over $2 billion, or 20 percent of revenues for R&D and capital expenditures. Motorola also spent tens of millions of dollars each year on employee training. The result of this strategy was that overall product defects have been slashed from nearly 3,000 per million in 1983 to under 200 today. Customers responded favorably. Motorola's global sales rose 13 percent.

Thus far, Motorola's success stems partly from a team atmosphere generated among employees who produce the highest quality products possible. Motorola spends half a billion dollars annually to ensure that new technologies keep their plants efficient and productive. Continuous training ensures that employees learn to use these new technologies effectively. Motorola motivates employees to produce quality products by creating and monitoring a team atmosphere; employees set their own goals in terms of achieving quality and meeting delivery schedules.

On October 3, 1991, Motorola went one step further in their quest for excellence. They announced the formation of Motorola Lighting Inc. (MLI). This subsidiary is the test bed for their adaptation of the Japanese approach to simultaneous design and construction of the product and the factory. The company seems committed to gaining a manufacturing edge.

Simultaneous design and manufacturing involves teams from engineering, marketing, and manufacturing joining together to design the product. Twenty-two employees from the MLI subsidiary worked together in a single room at Motorola headquarters. According to manufacturing manager Russ Intravartolo, "Everybody's business was everybody's business." Working closely together permitted the most critical element in efficiency: "simultaneous design and construction of the product and factory." Although widely used in Japan, the technique is still catching on among U.S. manufacturers. However, Motorola is embracing the concept. Rather than design the product and then test whether it can be manufactured, the MLI process makes manufacturing seamless. Redesign work that would have taken three weeks elsewhere is done in only two days because everyone is in on product design meetings. Therefore, the staff simply meets and solves problems whenever they occur. When defects occur, engineers gather for an "E2," Motorola jargon for a quick meeting to figure out what steps to take to address the problem.

Motorola is committed to "Six Sigma" quality, statistical jargon for defect-free manufacturing, and appears intent to do whatever it takes to accomplish this goal. Under the current leadership, Motorola has increased its quality 100 fold and has achieved a statistical margin of nearly 3.4 defects per million parts produced—close to their goal of 99.9997 percent perfection. However, for a company to be truly on a par with competitors like the Japanese, excellence in product design and quality is only one factor. On-time delivery, full customer support, timely introduction of products, and competitive pricing must be "nothing less than consistently perfect."[1]

Production and operations

The application of objective, especially quantitative, techniques to the design and operation of any system that transforms inputs into outputs.

Operations management

The management of the complex activities relating to planning production, organizing resources, directing operations and human resources, and monitoring system performance.

Only a few years ago, production management was taught exclusively in relation to factory environments such as that of Motorola. Today, the expanded field of production and operations management applies to all organizations, including banks, hospitals, schools, and government agencies. **Production and operations** is *the application of objective, especially quantitative, techniques to the design and operation of any system that transforms inputs into outputs.* Most production and operations techniques are equally applicable to manufacturing and service industries. **Operations management** is *the management of the complex activities relating to planning production, organizing resources, directing operations and human resources, and monitoring system performance.*

In this chapter, we will first discuss the evolution of production and operations management. Then, we will review a number of traditional techniques, including graphic methods, labor measurement, site selection, physical facility layout, maintenance control, and learning curves. This will be followed by a brief look at factories of the future. Next, we will discuss financial planning techniques. In the final sections of the chapter, we will examine simulation as it relates to production and operations management and a global perspective of production.

The Evolution of Production and Operations Management

The quality and cost of a product are determined largely by the effectiveness and efficiency of the production system. A substantial body of knowledge has accumulated on the use of statistics, computers, engineering, and behavioral science techniques in manufacturing environments since the Industrial Revolution. Application of these techniques helped make America the most productive nation in the world, a distinction it retained through the 1980s. But recent cost-cutting efforts by U.S. manufacturers have typically relied on such approaches as plant closings, downsizing (reducing the size of the entire operation), laying off production workers, and selling off failing, unwanted, or unprofitable businesses. This was especially true during the takeover craze of the late 1980s.

Also in the 1980s, perhaps as a result of the decreasing willingness of U.S. managers to invest in new technology, productivity in the United States grew more slowly than in most other industrialized countries. The United States lagged behind Japan, South Korea, Great Britain, West Germany, Sweden, France, and Canada in productivity growth.

Experts argue that American firms focus on capital investment as a means of reducing labor costs and consequently ignore the huge benefits to be gained from improving quality, reducing inventories, and tapping the hidden productivity of the labor force. Basically, American managers have been underutilizing their human capital—pouring hundreds of billions of dollars into equipment and technological advancements rather than keeping and retraining valuable employees and gearing their efforts to improve the relationship between work and productivity.

MANAGEMENT IN PRACTICE: A Skill-Building Exercise

You have a boss who simply will not listen. Last week, you hired the two technical operators who will run the new $600,000 laser micro-milling (cutting) machine. The machine must be attended at all times in order to keep it operating to the precise tolerances that the titanium nose cones require. For two of the six operating steps, the process requires both workers. However, those two processes take only twelve minutes of the eighty-minute cutting time. Both employees have four-year technical degrees. Your boss, the department manager, has just told you that the two employees will be in charge of the machine on alternate days. On each one's off day, that one will assist the other worker during the critical twelve-minute period. For the other sixty-eight minutes, the idle employee will clean up around the shop floor and help load and unload trucks.

You personally recruited both employees, and you realize that they won't stand still for clean-up duty and loading and unloading trucks. You can either try to force them to do so, and risk losing them, or you can go over your boss's head.

What would you do or say?

U.S. companies are beginning to follow and extend the Japanese method of worker involvement. Although the Japanese have a group-oriented culture, where workers help find and solve problems, activities are directed by managers and engineers. In the U.S., the evolution has gone beyond mere group decision making to a point of American teamwork. American teamwork involves group members in management activities such as determining the appropriate method of work or rating other group members' performance; some groups even have the authority to fire loafers.[2] Remember that Motorola motivates employees to produce quality products by creating and monitoring a team atmosphere in which employees set their own goals in terms of achieving quality and meeting delivery schedules.

Fortunately, American managers are beginning to balance their capital and human investments to improve the production system. Managers also appear to be more interested in any suggestions that can improve the production process. Maytag Company was so committed to improving their production operation that they solicited suggestions from nonsupervisory personnel. A total of 6,346 suggestions

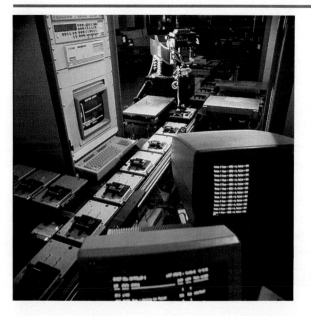

Fortunately, American managers are beginning to balance their capital and human investments to improve the production system. Motorola's flexible "factory of the future" in Boynton Beach, Florida, produces high-quality Bravo® pages in minutes instead of several days. Programmable robots are controlled by an integrated computer network.

Source: Photograph courtesy of Motorola, Inc.

were turned in, an average of 3 per employee. More than 2,700 of these ideas were actually implemented. Maytag management gave employees awards ranging up to $7,500 and totaling $200,322 for suggestions used.[3]

Other companies are approaching production problems by developing a "new math" formula for productivity. Traditional cost accounting methods are out at many firms such as Calcorp, Inc. Managers at Calcorp, a maker of graphic plotters, are making capital investment decisions in fresh and innovative ways. For example, instead of automating to cut costs, they invest in equipment to cut lead times, boost quality, reduce inventories, and increase flexibility. Management de-automated the shop by eliminating the traditional assembly line and using carts to push work around. The new system takes a fraction of the former space and output has tripled. It appears that this approach to productivity can benefit corporations by providing both structural changes and innovative approaches to technology, thereby improving the effectiveness and efficiency of the production system.[4] Because of the need to revitalize production systems, production and operations management has reemerged as a challenge to all organizations.

Graphic Methods

Several graphic techniques have been developed to assist in production and operations methods analysis. The techniques in and of themselves do not improve the way a task is done. Instead, they permit a person with an inquiring mind and knowledge of the subject to improve the production process. Four of these techniques are the flow process chart, the operation chart, the worker-machine chart, and the activity chart.

Flow Process Chart

Flow process chart

A chart illustrating the activities involved in an entire process, showing the sequence in which they are performed.

A chart illustrating the activities involved in an entire process, showing the sequence in which they are performed, is a **flow process chart.** Standard symbols have been developed to serve as a type of shorthand in recording activities. Each task to be accomplished is identified, along with the time it will take. A manager can then study the sequence of tasks to determine if there is a better way to accomplish the job. Figure 19–1 is the flow process chart for a cylinder head (the top part of a gasoline engine), which is to be ground and inspected prior to its assembly onto a tractor engine. Only the activities related to the grinding department are shown.

Operation Chart

Operation chart

A chart showing an operator's activities while one operation in a process is performed.

A chart showing an operator's activities while one operation in a process is performed is an **operation chart.** It might show the motions of the left hand and right hand of an operator. Its use is essential when the time from start to finish of an operation (the cycle time) is fairly short. Operations are usually broken down into smaller categories than those used with a flow process chart. A major benefit of an operations chart is that it permits a manager to view a task to see if it is being done the best way.

Description of Activity	Chart	Standard Time (Minutes)
Remove from storage		2
Grind surface		27
Inspect and eye-check		17
Transport to Assembly Department		5
	To next stage	

FIGURE 19–1

Flow Process Chart

Worker-Machine Chart

A chart showing if there is excessive idle time associated with either the worker or the machine is a **worker-machine chart.** These charts are beneficial when both a worker and a machine are used to perform a particular task. An idle worker may be assigned an additional machine to control. On the other hand, if the machine is expensive and needs to be kept operating, this may justify the cost of an additional operator even though the idle time of the worker goes up.

Worker-machine chart

A chart showing if there is excessive idle time associated with either the worker or the machine.

Activity Chart

In both the manufacturing and the service industries, efficient accomplishment of objectives requires the use of teams. An activity chart, which is similar to a worker-machine chart, is useful for this purpose. An activity chart can show the interaction of members of the group in performing a task. For example, in a hospital, the activities of a surgical team in performing an emergency operation must be carefully controlled. If any member of the team fails to act correctly at the right time, the results could be disastrous. An activity chart allows the actions of each team member in relation to those of other members to be graphically displayed.

Labor Measurement

The most critical factor in the production process is labor. If management is to manage labor resources effectively, there must be some way of measuring their use. Labor standards specify the amount of time necessary to perform a certain task. Standards are used to set up incentive plans and to compare the performance of individuals doing similar tasks. They are also used in preparing bids on contracts and in estimating completion dates. There are three primary labor measurement methods: time study, predetermined time standards, and work sampling.

Time Study

Time study

The systematic measurement and analysis of the time required to do work.

The systematic measurement and analysis of the time required to do work is **time study.** The most common approach to time study is patterned after the approach developed by Frederick W. Taylor in 1881. Under this procedure, a stopwatch is used to measure one worker's performance, and then the results become a standard for all workers. The following steps are normally included in a time study:

1. Describe the task to be performed.
2. Break the task down into a number of simple subtasks.
3. Measure the time required to perform each subtask and note operator performance. (This should be done over a number of work cycles.)
4. Compute the average time required to do the total task according to the following formula:

$$\text{Average time} = \frac{\text{Times recorded to perform all subtasks}}{\text{Number of cycles observed}}$$

5. Compute the normal time. The normal time is determined by computing a performance rating, that is, the percentage of reasonable working speed at which the observed worker is judged to be working. The formula for normal time is as follows:

Normal time = Average performance time × Rating factor

6. Calculate the standard time according to the following formula:

$$\text{Standard time} = \frac{\text{Normal time}}{1 - \text{Allowance fraction}}$$

The allowance fraction adjusts for personal needs, unavoidable work delays, and worker fatigue, among other variables. Suppose, for example, that an average time of five minutes was determined for painting a tractor wheel hub and that the time study analyst decided the worker was moving at 90 percent of normal speed. Assume further that the work methods department of the firm has a standard allowance for this kind of work of 15 percent. The standard time is computed as follows:

$$\text{Normal time} = \text{Performance time} \times \text{Performance rating}$$
$$= 5.0 \times .9$$
$$= 4.5 \text{ minutes}$$

$$\text{Standard time} = \frac{\text{Normal time}}{1 - \text{Allowance}}$$
$$= \frac{4.5}{1 - .15}$$
$$= \frac{4.5}{.85}$$
$$= 5.3 \text{ minutes}$$

Although the worker is moving at only 90 percent of normal speed, standard time can still be computed.

Predetermined Time Standards

An alternative to the measurement of the actual time required to do work is the use of **predetermined time standards**—*established estimates of the time that should be required to perform minute tasks.* In order to estimate how long a certain task will take, the time factors for each element are added together.

The most widely known approach to using predetermined time standards was developed by Frank and Lillian Gilbreth and is called methods time measurement (MTM). The Gilbreths called the basic work elements *therbligs* (if you reverse the last two letters of the Gilbreths' name and then spell it backward, you get *therblig*). Therbligs included such activities as selecting, grasping, positioning, assembling, reaching, holding, resting, and inspecting. Time values for various therbligs are available from the MTM Association for Standards and Research.

The use of predetermined time standards has several advantages. First, the standards may be established in a laboratory environment, avoiding interruption of normal production activities. Second, the standards can be known before a task is done, and this knowledge can aid in planning. Finally, the method is widely accepted by unions, perhaps because the association that sets the standards is independent of management.

Work Sampling

A way of measuring work that does not use a stopwatch is called **work sampling**—*the observation of a worker or workers at random times to determine the proportion of time that is being spent on various tasks.* If employees can be shown how to better accomplish their work and how to add to the overall team effort, they will benefit themselves, their team, and the corporation. A detailed procedure for work sampling was developed by L. Tippet in the 1930s. Statistical sampling techniques are used to determine the number of observations needed to obtain the desired degree of reliability.

Suppose that we wish to determine how much of a word processor operator's time is involved in the preparation of correspondence. If we observe the operator at one hundred randomly selected points and find that correspondence is being prepared at thirty of them, we can estimate that the operator works on correspondence 30 percent of the time.

Site Selection

Every firm has its own criteria for choosing a particular site for locating a new facility. In addition to cost considerations associated with purchasing and building a new site, many other factors must be evaluated, including the supply of skilled labor, union activities, quality of life, and local, state, and even international politics. For many reasons, a site that may be completely satisfactory for one company may be totally unacceptable for another. Many U.S. firms select plant sites in Mexico because of the low labor costs there. Cooper Tire provides an example.

Ivan Gorr, the head of Cooper Tire & Rubber Company, has always employed a strategy of expanding existing capacity by reequipping existing or older plants rather than building new ones. Some Cooper plants were purchased from major tire makers, such as Goodyear, and then refurbished. This resulted in low capital costs. Until recently, Cooper was also able to maintain the lowest labor costs in the industry, according to Gorr. But both capital and labor costs began to inch up in the late 1980s, and Cooper's profit margins slipped.

Cooper has never been a big supplier of original equipment tires bought by automobile manufacturers such as GM and Ford. Cooper's main business is making and selling replacement tires through retail dealers. Customers often choose tires on the basis of small differences in price. So Cooper was forced to seek new ways to lower costs.

The solution Cooper chose was to open a plant in Mexico, where labor costs per hour are a fraction of those in the United States. This is the first time that Cooper Tire has gone outside the United States. The experiment appears to have been a success. The company's sales and profits increased substantially, even though sales in the U.S. tire industry fell by 15 percent.[5]

A number of mathematical and computer-based techniques have been developed to assist in determining where to locate a physical facility. The most commonly used approach is to develop a set of criteria and rate each location on how well it meets the criteria. An example of this procedure is illustrated in Table 19–1. In this case, the most important factor for site selection is availability of skilled labor, so this factor is assigned a maximum score of 30. Availability of raw materials, with a maximum score of 20, is the next most important criterion. Third is access to transportation, with a top score of 15. In the example, three sites have been proposed and rated on each of the criteria. The total score for site 2 is significantly above the others, although site 2 ranks lowest on access to transportation. Often, there are many more factors than those shown in this simple illustration.

Physical Facility Layouts

For virtually any type of operation, management must determine the most effective way to lay out the physical facilities. Among the more traditional approaches are process layouts, product layouts, and fixed-position layouts. In a factory environment,

TABLE 19–1

Plant Location Scoring Model

	Maximum Score	Site 1	Site 2	Site 3
Availability of skilled labor	30	18	25	15
Availability of raw materials	20	12	18	10
Access to transportation	15	10	5	10
Total score		40	48	35

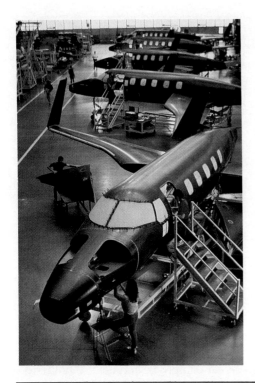

The overriding objective of physical facility layout is to maximize efficiency and effectiveness. After winning certification for its all-composite Starship, Beech Aircraft, a subsidiary of Raytheon Corporation, rolled its first production aircraft off this assembly line.

Source: Photograph courtesy of Raytheon Company

management might be concerned with the best placement for lathes and punch presses. Offices, desks, and computers might be of concern in an administrative setting. And in a hospital, the locations of operating rooms, laboratories, and nursing stations have a major impact on efficiency. The overriding objective of physical facility layout is to maximize efficiency and effectiveness.

Process Layouts

A wide variety of goods or services can be handled simultaneously when the process layout is used. A **process layout** is *an arrangement of the processing components according to the functions they perform.* A typical example of the use of the process layout is the job shop that produces different products, each by a different sequence of operations. Basically, there is no single best route through the system for all the goods or services produced. The product may be made one unit at a time or in batches (see Figure 19–2). The unit or batch moves from one department to another in a particular sequence.

A common example of the process layout is found in hospitals. Patients come to the hospital with a wide variety of problems. Depending on their ailment, they are routed through various departments—admissions, lab, x-ray, and so on. When the process layout is used, the objective is to arrange departments or work centers in the most economical manner. In most situations, an attempt is made to minimize material-handling costs.

A major advantage of the process layout is that it provides for flexibility in equipment and labor assignments. If one machine breaks down, for example, the entire

Process layout

An arrangement of the processing components according to the functions they perform.

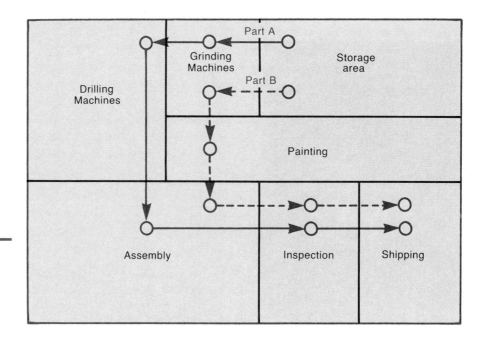

process may not have to be stopped. Work can simply be rerouted. Another advantage is that the process layout permits the economical manufacture of goods and services in small batches. It also permits a wide variety of outputs in different sizes and forms.

A disadvantage of the process layout is that it allows less specialized use of equipment and labor. Also, the items being processed require additional handling, since they must be moved to each process point. Finally, labor skill requirements are high, inventories must be large, and scheduling and coordination may present major problems.

Product Layouts

Product layout

The production arrangement that entails moving a product down an assembly line or conveyor and through a series of work stations until the product is completed.

The production arrangement that entails moving a product down an assembly line or conveyor and through a series of work stations until the product is completed is a **product layout.** Automobiles, television sets, and soft drinks are produced in this manner. When the product layout is used, the objective is to create a smooth, continuous flow along the assembly line with a minimum of idle time at each work station. The product layout presents a balancing problem. Time required at each work station needs to be balanced so that it is nearly the same as at the following one.

The main advantage of a product layout is manufacturing efficiency when large numbers of essentially identical items are produced. This is partly because automated and specialized equipment is used. Also, material handling is lower, inventories are reduced, and workers can usually be more quickly trained.

Product layouts have weaknesses too. First, assembly lines typically require a large investment. Second, a breakdown at one point on the assembly line can require the entire line to be stopped. Finally, an assembly line typically cannot handle a wide variety of products.

Fixed-Position Layouts

A method used in manufacturing large or heavy products is the **fixed-position layout**—*the production process in which the large or heavy product stays in one location, and people, tools, materials, and equipment are moved to the product as needed.* Basically, the production process occurs around the product because it is too large or too heavy to move along a production line. A military aircraft carrier is a product that, at a certain stage, is too large and too heavy to make a standard production line feasible. In order to complete the product, it is necessary to move the process to the location of the carrier.

Fixed-position layout

The production process in which the large or heavy product stays in one location, and people, tools, materials, and equipment are moved to the product as needed.

Maintenance Control

In a typical organization, the breakdown of even one machine can have severe effects. Workers may be idled, and in some instances entire facilities may have to be closed. Consider what will happen if the air-conditioning system in a large, modern office building fails or if the central computer system at General Motors is out of order for even a day.

Maintenance is *the sum of all activities involved in keeping a production system in working order.* In most organizations, it represents a significant part of total costs. *Routine inspection and other efforts aimed at preventing breakdowns and keeping equipment and facilities in good working order* are **preventive maintenance.** If a company is not willing to bear the costs of preventive maintenance, breakdowns tend to occur. Such breakdowns typically must be repaired on an emergency or priority basis, often at considerable expense. The purpose of preventive maintenance is to identify potential problems and make changes or repairs before breakdowns occur. For example, keeping a machine well oiled is a better alternative than replacing the machine because a bearing failure has caused it to break down.

A balance must be struck between preventive and breakdown maintenance. Notice in Figure 19–3 that as preventive maintenance costs rise, breakdown maintenance costs fall. The intersection of these two cost curves represents the lowest maintenance costs. Up to this point, putting more and more money into preventive main-

Maintenance

The sum of all activities involved in keeping a production system in working order.

Preventive maintenance

Routine inspection and other efforts aimed at preventing breakdowns and keeping equipment and facilities in good working order.

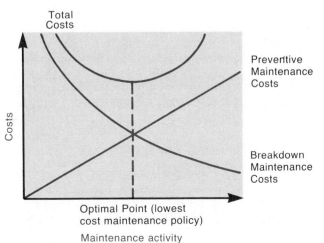

FIGURE 19–3

Preventive versus Breakdown Maintenance Costs

SOURCE: *Reprinted by permission from Ralph M. Stair, Jr., and Barry Render, Production and Operations Management: A Self-Correcting Approach (Boston: Allyn and Bacon, 1980), p. 350.*

A balance must be struck between preventive and breakdown maintenance. At some factories, such as the Defense Department's Savannah River Plant in South Carolina, the main emphasis is on preventive maintenance. This plant, managed by Westinghouse Corporation, is the only U.S. facility which produces radioactive tritium, an isotope considered essential to the nation's defense.

Source: Photograph courtesy of Westinghouse Corporation

tenance will reduce total maintenance-related costs. Beyond this point, though, the firm will be better off waiting for breakdowns to occur and repairing them when they do.

Learning Curves

Learning curve

A graphic representation of the decreasing time required to do a particular task as that task is repeated by a certain person.

A graphic representation of the decreasing time required to do a particular task as that task is repeated by a certain person is a **learning curve.** Essentially, the more times a person does a particular job, the easier the task becomes. Two basic principles are involved. First, the more times a task is done by a particular person, the less time it will take. Assume, for example, that a technician has just begun assembling a number of identical small components. If she needs twenty minutes to complete the first unit, by the time she has done four units, the time may be down to fifteen minutes. Second, the amount of time saved with each unit of experience normally decreases. The technician just mentioned has decreased the time required by five minutes in making just four units. Many additional repetitions may be needed to shave just one more minute off the time.

A mathematical relationship can be developed to determine how long it will take to produce any unit as a function of how many units have been produced before it. The implications of learning curve analysis are far-reaching. For instance, failure to consider the learning curve effect can result in running out of inventory and raw materials because the units produced are taking less and less time to finish. Also, considering the learning curve effect helps in labor planning and scheduling. It can keep managers from scheduling more time than is necessary for a project, thereby avoiding idleness or underemployment of workers.

Factories of the Future

Experts cite a long list of shortcomings when it comes to America's slippage as a real competitor in the world market for goods and services. They often mention outmoded and inflexible factories, inefficient organizations, a mass-production mind-set, low-skilled workers, technologically illiterate management, and behavior motivated by short-term profit. But much of U.S. industry has modernized in recent decades. General Electric's installation of flexible manufacturing at its Erie, Pennsylvania, locomotive factory is but one example.

● ●

"Here in this old Northeastern U.S. industrial community, we are giving an aging industrial complex an electronic heart transplant that will make it a world-class facility, competitive with the Japanese, Germans, or anyone else in the world." This is how a General Electric vice-president described GE's efforts to install flexible manufacturing systems at its diesel electric locomotive factory in Erie, Pennsylvania. It had taken five years and had cost $316 million, but the modernization program chief said that productivity had tripled and capacity could then be expanded by 100 percent. For example, production time for the heaviest motor frame had been reduced from sixteen days to sixteen hours.

Modernizing a Locomotive Factory

One flexible manufacturing system machines ten different locomotive components, ranging from a small gearbox weighing only 150 pounds to a large casting weighing more than a ton and containing as many as 140 machined surfaces. When a casting or welded frame enters the machining process, it is turned over to the central computer. This "executive computer" then orders an automatic transporter to take the piece to its first machining station. The proper program is automatically loaded into the individual machine computer. Parts being manufactured are shuffled among the various machines to make sure each machine is used efficiently. "Not a single nonrobotic hand will work on the frames until the computer is satisfied with the work and summons a human to take them away," said the individual in charge of technical systems at GE.

The executive computer also keeps track of tool life so tools can be replaced before they wear out and create defects. Some of the machines change their own tooling between jobs. On others, a robot situated nearby makes the tool changes. As modern as this may sound, a GE engineer points out that the technology in the plant is at least two years old because of the necessary construction time.[6]

● ●

American managers are sometimes faced with high-cost capital, difficult government regulations, and a refusal by management to refine the breakthroughs already in production.[7] What America may need to retain its competitive position are topnotch factories that properly balance technology, people, and innovation. The factories of yesteryear are being virtually reinvented through high technology. Rapidly moving into oblivion is the once-familiar scene of the blue-collar worker with dirty hands in front of a drilling or stamping machine. An almost antiseptic atmosphere now often appears to exist in some factories. Robots and other computer-controlled machinery manufacture items while technicians stand by the computer controls monitoring activities. For example, IBM's Lexington, Kentucky, plant manufactures computers that are untouched by human hands.[8]

The factories of the future are being put in place today. Just a few years ago, advances such as computer-aided design (CAD), computer-aided engineering (CAE), computer-aided manufacturing (CAM), and computer-integrated manufacturing (CIM) were touted as the wave of the future. With them, a customized order that comes in today can be ready for shipment tomorrow morning. Computer-integrated manufacturing is a sophisticated form of CAD/CAM. With the CIM system, companies have been able to make different versions of a product at mass-production speeds in lots as small as one unit.

More than ever before, managers are *not* looking to a technological fix to solve productivity problems. They are starting to redefine the design and manufacturing process. Some fresh ideas are starting to help U.S. companies go well beyond computer-aided manufacturing. Some companies are utilizing new math (described earlier in the chapter), design for manufacturability (DFM), and concurrent engineering.

With design for manufacturability, the product is engineered for easy assembly by reducing the number of parts or shunning the use of screws for quicker snap-on fasteners. NCR Corporation uses DFM on its latest point-of-sale terminal, and the system "can be put together in less than two minutes—blindfolded."[9]

Simultaneous design and manufacturing is somewhat similar to design for manufacturability. Teams from engineering, marketing, and manufacturing join together to design the product. Working closely together permits perhaps the most critical element in efficiency: "Simultaneous design and construction of the product and factory." Rather than design the product and then test whether it can be manufactured, the process is seamless. Redesign work can be done quickly because everyone involved is in on product design meetings. Subsequently, the staff can simply sit down and solve problems whenever they occur. Motorola has adopted this seamless process. Remember that when defects occur at Motorola, engineers gather for an "E2," Motorola jargon for a quick meeting designed to figure out what steps to take to address the problem.[10] To improve some processes concurrent engineering is used.

Concurrent engineering involves the simultaneous development of both the product and the process to make it. The factory evolves as the product does. Northrop Corporation is even giving manufacturing engineers veto power over designers. Ford Motor Company is also a big proponent of concurrent engineering. According to Ford's vice-president for research, John P. McTague, "The more design and production become seamless the better [off] we'll be."[11]

Also, interdepartmental barriers are beginning to fall because of the spread of shared databases in computer-integrated enterprises. Closer cooperation among workers is growing rapidly. Because of interdepartmental cooperation, Lockheed Corporation's Calfab sheet-metal facility slashed design and production time by 96 percent.[12]

With flexible manufacturing and more enlightened management-labor attitudes, many large companies—including IBM, Hewlett-Packard, John Deere, and 3M—have been able to reduce their total cost by 30 to 40 percent in a few years. Even small and medium-size companies can employ this strategy. CalComp, Inc., used this approach and substantially decreased its total cost with an investment of only $300,000.[13]

Ford's success can also be traced directly to the factory floor. There, teamwork, careful attention to detail, and proper utilization of technology have allowed Ford to increase productivity, quality, and consumer satisfaction. The blend of the techniques just discussed and a greater emphasis on employee involvement at all levels, including management, has allowed Ford to become the nation's low-cost automaker.[14]

American managers are beginning to realize that the factory is a dynamic place—an evolving entity that must properly balance technology, people, and innovation to meet the challenges of the future. One goal for factories of the future is unattended assembly. A new Ford plant in Lansdale, Pennsylvania, represents a big step in that direction for U.S. industry."It will be better than anything I've seen in Japan, and at least as good as GM's best." The plant manager was talking about Ford Motor Company's new Lansdale, Pennsylvania, circuit card factory. The cards control production of the 3 million car engines the plant is designed to make each year. Cimflex Teknowledge Corp. was hired to tie together the $100 million worth of computerized equipment at Lansdale.

Cimflex chief Romesh Wadhwani claimed the factory represented a big step toward "lights out" shifts for U.S. manufacturing. "In terms of tightness of integration," said Wadhwani, "it's ahead of world class." He said Japanese factories that operated unattended during night shifts only do machining, not assembly, and are slowed down to prevent problems. On the other hand, said Wadhwani, Ford's Lansdale plant would do machining and assembly without human oversight. Of course, circuit cards are not comparable in manufacturing complexity to some of the robots, for example, in Japan's most automated factories. The general assessment of the potential for unattended assembly at Lansdale was not as glowing as Wadhwani's, but both illustrate future possibilities.

Still, the advances made by expert-systems companies like Cimflex are offering a potential edge for U.S. manufacturing. Expert systems is a subfield of artificial intelligence (AI), which tries to simulate human cognitive processes. Wadhwani gave a glimpse of the world to come in manufacturing. "Until now," he said, "we've been focused on the shop floor. Now we're integrating up, into design for manufacturability and engineering analysis, to manufacturing planning and scheduling. Next, we will migrate downstream, into linking the factory to customer service."[15]

ETHICAL DILEMMA

The milling company you run has developed a computer-aided milling process. The process yields a wheat flour that, when used for bread, provides a lighter, more uniform texture than conventionally milled wheat flour. And the production process requires less expensive labor. The new flour can be sold for more profit because it requires less time to produce, is viewed by customers who have sampled it as a superior product, and has a labor cost advantage of 20 to 30 percent.

Unfortunately, the process gives off more dust than the emissions control equipment presently installed can handle and still maintain emissions within legal limits. Because of a lack of availability, your company will be unable to install new emissions control equipment for at least two years. If you wait that long to use the new process, your larger competitors may squeeze your company out of the market.

You must decide whether or not to use the new process during the third shift, which runs from 10 P.M. to 6 A.M. By using the process at that time, you could introduce the new flour; and the dust released by the process would not be detected in the dark. By the time demand becomes great enough to put on a second shift, the new emissions control equipment should be available. You can process the new type of flour during the third shift, from 10 P.M. to 6 A.M., or you can shut down the unit that processes the new type of flour and wait for the new emissions control equipment.

What would you do?

Financial Planning Techniques

One of the most valuable tools for a business planner is financial modeling. This tool is especially useful in making capital investment decisions. Factors related to profit and loss are so vital to the growth, and even survival, of a firm that it is advantageous for any planner to understand the available techniques. Some of the basic financial approaches are the payback method, break-even analysis, discounted cash flow, make/buy decisions, and purchase/lease decisions.

Payback Method

Payback method

The method of financial analysis by which investments are ranked according to the payback period, the time it takes an investment to pay back the initial capital in profits.

The most common and easiest method of financial analysis is the **payback method**— *the method of financial analysis by which investments are ranked according to the payback period, the time it takes an investment to pay back the initial capital in profits.* For example, if the initial investment is $1,000 and the return is $200 per year, the payback period is five years.

Although easy to understand, the payback method has major limitations. First, returns after the payback period are not considered. In the example, the investment might keep returning $200 for five more years. Second, the time value of money is not considered. A dollar today is not the same as a dollar ten years from now. To overcome the inaccuracy of this approach, many companies use it in a very conservative manner. For example, Lincoln Electric Company, the world's largest maker of arc welding products, has a maximum payback period for new projects of only two years. Thus, if a machine will not pay for itself during the first two years of operations, Lincoln will not buy it.

Break-Even Analysis

Break-even analysis

The financial analysis method used to determine the amount of a particular product that must be sold if a firm is to generate enough revenue to cover costs.

The financial analysis method used to determine the amount of a particular product that must be sold if a firm is to generate enough revenue to cover costs is **break-even analysis.** Fixed and variable costs and total revenue (total income) are charted according to the number of units produced in order to determine the point at which revenue and costs are equal and the operation begins to make money. In order to progress in a break-even study, one must be capable of identifying the following elements:

- Fixed costs.
- Variable costs.
- Price of the item.

Fixed costs are *costs that do not change with the level of output.* Costs that normally are considered fixed are the salaries of top management, rent, property taxes, and other similar expenses. **Variable costs** are *costs that are directly related to changes in output.* Costs that might be included as variable costs are direct material and labor expenses incurred in manufacturing a particular product.

The distinction between fixed and variable costs is not always as clear-cut as we might like it to be. Often, there is a gray area in which some costs can be considered either fixed or variable.

The break-even point for selling a product is arrived at by dividing total fixed costs by price minus variable costs. To illustrate: Suppose a product is priced at $15, total fixed costs are $1,000, and variable costs are $10 per unit. Using the following formula to determine the break-even point in units of output, we have:

$$\text{Break-even point in units} = \frac{\text{Total fixed costs}}{\text{Price} - \text{Variable costs}}$$

$$= \frac{\$1,000}{\$15 - \$10} = 200$$

Thus, we would have to sell 200 units before we could begin making a profit.

Figure 19–4 shows graphically how break-even analysis is used. The vertical axis is costs and revenue, and the horizontal axis is units of output.

The $1,000 in fixed costs is represented on the graph by a straight line. Variable costs change with the level of production, so the variable cost line slopes upward. Variable costs are added to fixed costs to determine total cost, so the variable cost line starts at the point where the fixed cost line intercepts the vertical axis. The total

Fixed costs

Costs that do not change with the level of output.

Variable costs

Costs that are directly related to changes in output.

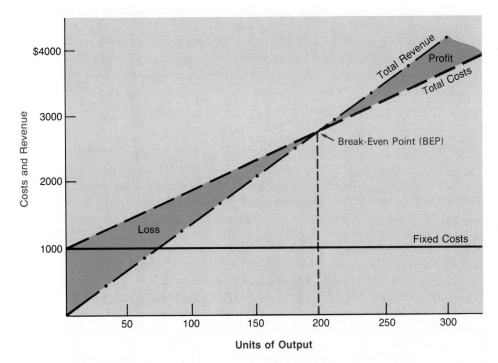

FIGURE 19–4

Break-Even Analysis

Year	Savings per Year Machine A	Savings per Year Machine B	Present Value of $1	Present Value of Savings Machine A	Present Value of Savings Machine B
1	$50,000	$60,000	0.870	$43,500	$52,200
2	50,000	60,000	.756	37,800	45,360
3	50,000	60,000	.658	32,900	39,480
4	50,000	60,000	.572	28,600	34,320
5	50,000		.497	24,850	
6	50,000		.432	21,600	
7	50,000		.376	18,000	
				208,050	171,360
		Less cost of equipment		200,000	150,000
		Net discounted cash flow		8,050	21,360
		Difference in net discounted cash flow		└─$13,310─┘	

TABLE 19–2

Purchase Decision

Note: Machine A costs $200,000; Machine B costs $150,000.

revenue line is price times number of units sold. The break-even point of 200 units is at the intersection of the total revenue and total cost lines.

How reliable is break-even analysis? Would you bet your firm's survival on it? Probably not, but the benefits can be substantial if break-even analysis is used with full appreciation of its weaknesses. If you drew a bead on the break-even point with a shotgun and fired, the pattern of the shots would spread out around the break-even point. This is about as accurate as you might expect to be because of the difficulty of correctly identifying fixed and variable costs. But break-even analysis certainly forces a manager to plan. And an individual who plans is in a position to make better decisions than a nonplanner.

Discounted Cash Flow

Discounted cash flow
technique

The way of valuing an investment that uses an interest rate or discount rate to calculate the present value of the income the investment is expected to produce.

One of the disadvantages of the payback method is that it does not consider the time value of money. A common approach to considering the time value of money in business decision making is the **discounted cash flow technique**—*the way of valuing an investment that uses an interest rate or discount rate to calculate the present value of the income the investment is expected to produce*. Most of the uses of this technique involve capital investment decisions. Taking into consideration the time value of money can mean the difference between profit and loss.

Assume that the vice-president of production must decide which of two machines should be purchased. One machine costs $200,000 and will generate a savings of $50,000 a year over the next seven years. The other machine costs $150,000 but will generate $60,000 in savings over the next four years. The discount rate is 15 percent. Referring to Table 19–2, notice that the net discounted cash flow (the amount saved) for Machine B is $21,360, whereas that for Machine A is only $8,050, a difference of $13,310. Therefore, Machine B is clearly the better choice, even though the total amount of cash saved over a seven-year period is greater for Machine A. When time value of money is taken into consideration, decisions are improved.

Make/Buy Decisions

Decisions concerned with evaluating the benefits of making a product in-house or going outside to another manufacturer are make/buy decisions. The main factor in such decisions is whether the manufacturing costs in-house are lower than those outside. But this is not the only factor to consider. The manager must also ask whether the space that will be used to manufacture the product in-house could be used more advantageously. If the space could be used to make more money through manufacturing other things, the decision might be made to produce the product outside the firm.

Purchase/Lease Decisions

Another important financial decision is whether to purchase or lease (rent) equipment. Discounted cash flow methods are often used in making such decisions. In evaluating the purchase option, such items as interest expense, depreciation, and salvage value must be considered. However, leasing may involve only the lease payment.

Simulation

Businesses have found simulation a valuable tool to use in the planning and decision-making process. **Simulation** is *the technique for experimenting with a real-world situation through an artificial model that represents that situation.*[16] A model is an abstraction of the real world. Thus, a simulation model represents a real-world situation through mathematical logic in an attempt to predict what will occur in an actual situation. Its uses are many and widespread.

Simulation transcends the boundaries of many of the other quantitative techniques. As such, it is not a separate quantitative tool; rather, it is a procedure that has been used effectively in conjunction with other mathematical tools, such as inventory control and quality control. A manager who operates in an uncertain environment may consider simulation.

The general steps associated with developing a simulation model are presented in Figure 19–5. Once the problem has been identified, a simulation model is

Simulation

The technique for experimenting with a real-world situation through an artificial model that represents that situation.

FIGURE 19–5

Steps in Simulation

developed and run. The results are then analyzed. If the manager wants to ask other "what if" questions about the problem, they can be asked. The manager is in a position to ask many questions about the other factors that could affect the problem.

Railroads have found simulation particularly beneficial. Have you ever wondered why more trains don't arrive at the same time on a single track? Trains are different lengths and weights; they travel at different speeds and typically must share a common track to get from one place to another. At times there are two or more tracks that the cars could travel on, but the majority of the time there is only one. Simulation provides the manager with the ability to recognize the many variables that are involved with activities such as train scheduling and to ask questions regarding solutions to the problem.

Procter & Gamble utilizes simulation to assist in solving some unusual problems. P&G provides the following example of how the company uses simulation:

> Pulp forms the basic raw ingredient for manufacturing paper and can be made in a variety of grades that are dependent on the chemical processing and the blend of wood species. Procter & Gamble refines pulp from trees, and they use simulation to aid in the design of a woodyard, assuring maximum operating efficiency with a minimum of capital investment.
>
> A woodyard serves as a surge area for wood arriving from various sources by unscheduled railcars and trucks. The wood is in the form of short and long logs and must be stored until used in the pulp mill. Naturally, railcars require different unloading equipment than trucks and the simulation helps determine the optimum number of unloading stations for both. Additionally, different equipment is needed to handle long logs than short logs for both railcars and trucks. After long logs are unloaded, they are cut into short logs before they can be stored, an operation that requires other special equipment. Finally, the operation of the pulp mill needs a constant feed of a well-controlled blend of wood species to be efficient. Wood must be stockpiled sufficiently to assure a constant feed regardless of the weather, which can bring the tree cutting operations to a standstill for a couple of weeks, or equipment failures in the woodyard. In net, the simulation of the flow of materials through the woodyard helps size equipment and stockpiles of logs to assure constant availability of the proper wood species for input to the pulp mill.

This example is but one of the ways simulation has been used effectively. If the risk of making a decision is great, the manager will need to evaluate many options before making a commitment to allocate resources. Simulation provides an excellent tool for evaluating alternatives and finding solutions to problems.

A Global Perspective

The quality and cost of a product are determined largely by the effectiveness and efficiency of the production system. In order to be competitive globally, American firms must produce quality products at competitive prices. Manufacturing systems in the United States are now undergoing revitalization to assist American manufacturers in their attempt to be competitive in the global business environment of the next decade. Production systems that will allow American firms to be globally competitive will probably require adaptation to the most recent behavioral and technological changes.

American managers are beginning to balance their capital and human investments to improve their production systems. Managers also appear to be more interested in any suggestions that can improve the production process. Companies are beginning to follow, and extend, the Japanese method of worker involvement. American teamwork involves group members in management activities, such as determining the appropriate method of work and rating other group members' performance.[17]

Some companies are approaching production problems by developing a "new math" formula for productivity. Traditional cost accounting methods are out. Managers are making capital investment decisions in fresh and innovative ways. For example, instead of automating to cut costs, they may invest in equipment to cut lead times, boost quality, reduce inventories, and increase flexibility. At Ford Motor Company, design for manufacturability and assembly (DFMA) allows products to be designed with regard to ease of manufacturing and assembly. This approach helped Ford trim manufacturing costs by $1.2 billion.[18] Because of the need to compete globally, American firms must reenergize production systems by balancing their capital and human investments and by using new approaches to production.

● ●

Self-Assessment Exercise

How Well Will You Work in a Production and Operations Management Environment?

1. Are you willing to learn the importance of balancing both your capital and human investments to improve the production system?

   ☐ Yes   ☐ No

2. Are you willing to remember that operating in a service-producing industry as opposed to a goods-producing industry creates different problems?

   ☐ Yes   ☐ No

3. Are you willing to recognize and be able to use the production and operations management techniques?

   ☐ Yes   ☐ No

4. Are you willing to learn to use the principles of motion economy to improve efficiency and reduce fatigue?

   ☐ Yes   ☐ No

5. Are you willing to remember that if you are to manage labor resources effectively you must have some way of measuring their use?

   ☐ Yes   ☐ No

(continued)

Summary

Several graphic techniques have been developed to assist in production and operations methods analysis. A flow process chart is an illustration of the activities involved in an entire process, showing the sequence in which they are performed. The operation chart shows an operator's activities while one operation in a process is performed. Through studying worker-machine charts, a manager is able to determine if there is excessive idle time associated with either the worker or the machine. An activity chart is useful to show the interaction of members of a group in performing a task.

There are three primary labor measurement methods: time studies, predetermined time standards, and work sampling. Time study is the systematic measurement and analysis of the time required to do work. Predetermined time standards are established estimates of the time that should be required to perform minute tasks. Work sampling is the observation of workers at random times to determine the proportion of time that is being spent on various tasks.

A number of mathematical and computer-based techniques have been developed to assist in determining where to locate a physical facility. However, the most commonly used approach is to develop a set of criteria and rate each location on how well it meets the criteria.

There are three basic approaches to arranging physical facilities: process layouts, product layouts, and fixed-position layouts. A process layout is an arrangement of the processing components according to the functions they perform. The production arrangement that entails moving a product down an assembly line or conveyor and through a series of work stations until the product is completed is a product layout. A fixed-position layout is the production process in which the large or heavy product stays in one location, and people, tools, materials, and equipment are moved to the product as needed.

Maintenance is the sum of all activities involved in keeping a production system in working order. A learning curve is a graphic representation of the decreasing time required to do a particular task as that task is repeated by a certain person.

The most commonly used and easiest method of financial analysis is the payback method, by which investments are ranked according to the time it takes an investment to pay back the initial capital in profits. The method used to determine the amount of a particular product that must be sold if a firm is to generate enough revenue to cover costs is break-even analysis. The discounted cash flow technique is the way of valuing an investment that uses an interest rate or discount rate to calculate the present value of the income the investment is expected to produce.

Simulation is the technique for experimenting with a real-world situation through an artificial model that represents that situation. Simulation transcends the boundaries of many of the other quantitative techniques.

Review Questions

1. Define each of the following terms:
   a. flow process chart
   b. operation chart
   c. worker-machine chart
2. Distinguish between time studies and work sampling.
3. Describe a process layout, a product layout, and a fixed-position layout.
4. What is the purpose of preventive maintenance?
5. What are the basic principles associated with the learning curve?
6. What are the costs involved in break-even analysis? Define each.
7. Why might a manager want to use the discounted cash flow technique of evaluating investment decisions as opposed to the payback method?
8. Explain what is meant by this statement: Simulation transcends the boundaries of many of the other quantitative techniques.

Key Terms

Production and operations
Operations management
Flow process chart
Operation chart
Worker-machine chart
Time study
Predetermined time standards

Work sampling
Process layout
Product layout
Fixed-position layout
Maintenance
Preventive maintenance
Learning curve

Payback method
Break-even analysis
Fixed costs
Variable costs
Discounted cash flow technique
Simulation

MATERIALS MANAGEMENT AT NEWCO

Tom Johnson, the new materials manager for the Newco Manufacturing Company, was concerned about the disorganization in his department. Newco had 250 employees and manufactured small electrical motors. Tom reported to the vice-president of manufacturing, Charles McDowell. Tom's fifteen subordinates performed such functions as stocking, receiving, inventory control, purchasing, and outside sales.

The previous materials manager had allowed the employees to do whatever job they thought necessary at the time. They had often shifted from job to job—working the parts-issue window while mechanics ordered parts, stocking the parts bin when time permitted, receiving parts when deliveries were made, and shipping orders to customers. The same employees answered the phone and handled outside sales as required. Employee complaints over matters such as inadequate pay, unclear work assignments, and lack of competent leadership had been frequent.

Charles gave Tom a detailed account of the past performance of the materials operation. He said the department performed very poorly, and he attributed this to a lack of overall direction, ineffective organization, and incompetent personnel. He said several of the employees were lazy and did as little work as possible. The turnover rate had been in excess of 200 percent per year for the past three years. Charles suggested that Tom "clean house" by firing most of the employees in the department and starting with a fresh crew.

Tom was shaken by what Charles had told him and by the complaints of the employees, and he considered finding a new position. He decided, however, to give the assignment his best efforts for at least a few months.

Questions

1. Would a flow process chart assist Tom? Discuss.
2. How should Tom handle the human situation he faces? Justify your answer.

WAVING THE SCHOOL FLAG

Phyllis Stevens, a junior management major at Western Kentucky University (WKU) was treasurer of the university's chapter of the Society for the Advancement of Management (SAM). The chapter had only $250 in its bank account, and Phyllis was asked to come up with a way to raise money. The first feasible idea she had was selling small WKU flags at football games. The team had been doing well and was expected to have a winning season. Still, Phyllis was concerned about getting the chapter into a venture that might not pay off.

Phyllis contacted a local seamstress, who agreed to make up 1,000 flags for $200, provided the SAM chapter would furnish the materials. The materials were available at a cost of 50 cents per flag. Since the flags would be sold by SAM members, there were expected to be no other costs. After lengthy discussion, the chapter decided to sell the flags for $1 each.

Questions

1. How many flags must the SAM chapter sell in order to break even?

2. How many flags must they sell to make a profit of $100?

3. If Phyllis thinks the maximum number of flags the SAM chapter can sell is 500, should the group take on the project? Discuss.

Notes

1. This case is a composite of a number of published accounts, among them: Kevin Kelly, "Motorola Wants to Light up Another Market," *Business Week*, October 14, 1991, p. 50; B. G. Yovovich, "Motorola's Quest for Quality," *Business Marketing*, September 1991, pp. 14–29; Jim Impoco, "Fighting Japan on Its Home Turf," *U.S. News & World Report*, June 24, 1991, pp. 50–52; and Kent Banning and Dick Wintermantel, "Motorola Turns Vision to Profits," *Personnel Journal* (February 1991): 51–55.

2. John Hoerr, "The Payoff from Teamwork," *Business Week*, July 10, 1989, pp. 56–62.

3. S. Feinstein, "Labor Letter," *Wall Street Journal*, March 15, 1988, p. 1.

4. Karen Pennar, "The Productivity Paradox," *Business Week*, June 6, 1988, pp. 100–114; Bruce Nussbaum, "Needed: Human Capital," *Business Week*, September 19, 1988, pp. 100–103.

5. INSIDE BUSINESS: Mr. Ivan Gorr discusses his very aggressive plans for the future, emphasizing many aspects of production and operations management, with CNN business news correspondent Grant Perry.

6. John A. Byrne, "Is Your Company Too Big?" *Business Week*, March 27, 1989, pp. 84–94; Anderson Ashburn, "GE Puts FMS in an Aging Plant," *American Machinist*, May 1983, pp. 104–105; B. H. LeCerf, "GE Pumps New Life into an Aging Factory," *Iron Age* (May 1983): 74–77; "Here Are GE's Latest Advances in Robotic Welding Systems," *Purchasing* (December 19, 1985): 18; and "GE to Test Core for Production UDF," *Aviation Week and Space Technology*, March 3, 1989, p. 67; and Standard and Poor's Corporation, "General Electric," *Standard NYSE Stock Reports* 56, no. 230 (May 2, 1989), sec. 12.

7. Otis Port, "A New Vision for the Factory," *Business Week*, Innovation 1989, p. 146.

8. Zachary Schiller, "Big Blue's Big Overhaul," *Business Week*, Innovation 1989, p. 147.

9. Port, "A New Vision for the Factory," p. 146.

10. Kelly, "Motorola Wants to Light up Another Market," p. 50.

11. Port, "A New Vision for the Factory," p. 146.

12. Ibid.

13. Ibid.

14. James B. Treece, "How to Teach Old Plants New Tricks," *Business Week Innovation* 1989, p. 130.

15. "A Factory That Practically Runs Itself," *Business Week*, May 8, 1989, p. 145.

16. Jack R. Meredith, *The Management of Operations*, 3d ed. (New York: Wiley, 1987), p. 669.

17. Hoerr, "The Payoff from Teamwork," pp. 56–62.

18. Karen Pennar, "The Productivity Paradox," pp. 100–114; Bruce Nussbaum, "Needed: Human Capital," pp. 100–103; Otis Port and Wendy Zellner, "Pssst! Want a Secret for Making Superproducts?" *Business Week*, October 2, 1989, p. 106.

Management
Information Systems

LEARNING OBJECTIVES

After completing this chapter students should be able to

- Explain the types of information needs firms have.

- Describe the characteristics of an effective MIS and explain the MIS at different organizational levels.

- Describe the steps involved in creating the MIS and offer guidelines for effective MIS design.

- Explain what is involved in the implementation of the MIS and the types of computers that are available for it.

- Describe the various types of information subsystems that are available for use by management and discuss the advantages of an integrated system.

- Describe major computer advancements and how they can affect productivity.

"I am not sure we have fewer meetings, but they are more productive," said Xerox president Paul Allaire. "We very rarely have a meeting at which we don't have enough information to make a decision." In 1985, Ken Soha, Xerox information systems director, began converting the company's top executives to computerized information management. The arrangement of work stations, networks, and software Soha designed was soon called the Executive Support System, or ESS. Currently the top 100 managers at Xerox are tied into ESS and Soha is extending it to 500 users. *Fortune* called the Xerox system "probably the most far-reaching in any company."

Allaire explained how ESS has improved meetings: "We had what's called the extended management committee meeting. When I was in Britain, I had to come to the United States for these meetings once a month. The reading material I had for the meeting was supposed to come a week in advance, but sometimes it was only three days. I still needed time to analyze it and comment on it, have my staff go over it. So I sometimes faced the prospect of reading it in a hotel room the night before the meeting, which was clearly ridiculous. Now, it's all on the ESS."

Allaire commissioned Soha to improve the effectiveness of the headquarters's staff and cut costs. Soha hired Jim Carlisle, managing director of Office of the Future Inc., to help. "Compared to people, technology is cheap," said Allaire. "I felt sure that technology could help reduce staff, the big expense item. But we realized we couldn't just present the system and say, 'Here's the answer to your prayers, and, by the way, take a 10 percent cut in your people.' You have to provide tools and let people decide how to use them most efficiently." He added, "But we had to start at the top."

Soha quickly ran into a problem created by nonstandardized reports and terminology. For example, two strategic business units might have different definitions for revenue. And the annual business plans were in varying formats, often depending on where the preparer previously worked or attended business school. Working with Allaire and other executives, Soha designed a standard five-page business plan. Each business unit put its plan on ESS five days before the annual planning meeting. Security safeguards in the system limited access to executives with a "need to know." But Xerox managers all over the world could see the proposed plans immediately. Such information could be downloaded from ESS and called up on laptop computers even during airline flights.

ESS is central to execution of Xerox's overall strategic plan for the 1990s. Former chief executive David Kearns was instrumental in turning the big marketer of document processing equipment into a customer-focused organization with "high expectations" of itself and "total quality control" (TQC). Kearns focused on reducing manufacturing costs and overhead and making the company less complicated. Kearns also keyed in on understanding what their customers really needed—not just wanted—from Xerox. Among the elements of Kearns's plan were a "quality vice president" to act as change agent, "standards and measurements," training which would "cascade" down from senior managers, "recognition and rewards," and pervasive communication.

After putting the plan into effect, Xerox nearly doubled its return on assets and generated $1 billion in surplus cash. The prevalence of pervasive communication increased even more when Kearns retired from Xerox to become the number 2 person at the United States Department of Education. Now the biggest advocate of the current Xerox executive support system, Paul Allaire is in charge. Allaire knows how effective the communication system has been and how important it will continue to be. Effective communication and an emphasis on quality have become integral parts of the Xerox way of doing things, which may account for what appears to be a bright future for the company.[1]

The Xerox story illustrates how one leading company has progressed into the information-processing age. A multitude of similar stories may be told of businesses across the nation—in fact, the world is in the midst of both an information and a high-tech revolution. Information for use in business continues to expand rapidly. Managers now have various types of computers and technology that allow them to more effectively use this information. The high-tech revolution is creating unlimited possibilities for managers, and managers are now able to implement what had only been dreamed of before—an effective management information system.

Management information system (MIS)

Any organized approach for obtaining relevant and timely information on which to base management decisions.

A **management information system (MIS)** is *any organized approach for obtaining relevant and timely information on which to base management decisions.* In all probability, no attribute of an organization so significantly affects decision making as does the management information system. Remember from Chapter 12 that the Chrysler Corporation and Maserati joint venture to build the Chrysler TC automobile was continually hindered by lack of information needed for decision making.[2] Such occurrences are often very expensive and virtually always disruptive. An effective MIS typically employs computers and other sophisticated technologies to process data that reflect the day-to-day operations of a company, organized in the form of information to facilitate the decision-making process.

Because of the importance of the management information system, an entire chapter is needed to review the topic and discuss future information trends. This discussion begins with a presentation of the information needs of a firm and characteristics of an effective MIS. Then, the different roles of the MIS at various organizational levels are examined. This is followed by a discussion of the steps in creating the MIS. Guidelines for effective MIS design are then given. They are followed by a presentation on the implementation of the MIS. Computer selection and information subsystems available for use by management are next reviewed. Finally, MIS advancements are examined with regard to their effect on productivity.

Information Needs of a Firm

As can be seen in Figure 20–1, both internal and external factors affect the organization and therefore must be accounted for in the MIS. Each component of the internal and external environment creates information needs for managers. A properly designed MIS assists in satisfying these needs. For example, Phillips 66 Company developed a management information system to help keep track of data and then was able to eliminate 40 percent of its management jobs.[3]

Notice in Figure 20–1 that the MIS draws information from the various internal functional areas, such as marketing, production, and finance, and integrates this information with that of the external environment, resulting in the creation of an information system. Both types of information are needed if managers are to perform effectively. For example, the marketing function will probably not operate properly without knowledge of the types of customers the firm is attempting to serve. Certainly, Xerox wants to know the types of customers that will ultimately purchase its products. And production may be hampered without an appreciation of the nature of the labor force available in certain areas. A multitude of internal and external interrelationships exist and must be reflected in the information system in order to satisfy the information needs of managers. For the MIS to provide maximum

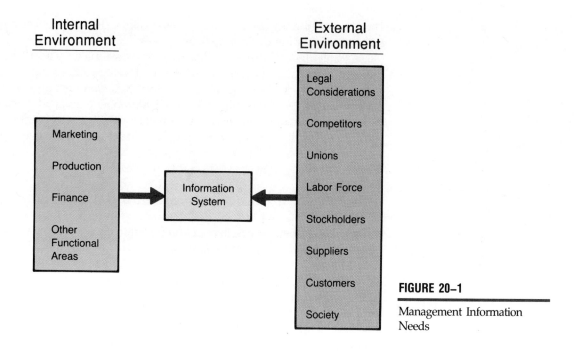

FIGURE 20–1

Management Information
Needs

benefit, however, it must be designed in the manner that offers the most beneficial information possible.

Characteristics of an Effective MIS

Any MIS, whether computerized or manual, should be designed to provide information with the following characteristics in order to afford managers the maximum utility from the information. Information should be

- *Timely—up-to-date.* Sound decisions cannot be based on outdated information. For example, a person desiring to invest in the stock market is at a severe disadvantage if decisions are made based on week-old or even day-old data.

- *Accurate—correct.* Managers must be able to rely on the accuracy of the information. Incorrect data probably will cause bad decisions to be made.

- *Concise—essential.* A manager can absorb only so much information during any one period. Therefore, the information should be limited to only the most necessary.

- *Relevant—what the manager needs to know.* Computers can provide managers with volumes of information. However, because only a small portion of available data is useful in a given situation, it is important to single out only the most relevant data to analyze.

- *Complete—everything that is needed.* Having no information is sometimes better than having partial information. A manager could draw false conclusions with incomplete information.

The absence of even one of these characteristics reduces the effectiveness of the MIS and complicates the decision-making process.

The Kraft, Inc., Grocery Products Group desperately needed an effective management information system. The Grocery Products Group was having a difficult time keeping track of business. Its top executives were getting stacks of paper with the previous day's sales results at 3:00 each afternoon. Now, with personal computers, the executives get the same information as early as 8:30 A.M., organized geographically and by product line. Basically, managers conduct their work lives differently now.[4]

The MIS at Different Organizational Levels

William H. Gruber once stated that: "The difference between now and five years ago is that [information] technology had limited function then. You weren't betting your company on it. Now you are."[5] This statement was true then, and it is even more relevant today. Basically, regardless of the managerial level, an effective management information system is essential for managers to cope with the complex and competitive environment they face.

Managers at each organizational level make particular demands on the MIS. Top-level managers often need information with which to make far-reaching decisions. Usually, they require extensive information relating to the external environment. For example, top-level managers at Xerox need to know about government legislation, economic trends and forecasts, and competitors' activities. On the other hand, Xerox's lower-level managers depend primarily on internal data. These managers typically need information in functional areas such as inventory reorder points and the number of workers to be assigned to a specific project. Top-level managers usually will want only product data that is summarized, perhaps by quarter. The Executive Support System (ESS) at Xerox is currently "empowering top executives to view critical information unfiltered by management layers, to communicate and coordinate in lightning speed with anyone in the organization, to analyze business scenarios as never before, like a master puppeteer, to control and shape decisions made in the far reaches of the corporation."[6] Lower-level managers are more likely to need production data on a daily or even hourly basis. Thus, each level of management benefits from information available from the MIS, but from different perspectives.

Whether used by top-, mid-, or lower-level managers, a successful MIS must produce several types of output related to business operations, such as the following:

- *Routine reports.* Business data summarized on a scheduled basis are routine reports. For example, weekly and monthly production reports may be sent to the general manager, whereas quarterly reports may be forwarded to upper-level managers.

- *Exception reports.* Reports that highlight major variations requiring management's attention are exception reports. An example is the quality exception report, completed when the number of defects increases beyond a predetermined maximum.

- *On-demand reports.* Information provided in response to a specific request is an on-demand report. The number of defects created by each worker in the plant is an example of an on-demand report that management could request.

- *Forecasts.* Reports on the results of applying predictive models to specific situations are forecasts. Managers may want to forecast the number and types of employees needed to satisfy projected demand for a firm's product.

Creating the MIS

In designing the MIS, managers must carefully consider four recommended steps that will provide the needed output and that will conform to the MIS criteria discussed earlier. These steps (see Figure 20–2) are not separate and distinct; considerable overlapping exists. The development of the MIS is not merely a matter of properly designing the system. Without a major commitment from top management, it is virtually impossible for any MIS to become smooth functioning and operational.

Study the Present System

In assessing the existing information system, the following questions might be asked: (1) What is the present flow of information? (2) How is the information used? (3) How valuable is this information in terms of decision making? There needs to be a thorough assessment of the organizational capabilities and strategic objectives and of any major external factors relevant to the organization's correct functioning. From this assessment, the determination of the informational, operational, and functional objectives can be realized, and the system can be designed to accomplish them.[7]

At one stage in his career, one of the authors was a team member in charge of developing one of the first integrated state highway information systems. Detailed analysis was done of the information flows and uses. One of the agencies involved was the state highway patrol. In conversations with local troop members, the author

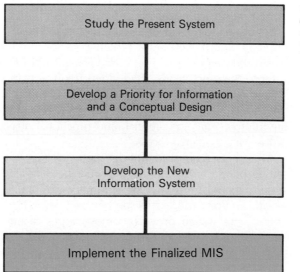

FIGURE 20–2

Creating the Management Information System

discovered that a weekly report to headquarters caused special difficulty. For each troop (there were thirteen), it took one officer about four hours to prepare the report. The author went to headquarters to determine how the data were used in decision making. He found that the reports were neatly filed by a secretary and that the data were never used. When one of the reports was not submitted on time, however, the secretary was directed to prepare a letter of reprimand to the unit commander. Identifying this kind of deficiency is the reason for asking the third question in the assessment.

Develop a Priority for Information and a Conceptual Design

Once the current system is thoroughly understood, it is used to develop a priority for needed information. There is certain information a manager must have if proper decisions are to be made, but some is merely nice to have, not critical to the manager's job performance. The MIS design must ensure provision of high-priority information; data lower on the priority list should be generated only if their benefits exceed the costs of producing them. The weekly report just described should not have had the priority it was accorded. Once the information needs are determined, a conceptual design of the management information system is developed.[8]

To set priorities for information needs, individual managers should develop their own priority lists and the lists should be integrated into a single list for the entire organization. Certain departments may discover that the information they identify as top priority will be far down on the organization's list. The needs of the entire organization must be the controlling factor.

Develop the New Information System

The organization's priority list for information needs should govern the detailed design of the new MIS. A system of required reports should be developed and diagrammed. Treating the whole organization as a unit allows the elimination of duplicate information. At a certain point on the priority list, the information is not worth the cost of providing it and should not be included.

Once the exact needs are decided upon, a plan for the management information system can be established. Then, a model of the system is created, tested, and refined until it meets specified performance levels. This model should be capable of achieving the informational, operational, and functional objectives established in the first step of the MIS creation process.[9]

After thoroughly studying the highway information system discussed earlier and setting priorities, the author prepared the diagram in Figure 20–3 to show how the system should function. The summary diagram was supported by many detailed reports and procedures. As can be seen, several types of input data are needed. For output, the system provides various types of information for both administration and operations. All departments are tied together. Data that come in from one department of the state can provide the information used in another department. If a person has a car wreck and is given a ticket, this information not only is used by

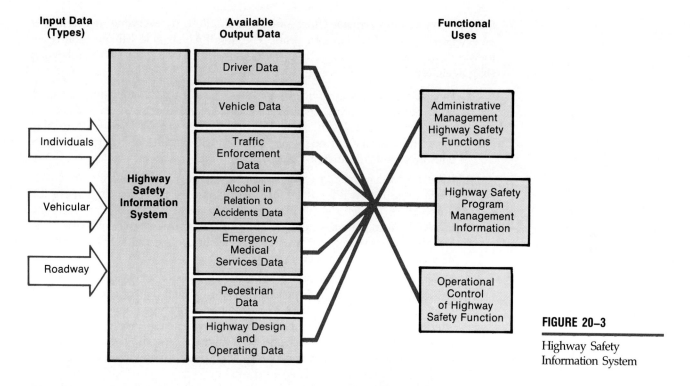

FIGURE 20–3

Highway Safety
Information System

law enforcement agencies but also becomes part of a database to identify high-accident locations. When the MIS is properly designed, the important information an organization needs in the decision-making process is available.

Implement the Finalized MIS

Once the formal model is finalized, the new management information system is ready to be implemented. At this point, the system must be made operational. Space allocations are made, computer equipment is selected, and all structural aspects of implementation are finalized. Once these decisions are made, the training program must commence. MIS support software is completed, and the organization's databases are entered into the system.

After all of this is completed and final checks are made, the management information system is ready for implementation.[10] Naturally, once the system is in place and functioning, it must be maintained to ensure that continuous "enhancements and changes to the system" are made to keep the system effective.[11]

Guidelines for Effective MIS Design

REVIEW QUESTION 5: The answer to Review Question 5 starts here.

Designing an appropriate management information system is a long-term, complex, and often tedious project. It requires the skills of a variety of specialists and of managers responsible for the design, implementation, and eventual use of the system.

MIS creation requires a major effort, often a team effort, by everyone involved over an extended period of two to four years. The first three steps in MIS creation relate to MIS design, which can most effectively be carried out by a focus on the following six guidelines:

1. *Form a design team of operating managers and system designers.* Operating managers must be involved because they best understand the information needs of various managerial levels. A system designed by such a team will probably satisfy the information needs of managers without burdening the managers with irrelevant information.[12]

2. *Balance the value and cost of the system by designing and installing it on a cost-benefit basis.* This will help eliminate cost overruns. Designing to achieve the purposes of the MIS should always be the primary objective of everyone involved. Also, software must be appropriate to support the envisioned system. In order to limit cost overruns, seek out commercial software that can be adapted to the proposed system.[13]

3. *Design a system that can provide relevant, high-quality information, rather than producing large quantities of information.* Providing high-quality information and limiting the quantity of information that has little value should increase the effectiveness of the management information system. A properly designed system does not supply middle- or top-level managers with the routine details of the organization's daily functioning, but it does provide top-level managers with critical information related to overall organizational effectiveness.[14] Basically, the MIS evaluates information to assure that it is relevant, condenses the information so it can be quickly absorbed and utilized, and sends it to the correct individuals.[15]

4. *Conduct a thorough pretest prior to final installation.* Make sure that omissions and errors in system design are detected, so such operational problems do not cause expensive changes in the final system.

5. *Provide adequate training and manuals for both users and operators of the system.* This is necessary to assure proper implementation of the system. It will also help make the system more effective. It should be made clear how the system will affect the organizational structure, the task responsibilities, and the jobs of each manager and employee.

6. *Make sure the management information system continually evolves, as the total business system does.* A management information system that fails to change will, in time, lose its effectiveness.

MANAGEMENT IN PRACTICE: A Skill-Building Exercise

You have been appointed to the design team assigned the formidable task of developing the new management information system. A design engineer is in charge of the project, and she has the responsibility of developing the entire system. You were selected to be on the team because you have had some experience in designing a management information system for your previous employer. However, your current company is a manufacturing firm, and the one you were previously employed by was a service firm.

You have just reviewed the list of team members and found that you are the only manager on the team. Everyone else is either a systems analyst or an engineer. Also, the time frame for development and implementation of the system has been estimated to be only nine months. You mention that in the firm you worked for before, the team composition was totally different and the project took a lot longer than nine months. The design engineer tells you that you aren't dealing with managers now and that technical people are faster and better at management information system design.

What would you do or say?

Implementation of the MIS

Since today's management information systems are certain to utilize computers, the discussion of the implementation of these systems will assume that computers will be part of them. Although technical problems do occur in implementing any MIS, the concern here will be with the people problems associated with implementation. These are the problems that the majority of managers are likely to encounter. Basically, managers must be aware of the causes of resistance to MIS implementation and the means of overcoming this resistance.

Resistance to Implementation of the MIS

Five major factors can cause resistance to the implementation of a management information system:

1. *Disruption of established departmental boundaries.* Department members may resist changing how their department operates, and they may resent altering the work relationships that have been established over the years.

2. *Disruption of the informal system.* If the informal system is powerful and effective, those who are part of it may resist anything that would threaten their informal position.

3. *Specific individual characteristics.* People who know how to do their present job in a satisfactory manner frequently resist change to a new procedure.

4. *The existing organizational culture.* An organization that maintains open and honest communications and has a high-trust relationship with its employees will have a less difficult time with implementation, and vice versa.

5. *How the change is implemented.* Everyone involved in the change should have a say as to how the change will evolve. The less involved employees are, the greater the level of resistance that will normally be encountered.[16]

Although employees at different levels of the organization are affected by implementation in different ways, most people are affected to some degree. When the inevitable resistance occurs, management must be prepared to overcome it.

Everyone involved in a major change should have some say in how the change will evolve. The less involved affected people are in decision making, the greater the level of resistance. Most companies have meeting rooms, such as the one shown here, and make these rooms available for meetings among managers from various departments.

Source: © Jim Pickerell

Overcoming Resistance to Implementation of the MIS

No single approach will overcome all resistance to implementation of the management information system. Implementation problems can be limited, however, if managers observe the following guidelines:

1. Resistance is limited to some degree if the system is user oriented. This is perhaps the most critical element in avoiding most of the resistance that is likely to occur.

2. If participation is encouraged and required of users, they must learn the system. Many of their fears will be alleviated when they become competent in using the system. Future users should be made part of the MIS team, so everyone who joins the firm immediately becomes oriented to the system.

3. Open and effective lines of communication should be established to make all users aware of the aims and characteristics of the system.

4. Individual performance measurements should be redefined to allow workers with changing roles to benefit as they gain new abilities and become adapted to the changes caused by the implementation.

5. Everyone concerned with the system should know that the computer is a tool that can handle many boring and routine tasks. By allowing managers to access information quicker and more thoroughly, the system gives managers the opportunity to use information in more creative and productive ways.[17]

Computer Selection

Because of the ever-expanding use of computers, it is becoming increasingly important for managers to be computer literate. Managers need not be data-processing experts, just as they need not be skilled accountants. Of course, they do need some accounting knowledge to understand and interpret financial reports, and they need to know what computers can and cannot do. Computers certainly should not be feared. Their presence is far too pervasive and their usefulness far too great.

If a computer is needed, the one chosen should provide the best capability of processing the needed data as accurately and quickly as possible. Users in the organization are being involved in the computer selection decision more than ever before.[18] Therefore, they must have an appreciation of the types of computers available to support their management information system. Because there are many types of computers and the capabilities of different types vary, they must review the possibilities and select the most beneficial one. Before choosing a computer, some managers have a systems analyst evaluate the choices with regard to how they can improve the management system. Computers are classified as super computers, mainframes, minicomputers, and microcomputers (or desktop computers) (see Figure 20–4).

Super Computers

At the upper end of the spectrum are super computers that cost millions of dollars and are capable of handling vast amounts of data. Included in this category are the Cray and the CYBER computers. Depending on its configuration, a Cray may sell for up to $29 million. It requires specially constructed subflooring to support its weight and needs special pumps to carry the fluorocarbon fluid that cools it. Included in the purchase price is the cost of two full-time engineers to maintain it for the life of the system.

As might be expected, the demand for super computers has been relatively small. However, it is expected to increase in the next few years. Also, a new breed of interactive super computers is currently being developed. These computers will allow

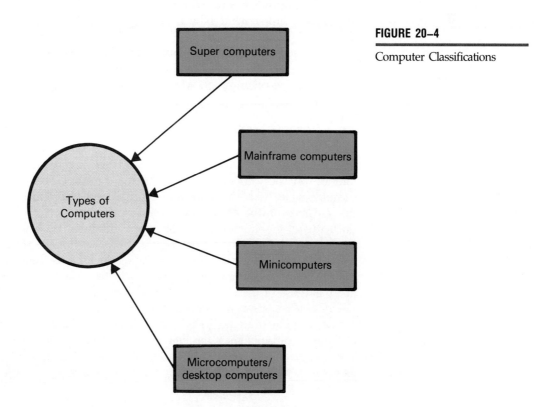

FIGURE 20–4

Computer Classifications

humans to interact with them during problem solving. The applications for which super computers are used include work with nuclear physics, meteorology, and the military. But because of their cost and the availability of more applicable systems, these computers are not expected to be used extensively in the typical management information system.[19]

Mainframe Computers

Most of the data-processing work for large organizations is done on mainframe computers. Mainframes are normally housed in special rooms and are maintained by data-processing specialists. A data-processing manager is typically in charge of various computer specialists, such as systems analysts, programmers, and machine operators, who support the system. Because mainframes can support large networks of individual terminals and remote job-entry locations, most large firms and many government agencies are equipped with them. Simulation, design, engineering, and applications requiring large databases are well within the capabilities of mainframe computers. Because of their capabilities, a high percentage of management information systems are supported by such computers. However, these systems are expensive, often costing as much as $1 million.

Minicomputers

These medium-sized computers are smaller, slower, and less expensive than mainframes and do not require special power hookups or environmental controls. They are usually supplemented by a large number of terminals and other peripheral devices. A prime advantage of minicomputers is the ability to enlarge a system to meet the needs of a growing organization. Minis were developed because they could meet particular needs at significantly lower costs than could large mainframes at locations in the organization where processing requirements were the greatest.

Microcomputers/Desktop Computers

Microcomputers have gained widespread favor in research and development laboratories, on shop floors, and in office management operations, as well as in the executive suite. Rod Canion, co-founder of Compaq Computers, supports the concept that advances in the area of microcomputer technology can significantly affect productivity. Of the four categories of computers discussed here, micros operate at the slowest speed; but they are getting faster and faster. The Intel 486 microprocessor, featuring reduced-instruction-set computing (fewer instructions and more computing power), offers speed and processing capabilities that, for many applications, are as good as those of minicomputers.[20] The disadvantage of the slowness of microcomputers is often offset by their ease of operation and low cost.

Microcomputers are not just for small businesses. Large corporations use thousands of them. Because of their flexibility, micros simplify many aspects of management. The microcomputer, often called a PC (for personal computer), can be a stand-alone tool able to show financial trends, answer "what if" questions, and even maintain the executive's calendar. Some managers who previously wrote memorandums in longhand now zip them out on the keyboard. Micros may interact with mainframes to give executives access to corporate databases or sophisticated programs.

In addition, microcomputers are becoming even more versatile, with such additions as faxboards. Today, faxboards allow those with microcomputers to "transmit text and graphics and handle the details of data communications."[21] In addition, portable, laptop and notebook (very lightweight laptops) personal computers are becoming more advanced. They now have better monitors, standard hard drives, and longer battery life, and they are lighter (some notebooks weigh under five pounds) and faster. With the addition of docking stations to hook them up to the primary microcomputer network in the office, portables, laptops, and notebooks are becoming even more useful.[22]

The main computing component of the microcomputer is located on an integrated circuit or chip, such as the Intel 486. Micros are capable of acquiring data, taking measurements, and controlling all kinds of processes in ways that greatly simplify manufacturing and production. They can be used in remote locations such as offshore oil-well platforms. They also work well in adverse environments such as on ships and airplanes. Micros can automatically change the settings of valves and other control devices in response to changes in physical conditions such as pressures and temperatures. Industrial robots often depend on microcomputers to help them do factory assembly operations formerly too complex for mechanization.

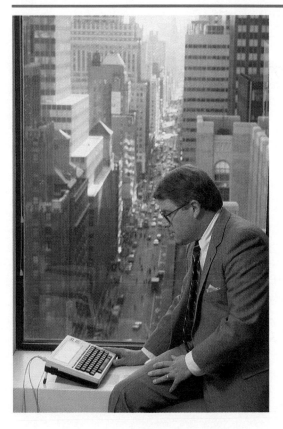

Portable personal computers are becoming increasingly advanced. They now have better monitors and hard drives, improved battery life, and they are lighter and faster. Many executives, like the one shown here, use portable computers to stay in touch with headquarters and to access their companies' mainframes.

Source: © Jim Pickerell

Many engineering firms today specialize in computer-aided design and computer-aided manufacturing (CAD/CAM) systems. These systems permit designers and engineers to develop a product, test it, and then program the equipment that makes it. The cost of CAD/CAM has been greatly reduced through the use of powerful microcomputers, some of which even small engineering and machine shops can afford. Because of their application to each stage of the product development cycle, microcomputers have made major contributions toward meeting the productivity challenge.

In every kind of organization and at every level, microcomputers simplify the job of administration. Traditional office paperwork is created and processed with the help of computers. Because micros can communicate with one another, many written reports and other types of written documentation have been eliminated. Word-processing software is available to assist in entering, arranging, correcting, retrieving, and printing all types of business information and correspondence.

It is obvious that microcomputers are gaining widespread favor, but managers should realize that computers are not a panacea for productivity problems. Some service companies are finding that computers do not always improve productivity.[23] For example, the quality of a letter may be improved because a manager can easily make changes using word processing. However, productivity itself may not have improved because of the extra time spent in editing and reediting the letter.

Possible Information Subsystems for Managers

Management uses various information subsystems; among them are accounting information systems, office management systems, manufacturing systems, marketing systems, and human resource information systems. They are called subsystems here because, taken separately, they do not constitute a management information system. In addition, some firms may have only one or perhaps two of these subsystems.

Accounting Information Systems

The processing of accounting data is traditionally the first area to receive much attention. Accounting information systems provide managers with much of their control information. Accuracy and speed are stressed in the processing of profit-and-loss information, taxes, and a multitude of other accounting-related activities. Subsets of a typical accounting system include accounts payable, payroll, accounts receivable, sales and invoices, inventory control, and financial reporting.

Office Management Systems

Only a few years ago, the typical office management system involved filing cabinets; letters dictated to secretaries, who then typed and mailed them; and telephone messages placed on the manager's desk to be answered at a later time. The potential for totally restructuring these systems is now a reality. Managers may now sit in front of their desktop computers and send messages to other company employees at distant points through electronic mail—messages that appear on the recipients' monitors.

Word processing has had a major impact on the modern office management system. Copies of correspondences that once filled a multitude of filing cabinets can now be conveniently stored on small floppy disks for rapid retrieval at a later date. Corrections, additions, and deletions can now be quickly accomplished without the need for a secretary to retype the document each time a change is made. Many managers have found it easy to learn word processing themselves. Often, they find it much quicker to type up correspondence themselves than to delegate this duty to others in the organization.

In addition, computer firms have introduced the concept of the desktop publishing work station. The software used for that purpose permits offices to turn out brochures and reports that look as though they were professionally printed.[24] The impact of these and other forms of modern technology is changing forever the way offices are run.

Manufacturing Systems

Not long ago, managers at an automobile assembly plant supervised long lines of workers attaching parts to each unfinished car as it passed separate work stations. Managers and workers using computer terminals can now determine the exact equipment configuration of each car as it passes by. The manufacturing process of production scheduling, inventory control, design, equipment control, and cost accounting is tied together through the use of computers. Computer innovations such as VANs now provide even small firms with the capability of using modern production control and scheduling methods.

You have accepted a job with an aggressive microcomputer manufacturer that recently entered the market. Microcomputer manufacturers are engaged in intense competition in an effort to become the first in the market with a software package that will enable their computers to recognize spoken instructions, which will make the computers easier for the average consumer to use. Your former employer is rumored to be the leader in this area of development.

When you were hired, you were led to believe that your selection was based on your management potential. At the beginning of the third week on the new job, you receive the following memo from the president: "Please meet with me tomorrow at 8:15 for the purpose of discussing the developments your former employer has made in microcomputer software." You can provide the information, or you can refuse to provide the information, possibly jeopardizing your career with the new firm.

What would you do?

A value-added network (VAN) links manufacturers with their customers and suppliers. Through the VAN system, products can be automatically shipped from the factory to retailers when inventory levels become low. This helps retailers maintain inventories at a minimum level and results in considerable cost savings for them.[25]

The latest technique for improving the manufacturing process is statistical quality control (SQC). Basically, SQC gauges the performance of the manufacturing process by carefully monitoring changes in whatever is being produced. The goal is to detect potential problems before they result in off-quality products, then pinpoint the reason for deviation and adjust the process to make it more stable.[26]

Marketing Systems

The purpose of marketing is to ensure that the proper product is offered to the customer at the right price and location and with the correct amount of promotion. In the past, the complexity of this task was often overwhelming. Tying together a marketing system consisting of product analysis and development, marketing research, place analysis, price analysis, promotional analysis, and sales was often difficult without the benefits of the computer. Through computerized marketing systems, information is made available to the marketing manager about such vital areas as product profitability and advertising effectiveness.

Human Resource Information Systems

Whereas the accounting system was typically the first system to be installed in a firm, the human resource information system was often the last. Firms are now realizing that a properly developed human resource information system can provide tremendous benefits. Figure 20–5 presents an overview of a system that was prepared for one organization. Note that numerous types of input data, from many sources,

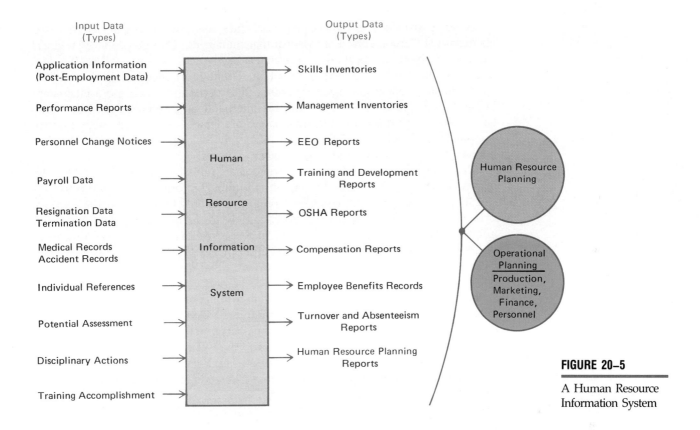

Input Data (Types)

- Application Information (Post-Employment Data)
- Performance Reports
- Personnel Change Notices
- Payroll Data
- Resignation Data Termination Data
- Medical Records Accident Records
- Individual References
- Potential Assessment
- Disciplinary Actions
- Training Accomplishment

Human Resource Information System

Output Data (Types)

- Skills Inventories
- Management Inventories
- EEO Reports
- Training and Development Reports
- OSHA Reports
- Compensation Reports
- Employee Benefits Records
- Turnover and Absenteeism Reports
- Human Resource Planning Reports

Human Resource Planning

Operational Planning Production, Marketing, Finance, Personnel

FIGURE 20–5

A Human Resource Information System

are necessary. Through this system, considerable amounts of output data become available. They may have far-reaching value in uses ranging from human resource planning to operations.

The human resource information system permits all human resource areas to be tied together into a single information system. Data from several input sources are integrated to provide needed output data. Information critical to the firm's human resource decision-making process is readily available when the system is properly designed. For instance, many firms are now studying historical trends to determine the best ways of securing qualified applicants. In addition, it would be difficult to comply with the many laws and government rules if not for these modern systems. As the human component of the firm gains greater importance, it is likely that we will see continued growth in human resource information systems.

A Global Approach to HRIS

Developing an effective global HRIS is virtually essential because of the complexity involved in managing a global labor force. The degree to which a human resource professional can globalize his or her function is dependent on many factors, and one of the most important is an effective HRIS. Information concerning the many variables affecting human resources must be shared; it must be relevant and timely to assure that the best human resource decisions are made.

According to a vice-president of personnel and employee relations at Denver-based Hamilton Oil Corporation, it is essential that human resource people in each global location be experts on local laws, customs, salary structures, and the like. It is also essential that they have quality information. Through an effective HRIS, Hamilton Oil's human resource management approach is becoming much more integrated. Presently, he shares information with his international counterparts by telephone, fax, and telex. All human resource managers are linked electronically with a micro-computer-based network. This system allows the establishment of a database of human resource statistics and other relevant material.[27]

Other companies have developed ways to share human relations information. An organized approach for obtaining relevant and timely information on which to base global human resource decisions has become a top priority for Dow's chemical group. Dow is conducting an extensive feasibility study to determine whether, and how, human resource managers worldwide might be electronically linked to provide greater access to international personnel records and other data. Presently, however, Dow has so much information restricted by local laws that developing an effective HRIS will be complicated.[28]

Sharing information from a centralized database is only one way human resource professionals worldwide share data. For example, McDonald's developed "Best Bets," a program that encourages regional human resource professionals to share innovative plans with their counterparts in other nations. The P-Factor established by Canadian managers is a perfect example of the concept. The P-Factor, a means of measuring the effectiveness of local personnel practices, was adopted by McDonald's human resource managers throughout the world.[29]

Using the MIS

A true management information system has the capability of integrating the various subsystems in order to provide managers at all levels with better decision-making capabilities. For example, information from the human resource information system may provide the manager with knowledge about the feasibility of plant expansion in relation to specific human resource requirements. The accounting system may be consulted to determine if the anticipated plant expansion will be cost-effective. Rather than each subsystem acting as a separate entity, all are tied together in the MIS to give management an extra edge in making decisions.

Previous chapters identified the basic functions of management: planning, orga-nizing, influencing, and controlling. The purpose of an effective and useful man-agement information system is to help accomplish these functions, and each of the subsystems mentioned may assist in that effort. When all the subsystems are inte-grated into a total management information system, the power of the information available for decision making is greatly enhanced.

Technology Affecting Management[30]

Technological advances in computer hardware and software occur virtually every day. These developments have the potential of improving management and raising employee productivity. It's impossible to foresee all the new uses for each technological breakthrough. The only certainty is that managers must be aware of these innovations and alert to their capabilities. An executive for United Services Automobile Association (USAA) noted that even during tough economic times, technological changes must be tracked to maintain a competitive edge.[31] Failure to keep up with developments in this rapidly changing area can threaten a firm's competitive position and possibly even its survival. We next discuss some of the uses of computer technology that most significantly affect management.

Application and Communication Software

Several types of existing software continue to impact management. This software includes data communication, word processing, computer graphics, spreadsheets, decision support systems, and database management systems.

Data Communication *The sending of data produced by a computer over some form of communication medium, such as phone lines,* is referred to as **data communication.** This form of communication is becoming increasingly important in the business world. Caterpillar, Inc. owns its own communications satellite and places a heavy emphasis on advanced data communications to better serve its global market.[32] Managers can transmit documents or messages over phone lines and eliminate wasted time and possible misunderstandings, thereby facilitating decision making. For example, prior to a teleconference, it is often useful to transmit electronic mail so that everyone involved can become familiar with the exact nature of the discussion.

Electronic mail capabilities also include the ability to schedule a meeting for an entire work group, automatically sending messages to meeting attendees and even spell checking that message.[33] The use of facsimile to make a copy of a document and send it electronically to another location has been revitalized by faster, lower-cost personal computer systems.[34] Cellular radio is another important communications medium for mobile voice and data communications.[35]

Word Processing *A computer application that permits an operator to create and edit written material* is referred to as **word processing.** Word processing allows simplified editing of manuscripts and correspondence. For example, inserting a new paragraph at the beginning of a ten-page manuscript no longer requires retyping the entire document. Managers, too, can use word processing. The manager types out the memo, edits it on the screen, and with a few commands, prints it out or routes it using electronic mail. Word processing has become one of today's most significant communication enhancement tools. Word processing also allows managers to develop sensitive documents, such as workforce reduction plans or performance appraisal reports, without risking a breech of security.

Computer Graphics "A picture is worth a thousand words." Managers can use computer programs to produce various kinds of graphs and charts in both black and white and color. These graphics represent a large amount of data reduced to a single image.[36] Managers continually process data that can be graphically presented, thereby illustrating the message much more effectively than simple text could.

Spreadsheet Programs Spreadsheet programs provide a column-row matrix on which numbers or words can be entered and stored, and calculations performed on

Data communication

The sending of data produced by a computer over some form of communication medium, such as phone lines.

Word processing

A computer application that permits an operator to create and edit written material.

that data. Predefined statistical, financial, and mathematical functions make "what if" questions quickly and easily answered. Graphics functions are also included to illustrate the cell data.[37] Spreadsheet analysis is particularly beneficial in activities such as planning.

Decision Support Systems   Often computer departments are backed up with demands for urgently needed information. To overcome this problem, many managers have acquired their own **decision support system (DSS),** *an information system that allows users to quickly process and retrieve information.* Normally DSSs are sophisticated database systems capable of retrieving, displaying, and processing a wide variety of information. Graphics, simulation, modeling, and quantitative analysis are also typically available through decision support systems. Obviously, DSSs can be very useful in planning.

Database Management   Information subsystems are commonly developed for accounting, office management, manufacturing, marketing, and human resources. Often the data and programs in these subsystems are considered separate and distinct, resulting in a tremendous amount of redundant data. For example, the accounting system would normally contain names and social security numbers of all employees—and so would the human resource files. The purpose of **database management** is to reduce such redundancies insofar as possible. The term thus refers to *the integration of information subsystems in order to reduce the duplication of information, effort, and cost and to provide controlled access to this information.* When Toyota sought to staff its manufacturing plant in Georgetown, Kentucky, more than 60,000 people applied. An intensive eight-phase hiring process was used and tracked through a computer tracking system.[38]

Teleconferencing

Partly because of the high cost of business travel, in terms of both time and money, teleconferencing is becoming increasingly popular. **Teleconferencing** is a method of conducting or participating in multiparty discussions by telephone or videophone. Teleconferencing may become a major means not only of improving managerial communication and productivity, but also of lowering their cost. Such systems could allow managers to resolve many problems without ever meeting in person with other parties, thus saving both time and money.

Voice Mail

Voice mail is *spoken messages transmitted electronically and stored for delivery to the recipient at a later time.* When a voice mail system is used, an individual gains access by dialing a special number and providing a password and user identification number. The user may then listen to any new messages, replay old messages, eliminate messages, and/or record messages for others. Managers can place confidential information in the system and know that the message will be received in the exact manner that it was sent. Voice mail could prove useful when managers are dealing with sensitive matters, such as layoffs, and want to avoid phone communications that could be overheard. J. P. Stevens and Company uses voice mail extensively.

Decision support system (DSS)

An information system that allows users to quickly process and retrieve information.

Database management

The integration of information subsystems in order to reduce the duplication of information, effort, and cost and to provide controlled access to this information.

Teleconferencing

A method of conducting or participating in multiparty discussions by telephone or videophone.

Voice mail

Spoken messages transmitted electronically and stored for delivery to the recipient at a later time.

"It's a medium for exchanging information that has proven to be an effective productivity tool." A senior telecommunications analyst at J. P. Stevens was describing the company's new voice mail system. Voice mail was just one aspect of Stevens's sophisticated management information system, called BSP, for Business System Plan. With ten textile divisions, Stevens was the second-largest U.S. textile manufacturer, behind Burlington Industries. The system, built around a Northern Telecom SL-1 PBX, allows recorded messages to be sent and accessed by telephone 24 hours a day. Each authorized user had to enter a personal security code to send or check "mail."

One manager who used the system regularly was John T. English, a customer service director in Stevens's converter and industrial fabrics division. "If I'm caught at a meeting," English said, "I'm confident that messages are accurate because they are what a person said, not a translation. I've detected in messages how strongly someone feels about something by his or her voice." English used the system, for example, to pass along confidential information to his accounting group. "They need certain information from me," said English, "and voice messaging saves me from having to travel to a different part of the building, hoping the person is there to deliver confidential information to. Now I know the information remains confidential and I know when it's received." English concluded, "I'm sure there's a reduction of memo writing. I used to have a stack of pink confidential envelopes. I don't use them anymore—I use voice messaging."[39]

Telecommuting

As previously mentioned in Chapter 13, many firms have turned to telecommuting as a way of meeting particular management needs. *When workers at home or temporarily away from the office perform their work over telephone lines tied to a computer, as if they were at the office*, the procedure is called **telecommuting.** Telecommuters generally are information workers. They perform jobs that require, for example, analysis, research, writing, budgeting, data entry, or computer programming.[40] Working at home is not for everyone, but certain people such as writers, reservation agents, researchers, and computer programmers can easily adapt to this style of work. One computer programmer quit his job in San Diego and moved to the island of St. John, agreeing to "help out" his former employer if needed. Within two weeks, the programmer had established a consulting firm and was working his own hours. An editor of *Telecommuting Review,* described this exotic setup as "feasible only if the employee is highly trained, can do virtually all of the job long distance and possesses a hard-to-find skill."[41] Telecommuters often have more productive time since they do not drive to and from work. Also, handicapped people who cannot easily get to an office find telecommuting an excellent alternative.

Although the concept of telecommuting has many positive aspects, managers often have difficulty coping with it in practice. The question they often ask is, "How do I supervise a person that I never see?" And some workers dislike telecommuting because they miss the friendly association with co-workers. Pacific Bell has a

Telecommuting

When workers are able to remain at home or at least temporarily away from the office and perform their work over telephone lines tied to a computer, as if they were at the office.

systematic procedure for selecting the types of jobs and the types of people who would benefit from telecommuting. In 1991, an estimated 4.4 million people were working at home during normal business hours.[42] Subsequently, managers must be prepared to deal with this alternative type of work. At Pacific Bell, telecommuting has already become a way of life.

Telecommuting at Pacific Bell

Pacific Bell is one of two main subsidiaries of Pacific Telesis Group. PacBell was one of about 500 companies in the United States that had formal telecommuting programs. It even had a telecommuting manager, Kathy Nolan.

When PacBell decided to move most of its operation from San Francisco to Ramon, 35 miles away, some employees did not want to go. For several years, the company had been encouraging certain people to work at home, with their computer terminals connected to the office. The move to Ramon offered a chance to test a new kind of telecommuting, involving the use of satellite offices. The company set up such an office in San Francisco and allowed 15 of the employees to remain there while the others transferred to Ramon. Several marketing executives among the 15 had business reasons for wanting to stay in San Francisco, because some big clients were headquartered there.

Later, a satellite telecommuter office was established in San Diego, again because a larger operation had to be moved. In that case, the workers involved were fiber-optics specialists, exceptionally hard to find or replace. Some individuals believed the company would have lost these specialists if they had been required to move.

Whether at satellite offices or at home, telecommuters, according to Nolan, tended to have flexible working hours. "If you manage by objective," said Nolan, "it doesn't make any difference where the job gets done." Because they are not physically present at the main workplace, telecommuters must be managed differently from other workers. One Pacific Bell manager said of a telecommuting subordinate, "I really have to make an extra effort to plan better because I won't be running into him at the water cooler." A UCLA researcher who helped Pacific Bell in its telecommuting program said, "The mental wrench of coping with employees who aren't physically around you is by no means easy to overcome." He later remarked that such employees and their managers "become better communicators out of necessity."[43]

Expert Systems

Expert system

A system that uses knowledge about a narrowly defined, complex area to act as a consultant to a human.

An **expert system** is *a system that uses knowledge about a narrowly defined, complex area to act as a consultant to a human.*[44] In some instances, an organization may rely significantly on the knowledge of one or more individuals in particular areas that may be captured in an expert system.[45] This captured expertise may then be used for training or may be disseminated throughout the organization for other employees to use. Mrs. Fields Cookies, Inc. uses an expert system to develop a profile of prospective applicants that is compared with the desired employee profile and reports the results to the store manager.[46] Other typical expert systems in the area of human resource management include employee performance evaluation, education scheduling, and employee benefits.[47]

Graphical User Interfaces

Graphical user interfaces (GUIs) *represent a move to truly make software applications easy to use. Computer users touch or aim at graphic figures (icons) or framed written commands to communicate with the computer program.* No longer are keys depressed on the keyboard. Popular GUIs include Microsoft's "Windows," the IBM/Microsoft "Presentation Manager," Open Software Foundation's "Motif," and the Macintosh GUI.[48]

Multimedia

Multimedia is *a computer application that produces presentations combining automation, stereo sound, full-motion video, and graphics.* Because users are immediately drawn to these presentations, they are useful in sales presentations and in training and development. Lotus used multimedia when it introduced "Release 3.0," and American Airlines uses it to train thousands of employees annually. Managers can incorporate photographs, voice, and document images into database files. The manager can access an employee's photograph, social security card, and signed year-end appraisals.[49]

A Global Perspective

A global management information system is an organized approach for obtaining relevant and timely information on which to base management decisions. An ideal management information system exists when users are supplied with all the information they need when they need it. Such a utopian situation has not yet arrived for most companies, especially those with global operations. To help offset less effective global management information systems, companies are developing decision support systems that allow users to interact directly with a computer to get information quickly. A decision support system lets managers call up a menu of available programs. Normally decision support systems are sophisticated database systems capable of retrieving, displaying, and processing information. Graphics, simulation, modeling, and quantitative analysis are also typically available through decision support systems.

At Midland, Michigan-based Dow Chemical Company, a diversified chemical manufacturer with facilities throughout the world—and with about 1,000 of the firm's employees on assignment outside their country of origin—a decision support system is being considered. The decision support system would allow global managers to share data with one another to facilitate the planning and decision making process. Sharing data is essential if global managers are going to perform to their maximum potential. Dow is conducting an extensive feasibility study to determine whether, and how, managers worldwide might be linked electronically to provide greater

Graphical user interfaces (GUI's)

Represent a move to truly make software applications easy to use. Computer users touch or aim at graphic figures (icons) or framed written commands to communicate with the computer program.

Multimedia

A computer application that produces presentations combining automation, stereo sound, full-motion video, and graphics.

access to international records and other computerized data. One major problem encountered when attempting to develop such a system is the vast amount of information normally accumulated in a global company. However, sharing information from computer files is not the only way managers worldwide share data.

While an effective decision support system is an important part of the global management information system, it is often necessary to supplement the system to satisfy the information needs of those in the organization. McDonald's "Best Bets" program encourages managers to share their innovative plans with their counterparts in other nations. *World* is a publication of Milwaukee-based GE Medical Systems (GEMS), a division of the General Electric Company, which has several thousand employees, half of whom are located outside the United States. *World*, a quarterly newsletter for employees worldwide, is specifically designed to promote global integration. It is also very important to supplement the information system with global meetings, seminars, and conferences that bring managers together.

The importance of an effective global decision support system, supplemented by other information sources, cannot be overstated. An ineffective global management information system can impede understanding, coordination, and decision making. With information missing, managers become less effective. Effective global management often depends on good, quick, complete, and concise information from a well-designed management information system.[50]

•••

Self-Assessment Exercise

How Well Will You Deal with Information Systems?

1. Are you willing to recognize that sound decisions cannot be based on outdated information?

   ☐ Yes   ☐ No

2. Are you willing to recognize that employees must be able to rely on the accuracy of the information provided to them?

   ☐ Yes   ☐ No

3. Are you willing to remember that workers can absorb only so much information during any one period?

   ☐ Yes   ☐ No

4. Are you willing to make sure that the information you provide employees is relevant?

   ☐ Yes   ☐ No

5. Are you willing to attempt to provide workers with complete information?

   ☐ Yes   ☐ No

6. Are you willing to learn how an MIS is useful to managers at all levels?

   ☐ Yes   ☐ No

(continued)

7. Are you willing to remember that the MIS should be designed to assist in the accomplishment of the objectives of the organization?

   ☐ Yes   ☐ No

8. Are you willing to learn that in designing an MIS, the most important information needs should be considered first?

   ☐ Yes   ☐ No

9. Are you willing to learn that the information needs of the firm are constantly changing?

   ☐ Yes   ☐ No

10. Are you willing to recognize that there may be some initial resistance to the implementation of an MIS?

    ☐ Yes   ☐ No

Summary

A management information system (MIS) is any organized approach for obtaining relevant and timely information on which to base management decisions. An effective MIS typically employs computers and other sophisticated technologies. It draws information from various internal functional areas, such as marketing and finance, and integrates this information with that of the external environment. Both internal and external information is needed, and it should be timely, accurate, concise, relevant, and complete. If not, effectiveness is reduced, complicating the decision-making process.

Managers at each organizational level make unique demands on the MIS. Top-level managers need to make far-reaching decisions that usually require extensive information relating to the external environment. Lower-level managers depend primarily on internal data. In designing the MIS, all managers must carefully consider four recommended steps: study the present system, develop a priority for information and a conceptual design, develop the new information system, and implement the finalized MIS.

MIS design can most effectively be carried out by a focus on the following six guidelines: (1) Form a design team of operating managers and system designers; (2) balance the value and cost of the system by designing and installing it on a cost-benefit basis; (3) design a system that can provide relevant, high-quality information, rather than producing large quantities of information; (4) conduct a thorough pretest prior to final installation; (5) provide adequate training and manuals for both users and operators of the system; and (6) make sure the management information system continually evolves, as the total business system does. Managers must be aware of the causes of resistance to MIS implementation and the means of overcoming this resistance.

Because there are many types of computers and the capabilities of different types vary, users must review the possibilities and select the most beneficial computer. Before choosing a computer, some managers have a systems analyst evaluate the choices with regard to how they can improve the management system. Computers are classified as super computers, mainframes, minicomputers, and microcomputers.

Management also uses various information subsystems, including accounting, office management, manufacturing, marketing, and human resource systems. A true MIS integrates these subsystems in order to provide managers at all levels with better decision-making information.

New developments in computer hardware and software occur virtually every day. Among them are data communication, word processing, computer graphics, spreadsheet programs, decision support systems, database management, teleconferencing, voice mail, telecommuting, expert systems, graphical user interfaces, and multimedia.

Review Questions

1. Define *management information system*. What are the information needs of a firm?
2. What are the basic characteristics required of the MIS?
3. Briefly describe the types of reports an effective MIS should produce.
4. Briefly describe the steps involved in creating the MIS.
5. List the guidelines for effective MIS design.
6. What are the factors that can interfere with implementation of the MIS?
7. Distinguish among the following general types of computers:
   a. super computers
   b. mainframes
   c. minicomputers
   d. microcomputers
8. Briefly describe the various information subsystems available to managers.
9. Briefly describe the new developments in computer hardware and software that can be used to enhance productivity.

Key Terms

Management information system (MIS)
Data communication
Word processing
Decision support system (DSS)

Database management
Teleconferencing
Voice mail
Telecommuting

Expert system
Graphical user interfaces (GUI's)
Multimedia

David McNeil was CEO of the McNeil Company, which he had founded. The company was involved in three businesses. The medical division, Procare, offered extended care to the elderly through four facilities similar to nursing homes. Procare also operated two pharmacies. The second business was toys. McNeil had seven leased toy stores in malls. The third and biggest operation was shoes. McNeil ran ten shoe stores, mostly in malls, and twelve shoe departments in department stores. He was asked to tell of his recent experience with computerization.

He began: "When I bought the medical division five years ago, it had its own IBM mainframe computer system. John Seeger, previous owner and still president of Procare, is something of a computer whiz. So I asked him to help computerize Shoes and Toys and gave him a free rein about how to do it. Two years and $400,000 later, we had a Prime computer in the main office with point-of-sale terminals in all our stores. The system cranked out daily, weekly, and monthly reports on every topic imaginable. Procare was never hooked into the Prime since it already had a good system.

"The year before last, Procare got into financial trouble and John had to start spending all his time trying to get it back on track. However, his systems analyst, who had been with Procare for years, helped the people in Medical and Shoes when he could. Prime had no local office but quickly sent a maintenance person by plane when we called and was able to diagnose some problems through a modem hookup. Still, the system stayed down quite a bit after John went back to Procare.

"I soon realized that the stacks of computer paper on all my managers' desks were not being used. I don't know much about computers, but I do know how much useless paperwork costs. So I began to eliminate reports, waiting for someone to yell. No one ever yelled. Before long, the Prime was being used just for payroll, accounts receivable and payable, and general ledger. The point-of-sale terminals are still connected to the Prime, which costs a lot in phone charges, but the terminals are used just as cash registers. It's a good thing my managers kept their manual reporting and accounting system as a backup to the computer.

"This has been a fiasco," McNeil concluded. "We have all agreed that it will be a long time before we spend that much money and time again without knowing what we're doing."

Questions

1. Was McNeil's computerization effort doomed from the start? Explain.
2. What alternatives concerning his MIS did McNeil have after Procare got into financial trouble? What should he have done?

"I don't know how we managed before we got our computer," said Martha Tolpin. Tolpin is the owner of Fort Steel Products, Inc., in Fort Collins, Colorado. Fort Steel makes a line of metal patio furniture that is marketed through lawn and garden stores and furniture stores in the Southwest. Selling is mainly by telephone. Each Fort Steel salesperson has an interactive terminal that provides up-to-date information on inventory levels, prices of items, shipping availability and costs, customer credit status, and so forth. Of course, the system also performs all the usual accounting functions, such as payroll, accounts payable, and general ledger. Tolpin gets a single weekly report, which gives her summarized information for the week, the previous quarter, and the year to date.

Tolpin had decided early on that computers represented the wave of the future, but she shopped around several years before deciding on a system for Fort Steel. In the meantime, she became competent on an IBM PC she had bought, using it for word processing and for some spreadsheet calculations.

One of many computer salespeople who called on

Fort Steel over the years was Ivan Pierson. Pierson was with Darkar, a consulting firm in New Orleans. After hearing Pierson's presentation and checking with several of his clients, Tolpin purchased a complete hardware and software package from Darkar. The system was designed especially for small manufacturers and cost $73,000, including fifty hours of programming and maintenance time. The initial price also included a three-day course on the system for Fort Steel's head bookkeeper and a clerk. Tolpin knew she could have bought the hardware locally for about $12,000. Spending the extra $60,000 or so just for software and support was a difficult decision.

Because she was "intrigued" with computers, as she put it, Tolpin went to New Orleans to sit through the course with her two employees. While she was in New Orleans, Pierson and his boss treated her to a Cajun dinner at K-Paul's Kitchen (owned by world-famous chef Paul Prudhomme) and a tour of Bourbon Street and the French Quarter.

During the two years since the system was installed, Tolpin has continued the friendship. She has recommended Darkar to several acquaintances, two of whom have made purchases. She also was instrumental in promoting the Darkar system through the Southwest division of the American Association of Manufacturers, a trade association to which Fort Steel belongs. Tolpin received no commission on the sales, but Darkar has improved the basic system markedly since she bought hers, and Pierson has ensured that each improvement was installed at Fort Steel at no charge. In fact, says Tolpin, "I haven't gotten any bill at all from Darkar in over a year."

Questions

1. Did Tolpin pay too much for her system? Justify your answer.
2. Discuss the human aspects of the case.

Notes

1. This case is a composite of a number of published accounts, among them: David T. Kearns, "Xerox: Satisfying Customer Needs with a New Culture," *Management Review* (February 1989): 61–63; Barbara Hetzer, "How Xerox Zapped the Japanese," *Business Month*, June 1989, pp. 81–82; Lou Wallis, "Power Computing at the Top," *Across the Board*, January–February 1989, pp. 42–51; James R. Norman, "Xerox Rethinks Itself—And This Could Be the Last Time," *Business Week*, February 13, 1989, pp. 90–93; Jeremy Main, "At Last, Software CEOs Can Use," *Fortune*, March 13, 1989, pp. 77–83; Russell Mitchell, "How Top Brass Is Taking to the Keyboard at Xerox," *Business Week*, June 27, 1988, p. 86; James R. Norman, "Xerox on the Move," *Forbes*, June 10, 1991, pp. 70–71; and Standard and Poor's Corporation, "Xerox Corporation," *Standard NYSE Stock Reports* 56, no. 128 (July 6, 1989): sec. 24.

2. John Rossant and Wendy Zeller, "How Chrysler's $30,000 Sports Car Got Sideswiped," *Business Week*, January 23, 1989, p. 68.

3. Susan M. Gelford, "The Computer Age Dawns in the Corner Office," *Business Week*, June 27, 1988, pp. 84–86.

4. Ibid.

5. Catherine L. Harris, "Information Power," *Business Week*, October 14, 1985, p. 108.

6. Gary K. Gulden and Douglas E. Ewers, "Is Your ESS Meeting the Need?" *Computerworld*, July 10, 1989, p. 85.

7. Robert G. Murdick, "MIS Development Procedures," *Journal of Systems Management* 21 (December 1970): 22–26.

8. Ibid.

9. Ibid.

10. Ibid.

11. Harry C. Benham, R. Leon Price, and Jennifer L. Wagner, "Comparison of Structured Development Methodologies," *Information Executive* 2 (Spring 1989): 19.

12. Arnold Barnett, "Preparing Management for MIS," *Journal of System Managements* 23 (January 1972): 40–43.

13. Michael Potter and Robin McNeill, "The New Programmer—The Next Wave of Computer Innovation in North American Business," *Business Quarterly* 48 (Winter 1983): 132–134.

14. John P. Murry, *Managing Information Systems as a Corporate Resource* (Homewood, IL: Dow Jones–Irwin, 1984).

15. John F. Rockart, "Chief Executives Define Their Own Data Needs," *Harvard Business Review* 57 (March–April 1979): 81–93.

16. G. W. Dickson and John K. Simmons, "The Behavioral Side of MIS," *Business Horizons* 13, no. 4, August 1970, pp. 59–71.

17. Ibid.

18. Michael Alexander, "Who Gives Final Nod to IS Buys?" *Computerworld*, June 12, 1989, p. 45.

19. Dave Evans, "An Old Idea Gets a New Twist," *Computerworld*, May 29, 1989, p. 63.

20. Richard Brandt, "It Takes More than a Good Idea," *Business Week*, June 16, 1989, p. 123.

21. M. David Stone, "PC to Paper Fax Grows Up," *PC Magazine*, April 11, 1989, p. 95.

22. Bill Howard, "286 Laptops Compute en Route," *PC Magazine*, July 1989, pp. 95–97.

23. Stephen Kreider Yoder, "IBM Tries to Woo Back Buyers in Japan," *Wall Street Journal*, April 4, 1988, p. 37.

24. "The Passion Is Back at Apple Computer," *Fortune*, January 19, 1987, p. 8.

25. Joel Dreyfuss, "Networking: Japan's Latest Computer Craze," *Fortune* (July 7, 1986): 94.

26. Otis Port, "The Push for Quality," *Business Week*, June 8, 1987, p. 132.

27. Ellen Brandt, "Global HR," *Personnel Journal* 70 (March 1991): 38–39.

28. Ibid., p. 42.

29. Ibid., p. 43.

30. This section written by Dr. Judy A. Mondy, Department of Management and Marketing, McNeese State University.

31. Alice Laplante, "The Needing Edge," *Computerworld*, March 18, 1991, p. 65.

32. Michael Fitzgerald, "IS Helps 'Cat' Stay on Its Feet," *Computerworld Premier 100*, October 9, 1990, sec. 2, p. 60.

33. Richard Brady, Rod Chapin, Steve Irvin, Patrick Lyons, and Sebastian Rupley, "Product Comparison: Meeting the Mail," *Infoworld*, October 29, 1990, p. 71.

34. James A. O'Brien, *Introduction to Information Systems in Business Management*, 6th ed. (Homewood, IL: Irwin, 1991), p. 257.

35. Ibid., p. 181.

36. James A. Senn, *Information Systems in Management*, 4th ed. (Belmont, CA: Wadsworth, 1990), p. 265.

37. Ibid.

38. Chuck Cosentino, John Allen, and Richard Wellins, "Choosing the Right People," *HR Magazine* 35 (March, 1990): 66–70.

39. "Voice Mail Boosts Sales, Management Efficiency," *Textile World*, May 1986, pp. 77–78; Harvard Business School, "J. P. Stevens & Co., Inc." (HBS Case Services, case 9-184-022, rev. November 1984); Larry Ward, "The J. P. Stevens MIS" (student paper at Bentley College, January 1987); and J. P. Stevens and Company, *Annual Report* (various years).

40. Michael Alexander, "Travel-Free Commuting," *Nation's Business* 78 (December 1990): 33.

41. Carol Hildebrand, "Give This Programmer Sun, Surf and Software," *Computerworld* 25 (March 11, 1991): 1–16.

42. Mitch Betts, "Bush to Push Work-at-Home," *Computerworld* 24 (November 26, 1990): 1.

43. Roxane Farmanfarmaian, "Making Telecommuting Succeed," *Working Women*, February 1989, pp. 46–52; John Lamb, "At Home in the Electronic Cottage," *New Scientist*, May 5, 1988, p. 63; Susan F. Rasky, "Bill to Benefit Baby Bells Is Proposed," *New York Times*, April 28, 1989, p. D12; Robert D. Hof, "The Baby Bells Toddle toward Cable," *Business Week*, May 8, 1989, p. 40; Standard and Poor's Corp., "Pacific Telesis," *Standard NYSE Stock Reports* 56, (May 17, 1989), sec. 16.

44. O'Brien, *Introduction to Information Systems in Business Management*, p. 325.

45. Fritz H. Grupe, "Planning Your Expert System Strategy," *Information Executive* 4 (Winter 1991): 47.

46. Michael Fitzgerald, "Cooking with Expert Systems," *Computerworld* 24 (October 15, 1990): 45.

47. O'Brien, *Introduction to Information Systems in Business Management*, pp. 325–330.

48. William A. Newman and Floyd J. Brock, "Moving into the Graphical Decade: Graphical User Interfaces in the '90's," *Information Executive* 4 (Winter 1991): 28–32.

49. Robert Sadarini, "The Art of Imagineering," *Information Executive* 4 (Summer, 1991): 6–7.

50. Oded Shenkar and Yoram Zeira, "International Joint Ventures: A Tough Test for HR," *Personnel*, January 1990, p. 28; Ellen Brandt, "Global HR," pp. 38–44.

Management Skills

How well you would adapt and function in a multinational environment depends to some extent on the nature of your cultural makeup. If you are rather inflexible and insensitive in relation to other cultures, you may have problems adapting to new cultures. If you are to function effectively in the global economy, you will need to develop a certain degree of cultural sensitivity. To assess the makeup of your cultural attitudes, take the self-assessment exercise "What Is the Makeup of Your Cultural Attitudes?" Then, turn to page 635 to evaluate yourself.

What Is the Makeup of Your Cultural Attitudes?

INSTRUCTIONS: Indicate the extent to which you agree or disagree with each of the following statements. Answer each statement by circling the appropriate number; for example, if you strongly agree with a particular statement, you would circle the "5" next to that statement.

5 = Strongly agree   **3** = Neither agree nor disagree   **2** = Disagree
4 = Agree   **1** = Strongly disagree

	STRONGLY AGREE		STRONGLY DISAGREE	
1. It is important to have job requirements and instructions spelled out so people always know what they are expected to do.	5	4 3	2	1
2. Managers expect workers to closely follow instructions and procedures.	5	4 3	2	1
3. Rules and regulations are important because they inform workers what the organization expects of them.	5	4 3	2	1
4. Standard operating procedures are helpful to workers on the job.	5	4 3	2	1
5. Instructions for operations are important for workers on the job.	5	4 3	2	1
6. Individual rewards are not as important as group welfare.	5	4 3	2	1
7. Group success is more important than individual success.	5	4 3	2	1
8. Being accepted by the group is more important than working on your own.	5	4 3	2	1

9. An individual should not pursue his or her own objectives without considering the welfare of the group.	5	4	3	2	1
10. It is important for a manager to encourage loyalty and a sense of duty to the group.	5	4	3	2	1
11. Managers should make most decisions without consulting subordinates.	5	4	3	2	1
12. It is often necessary for a supervisor to emphasize his or her authority and power when dealing with subordinates.	5	4	3	2	1
13. Managers should be careful not to ask the opinions of subordinates too frequently.	5	4	3	2	1
14. A manager should avoid socializing with his or her subordinates off the job.	5	4	3	2	1
15. Subordinates should not disagree with their manager's decisions.	5	4	3	2	1
16. Managers should not delegate difficult and important tasks to their subordinates.	5	4	3	2	1
17. Meetings are usually run more effectively when they are chaired by a man.	5	4	3	2	1
18. It is more important for men to have a professional career than it is for women to have a professional career.	5	4	3	2	1
19. Women do not value recognition and promotion in their work as much as men do.	5	4	3	2	1
20. Women value working in a friendly atmosphere more than men do.	5	4	3	2	1
21. Men usually solve problems with logical analysis; women usually solve problems with intuition.	5	4	3	2	1
22. Solving organizational problems usually requires the active forcible approach, which is typical of men.	5	4	3	2	1
23. It is preferable to have a man in a high-level position rather than a woman.	5	4	3	2	1
24. There are some jobs in which a man can always do better than a woman.	5	4	3	2	1
25. Women are more concerned with social aspects of their job than they are with getting ahead.	5	4	3	2	1

Source: This questionnaire is part of a larger instrument currently under development by Professors Peter W. Dorfman and Jon P. Howell, both of New Mexico State University. Reprinted by permission of the authors.

Management Skills
Self-Assessment

How Do Your Ethics Stack Up? (Part I) page 102

Scoring Procedure

Strongly Agree:	3 points
Agree:	2 points
Disagree:	1 point
Strongly Disagree:	0 points

According to the author of the exercise, interpret the total score as follows:

0 points:	Prepare for canonization ceremony
1–5 points:	Bishop material
6–10 points:	High ethical values
11–15 points:	Good ethical values
16–25 points:	Average ethical values

26–35 points:	Need moral development
36–44 points:	Slipping fast
45 points:	Leave valuables with the warden

Recommendation to Improve Student Ethics

If you score at, or below, *average ethical values* (16 points or above), you are encouraged to carefully review Chapter 3, specifically the sections "A Model of Ethics" and "Business Ethics." Also, if you score in this range, you should carefully review the "Management Tips" section in Chapter 3.

Are You a Good Decision Maker? (Part II) page 192

Scoring Procedure

Rating for Questions 4, 9, and 11:

Yes:	3 points
No:	1 point

Rating for the Remaining Questions:

No:	3 points
Yes:	1 point

The exercise should be interpreted on the basis of the total score, as follows:

Score of 32 and above:	Very good decision maker

Score of 23–30:	Average decision maker
Score of 22 or below:	Poor decision maker

Recommendation to Improve Student Decision-Making Ability

If you score at, or below, the level of an *average decision maker* (30 points or below), you are encouraged to carefully review Chapter 4, specifically the section "Decision-Making Requirements." Also, if you score in this range, you should carefully review the "Management Tips" section in Chapter 4.

How Well Would You Fit in a Bureaucracy? (Part III) page 290

Scoring Procedure

Question Number	Response	Point Value
1.	Mostly Agree	2
2.	Mostly Agree	2
3.	Mostly Disagree	2
4.	Mostly Agree	2
5.	Mostly Disagree	2
6.	Mostly Disagree	2
7.	Mostly Agree	2
8.	Mostly Agree	2
9.	Mostly Disagree	2
10.	Mostly Agree	2
11.	Mostly Agree	2
12.	Mostly Disagree	2
13.	Mostly Disagree	2
14.	Mostly Agree	2
15.	Mostly Disagree	2
16.	Mostly Agree	2
17.	Mostly Disagree	2
18.	Mostly Agree	2
19.	Mostly Agree	2
20.	Mostly Disagree	2

The exercise should be interpreted on the basis of the total score, as follows:

Score of 30 and above: Very high bureaucratic orientation

Score between 29 and 10: Average bureaucratic orientation

Score of 9 and below: Very low bureaucratic orientation

An individual with a rating of *very high* will probably enjoy working in a bureaucratic environment. However, an individual with a rating of *very low* will probably be better off avoiding a bureaucratic environment. Individuals with an *average* rating may survive and thrive to a similar degree in either type of organization. But scoring at the higher range still indicates a greater bureaucratic orientation.

Recommendation to Refine Student Perceptions Regarding a Bureaucracy

If you score at, or below, an *average bureaucratic orientation* (29 points or below), you are encouraged to carefully review Chapter 8 to make sure that your perception of what a bureaucracy is all about is correct.

What Kind of Leader Are You? (Part IV) page 486

Scoring Procedure

In order to compute your leadership style, use the following guidelines:

1. Circle the item numbers for items 8, 12, 17, 18, 19, 30, 34, and 35.

2. Write a "1" in front of the *circled items* to which you responded S (Seldom) or N (Never).

3. Write a "1" in front of *items not circled* to which you responded A (Always) or F (Frequently).

4. Circle the "1's" you have written in front of the following items: 3, 5, 8, 10, 15, 18, 19, 22, 24, 26, 28, 30, 32, 34, and 35.

5. Count the circled "1's." This is your score for having a participation orientation. Record the score in the blank following the "P Score" at the end of the questionnaire.

6. Count the uncircled "1's." This is your score for having

an autocratic orientation. Record this number in the blank following the "A Score."

Interpretation of your scores: Three leadership categories will be addressed here:

Autocratic leadership
Participative leadership
Democratic/laissez-faire leadership

Autocratic Leadership: An *autocratic leader* is a person who tells subordinates what to do and expects to be obeyed without question.

Score of 16 and above: Highly autocratic leader
Score of 10–15: Somewhat autocratic leader
Score of 0–9: Nonautocratic leader

Participative Leadership: A *participative leader* is a person who involves subordinates in decision making but may retain the final authority.

Score of 12–15:   Highly participative leader
Score of 9–11:   Participative leader
Score of 0–8:   Nonparticipative leader

Democratic/Laissez-Faire Leadership: A *democratic leader* is a person who tries to do what the majority of subordinates desire. A *laissez-faire leader* is a person who is uninvolved in the work of the unit.

A Score: Score of 10–15:   Somewhat autocratic leader
P Score: Score of 9–11:   Participative leader

Recommendation to Improve Student

In Chapter 11, four basic leadership styles were identified: autocratic, participative, democratic, and laissez-faire (see Figure 11–1). You are encouraged to read Chapter 11 carefully, especially the sections dealing with these types of leadership. If you are rated as overly autocratic or overly participative, you are encouraged to carefully review and study the advantages and disadvantages of each type of behavior.

Do You Manage Time Effectively? (Part V) page 488

Scoring Procedure

All of these questions, 1–7, are evidence of ineffective time management.
   The exercise should be interpreted on the basis of the total score, as follows:

1 or 2 boxes checked: Average time management ability
3 boxes checked: Below average time management ability
4 or more boxes checked: Extremely poor time management ability

All of these questions illustrate the *extreme*, where time is out of the respondent's control. Each question illustrates some aspect of poor time management. Some comments regarding the seven questions are:

Question 1: A person who is continually tired probably is working improperly, is doing someone else's work, or is in the wrong line of work.
Question 2: It is not your responsibility to take on the work of others. Some people lack the ability to say no. When you are asked to do something, answer this question: If I accept, will this improve the productivity of my unit, help me in some way, or be of great service to others? In many instances, the answer will be no, so just say no.
Question 3: If work controls your life, you will probably not be as effective as you would be if you scheduled some time for recreation and some social activities.

Question 4: Although managers must adhere to a schedule, lack of flexibility can create productivity problems. Lack of organization wastes time, but rigidity may cause problems when unusual situations occur.
Question 5: Managers must be able to clear away work and set priorities. Don't allow yourself to put off work until you have so much to do that you do not do anything. It is best to complete both desirable and undesirable tasks as they come up rather than to continuously put them off. It may even be better to do the distasteful tasks first.
Question 6: Details are sometimes important, but managers must not get caught up in a web of details.
Question 7: Managers who do not delegate often achieve limited success and always feel overwhelmed.

Recommendation to Improve Student Time Management Ability

Basically, even if you are rated as *average* (one or two boxes checked), you probably have a time management problem. If you are rated *below average* or *extremely poor* you need to enhance your time management ability. You are encouraged to carefully review Chapter 16 to help improve your time management skills. Specifically, you should review the sections "How Managers Can Control Their Time Better" and "Management Tips."

What Is the Makeup of Your Cultural Attitudes? (Part VI) page 630

Scoring Procedure

Sum up items 1 through 5 and divide by 5. This is your mean **uncertainty avoidance** score.

Sum up items 6 through 10 and divide by 5. This is your mean **individualism/collectivism** score.

Sum up items 11 through 16, and divide by 6. This is your mean **power distance** score.

Sum up items 17 through 25 and divide by 9. This is your mean **masculinity/femininity** score.

The exercise should be interpreted on the basis of the mean scores, as follows:

1. **Uncertainty avoidance**—Defines the extent to which people in a culture feel threatened by uncertainty and ambiguous situations and try to avoid such situations. The higher the mean score (5 is the maximum mean score), the more likely the manager is to feel threatened in new cultures.

2. **Individualism/collectivism**—Individualism implies a loosely knit social framework in which people are supposed to take care of themselves (as opposed to collectivist cultures characterized by "individual groups" that are expected to take care of their members). The higher the mean score, the more likely a manager will be productive in a team or group environment.

3. **Power distance**—Defines the extent to which the less powerful person in a society accepts inequality in power and considers it normal. The higher the mean score, the more likely that a person will be power oriented and may have difficulty working in an environment where power is distributed among many individuals or groups. This type of person may even be manipulative and overemphasize control.

4. **Masculinity/femininity**—Defines the extent to which the dominant values of society are "masculine" (e.g., assertive and competitive) or feminine (e.g., less assertive and less competitive). The higher the mean score, the more likely that masculine traits are dominant. In a country such as present-day Japan, a feminine type may have trouble coping.

You can compare your scores with a sample of U.S. and Mexican students to see how well you would embrace their cultures. The closer your mean score is to their mean scores, the greater the likelihood that you would mesh with their culture.

Dimension	U.S. Students	Mexican Students
Uncertainty avoidance	3.41	4.15
Individualism/collectivism	2.19	3.33
Power distance	1.86	2.22
Masculinity/femininity	2.78	2.75

Recommendation to Improve Cultural Sensitivity

Basically, if you have a mean rating approaching 5, you probably are not very flexible and may find it difficult to adapt to new cultures. To enhance your skills in relation to cultural sensitivity, you should read Chapter 15 carefully. You should also read the section of Chapter 14 dealing with power.

Glossary

ABC inventory method: The classification of inventory items, for control purposes, into three categories, according to unit costs and number of items kept on hand.

Acceptance sampling: The inspection of a portion of the output or input of a process to determine acceptability.

Accountability: Any means of ensuring that the person who is supposed to perform a task actually performs it and does so correctly.

Action planning: The establishment of performance objectives and standards for individuals.

Affirmative action: Performance required to ensure that applicants are employed, and that employees are treated appropriately during employment, without regard to race, creed, color, or national origin.

Alternatives: Choices that the decision maker has to decide on.

Analyzer strategy: The business-level strategy of attempting to maintain a stable business while innovating on the fringe.

Arbitration: The process in which a dispute between two parties is submitted to a third party to make a binding decision.

Authority: The right to decide, to direct others to take action, or to perform certain duties in achieving organizational objectives.

Autocratic leader: A leader who tells subordinates what to do and expects to be obeyed without question.

Backward integration: A company's taking control of any of the sources of its inputs, including raw materials and labor.

Body language: The nonverbal method of communication in which physical actions such as motions, gestures, and facial expressions convey thoughts and emotions.

Brainstorming: The idea-generating technique wherein a number of persons present alternatives without regard to questions of feasibility or practicality.

Break-even analysis: The financial analysis method used to determine the amount of a particular product that must be sold if a firm is to generate enough revenue to cover costs.

Budget: A statement of planned allocation of resources expressed in financial or numerical terms.

Burnout: The state of fatigue or frustration that stems from devotion to a cause, a way of life, or a relationship that does not provide the expected reward.

Business ethics: The application of ethical principles to business relationships and activities.

Business-level strategic planning: The planning process concerned primarily with how to manage the interests and operations of a particular business.

Capital budget: A statement of planned expenditures of funds for facilities and equipment.

Carrying costs: The expenses associated with maintaining and storing products before they are sold or used.

Centralization: The degree to which authority is retained by higher-level managers in an organization rather than being delegated.

Chain of command: The line along which authority flows from the top of the organization to any individual.

Change: Moving from a known to an unknown.

Change agent: The person or group responsible for ensuring that the planned change in organizational development is properly implemented.

Change sequence: The sequence of events that is needed to bring about change in an organization.

Closed system: An organization or assemblage of things that neither affects nor is affected by outside events.

Coalescing: The process of individuals or groups combining their resources to pursue common objectives.

Coercive power: The power that is derived from the ability to punish or to recommend punishment.

Cohesiveness: The degree of attraction the group has for each of its members.

Committee: A group of people assigned to work together to do something not included in their regular jobs.

Communication: The transfer of information, ideas, understanding, or feelings among people.

Communication channels: The means by which information is transmitted in organizations.

Communication networks: The pathways through which messages between and among people in organizations flow.

Comparable worth: The concept that requires the value for dissimilar jobs to be compared under some form of job evaluation and pay rates to be assigned according to their evaluated worth.

Compensation: All rewards individuals receive as a result of their employment.

Compressed workweek: Any arrangement of work hours that permits employees to fulfill their work obligation in fewer days than the typical five-day workweek.

Concentric diversification: The development of businesses related to the firm's current businesses.

Conceptual skill: The ability to comprehend abstract or general ideas and apply them to specific situations.

Conflict: Antagonism or opposition between or among persons.

Conglomerate diversification: The development of businesses unrelated to the firm's current businesses.

Consideration: The extent to which leaders' relationships with subordinates are characterized by mutual trust and respect for employees' ideas and feelings.

Contact chart: A diagram showing various individuals in the organization and the numbers of interactions they have with others.

Contingency planning: The development of plans to be placed in effect if certain events occur.

Control chart: The graphic record of how closely samples of a good or service conform to standards over time.

Control tolerances: Specifications of how much deviation will be permitted before corrective action is taken.

Controlling: The process of comparing actual performance with standards and taking any necessary corrective action.

Co-opting: The method of increasing power and creating alliances in which individuals or groups whose support is needed are absorbed into another group.

Coordination: The process of ensuring that persons who perform interdependent activities work together in a way that contributes to overall objective attainment.

Corporate culture: The system of shared values, beliefs, and habits within an organization that interacts with the formal structure to produce behavioral norms.

Corporate-level strategic planning: The process of defining the overall character and purpose of the organization, the businesses it will enter and leave, and how resources will be distributed among those businesses.

Cost leadership strategy: The business-level strategy in which the organization aggressively seeks efficient facilities, pursues cost reductions, and uses tight cost controls to produce products more efficiently than competitors.

Creativity: The ability to generate ideas that are both innovative and functional.

Critical path method (CPM): The planning and control technique that involves the display of a complex project as a network, with one time estimate used for each step in the project.

Data communication: The sending of data produced by a computer over some form of communication medium, such as phone lines.

Database management: The exchange of information with people who are higher or lower in the organization but who are directly in the formal chain of command.

Decentralization: The condition that exists when a significant amount of authority is delegated to lower levels in the enterprise.

Decision making: The process of generating and evaluating alternatives and making choices among them.

Decision risk: Exposure to the probability that an incorrect decision will have an adverse effect on the organization.

Decision support system (DSS): An information system that allows users to quickly process and retrieve information.

Defender strategy: The business-level strategy that seeks to maintain current market share by holding on to current customers.

Delegation: The process of assigning responsibility along with the needed authority.

Delphi technique: The formal procedure for obtaining the consensus of a number of experts through the use of a series of questionnaires.

Democratic leader: A leader who tries to do what the majority of subordinates desires.

Departmentation: The process of grouping related work activities into manageable units.

Diagonal communication: The exchange of information with people who are higher or lower in the organization but who are not directly in the formal chain of command.

Differentiation strategy: The business-level strategy that involves an attempt to distinguish the firm's goods or services from others in the industry.

Directing: The process of telling a person what to do.

Disciplinary action: Action taken to correct unacceptable behavior.

Discipline: The state of employee self-control and orderly conduct present in an organization.

Discipline without punishment: A process whereby a worker is given time off with pay to think about whether he or she really wants to follow the rules and continue working for the company.

Discounted cash flow technique: The way of valuing an investment that uses an interest rate or discount rate to calculate the present value of the income the investment is expected to produce.

Diversification: Increasing the variety of goods or services made or sold.

Dominant culture: The corporate culture that expresses the shared views of the majority of the organization's members.

Economic order quantity (EOQ) inventory control method: The procedure for balancing ordering costs and carrying costs so as to minimize total inventory costs.

Effectiveness: The capability of bringing about an effect or accomplishing a purpose, sometimes without regard to the quantity of resources consumed in the process.

Efficiency: The capability of producing desired results with a minimum of energy, time, money, materials, or other costly inputs.

Empathy: The ability to identify with the feelings and thoughts of another person.

Employee assistance program: A coordinated effort by an organization to help employees deal with special problems and needs.

Employee-centered work redesign: An innovative concept designed to link the mission of the company with the job satisfaction needs of employees.

Employee orientation: The formal process of helping new employees adjust to the organization, job, and work group.

Employment requisition: A form issued to activate the recruitment process, typically including such information as the job title, starting date, and pay scale and a brief summary of principal duties.

Equity theory: The motivation theory that people assess their performance and attitudes by comparing both their contribution to work and the benefits they derive from it to the contributions and benefits of "comparison oth-ers" whom they select—and who in reality may be like or unlike them.

Ethics: The discipline dealing with what is good and bad, or right and wrong, or with moral duty and obligation.

Executive Orders: Directives issued by the President that have the force and effect of laws enacted by Congress.

Expectancy theory: The approach to motivation that attempts to explain behavior in terms of an individual's objectives and choices and the expectations of achieving the objectives.

Expert (knowledge) power: The power that comes from a person's possessing special knowledge or skills.

Expert system: A system that uses knowledge about a narrowly defined, complex area to act as a consultant to a human.

External environment: Those factors that affect a firm from outside its organizational boundaries.

Extrinsic motivation: Motivation by factors outside the job, such as pay, job title, and tenure.

Fixed costs: Costs that do not change with the level of output.

Fixed-position layout: The production process in which the large or heavy product stays in one location, and people, tools, materials, and equipment are moved to the product as needed.

Flextime: The practice of permitting employees to choose, with certain limitations, their own working hours.

Flow process chart: A chart illustrating the activities involved in an entire process, showing the sequence in which they are performed.

Focus strategy: The business-level strategy in which the organization concentrates on a specific regional market, product line, or buyer group.

Formal communication channels: The communication channels that are officially recognized by the organization.

Forward integration: Integration toward the final users of a company's goods or services.

Function: A type of work activity that can be identified and distinguished from other work.

Functional authority: The right of staff specialists to issue orders in their own names in designated areas.

Functional authority organizations: Organizations whose staff departments have authority over line personnel in narrow areas of specialization (a modification of line and staff organizations).

Functional-level strategic planning: The process of determining policies and procedures for relatively narrow areas of activity that are critical to the success of the organization.

Glass ceiling: The invisible barrier in organizations which prevents many women from achieving top-level management positions.

Grapevine: The informal means by which information is transmitted in an organization.

Graphical User Interfaces (GUIs): Represent a move to truly make software applications easy to use. Computer users touch or aim at graphic figures (icons) or framed written commands to communicate with the computer program.

Grievance procedure: A systematic process through which employees complain about matters affecting them.

Group: Two or more people having a unifying relationship, such as common objectives or physical proximity.

Group structure process: The interpersonal interactions needed to accompany and accomplish task activities.

Health: The condition of being physically and emotionally able to perform vital functions normally or properly.

Horizontal differentiation: The process of forming additional units at the same level in the organization.

Horizontal integration: Buying or taking control of competitors at the same level in the production and marketing process.

Host country: The country where an operational unit of a multinational company resides.

Human resource management (HRM): The wide range of organizational activities involved in staffing, training and development, compensation, health and safety, employee and labor relations, and human resource research.

Human resource planning (HRP): The development of strategies and tactics to ensure that the required numbers of employees with the required skills are on the job when they are needed.

Human skill: The ability to understand, motivate, and get along with other people.

Influencing: The process of determining or affecting the behavior of others.

Informal communication channels: Ways of transmitting information within an organization that bypass formal channels.

Informal group: Two or more persons associated with one another in ways not prescribed by the formal organization.

Informal organization: The set of evolving relationships and patterns of human interaction within an organization that are not officially prescribed.

Information filtering: The process by which a message is altered through the elimination of certain data as the communication moves from person to person in the organization.

Information overload: The condition that exists when an individual is presented with too much information in too short a time.

Initiating structure: The extent to which leaders establish objectives and structure their roles and the roles of subordinates toward the attainment of the objectives.

Integration: The unified control of a number of successive or similar operations.

Internal environment: Those factors inside an organization that affect the organization's management.

Intimidation: The compelling of action or inaction through fear or awe.

Intrinsic motivation: Motivation by factors within the job, such as creativity, autonomy, and responsibility.

Inventory: The goods or materials available for use by a business.

Iron law of responsibility: The rule, first stated by Keith Davis, that "in the long run, those who do not use power in a manner society considers responsible will tend to lose it."

Jargon: The special language that group members use in their daily interactions.

Job analysis: The systematic process of determining the skills and knowledge required for performing jobs in the organization.

Job description: A document that describes the tasks and responsibilities of a job and its relationships to other jobs.

Job design: The process of determining the specific tasks to be performed, the methods used in performing these tasks, and how the job relates to other work in the organization.

Job enlargement: Changes in the scope of a job so as to provide greater variety for the worker.

Job enrichment: Basic changes in the content and level of responsibility of a job so as to provide greater challenge to the worker.

Job sharing: Two part-time people splitting the duties of one job in some agreed-on manner and being paid according to their contributions.

Job specification: A statement of the minimum acceptable qualifications a person should possess to perform a particular job.

Just-in-time (JIT) inventory method: The practice of having inputs to the production process delivered precisely when they are needed, thereby assigning to suppliers the responsibility for keeping inventories to a minimum.

Laissez-faire leader: A leader who is uninvolved in the work of the unit.

Lateral communication: Communication by managers at the same organizational level.

Leadership (leading): Influencing others to do what the leader wants them to do.

Leadership continuum: The graphical representation, developed by Robert Tannenbaum and Warren H. Schmidt, of the trade-off between a manager's use of authority and the freedom that subordinates experience as the leadership style varies from boss-centered to subordinate-centered.

Learning curve: A graphic representation of the decreasing time required to do a particular task as that task is repeated by a certain person.

Leased employees: Individuals provided by an outside firm at a fixed hourly rate, similar to a rental fee, often for extended periods.

Legitimate power: The power that results from a person's being placed in a formal position of authority.

Line and staff organizations: Organizations that have direct, vertical relationships between different levels and also specialists responsible for advising and assisting other managers.

Line departments: Departments directly involved in accomplishing the primary purpose of the organization.

Line organizations: Organizations that have only direct, vertical relationships between different levels in the firm.

Maintenance: The sum of all activities involved in keeping a production system in working order.

Management: The process of getting things done through the efforts of other people.

Management by objectives (MBO): The philosophy of management that emphasizes the setting of agreed-on objectives by managers and their subordinates and the use of these objectives as the primary bases of motivation, evaluation, and control efforts.

Management development programs: Formal efforts to improve the skills and attitudes of present and prospective managers.

Management information system (MIS): Any organized approach for obtaining relevant and timely information on which to base management decisions.

Managerial Grid: The two-dimensional matrix developed by Robert Blake and Jane Mouton that shows concern for people on the vertical axis and concern for production on the horizontal axis.

Managing diversity: Having an acute awareness of characteristics common to a culture, race, gender, age, or sexual preference, while at the same time managing employees with these characteristics as individuals.

Mathematical models: Mathematical equations that define and represent the relationships among elements of a system.

Matrix departmentation: The form of departmentation that occurs when project departmentation takes on a permanent status designed to achieve specific results by using teams of specialists from different functional areas of the organization.

Matrix organization: A permanent organization designed to achieve specific results by using teams of specialists from different functional areas in the organization.

Mediation: The process in which a third party enters a dispute between two parties for the purpose of assisting them in reaching an agreement.

Middle managers: Managers above the supervisory level but subordinate to the firm's most senior executives.

Mission: A unit's continuing process, or reason for being.

Mission statement: A broadly stated definition of the basic purpose and scope of a unit.

Model: An abstraction of a real-world situation.

Motivation: The desire to put forth effort in pursuit of organizational objectives.

Multimedia: A computer application that produces presentations combining automation, stereo sound, full-motion video, and graphics.

Multinational company (MNC): A firm that is based in one country (the parent, or home, country) and produces goods or provides services in one or more foreign countries (host countries).

Networking: The cultivating of relationships with the right people for the purpose of obtaining power.

Noise: Anything that interferes with the accurate transmission or reception of messages.

Nominal grouping: The approach to decision making that involves idea generation by group members, group interaction only to clarify ideas, member rankings of ideas presented, and alternative selection by summing up the rankings.

Nonroutine decisions: Decisions that are designed to deal with unusual problems or situations.

Norm: A standard of behavior expected of informal group members.

Objectives: The desired end results of any activity.

Ombudsperson: A complaint officer with access to top management who hears employee complaints, investigates, and recommends appropriate action.

Open-door policy: An established guideline that allows workers to bypass immediate supervisors in regard to substantive matters without fear of reprisal.

Open system: An organization or assemblage of things that affects and is affected by outside events.

Operating budget: A statement of the planned income and expenses of a business or unit.

Operation chart: A chart showing an operator's activities while one operation in a process is performed.

Operations management: The management of the complex activities relating to planning production, organizing resources, directing operations and human resources, and monitoring system performance.

Ordering costs: Administrative, clerical, and other expenses incurred in obtaining inventory items and placing them in storage.

Organization: Two or more people working together in a coordinated manner to achieve group results.

Organizational behavior modification: The application of B. F. Skinner's reinforcement theory to organizational change efforts.

Organizational constituency: Any identifiable group that organizational managers either have or acknowledge a responsibility to represent.

Organizational development (OD): Planned and systematic attempts to change the organization, typically to a more behavioral environment.

Organizational stakeholder: An individual or group whose interests are affected by organizational activities.

Organizational strategists: The people who spend a large portion of their time on matters of vital or far-ranging importance to the organization as a whole.

Organizational structure: The formal relationships among groups and individuals in the organization.

Organizing: The process of prescribing formal relationships among people and resources to accomplish objectives.

Parent country: The country where the headquarters of a multinational company is located.

Participative leader: A leader who involves subordinates in decision making but may retain the final authority.

Path-goal theory: The proposition that managers can facilitate job performance by showing employees how their performance directly affects their receiving desired rewards.

Payback method: The method of financial analysis by which investments are ranked according to the payback period, the time it takes an investment to pay back the initial capital in profits.

Payoff relationship: Evaluating alternatives in terms of their potential benefits or costs.

Perception set: A fixed tendency to interpret information in a certain way.

Performance appraisal: The formal and systematic measurement and evaluation of job performance.

Physical models: Models that generally look like the systems they represent.

Planning: The process of determining in advance what should be accomplished and how it should be realized.

Plans: Statements of how objectives are to be accomplished.

Policy: A predetermined guide established to provide direction in decision making.

Political action committees (PACs): Tax-favored organizations formed by special interest groups to accept contributions and influence government action.

Politics: A network of interactions by which power is acquired, transferred, and exercised on others.

Portfolio strategy: The process of determining how an SBU will compete in a particular line of business, with a concentration on the mix of business units and product lines that fit together in a logical way to provide synergy and competitive advantage for the corporation.

Power: The ability to influence behavior.

Predetermined time standards: Established estimates of the time that should be required to perform minute tasks.

Preliminary interview: The type of interview used to eliminate any obviously unqualified job applicants.

Preventive maintenance: Routine inspection and other efforts aimed at preventing breakdowns and keeping equipment and facilities in good working order.

Primary groups: Small groups characterized by relatively close associations among members.

Proactive response: Taking action in anticipation of environmental changes.

Problem content: The environment in which the problem exists, the decision maker's knowledge of that environment, and the environment that will exist after a choice is made.

Procedure: A series of steps for the accomplishment of some specific project or endeavor.

Process layout: An arrangement of the processing components according to the functions they perform.

Product layout: The production arrangement that entails moving a product down an assembly line or conveyor and through a series of work stations until the product is completed.

Production and operations: The application of objective, especially quantitative, techniques to the design and operation of any system that transforms inputs into outputs.

Productivity: A measure of the relationship between inputs (labor, capital, natural resources, energy, and so forth) and the quality and quantity of outputs (goods and services).

Program evaluation and review technique (PERT): The planning and control technique that involves the display of a complex project as a network of events and activities with three time estimates used to calculate the expected time for each activity.

Progressive discipline: The disciplinary action approach designed to ensure that the minimum penalty appropriate to the offense is imposed.

Project organization: A temporary organization designed to achieve specific results by using teams of specialists from different functional areas in the organization.

Prospector strategy: The business-level strategy that involves innovation through seeking out new opportunities, taking risks, and expanding.

Quality: The degree of excellence of a good or service.

Quality circles: Small groups of employees who get together on company time to develop ways to improve the quality and quantity of work.

Reactive response: Reacting to environmental changes after they occur.

Recruitment: The process of attracting individuals—in sufficient numbers and with appropriate qualifications—and encouraging them to apply for jobs with the organization.

Referent power: The power that is based on a liking for, or a desire to be liked by, the power holder.

Reinforcement theory: The idea that human behavior can be explained in terms of the previous positive or negative outcomes of that behavior.

Responsibility: The obligation to perform work activities.

Retrenchment: The reduction of the size or scope of a firm's activities.

Reward power: The power that is derived from a person's ability to reward another individual.

Role: Total pattern of expected behavior of an individual.

Rule: A specific and detailed guide to action set up to direct or restrict action in a fairly narrow manner.

Safety: Freedom from danger.

Scalar principle: The philosophy that authority and re-

sponsibility should flow from top management downward in a clear, unbroken line.

Schematic models: Line drawings, flowcharts, graphs, maps, organization charts, and similar items that represent the major features of a particular system.

Secondary groups: Groups that are larger and less intimate than primary groups.

Selection: Determining which individual to hire for a particular job.

Self-fulfilling prophecy: The idea that the manager's positive or negative expectations will have a significant influence on employee motivation and performance.

Sensitivity training: The organizational development technique that uses leaderless discussion groups to develop awareness of and sensitivity to oneself and others. (Also called T-group training and laboratory training.)

Simulation: The technique for experimenting with a real-world situation through an artificial model that represents that situation.

Social audit: A systematic assessment of a company's activities in terms of their social impact.

Social contract: The set of written and unwritten rules and assumptions about acceptable interrelationships among the various elements of society.

Social responsibility: The implied, enforced, or felt obligation of managers, acting in their official capacity, to serve or protect the interests of groups other than themselves.

Source (sender): The person who has an idea or message to communicate to another person or persons.

Span of management (control): The number of direct subordinates reporting to any manager.

Specialization of labor: The division of a complex job into simpler tasks so that one person or group may carry out only identical or related activities.

Staff departments: Departments that provide line people with advice and assistance in specialized areas.

Staffing: The formal process of ensuring that the organization has qualified workers available at all levels to meet its short- and long-term business objectives.

Standard operating procedures (SOPs): The stable body of procedures, written and unwritten, that govern an organization.

Standards: Established levels of quality or quantity used to guide performance.

Standing plans: Plans that remain roughly the same for long periods of time.

States of nature: The various situations that could occur and the probability of each of them occurring.

Statistical process control: Gauging the performance of the manufacturing process by carefully monitoring changes in whatever is being produced.

Status symbol: A visible, external sign of one's social position.

Stockholders (shareholders): The owners of a corporation's stock.

Strategic business unit (SBU): Any part of a business organization that is treated separately for strategic planning purposes.

Strategic control points: The critical points selected for monitoring in the process of producing goods or services.

Strategic planning: The process by which top management determines overall organizational purposes and objectives and how they are to be achieved.

Strategic planning staff specialists: Specialists who assist and advise managers in strategic planning.

Stress: The body's reaction to any demand made on it.

Stress audit: A review that helps identify the symptoms and causes of stress.

Strong corporate culture: The dominant corporate culture that is widely and ardently adhered to by members of the organization.

Subcultures: Corporate cultures characteristic of various units in an organization.

Supervisory managers: The managers who directly oversee the efforts of those who actually perform the work.

Survey feedback method: The organizational development method of basing change efforts on the systematic collection and measurement of subordinates' attitudes through anonymous questionnaires.

Synergism: The cooperative action of two or more persons working together to accomplish more than they could working separately.

Systems approach: The viewing of any organization or entity as an arrangement of interrelated parts that interact in ways that can be specified and to some extent predicted.

Tactical plans: Plans designed to implement the strategic plans of top management.

Task activity: The steps used to perform a task, not including the procedures and materials required to accomplish it.

Task (functional) groups: Groups determined by prescribed job requirements.

Team building: A conscious effort by management to develop effective work groups throughout the organization.

Technical skill: The ability to use specific knowledge, methods, and techniques in performing work.

Telecommuting: When workers at home or temporarily away from the office perform their work over telephone lines tied to a computer as if they were at the office.

Teleconferencing: A method of conducting or participating in multiparty discussions by telephone or videophone.

Theory X: The assumption that people dislike work and responsibility, lack ambition and creative ability, and mainly want security and money.

Theory Y: The assumption that expending physical and mental effort is natural, that people can be self-directed if achievement brings rewards, and that most can exercise imagination, ingenuity, and creativity and learn to seek responsibility.

Theory Z: The belief that a high degree of mutual responsibility, loyalty, and consideration between companies and their employees will result in higher productivity and improved employee welfare.

Time study: The systematic measurement and analysis of the time required to do work.

Timing: The determination of when a message should be communicated.

Top managers: The organization's most senior executives.

Total quality management: A commitment to excellence by everyone in an organization that emphasizes excellence achieved by teamwork and a process of continuous improvement.

Training and development programs: Formal efforts to help employees learn new skills, improve existing skills, or otherwise improve their ability to perform in the organization.

Trait approach to leadership: The evaluation and selection of leaders on the basis of their physical, mental, social, and psychological characteristics.

Transformational leader: A person who has the special ability to lead an organization through major strategic change.

Transnational company: A firm that views the world as one market, conducts operations in many countries, and makes decisions as if national boundaries do not exist.

Tunnel vision: The extremely narrow viewpoint of people who have mental blinders, such as individual biases, that restrict the search for a solution to a narrow range of alternatives.

Type I ethics: The strength of the relationship between what an individual or an organization believes to be moral and correct and what available sources of guidance suggest is morally correct.

Type II ethics: The strength of the relationship between what one believes and how one behaves.

Union: A group of employees who have joined together for the purpose of dealing with their employer.

Unity of command principle: The belief that each person should answer to only one immediate superior.

Variable costs: Costs that are directly related to changes in output.

Vertical differentiation: The process of creating additional levels in the organization.

Voice mail: Spoken messages transmitted electronically and stored for delivery to the recipient at a later time.

Word processing: A computer application that permits an operator to create and edit written material.

Work sampling: The observation of a worker or workers at random times to determine the proportion of time that is being spent on various tasks.

Worker-machine chart: A chart showing if there is excessive idle time associated with either the worker or the machine.

Worker participation: The process of involving workers in the decision-making process.

Zero base budgeting: The system of budgeting that requires management to take a fresh look at all programs and activities each year, rather than merely building on last year's budget.

References

Adler, Paul S. "Managing Flexible Automation." *California Management Review* 30 (Spring 1988): 34–56.

Agor, Weston H. "Nurturing Executive Intrapreneurship with a Brain-Skill Management Program." *Business Horizons* 31 (May–June 1988): 12–15.

Akers, John R. "Ethics and Competitiveness—Putting First Things First." *Sloan Management Review* 30 (Winter 1989): 69–71.

Albert, Michael. "Transmitting Corporate Culture through Case Stories." *Personnel* (August 1987): 71–73.

Albrecht, W. Steve, and David W. Schmoldt. "Employee Fraud." *Business Horizons* 31 (July–August 1988): 16–18.

Alderfer, C. P. *Existence, Relatedness, and Growth: Human Needs in Organizational Settings.* New York: Free Press, 1972.

Alexander, John W. "Sharing the Vision." *Business Horizons* 32 (May–June 1989): 56–59.

Allaire, Yvan, and Mihaela E. Firsirotu. "Coping with Strategic Uncertainty." *Sloan Management Review* 30 (Fall 1988): 7–15.

Allen, L. A. "Managerial Planning: Back to the Basics." *Management Review* 70 (April 1981): 15–20.

Anderson, Joyce S. "Real Open-Door Communication." *Personnel Journal* 68 (May 1989): 32–37.

Applegate, Lynda A., James I. Cash, Jr., and D. Quinn Mills. "Information Technology and Tomorrow's Manager." *Harvard Business Review* 66 (November–December 1988): 128–136.

Aram, John D. "The Paradox of Interdependent Relations in the Field of Social Issues in Management." *Academy of Management Review* 14 (April 1989): 266–283.

Arnold, John D. "The Why, When, and How of Changing Organizational Structures." *Management Review* (March 1981): 17–20.

Arogyaswamy, Bernard, and Charles M. Byles. "Organizational Culture: Internal and External Fits." *Journal of Management* 13 (Winter 1987): 647–658.

Ashton, J. E., and F. X. Cook, Jr. "Time to Reform Job Shop Manufacturing." *Harvard Business Review* 67 (March–April 1989): 106–111.

Astley, W. G., and A. H. van de Ven. "Central Perspectives and Debates in Organization Theory." *Administrative Science Quarterly* (June 1983): 248.

Atkinson, Lisa, and Joseph Galaskiewicz. "Stock Ownership and Company Contributions to Charity." *Administrative Science Quarterly* 33 (March 1988): 82–100.

Attaran, Mohsen. "The Automated Factory: Justification and Implementation." *Business Horizons* 32 (May–June 1989): 80–86.

Axline, Larry L. "Business Ethics: Blackjack or Bust?" *Management Review* 79 (October 1990): 64.

Bahrami, Bahman. "Productivity Improvement through Cooperation of Employees and Employers." *Labor Law Journal* 39 (March 1988): 167–178.

Bahrami, Homa, and Stuart Evans. "Strategy Making in High-Technology Firms: The Empiricist Mode." *California Management Review* 31 (Winter 1989): 107–128.

Baird, Lloyd, and Ilan Meshoulam. "Managing Two Fits of Strategic Human Resource Management." *Academy of Management Review* 13 (January 1988): 116–128.

Bales, R. F., and F. L. Strodtbeck. "Phases in Group Problem Solving." *Journal of Abnormal and Social Psychology* 46 (1951): 485–495.

Barczak, Gloria, Charles Smith, and David Wilemon. "Managing Large-Scale Organizational Change." *Organizational Dynamics* 16 (Autumn 1987): 22–35.

Barley, Stephen R. "Cultures of Culture: Academics, Practitioners and the Pragmatics of Normative Control." *Administrative Science Quarterly* 3 (March 1988): 24–60.

Barnes, Louis B., and Mark P. Kriger. "The Hidden Side of Organizational Leadership." *Sloan Management Review* 28 (Fall 1986): 15–25.

Barnlund, Dean C. "Public and Private Self in Communicating with Japan." *Business Horizons* 32 (March–April 1989): 32–40.

Baron, Jonathan, and John C. Hershey. "Outcome Bias in Decision Evaluation." *Journal of Personality and Social Psychology* 51 (April 1988): 569–579.

Bart, Christopher K. "Budgeting Gamesmanship." *Academy of Management Review* 4 (November 1988): 285–294.

Bartlett, Christopher A., and Sumantra Ghoshal. "Organizing for Worldwide Effectiveness: The Transnational Solution." *California Management Review* 31 (Fall 1988): 54–74.

Batten, Joe D. "Leading by Expectation." *Management World* 17 (January–February 1988): 35–36.

Bavaria, Steve. "Corporate Ethics Should Start in the Boardroom."

Business Horizons 34 (January–February 1991): 9–12.

Beilinson, Jerry. "Workforce 2000: Already Here?" *Personnel* 67 (October 1990): 3–4.

Benfari, Robert C., and Harry E. Wilkinson. "Intelligence and Management." *Business Horizons* 31 (May–June 1988): 22–28.

Benne, K. D., and P. Sheats. "Functional Roles of Group Members." *Journal of Social Issues* 4 (1948): 41–49.

Bennis, W. "Leadership: A Beleaguered Species?" *Organizational Dynamics* 5 (Summer 1976): 13–14.

Berger, Raymond M., and Donna H. Tucker. "How to Evaluate a Selection Test." *Personnel Journal* 66 (February 1987): 88–90.

Berry, Leonard L., A. Parasuraman, and Valarie A. Zeithaml. "The Service-Quality Puzzle." *Business Horizons* 31 (September–October 1988): 35–43.

Bertrand, Kate. "Marketers Rush to Be First on the Bloc." *Business Marketing* 75 (October 1990): 20–23.

Beyer, Janice M. "How an Organization's Rites Reveal Its Culture." *Organizational Dynamics* 15 (Spring 1987): 4–25.

Bhide, Amar, and Howard H. Stevenson. "Why Be Honest if Honesty Doesn't Pay." *Harvard Business Review* 66 (September–October 1990): 121–129.

Bills, David B. "Costs, Commitment, and Rewards: Factors Influencing the Design and Implementation of Internal Labor Markets." *Administrative Science Quarterly* 32 (June 1987): 202–221.

Blair, John. "Not Again! The Messy Business of Planning." *Computerworld* 21 (November 30, 1987): 69–73.

Blake, Robert R., and Jane S. Mouton, "Theory and Research for Developing a Science of Leadership." *Journal of Applied Behavioral Science* 18 (March 1982): 275–291.

Bobbitt, H. R., Jr., and J. D. Ford. "Decision-Maker Choice as a Determinant of Organizational Structure." *Academy of Management Review* 5 (January 1980): 13–23.

Bommer, Michael, Clarence Gratto, Jerry Gravender, and Mark Tuttle. "A Behavioral Model of Ethical and Unethical Decision Making." *Journal of Business Ethics* 6 (May 1987): pp. 265–280.

Boone, Louis E., and David L. Kurtz. "CEOs: A Group Profile." *Business Horizons* 31 (July–August 1988): 38–42.

Boone, Louis E., David L. Kurtz, and Patrick Fleenor. "CEOs: Early Signs of a Business Career." *Business Horizons* 31 (September–October 1988): 20–24.

Bowen, David E., Caren Siehl, and Benjamin Schneider. "A Framework for Analyzing Customer Service Orientations in Manufacturing." *Academy of Management Review* 14 (January 1989): 75–95.

Briscoe, Dennis R. "Organizational Design: Dealing with the Human Constraint." *California Management Review* 23 (Fall 1980): 71–80.

Briscoe, Dennis R., and Susan Harwood. "Improving the Interview Process." *Personnel* 61 (September 1987): 18–20.

Brockner, Joel, and Tod Hass. "Self-Esteem and Task Performance in Quality Circles." *Academy of Management Journal* 29 (September 1986): 17–22.

Brown, J. L., and N. M. Agnew. "The Balance of Power in a Matrix

Structure." *Business Horizons* 25 (November–December 1982): 51–54.

Buffa, Elwood S. *Modern Production-Operations Management*. 8th ed. New York: Wiley, 1987.

Buller, Paul F. "For Successful Strategic Change: Blend OD Practices with Strategic Management." *Organizational Dynamics* 16 (Winter 1988): 42–55.

Burchman, Seymour, Barbara Dewey, and Craig Eric Schneier. "Unlocking Employee Performance: Pay for Performance." *Management Solutions* (March 1988): 23–29.

Burge, Benjamin D. "Producing a Quality Product." *Journal of Systems Management* 41 (November 1990): 7–9.

Byrd, Richard E. "Corporate Leadership Skills: A New Synthesis." *Organizational Dynamics* 16 (Summer 1987): 31–40.

Camillus, John C. "Six Approaches to Preventive Management Control." *Financial Executive* 48 (December 1980): 28–31.

Campbell, Donald J. "Task Complexity: A Review and Analysis." *Academy of Management Review* 13 (January 1988): 40–52.

Campion, Michael A., and Paul W. Thayer. "Job Design: Approaches, Outcomes, and Trade-Offs." *Organizational Dynamics* 15 (Winter 1987): 66–79.

Carr, Clay. "Expert Support Environments." *Personnel Journal* 68 (April 1989): 117–126.

Caruth, Don. "Words: A Supervisor's Guide to Communications." *Management Solutions* 31 (June 1986): 34–35.

Chase, R. B., and D. A. Garvin. "The Service Factory." *Harvard Business Review* 67 (July–August 1989): 61–69.

Cheng, J. L. C. "Interdependence and Coordination in Organizations: A Role-System Analysis." *Academy of Management Journal* 26 (March 1983): 156–162.

Chew, W. Bruce. "No-Nonsense Guide to Measuring Productivity." *Harvard Business Review* 66 (January–February 1988): 110–119.

Child, John. "Information Technology, Organization, and Response to Strategic Challenges." *California Management Review* 30 (Fall 1987): 33–50.

Clark, Kim B., and Robert H. Hayes. "Recapturing America's Manufacturing Heritage." *California Management Review* 30 (Summer 1988): 9–33.

Clegg, Stewart R. "The Language of Power and the Power of Language." *Organization Studies* 8 (Winter 1987): 60–69.

Coate, L. Edwin. *An Analysis of Oregon State University's Total Quality Management Pilot Program*. Oregon State University Press, 1990.

Cobb, A. "Informal Influence in the Formal Organization: Perceived Sources of Power among Work Unit Peers." *Academy of Management Journal* 23 (March 1980): 155–161.

Coccari, Ronald L. "How Quantitative Business Techniques Are Being Used." *Business Horizons* 32 (July–August 1989): 70–74.

Coch, L., and J. French, Jr. "Overcoming Resistance to Change." *Human Relations* 1 (1984): 512–532.

Cohen, Allan R., and David L. Bradford. "Influence without Authority." *Organizational Dynamics* 17 (Winter 1989): 5–17.

Collins, Paul E., Jerald Hage, and Frank M. Hull. "Organizational and Technological Predictors of Change in Automaticity." *Academy of Management Journal* 31 (December 1988): 512–543.

Conger, Jay A. "Leadership: The Art of Empowering Others." *Academy of Management Executive* 3 (February 1989): 17–24.

Conger, Jay A., and Rabindra N. Kanungo. "The Empowerment Process: Integrating Theory and Practice." *Academy of Management Review* 13 (July 1988): 471–482.

Cooper, Robin. "You Need a New Cost System When . . ." *Harvard Business Review* 67 (January–February 1989): 77–82.

Cooper, Robin, and R. S. Kaplan. "Measure Costs Right: Make the Right Decisions." *Harvard Business Review* 66 (September–October 1988): 96–105.

Cosier, R. A., and D. R. Dalton. "Equity Theory and Time: A Reformulation. *Academy of Management Review* 8 (1983): 311–319.

Cotton, John L., David A. Vollrath, Kirk L. Froggatt, Mark L. Lengnick-Hall, and Kenneth R. Jennings. "Employee Participation: Diverse Forms and Different Outcomes." *Academy of Management Review* 13 (January 1988): 8–22.

Crandall, Lin P., and Mark I. Phelps. "Pay for a Global Work Force." *Personnel Journal* 70 (February 1991): 28–33.

Cross, Richard Hunter, III. "Strategic Planning: What It Can and Can't Do." *SAM Advanced Management Journal* 52 (Winter 1987): 13–16.

Cummings, L. L. "Compensation, Culture, and Motivation: A Systems Perspective." *Organizational Dynamics* (Winter 1984): 33–44.

Cusumano, Michael A. "Manufacturing Innovation: Lessons from the Japanese Auto Industry." *Sloan Management Review* 39 (Fall 1988): 29–39.

d'Amboise, Gerald, and Marie Muldowney. "Management Theory for Small Business: Attempts and Requirements." *Academy of Management Review* 13 (April 1988): 226–240.

Dalton, Dan R., and William D. Todor. "Win, Lose, Draw: The Grievance Process in Practice." *Personnel Administrator* 26 (March 1981): 25–29.

Dalton, Dan R., William D. Todor, J. Spendelini, J. Fielding, and L. W. Porter. "Organization Structure and Performance: A Critical Review." *Academy of Management Review* 5 (January 1980): 61–64.

Davenport, Thomas H., Michael Hammer, and Tauino J. Metsisto. "How Executives Can Shape Their Company's Information Systems." *Harvard Business Review* 67 (March–April 1989): 130–134.

Davis, T. R. V., and F. Luthans. "Leadership Reexamined: A Behavioral Approach." *Academy of Management Review* 4 (1979): 237–248.

Dean, J. W., Jr., and G. I. Susman. "Organizing for Manufacturable Design." *Harvard Business Review* 67 (January–February 1989): 28–37.

DiPrete, Thomas A. "Horizontal and Vertical Mobility in Organizations." *Administrative Science Quarterly* 32 (September 1987): 422–444.

Dodd-McCue, Diane, J. Matejka Kenneth, and D. Neil Ashworth. "Deep Waders in Muddy Waters: Rescuing Organizational Decision Makers." *Business Horizons* 30 (September–October 1987): 54–57.

Dolan, Shimon, and Aharon Tziner. "Implementing Computer-Based Automation in the Office: A Study of Experienced Stress." *Organizational Behavior Management* 9 (April 1988): 183–187.

Donovan, John J. "Beyond Chief Information Officer to Network Manager." *Harvard Business Review* 66 (September–October 1988): 134–143.

Drucker, Peter F. "Management and the World's Work." *Harvard Business Review* 66 (September–October 1988): 65–76.

Duchessi, Peter, Charles M. Schaninger, and Don R. Hobbs. "Implementing a Manufacturing Planning and Control System." *California Management Review* 31 (Spring 1989): 75–90.

Dugan, Kathleen Watson. "Ability and Effort Attributions: Do They Affect How Managers Communicate Performance Feedback Information?" *Academy of Management Journal* 32 (March 1989): 87–114.

Duncan, W. Jack, Peter M. Ginter, Andrew C. Rucks, and T. Douglas Jacobs. "Intrapreneurship and the Reinvention of the Corporation." *Business Horizons* 31 (May–June 1988): 16–21.

Durack, Elmer, II. "Corporate Business and Human Resources Planning Practices: Strategic Issues and Concerns." *Organizational Dynamics* 15 (Summer 1986): 73–87.

Dutton, Jane E., and Susan E. Jackson. "Categorizing Strategic Issues: Links to Organizational Action." *Academy of Management Journal* 12 (January 1987): 76–90.

Earley, P. Christopher. "Trust, Perceived Importance of Praise and Criticism, and Work Performance: An Examination of Feedback in the United States and England." *Journal of Management* 12 (Winter 1986): 457–473.

Eckley, Robert S. "Caterpillar's Ordeal: Foreign Competition in Capital Goods." *Business Horizons* 32 (March–April 1989): 80–86.

Eisenhardt, Kathleen M., and L. J. Bourgeios, III. "Politics of Strategic Decision Making in High-Velocity Environments: Toward a Midrange Theory." *Academy of Management Journal* 31 (December 1988): 737–770.

Ernz, M., P. C. Earley, and C. L. Hulin. "The Impact of Participation on Goal Acceptance and Performance: A Two-Step Model." *Academy of Management Journal* 28 (1985): 50–66.

Etzioni, Amitai. "Normative-Affective Factors: Toward a New Decision-Making Model." *Journal of Economic Psychology* 9 (June 1988): 125–150.

Ewing, David W., and Pamela M. Banks. "Listening and Responding to Employees' Concerns." *Harvard Business Review* 58 (January–February 1980): 101–114.

Feild, Hubert S., and Robert D. Gatewood. "Matching Talent with the Task: To Find the Right People, First Define the Jobs You Want Them to Do." *Personnel Administrator* 32 (April 1987): 113–123.

Feldman, Davis C. "The Development and Enforcement of Group Norms." *Academy of Management Review* 9 (1984): 47–53.

Feldman, Steven P. "How Organizational Culture Can Affect Innovation." *Organizational Dynamics* 17 (Summer 1988): 57–68.

Ferris, Rodney. "How Organizational Love Can Improve Leadership." *Organizational Dynamics* 16 (Spring 1988): 40–51.

Fiedler, F. E. *A Theory of Leadership Effectiveness*. New York: McGraw-

Hill, 1967.

Fiedler, F. E., and M. M. Chemers. *Leadership and Effective Management*. Glenview, Ill.: Scott, Foresman, 1974.

Fiegenbaum, Avi, John McGee, and Howard Thomas. "Exploring the Linkage between Strategic Groups and Competitive Strategy." *International Studies of Management and Organization* 18 (Spring 1988): 6–25.

Field, R. H. G. "A Critique of the Vroom-Yetton Contingency Model of Leadership Behavior." *Academy of Management Review* 4 (1979): 249–253.

Fiorelli, Joseph S. "Power in Work Groups: Team Member's Perspectives." *Human Relations* 11 (January 1988): 1–12.

Fisher, K. Kim. "Managing in the High-Commitment Workplace." *Organizational Dynamics* 17 (Winter 1989): 31–50.

Fitzgerald, Thomas H. "Can Change in Organizational Culture Really Be Managed?" *Organizational Dynamics* 16 (Autumn 1988): 4–15.

Fleming, Mary M. K. "Keys to Successful Project Management." *CMA—The Management Accounting Magazine* 60 (November–December 1986): 58–61.

Folger, Robert, and Mary Konovsky. "Effects of Procedural and Distributive Justice on Reactions to Pay Raise Decisions." *Academy of Management Journal* 32 (March 1989): 115–131.

Fombrun, Charles J. "Structural Dynamics within and between Organizations." *Administrative Science Quarterly* 31 (September 1986): 103–121.

Ford, J. D., and W. H. Hegarty. "Decision Makers' Beliefs about the Causes and Effects of Structure: An Exploratory Study." *Academy of Management Journal* 27 (June 1984): 271–291.

Fredericks, Peter, and N. Venkatraman. "The Rise of Strategy Support Systems." *Sloan Management Review* 29 (Summer 1988): 47–54.

Frederickson, James W. "The Strategic-Decision Process and Organizational Structures." *Academy of Management Review* 11 (April 1986): 280–297.

Freudenberger, Herbert J. *Burnout: The High Cost of High Achievement*. Garden City, N.Y.: Anchor Press, 1980.

Friedman, Milton. *Capitalism and Freedom*. Chicago: University of Chicago Press, 1962.

Fry, L. W., and J. W. Slocum, Jr. "Technology, Structure, and Workgroup Effectiveness: A Test of a Contingency Model." *Academy of Management Journal* 27 (June 1984): 221–246.

Fulks, Fred T. "Total Quality Management." *Food Technology* 45 (June 1991): 96–101.

Garsombke, Diane J. "Organizational Culture Dons the Mantle of Militarism." *Organizational Dynamics* 17 (Summer 1988): 46–56.

Garvin, David A. "Quality on the Line." *Harvard Business Review* (September–October 1983): 67.

Gellerman, Saul W. "Managing Ethics from the Top Down." *Sloan Management Review* 30 (Winter 1989): 73–79.

Gersick, Connie J. G. "Marking Time: Predictable Transitions in Task Groups." *Academy of Management Journal* 32 (June 1989): 274–309.

Ghertman, Michel. "Foreign Subsidiary and Parents' Roles during Strategic Investment and Divestment Decisions." *Journal of International Business Studies* 19 (Spring 1988): 17–37.

Giacalone, Robert A., and Stephen B. Knouse. "Reduce the Need for Defensive Communication." *Management Solutions* (September 1987): 20–25.

Gist, Marilyn E., Edwin A. Locke, and M. Susan Taylor. "Organizational Behavior: Group Structure, Process, and Effectiveness." *Journal of Management* 13 (Summer 1987): 237–257.

Goddard, Robert W. "Effective Language." *Personnel Journal* 68 (April 1989): 32–37.

Gold, Bela. "Charting a Course to Superior Technology Evaluation." *Sloan Management Review* 39 (Fall 1988): 19–27.

Gold, Ben. "Computerization in Domestic and International Manufacturing." *California Management Review* 31 (Winter 1989): 129–143.

Goldstein, Jeffrey. "A Far-from-Equilibrium Systems Approach to Resistance to Change." *Organizational Dynamics* 16 (Autumn 1988): 16–26.

Gomes-Casseres, Benjamin. "Joint Ventures in the Face of Global Competition." *Sloan Management Review* 30 (Fall 1988): 17–26.

Goodpaster, Kenneth E., and John B. Matthews, Jr. "Can a Corporation Have a Conscience?" *Harvard Business Review* 60 (January–February 1982): 132–141.

Gorry, G. Anthony, and Michael S. Scott Morton. "A Framework for Management Information Systems." *Sloan Management Review* 30 (Fall 1988): 49–61.

Govindaragan, Vijay. "A Contingency Approach to Strategy Implementation at the Business-Unit Level: Integrating Administrative Mechanisms with Strategy." *Academy of Management Journal* 31 (December 1988): 828–853.

Graeff, C. L. "The Situational Leadership Theory: A Critical View." *Academy of Management Review* (April 1983): 285–291.

Grant, Rebecca A., Christopher A. Higgens, and Richard H. Irving. "Computerized Performance Monitors: Are They Costing You Customers?" *Sloan Management Review* 29 (Summer 1988): 39–45.

Green, Stephen G., and M. Ann Welsh. "Cybernetics and Dependence: Reframing the Control Concept." *The Academy of Management Review* 13 (April 1988): 287–301.

Greenfield, Sue, Robert C. Winder, and Gregory Williams. "The CEO and the External Environment." *Business Horizons* 31 (November–December 1988): 20–25.

Greiner, Ann Claire. "Quality Counts." *Technology Review* 93 (July 1990): 19–20.

Griffin, Ricky W. "Consequences of Quality Circles in an Industrial Setting: A Longitudinal Assessment." *Academy of Management Journal* 31 (June 1988): 338–358.

Griggs, Walter S., and Wallace R. Johnson. "Truth-in-Doors." *Management Solutions* (October 1988): 22–24.

Grinblatt, Mark, and Sheridan Titman. "Adverse Risk Incentives and the Design of Performance-Based Contracts." *Management Science* 35 (July 1989): 807–822.

Gross, Andrew C. "The Information Vending Machine." *Business*

Horizons 31 (January–February 1988): 24–33.

Hackman, J. D. "Power and Centrality in the Allocation of Resources in Colleges and Universities." *Administrative Science Quarterly* 30 (March 1985): 61–77.

Hahn, Chan K., Daniel J. Bragg, and Dongwook Shin. "Impact of the Setup Variable on Capacity and Inventory Decisions." *Academy of Management Review* 13 (January 1988): 91–103.

Haley, Michael. "The Economic Dynamics of Work." *Strategic Management Journal* 7 (September–October 1986): 459–472.

Hambrick, Donald C. "The Top Management Team: Key to Strategic Success." *California Management Review* 30 (Fall 1987): 88–108.

Hampden-Turner, Charles. "The Boundaries of Business: The Cross-Cultural Quagmire." *Harvard Business Review* 69 (September–October 1991): 94.

Handy, C. "Through the Organizational Looking Glass." *Harvard Business Review* 58 (January–February 1980): 115–121.

Harper, Stephen C. "Intuition: What Separates Executives from Managers." *Business Horizons* 31 (September–October 1988): 13–19.

Harrell, Adrian, and Michael Stahl. "Additive Information Processing and the Relationship between Expectancy of Success and Motivational Force." *Academy of Management Journal* 29 (June 1986): 424–433.

Harris, Robert G. "Telecommunications Policy in Japan: Lesson for the U.S." *California Management Review* 31 (Spring 1989): 113–131.

Hart, S., M. Boroush, G. Enk, and W. Hornick. "Managing Complexity through Consensus Mapping: Technology for the Structuring of Group Decisions." *Academy of Management Review* 10 (1985): 587–600.

Haspeslagh, Philippe. "Portfolio Planning: Uses and Limits." *Harvard Business Review* 60 (January–February 1982): 58–73.

Hauser, John R., and Don Clausing. "The House of Quality." *Harvard Business Review* 66 (May–June 1988): 63–73.

Hax, Arnoldo C., and Nicolas S. Mailuf. "The Concept of Strategy and the Strategy Formation Process." *Interfaces* 18 (May–June 1988): 99–109.

Hayes, Robert H., and Ramchandran Jaikumar. "Manufacturing's Crisis: New Technologies, Obsolete Organizations." *Harvard Business Review* 66 (September–October 1988): 77–85.

Heiner, Ronald A. "Imperfect Decisions in Organizations: Toward a Theory of Internal Structure." *Journal of Economic Behavior and Organization* 9 (January 1988): 25–44.

Heneman, Robert L., David B. Greenberger, and Chigozie Anonyuo. "Attributions and Exchanges: The Effects of Interpersonal Factors on the Diagnosis of Employee Performance." *Academy of Management Journal* 32 (June 1989): 466–476.

Herbert, Theodore T. "Strategy and Multinational Organization Structure: An Interorganizational Relationships Perspective." *Academy of Management Review* 9 (1984): 259–271.

Herbert, Theodore T., and Helen Deresky. "Should General Managers Match Their Business Strategies?" *Organizational Dynamics* 15 (Winter 1987): 40–51.

Hersey, P., and K. H. Blanchard. *Management of Organizational Behavior.* 4th ed. Englewood Cliffs, N.J.: Prentice-Hall, 1982.

Herzberg, Frederick. "One More Time: How Do You Motivate Employees?" *Harvard Business Review* 65 (September–October 1987): 109–120.

Hill, Charles W. L. "Differentiation versus Low Cost or Differentiation and Low Cost." *Academy of Management Review* 13 (July 1988): 401–412.

Hiromoto, Toshiro. "Another Hidden Edge—Japanese Management Accounting." *Harvard Business Review* 66 (July–August 1988): 22–27.

Hixon, Allen L. "Why Corporations Make Haphazard Overseas Staffing Decisions." *Personnel Administrator* 31 (March 1986): 91–94.

Holloway, Clark, and Herbert H. Hand. "Who's Running the Store, Anyway? Artificial Intelligence!!!" *Business Horizons* 31 (March–April 1988): 70–75.

Hornstein, Harvey A., Madeline E. Heilman, Edward Mone, and Ross Tartell. "Responding to Contingent Leadership Behavior." *Organizational Dynamics* 15 (Spring 1987): 56–65.

Hosmer, LaRue Tone. "Adding Ethics to the Business Curriculum." *Business Horizons* 31 (July–August 1988): 9–15.

House, R. J. "A Path-Goal Theory of Leader Effectiveness." *Administrative Science Quarterly* 16 (1971): 321–338.

Howard, Patricia Digh. "World Shrink." *HRMagazine* 36 (January 1991): 42–43.

Howard, Robert. "The Designer Organization: Italy's GFT Goes Global." *Harvard Business Review* 69 (September–October 1991): 28–44.

Huber, Vandra L., Margaret A. Neale, and Gregory B. Northcraft. "Decision Bias and Personnel Selection." *Organizational Behavior and Human Decision Processes* 40 (August 1987): 136.

Hunt, Bradley D., and Judith F. Vogt. "What Really Goes Wrong with Participative Work Groups?" *Training and Development Journal* 42 (May 1988): 96–100.

Hyman, Michael R. "Ethical Codes Are Not Enough." *Business Horizons* 33 (March–April 1990): 15–22.

Ireland, Karin. "The Ethics Game." *Personnel Journal* 70 (March 1991): 72–75.

Isenberg, Daniel J. "The Tactics of Strategic Opportunism." *Harvard Business Review* 65 (March–April 1987): 92–97.

Jacobs, Dorri. "Exploring Causes of Problem Performance." *Management Solutions* (December 1988): 10–17.

Jacobs, Raymond A., and Harvey M. Wagner. "Reducing Inventory System Costs by Using Robust Demand Estimators." *Management Science* 35 (July 1989): 771–787.

Jaikumar, Jay. "The Boundaries of Business: The Impact of Technology." *Harvard Business Review* 69 (September–October 1991): 100–101.

Jamson, W. A. "A Theory of Coalition Formation." *American Sociological Review* 26 (1961): 372–382.

Joiner, C. W., Jr. "Making the 'Z' Concept Work." *Sloan Management Review* 26 (September 1985): 57–63.

Jordan, Paul C. "Effects of an Extrinsic Reward on Intrinsic Motivation: A Field Experiment." *Academy of Management Journal* 29 (June 1986): 405–412.

Joyce, William F. "Matrix Organization: A Social Experiment." *Academy of Management Journal* 29 (September 1986): 537.

Juran, J. M., Frank M. Gryna, and R. S. Bingham, *Quality Control Handbook.* New York: McGraw-Hill Book Company, 1974.

Kahn, R. L., and E. Boulding. *Power and Conflict in Organizations.* New York: Basic Books, 1964.

Kantrow, Alen M. "Why Read Peter Drucker?" *Harvard Business Review* 58 (January–February 1980): 74–83.

Kaplan, Robert S. "One Cost System Isn't Enough." *Harvard Business Review* 66 (January–February 1988): 61–66.

Katz, Jerome, and William B. Gartner. "Properties of Emerging Organizations." *Academy of Management Review* 13 (July 1988): 429–441.

Katz, R., and M. L. Tushman. "A Longitudinal Study of the Effects of Boundary Spanning Supervision on Turnover and Promotion in Research and Development." *Academy of Management Journal* 26 (1983): 437–456.

Keil, E. C. "Corporate Culture; Fashion or Fact?" *Colorado Business Magazine* 15 (May 1988): 105–109.

Keller, Robert T. "Cross-Cultural Influences on Work and Nonwork Contributors to Quality of Life." *Group and Organization Studies* 12 (September 1987): 304–318.

Kelly, Charles M. "Remedial MBO." *Business Horizons* (September–October 1983): 62–67.

Kelly, Robert E. "In Praise of Followers." *Harvard Business Review* 66 (November–December 1988): 142–148.

Kenny, Graham K., Richard J. Butler, David J. Hickson, David Gray, Geoffrey R. Mallory, and David D. Wilson. "Strategic Decision Making: Influence Patterns In Public and Private Sector Organizations." *Human Relations* 10 (September 1987): 613–622.

Kerr, Jeffrey, and John W. Slocum, Jr. "Managing Corporate Culture through Reward Systems." *Academy of Management Executive* 1 (May 1987): 99–108.

Kester, W. Carl, and Robert A. Taggart, Jr. "Capital Allocation—Hurdle Rates, Budgets, or Both?" *Sloan Management Review* 30 (Fall 1988): 83–90.

Kets de Vries, Manfred F. R. "Leaders Who Self-Destruct." *Organizational Dynamics* 17 (Spring 1989): 5–11.

Kipnis, David. *The Powerholders.* Chicago: University of Chicago Press, 1976.

Kipnis, David, and Stuart M. Schmidt. "Upward-Influence Styles: Relationship with Performance Evaluation, Salary, and Stress." *Administrative Science Quarterly* 33 (December 1988): 528–541.

Klaas, Brian S. "Determinants of Grievance Activity and the Grievance System's Impact on Employee Behavior: An Integrative Perspective." *Academy of Management Review* 14 (July 1989): 445–458.

Klein, Howard J. "An Integrated Control Theory Model of Work Motivation." *Academy of Management Review* 14 (April 1989): 150–172.

Kleinman, Dan. "What to Look for in Tomorrow's Employee." *Personnel Journal* 66 (October 1987): 192–106.

Kleinschrod, Walter A. "Where Have All the Workers Gone?" *Administrative Management* 48 (February 1987): 45.

Knotts, Rose. "Cross Cultural Management: Transformations and Adaptations." *Business Horizons* 32 (January–February 1989): 29–33.

Koehler, Kenneth G. "Link Budget to Overall Plan." *CMA—The Management Accounting Magazine* 61 (May–June 1987): 17.

Krubasik, Edward G. "Customize Your Product Development." *Harvard Business Review* 66 (November–December 1988): 46–53.

Kuhlmann, Torsten M. "Adapting to Technical Change in the Workplace." *Personnel* 65 (August 1988): 67–69.

Kulik, Carol T. "The Effects of Job Categorization on Judgments of the Motivating Potential of Jobs." *Administrative Science Quarterly* 34 (March 1989): 68–90.

Laabs, Jennifer J. "The Global Talent Search." *Personnel Journal* 70 (August 1991): 38–44.

Langowitz, Nan S. "Managing New Product Design and Factory Fit." *Business Horizons* 32 (May–June 1989): 76–79.

Larsson, Rikard, and David W. Bowen. "Organization and Customer: Managing Design and Coordination of Services." *Academy of Management Review* 14 (April 1989): 213–233.

Lawler, Edward E., III. "Choosing an Involvement Strategy." *Academy of Management Executive* 2 (August 1988): 197–204.

Lawrence, Barbara S. "New Wrinkles in the Theory of Age: Demography, Norms, and Performance Ratings." *Academy of Management Journal* 31 (June 1988): 309–337.

Lawrence, P. R., and J. W. Lorsch. "Differentiation and Integration in Complex Organizations." *Administrative Science Quarterly* 12 (June 1967): 1–47.

Lederer, Albert L., and Aubrey L. Mendelow. "Information Systems Planning: Top Management Takes Control." *Business Horizons* 31 (May–June 1988): 73–78.

Lee, Dixie, and Richard Brostrom. "Managing the High-Tech Professional." *Personnel* 65 (June 1988): 12–17.

Lee, James A. "Changes in Managerial Values, 1985–1986." *Business Horizons* 31 (July–August 1988): 29–37.

Lengel, Robert H., and Richard L. Daft. "The Selection of Communication Media as an Executive Skill." *Academy of Management Executive* 2 (August 1988): 225–234.

Levinthal, Daniel A., and Mark Fichman. "Dynamics of Interorganizational Attachments: Auditor-Client Relationships." *Administrative Science Quarterly* 33 (September 1988): 345–369.

Levitt, Barbara, and Clifford Nass. "The Lid on the Garbage Can: Institutional Constraints on Decision Making in the Technical Core of College-Text Publishers." *Administrative Science Quarterly* 34 (June 1989): 190–206.

Lewis, John C. "Issues Concerning High Technology Managers from Multiple Cultural Backgrounds." *Journal of Management Development* 6 (Fall 1987): 73–86.

Lieberman, S. "The Effects of Changes in Roles on the Attitudes of Role Occupants." *Human Relations* 9 (1956): 385–417.

Liebowitz, S. Jay, and Aubrey L. Mendelow. "Directions for Development: Long-Term Organizational Change Requires Corporate Vision and Patience." *Personnel Administrator* 33 (June 1988): 116

Linsay, W. M., and L. W. Rue. "Impact of the Organization Environment on the Long-Range Planning Process: A Contingency View." *Academy of Management Journal* 23 (September 1980): 385–404.

Longenecker, Clinton O., Dennis A. Gioia, and Henry P. Sims, Jr. "Behind the Mask: The Politics of Employee Appraisal." *Academy of Management Executive* 1 (August 1987): 183–194.

Longenecker, Justin G., Joseph A. McKinney, and Carlos W. Moore. "Ethics in Small Business." *Journal of Small Business Management* 27 (January 1989): 27–31.

LoPresto, Robert. "Ethical Recruiting." *Personnel Administrator* 31 (November 1986): 90–92.

McArthur, Jerie, and D. W. McArthur. "The Pitfalls (and Pratfalls) of Corporate Communications." *Management Solutions* (December 1987): 15–21.

McCullers, John C., Richard A. Fabes, and James D. Moran, III. "Does Intrinsic Motivation Theory Explain the Adverse Effects of Rewards on Immediate Task Performance?" *Journal of Personality and Social Psychology* 52 (May 1987): 1027–1033.

McGregor, Douglas. *The Human Side of Enterprise.* New York: McGraw-Hill, 1961.

McGuire, Jean B., Alison Sundgren, and Thomas Schneeweis. "Corporate Social Responsibility and Firm Financial Performance." *Academy of Management Journal* 31 (December 1988): 854–872.

McKenzie, C. L., and C. J. Qazi. "Communication Barriers in the Workplace." *Business Horizons* 26 (March-April 1983): 70–72.

MacMillan, Ian C., Donald C. Hambrick, and Diana L. Day. "The Product Portfolio and Profitability: A PIMS-Based Analysis of Industrial-Product Businesses." *Academy of Management Journal* 25 (December 1982): 733–755.

Maddox, Robert C., and Douglas Short. "The Cultural Integrator." *Business Horizons* 31 (November–December 1988): 57–59.

Magnus, Margaret. "Is Your Recruitment All It Can Be?" *Personnel Journal* 66 (February 1987): 54–63.

Main, Jeremy. "Making Global Alliances Work." *Fortune*, December 17, 1990, pp. 121–126.

Mainiero, Lisa A. "Coping with Powerlessness: The Relationship of Gender and Job Dependency to Empowerment-Strategy Usage." *Administrative Science Quarterly* 31 (December 1986): 633–653.

Malik, S. D., and Kenneth N. Wexley. "Improving the Owner/Manager's Handling of Subordinate Resistance to Unpopular Decisions." *Journal of Small Business Management* 24 (July 1986): 22–28.

Mann, Carl P. "Transformational Leadership in the Executive Office." *Public Relations Quarterly* 33 (Spring 1988): 19–23.

Mansfield, Edwin. "Technological Creativity: Japan and the United States." *Business Horizons* 32 (March–April 1989): 48–53.

Manz, Charles C., and Henry P. Sims, Jr. "Leading Workers to Lead Themselves: The External Leadership of Self-Managing Work Teams." *Administrative Science Quarterly* 32 (March 1987): 106–129.

Marash, Stanley A. "Blueprint for Quality." *Personnel Journal* 68 (March 1989): 120–123.

March, James G., and Martha S. Feldman. "Information in Organizations as Signal and Symbol." *Administrative Science Quarterly* 26 (June 1981): 171–186.

Marcus, Alfred A. "Responses to Externally Induced Innovation: Their Effects on Organizational Performance." *Strategic Management Journal* 9 (July–August 1988): 387–402.

Markowitz, Jarroid. "Managing the Job Analysis Process." *Training and Development Journal* 41 (August 1987): 64–67.

Martin, Bob, and Stephanie Lawrence. "Personnel Executives Respond to Reaffirmation of Affirmative Action." *Personnel Journal* 66 (May 1987): 9–15.

Martin, Robin, and Toby D. Wall. "Attentional Demand and Cost Responsibility as Stressors in Shopfloor Jobs." *Academy of Management Review* 31 (March 1989): 69–86.

Mascarenhas, Briance. "Strategic Group Dynamics." *Academy of Management Journal* 32 (June 1989): 333–352.

Maslow, Abraham H. *Motivation and Personality.* New York: Harper & Bros., 1954.

Meindl, James R. "Managing to Be Fair: An Exploration of Values, Motives, and Leadership." *Administrative Science Quarterly* 34 (June 1989): 252–276.

Mendenhall, Mark E., and Gary Oddou. "The Overseas Assignment: A Practical Look." *Business Horizons* 31 (September–October 1988): 78–84.

Meyer, Alan D. "Mingling Decision-Making Metaphors." *Academy of Management Review* 9 (January 1984): 6–17.

Meyer, Alan D., and James B. Goes. "Organizational Assimilation of Innovations: A Multilevel Contextual Analysis." *Academy of Management Journal* 31 (December 1988): 897–923.

Meyer, Marc H., and Edward B. Roberts. "Focusing Product Technology for Corporate Growth." *Sloan Management Review* 29 (Summer 1988): 7–16.

Michael, Steven R. "Feedforward versus Feedback Controls in Planning." *Managerial Planning* 29 (November–December 1980): 34–38.

Middaugh, J. Kendall, II. "Management Control in the Financial-Services Industry." *Business Horizons* 31 (May–June 1988): 79–86.

Miles, Raymond E. "Adapting to Technology and Competition: A New Industrial Relations System for the 21st Century." *California Management Review* 31 (Winter 1989): 9–28.

Miller, William B. "Motivation Techniques: Does One Work Best?" *Management Review* (February 1981): 47–52.

Miner, Anne S. "Idiosyncratic Jobs in Formalized Organizations." *Administrative Science Quarterly* 32 (September 1987): 327–351.

Mintzberg, Henry. *Power in and around Organizations.* Englewood Cliffs, N.J.: Prentice-Hall, 1983.

Mizock, Murray. "What You Aren't Saying May Be Everything." *Data Management*, September 1986, p. 33.

Moad, Jeff. "Tools to Automate Quality Production." *Datamation*, April 15, 1991, pp. 63–66.

Moffat, Susan. "To Be a Leader in Technology, You Must Share It." *Fortune*, January 14, 1991, pp. 34–35.

Mondy, R. Wayne, and Robert M. Noe, III. *Human Resource Man-*

agement. 5th ed. Newton, Mass.: Allyn and Bacon, 1993.

Mondy, R. Wayne, Robert M. Noe, III, and Robert E. Edwards. "What the Staffing Function Entails." *Personnel* 63 (April 1986): 55–58.

Mondy, R. Wayne, Shane R. Premeaux, and Arthur Sharplin. "Motivation in Practice." *Manage* 39 (Second Quarter 1986): 13, 22–23.

Moorhead, Gregory, and John R. Montanari. "An Empirical Investigation of the Groupthink Phenomenon." *Human Relations* 30 (May 1988): 300–311.

Moriarty, R. T., and G. S. Swartz. "Automation to Boost Sales and Marketing." *Harvard Business Review* 67 (January–February 1989): 100–109.

Morley, Donald Dean, and Pamela Schockley-Zalabak. "Conflict Avoiders and Compromisers: Toward an Understanding of Their Organizational Communication Style." *Group and Organization Studies* 11 (December 1986): 387–402.

Morris, Barry G. "The Executive: A Pathfinder." *Organizational Dynamics* 16 (Spring 1988): 62–77.

Morris, Richard M., III. "Management Control and Decision Support Systems—An Overview." *Industrial Management* 28 (January–February 1986): 8–15.

Morrisey, George L. "Who Needs a Mission Statement? You Do." *Training and Development Journal* 42 (March 1988): 50–52.

Murphy, Patrick E. "Creating Ethical Corporate Structures." *Sloan Management Review* 30 (Winter 1989): 81–87.

Naisbitt, John. *Megatrends.* New York: Warner Books, 1982.

Nardone, Thomas. "Decline in Youth Population Does Not Lead to Lower Jobless Rates." *Monthly Labor Review*, June 1987, 37–42.

Nardoni, Ren. "Integrated Staffing Systems." *Personnel Journal* 68 (May 1989): 106–110.

Neider, L. L. "Experimental Field Investigation Utilizing an Expectancy Theory View of Participation." *Organizational Behavior and Human Performance* 26 (December 1980): 425–442.

Nelson, Reed E. "The Strength of Strong Ties: Social Networks and Intergroup Conflict in Organizations." *Academy of Management Journal* 32 (June 1989): 377–401.

Nelton, Sharon. "Beyond Body Language." *Nation's Business* (June 1986): 73–74.

Nicholson, P. J., Jr., and S. C. Goh. "The Relationship of Organization Structure and Interpersonal Attitudes to Role Conflict and Ambiguity in Different Work Environments." *Academy of Management Journal* (March 1983): 148.

Nielsen, Richard P. "Changing Unethical Organizational Behavior." *Academy of Management Executive* 2 (May 1989): 123–130.

Nitcoki, Joseph Z. "In Search of Sense in Common Sense Management." *Journal of Business Ethics* 6 (November 1987): 639–647.

Norwood, Janet L. "The Labor Force of the Future." *Business Economics* 22 (July 1987): 9–14.

O'Connor, John T. "The Well-Designed Office." *Harvard Business Review* 67 (March–April 1989): 125–129.

O'Donnell, Joseph. "The Creative-Rational Manager." *Manage* 10 (July 1988): 1–3.

O'Reilly, Charles A., III, David F. Caldwell, and William P. Barnett. "Work Group Demography, Social Integration, and Turnover." *Administrative Science Quarterly* 34 (March 1989): 21–37.

Ogilvis, John R., Michael F. Pohlen, and Louise H. Jones. "Organizational Information Processing and Productivity Improvement." *National Productivity Review* 7 (Summer 1988): 229–237.

Ohmae, Kenichi. "Managing in a Borderless World." *Harvard Business Review* 67 (May–June 1989): 152–161.

Olson, D., and R. Bangs. "No-Fault Attendance Control: A Real World Application." *Personnel Administrator* 29 (June 1984): 53–56.

Olson, Philip D. "Entrepreneurship and Management." *Journal of Small Business Management* 25 (July 1987): 7–13.

Ono, Karou, and James H. Davis. "Individual Judgment and Group Interaction: A Variable Perspective Approach." *Organizational Behavior and Human Decision Processes* 11 (April 1988): 211–232.

Ordiorne, G. S. "Uneasy Look at Motivation Theory." *Training and Development Journal* 34 (June 1980): 106–112.

Ornstein, Suzyn. "The Hidden Influences of Office Design." *Academy of Management Executive* 2 (May 1989): 144–148.

Orth, Charles D., Harry E. Wilkinson, and Robert C. Benfari. "The Manager's Role as Coach and Mentor." *Organizational Dynamics* 15 (Spring 1987): 66–74.

Ouchi, William G. "Relationship between Organizational Structure and Organizational Control." *Administrative Science Quarterly* 22 (March 1981): 95–113.

Paquette, Laurence, and Thomas Kida. "The Effect of Decision Strategy and Task Complexity on Decision Performance." *Organizational Behavior and Human Decision Processes* 41 (February 1988): pp. 128–142.

Pasewark, William R. "A New Approach to Quality Control for Auditors: Quality Circles." *The Practical Accountant* 24 (March 1991): 68–71.

Peters, Thomas J. "Facing Up to the Need for a Management Revolution." *California Management Review* 30 (Winter 1988): 7–38.

Peters, Thomas J., and Robert H. Waterman, Jr. *In Search of Excellence.* New York: Harper & Row, 1982.

Philbrick, Jane Hass, and Marsha E. Hass. "The New Management: Is It Legal?" *Academy of Management Executive* 4 (November 1988): 325–330.

Porter, L. W. "A Study of Perceived Need Satisfactions in Bottom and Middle Management Jobs." *Journal of Applied Psychology* 45 (1961): 1–10.

Powell, Gary N. "The Effects of Sex and Gender on Recruitment." *Academy of Management Review* 12 (October 1987): 731–743.

Powell, Walter W. "Hybrid Organizational Arrangements." *California Management Review* 30 (Fall 1987): 67–87.

Premeaux, Shane R., R. Wayne Mondy, and Art Bethke. "Decertification: Fulfilling Unions' Destiny?" *Personnel Journal* 66 (June 1987): 144–148.

Pryor, Austin K., and William K. Foster. "The Strategic Management of Innovation." *Journal of Business Strategy* 7 (Summer 1986): 38–42.

Quick, James Campbell, Debra L. Nelson, and Jonathan D. Quick. "Successful Executives: How Independent?" *Academy of Management Executive* 1 (August 1987): 139–146.

Ragozzino, Pat P. "IS Quality—What Is It?" *Journal of Systems Management* 41 (November 1990): 15–16.

Randolph, W. Alan, and Barry Z. Posner. "What Every Manager Needs to Know about Project Management." *Sloan Management Review* 29 (Summer 1988): 65–73.

Rapoport, Carla. "Mazda's Bold New Global Strategy." *Fortune*, December 17, 1990, pp. 109–113.

Rechner, Paula L. "Corporate Governance: Fact or Fiction?" *Business Horizons* 32 (July–August 1989): 11–15.

Reilly, Bernard J. "Ethical Business and the Ethical Person." *Business Horizons* 33 (November–December 1990): 23–27.

Reimann, Bernard C., and Yoash Wiener. "Corporate Culture: Avoiding the Elitist Trap." *Business Horizons* (March–April 1988): 36–42.

Risman, Barbara J., and Donald Tomaskovic-Devey. "The Social Construction of Technology: Microcomputers and the Organization of Work." *Business Horizons* 32 (May–June 1989): 71–75.

Roberts, Nancy C., and Paula J. King. "The Stakeholder Audit Goes Public." *Organizational Dynamics* 17 (Winter 1989): 63–79.

Robin, Donald, Michael Giallourakis, Fred R. David, and Thomas E. Moritz. "A Different Look at Codes of Ethics." *Business Horizons* 32 (January–February 1989): 66–73.

Robin, Donald P., and Eric Reidenbach. "Balancing Corporate Profits and Ethics." *Business* 40 (October–November–December 1990): 11–14.

Rockart, John F. "The Line Takes the Leadership—IS Management in a Wired Society." *Sloan Management Review* 29 (Summer 1988): 57–64.

Rockart, John F., and James E. Short. "TT in the 1990s: Managing Organizational Interdependence." *Sloan Management Review* 30 (Winter 1989): 7–17.

Runcie, John F. "By Days I Make the Cars." *Harvard Business Review* (May–June 1980): 106–115.

Sass, C. Joseph, and Teresa A. Keefe. "MIS for Strategic Planning and a Competitive Edge." *Journal of Systems Management* 39 (June 1988): 14–17.

Schein, Edgar H. "Organizational Socialization and the Profession of Management." *Sloan Management Review* 30 (Fall 1988): 53–65.

Schenkel-Savitt, Susan, and Steven P. Seltzer. "Recruitment as a Successful Means of Affirmative Action." *Employee Relations Law Journal* 13 (Winter 1987): 165–179.

Scheuing, Eberhard E. "How to Build a Quality-Conscious Team." *Supervisory Management* 35 (January 1990): 6.

Schilit, Warren Keith. "Upward Influence Activity in Strategic Decision Making." *Group and Organization Studies* 12 (September 1987): 343–368.

Schmenner, Roger W. "Escaping the Black Holes of Cost Accounting." *Business Horizons* 31 (January–February 1988): 66–72.

Schriber, Jacquelyn, and Barbara A. Gutck. "Some Time Dimensions of Work: Measurement of an Underlying Aspect of Organization Culture." *Journal of Applied Psychology* 72 (November 1987): 642–650.

Schuler, Randall S., and Susan E. Jackson. "Linking Competitive Strategies with Human Resource Management Practices." *Academy of Management Executive* 1 (August 1987): 207–220.

Schwartz, Andrew E. "The Why, What, and to Whom of Delegation." *Management Solutions* (June 1987): 31–38.

Schweiger, David M., William R. Sandberg, and James W. Ragan. "Group Approaches for Improving Strategic Decision Making: A Comparative Analysis of Dialectical Inquiry, Devil's Advocacy, and Consensus." *Academy of Management Journal* 29 (March 1986): 51–71.

Seltzer, Joseph, and Rita E. Numerof. "Supervisory Leadership and Subordinate Burnout." *Academy of Management Journal* 31 (June 1988): 439–446.

Shaffer, James C. "Mission Statements: Why Have Them? (Corporate Mission Statements)." *Communication World* 4 (June 1987): 14–16.

Sheehy, James W. "New Work Ethic Is Frightening." *Personnel Journal* 69 (June 1990): 28–36.

Sherman, J. D., and H. L. Smith. "The Influence of Organization Structure on Intrinsic versus Extrinsic Motivation." *Academy of Management Journal* 27 (December 1984): 877–884.

Shetty, Y. K. "Guidelines for Managing in Service Business." *Management Solutions* (February 1987): 38–42.

Sievers, Burkard. "Beyond the Surrogate of Motivation." *Organization Studies* 7 (Fall 1986): 335–351.

Silver, P. G., and Craig Jurgenson. "The Disabled Employee: A Supervisory Challenge." *Thrust: Journal for Employment and Training Professionals* 7 (Fall/Winter 1986): 65–70.

Simon, Ruth, and Graham Button. "What I Learned in the Eighties." *Forbes*, January 8, 1991, pp. 100–114.

Sinclair, J. M. "Is the Matrix Really Necessary?" *Project Management Journal* 15 (March 1984): 49–55.

Sinetar, Marsha. "The Informal Discussion Group—A Powerful Agent for Change." *Sloan Management Review* 29 (Summer 1988): 61–65.

Singh, Jitendra V. "Performance, Slack, and Risk Taking in Organizational Decision Making." *Academy of Management Journal* 29 (September 1986): 562–585.

Skinner, B. F. *The Behavior of Organisms: An Experimental Approach.* New York: Appleton-Century, 1938.

Skinner, Wickham. "What Matters to Manufacturing." *Harvard Business Review* 66 (January–February 1988): 10–17.

Smart, Bradford D. "Progressive Approaches for Hiring the Best People." *Training and Development Journal* 41 (September 1987): 46–53.

Smith, Gerald F. "Defining Managerial Problems: A Framework for Prescriptive Theorizing." *Management Science* 35 (August 1989): 963–981.

Smith, Harold Ivan. "Singles in the Workplace." *Personnel Administrator* 33 (February 1988): 76–81.

Smith, Kenwyn K. "The Movement of Conflict in Organizations: The Joint Dynamics of Splitting and Triangulation." *Administrative Science Quarterly* 34 (March 1989): 1–20.

Smith, Kenwyn K., and David N. Berg. "A Paradoxical Conception of Group Dynamics." *Human Relations* 10 (October 1987): 633–657.

Smith, Martin A. "Improving Product Quality in American Industry." *Academy of Management Executive* 1 (August 1987): 243–246.

Snyder, Neil H., Bernard A. Morin, and Marilyn A. Morgan. "Motivating People to Build Excellent Enterprises." *Business* 38 (April–June 1988): 14–19.

Srivastva, Suresh, and Frank J. Barrett. "The Transforming Nature of Metaphors in Group Development: A Study in Group Theory." *Human Relations* 11 (January 1988): 31–63.

Standing, Guy. "Unemployment and the Recomposition of Labor Reserves." *Annals of the American Academy of Political and Social Science* 492 (July 1987): 80–96.

Steffy, Brian D., and Steven D. Maurer. "Conceptualizing and Measuring the Economic Effectiveness of Human Resource Activities." *Academy of Management Review* 13 (April 1988): 271–286.

Steingraber, "Total Quality Management: A New Look at a Basic Issue." *Vital Speeches of the Day*, April 15, 1991, pp. 415–416.

Strolle, Alfred. "Creating a Total Quality Management Culture Is Everyone's Business." *Research Technology Management* 34 (July–August 1991): 8–9.

Sullivan, Jeremiah J. "Three Roles of Language in Motivation Theory." *Academy of Management Review* 13 (January 1988): 104–115.

Swann, James P., Jr. "Formal Grievance Procedures in Nonunion Plants." *Personnel Administrator* 26 (August 1981): 66–70.

Tavernier, Gerard. "Improving Managerial Productivity: The Key Ingredient Is One-on-One Communication." *Management Review* 70 (February 1981): 13–16.

Taylor, Alex, Jr. "Why Women Managers Are Bailing Out." *Fortune*, August 18, 1986, pp. 16–23.

Taylor, R. L., and R. A. Zawachi. "Trends in Performance Appraisal: Guidelines for Managers." *Personnel Administrator* 29 (March 1984): 71–80.

Thackray, John. "The Fall of Corporate Planning." *Management Today* (July 1986): 17.

Thibaut, J. W., and H. H. Kelley. *The Social Psychology of Groups.* New York: Wiley, 1959.

Thompson, J. D. *Organization in Action.* New York: McGraw-Hill, 1967.

Tjosvold, Dean. "Effects of Crisis Orientation on Managers' Approach to Controversy in Decision Making." *Academy of Management Journal* 27 (March 1984): 130–138.

Tobin, Lawrence M. "The New Quality Landscape: Total Quality Management." *Journal of Systems Management* 41 (November 1990): 10–14.

Trice, H. M., and J. M. Beyer. "Studying Organizational Cultures through Rites and Ceremonials." *Academy of Management Review* 9 (October 1984): 653–669.

Tung, Rosalie L. "Career Issues in International Assignments." *Academy of Management Executive* 2 (August 1988): 241–244.

Turino, Jon. "Test Strategies that Cut Manufacturing Costs." *SAM Advanced Management Journal* 49 (Winter 1984): 42–53.

Turney, Peter, and Bruce Anderson. "Accounting for Continuous Improvement." *Sloan Management Review* 30 (Winter 1989): 37–47.

Tylecote, Andrew. "Time Horizons of Management Decisions: Causes and Effects." *Journal of Economic Studies* 14 (November 1987): 51–64.

Ulrich, David, and Margaret F. Wiersema. "Gaining Strategic and Organizational Behavior." *Academy of Management Executive* 2 (May 1989): 115–122.

Van de Vliert, E. "Escalative Intervention in Small-Group Conflicts." *Journal of Applied Behavioral Science* 21 (February 1985): 19–36.

Veglahn, Peter A. "The Five Steps in Practicing Effective Discipline." *Management Solutions* (November 1987): 24–29.

Venkatraman, N. "The Concept of Fit in Strategy Research: Toward Verbal and Statistical Correspondence." *Academy of Management Review* 14 (July 1989): 423–444.

Victor, Bart, and John B. Cullen. "The Organizational Bases of Ethical Work Climates." *Administrative Science Quarterly* 33 (March 1988): 101–125.

Voluck, Philip R. "Recruiting, Interviewing and Hiring: Staying within the Boundaries." *Personnel Administrator* 32 (May 1987): 15–19.

Vroom, Victor H. *Work and Motivation.* New York: Wiley, 1964.

Vroom, Victor H., and A. J. Jago. "Decision-Making as a Social Process: Normative and Descriptive Models of Leader Behavior." *Decision Sciences* 5 (1974): 743–769.

Vroom, Victor H., and P. W. Yetton. *Leadership and Decision-Making.* Pittsburgh, Pa.: University of Pittsburgh Press, 1973.

Wagel, William H. "An Unorthodox Approach to Leadership Development." *Personnel* 63 (July 1986): 1–3.

Walker, A., and J. Lorsch. "Organizational Choice: Product versus Function." *Harvard Business Review* 46 (November–December 1968): 129–138.

Walsh, James P. "Selectivity and Selective Perception: An Investigation of Managers' Belief Structures and Information Processing." *Academy of Management Journal* 31 (December 1988): 873–896.

Walton, Mary. *The Dimming Management Method.* New York: Perigee Books, 1986.

Wanous, J. P., A. E. Reichers, and S. D. Malik. "Organizational Socialization and Group Development: Toward an Integrative Perspective." *Academy of Management Review* 9 (1984): 670–683.

Warner, Timothy N. "Information Technology as a Competitive Burden." *Sloan Management Review* 29 (Fall 1987): 55–61.

Waterman, H., Jr., J. Peters, and R. Phillips. "Structure Is Not Organization." *Business Horizons* 23 (June 1980): 14–26.

Webber, Alan M. "Ricochet Change across the Pacific." *Harvard Business Review* 66 (September–October 1988): 144–152.

Weigelt, Keith, and Ian MacMillan. "An Interactive Strategic Analysis Framework." *Strategic Management Journal* 9 (Summer 1988): 27–40.

Weihrich, Heinz, and Diethard Buhler. "Training Managers for the Global Market." *Business* 40 (July–September 1990): 40–42.

Weisbord, Marvin R. "Toward Third-Wave Managing and Consulting." *Organizational Behavior* 15 (Winter 1987): 4–25.

Weiss, Alan. "Seven Reasons to Examine Work Place Ethics." *HRMagazine* 36 (March 1991): 69–74.

Welsh, M. Ann, and Gordon E. Dehler. "Political Legacy of Administrative Succession." *Academy of Management Journal* 31 (December 1988): 948–961.

Weston, Frederick C., Jr. "Computer Integrated Manufacturing Systems: Fact or Fantasy?" *Business Horizons* 31 (July–August 1988): 64–68.

Wheelock, Keith. "A Tough Job Market Ahead, Especially for Working Mothers." *Personnel Administrator* 31 (April 1986): 119–128.

Wheelwright, Steven C., and W. Earl Sasser, Jr. "The New Product Development." *Harvard Business Review* 67 (May–June): 112–127.

White, John A. "TQM: It's Time, Academia!" Paper based on a presentation given July 18, 1990, at the First National Symposium on the Role of Academia in National Competitiveness and Total Quality Management, hosted by West Virginia University.

Whitehill, Arthur M. "American Executives through Foreign Eyes." *Business Horizons* 32 (May–June 1989): 42–48.

Whyte, Glen. "Groupthink Reconsidered." *The Academy of Management Review* 14 (January 1989): 40–56.

Wilson, Ian. "The Strategic Management Technology: Corporate Fad or Strategic Necessity." *Long Range Planning* 19 (April 1986): 21–22.

Wright, Phillip C. "Management by Objectives—One More Time." *Supervision* (January 1984): 3–5.

Wueste, Richard A. "A Matter of Inconsequence: Mastering the Art of Executive Triviality." *Management World* 17 (March–April 1988): 40–41.

Yasai-Ardekani, Masoud. "Effects of Environmental Scarcity and Munificence on the Relationship of Context to Organizational Structures." *Academy of Management Journal* 32 (March 1989): 131–156.

Zaleznik, A., C. R. Christensen, and F. J. Roethlisberger. *The Motivation, Productivity, and Satisfaction of Workers*. Boston: Harvard Business School, Division of Research, 1958.

Zarembra, Alan. "Communicating Upward." *Personnel Journal* 68 (March 1989): 34–39.

Zauderer, Donald, and Joseph Fox. "Resiliency in the Face of Stress." *Management Solutions* (November 1988): 30–35.

Zeltmann, Steven M. "Communications Networks for Managing Global Operations." *Business Perspectives* 4 (Fall 1990): 20–22.

Zenger, Rodd R., and Barbara S. Lawrence. "Organizational Demography: The Differential Effects of Age and Tenure Distributions on Technical Communication." *Academy of Management Journal* 32 (June 1989): 353–376.

Zierden, William E. "Leading through the Follower's Point of View." *Organizational Dynamics* 8 (Spring 1980): 27–46.

Index

NAME INDEX

Abshire, Roger D., 534
Achachter, Victor, 281
Adair, "Red", 427
Adams, J. Stacy, 308
Akers, John F., 238, 331, 332, 334
Alderfer, Clayton, 299, 305–306
Allaire, Paul, 601
Allen, Robert, 135–137, 153, 209, 229
Anderson, Warren, 98
Argyris, Chris, 296–297, 311, 474
Armstrong, Neil, 248
Asch, Solomon, 397
Athos, Anthony, 321

Bales, Robert F., 68
Bamforth, K.W., 69
Barnard, Chester I., 66
Barney, Robert, 3, 6, 9, 14
Beech, Olive Ann, 169
Bennett, Patrick, 333, 334
Bennis, Warren, 474
Bergeman, Richard P., 567
Bieber, Owen, 45
Blake, Robert R., 339, 478
Blanchard, Kenneth, 340, 346–349
Blanchflower, David, 555
Boesky, Ivan, 91
Booker, Beatrice, 188
Bowen, Murphy, 253
Brennan, Edward A., 236
Buckley, William F., 111
Burns, Robert, 151
Burns, Tom, 71
Burr, Donald, 24
Busch, August, III, 11
Bush, George, 44, 429

Calloway, James, 257
Canion, Rod, 501, 612
Carlisle, Jim, 601
Carroll, Archie B., 78
Cary, Frank, 331
Chase, Rex, 195
Coch, Lester, 68
Conway, Earl C., 523, 524
Costello, Robert, 527
Cowper, Steve, 81

Crane, Russell L., 456
Crosby, Philip B., 525, 531, 535
Crown, Marc, 132

Daniel, Fluor, 567
Davis, Jim, 253
Davis, Keith, 86, 96
Davis, Ralph C., 116
DeLuca, Fred, 35, 36, 38, 48
Deming, W. Edwards, 516, 524, 525, 527, 531, 532, 535, 539
Dickson, William J., 67
Djurdjevic, Bob, 331
Donaldson, Gordon, 466
Drucker, Peter, 79, 154, 173
Duncan, Paul, 561

Eaton, Robert J., 106
Emerson, Harrington, 64, 66
Emery, F. E., 69
English, John T., 621

Fayol, Henri, 66
Feigenbaum, Armand V., 528, 532
Ferrer-Westrop, Sterling, 534
Fiedler, Fred E., 340, 343–344
Fisher, M. C., 523
Ford, Henry, 197, 341, 389
Franklin, Benjamin, 28
Freeman, Richard, 555
French, John R. P., Jr., 68, 425
Friedman, Milton, 87

Galusha, Joe, 405
Galvin, Robert, 575
Gantt, Henry L., 64, 65
Gault, Stanley C., 367
Ghiselli, Edwin, 335
Gilbreth, Frank, 64, 65, 581
Gilbreth, Lillian, 64, 65, 581
Giuliani, Rudolph, 91
Gluck, Frederick W., 335
Goizueta, Robert, 105–108, 110, 113, 122, 169
Gordon, Judith, 337
Gorr, Ivan, 582
Graicunas, V.A., 236, 237
Gross, Joe, 210–211, 213

Gruber, William H., 604
Guadagno, Louis A., 523

Hackman, J. Richard, 317, 401
Hammond, Josh, 529
Harbour, James, 516
Harris, Betty, 113
Harris, Louis, 78
Hart, Alex W., 528
Hefner, Christie, 452
Hefner, Hugh, 451
Hersey, Paul, 340, 346–349
Herzberg, Frederick, 299, 302, 303, 311, 318, 460, 478
Hicks, Wayland, 238
Honeycutt, Gloria, 223
Hornsby, Gerald, 566
House, Robert, 337, 340
Hustead, Bill, 189
Hustead, Ted, 189

Iacocca, Lee, 106, 111, 115, 337
Icahn, Carl, 227
Inamori, Kazuo, 143
Intravartolo, Russ, 575
Ishikawa, Kaoru, 526, 532
Iverson, Kenneth, 160

Jasinowski, Jerry, 259
Jay, Anthony, 450
Jobs, Steve, 449, 450
Johnson, Lyndon B., 266
Juran, J. M., 525, 531, 535

Kahn, Robert L., 70
Katz, Daniel, 70
Kavner, Robert, 341
Kearns, David, 472, 601
Kennedy, John F., 248, 428
King, Martin Luther, Jr., 90
King, Olin, 427
King, W. Frank, III, 8
Kinnear, James W., 227, 228, 233, 234, 239
Kondrasuk, Jack N., 157
Koontz, Harold, 69
Kotter, John, 424

659

Kravner, Robert, 464
Kroc, Ray, 451, 509

Lawler, Edward, 313, 314
Learson, T. Vincent, 331
Leaveitt, Harold, 108
Levin, Doron P., 421
Lewin, Kurt, 465
Lewis, Shelton, 223
Likert, Rensis, 338, 462
Lincoln, James F., 88
Livingston, J. Sterling, 297
Loren, Allan Z., 449
Lorsch, Jay, 466
Lutz, Robert A., 106

McCause, Anne Adams, 339
McClelland, David, 299, 306, 307, 311, 424, 425, 433, 554
McColl, Hugh, Jr., 316
McGregor, Douglas, 68–69, 296–297, 311, 333, 460
Mackay, Harvey, 15
Macke, Kenneth A., 79
McKinnen, Dan, 59
McNealy, Scott G., 11
McTague, John P., 588
Manzi, Jim P., 8
Maples, Mike, 242
March, James G., 66
Marriott, Bill, 352
Martin, Leroy, 24
Maslow, Abraham, 299–306, 311, 460, 560
Maxwell, Leon C., 366
Mayo, Elton, 67, 294
Miles, Raymond, 181
Mintzberg, Henry, 71, 363, 429
Monaghan, Tom, 293, 294
More, Sir Thomas, 84
Morita, Akio, 56, 353
Morris, Charles, 401
Morris, Ernie, 40
Moses, 62
Mouton, Jane Srygley, 339, 478

Nagel, Russell A., 334
Nemeth, Lane, 46

Nolan, Kathy, 622
Nowlin, Dennis L., 51

Oldham, Greg R., 317
Oliver, William H., 539
Olson, James, 135, 229
Opel, John, 331
Ouchi, William, 295, 321

Pagano, Anthony M., 92
Pascale, Richard, 321
Perez, Geraldo, 489
Perot, H. Ross, 8, 9, 14, 170, 337, 341, 352, 421–423, 425, 426, 433
Peters, Thomas J., 203, 400
Popoff, Frank, 547
Porter, Michael E., 183, 184

Quinlan, Michael R., 451, 489, 490, 509

Rabinowitz, Nan, 131
Raven, Bertram, 425
Reagan, Ronald, 59, 88, 263
Rice, A. K., 69
Roethlisberger, Fritz (F.J.), 67
Rogers, Carl, 379
Rumack, Frederick M., 305

Sanders, Colonel Harland, 3
Sanderson, Roy, 198
Sarni, Vincent A., 359, 455–456
Schein, Edgar, 27
Schmidt, Warren H., 340, 342–343
Schott, Marge, 425
Sculley, John, 145, 449, 450, 451
Selye, Hans, 437
Shapiro, Robert, 163
Shepard, Woodrow, 210–213
Shewart, Walter A., 524
Simon, Herbert, 66, 173
Skinner, B. F., 310
Smeltzer, George, 254
Smith, Adam, 62, 86, 200
Smith, Frederick W., 7, 38, 129
Smith, Roger B., 9, 170
Smith, Roland, 558
Smith, Sam, 253

Snekiker, David K., 526
Snow, Charles, 181
Soha, Ken, 601
Sower, Victor E., 534
Spindler, Michael H., 449, 450, 451
Stalker, George, 71
Staw, Barry, 312
Stempel, Robert C., 9, 236
Stevens, Ralph W., 566

Taguchi, Genichi, 529, 532
Tannenbaum, Robert, 340, 342–343
Taylor, Frederick W., 62, 64, 66, 294, 580
Thomas, Clarence, 429
Thomas, R. David, 3–5, 9, 13
Thornton, Dean D., 259
Thorpe, Larry, 154
Tippet, L., 581
Tomaso, Alejandro de, 111
Treacher, Arthur, 3
Trist, E. L., 69
Truman, Harry, 122
Trump, Donald, 59, 432–433

Valladao, Dick, 254
Van Der Klugt, Cornelius, 18, 550
Verdin, Jo Ann, 92
Vittoria, Joseph V., 303, 304
Vroom, Victor, 311–312, 344–346

Wadhwani, Romesh, 589
Walton, Sam, 75, 195, 334, 341
Watson, Thomas J., 331, 471
Watson, Thomas J., Jr., 331
Weber, Max, 66
Wilkinson, Barry, 553
Williams, Monci Jo, 432
Wilson, T. A., 169
Woodward, Joan, 71, 238
Woolard, Edgar S., Jr., 382
Wozniak, Steve, 449

Yakushiji, Taizo, 556
Yetton, Philip, 344–346

COMPANY INDEX

AFG Industries, 403
Alcoa, Inc., 509, 549
Allied Chemical, 77
Allied Corporation, 165
American Airlines, 623
American Express, 59, 528
American Motors Corporation, 111
American West Airlines, 185
Amoco Corporation, 227

Anheuser-Busch, 11, 182
Apple Computer Inc., 145, 242, 449–451, 458, 466, 513
Armco, 147–148
AT&T Corporation, 46, 77, 135–138, 141, 142, 146, 151, 153, 172, 177, 209, 220, 229, 282, 283, 318, 341, 452, 464, 466, 478, 494, 531, 558
Avis, 303, 304

Baker Hughes, Inc., 178
Baldor Electric, 525, 526
BankAmerica, 5, 77, 78
Bausch & Lomb, 184
BayBank Middlesex, 132
Bell Telephone, 282. *See also* AT&T Corporation
Berlitz International, 383
Bethlehem Steel Company, 64, 160

SUBJECT INDEX